SMO6001005
6/07
£13.99
320.092(Fre)

D1145432

Rawls

"sympathetic, comprehensive, thorough, and accessible"
Leif Wenar, University of Sheffield, UK

"A monumental study of a monumental theorist. This invaluable resource engages with Rawls's work at every level: it's an exposition, it's a critique, and most important it projects an understanding of Rawls's work into the future of political philosophy. On every page, Professor Freeman's attention to detail is suffused by his awareness of the overall structure of the theory and the philosophical significance of Rawls's grand strategy."
Jeremy Waldron, New York University School of Law, USA

ST MARTIN'S COLLEGE
LANCASTER LIBRARY

Routledge Philosophers

Edited by Brian Leiter
University of Texas, Austin

Routledge Philosophers is a major series of introductions to the great
Western philosophers. Each book places a major philosopher or thinker
in historical context, explains and assesses their key arguments, and
considers their legacy. Additional features include a chronology of major
dates and events, chapter summaries, annotated suggestions for further
reading and a glossary of technical terms.

An ideal starting point for those new to philosophy, they are also essential
reading for those interested in the subject at any level.

Hobbes	A. P. Martinich
Leibniz	Nicholas Jolley
Locke	E. J. Lowe
Hegel	Frederick Beiser
Rousseau	Nicholas Dent
Schopenhauer	Julian Young
Freud	Jonathan Lear
Kant	Paul Guyer
Husserl	David Woodruff Smith
Darwin	Tim Lewens
Rawls	Samuel Freeman
Aristotle	Christopher Shields

Forthcoming:

Spinoza	Michael Della Rocca
Hume	Don Garrett
Fichte and Schelling	Sebastian Gardner
Merleau-Ponty	Taylor Carman
Heidegger	John Richardson
Aquinas	Christopher Hughes
Wittgenstein	Bill Child
Adorno	Brian O'Connor
Foucault	Béatrice Han-Pile
Kierkegaard	Andrew Cross

Samuel Freeman

Rawls

Routledge
Taylor & Francis Group

LONDON AND NEW YORK

First published 2007
by Routledge
2 Park Square, Milton Park, Abingdon, Oxon OX14 4RN

Simultaneously published in the USA and Canada
by Routledge
270 Madison Ave, New York, NY 10016

*Routledge is an imprint of the Taylor & Francis Group, an
informa business*

© 2007 Samuel Freeman

Typeset in Johanna MT by Taylor & Francis Books
Printed and bound in Great Britain by
The Cromwell Press, Trowbridge, Wiltshire

All rights reserved. No part of this book may be reprinted or
reproduced or utilized in any form or by any electronic,
mechanical, or other means, now known or hereafter
invented, including photocopying and recording, or in any
information storage or retrieval system, without permission in
writing from the publishers.

British Library Cataloguing in Publication Data
A catalogue record for this book is available from the British
Library

Library of Congress Cataloging in Publication Data
Freeman, Samuel Richard.
   Rawls / Samuel Freeman.
     p. cm. – (Routledge philosophers)
   Includes bibliographical references and index.
   1. Rawls, John, 1921–2002. 2. Justice. 3. Political
science – Philosophy. I. Title.

   JC578.F6975   2006
   320.092–dc22   2006032203

ISBN10: 0–415–30108–4 (hbk)
ISBN10: 0–415–30109–2 (pbk)
ISBN10: 0–203–08660–0 (ebk)

ISBN13: 978–0–415–30108–4 (hbk)
ISBN13: 978–0–415–30109–1 (pbk)
ISBN13: 978–0–203–08660–5 (ebk)

For Annette
and
in memory of John Rawls

In memory of John Hawk

viii **Contents**

Preface and Acknowledgments

The aim of this book is to explain the main ideas in John Rawls's political and moral philosophy. Rawls is the foremost political philosopher of the twentieth century, and is recognized by many as one of the great political philosophers of all time. His main work, *A Theory of Justice*, has now been translated into more than thirty languages. Rawls devoted his entire career to one general philosophical topic and as a result wrote more on the subject of justice than any other major philosopher. The general features of his vision of a just society are familiar – a constitutional democracy that gives priority to certain fundamental rights and liberties, while expanding equal opportunities among all persons and guaranteeing a minimum social income for all. Other than his "difference principle," what is most distinctive about his position are not his principles of justice – the principles of equal basic liberties and fair equal opportunities resemble in many important respects ideas found in Kant, J.S. Mill, and other representatives of the high liberal tradition. It is rather his philosophical argument for these social and political institutions. Rawls revived the natural rights theory of the social contract found in Locke, Rousseau, and Kant, and joined it with an account of moral justification that is more suited to the modern sensibilities of a more secular, democratic, and scientific age.

The guiding purpose of Rawls's work is to justify the primary institutions of a liberal and democratic society in terms of a conception of justice that democratic citizens themselves can accept and rely upon to guide their deliberations and to justify to one another the basic institutions and laws governing a democratic society. The goal of providing a "public charter" for a democratic society, or (as he also called it) a "public basis for political justification," becomes especially prominent in Rawls's later works. This goal connects with his early reliance on the liberal and democratic social contract traditions of Locke, Rousseau, and Kant. For the basic idea of their doctrine is that the members of society ought to be able to freely accept and generally endorse the main political and social institutions that regulate and shape their everyday lives. Rawls's well-known version of the social contract – an impartial agreement on principles of justice behind a "veil of ignorance" that deprives the parties of knowledge of all particular facts about themselves and their society – is but one part of his extended contractarian argument. Equally important is a second contractarian argument, that free and equal citizens situated in a "well-ordered society" who are morally motivated by their sense of justice can also accept and agree to the same principles of justice. The idea of a well-ordered society is the controlling influence behind Rawls's contractarianism, including the original position.

Central to the justification of principles of justice for Rawls is the realistic possibility of a well-ordered society in which all reasonable and rational persons agree to and generally comply with the same principles of justice. Rawls's political liberalism is specifically designed to show how the basic contractarian ideal of reasonable agreement among all free and equal citizens is a feasible social ideal, compatible with human nature and the constraints of social cooperation. His accounts of public reason, a political conception of justice, and a public basis for political justification take social contract doctrine one step further than his illustrious predecessors. Rawls thought that citizens' acceptance of both the principles of justice behind the constitution and also of their justification are necessary if we are to take seriously freedom and equality as the foundational political values of a democratic society. A guiding theme in this book is the centrality of the ideal of a well-ordered society to Rawls's contractarianism and the development of his theory of justice.

It is often said that Rawls sought to justify a constitution resembling the U.S. Constitution, with a bill of rights, separation of powers, and judicial review. While this was not a specific aim, it is true that he thought highly of these institutions and saw them as more likely to realize the equal basic rights and fair opportunities of citizens than other democratic alternatives. The main respect in which justice as fairness departs from the American constitutional system is its account of economic justice, including fair equal opportunities and the difference principle's requirement that the economy be organized to maximize the benefits going to society's least advantaged members. Currently, social and political policies in the U.S. increasingly focus on its most wealthy members and allows wealth to "trickle-down" to those less advantaged. (This is apparent in proposals to eliminate the estate tax and not to tax unearned investment income, including capital gains, while leaving taxes on workers' earned income undisturbed.) Rawls himself is sometimes accused of endorsing a "trickle-down" economy because his difference principle allows for inequalities of income and wealth in order to provide people with incentives to educate their capacities, work longer hours, take risks, and so on.[1] But if by "trickle-down" is meant an economy that maximally or even predominantly benefits the more advantaged in hopes that it will coincidentally benefit the least, then Rawls's position is exactly the opposite: the difference principle requires societies to focus on the economically *least* advantaged first and take measures to maximize their economic prospects (including opportunities to exercise influence and control in their work). Under the difference principle only incentives designed to maximally benefit the least advantaged, not the most advantaged, are permitted; permissible incentives and inequalities are those that leave the least advantaged better situated than all other workable alternatives. In this regard it is more accurate to say that under the difference principle wealth and income are allowed to "suffuse upwards" from the less advantaged, rather than "trickle down" from the more advantaged. The general point is that, assuming that inequalities can work to everyone's benefit, no other principle allowing for inequalities benefits the least advantaged more than does the difference principle.

Rawls says in his *Lectures on the History of Political Philosophy* that a moral theory is best understood when considered in its best light, and that there is no point in criticizing a theory otherwise

(LHPP, xiii, 105). I have tried to present Rawls's theory of justice at its best. Accordingly, one of my aims is to clear up some of the more frequent misunderstandings of his position. But I also discuss what (I believe) are some genuine problems and obscurities. Primary among these are his several efforts to formulate a conception of justice that can be publicly accepted by all reasonable persons within the feasible social world he calls a "well-ordered society." Rawls's account in *A Theory of Justice* of how such a well-ordered society is realistically possible ultimately encounters difficulties, and this leads him to the revisions made in *Political Liberalism* (see Chapter 7 below). But in his final work, "The Idea of Public Reason Revisited," Rawls seems to have accepted that general agreement by all citizens on justice as fairness is an unrealistic possibility. This must have been an enormous disappointment for him, for he had worked for nearly forty years trying to show how a well-ordered society where everyone accepts justice as fairness as its public charter is a realistic possibility, compatible with human nature and general facts about social cooperation. He remained confident to the end, however, that, whatever the shortcomings of human nature, reasonable people are still capable of an effective sense of justice and morally endorsing a liberal conception that protects basic liberties, provides equal opportunities, and secures a social minimum for all citizens. Whether or not Rawls's confidence in the human condition is justified or misplaced, his works will remain a major accomplishment in the history of moral and political thought for generations to come.

The book is organized chronologically, to accord with the order of publication of Rawls's three main books and their main parts. The first chapter consists of a short biography of Rawls's life, followed by a discussion of the major philosophers who influenced his works and his interpretations of them. The chapter concludes with a discussion of Rawls's account of justification as a "reflective equilibrium" of our considered convictions, an idea which informs all his works. (For readers less interested in historical influences or philosophical issues of justification, these sections can be skipped without too much loss of understanding.) Chapters 2–6 cover Rawls's major work, *A Theory of Justice*. Chapters

2–4 are the most central to an initial understanding of Rawls's main contributions, since they explain Part I of *A Theory of Justice* on the principles of justice (chs. 2–3) and Rawls's argument for these principles from the original position (ch. 4). Chapter 5 covers material in *A Theory of Justice*, Part II and elsewhere, and discusses the institutions required by justice as fairness. Chapter 6 then takes up *A Theory of Justice*, Part III, on goodness as rationality, the sense of justice, and stability, and discusses Rawls's congruence argument, that justice is essential to the human good. Chapter 7 is a transition chapter, discussing the interim between *A Theory of Justice* and *Political Liberalism*, and includes Rawls's accounts of Kantian Constructivism and the independence of moral theory. (These discussions are of more interest to specialists.) It concludes with a discussion of some of the main problems Rawls found with his arguments in Part III of *A Theory of Justice*, which led him to formulate the doctrine of political liberalism. The main ideas in *Political Liberalism* are covered in the next two chapters, with Chapter 8 discussing lectures I–III and the ideas of a political conception of justice and political constructivism, and Chapter 9 discussing lectures IV and VI, including the ideas of overlapping consensus and public reason. Finally, Chapter 10 takes up Rawls's final work, his account of international justice in *The Law of Peoples*, and discusses how it is part of political liberalism and the basis for the foreign policy of a liberal constitutional democracy.

I am grateful to many friends and colleagues over the years for their comments, advice, criticisms, and discussions; especially to Joshua Cohen, Amy Gutmann, Paul Guyer, Rahul Kumar, Stephen Perry, Andrews Reath, Thomas Ricketts, T.M. Scanlon, Samuel Scheffler, K.C. Tan, and R. Jay Wallace. To Andrews Reath and K.C. Tan I am especially grateful for devoting the time and effort required to read the manuscript, and providing many hours and many pages of critical feedback. Extensive comments by four anonymous reviewers for Routledge helpfully led to many needed revisions. Mark Kaplan read Chapter 4 and provided much helpful advice regarding my discussion of decision theory. Matt Lister and Mark Navin provided many helpful comments too. I am especially grateful to my former student and good friend Joseph Farber, who before his tragic death in May 2006 read much of this manuscript and gave me many helpful comments while undergoing treatments for cancer. Other students who have worked with me and from whom I have learned much about Rawls and political philosophy over the years include Melina Bell, Ned Diver, John Oberdiek, Paul Litton, Tom Sullivan, Maria Morales, and Jennie Uleman. I am very grateful to Mardy Rawls for correcting the page proofs and providing biographical information and editorial suggestions. Many thanks to Betsy Freeman Fox, who corrected all page proofs, and to Matt Lister and Erin Lareau. I am also grateful to the contributors to the *Cambridge Companion to Rawls*, from whom I learned a good deal in the process of editing that volume.

Among my greatest debts are those owed to Rawls's most conscientious and trenchant critics and commentators: including my teachers Ronald Dworkin, Martha Nussbaum, as well as Robert Nozick, and Burton Dreben, both now deceased; then to G.A. Cohen, Joseph Raz, Brian Barry, Amartya Sen, Thomas Nagel, Jürgen Habermas, Thomas Pogge, Charles Beitz, Jeremy Waldron, Will Kymlicka, Michael Sandel, Philippe van Parijs, and others too numerous to mention whose work is discussed or touched on herein. I have tried to address their criticisms and assessments to some degree, no doubt not satisfactorily enough. Reflection on their criticisms and remarks on Rawls has helped me perhaps more than anything to become clear in my own mind about the ramifications, obscurities, and occasional lacunae in Rawls's positions.

Kathleen Moran, my research assistant, spent many hours formatting and helping me to edit the manuscript and prepare the index; I am especially thankful for her invaluable assistance during the past two years on this and two other manuscripts. I appreciate all the attention that my production editor, Annamarie Kino of Routledge gave to the manuscript, and I am most grateful for her help and advice. Thanks to Brian Leiter for his invitation to write this book. I am grateful to the School of Arts and Sciences at the University of Pennsylvania and to Deans Samuel Preston and Rebecca Bushnell for providing a year's leave in 2005–6, so that I could write the second half of the book. Thanks also to Barbara Fried, Larry Kramer, and the Law School at Stanford University for

providing an office during that year; to Debra Satz, Michael
Bratman, and the Stanford Philosophy Department for their hospi-
tality and accommodations; to Samuel Scheffler, Eric Rakowski,
and Sandy Kadish of the JSP Program at the Law School at UC-
Berkeley for allowing me to be a Kadish Fellow and participate in
their seminars for the year; and finally to my good friend Jay
Wallace of the Philosophy Department at Berkeley, who allowed
me to take over his office to work on this manuscript during my
weekly visits that year.

My wife, Annette Lareau-Freeman, has for years provided me
with sound and sensible advice about how to write this book. She
emphasized the kinds of questions and objections I should
address, as well as those I should avoid. She painstakingly read the
manuscript and urged me to clarify ideas for the benefit of non-
specialists. Above all I appreciate her optimism, and her constant
encouragement and moral support; and for this and so much else I
dedicate this book to her.

Finally, my greatest debt is to John Rawls, who was my teacher
and friend for over twenty-five years. I was a third-year law
student in the mid-1970s when I first read A Theory of Justice, and,
like many people, I felt the book gave philosophical expression to
my most deeply held moral convictions. I decided then (foolishly
perhaps at the time since I had a one-year-old daughter) to give
up a legal career and study political and moral philosophy. After
serving as a law clerk in federal and state courts, I applied to graduate schools, and much to my surprise and good fortune I was
able to study under Jack at Harvard. Thereafter, I regularly talked
with Jack and traveled from Philadelphia to Lexington to visit with
Jack and Mardy at their home two or three times each year. Upon
Jack's request I had the great honor to edit his Collected Papers and,
with Mardy's help, his Lectures on the History of Political Philosophy. He
was a genuinely singular individual. For in addition to being a
world-historical thinker, he was generous and unassuming, and
completely decent and fair-minded, a rare combination of attributes.
Jack's modesty was evident in his self-effacing sense of humor.
For example, towards the end of his life he composed a short
autobiography for his friends, called "Just Jack." Its title derives

from a true story he relates therein, told him by Paul Freund of Harvard Law School. There were once two local judges on the federal courts in Chicago named "Julius Hoffman." To distinguish them Chicago lawyers called one, who was highly respected, "Julius the Just." The other Judge had notoriously presided over the Chicago Seven trial in the 1970s.[2] They called him "just Julius." So Jack took to signing letters and inscribing books for his friends "just Jack." However much he thought of himself, and wanted others to think of him, as "just Jack," he was indeed Jack the Just, the preeminent theorist of justice in the modern era. This book is devoted to his memory.

Abbreviations

The following abbreviations for Rawls's work appear throughout the text.

CP   *Collected Papers*, edited by Samuel Freeman, Cambridge, MA: Harvard University Press, 1999.

JF   *Justice as Fairness: A Restatement*, edited by Erin Kelley, Cambridge, MA: Harvard University Press, 2001.

LHMP   *Lectures on the History of Moral Philosophy*, edited by Barbara Herman, Cambridge, MA: Harvard University Press, 2000.

LHPP   *Lectures on the History of Political Philosophy*, edited by Samuel Freeman, Cambridge, MA: Harvard University Press, 2007.

LP   *The Law of Peoples*, Cambridge, MA: Harvard University Press, 1999.

PL   *Political Liberalism*, New York: Columbia University Press, 1993; revised paperback edition, 1996; expanded edition, 2005.

TJ   *A Theory of Justice*, Cambridge, MA: Harvard University Press, 1971; revised edition, 1999.

1921   born on February 21 in Baltimore, MD, U.S.A., to William Lee Rawls, an attorney, and Anna Abell Stump Rawls

1935–39   attends and graduates from Kent School, an Episcopal preparatory school for boys in Western Connecticut

1943   completes B.A. in Philosophy at Princeton University (Princeton, NJ) in January, and immediately enlists in U.S. Army

1943–46   serves in the US infantry in the Pacific; fights in 36-day battle at Leyte (New Guinea) and 120-day battle at Luzon (Philippines). Serves four months in occupied Japan

1949   marries Margaret Warfield Fox of Philadelphia upon her graduation from Pembroke College at Brown University; four children are born to their marriage of 53 years

1950   receives Ph.D. from Princeton; W.T. Stace supervisor of dissertation on moral worth and moral knowledge, which begins formulation of idea of "reflective equilibrium"

1950–52   instructor at Princeton

1952–53   receives a Fulbright Fellowship to Oxford University (Oxford, U.K.) where he studies with H.L.A. Hart, Isaiah Berlin, and Stuart Hampshire

1953   Assistant and later Associate Professor at Cornell University

1957   publication of the paper "Justice as Fairness" where at the age of thirty-four, Rawls first presents the arguments later developed in *A Theory of Justice*

1959–60 Visiting Associate Professor at Harvard

1960 joins Massachusetts Institute of Technology (MIT, Cambridge, MA) as Professor of Philosophy

1962 joins the Philosophy Department at Harvard University (Cambridge, MA)

1963 publishes "The Sense of Justice," his account of moral psychology later developed as chapter 8 of *A Theory of Justice*

1967 publishes "Distributive Justice," initial account of the difference principle

1969 publishes "The Justification of Civil Disobedience," later revised to appear in chapter 6 of *A Theory of Justice*

1971 publication of *A Theory of Justice*, his most famous work, presenting his well-known accounts of the "original position," "veil of ignorance," "equal basic liberties," and "difference principle." Goes on to sell over half a million copies and is translated into more than 30 languages

1974–75 serves as President of the Eastern Division of the American Philosophical Association

1979 becomes James Bryant Conant University Professor of Philosophy at Harvard

1980 presents three Dewey Lectures at Columbia University, "Kantian Constructivism in Moral Theory," which emphasize centrality of the idea of free and equal moral persons to justice as fairness

1981 presents the Tanner Lectures at University of Michigan, "The Basic Liberties and Their Priority," a significant development of his first principle of justice

1985 publishes "Justice as Fairness: Political, not Metaphysical," a significant stage in development of his doctrine of political liberalism

1987 publication of "The Idea of an Overlapping Consensus," originally presented as the Hart Lecture in Jurisprudence and Moral Philosophy at Oxford University in 1986, in honor of H.L.A. Hart

1989 publishes "Themes in Kant's Moral Philosophy," the initial presentation of his lectures on Kant later published in full in 2000

1991 retires from full-time position at Harvard; continues teaching yearly course in Modern Political Philosophy until 1995

1993   publication of *Political Liberalism*, where Rawls develops the
        ideas of "political constructivism," "overlapping consensus,"
        "public reason," and "public justification." Delivers and
        publishes Amnesty International Lecture, "The Law of
        Peoples," the initial account of his theory of international
        justice

1995   suffers first stroke in October and retires from teaching
        and public lectures, but continues writing

1997   publishes "The Idea of Public Reason Revisted," which he
        regarded as final statement of political liberalism

1999   publication of *The Law of Peoples*, *Collected Papers*, and the
        revised edition of *A Theory of Justice*. Awarded National
        Humanities Medal by President Clinton, and also Rolf
        Schock Prize in Logic and Philosophy

2000   publication of *Lectures on the History of Moral Philosophy*, with
        lectures on Leibniz, Hume, Kant, and Hegel

2001   publication of *Justice as Fairness: A Restatement*, which was
        originally part of his lectures on Modern Political
        Philosophy at Harvard

2002   dies November 22 at home in Lexington, Massachusetts,
        at age 81; buried in Mt. Auburn Cemetery, Cambridge,
        Massachusetts

2007   publication of *Lectures on the History of Political Philosophy*, with
        lectures on Hobbes, Locke, Hume, Rousseau, Mill, Marx,
        Sidgwick, and Butler

One

Introduction

BIOGRAPHY

John Rawls was born in Baltimore, Maryland, 21 February 1921, to William Lee and Anna Abele Stump Rawls. He was the second of five sons, two of whom died in childhood. He grew up in Baltimore, where his father practiced law. John Rawls's mother came from an established and once well-to-do Baltimore family. She was an intelligent and accomplished woman, and an early President of the new League of Women Voters in Baltimore.

His father came from eastern North Carolina, in the area near Greenville. Ill with tuberculosis, his grandfather left North Carolina for Baltimore to be near Johns Hopkins Hospital when Rawls's father was 12. Needing to help the family financially, his father left school at 14 and took a job as "runner" for a law office. Making use of the firm's law library in his free time, Rawls's father taught himself law. With no further formal education, he passed the state bar exam and became a practicing lawyer in 1905, at age 22. In 1911 he became a partner in the law firm of Marbury, Gosnell, and Williams, one of the oldest law firms in the U.S.A. Its founder was the Marbury of the famous Supreme Court case *Marbury v. Madison* (1813), in which Chief Justice Marshall held that the Supreme Court had the power to judicially review the constitutionality of acts of Congress and the Executive branch.

Despite his lack of academic training, Rawls's father was learned, cultivated, and a highly respected lawyer. As early as 1909, he argued before the U.S. Supreme Court a border dispute between West Virginia and Maryland, and in 1930 he was appointed by the Supreme Court as Special Master in a boundary dispute between New Jersey and Delaware. His report was adopted by the Court with high commendation. In 1919 he was elected President of the Bar Association of Baltimore City, probably the youngest man chosen for that office up to that time.

While Rawls's father was a highly successful lawyer, and the family was sufficiently well-to-do to provide the children with excellent educations, he did not handle money well. Upon his death in 1946 he left no will and almost no money. Mrs. Rawls was left quite destitute. Her mental health was affected, and she and her 12-year-old son Richard were thereafter provided for until her death in 1954 by two of her nephews and Rawls's older brother, Bill.

John Rawls attended the Calvert School in Baltimore for six years, then a public school, Roland Park Junior High for two years, while his father was President of the School Board of Baltimore City, after which he attended high school from 1935 to 1939 at the Kent School in western Connecticut, an Episcopal school for boys. He graduated in 1939, and entered Princeton University.

Regarding his reasons for majoring in philosophy at Princeton, Rawls said:

> I never thought of the law, the chosen career of my father and my brother, as I felt that my stammering would prevent that; and besides it never appealed to me any more than business did. In succession I tried various subjects. Chemistry, which I began with, soon proved beyond me, as did mathematics, even more so. I experimented with painting and art. I took a course in music and was told gently by my greatly talented teachers, Roger Sessions and Milton Babbitt, whose talent was really wasted on me, that I should do something else instead. This advice would have gained A.W. Tucker's approval, had he cared; for he muttered, when I told him I had given up the idea of studying mathematics, "I hope you find something you can do, Rawls," as if he couldn't imagine what it might be. Nor at that time could I, but I kept trying and eventually ended up in Philosophy.

Upon graduating from Princeton in January 1943, Rawls promptly joined the U.S. Army as a Private in the Infantry; after basic training he was sent to fight in the Pacific with the 32d Infantry Division (the "Red Arrow Division") in its 128th Infantry Regiment. He fought at the 36-day battle of Leyte in New Guinea, and then fought again at the 120-day Battle of Luzon in the Philippines. Upon drinking from a stream one day without his helmet, an enemy bullet grazed his head, leaving a scar for the rest of his life. As a radio operator Rawls often had to go on dangerous patrols behind enemy lines along the treacherous Villa Verde Trail on Luzon, for which he was awarded a Bronze Star. When General Yamashita, head of the Japanese forces, surrendered on Luzon, around August 21, 1945, Rawls volunteered to take part in a party of about 25 men who were sent deep into the jungle to lead the General out. Since many Japanese soldiers did not know that the war was over, it was a dangerous hike, but Rawls said that he felt he needed to be there on that particular mission. Rawls entered Japan with the occupying forces in September 1945. His troop train went through the remains of Hiroshima soon after its atomic destruction in August 1945, which, together with word of the Holocaust in Europe, had a profound effect upon him. Many of Rawls's friends in his regiment and classmates from Calvert, the Kent School, and Princeton were killed during the war.

Upon completing military service in January 1946, Rawls entered graduate studies in Philosophy at Princeton University on the GI Bill, spending the year 1947–48 at Cornell. He completed and defended his thesis in 1949, just before his marriage, and received the Ph.D. Degree in June 1950. He wrote his dissertation under W.T. Stace, on moral knowledge and judgments on the moral worth of character. Rawls then taught for two years as an Instructor at Princeton (1950–52), after which his contract was not renewed.

Rawls went to Oxford on a post-doctoral Fulbright Fellowship for the academic year 1952–53, where he was a member of the High Table at Christ Church College. Rawls's year at Oxford was one of the most formative of his long career. While at Oxford Rawls was especially influenced by lectures by H.L.A. Hart on the philosophy of law, as well as seminars by Isaiah Berlin and Stuart

Hampshire, and he took part in a periodic discussion group held in Gilbert Ryle's living quarters.

Rawls returned to the U.S.A. in 1953 and went to Cornell University in Ithaca, New York, as Assistant Professor of Philosophy, where he joined his former teacher Norman Malcolm on the faculty, as well as his former Princeton classmates and life-long friends Rogers Albritton and David Sachs. Rawls was soon promoted to tenure, and remained at Cornell until 1959, when he visited Harvard University for one year. He then joined the faculty at MIT (Massachusetts Institute of Technology) in Cambridge, Massachusetts, in 1960. Two years later Rawls assumed a Professorship at Harvard. He remained a member of the standing faculty at Harvard until his retirement in 1991, and continued teaching his course in political philosophy until 1995.

At Harvard Rawls occupied the John Cowles Chair in Philosophy until 1978, when he succeeded Kenneth Arrow as James Bryant Conant University Professor, one of the most prestigious positions at Harvard. *A Theory of Justice* was published in 1971 and was awarded the Phi Beta Kappa Ralph Waldo Emerson Prize in 1972. He was Chairman of the Harvard Philosophy Department from 1970 to 1974, and in 1974–75 was President of the American Philosophical Association, Eastern Division. Rawls was a member of the Harvard Philosophy Department during its greatest years. Among his colleagues were W.V. Quine, Nelson Goodman, Hilary Putnam, Stanley Cavell, Robert Nozick, Rogers Albritton, G.E.L. Owen, Roderick Firth, Israel Scheffler, and his good friend, especially in his later years, the logician Burton Dreben. Rawls's students Martha Nussbaum, Warren Goldfarb, T.M. Scanlon, and then Christine Korsgaard became colleagues in the latter half of his career at Harvard.

In 1999, Rawls was awarded a National Humanities Medal by President Clinton. He was awarded the Rolf Schock Prize in Logic and Philosophy the same year. He received honorary degrees from Oxford, Princeton, and Harvard universities, which were the universities to which he felt a special attachment. A quiet, witty, and modest man, Rawls taught and influenced a great many of America's best-known contemporary philosophers. He was a private person who spent his time either at his work, or with his family and close friends. He regularly declined requests for interviews, and chose not to take an active role in public life. He conscientiously avoided a celebrity status. Rawls believed that philosophers are normally misunderstood when they address the public, and that though philosophy has a major influence on political life, its influence is indirect, taking many years before it becomes a part of a community's moral consciousness.

Rawls's lifelong interest in justice developed out of his early concern (discussed in greater detail in the next section) with the basically religious question: Why is there evil in the world and is human existence redeemable in spite of it? This question eventually led him to inquire whether a just society is realistically possible. His life's work is directed towards discovering what justice requires of us, and showing that it is within human capacities to realize a just society and a just international order.

In his later years Rawls was especially interested in history, particularly books on World War II and on Abraham Lincoln, whom he especially admired as a statesman who did not compromise with evil. These interests are evident in Rawls's late works on justice between nations. Of Rawls, Rogers Albritton of UCLA was quoted in the magazine *Lingua Franca* as saying: "Jack is . . . a man who has an incredibly fine moral sense in his dealings with other human beings. He is not just the author of a great book, he is a very admirable man. He is the best of us."

In 1949 Rawls married Margaret Warfield Fox of Baltimore, upon her graduation from Pembroke College in Brown University. Mrs. Rawls is an artist, has been active in local politics in Lexington, Massachusetts, and has worked in Environmental Planning for the state. Among her many portraits are several of John Rawls. She assisted in the editing and production of John Rawls's final books. Four children were born to John and Margaret Rawls. The Rawls family lived in a large nineteenth-century white-frame house in Lexington, Massachusetts, beginning in 1960, where Mrs. Rawls continues to reside.

In 1995 Rawls suffered the first of a series of strokes. In spite of declining health, he continued to work for most of the remaining seven years of his life. With the help of Mrs. Rawls and his friend Burton Dreben, he completed the important Second Introduction to *Political Liberalism*, 'The Idea of Public Reason Revisited," and his short book *The Law of Peoples*. Rawls also oversaw the editing and publication of his *Collected Papers* and two sets of his lectures in philosophy, *Lectures on the History of Moral Philosophy* and *Justice as Fairness: A Restatement*. His *Lectures on the History of Political Philosophy* will appear in 2007. With Rawls's approval Mrs. Rawls did considerable preliminary copy-editing on the latter two books. John Rawls died at home on November 24, 2002, three months before his 82nd birthday.

In an interview in 1990 Rawls said about *A Theory of Justice*: "Its size and scope was a little mad, actually. In writing it I guessed it was about 350 pages; when it was put in galleys and the Press told me it was nearly 600 pages (587 to be exact) I was astounded." He said that after completing that book, "I had planned on doing some other things mainly connected with the third part of the book, which was the part I liked best, the part on moral psychology. . . . I have never gotten around to that." In some yet-to-be-published remarks on "My Teaching" (1993), Rawls says:

> The part of the book I always liked best was the third, on moral psychology. The reception of my book, though, took me by surprise and I looked for an explanation. I suppose it has some merit, but I have always believed that most of its wider appeal lay in the situation at that time, the time of the Vietnam war and the state of academic and political culture then. For a long period there had been but few works of that kind – I think of Berlin and Hart, Barry and Walzer – hence there was, it seems, a felt need for them. The book gave a demonstration, however faulty, that its subjects could be talked about as a coherent part of philosophy, supported by quite reasonable arguments, and not simply as the expression of one's opinions and sentiments. I decided I should study many of the criticisms, as there were very good objections from people such as Arrow, Sen, and Harsanyi, as well as from Hart and Nagel, Nozick and Scanlon, to mention a few. I wanted

to find ways to strengthen the idea of justice as fairness and to meet their objections.

Of his teaching Rawls said:

> [One] thing I tried to do was to present each writer's thought in what I took to be its strongest form. I took to heart Mill's remark in his review of [Adam] Sedgwick: "A doctrine is not judged at all until it is judged in its best form" (*CW*: X, 52). So I tried to do just that. Yet I didn't say, not intentionally anyway, what to my mind they should have said, but what they did say, supported by what I viewed as the most reasonable interpretation of their text. The text had to be known and respected, and the doctrine presented it in its best form. Leaving aside the text seemed offensive, a kind of pretending. If I departed from it – no harm in that – I had to say so. Lecturing that way, I believed that a writer's views became stronger and more convincing, and would be for students a more worthy object of study.
>
> Several maxims guided me in doing this. I always assumed, for example, that the writers we were studying were always much smarter than I was. If they were not, why was I wasting my time and the students' time by studying them? If I saw a mistake in their arguments, I supposed they saw it too and must have dealt with it, but where? So I looked for their way out, not mine. Sometimes their way out was historical: in their day the question need not be raised; or wouldn't arise or be fruitfully discussed. Or there was a part of the text I had overlooked, or hadn't read.
>
> We learn moral and political philosophy, and indeed any other part of philosophy by studying the exemplars – those noted figures who have made cherished attempts – and we try to learn from them, and if we are lucky, to find a way to go beyond them. My task was to explain Hobbes, Locke and Rousseau, or Hume, Leibniz and Kant as clearly and forcefully as I could, always attending carefully to what they actually said.

The result was that I was loath to raise objections to the exemplars – that's too easy and misses what is essential – though it was important to point out objections that those coming later in the same tradition sought to correct, or to point to views those in another tradition thought were mistaken. (I think here of the social contract view and utilitarianism as two traditions.) Otherwise philosophical thought can't progress and it would be mysterious why later writers made the criticisms they did.

MOTIVATIONS UNDERLYING RAWLS'S LIFEWORK

It is difficult to say what a great philosopher's motivations are in setting forth a philosophical position. Fortunately some philosophers are explicit about their aims. In his lectures Rawls emphasized the importance of reading the preface to any philosophical work, to gain an understanding of a philosopher's reasons for writing the book. In the Preface to *A Theory of Justice*, Rawls indicates that one of his primary aims is to set forth the most appropriate moral conception of justice for a democratic society, a moral conception that was better suited to interpreting the democratic values of freedom and equality than the reigning utilitarian tradition. For this reason, Rawls says, he sought to revive the philosophical doctrine of the social contract that stems from _ Locke, Rousseau, and Kant. Rawls's concern with democratic justice increasingly came to dominate his aims in the latter half of his career, in working out the position he called "political liberalism." But prior to his nearly exclusive focus on democratic justice, Rawls was led to political philosophy by a concern for more general questions.

In his junior and senior years at Princeton Rawls became deeply interested in theology and its relation to ethics. Rawls's undergraduate honors thesis at Princeton was on the religious problems of humanity's sinfulness and the possibility of community.[1] His interest led to his career plans to attend Divinity School and enter the Episcopal ministry. But service in World War II intervened. The war and his experience as a soldier caused him to rethink his religion and particularly the possibility of human goodness.

Horrendous evil leads people to have strikingly different convictions about humanity and religion. Orthodox Christian doctrine is in many respects built around an assumption of the corruption of human nature, which purportedly explains why there is such great evil in the world.[2] "Original sin" was not just Adam's and Eve's Fall, but a pronouncement of the original flawed character that resides in all human beings and motivates their actions. The mass carnage of World War II led Rawls to question these and other religious beliefs. Why would a benevolent God create humans so that they were *naturally* inclined to accept, not to mention engage in, such mass slaughter and destruction of other humans? Rather than inspiring Rawls to reaffirm Christian doctrine, the horrendous evil of World War II led him to renounce it. He abandoned Christianity because the morality of God (as opposed to the morality of mankind) made no sense to him. In his unpublished remarks on his religion, Rawls said:

> When Lincoln interprets the Civil War as God's punishment for the sin of slavery, deserved equally by North and South, God is seen as acting justly. But the Holocaust can't be interpreted in that way, and all attempts to do so that I have read of are hideous and evil. To interpret history as expressing God's will, God's will must accord with the most basic ideas of justice as we know them. For what else can the most basic justice be? Thus, I soon came to reject the idea of the supremacy of the divine will as also hideous and evil.

The problem Rawls found with Christianity was not simply that God allowed to happen such evils as the Holocaust and the indiscriminate bombing and destruction of German and Japanese cities and their civilian populations. Rawls questioned how a benevolent God worthy of veneration could exist who *created* the human species so that its will was naturally corrupt and predestined to commit evils, large and small. Rawls also could not make sense of a God who selectively intervenes in the world in response to prayers, and even then only in response to prayers by Christian believers. Surely the prayers of the millions who died in the

Holocaust should have moved God to do something in response? For these and other reasons the actions of the Christian God seemed completely arbitrary to Rawls. Such an arbitrary Being was not worthy of faith and veneration by us. Rawls said:

> These doctrines all became impossible for me to take seriously, not in the sense that the evidence for them was weak or doubtful. Rather, they depict God as a monster moved solely by God's own power and glory. As if such miserable and distorted puppets as humans were described could glorify anything!

Finally, Rawls believed that Christianity and religion generally had the wrong attitude towards morality. The great religions say a god is necessary, not simply to enforce justice and counter human immorality, but in order to create morality and the realm of value. But if God were to be conceived as good and worthy of veneration, then morality and value must have some original source other than God's will. Surely God must have reasons for the moral laws He issues; and if so then morality and justice must have their basis in reasons accessible to rational beings like us. Rawls said in his unpublished remarks on "My Religion":

> Reasoning in its most basic forms is invariant with respect to the various kinds of beings that exercise it. Hence God's being, however great the divine powers, does not determine the essential canons of reason. Moreover . . . the basic judgments of reasonableness must be the same, whether made by God's reason or by ours. This invariant content of reasonableness – without which our thought collapses – doesn't allow otherwise, however pious it might seem to attribute everything to the divine will.

Rawls believed that morality had no need for a god to justify it. Instead, if there is to be justified belief in any god's existence it depends upon the needs of morality. Like Kant, Rawls believed that, if God were needed for morality, it would be in order to provide us with the confidence that the "realistic utopia" of a just society and just world are possible. For without the confidence that justice can be achieved on earth, reasonable people might become skeptical, lose their sense of justice, and eventually lapse into cynicism and injustice. For Kant, this possibility led to the Postulate that God exists in order to guarantee that the human good (happiness) is "congruent" with a person's justice and moral virtue. Rawls resorted to non-religious argument to show that justice and the human good were "congruent" and hence that a fully just or "well-ordered" society is a "realistic utopia."

Rawls's concern for the possibility of achieving justice and its compatibility with human nature and the human good were driving influences behind his written work. It explains in large part his focus in *A Theory of Justice* on moral psychology and the development of the sense of justice, as well as the problems of the feasibility and "stability" of a conception of justice and whether justice is a rational way of life. It also underlies Rawls's subsequent revisions to justice as fairness and his transition to political liberalism. Finally, it is behind his rejection of cosmopolitanism and a global distribution principle and other elements of his account of the Law of Peoples. All this will be discussed in due course. The biographical point deserving emphasis here is that, in rejecting Christian doctrine, Rawls was rejecting Christianity's pessimism about human nature and its skepticism of humanity's capacities for justice, to find meaning in this life, and to redeem itself. Rawls attests to the centrality of this concern in the concluding paragraph of his last publication, *The Law of Peoples*:

> If a reasonably just Society of Peoples whose members subordinate their power to reasonable aims is not possible, and human beings are largely amoral, if not incurably cynical and self-centered, one might ask, with Kant, whether it is worthwhile for human beings to live on the earth.[3]
>
> (*LP*, 128)

A fundamental assumption of Rawls's moral psychology is that humans are not naturally corrupt, amoral, or moved purely by selfish motives but have genuine dispositions to sociability. If social cooperation – as opposed to efficiently coordinated behavior – is to be possible, humans must normally have an effective sense of justice, or willingness to abide by fair terms of cooperation. Rawls believed that humans are capable of regulating their pursuits according to justice's requirements and are able to will and to do justice for its own sake even when it imposes demands that conflict with our most important aims. Justice is compatible with human nature – we are not prone to religious or secular versions of original sin. Moreover, Rawls long sought to show how appropriate exercise of our sense of justice is compatible with the human good, and how justice is worth realizing for its own sake. It is difficult to understand Rawls without these assumptions and aspirations.

HISTORICAL INFLUENCES

Contemporary Influences

Rawls's research agenda was only mildly influenced by the contemporary discussions in moral and political philosophy. In the 1950s and 1960s, moral philosophy was largely focused on "meta-ethical" questions regarding the meaning of moral terms and the possibility of true moral statements. Conceptual analysis, largely inspired by Oxford ordinary language philosophy, held sway in philosophical discussions in moral philosophy. However much he was influenced early on by Wittgenstein and Oxford philosophy in other ways, Rawls believed that the analysis of moral concepts, though it could prove useful, by itself reveals little about the substance of moral principles. "The analysis of moral concepts and the a priori . . . is too slender a basis," he says, for developing a moral theory (TJ, 51/44 rev.).

Rawls developed the idea of the original position independently in the early 1950s, starting from an idea in his doctoral thesis, part of which was published as his first paper, "Outline for a Decision Procedure in Ethics" (1951).[4] In this paper Rawls suggests an account of moral justification of "reasonable principles" for resolving conflicts of interests. This account is framed in terms of a hypothetical "reasonable decision procedure" in which "competent judges," who are reasonable and have "sympathetic knowledge of human interests," seek principles of resolution that account for their "considered moral judgments." "Reasonable principles" are those that are "acceptable to all, or nearly all, competent judges" (CP, 11). Rawls says in his 1990 interview with *The Harvard Review of Philosophy* that he started collecting notes that later evolved into *A Theory of Justice* in Fall 1950, after completing his thesis. During this period he studied economics with W.J. Baumol, and read closely Paul Samuelson on general equilibrium theory and welfare economics, J.R. Hicks's *Value and Capital*, Walras's *Elements*, Frank Knight's *Ethics of Competition*, and Von Neumann and Morgenstern's seminal work in game theory.

> As a result of all these things, somehow – don't ask me how – plus the stuff on moral theory which I wrote my thesis on – it was out of that, in 1950–51, that I got the idea that eventually turned into the original position. The idea was to design a constitution of discussion out of which would come reasonable principles of justice. At that time I had a more complicated procedure than what I finally came up with.
>
> *HRP*: Did you publish that original more complicated formula?
>
> No, I couldn't work it out.[5]

Rawls was largely self-taught in political philosophy. The only course he had in political philosophy was as an undergraduate at Princeton, taught by the Wittgenstein student and philosopher of language Norman Malcolm. Rawls nowhere mentions the influence of his thesis supervisor, the Hegel scholar W.T. Stace. For the most part Rawls seems to have learned the great classics in political and moral philosophy on his own. He sought to engage and critically come to terms with the works of the major moral and political philosophers since Plato and Aristotle. In many respects his philosophy is a continuing conversation with them. Rawls's interpretations of the major modern political and moral philosophers since Hobbes are available in his published lectures, and a reader can gain invaluable insight into Rawls's works on justice through these lectures. In moral philosophy these include extensive lectures on Kant, as well as on Leibniz's perfectionism and Hume's utilitarianism, and Hegel's philosophy of right, all collected in Rawls's *Lectures on the History of Moral Philosophy*, as well as lectures on Joseph Butler's moral psychology in Rawls's *Lectures on the History of Political Philosophy*. The latter book contains lectures on the political and moral philosophy of the social contractarians Hobbes, Locke, and Rousseau, the utilitarians Hume, Sidgwick, and J.S. Mill, and on Karl Marx. There is not the space here to dwell at length on Rawls's lectures on the great historical figures that so profoundly influenced him. At most I can only touch upon some highlights.

Rawls and the Social Contract Tradition

Rawls says that his aim in *Theory* is to "generalize and carry to a higher order of abstraction the traditional theory of the social contract as represented by Locke, Rousseau, and Kant" (TJ, viii/xviii rev.). One of the major philosophical accomplishments of Rawls's work has been to revive this long-moribund but still world-historical tradition in political philosophy. Social contract doctrine once provided the primary justification for the democratic and republican revolutions of the eighteenth century, including the American Declaration of Independence and the French Declaration of the Rights of Man. But since David Hume's and Jeremy Bentham's utilitarian arguments against it, social contract doctrine was not taken seriously among political and moral philosophers, even though the idea of a "social contract" was celebrated in popular political lore.

The basic idea of this "natural rights" theory of the social contract (as Rawls terms it, see TJ, 32/28 rev.) is that a legitimate constitution is one that could be agreed to among free and equal persons from a position of equal right and equal political jurisdiction. What primarily distinguishes this natural rights tradition from Hobbes and Hobbesian contract views is that natural rights theories made certain moral assumptions about individuals' rights and duties from the outset, which function as moral conditions and constraints upon the social contract and any resulting laws agreed to. In this tradition rational persons are assumed to be equally free by natural right (*de jure*) and to have equal rights of political jurisdiction to govern themselves, as well as certain personal rights (freedom of conscience, for example) which they cannot alienate. Locke assumes that an "equal right to natural freedom" is a "Law of Nature," while Kant says that the "Innate Right of Freedom" is the sole original right that belongs to all persons by virtue of their humanity, and that this right contains within itself the "Innate Equality" of mankind.[6] On Rawls's interpretation of Locke's social contract, a legitimate constitution is one that could be contracted into by free persons from a position of equal right and equal political jurisdiction (defined by a state of nature), without anyone violating another's, or alienating his or her own, natural rights, or without anyone having to violate any of the duties owed to God to preserve oneself and the rest of mankind, or without doing anything irrational that would make oneself worse off than in a state of nature.[7]

By contrast Hobbesian contract doctrines assume that rational persons are either self-interested, or at most aim to advance only their own interests and conceptions of the good; there are no moral constraints, such as others' moral rights, on their rational pursuit of their interests prior to the social contract. The Hobbesian social contract is a rational compromise among essentially conflicting interests, where all parties agree to cooperate by observing certain reasonable constraints on condition that others abide by them too, in order that all may effectively pursue their own interests. In Hobbes's account purely rational individuals are moved to secure their fundamental interests in their own self-preservation, their conjugal affections, and procuring the means for commodious living; to do so they agree to authorize one person, the Sovereign, to exercise whatever political power the Sovereign deems necessary to enforce the Articles of Peace. Hobbes's social contract is an Authorization Agreement whereby one person is authorized by everyone to exercise nearly absolute power *de jure* (and absolute power in fact) to maintain peace and promote conditions of prosperity.[8]

Rawls's original position in effect combines elements from both the natural right theory and the Hobbesian theory of the social contract. Like Hobbesian views, the parties to Rawls's social contract – the "original position" – make a purely rational choice: they are not morally motivated, but aim only to choose terms of cooperation that best advance their own particular good and their fundamental interests (which Rawls defines differently than Hobbes). Still, Rawls's social contract position differs considerably from Hobbesian views in that he denies that moral principles of justice are simply the product of a purely rational choice designed to promote individual interest. Like Locke's, Rousseau's, and Kant's natural rights positions, Rawls structures his social contract so that its parties' judgments are constrained by moral conditions, primarily the "veil of ignorance" and the five formal constraints of Right. The veil renders Rawls's contractors ignorant of all facts about themselves and society; thereby they are led to an impartial decision. As Locke's parties are explicitly prohibited from agreeing to anything that would compromise anyone's equal rights to freedom of conscience, so Rawls's parties are prohibited, in effect, from agreeing to principles of justice that would compromise this and other basic liberties.

The hypothetical nature of Rawls's agreement in the original position resembles Kant's idea of the Original Contract, which Kant says is a hypothetical, and not a real, social contract. On Rawls's reading, *all* the major proponents of the social contract tradition, from Hobbes through Locke, Rousseau, and down to Kant, regard the social contract as a hypothetical thought experiment that is designed to show what are the most reasonable terms of cooperation among rational persons who are regarded as equals. It is not essential to the argument of any of the major proponents of social contract doctrine whether there has been or will ever be any actual social contract by all (adult) members of a society. The fact that people actually agree to something, even if they do so unanimously, is of no moral import by itself, unless their agreement first satisfies various reasonable (moral) and rational (evaluative) conditions, they have adequate knowledge, appreciate relevant facts, reason correctly, and so on.

Consider now Hume's and Bentham's utilitarian criticism of social contract doctrine. Hume's basic criticism of Locke and the "Whig doctrine of consent" is that the legitimate exercise of political power, and individuals' duties of allegiance to respect it and obey the laws, cannot be justified by people's consent. For not only has no such consent ever been given anywhere, but even if it had sometime in the distant past, we cannot be bound by the promises of our forebears. And even if people now consent to government's powers, still we need ask: Why should people be held to their promises and agreements to respect the laws and obey political authority? For surely there is nothing sacrosanct about such agreements when they result in great harm to others or to those who make them. Hume says that the only justification for keeping our promises and agreements is that it promotes public utility, "the convenience and necessities of mankind."9 But the legitimacy of governments, our duty of allegiance, and the duty to obey laws, have the same foundation, in public utility. It is then an unnecessary shuffle to seek to justify these duties by appeal to the duty to keep our promises. Social contract doctrine, Hume concludes, is superficial and unnecessary; it does not represent the true reasons for our political duties.

Hume's criticism has been generalized and applied to Rawls's and other contemporary contractarian views (such as T.M. Scanlon's).10 We will later consider how Rawls's contract doctrine fares in the face of this forceful objection. In Rawls's lectures on Hume's "Of the Original Contract," Rawls says that Hume misreads Locke in several respects. To begin with, as a test for the legitimacy of political constitutions, Locke's social contract does not require actual consent. Even if our forebears had entered into a social contract and agreed to the constitution, this is not what makes our constitution legitimate now. Instead, Locke's social contract doctrine says (says Rawls) that no government is legitimate unless it could have been agreed to by rational individuals, starting from a position of equal right and equal political jurisdiction, without anyone's violating their duties to God or mankind, or alienating their fundamental moral rights, or agreeing to anything that would make them worse off than in a (somewhat benign Lockean) state of nature. Whether a constitution passes this test of constitutional legitimacy is a philosophical and not a historical question.

By contrast with Locke's contractarian account of political legitimacy, Locke's account of *individuals' political obligations*, including their duties of allegiance towards particular regimes, *does* say that actual express consent is required for anyone to become a permanent member of a society. The mere fact that I was born in the U.S. should not make me a citizen; citizenship should depend upon my giving my express consent to join this political society and undertaking the duties of citizenship that it imposes (fighting its just wars, serving on juries, etc.). Of course, our duty to obey the laws of a society is something different, and should not require our having given our consent, for this would give people leeway to disobey the law at will. But contrary to Hume's reading, Locke never says that actual consent is required for this duty. For Locke our duty to obey the laws of a legitimate constitution stem from our natural duties to God to preserve ourselves and the rest of mankind, which include duties to respect others' persons and property. But whatever Locke's positions on the duties to obey the laws and bear allegiance towards particular governments, they should not be confused with his social contract thesis. That thesis is a hypothetical test for determining, not these or other duties of individuals, but the legitimacy of political constitutions and the duties of governments who are their agents.

If this is a fair response to Hume, then, as Rawls contends, Hume's substantive criticism that Locke's social contract is an unnecessary shuffle can only be assessed by applying both Hume's principle of utility and Locke's social contract to see whether they identify the very same types of government as legitimate and illegitimate. Only if they do is Hume's argument against Locke successful. The problem is that it is difficult to see why the constitutions that *could* be agreed to from a position of equal right (Locke's standard) should exactly correspond with the constitutions that best promote public utility (Hume's standard). Hume himself had reservations about resistance to absolute monarchies, the very form of government Locke condemns via his social contract theory. Unless it can be shown that Hume's test of public utility justifies the very same constitutions justified by Locke's social contract doctrine, then Hume's criticism that Locke's doctrine is redundant fails. One begins to suspect that the traditional utilitarian argument against social contract doctrines is based upon misunderstanding the point.

Rousseau

While Locke's contract doctrine is among the most significant philosophical defenses of liberalism, Rousseau's contract doctrine is one of the most impassioned, brilliant, and yet enigmatic philosophical defenses of democracy. There are at least three important aspects of Rousseau's position that have parallels in Rawls.

First, there is Rousseau's doctrine of natural goodness, including his rejection of the Christian doctrine of original sin and the Hobbesian account of human nature as purely self-interested and naturally indifferent to others' fates.[11] Rawls largely accepted the Rousseauian position that the kind of person we are is partially determined by the social and political institutions we create and maintain. Humans, like all creatures, are motivated by "self-love" and a concern for their own good, but this is not our only motivation. Humans also have natural social inclinations, including a natural capacity for sympathy and compassion with their fellow beings, which can be either encouraged or extinguished by their social circumstances. Moreover, humans are capable of justice and under normal circumstances of social life they develop a sense of justice directed towards those with whom they stand in cooperative relations. Rawls mentions the account of moral learning in Rousseau's *Emile* as the beginning of a tradition in moral psychology that profoundly influenced his account of the stages of moral development and the sense of justice (TJ, 459–60/402–3 rev.).

Second, Rawls affirms Rousseau's idea that equal rights of political participation are central to individual freedom. In Locke's social contract it is envisioned that the large majority of people will alienate their natural political rights in order to gain the benefits of political society. Equal political rights are then not among the inalienable liberties; Locke was a liberal but not a democrat. Rawls accepts Rousseau's position that to alienate one's political liberties is to give up a large part of one's freedom, including the primary bases for individual self-respect (proper *amour propre*). Rawls did not endorse Rousseau's romantic conception of direct democracy, requiring that citizens actively take part in legislating the laws. Except for citizens' direct participation in local government affairs (town meetings, etc.), it is impractical for most purposes in modern societies. But like Rousseau, Rawls regarded the realization of one's status as an equal citizen of fundamental significance and essential to a person's good. Democratic engagement and participation is the primary activity for development and exercise of the capacity for the sense of justice.

Third, Rousseau's doctrine of the General Will influenced Rawls's account of voting and also his account of public reason. For Rousseau it is citizens' and legislators' duty to vote, not their "particular will" or personal preferences of a majority, but instead their conscientious and informed judgments regarding the common good. The common good for Rousseau is justice, which consists in the measures needed to achieve the freedom and equality of citizens. To vote the general will is then to vote what is required by justice. Rawls endorses this position in his account of democracy. Legislators are to vote their considered judgments regarding the laws mandated by the principles of justice (TJ, sect. 54). "The legislative discussion must be conceived not as a contest between interests, but as an attempt to find the best policy as defined by the principles of justice. . . . An impartial legislator's only desire is to make the correct decision in this regard . . . " (TJ, 357/314 rev.). Rawls's account of democracy has stimulated much of the current discussions on "deliberative democracy."[12] Connected with deliberative democracy is Rawls's idea of public reason, an idea also found initially in Rousseau and then Kant.[13] For Rawls, public reasons are the considerations that citizens and legislators should rely upon in coming to a decision on laws and public policies. We should not vote on the basis of what Rousseau calls our "private reasons," but only the balance of public reasons. One role of a liberal conception of justice is to provide the "content of public reason."

Kant

Rawls's lengthy lectures on Kant (nearly 200 pages in LHMP) indicate that Kant is the philosopher who most profoundly influenced him. From the idea of "the priority of right over the good" and the Kantian interpretation of justice as fairness in *A Theory of Justice*, to Kantian (and later Political) Constructivism and the Independence of Moral Theory, then the conception of moral personality and the distinction between the Reasonable and the Rational in *Political Liberalism*, and finally the rejection of a world state and the idea of a "realistic utopia" in Rawls's *Law of Peoples*, one can discern that many of Rawls's main ideas were deeply influenced by his understanding of Kant.

Rawls is often interpreted as grounding his conception of justice in an interpretation of Kant's idea of respect for persons. But here again, Rawls insists that it is a mistake to think that a moral conception can be arrived at by analyzing or interpreting the ideas of "respect or of the inherent worth of persons (or any other fundamental ideas). It is precisely these ideas that call for interpretation" (TJ, 586/513 rev.). It might be said that Rawls's work elucidates the idea of "respect for persons as free and equal moral persons who are both reasonable and rational." But even this does not say much until one begins to fill in Rawls's definitions of these obscure concepts and the principles that are associated with these and other central ideas in his theory. Just as Kant thought that to respect humanity as an end-in-itself requires that we abide by the categorical imperative, for Rawls to respect persons fully as free, equal, reasonable, and rational requires that we cooperate with them on terms specified by the principles of justice. So far as we aim to uncover the meaning of respect for persons for Rawls, it is explicated by justice as fairness.

Kant had little direct influence on Rawls's initial drafts of *A Theory of Justice* in the 1950s and 1960s (most of the first six chapters and chapter 8 on the sense of justice). The Kantian interpretation of justice as fairness (TJ, sect. 40) was written relatively late and was incorporated into *A Theory of Justice* primarily to show how justice as fairness is "congruent" with the good (TJ, sect. 86). After *Theory* Rawls increasingly came to be influenced by Kant. Only in Rawls's final works did he seek to distance himself from Kant, to avoid controversial foundations for political liberalism (LP, 86–87).

Kant's moral philosophy, not so much his political philosophy, influenced Rawls. Most of what he regarded as important in Kant's political philosophy he attributed to Locke and Rousseau, and involved Kant's development of their views (e.g., the innate right of freedom, the original contract, the general will, and so on). The exception is Kant's writings on international justice, which influenced Rawls's *The Law of Peoples*. Compare the concluding paragraph of *The Law of Peoples* (set forth at the end of the third section above) with Rawls's explanation of Kant's idea of "reasonable faith": "Reasonable political faith . . . is the faith that such a peaceful international society of peoples is possible and favored by forces of nature. To abandon this faith is to give up on peace and democracy; and that we can never do as long as we affirm both the moral law and human freedom" (LHMP, 321). The parallel between Kant's idea of the Kingdom (or Realm) of Ends and Rawls's idea of a well-ordered society deserves mention. As Kant's realm of ends is a social world in which everyone accepts and complies with the categorical imperative, Rawls's well-ordered society is a social world where all accept and normally satisfy the principles of justice. Moreover, as conscientious moral agents apply the categorical imperative by reasoning about maxims that are generally acceptable in a realm of ends, Rawls's parties in the original position choose principles of justice that will be generally acceptable among members of a well-ordered society (TJ, 453–54/397–98 rev.).

Utilitarianism: Hume, Sidgwick, and Mill

Hume's account of the convention of justice was one of the first major historical influences upon Rawls. Rawls's second article, "Two Concepts of Rules," attempts to make sense of utilitarianism largely along lines that Hume suggests, defending it against common objections to utilitarianism. Rawls suggests that we should conceive of justice in terms of the rules of a social practice, or "convention," as Hume says. With Hume, Rawls contends that promising and contractual agreements, property, punishment, and political constitutions are all social practices that can be designed in different ways, and which can only be understood by reference to the rules constituting these practices. To justify actions within such a practice – for example, a decision whether or not to keep one's promise – one appeals to the rules of the practice and what it forbids or allows: appealing to these rules is what is involved in giving a moral justification of the action. By contrast, to justify the practice itself, or changes to the rules of the practice, one is to appeal to some more abstract principle. Rawls suggests, following Hume, that this is how to understand the role of the principle of utility. It misunderstands utilitarianism as a social doctrine to regard it as appropriate to appeal to the principle of utility in deciding whether to follow the rules of a practice or how to act within the practice. The principle of utility is not best conceived as a rule for directly guiding individual choices in particular actions. It is sensibly applied only indirectly to actions, via its role in determining and justifying the social rules individuals ought to follow and appeal to in the normal course of daily life.

Hume's account of justice, joined with Wittgenstein's idea of a practice, influenced Rawls's later account of social institutions, as well as Rawls's idea that principles of justice apply in the first instance, not directly to determine individual actions, but to the rules of institutions constituting the basic structure of society. As Hume regarded a just person as one who regularly complied with the rules of the conventions of justice, for Rawls, to act justly is to comply with the rules of basic institutions that conform to principles of justice. Here too Hume's account of the sense of justice, as a disposition to comply with rules of justice, also influenced Rawls's account of that moral sentiment.

Henry Sidgwick's *Methods of Ethics* (7th ed., 1907) was for Rawls the major statement and defense of the classical utilitarian tradition. It provides the canonical statement of classical utilitarianism against which Rawls argues in *A Theory of Justice*. Sidgwick also substantially influenced two other important features of Rawls's position. First, there is Sidgwick's methodology, which involved the comparative study of the major traditions in moral philosophy in order to determine which position best met the criteria of a "rational method" of ethics. Like Sidgwick's criteria for a rational method, the original position is designed to incorporate "all the relevant requirements of practical reason," (PL, 90) so that it may serve as a method of selection to decide upon the most reasonable conception of justice from among an array of alternatives. Rawls also follows Sidgwick in regarding Intuitionism and Perfectionism as among the "methods" of ethics that are to be compared with utilitarianism. Unlike Sidgwick, Rawls did not see Rational Egoism as a moral conception at all. Sidgwick's account of rational individual choice provided Rawls with many elements for his account of a person's good, as well as suggesting to Rawls the point of view of "deliberative rationality" from which a person is to reflect upon and determine his or her own rational plan of life.

At the same time, Rawls adamantly rejects Sidgwick's hedonism and his view that pleasurable experiences are the final aim of all rational desire; Rawls argues instead for a plurality of intrinsic human goods. The semi-perfectionist account of the human good implicit in Rawls's account of the Aristotelian Principle is influenced by Mill's rejection of hedonism and his argument that the "higher pleasures" are qualitatively superior in kind to the "lower pleasures." Like Mill, Rawls contends that it is a fact of human nature that, when people take advantage of opportunities to develop and educate their natural abilities, they normally prefer ways of life that involve the development and exercise of their higher capacities. From the point of view of deliberative rationality Rawls contends that it is rational for a person to incorporate the realization of certain higher activities into his or her plan of life. As in Mill's account of individuality, for Rawls a condition of realizing one's rational good is that the plan of life that a person leads be one that is freely chosen by that person. This explains his curious claim that, in spite of the Aristotelian Principle, still it is possible that a person's *rational* good involves living a life plan devoting enormous time and energy to counting blades of grass. However wasteful and irrational such a life might otherwise seem for perfectionists, it could be rational for a person to live that life so long as it is a fully informed life plan that is *freely* chosen and affirmed in deliberative rationality. It is for this reason that I call Rawls a "semi-perfectionist" in his account of a person's good: *autonomous choice* of a life plan is a necessary condition of living a good life, even if one's life is otherwise wasted in trivial, indeed worthless, activity. But this, as I understand him, is also Mill's view.

Finally, J.S. Mill's principle of liberty bears obvious resemblances to Rawls's first principle of justice. This becomes especially apparent in Rawls's lectures on Mill, where he interprets Mill's principle of liberty as protecting, not "liberty as such," but roughly the same basic liberties that are part of Rawls's first principle. Also Mill's defense of representative democracy influenced Rawls's justification of political rights of participation in *A Theory of Justice* (TJ, 233–34/204–06 rev.). Two main arguments Rawls gives for democracy are based in Mill's contention that equal political rights enable persons to politically defend their basic rights and liberties, and also that democratic participation requires that people take into account interests that are not their own, and thereby broadens their sympathies and educates their moral sentiments. Rawls later relies upon the latter argument as one of the main reasons for equal political rights, to emphasize the central role of participation in democratic public life in the development and exercise of the sense of justice.

Hegel and Marx

Hegel had little direct influence on Rawls's initial working out of the main ideas of *A Theory of Justice*. He is mentioned three times, and each time he is said to hold a position that Rawls rejects.[14] But after *Theory* Rawls emphasized certain parallels between his position and Hegel's, in contrast with Kant's view.[15] First, like Hegel, Rawls says he rejects the dualisms implicit in Kant's transcendental philosophy (CP, 303–4) – between the analytic and synthetic, a priori vs. a posteriori, and reason in its pure vs. empirical uses, for example.[16] This is most evident in Rawls's position that natural facts and regularities are highly relevant to justifying first principles of justice. Rawls calls upon the findings of psychology, economics, sociology, biology, history, and other empirical inquiries to justify his principles of justice. It was important for him to set forth principles of justice that are attuned to the requirements and limitations of human nature and the possibilities of social life. As we shall see, this is due, among other reasons, to Rawls's concern that justice be compatible with the human good.

Rawls also resembles Hegel and departs from Kant in emphasizing the social bases of moral principles of justice. One of Hegel's "great contributions," Rawls says, is to discern the "deep social rootedness of people within an established framework of their political and social institutions . . . A Theory of Justice follows Hegel in this respect when it takes the basic structure of society as the first subject of justice."[17] Like Hegel too, Rawls's position implies that moral and political autonomy can only be achieved within an appropriate social framework. He says of Hegel, "It is only within a rational (reasonable) social world, one that by the structure of its institutions guarantees our freedom, that we can lead lives that are fully rational and good."[18] A similar position is implicit in Rawls's argument for the congruence of the right and the good in A Theory of Justice: It is only within a well-ordered society of justice as fairness that free and equal individuals can achieve their full autonomy as reasonable and rational beings.

Related to the social bases of justice and individuals' freedom, Rawls finds parallels in Hegel's idea of justification with his (Rawls's) own emphasis upon the social and public role of a political conception of justice in providing a public basis for justification (see CP, 426, 426n.). The idea of the social role of a conception of justice bears some resemblance to Hegel's idea of philosophy as reconciliation. Hegel says: "What it ["the truth about right" or justice] needs is to be comprehended so that the content which is already rational [vernünftig, which Rawls translates as "reasonable"] in itself may also gain a rational [reasonable] form and thereby appear justified to free thinking." Of this passage Rawls says:

> To become reconciled to our social world does not mean to become resigned to it. . . . Rather, reconciliation means that we have come to see our social world as a form of life in political and social institutions that realizes our essence – that is, the basis of our dignity as persons who are free. It will "thereby appear justified to free thinking."
>
> (*LHMP*, 331)

Rawls's accounts of moral and political autonomy both require (like Hegel, and Rawls says like Marx too) that people publicly know and accept the bases of their political and social relations, which in turn realize their status as free persons (CP, 326). "Being in this position is a precondition of freedom; it means that nothing is or need be hidden" (ibid.). For Rawls (unlike Hegel) such "reconciliation" cannot take place in the current social world as it now is, but only in a well-ordered society of justice as fairness where reasonable persons generally publicly accept this liberal egalitarian conception of justice.

In A *Theory of Justice* and later works Rawls was acutely aware of Marx's and other socialists' criticisims of liberalism, constitutional democracy, and of capitalism and markets. I just mentioned Rawls's later emphasis on the requirement of the "full publicity" of a society's conception of justice, which is partly a response to Marx's account of ideology, or false consciousness, and the role of conceptions of justice in obscuring the true nature of social relations. In addition, Rawls's focus on the "background justice" of the "basic structure of society" is in part responsive to Marx's critique of capitalism and the structure of property relations (TJ 259, 309n./ 229, 271–2n. rev.). Moreover, Rawls distinguishes between the allocative and distributive function of markets (TJ, 270–74/239–42 rev.). The former refers to the crucial role of markets in allocating factors of production efficiently in order to promote greater productivity and minimize waste of resources. Any rational and just economic system, Rawls believes, should endorse the allocative role of markets and prices. But this does not entail markets' distributive role, or relying on markets and the price system for the the distribution of income and wealth. The injustice of capitalism in large part consists in its nearly exclusive reliance on markets and prices for distribution of income and wealth, thereby excessively rewarding those with property in means of production at the expense of workers who labor to produce wealth. Finally, Rawls in later works argues that distributive justice requires either a property-owning democracy or a liberal socialist system, both of which eliminate the wage-relationship with capitalist owners and provide workers with real opportunities to control their work environment and their means of production. (See below, Chapter 5 on property-owning democracy.)

Conclusion

I have sought to convey in this section Rawls's connections with the major historical predecessors that influenced his work. Though raised within the Anglo-American analytic tradition in philosophy, Rawls is mainly responding to problems set forth by the major moral and political philosophers since Hobbes. For this reason, Rawls's lectures on the history of moral and political philosophy provide valuable insight into Rawls's own work, in addition to being among the best summaries available of the works of these important historical figures. Rawls is as systematic as any of the great European philosophers of former centuries, and thus it is difficult to understand and appreciate his arguments without seeing their place within the larger context of his entire theory and its relationship to his historical predecessors. Both methodologically and stylistically he departs from the analytic tradition. (His friend Burton Dreben once compared Rawls's methodological holism with Hegel's, and said of *A Theory of Justice*, "It reads like it was translated from the original German.") On the other hand Rawls is as meticulous as any other analytic moral philosopher in setting forth the premises and assumptions supporting his main conclusions. He was especially attentive to the question of justification in moral and political philosophy, a subject to which we now turn.

RAWLS ON JUSTIFICATION IN MORAL PHILOSOPHY:
REFLECTIVE EQUILIBRIUM

Before discussing Rawls's principles of justice and their contractarian justification, it is helpful to understand his more general ideas about justification in moral philosophy. Moral justification was the topic of Rawls's doctoral dissertation and his first publication,[19] and it occupied him throughout his life. Rawls's *Political Liberalism* is largely driven by a conception of the kind of justification that is appropriate for and within a democratic society. The idea of reflective equilibrium is one of several key ideas about justification in Rawls's theory of justice. Others are the original position, constructivism, and public reason, which will all be discussed in due course. But reflective equilibrium is the most general idea of justification, and it provides the framework for understanding these other ideas.

In general, the idea of justification is an epistemological concept, connected with our knowledge of some domain (of empirical facts, mathematical theorems, moral principles, etc.), how we come to know or at least can claim to know what we do, and our reasons for our beliefs and judgments regarding what is true. To provide a justification for some claim or action is to provide reasons for believing that the claim is true or that the action is right or reasonable. Justification is connected with the idea of the *objectivity* of judgments and there being some method of argument (in some cases, proof) which rational and/or reasonable people can apply to reach the same correct conclusion. Many people (e.g., moral skeptics and nihilists) and many philosophers with a scientistic attitude (e.g., logical positivists) believe that, while there are empirical justifications in the sciences and logical justifications in mathematics and like fields, nonetheless justification in ethics is not possible, since there is no moral or ethical truth. Moral statements are said to be expressions of our emotions, preferences, or attitudes, or universalizable commands, or individual or social efforts to gain power over people's will and actions. Rawls, however, like many other philosophers, believes in the objectivity of moral judgments and in their capacity to be more or less reasonable. He also believes in moral judgments' capacity for correctness, including truth or falsity. But he has a distinct way of accounting for the objectivity of moral judgments and the justifiability of moral statements and their reasonableness or truth.

A longstanding position on the justification of moral judgments and principles, which perhaps goes back to Plato, is that they are inferable in some way (ideally by logical deduction) from the most abstract moral principles, which themselves are fundamental truths that are not subject to logical proof, but are instead knowable to our reason via a philosophical intuition. Rawls has this position in mind when he says:

> A conception of justice cannot be deduced from self-evident premises or conditions on principles; instead, its justification is the matter of the mutual support of many considerations, of everything fitting together into one coherent view.
>
> (*TJ*, 21/19 rev.)

> Justification rests upon the entire [moral] conception and how it fits in with and organizes our considered judgments in reflective equilibrium.
>
> (*TJ*, 579/507 rev.)

For Rawls, the "mutual support of many considerations" exists when principles of justice stand in "general and wide reflective equilibrium" with our "considered convictions" of justice at all levels of generality.

Rawls's idea of reflective equilibrium presupposes an idea of "considered judgments" and "considered moral convictions." These are what are brought into an "equilibrium" with each other upon due reflection. "Considered judgments are simply those rendered under conditions favorable to the exercise of the sense of justice, and therefore in circumstances where the more common excuses and explanations for making a mistake do not obtain" (*TJ*, 47–48/42 rev.). Considered judgments are the moral judgments "in which we have the greatest confidence" (*TJ*, 19/17 rev.). The examples Rawls initially provides are our judgments that "religious intolerance and racial discrimination are unjust" (ibid.). Later Rawls says that Lincoln's assertion that "If slavery is not wrong, nothing is wrong" is a good example of people's considered convictions of justice (JF, 29). "These convictions are . . . fixed points which we presume any conception of justice must fit" (TJ, 20/18 rev.). Rawls seems to regard our fixed considered convictions as a kind of "data" that principles are to be made compatible with so far as possible. The "initial aim" of a theory of justice, Rawls says, is to find the conception of justice that "best fits" with our considered moral convictions. Later we'll consider what Rawls means by "best fit"; it is not simply a matter of intuitive balancing or feeling comfortable with one's judgments, but rather is explicated in part by Rawls's constructivism and the original position.

For Rawls reflective equilibrium is not a general theory of justification suitable for all judgments. It is often thought that Rawls's idea of reflective equilibrium is based in the holistic epistemology of his colleagues at Harvard, Willard Van Quine and Nelson Goodman. Rawls indeed cites parallels with Goodman's account of deductive and inductive inference when he first mentions reflective equilibrium (TJ, 20n./18n. rev.), and also the influence of Quine (TJ, 579n./507n. rev.).[20] Rawls was always generous in citing influences on his work. But Rawls developed the idea of "considered judgments" and bringing them into a reflective equilibrium over twenty years before he wrote *A Theory of Justice*, in his doctoral dissertation, and then in "Outline for a Decision Procedure in Ethics" (1951) (CP, ch.1). As evident in that article, Rawls sees reflective equilibrium, not as part of a more general epistemological account of justification; rather it is as an account of justification appropriate to moral philosophy, for the justification of moral principles. Rawls says, "Reflective equilibrium . . . is a notion characteristic of the study of principles which govern actions shaped by self-examination. Moral philosophy is Socratic" (TJ, 48–49/paragraph deleted in revised ed.).

One distinctive feature of reflective equilibrium is that it requires that considered moral judgments at all levels of generality be regarded as relevant in arguing for and justifying moral principles. It privileges neither the general nor the particular. To clarify: We can distinguish moral judgments at three levels of generality. First there are particular moral judgments; for example, the judgments that A harmed or wronged B, or (more generally) that the U.S. government is wrong to imprison aliens merely on grounds of suspicion and without a fair hearing. Then there are more abstract judgments, which include (but are not limited to) commonly accepted moral rules and principles: People ought to keep their promises, slavery is wrong, or democratic citizens ought to have a right of freedom of expression. Third, there are the most abstract moral considerations and principles, which are appealed to in justification of moral rules. Here would be such generalizations as persons ought to be treated with equal respect, or as "ends-in-themselves," or Sidgwick's principle of benevolence, that we ought to maximize the good, impartially construed.

"Philosophical intuitionism" is found in Sidgwick and others; it says that the most fundamental level of justification is abstract principle. Certain abstract principles (for Sidgwick the principles of impartial benevolence, of equity, and of prudence) are knowable as self-evidently true by a rational or "philosophical intuition." Sidgwick provides certain criteria for recognizing the self-evidence and philosophical certainty of these principles.[21] With these unquestionable truths, Sidgwick proceeds to argue that utilitarianism and rational egoism are the most rational "methods of ethics." One of the important features of Sidgwick's Methods is that he tried to show that the principle of utility was compatible with many of our ordinary moral convictions, "the morality of common sense." Still, the philosophical intuitions that Sidgwick relied upon for the foundation of morality were not open to being questioned by common-sense morality. They were "self-evident," and met all the relevant criteria of practical reason for a rational "philosophical intuition."

In his earlier explications, Rawls seems to present reflective equilibrium as an alternative to philosophical intuitionism (as well as naturalism in ethics – see below). (See again his claim above, "A conception of justice cannot be deduced from self-evident premises or conditions on principles" (TJ, 21/19 rev.).) According to reflective equilibrium, the most abstract moral considerations of the kind that Sidgwick relies upon do not have any special priority in justification of moral principles. In this regard, reflective equilibrium is "non-foundationalist": it does not attempt to "ground" moral principles in other principles or abstract judgments that are taken as axiomatic, self-evident, and not open to revision. Instead, considered moral convictions at all levels of generality must "fit" with moral principles if principles are to be justified. But since we have many different kinds of moral convictions, reflective equilibrium assumes that some of our moral convictions will be subject to revision once we try to make them consistent with moral principles in reflective equilibrium. Here, importantly, our more abstract "philosophical intuitions" are to be given no priority in this process of reflection. "It is a mistake to think of abstract conceptions and general principles as always overriding our more particular judgments" (PL, 45). Indeed, perhaps we will be led to abandon the most general conviction (assuming we endorse it) that we ought to promote the good impartially construed, if it cannot be accommodated with the principles of justice most compatible with the great bulk of other considered moral convictions. This is what Rawls's principles of justice imply — that we cannot always impartially promote the good (for example, human welfare) when this requires us to undermine requirements of justice. Whether or not the principle of impartial benevolence withstands reflective equilibrium, the example indicates how the method differs from philosophical intuitionism.

Beginning with *Political Liberalism*, Rawls offers another more moderate way to understand reflective equilibrium. Reflective equilibrium becomes a methodological claim that a justification of a moral conception requires showing that it "fits" (in some to-be-specified sense) with our considered moral convictions at all levels of generality. On this moderate account reflective equilibrium does not necessarily exclude Sidgwick's and Moore's rational intuitionism, or other "foundationalist views." Upon reflection, it may well be that, all things considered, our considered moral convictions do have a deductive basis in highly abstract moral principles, and that these abstract principles ("treat similar cases similarly," "maximize the good impartially construed," "right conduct promotes human welfare," etc.) are self-evident. On this moderate account of reflective equilibrium, to show that our moral convictions "fit together in reflective equilibrium" requires that we demonstrate how our most considered convictions about right and wrong are derivable from a moral conception which itself has a deductive basis in these abstract rational intuitions. Rather than contrasting reflective equilibrium with foundationalist positions like rational intuitionism, Rawls in later works instead contrasts such positions with constructivism in moral and political philosophy.[22]

When understood as potentially compatible with a foundationalist view such as rational intuitionism, it may seem that reflective equilibrium does not exclude much. But it does exclude moral skepticism and other metaphysical views which would question moral judgments en masse as illusory, or as ideological and not worth taking seriously. It also excludes philosophical views which try to derive a moral conception largely from outside moral judgment. Of positions which seek to ground moral theory in conceptual analysis or analysis of meanings, Rawls says: "It is obviously impossible to develop a substantive theory of justice founded solely on truths of logic and definition. The analysis of moral concepts and the a priori, however traditionally understood, is too slender a basis" (TJ, 51/44 rev.).

Notice here also Rawls's assertion that "One may think of moral philosophy at first [provisionally] as the attempt to describe our moral capacity; or, in the present case, one may regard a theory of justice as describing our sense of justice" (TJ, 46/41 rev.). He goes on to compare moral philosophy's search for principles compatible with our considered moral convictions with Chomskian linguistics' search for grammatical principles that account for our sense of grammaticalness of sentences. It is easy to read too much into these remarks. I do not think Rawls is suggesting that moral principles are a priori and implicit in our capacities for moral reasoning (though at times his Kantian affinities might seem to suggest this). Rather he is best understood as suggesting that we can rely on our capacities for moral reasoning under appropriate conditions, and that our moral judgments are not always arbitrary but are capable of discerning and being guided by objective moral principles. Reflective equilibrium does not presuppose that we should take all considered moral convictions as given and beyond revision. On the contrary, it requires that we critically assess our convictions, and assumes that none are taken as unrevisable. Rawls says, "Moral philosophy is Socratic: we may want to change our present considered judgments once their regulative principles are brought to light."[23] Indeed, upon reflection "a person's sense of justice may or may not undergo a radical shift" (TJ, 49/43 rev.).

Some have criticized reflective equilibrium on grounds that it is conservative or biased in favor of the status quo, since it works from our existing considered moral convictions. But how could we make moral judgments and do moral philosophy otherwise? We have to begin somewhere in moral thinking, and reliance upon considered moral convictions is unavoidable in so far as we do. Unless the critic is prepared to reject moral thinking as illusory, at least under current conditions, this criticism carries no force, at least not until we are provided with a convincing explanation why our moral convictions are, en masse, unreliable. The method of reflective equilibrium does not deny that people's moral sensibilities can be biased or distorted by their social and political circumstances. But Rawls assumes that under current conditions of a constitutional democracy where the values of freedom and equality are widely affirmed (even if construed differently), our considered moral convictions are sufficiently reliable to proceed with a moral theory of justice that at least approximates the correct or most reasonable view. It is only the nihilistic idea that our moral capacities themselves are unreliable no matter what the circumstances, and that morality and justice are simply illusory, that is incompatible with reflective equilibrium. But reflective equilibrium assumes that free and equal persons are as entitled to have as much confidence in the deliberated conclusions of reflective moral reasoning as we are in any other forms of critical philosophical or scientific reflection. A skeptical view which denies this – therewith questioning or denying the wrongness of cruelty, torturing the innocent, enslaving people, and other entrenched considered moral convictions – has to rely on metaphysical assumptions that are far more questionable than the judgments they would refute.[24]

The confidence Rawls expresses in moral thinking also explains his view that purely metaphysical (including naturalistic or linguistic) arguments for moral principles are insufficient to provide justification. These provide "too slender a basis" for developing or justifying a substantive moral theory (TJ, 51/44 rev., 578–79/506–07 rev.). Rawls rejects the idea that a naturalist metaphysics uniquely speaks in favor of one moral theory over all others. For example, some suggest that economics and rational choice theory and/or evolutionary theory provide evidence for the truth of utilitarianism, or alternatively for a Hobbesian view, since they are among the best explanations and tools we have in the sciences. Granting, for the sake of argument, that neo-classical price theory provides a good account of the behavior of economic agents under free-market competitive conditions, it is not clear why the utility-maximizing behavior of individual agents in economic and other contexts lends support to the idea that we ought to maximize either individual or aggregate utility.[25] Rawls thinks moral philosophy must take into account the general facts of natural and social sciences to decide what principles are practically possible and stable. But his account of the "independence of moral theory" (CP, ch. 15, discussed in ch. 7 below) implies that modern economics and rational choice theory, along with Darwinian theory, are compatible with any number of moral conceptions of justice.

To sum up the "moderate" view of reflective equilibrium that Rawls endorses in his later works: (1) Reflective equilibrium is a thesis about justification in moral philosophy; it is not a metaphysical theory about the nature of truth (a "coherentist theory"), or a general epistemological thesis about the nature of justification in general. It assumes: (2) that, however questionable particular moral convictions might be, we can have confidence in our capacities for moral reasoning and judgment; they are not like religious sensibilities or capacities for "spirituality," which (most philosophers believe) may be groundless and based on illusions. Moreover, (3) justification in moral philosophy must work within moral reasoning; it is necessary (if not also sufficient) to the justification of a moral conception that it "fit" with our considered moral convictions, at all levels of generality, and after consideration of alternative moral views ("wide reflective equilibrium"). This "moderate" understanding does not rule out any of the traditional moral conceptions – Kantianism, utilitarianism, perfectionism, or intuitionism (pluralism) – but it does rule out moral skepticism and nihilism and other doctrines that doubt our capacities for morality altogether, as well as naturalism and other reductionist efforts to justify moral principles purely on the basis of factual, linguistic, or metaphysical claims.

Rawls also suggests the more robust understanding of reflective equilibrium earlier in his career, up to and including Theory, one that fits with his Kantian orientation. This robust, or "Kantian interpretation" of reflective equilibrium (as I will term it), is suggested by the claim, "We may suppose that everyone has within himself the whole form of a moral conception" (TJ, 50/44 rev.). One role of moral philosophy is to discover the moral conception implicit in our moral capacities (see TJ, 46/41 rev.). We are not just to find the moral conception that "best fits" with our existing considered convictions, but are to critically examine them, in light of a range of more abstract moral principles and considerations. Again, reflective equilibrium "is Socratic" (TJ, 49/ deleted in rev. ed.) and involves a kind of critical "self-examination" of our sense of justice, to discover the principles that regulate and reflect our (considered) moral judgments. Part of this process is to be open "to change our present considered judgments once their regulative principles are brought to light" (TJ, 48–49/deleted in rev. ed.).

This more robust understanding of reflective equilibrium is "Kantian" in that, first, it parallels Kant's idea that morality and the categorical imperative are implicit in moral awareness, and that they are to be discovered by a kind of practical reasoning that is Socratic, and so involves the critical examination of our considered moral convictions.[26] Second, being implicit in moral awareness means (for Kant and early Rawls) that moral principles are not "facts" that are prior to and independent of practical reasoning, but that they are, in some manner, a product of practical reasoning itself. This connects morality with the idea of autonomy, including the autonomy of practical reason, and connects reflective equilibrium with what Rawls eventually calls "Kantian Constructivism in Moral Theory."[27]

On this Kantian reading, reflective equilibrium is incompatible with rational intuitionism and other positions (e.g., divine command doctrines) that regard moral principles as existing prior to and independent of our moral reasoning (cf. TJ, 578/507 rev.). There are no "moral facts" or first principles prior to and independent of moral reasoning that are somehow "given" to us (by intuition or any other way) and to which our moral judgments reflect or correspond. Instead, reflective equilibrium is a way to discover the moral principles that are already "implicit in practical reasoning." It assumes these principles are accessible in no other way – not by rational intuition, or any other means of self-evident access.

On this robust reading, Kantian constructivism is an essential component of reflective equilibrium. A "procedure of construction" (for Rawls, the original position) works "within reflective equilibrium" (Rawls says) to enable us to discover and justify the principles of justice that are regulative of our capacities for justice. I have more to say about Rawls's account of constructivism later, and its relation to reflective equilibrium (see Chapter 7 below). For Rawls prior to political liberalism, Kantian constructivism is a way to give content to Kant's idea of moral autonomy, understood as reason giving principles to itself out of its own resources. Constructivism is a method of practical reasoning and justification that enables us to "fit" together our considered moral convictions at all levels of generality in reflective equilibrium. In large part, constructivism defines what Rawls means by "fit together" our considered moral convictions in reflective equilibrium. The important point here is that, seen as part of reflective equilibrium,

Kantian constructivism displaces the need for justifying moral principles by showing that they have their origins anywhere "outside" of practical reasoning itself. As such, reflective equilibrium, on this robust Kantian interpretation, competes with rational intuitionism and any other doctrine of moral justification that regards moral principles as deriving from a source other than practical reason itself.

Because it incorporates a constructivist procedure, Rawls's reflective equilibrium is able to withstand the following objection: "If all that reflective equilibrium says is that our moral judgments should 'fit' or be compatible among themselves and with other considered beliefs, what prevents the idea from collapsing into the triviality that sound moral principles are those that are supported by the best reasons?" In response: The original position gives content to the idea of how a "fit" of considered convictions with principles is to be achieved. Reflective equilibrium works "through the original position." This is not to rule out the possibility that some other constructivist procedure might do a better job of bringing our considered judgments into reflective equilibrium. But the point is that *some* constructivist procedure of deliberation is integral to reflective equilibrium as Rawls conceived it. Even in *Political Liberalism*, "political constructivism" provides Rawls's preferred method of what it means for our considered judgments of political justice to "fit" together in general and wide reflective equilibrium. But here he seems to concede that reflective equilibrium can be detached from constructivism, and that other methods of reasoning might be used to make sense of the ideas of "fit" and of bringing our considered convictions into reflective equilibrium.

I have presented reflective equilibrium as an account of moral justification without considering its relationship to the justification of other kinds of claims. It has been argued that, if reflective equilibrium is to be convincing, it must not only bring our moral judgments into equilibrium, but that moral principles must also be brought into equilibrium with our other judgments, including scientific and other theoretical judgments as well as practical judgments. On this broader reading, reflective equilibrium is a general theory of justification, which holds for all our judgments, not just moral convictions.[28]

Clearly, Rawls thought a moral conception of justice should be compatible with what is scientifically or otherwise empirically settled. Indeed he went to great lengths to insure that the principles of justice did "fit" with what we know about psychology, biology, evolutionary theory, economics, and other social and natural sciences. But of course the kind of "fit" that empirical judgments have with moral principles was not to be defined by choice in the original position, unlike the "fit" between our fixed considered moral convictions and principles of justice. The main point of the argument for stability in Part III of *A Theory of Justice* is to show that justice as fairness is compatible with human nature and general facts about social cooperation and institutions. For example, if principles of justice demand of us more than most people are normally capable of (as impartial benevolence does, for example), this indicates that these principles do not "fit" well with human nature.

Second, it is equally clear that Rawls does not believe that any particular conception of justice is implied by or uniquely "fits" with considered scientific judgments. While Rawls thinks that natural facts are relevant to the justification of a conception of justice, he rejects "naturalism" in moral philosophy, in so far as it says that moral principles are reducible to or in some way derivable from natural facts and scientific theories. There is in his view no moral conception that is uniquely favored by evolutionary psychology or biology, or by any other natural or social science. Rather, most if not all of the traditional moral conceptions are capable of being realized in societies that are, to some degree or other, feasible. For example, Rawls does not argue, in his account of stability, that a utilitarian society is not feasible, or that impartial benevolence is impossible for us and entirely incompatible with human nature. Rather he suggests (1) that because of certain facts about human nature, impartial benevolence is very difficult for humans, and is not reliable as a widespread moral motivation capable of stabilizing a system of justice. For this and other reasons, (2) a well-ordered utilitarian society in which the principle of utility is publicly known and generally accepted by the members of society is prone to instability. This does not mean that a society ordered according to the principle of utility is not compatible with human nature or otherwise feasible. But it is a society in which many people will openly reject that very principle, because of the extreme sacrifices that it imposes on them for the sake of greater aggregate utility.

Third, in *Political Liberalism*, it becomes important for Rawls that justice as fairness can be made compatible with many metaphysical, epistemological, theological doctrines that Rawls calls "reasonable comprehensive doctrines." This implies that several comprehensive doctrines can be brought into reflective equilibrium with justice as fairness. This is an essential idea in political liberalism. It underlies Rawls's account of a "freestanding" political conception of justice. It is also part of what he means by a "public justification" of a conception of justice – that it can be brought into reflective equilibrium with a number of reasonable comprehensive doctrines.[29]

Finally, I re-emphasize that Rawls sees reflective equilibrium as particularly a claim about moral justification, not justification in general. It may or may not be true of laws, theorems, or principles in other disciplines that their justification requires showing them to be in reflective equilibrium with general and particular considered judgments. Rawls takes no position on justification in general or other epistemological issues. Scientific disciplines have a kind of subject matter and data that have no parallel in moral inquiries. Our considered moral convictions are not representations or judgments regarding empirical facts in the world. They are rather judgments about what we ought to choose and do, or about what kinds of institutions or states of affairs we ought to put into place. Having such a different content from moral judgments, it may well be that the kind of justification appropriate to scientific and other theoretical inquiries is very different from the kind that is appropriate to ethics. Rawls regards reflective equilibrium as especially appropriate to ethics; again, it is "a notion characteristic of the study of principles which govern actions shaped by self-examination" (TJ, 48–49/deleted in rev. ed.).

To conclude, one noticeable characteristic of Rawls's method of argumentation is that he provides several separate strands of argument to support his conclusions. For example, there are at least four separate arguments for why the parties in the original position will choose the principles of justice, and there are five reasons that Rawls imposes the publicity condition on the parties' choice in the original position (see "The Independence of Moral Theory"). This plethora of arguments for the same conclusion is related to reflective equilibrium. Rawls does not see practical reason as grounded in fundamental principles, to which we can trace back and deduce all practical reasons and conclusions. There are a great number of relatively fixed moral convictions, both general and particular, that reasonable people have, and it cannot be said that the more general convictions have a more fundamental or certain status. If justification in moral philosophy is not a matter of deduction from foundational principles, but rather showing the compatibility of moral principles with our considered moral convictions, then it is only to be expected that a number of arguments from different premises will be required to justify moral principles and the most reasonable conception of justice.

FURTHER READING

"John Rawls: For the Record," an interview with The Harvard Review of Philosophy, vol. 1, no. 1 (1999): 38–47. (Rawls discusses his life and his interests in philosophy.)

Pogge, Thomas John Rawls, His Life and Theory of Justice, Oxford, UK: Oxford University Press, 2006, chapter 1. (A more extensive biography of Rawls's life.)

Rawls, John, Lectures on the History of Moral Philosophy, Barbara Herman, ed., Cambridge, MA: Harvard University Press, 2000.

Rawls, John, Lectures on the History of Political Philosophy, Samuel Freeman, ed., Cambridge, MA: Harvard University Press, 2007.

Scanlon, Thomas, "Rawls on Justification," in The Cambridge Companion to Rawls, Samuel Freeman, ed., New York: Cambridge University Press, 2003.

Two

Liberalism, Democracy, and the Principles of Justice

The origins of liberalism are disputed. Since Marx many have argued that liberalism had its origins in capitalism and its need for free markets in labor and private ownership and control of real capital, including the means of production. John Locke's account of the origins of private property in self-ownership in a state of nature is regarded by many on both the left and the right as the quintessential statement of the foundations of liberalism. Liberalism is thereby conceived primarily as an economic doctrine. Rawls regards Locke as a seminal figure in the history of liberalism too, but not because of Locke's supposed economic liberalism. Rather it is because of Locke's affirmation that all "men" are born free and equal with certain inalienable liberties; that governments have a duty to respect these liberties and tolerate different religious confessions; and that political power is to be exercised for the common good. Rawls sees the historical origins of liberalism primarily in the European Wars of Religion in the sixteenth and seventeenth centuries.[1] They gave rise to the idea that it should not be the role of governments to enforce a particular religious confession, but that different religious views should be tolerated. The core liberal freedoms of liberty of conscience and freedom of thought developed from this historical starting point. Locke's political writings were largely an attempt to provide a philosophical justification for a limited, constitutional government that respected religious and other liberties.

Modern democracy had an equally unsettling historical origin in the eighteenth-century American and French Revolutions. But the theoretical underpinnings of equal democratic rights of political participation were already latent in seventeenth-century liberalism. Once Locke recognized that all are born free and equal, it would be difficult for liberal theorists – try as they might – to avoid the idea that all members of society ought to have the status of equal citizen, without regard to their gender, race, religion, or property qualifications. Rousseau is the major theorist of democracy within the social contract tradition. Rousseau's idea of democracy as deliberation among equal citizens on justice and the common good, along with Mill's account of representative democracy, are the precursors to Rawls's account of equal rights of political participation and democratic deliberation upon justice.

Rawls's conception of social justice, "justice as fairness," is a *liberal* conception in that it protects and gives priority to certain *equal basic liberties*, which enable individuals to freely exercise their consciences, decide their values, and live their chosen way of life. Liberal governments and societies respect individuals' choices and tolerate many different lifestyles as well as religious, philosophical, and moral doctrines. Rawls's account is also liberal in that it endorses *free markets* in economic relations (vs. a planned economy), respects individuals' *free choices of occupations and careers*, and provides a *social minimum* for the least advantaged members of society. Rawls's conception of justice is *democratic* in that it provides for *equal political rights* and seeks to establish *equal opportunities* in educational and occupational choices. It is *egalitarian* in that it seeks to maintain the "fair value" of the political liberties, establishes "fair equality of opportunity," and determines the social minimum by aiming to maximally benefit the least advantaged members of society. These rights, liberties, and opportunities are subsumed under Rawls's two principles of justice. I discuss these principles here in the order of their priority, starting with the principle of equal basic liberties, then fair equality of opportunity, and finally the difference principle.

THE FIRST PRINCIPLE OF JUSTICE: THE BASIC LIBERTIES

Each person has an equal claim to a fully adequate scheme of equal basic rights and liberties, which scheme is compatible with the same scheme for all; and in this scheme the equal political

liberties, and only those liberties, are to be guaranteed their fair
value.

$$(PL, 5)^2$$

The main idea of the first principle is that there are certain basic
rights and freedoms of the person that are more important than
others, and that are needed to characterize the moral ideal of free
and equal persons. With the first principle Rawls aims first to define
a democratic ideal of free citizens who have equal civic status with
powers to fairly and effectively influence legislation and take part in
public political life. Here he works within a Rousseauian conception
of democracy as equal citizens' deliberation on justice and the
common good. Second, the first principle in *Theory* is part of Rawls's
liberal ideal of free self-governing persons who develop their
human capacities, and shape and pursue ways of life that are intrinsically rewarding. This is the ideal of the person that underlies the
"liberalisms of freedom" of the high liberal tradition. The high
liberal tradition traces its lineage back to Kant; through Humboldt
and the German Idealists, it had a major influence on J.S. Mill's
liberalism (including his ideal of "individuality"). Rawls contrasts
"liberalisms of freedom" with the "liberalisms of happiness" found
in classical liberalism.[3] Classical liberalism originates largely with
David Hume, Adam Smith, and the classical economists and developed in Britain together with utilitarianism. Classical liberalism
primarily differs from high liberalism in placing greater emphasis
upon economic rights of property, contract and trade, and the
freedom of consumption. Whereas the high liberal tradition sees
the freedom and independence of the person as the primary end of
justice, classical liberalism sees them more as means that are
instrumental to the primary end of individual happiness.

Rawls's first principle refers, not to "liberty" but to "basic liberties." He appeals to the commonly accepted idea that certain rights
and liberties are more important or "basic" than others. Most
people believe it is more important that they be free to decide their
religion, speak their minds, choose their own careers, and marry
and befriend only people that they choose, than that they have the
freedom to drive without safety belts and as fast as they please, use

their property without regulation, or enter into just any kind of financial dealing that is beneficial to them. Some freedoms of course deserve no protection at all – for example, driving while intoxicated, or entering others' houses without permission. Accordingly Rawls construes the liberal emphasis on protection of "liberty" primarily in terms of certain "basic liberties," and not the protection of just any sort of freedom or "liberty as such." There is nothing original here; the idea that certain rights and liberties are more "fundamental" than others and warrant special protection has long been recognized in American constitutional law. Moreover, J.S. Mill's Principle of Liberty is also designed to protect largely the same range of basic liberties found in Rawls's first principle.[4] What is original in Rawls's liberalism is his answer to the question, "How are we to decide which liberties are basic or fundamental, and which are not, and how are we to decide conflicts between the basic liberties?"

But first consider what liberties Rawls regards as basic. He mentions five sets of basic liberties: liberty of conscience and freedom of thought; freedom of association; equal political liberties; the rights and liberties that protect the integrity and freedom of the person (including freedom of occupation and choice of careers and a right to personal property); and finally the rights and liberties covered by the rule of law (PL, 291). Protections for the physical and psychological integrity and freedom of the person are the most obvious basic rights and liberties, for they forbid unjustified violence, coercion, and enslavement of persons (among other things). Any reasonable conception of justice, liberal or non-liberal, recognizes these as morally protected rights. Rawls's account of justice is *liberal* since it gives *equal* protection to these and other basic rights and liberties of the person, including liberty of conscience, freedom of thought, freedom of association, and the rights and liberties that are integral to the rule of law. His account is *democratic* since it also includes among equal basic rights the "equal political liberties," or equal rights of political participation (TJ, sect. 36). These include mainly the right to vote and hold office, freedom of political speech and discussion, freedom of assembly, freedom to make grievances against and criticize the government, and the right to form and join political parties. Rawls sees the basic liberties abstractly, as including within their reach numerous more specific rights and liberties. Liberty of conscience then includes not simply the freedom to decide one's religion but also the freedom to disregard or reject all religions. More generally it includes freedom of belief in ethical questions regarding morality, values, and the purposes of one's life, metaphysical questions of the nature of reality, and spiritual questions about what gives life its meaning. Each of us holds certain ideals, values and convictions that are authoritative for us in that they prescribe the orientation for our existence and pursuits. Traditionally these were a matter of religion for most people. It is a familiar idea that it is not the role of the State to prescribe, advocate, or even favor in its policies any particular religious confession or doctrine. Religious toleration, or the "free exercise" and the non-establishment of religion proclaimed by the first amendment of the U.S. Constitution, were the intellectual product of the Wars of Religion that transpired in the sixteenth and seventeenth centuries in Europe. Freedom of conscience, as Rawls understands it, generalizes this idea to include freedom of philosophical, evaluative, and moral beliefs as well. More controversially, freedom of conscience, as Rawls construes it, includes the "separation" or independence of political decisions from influence by not just religious doctrines, but other "comprehensive" philosophical and moral doctrines as well. This aspect of freedom of conscience is discussed more fully in Chapter 8 when Rawls's idea of public reason is taken up. The general idea is that in questions of values and morals the State's actions are limited to prescribing laws that enforce "political values of public reason," including a liberal conception of justice.

Freedom of thought is similar to liberty of conscience, but extends more broadly to include freedom of belief and the *expression* of belief on all subjects, be they political, literary, artistic, scientific, or philosophical. This basic liberty protects freedom of inquiry and discussion, as well as the freedom to communicate and express one's views on all subjects.

The third basic liberty Rawls mentions is freedom of association, the "liberty to associate with persons one chooses and to unite into groups of all kinds." This freedom works in tandem with freedom of conscience, for without it freedom of conscience is effectively denied (PL, 313). If a person cannot associate and share ideas with people of like-minded attitudes, convictions or faiths, then the freedom to practice one's conscientious convictions is of little value. An interesting question raised by this freedom is its role in family life, and in marital and other intimate relations, as well as its relationship to the right of privacy in American constitutional law (questions addressed in Chapter 5).

Regarding the freedoms specified by the liberty and integrity of the person, in addition to the obvious protections mentioned above, they also include freedom of movement and free choice of occupation,[5] as well as a right to (hold) *personal* property, which Rawls says is necessary for personal independence and a sense of self-respect.[6] Here it is interesting that Rawls does not define freedom of the person as expansively as Mill, who says it includes "liberty of tastes and pursuits, of framing the plan of life to suit our own character."[7] Perhaps Rawls thought this abstract freedom was already taken care of by the combination of the other basic liberties, especially freedom of conscience, thought, and association when combined with the freedom of the person. On the other hand, Rawls's liberalism may not be as permissive as Mill's, for he clearly sees certain exercises of the basic freedom of the person as warranting more protection than others.[8] This is implicit in his account of the "central range of application" of a basic liberty, discussed below. This leaves open restrictions on certain "self-regarding" conduct which Mill might have allowed (for example, self-destructive uses of narcotics, or unmotivated suicides, or perhaps prostitution).

Then again, Rawls resembles Mill in holding that freedom of occupation and choice of careers are protected as a basic freedom of the person, but that neither freedom of the person nor any other basic liberty includes other economic rights prized by classical liberals, such as freedom of trade and economic contract. Rawls says that freedom of the person includes having a right to hold and enjoy *personal* property. He includes here control over one's living space and a right to enjoy it without interference by the State or others. The reason for this right to personal property is that, without control over personal possessions and quiet enjoyment of one's own living space, many of the basic liberties cannot be enjoyed or exercised. (Imagine the effects on your behavior of the high likelihood of unknowing but constant surveillance.) Moreover, having control over personal property is a condition for pursuing most worthwhile ways of life. But the right to personal property does not include a right to its unlimited accumulation. Similarly, Rawls says the first principle does not protect the capitalist freedom to privately own and control the means of production, or conversely the socialist freedom to equally participate in the control of the means of production (TJ, 54 rev.; PL, 338; JF, 114). These are not, he says, freedoms needed for the adequate development and full exercise of the moral powers of free and equal citizens (JF, 114). This suggests that, for Rawls, the decision between capitalism and socialism is not a question of basic liberties at all, but is to be decided on other grounds (the second principle of justice). Rawls holds that the extent of economic liberties and rights of use of productive property are to be decided, and their scope settled, by the requirements of the difference principle. Economic liberties and efficiency in production and trade normally benefit the least advantaged; but the freedom to enter into economic contracts and use productive resources is to be regulated by their effects on the least advantaged, and are not basic liberties. Rawls calls economic liberties non-basic "liberties connected with the second principle" (PL, 363). They are important liberties to the degree that they benefit everyone beginning with the least advantaged. But they are not on a par with the basic liberties that are needed to specify the ideal of free and equal persons that Rawls employs.

The limits Rawls imposes on ownership and use of the means of production suggests that Rawls sees rights of property as complex. There is no right to "property as such" that gives people the freedom to do with their possessions whatever they please. Of course, no conception of justice allows people to do anything they please with their possessions. (As the libertarian Robert Nozick says, I cannot leave my knife in your chest (ASU, 171).) The problem for any conception is to define the limits on uses of property. Libertarianism is distinctive in that it imposes minimal limits on use: so long as usages do not violate others' (libertarian) rights, then they are permissible, no matter how much the value of others' freedom and well-being might be adversely affected by those usages. (For example, I may have a libertarian right to monopolize certain resources and refuse to sell them to ethnic groups I dislike, even if this has the effect of undermining the health and welfare of entire communities.)[9]

Rawls's basic right to hold personal property is then a limited right to hold personal belongings that are needed for personal independence and self-respect (JF, 114). Its purpose is to insure people the right to use and control the possessions needed to effectively exercise the basic liberties and freely pursue a wide range of permissible conceptions of the good. The right to personal property is not a substantive right to a guaranteed minimal income, but a formal right to hold and be secure in one's legitimate possessions. Society cannot deprive anyone (as it once did in the case of slaves and to a lesser degree married women) of the civil right to hold, use, and control personal property, as it is defined by law. Guarantees to income or minimal holdings of property are primarily covered by the difference principle in Rawls's account of social justice.[10] Moreover, rights to unlimited accumulation, absolute ownership of the means of production, and unregulated use and transfer of economic resources are not among the basic rights to hold personal property. Rawls sees economic usages of property as admitting of regulation by law in order to satisfy the requirements of justice and even public convenience and enjoyment. Ownership of a Dürer or Picasso does not mean you can destroy it. Also governments may restrict land usage for certain purposes (residential, business, or environmental zoning, for example). Of course, such restrictions on use may not be arbitrarily imposed and must be for a legitimate public purpose, and governments may have a duty to compensate fairly those whose once legitimate usages are restricted.

Under the rights and liberties of the rule of law, Rawls includes the regular and impartial administration of law ("justice as regularity"), and such liberties as freedom from arbitrary arrest and seizure of property (TJ, 61/53 rev.), fair and open trials, rational rules of evidence, a right against self-incrimination, and other due process rights. While the rule of law does not itself assure substantive liberties (since laws can be regularly enforced but still oppressive) it is a precondition for enjoying them, for without the rule of law the boundaries of liberties are uncertain, and people do not know when there will be interferences with their plans and actions (see TJ, sect. 38).

To say these liberties are "basic" does not simply mean they are more important than others and are to be given a special weight. It also means they are "inalienable" – "any undertakings to waive or to infringe them are void *ab initio*" (PL, 365–66; CP, 372n.). Not only are government agents and democratic majorities precluded from violating basic liberties, but also citizens themselves cannot transfer them to others or bargain them away. The idea of the inalienability of basic liberties is not peculiar to Rawls but is a fixed feature of liberalism. No liberal government would enforce a contract whereby a person attempted to sell himself into slavery, or give up freedom of religion or freedom of speech (by making oneself a permanent member of a religious confession, for example). People might forfeit some of their basic liberties as a result of committing serious crimes, but forfeiture is different from voluntary transfer. Inalienability is one consequence of the fact that freedom of contract and absolute rights of property are not absolute or basic liberties for Rawls. One cannot do with oneself just anything one pleases, as if one's person were fungible property. This is not because a person does not "own himself" and is owned by the State; the idea of self (or state) ownership of persons plays no role in Rawls. Rather it is because the basic liberties (and justice as fairness as a whole) are based in a moral ideal of persons as free and equal self-governing agents who have an essential interest in maintaining their freedom, equality, and independence. It is the primary role of democratic government to maintain the conditions for realizing this ideal of persons. To enforce contracts whereby citizens attempt to alienate their own or obtain ownership of others' basic liberties is a misuse of public political power. It fails to show respect for persons as equal citizens. This is perhaps the main regard in which Rawls, and liberals generally, differ from libertarianism. Libertarianism is a doctrine of self-ownership. Absolute rights of property and freedom of contract are its most fundamental liberties. As such, it rejects the idea of inalienability of basic rights and liberties. One's person is one's property, subject to alienation and mistreatment like anything else one owns. For Rawls, any such doctrine which allows persons to be alienated and treated against their will as property, even if done by their own prior consent, is an abuse of public political power and does not show respect for persons as free and equal.[11]

Finally, Rawls says that none of the basic liberties are absolute. This means that none of the basic liberties are singly more important than other basic liberties, outweighing them and all other political values when they come into conflict. Instead, conflicts among the basic liberties and with other important political values are to be decided so as to maintain a "fully adequate scheme" of basic liberties. ("Fully adequate" to what? I address this question below.) It might be thought that freedom of speech is absolute if any basic liberty is. But a moment's reflection will show that there are a number of necessary restrictions on freedom of speech to protect other rights and liberties. For example, people cannot incite others to riot or raise false alarms that endanger others' lives; nor can people engage in fraud, bribery, false advertising, or conspiracy to commit crimes, or threaten people's lives or libel them and destroy their reputation. These are all accepted restrictions on freedom of speech, normally recognized to protect other important rights, liberties, and interests. Rawls argues that there can even be restrictions on campaign advertisements, a form of political speech, if they are clearly needed to maintain the "fair value" of the political liberties. In this example, one basic liberty is being used to decide the limits of another. Importantly, for Rawls, the only legitimate reasons for restricting the basic liberties are to maintain a more extensive scheme, or "fully adequate scheme," of basic liberties. The basic liberties cannot be restricted for reasons other than to protect and maintain the basic liberties themselves. This is what Rawls means by the priority of liberty, which is discussed later.

Now turn to our second question: How is Rawls's list of basic liberties decided? What privileges some liberties over others? In particular, what warrants Rawls's contention that the economic liberties and rights of property are not as fundamental and important as other basic liberties? In *Theory* Rawls says the basic liberties are given by a list (*TJ*, 53 rev.), but he is rather unclear about where this list comes from. He seems to rely partly upon the history of constitutional law in the United States and other liberal democracies. He also suggests that the basic liberties, like other primary goods, are those that are needed to pursue a wide range of conceptions of the good. Still, Rawls clearly thinks the basic liberties are connected with the idea of equal citizens, for he calls them "the liberties of equal citizenship" (*TJ*, 197/173 rev., 204/178 rev.), and he says that the first principle is to be applied from "the standpoint of the representative equal citizen" to decide what is the most rational scheme for the equal citizen to prefer (*TJ*, 204/179 rev.).

This was not sufficient to forestall criticism from even sympathetic critics. In one of the few critical reviews to which Rawls explicitly responded, H.L.A. Hart commented on two gaps in Rawls's treatment of liberty in the first principle. First, the grounds upon which the parties in the original position adopt the basic liberties and agree to their priority are not adequately explained. Second, no satisfactory criterion is given by Rawls for specifying and adjusting the basic liberties to one another when they conflict.[12] Hart also contends that the idea of "the most extensive total system of basic liberties" in Rawls's first principle is problematic since it suggests maximizing the extent of liberty. But in some cases, Hart says, the idea of maximum liberty makes no sense, while in others it leads to absurd or unacceptable consequences. To take Sidgwick's example, if the aim is really to maximize liberty, this would seem to require an absence of private property; for others' private property rights place enormous restrictions on individuals' freedom of movement and rights to use and enjoy things as they please. In response to Hart's article, Rawls refined the argument for the basic liberties, basing them (and justice as fairness as a whole) in an ideal of democratic citizens as free and equal persons (see PL, VIII).

One of the main contributions to liberal theory that Rawls sees himself making is to uncover and explicitly utilize an ideal of the person that underlies the high liberal tradition and liberalism as a philosophical doctrine (see PL, 369). This is the ideal of free and equal persons with two "moral powers" and a freely adopted conception of the good. Rawls mentions this ideal of the person initially in Theory as providing the basis for equality (sect. 77). It also plays a central role in the Kantian interpretation of justice as fairness (sect. 40), and later in Part III of Theory it provides the basis for the congruence argument for stability (sect. 86). Finally, in the revised edition of Theory Rawls relies on this conception of persons to argue for the priority of liberty (TJ, sect. 82, 541–43/474–76 rev.). But as important as these occasional uses of the conception of free and equal persons were to the argument in Theory, they did not play the central role that they later acquired. Though Rawls did not fully expand upon the conception of citizens as free and equal persons until these later works,[13] I will rely on them here when appropriate to expound Rawls's understanding of the first principle of justice.

The two moral powers of free and equal persons are, first, a capacity to be "reasonable," which is a moral capacity for justice – the power to understand, apply, and cooperate with others on terms of cooperation that are fair; second is the capacity to be "rational," to have a rational conception of the good – the power to form, revise, and to rationally pursue a coherent conception of values, as based in a view of what gives life and its pursuits their meaning. The capacities to be reasonable and rational Rawls regards as the primary capacities for practical reasoning. In Rawls's subsequent Kantian terminology they are capacities for the Right and the Good, or the Reasonable and the Rational. These capacities form "the bases of equality," or the features of humans by virtue of which they warrant being treated as equals and respected as subjects of justice (TJ, sect. 77). By contrast with utilitarians, Rawls does not see the capacity for pleasure and pain, or the capacity for desire, as the primary feature of beings by virtue of which they deserve special moral consideration. Animals other than humans have the capacities for pleasure and pain, and this is morally significant in our treatment of them. Still, Rawls endorses the common-sense view that humans as a species deserve an exceptional kind of moral consideration, above and beyond that which we owe to other animals; for humans, unlike other species, have the moral powers to be reasonable and rational and other powers necessary for practical reasoning. This is what primarily distinguishes humans as the primary subjects of justice.

The ideal of free and equal persons with the moral powers is a Kantian ideal. Rawls distinguishes it from a metaphysical conception of the self, such as the idea of personal identity (CP, ch. 15). It is rather a "practical" conception of a person's agency that we presuppose in our moral and other practical dealings with one another. It is a fact about our practices of holding one another responsible that we do so only for people who have both moral powers. For example, the traditional test for legal insanity is that a person have the capacity to distinguish right from wrong, which is part of what is involved in the capacity for a sense of justice. Moreover, we do not hold young children or incompetents responsible for their actions, nor do we allow them to fully manage their affairs, mainly because they do not adequately possess the capacity to be rational and attend to their own good.

I return to the conception of the person later. It plays a significant role in the discussion of stability in Chapter 6 and in the account of the evolution of Rawls's political liberalism in Chapter 7. For now, it is relevant in that the conception of the person with two moral powers supplies the criterion for deciding what are the basic liberties. What makes a liberty basic for Rawls is that it is *an essential social condition for the adequate development and full exercise of the two powers of moral personality over a complete life* (PL, 293). In Rawls's response to Hart,[14] he explains in detail how each of the basic liberties is needed if free and equal individuals are to be in a position to exercise and develop one or the other moral power. He argues first that liberty of conscience and freedom of association are crucial to the exercise of the capacity for a rational conception of the good (PL, 310–15). For without these freedoms individuals could not examine different values or philosophical, religious, and moral doctrines, and come to a decision about which way of life is most suited to their characters. The basic idea here is that freedom of conscience and association are needed to come to an informed decision about the moral, philosophical, and religious principles that provide authoritative guidance for people in deciding and acting upon their fundamental beliefs and values, or "rational plans of life." Next, freedom of thought and the political liberties are needed if individuals are to adequately develop and fully exercise their capacity for a sense of justice (PL, 315–24). Having the freedom to discuss moral and political issues, criticize the government, and take an active role in public political life are all needed if a person is to realize his capacity to reason about justice and act on its demands. The exercise of these liberties thus warrants exceptional protection since they are needed for the adequate development and full exercise of one's capacity to understand, apply and act on requirements of justice, and to participate in "the public use of reason," the critical assessment and/or justification of actions and institutions according to reasons of justice. Finally, the rights and liberties that maintain the integrity and freedom of the person, and the rights and liberties that are needed for the rule of law, are instrumental to the exercise of all the preceding basic liberties, and therewith the exercise and development of both moral powers as well as the pursuit of a reasonable conception of the good. For example, having the right to hold personal property is necessary if a free and equal person is to develop his or her moral personality and pursue most any reasonable conception of the good. Perhaps the peripatetic ascetic who meditates in the desert and takes his meals from nature has little need for personal possessions (beyond his clothing). But no one can do this for a lifetime; access to possessions is needed at some period to develop capacities and acquire the beliefs that outfit one for asceticism. In any case, exceptionless generalizations are not required to demonstrate the importance of this basic liberty to most ways of living.

This account of the liberties needed to develop moral personality underlies Rawls's rejection of the libertarian and classical liberal idea that unrestricted economic freedoms are among the basic liberties. These economic liberties include absolute rights of economic contract, private ownership of the means of production, and the unregulated freedom to use and dispose of one's property as one pleases. J.S. Mill rejected Herbert Spencer's claim that economic liberties are equally important as other personal liberties, on grounds that economic activity is a social act which, though it benefits some, can also adversely influence others' prospects.[15] This is an important reason for economic regulation of contracts and uses of property. But here a libertarian might rejoin that freedom of speech has social consequences and can adversely affect others too (e.g., the neo-Nazi demonstrations in Jewish neighborhoods in Skokie, IL); nonetheless, adverse effects are only rarely a reason to limit the scope or content of freedom of speech. (As federal courts held, moral offense to Holocaust survivors was not sufficient reason to forbid the neo-Nazi march.) So why shouldn't economic freedom be among the basic liberties that cannot be limited except when needed to protect and maintain other basic liberties?

The implication of the libertarian claim – that economic liberties are equally fundamental along with other personal and political liberties – is that it limits considerably a liberal society's ability to regulate the uses of property, economic contracts, and business transactions and activities. For example, libertarians argue that environmental laws and zoning ordinances restricting uses of property violate basic economic liberties to use one's property as one pleases. Or that health and safety laws regulating working conditions, product safety provisions, minimum wage laws, and laws requiring overtime for more than a 40-hour week interfere with freedom of economic contract. Even taxation for purposes of providing a social minimum, emergency relief, and to fund public goods are said by libertarians to be a violation of basic rights of property. If unregulated freedom of contract and absolute rights of property are basic liberties, this limits considerably the political liberties and the range of legislation that democratic assemblies can enact. It is hardly surprising, then, that economic libertarians and many classical liberals are hostile to democratic government, or at least to democratic governments' "interference" with a free economy (hence the idea of *laissez-faire*).

But what would reasonably justify such expansive individual rights to make economic contracts and accumulate, use, and dispose of property without regard to the adverse consequences they have for those who are worse off? Of course libertarians and classical liberals have their arguments (ranging from appropriation of property in a semi-Lockean state of nature to social utility). Robert Nozick and other libertarians have suggested, without much visible argument, that individual autonomy underlies extensive libertarian property rights.[16] But what is the conception of autonomy that would allow, as libertarianism does, for conditions in which a small minority might monopolize the means of production while large numbers of people are either destitute and unemployed, or have lost economic independence since they have no alternative to a wage relationship with those who own and control the means of production? Whatever the libertarian conception of autonomy might be, it seems to have little in common with the Kantian and Millian accounts that inform Rawls's position in *Theory*. In Rawls's account none of the libertarian economic liberties are necessary for the adequate development and full exercise of the two moral powers or to pursue a wide range of reasonable conceptions of the good. Indeed, instituting the economic liberties as basic liberties would undermine the ability of many free and equal persons to achieve economic independence and enjoy income and wealth adequate to their leading a wide range of reasonable plans of life. Unregulated economic liberties then render practically impossible many persons' adequate development of their moral powers, and therewith freedom and equality and their having fair opportunities to pursue a reasonable conception of the good. This is the underlying message in Rawls's explicit rejection of basic economic liberties.

This does not mean that Rawls does not find the economic liberties to be of importance. They are very important when *appropriately regulated*, for they then can create social and economic conditions that enable free and equal persons to achieve independence and effectively pursue a reasonable conception of the good.

But the importance of the economic liberties then stems, not directly from the first principle of justice, but from reasons of economic justice as defined by fair equality of opportunity and the difference principle. Free markets in allocating the means of production are essential, Rawls believes, to economic efficiency, which is instrumental to creating a wide range of employment opportunities for citizens, and to effective economic production benefiting the less advantaged as it also benefits those better off. But this does not imply the libertarian and classical liberal positions that free markets also should be relied on more or less exclusively for the distribution of income and wealth. The allocative vs. distributive use of markets is a topic for the next chapter. Here the general point is simply that the nature and extent of economic liberties are determined for Rawls by the measures needed to realize economic justice as defined by the second principle of justice. They are not among the basic liberties protected by the first principle.

LIBERTY AND THE WORTH OF LIBERTY

A frequent criticism of liberalism from the Left is implicit in the quip (loosely adapted from Anatole France) that in France all are equals and are free, for the rich and the poor alike have the freedom to sleep under bridges. The point is that the kind of freedom and equality liberalism provides are empty legal abstractions, of no value to those without adequate means to enjoy them. After all, how much can equal political rights, and freedom of conscience, expression, and association be worth to a person who has to beg and scrounge for food in garbage dumps all day just to survive? Real liberty is not simply an empty formalism; rather it requires that people have the powers, opportunities, and resources that enable them to act as they freely choose.

Rawls would agree; without adequate resources the basic liberties are of little or no value to people: "The basic liberties are a framework of legally protected paths and opportunities. Of course, ignorance and poverty, and the lack of material means generally, prevent people from exercising their rights and from taking advantage of these openings" (PL, 325–26). But he does not respond to this problem by sacrificing liberalism's formal conception of a liberty as the absence of certain interferences and institutional restrictions on a person's freedom to act in certain ways. Instead Rawls distinguishes liberty from the "worth of liberty, that is, the usefulness to persons of their liberties" (PL, 326). He contends that justice as fairness aims to insure the worth of basic liberty for everyone, by maximizing its worth to the least advantaged (TJ, 205/179 rev.). For Rawls, to have a liberty is to be free from institutional (i.e. legal or social) constraints in order to act in a certain manner (TJ, 202/177 rev.). Generally Rawls sees liberty as a normative notion, mainly specified in legal and constitutional terms by a certain structure of institutions, or system of rules that define rights and duties. He does not understand liberty as Hobbes did, purely in physical terms and as the absence of effective constraints, whether institutional or physical. The difference is captured by the idea that while A is without (institutional) liberty to do x he may still be (physically) free to do x. For example, on Rawls's institutional account of liberty, while a thief does not have the legal liberty to use my car, still he might be physically free to drive away in it so long as he can avoid capture by police. Conversely, a person may have the institutional liberty to act in certain ways (e.g., freedom of movement), yet because of physical or social impediments (illness or poverty) he is not free, or is physically unable, to exercise that liberty. When Rawls speaks of a "fully adequate scheme" (or "most extensive total system") of basic liberties, he means liberties in the institutional sense.

Why doesn't Rawls's institutional definition of liberty just play into the Left critic's hands, since having an institutional liberty says nothing about a person's capacity to exercise it? Rawls contends that while the first principle guarantees basic liberties only in an institutional sense (except for the political liberties), the aim of the second principle is to guarantee the worth or value of the basic liberties for everyone, particularly the economically least advantaged. It does so by insuring that everyone has adequate all-purpose means (powers, opportunities, income, and wealth) needed to exercise the basic liberties effectively. Because of the difference principle's guarantee of a full "social minimum," there should not be a class of impoverished people in a well-ordered society of justice as fairness for whom the basic liberties are of little or no value. To be sure, there will be those who are "least advantaged," as there must be in any society with unequal incomes, but the least advantaged should have more than sufficient resources – more than they would in any other social system compatible with equal basic liberty – to effectively exercise their basic liberties and pursue their ends.

But here Rawls's Left critics may rejoin with the following: While Rawls's liberalism is surely more attuned to the needs of the poor than classical liberals or libertarians, still his promise of *equality* of basic liberty remains empty. For equal liberty is not possible without equal worth of liberty. But Rawls's difference principle allows for inequalities of resources, and these might be so large as to undermine the basic liberties of the least advantaged. Two examples should suffice. First the wealthy exercise enormous political influence on democratic processes, and there are no effective means for neutralizing the political effects of wealth in a capitalistic democracy. Given the corrupting influences that large concentrations of wealth have on politics, how can there be "equal rights of political participation" or any degree of equal political influence? Second, how can there be equal freedom of expression when those worse off are without the means to communicate their views to others? The wealthy control mass communications (TV, radio, newspapers, book publishing, etc.) and mainly publish positions that favor and indoctrinate others in their views. Equal liberty without equal worth of liberty is an empty abstraction.[17]

It is difficult to appreciate Rawls's response to this line of criticism without going into detail regarding the difference principle (see next chapter). But generally his response is as follows.

First, no principles of justice could insure the equal worth to people of many of the basic liberties. Since people differ in so many ways – in their primary aims and their religious views, in intelligence and natural talents, their upbringing, their friends and relatives, their careers, and so on – they will inevitably assign different values to one or another basic liberty. Freedom of thought and expression will often have greater worth for lawyers, academics, and political activists, than for carpenters or real-estate agents with few political or intellectual interests. Freedom of movement is normally worth more to truck drivers than to recluses or the disabled. Freedom of conscience is normally worth more to atheists than to members of a predominant religion (such as Christianity) who otherwise might politically enforce their religious views. Rather than equal worth, the most that principles of justice can do is seek to guarantee the *fair value* of the basic liberties. This is the role of the difference principle: it guarantees that all have income and wealth adequate to the fair and effective exercise of the basic liberties.

Second, it would not only be practically impossible, but also unfair and socially divisive to try to achieve equal worth of liberty, since it can result in great inequalities in income and wealth. To achieve equal worth of freedom of conscience would require lavishing resources on people whose religions require pilgrimages, elaborate rituals, costumes, and cathedrals, while withholding resources to those who silently meditate and practice self-denial (see PL, 325–26). Some people may never vote because they care little for equal political rights and freedom of speech: Are they to be compensated because these liberties are worth little to them? Rawls says that part of being a free person is that individuals are held *responsible for their ends* (PL, 33–34). Free persons do not conceive of themselves as saddled with aims and aspirations which they cannot revise or control. They are regarded as capable of adjusting their aims and aspirations in light of the resources that they can reasonably expect from society. Accordingly, it is not fair to expect others to underwrite one's religious way of life no matter how expensive its requirements may be in order to achieve an elusive equal worth of liberty of conscience.

Rawls's denial that equal worth of liberty is a requirement of justice suggests one way his conception is not welfare-based. Rawls does not see the egalitarian requirements of distributive justice as requiring equal or fair distributions of welfare (or happiness), but rather in terms of equal or fair distributions of certain resources, the "primary social goods" that are essential to individuals' freedom and self-respect: rights and liberties, powers and opportunities, income and wealth, and the bases of self-respect. His liberalism is a "liberalism of freedom" and not a "liberalism of happiness." It is not the role of just social institutions to engineer society so that it promotes the equal or fair distribution of happiness, but rather to fairly provide individuals with the resources they need to freely and fairly pursue ways of life they find worthwhile.

The one exception to Rawls's rejection of the equal worth of the basic liberties is the equal political liberties, the worth of which "must be approximately, or at least sufficiently equal, in the sense that everyone has a fair opportunity to hold public office and to influence the outcome of political decisions" (PL, 327; also TJ, 225–27/197–99 rev.). Rawls thinks that it is hard to realize the ideal of equal citizenship required by justice if the political liberties are of greatly unequal worth to citizens. Hence Rawls includes in the first principle the requirement that the "fair value" of the political liberties be guaranteed (PL, 327–28). "Unless the fair value of these liberties is approximately preserved, just background institutions are unlikely to be either established or maintained" (PL, 327–28). Moreover, the worth of political liberties to people is far more subject to their social position and place in the distribution of income and wealth than are other liberties (PL, 328). Among the measures for achieving the fair value of the political liberties are the provision of public financing of political campaigns and public forums for political debate, along with limits on private political advertising paid for by interested industries and other groups, and fair access to public broadcasting by participating political groups. Rawls nowhere mentions the greater equalization of wealth itself as a condition of maintaining equal political liberties, though others have suggested this. If the measures he suggests are inadequate for the fair value of the political liberties, his position would seem to require distributive measures that equalize the disparities that the difference principle might otherwise allow to the degree needed to establish the fair value of the political liberties for all citizens.

Finally, regarding the worth of the basic liberties, Rawls says: "Taking the two principles together, the basic structure is to be arranged to maximize the worth to the least advantaged of the complete scheme of equal liberty shared by all. This defines the end of social justice" (TJ, 205/179 rev., cf. PL, 326). To say that "the end of social justice" is to maximize the worth of the basic liberties to the least advantaged indicates that Rawls's liberalism is seriously concerned with insuring something other than simply the formal legal protection of basic liberal liberties. While the idea of equal worth of liberty may sound attractive, it is not a realistic ideal. A more realistic and less problematic ideal, he believes, is insuring the worth of everyone's basic liberties, to the degree that their worth to the least advantaged is maximized.

THE PRIORITY OF LIBERTY (TJ, SECTS. 39, 82)

> By the priority of liberty I mean the precedence of the principle of equal liberty over the second principle of justice. The two principles are in lexical order, and therefore the claims of liberty are to be satisfied first. . . . The precedence of liberty means that liberty can be restricted only for the sake of liberty itself.
>
> (*TJ*, 244/214 rev.; see also *PL*, 295)[18]

Liberalism for Rawls assigns precedence to maintaining the basic liberties over other social needs and aims, including the majority's will. A liberal constitution guarantees basic liberties first and above all else. This assumes that a society is ready to sustain a liberal constitution and that everyone's basic needs can be met (JF, 44 n. 7). Otherwise, in less favorable circumstances Rawls's "general conception of justice" applies. It says:

> All social values – liberty and opportunity, income and wealth, and the social bases of self-respect – are to be distributed equally unless an unequal distribution of any, or all, of these values is to everyone's advantage. Injustice, then, is simply inequalities that are not to the benefit of all.
>
> (*TJ*, 62/54 rev.)

The general conception does not give priority to the basic liberties over the fair distribution of other *primary social goods*. The primary social goods, once again, are the resources which Rawls's principle of justice are designed to distribute: rights and liberties, powers and opportunities, income and wealth, and the bases of self-respect (TJ, 62/54 rev.). Rawls in *Theory* describes these as all-purpose social means that any rational person should want whatever else he or she wants (TJ, 92/79 rev.), and of which it is rational to prefer more rather than less (TJ, 397/349 rev.). Their derivation will be discussed later. The general conception of justice regards all the primary goods as of equal significance and distributes them to benefit everyone equally, allowing for an inequality only if it is to the greater benefit of those who end up with the least. The general conception applies to the non-ideal case in conditions unfavorable to liberalism and democracy; once a society is able to sustain a liberal constitution the "special conception of justice" applies, giving priority to the equality of basic liberties over other social values, and equality of fair opportunity over the difference principle. Each society has a duty to seek to establish conditions in which the special conception of justice applies. As Rawls says, "The equal liberties can be denied only when it is necessary to change the quality of civilization so that in due course everyone can enjoy these freedoms" (TJ, 475 rev.). Rawls also thinks that giving priority (or primacy) to the basic equal liberties does not presuppose a high level of income and wealth in society (JF, 47n.). Relatively poor countries, such as India and Costa Rica, can sustain successful democratic governments and societies.

Rawls says "liberty can be restricted only for the sake of liberty itself" (TJ, 244/214 rev.). It is important to understand this to mean "basic liberty" to avoid being misled. Rawls surely does not mean that no restrictions on liberty whatsoever are allowed except to protect other liberties. The reason I cannot raucously party on neighborhood streets at 2 a.m. is not to protect your liberty, but in order that you may sleep. The priority of liberty means that the exercise of a *basic* liberty may be restricted only if this is needed to protect some other basic liberty, or leads to a greater overall liberty in the scheme of basic liberties. This means not simply that basic liberties cannot be restricted for the sake of reasons of public welfare or perfectionist values (already guaranteed by the priority of justice); it also means basic liberties may not be restricted for the sake of non-basic liberties (such as freedom of contract), or even to provide greater opportunities and resources for the poor under the second principle.

Rawls says there are two sorts of cases that violate the priority of liberty. The first is when everyone's basic liberties are restricted unduly or for the wrong reasons. Examples are familiar from American constitutional law. Freedom of political or literary expression cannot be restricted because certain kinds of speech or literature offend people's moral sensibilities. Or, the right to control one's procreation, which is one of the freedoms of the person, cannot be restricted because of religious objections to artificial birth control.[19] The second kind of case involves an inequality of basic liberty. Rawls gives two examples (PL, 295; JF, 47; cf. TJ, 247–48/217–18 rev.). The equal political liberties of some people cannot be restricted on grounds that their having these liberties enables them to defeat policies needed for economic efficiency, or even to provide greater benefits to the least advantaged. Suppose those better off attempt to strike a deal with the poor: "Give up your right to vote, and we'll increase your social minimum." The priority of liberty prohibits this sort of restriction of equal political liberties, for the first principle cannot be traded off for the benefits of the second except in conditions unfavorable to the special conception. The example indicates the importance Rawls assigns to the status of equal citizen.[20] A second example is military conscription. Congress enacted and maintained during the Vietnam War a discriminatory selective service that exempted college students from the military draft on grounds that excusing them from the draft furthered society's educational needs. Again, since the military draft is a serious limit on individuals' freedom, this exemption is an impermissible inequality of the basic liberty of the person (JF, 47).

What kinds of restrictions on basic liberties *are* permitted by the priority of liberty? Under freedom of thought and expression, consider Justice Holmes's example that falsely shouting fire in a dark crowded theater can be made an illegal form of speech, since its effects endanger people's lives. Better examples would be restrictions on speech inciting people to riot or retaliatory violence, or creating fear of bodily harm. Conspiracies to commit crimes can be restricted, as can violent threats to individuals, for they jeopardize freedom and integrity of the person. So-called "hate speech" is different, since, though offensive, it does not immediately endanger basic liberties.

Rawls also recognizes the legitimacy of legal restrictions on such illicit forms of speech as fraud and false advertising. Presumably fraud and false advertising can be restricted since they undermine the first principle's rights to personal property needed for individual independence. But here one might object as follows: "Surely protecting personal property is not the only reason to forbid fraud and misrepresentation. Not all property rights are protected by the first principle, but only by the second principle (for example, ownership rights in the means of production, in so far as that is justified by the difference principle). Commercial misrepresentations involving these rights are just as punishable as when they involve theft of personal property. Also, what about libel, intentionally misrepresenting the truth to undermine a person's character or reputation (so he loses his job, business opportunities, his friends and connections, and so on)? It should be legally actionable at least by civil suit, even if not made a crime. But is libel really an infringement on a basic liberty?"

It may be that libel can be restricted as a kind of infringement on the right of integrity of the person or even to personal property (one's character and good name), but this may involve stretching these concepts more than common sense allows. Still, libel of businesses and brand names would pose a different problem, since corporations are not natural persons and would not seem to be protected under this basic liberty. In any case, assuming restrictions on libel are justifiable under the first principle, it still seems that there are other reasonable restrictions on freedom of speech and expression which are hard to justify by Rawls's requirement that "liberty can be restricted only for the sake of liberty itself." For example, consider (again) yelling drunken obscenities at 2 a.m. at people outside their residence, or near hospitals or funeral homes during services, which are normally punishable as "disturbances of the peace." These annoyances do not violate anyone's *basic* liberties in Rawls's sense. However much some libertarians might allow for these exercises of freedom of speech, it was never Rawls's aim (I believe) to make his liberalism so permissive. But it is not altogether clear from *Theory of Justice* how these annoying utterances may be restricted. In the first edition of *Theory* Rawls addressed this sort of problem by distinguishing between "restrictions" versus "regulations" of speech, an idea which is familiar from the Supreme Court's distinction between impermissible restrictions on content and permissible regulations of the "time, place and manner" of expression.[21] It is not always a violation of freedom of thought and expression if the use of insults and obscenities, or boisterous behavior, are regulated as to their time, place, and manner of expression. Then there is no restriction on content of the message expressed or conveyed. So it may be okay to curse and yell obscenities at your neighbor during daylight hours but not when people in the neighborhood are trying to sleep, or when he's hospitalized or attending his mother's funeral.[22]

A problem remains, however, in deciding when such regulations on expression are reasonable and at what point regulation of time, place, and manner of speech shades over into impermissible restriction on the content of speech. (A time restriction on religious education limiting it to the evening hours so that children will spend daylight hours on non-religious learning would clearly violate freedom of expression and of conscience.) Moreover, in some cases, restrictions on content of speech are appropriate, even if not for the sake of some other basic liberty. Suppose advertisers, engaged in their usual "puffing up" of their products' benefits, cause people to be misled regarding the nutritional or other health values of products. ("This nutritional supplement can strengthen the heart and forestall the aging process!") This sort of near-misrepresentation, though it may not rise to the level of fraud, perhaps should still be limited, for its purpose is simply to dupe people for the sake of financial gain. (Such claims regarding the health-inducing qualities of food and drugs are often regulated and sometimes restricted in the U.S. by the FDA (Food and Drug Administration).) How can Rawls, given the absolute priority he assigns to basic liberties such as free speech, accommodate these sorts of restrictions on speech for the sake of less important interests such as public health and discouraging illicit financial gain?

In the revised edition of TJ Rawls says enigmatically: "These [basic] liberties have a central range of application within which they can be limited and compromised only when they conflict with other basic liberties" (TJ, 54 rev.). Even without further elaboration, this appears to be a major qualification to the priority of liberty set forth in Theory; for it means that not just any exercise of an abstract basic liberty has priority over all other social goods. Rather, it is only when a basic liberty is being exercised in its "central range of application" that it has priority and cannot be limited except for the sake of another basic liberty. But what is the central range of application of a basic liberty, and how is it decided? This is not discussed any further in Theory but is clarified in Lecture VIII of Political Liberalism, "The Basic Liberties and their Priority."

The *central range of application of a basic liberty* is the area of exercise of a liberty in which it is most essential to realize one of the *moral powers*. (Here Rawls speaks of the two fundamental cases, referring to the exercise of each of the moral powers.) The central range of application of *liberty of conscience* and *freedom of association* is in the "first fundamental case" of the exercise and development of the rational capacity for a conception of the good. We saw above that the exercise of these liberties warrants exceptional protection since they are needed to adequately develop and fully exercise the rational capacity to form, revise, and rationally pursue a conception of the good, including the values that give life its meaning for a person (PL, 310–15). Next, the central range of application of *freedom of thought and expression* and of *the political liberties* is in "the second fundamental case" of the exercise and development of the capacity for a sense of justice (PL, 315–24). These liberties are especially central to the informed application of the principles of justice and reasoning about what their institutional requirements (laws and other social norms) imply in particular cases. They are then necessary for democratic citizens' informed and rational deliberation about justice and the common good. Finally, Rawls says that the remaining basic liberties – *freedom and integrity of the person, and the rights and liberties of the rule of law* – are necessary preconditions of the exercise of both moral powers, since "they are necessary if the preceding basic liberties are to be properly guaranteed" (PL, 335).

Now, the *significance* of a particular liberty is the degree to which it is more or less essentially involved in the full and informed exercise of the moral powers in their central range of application in the two fundamental cases. Rawls means here simply that some exercises of a basic liberty have greater significance to realizing the moral powers than others. Political speech regarding matters of justice has extraordinary significance for the exercise of the capacity for justice. As a result Rawls sees political discussion and debate as deserving near-absolute protection. The main exceptions he recognizes are the use of incendiary political polemics or "hate speech" in circumstances that are highly likely to lead to imminent violent action (PL, 336) and limitations on political advertising in the interest of maintaining the fair value of the political liberties. Similarly Rawls sees literary, scientific, artistic, and philosophical speech and expression as significant to the exercise of the rational capacity for a conception of the good. But not all forms of expression are protected by the basic liberties. Commercial advertising, for example, has diminished or no significance for the exercise of the capacity of justice or the capacity to rationally form and pursue a conception of the good. This does not mean that commercial speech does not deserve any protection, only that it is not a basic liberty. Advertising is often relevant to achieving fair equality of opportunity (in advertising of positions and educational opportunities), and also the requirements of economic justice and the difference principle (in the advertising of price information). But as for the kind of "puffing" and near-misrepresentation that is typical of market-strategic advertising, where the sole aim is to beguile customers in order to increase market share, Rawls sees it as "socially wasteful and a well-ordered society that tries to preserve competition and to remove market imperfections would seek reasonable ways to limit it" (PL, 365). Moreover, libel and defamation of private persons has no justification or, as Rawls says, "no significance at all for the public use of reason to judge and regulate the basic structure, and it is in addition a private wrong" (PL, 336). It can be made a civil cause of action for damages.

What emerges from Rawls's later discussion of the basic liberties, and especially freedom of thought and expression, is then a complex multi-tiered account of the basic liberties. The complexity of the account comes out in two ways. First, none of the basic liberties is absolute or has strict priority over any other. There are occasions where any of the basic liberties may be limited for the sake of maintaining a more adequate scheme of basic liberties. For example, freedom of political speech is one of the most important liberties in a democracy. But as important as freedom of political speech is, it is a mistake to rigidly protect political advertising no matter what its harmful effects on the democratic process and the fair value of the political liberties to those less advantaged. Rawls argues then that it was a mistake for the Supreme Court to strike down laws regulating campaign contributions and political advertising, which were enacted to limit distortions of information and to maintain a balance of political views and thereby maintain the integrity of the electoral process (PL, 359–62). Here one basic liberty (freedom of thought and expression) should be restricted or regulated for the sake of another (equal political liberties), where the guiding aim always is to make adjustments in the basic liberties needed to achieve a scheme that is "fully adequate" to the exercise of development of the moral powers.

The second way the complexity of Rawls's account comes out is that not all exercises of an abstract basic liberty deserve the same degree of protection. Political speech deserves greater protection than commercial advertising; commercial advertising of jobs, consumer prices, and product specifications deserves greater protection than market-strategic "puffing"; and libel, defamation, and invasion of the privacy of private citizens should not be protected at all and even treated as civil wrongs. Rawls's account of freedom of expression accords with Supreme Court holdings from the 1960s and into the 1980s, before the ideological shift of the Court beginning in the Reagan presidency. One thing Rawls accomplished (whether intentionally or not) was to give a philo-sophical justification for the liberal Warren-Court era multi-tiered doctrine concerning freedom of speech.[23] His account does not support recent trends in Supreme Court decisions, which give corporate advertising nearly equal status and significance along with other forms of protected speech. And while Rawls never addressed issues such as "hate speech," or obscenity and the regu-lation of pornography, the tendency of his multi-tiered account would seem to permit certain restrictions or at least greater regu-lations on each than are now permitted in constitutional law. For it is unclear how either form of expression relates to the central range of application of the basic liberties in the adequate develop-ment and full exercise of the moral powers. Others, admittedly, might disagree about pornography particularly, and there is room for disagreement since Rawls did not address the issue.

SOME OBJECTIONS TO THE PRIORITY OF LIBERTY

The priority of liberty is one of the more distinctive features of justice as fairness. Rawls says that along with the requirement that all inequalities be justified to the least advantaged, the priority of liberty accounts for "the force of justice as fairness," and that "this pair of constraints distinguishes it from intuitionism and teleolog-ical theories" (TJ, 250/220 rev.). In *Political Liberalism*, Rawls contends that the priority of liberty is a central feature of any genuinely liberal view. But this priority has been widely criticized, even by other liberals, as "dogmatic" (Hart) and "outlandishly extreme" (Barry).[24] These objections are not without force when applied to the vague form in which Rawls left the first principle and the priority of liberty in *Theory of Justice*. There the first prin-ciple required that "Each person is to have an equal right to the *most extensive total system* of equal basic liberties compatible with a similar system of liberty for all" (TJ, 250/220 rev.). The priority rule that is part of the principles of justice said that "a less extensive liberty must strengthen the total system of liberty shared by all" (ibid.). But we all can imagine some restrictive regulation on a basic liberty we could support for the sake of something other than strengthening the scheme of basic liberties. Many liberal advocates of free speech would recognize the legal legitimacy of bans on unregulated obscenity and pornography or public nudity for example, or relieving oneself in public view. Or, assuming that a right of privacy in intimate relations is protected by freedom of the person, surely there are still legitimate (public) reasons for restricting necrophilia and bestiality that have nothing to do with protecting other basic liberties (e.g., public health, respect for the dead, protection of animals from abuse). We've seen that Rawls himself eventually endorses the restriction of certain kinds of speech for reasons other than protecting the basic liberties; for example, market-strategic advertising might be restricted, he suggests, on grounds that it is "socially wasteful."

One of the main problems with the first principle and its priority, particularly in Theory, lies in the "specification" of basic liberties for constitutional and legislative purposes. To return to Hart's question: How are we to decide what constitutional rights and liberties the first principle protects? Rawls states the basic liberties in highly abstract terms, and envisions that they will be further "specified" in the constitutional, legislative, and judicial stages of the "four-stage sequence" he sets forth for applying the principles of justice (TJ, sect. 31). The four-stage sequence consists of (1) the original position; (2) the constitutional stage, at which the principles of justice are applied to decide on a democratic constitution; (3) the legislative stage, where laws are decided in accordance with (1) and (2); and (4) what might be called "the judicial and administrative stage" involving the application of the rules and principles of the other three stages to particular cases. These four stages are all deliberative points of view we are to assume in reasoning about the choice and application of principles of justice. For example, to decide the constitutional rights and procedures the first principle requires, we are to ask ourselves, based on knowledge of general facts about our society, "What constitutional rights and procedures are required to specify the conditions needed to realize the basic liberties of justice?" Rawls lists some of the main constitutional liberties that are included under the basic liberties. For example, the political liberties include equal rights to vote and hold office, freedom of political speech, the right of assembly, the right to form and join political parties, and normally bare majority rule in enacting ordinary legislation (TJ, sects. 36–37). Still, we are often left uncertain about what liberties, if any, go unmentioned and should also be included. For example, Rawls indicates that freedom and integrity of the person include rights to life and against violence, psychological manipulation, and forced servitude, as well as freedom of movement, freedom of occupation, and choice of careers, and a right to hold personal property. But does freedom of the person or freedom of association include a "right of privacy" as understood in American constitutional law (including freedom in one's sexual relations and a right to control one's procreation, with a right to abortion)? Does freedom of conscience and of the person include a right to (assisted) suicide or euthanasia at some stage at the end of a life? Or can one commit suicide even if for no apparent reason? Do the basic liberties encompass a right to use mind-altering drugs, even in a self-destructive fashion? Does freedom of thought and expression include an unregulated right to produce, consume, and display pornography? In Theory Rawls said that the specification of the basic liberties need not be decided in the original position, but could wait until the constitutional and later stages, when more information was available to the parties to help decide what more specific liberties were protected by the first principle. This may only postpone the inevitable problem, for in Theory he provides little guidance of the kinds of considerations that hypothetical parties to the constitutional and later stages are to take into account in specifying the basic liberties. Moreover, the guidance he does provide appears potentially conflicting. Rawls says that we are to occupy the position of a representative equal citizen in applying the first principle, but this alone seems indeterminate without more information about the interests and aims of equal citizens. He also cites approvingly the reasons J.S. Mill gives for his principle of liberty, namely, to develop human capacities and powers and encourage "vigorous natures"; to enable people to have rational and informed preferences; and because people by nature prefer to live under free institutions (*TJ*, 184–85 rev.). But he does not make clear whether he intends the first principle to be as potentially wide-ranging as Mill's principle, for Mill would seem to allow for all kinds of self-destructive conduct so long as it does not "harm" others. Finally, in the revised edition of *Theory* Rawls, perhaps aware of criticisms of his account, adds that "the account of the basic liberties is not offered as a precise criterion that determines when we are justified in restricting a liberty, whether basic or otherwise. There is no way to avoid some reliance on our sense of balance and judgment . . . it may call upon our intuitive capacities" (*TJ*, 180 rev.).

Perhaps Rawls mainly aimed in *Theory* only to show that justice as fairness is a better democratic alternative than utilitarianism and similar teleological views. But it is hard to fully assess the force of Rawls's arguments in *Theory* for the priority of liberty until the problem of the constitutional specification of the basic liberties is resolved. For how can we know whether it is rational to give the abstract basic liberties of the first principle priority over all other social concerns, if we do not know first what the more specific liberties are that we are committed to giving priority to? Rawls implies in *Theory* that the parties run no risks by giving priority to basic liberties over other social values, since the basic liberties only insure the freedom to act and do not require people to exercise their liberties (e.g., their political liberties) if they do not want to. But this ignores the fact that, however much I may rationally prefer complete freedom of expression and action for myself, it is not always rational for me to want other people to have the same liberty that I have.[25] After all, they may abuse their liberty or act against my interests in exercising their liberties. Of course we can still go along with Rawls and agree that the clearest cases should have priority. He makes the most forceful case for liberty of conscience, by arguing that a person who is willing to gamble with and trade off for other primary goods the freedom to hold and practice religious, philosophical, and moral convictions and obligations does not take his convictions seriously; such a person does not even know what is involved in having conscientious convictions and obligations (TJ, 207/181–82 rev.; PL, 311). To agree to any such principle requiring one to sacrifice freedom to practice one's own religious or moral beliefs does not withstand *the strains of commitment* (TJ, 475 rev.), for a person cannot in good faith commit himself to willingly comply with such a restriction in the future. But Rawls himself admits that this argument for the priority of basic liberties applies most forcefully to liberty of conscience, and may not be as convincing with other basic liberties (TJ, 209/184 rev.).

These reasons, for example, would not seem to apply to the priority of the political liberties. Why wouldn't a rational less advantaged person agree to give up his right to vote in exchange for a larger social minimum? After all, what real effect does one person's vote have in a modern democracy? In *Theory* the main argument Rawls makes is that equality of political liberties, and the priority of the basic equal liberties more generally, are among the primary bases of self respect: "The basis for self-respect in a just society is not then one's income share but the publicly affirmed distribution of fundamental rights and liberties. And this distribution being equal, everyone has a similar and secure status" (TJ, 544/477 rev.). Rawls contends that the status required for self-respect in a well-ordered democratic society comes from having the status of equal citizenship, which in turn requires the equal basic liberties. It would not be rational for less advantaged persons to compromise this primary ground for their self-respect, by giving up their right to vote for example, for this would "have the effect of publicly establishing their inferiority as defined by the basic structure of society. This subordinate ranking in public life would indeed be humiliating and destructive of self-esteem" (TJ, 477 rev.). Perhaps so, but why isn't inequality of income and wealth also destructive of their self-esteem? Rawls denies above that having approximate equality of income and wealth is needed for self-respect in a well-ordered society. This is a controversial claim. In order for it to be convincing, Rawls has to tie the conditions of equal citizenship with a principle of distributive justice that expresses a conception of reciprocity. The connection between equal citizenship and the difference principle is discussed later in this chapter.

Another way to understand Rawls's grounds for the priority of liberty in Theory is to connect it with the Kantian interpretation of justice as fairness. Already in 1975, in the revised (German) edition of that book, Rawls says that the parties in the original position have a "highest-order interest in how their other interests . . . are shaped and regulated by social institutions" (TJ, 475 rev.). This is because "The parties conceive of themselves as free persons who can revise and alter their final ends and who give priority to preserving their liberty in this respect" (ibid.). This suggests that the parties to Rawls's social contract, as free persons, have a fundamental interest in (what Rawls later calls) their *rational autonomy*, i.e., their freedom to shape their life plans, revise their final ends, and rationally pursue a conception of the good that is of their choosing. This is one explanation why Rawls's parties in the original position assign priority to the basic liberties, since these liberties are essential conditions of an individual's rational autonomy and framing a life plan that suits his/ her particular character and capacities.[26]

Now it may be that the priority of basic liberty, conceived in maximizing terms of "the most extensive total system of basic liberties" in Theory (as the first principle there says), can only be justified on the Kantian assumption that (rational and moral) autonomy is essential to a person's good. This would accord with the reading of the first principle that likens it to Mill's wide-ranging principle of liberty, which also is (partly) grounded in "individuality," a similar idea to rational autonomy.[27] But this makes the priority of liberty too dependent on the Kantian interpretation, which later (as we'll see in Chapter 7) poses problems for Rawls's liberalism. He addresses these problems in Political Liberalism, but this requires that he give up the Kantian interpretation and narrow the scope of the priority of liberty.

But in fact, the narrowing of the priority of liberty already begins prior to Political Liberalism, in 1982 in "The Basic Liberties and their Priority" (PL, VIII). Here Rawls makes clear two things: first, as the revised first principle states, priority is to be given, not to "the most extensive scheme" (*Theory*), but to "a fully adequate scheme" of basic liberties. Second, the scheme of basic liberties is to be "fully adequate" to the exercise and development of the moral powers, not in just any circumstance, but in the "two fundamental cases" (that is, in applying the principles of justice, and in deliberating about one's conception of the good: PL, 332).

This narrowing of the scope of the priority of liberty implies that Rawls's first principle, post-*Theory*, is not as wide-ranging in the liberties it protects as is Mill's principle of liberty. Whereas Mill's principle of liberty seems to allow for much self-destructive conduct so long as it does not interfere with others' rights and liberties – unregulated rights to suicide and rights to use narcotics, for example (though not a right to sell oneself into slavery) – Rawls's first principle would not seem to protect such conduct and would allow it to be regulated and restricted for other reasons (for example, to maintain the integrity of people's moral powers).[28] Moreover, whereas Mill's principle would seem to allow for gambling, prostitution, and pornography so long as their supply, availability, and enjoyment do not violate others' rights, I believe Rawls again would allow these activities to be restricted for "*public reasons*" other than protecting basic liberties. Rawls says there is a "presumption" of liberty that applies to any action (PL, 292), which means that it may only be restricted for good and sufficient reasons. What are good and sufficient reasons? From Rawls's political liberalism we learn that liberty (non-basic as well as basic) may not be restricted for reasons that stem only from a "comprehensive doctrine" – hence liberty may not be restricted for religious or perfectionist reasons, or simply because others are offended by conduct. But (non-basic) liberties may be restricted for public reasons other than those recognized by Mill and Rawls in *Theory*, and even basic liberties may be restricted for good public reasons if their exercise is not necessary to the exercise and development of the moral powers in the two fundamental cases.

To take an example of Rawls's difference with liberals such as Mill and with his own earlier view: it is difficult to see how the widespread availability and public display of pornographic literature such as is common in many areas in the U.S. can be justified on grounds of the more limited account of priority of liberty Rawls develops post-*Theory*. For in what way does pornography enable the development and exercise of the moral powers? This does not mean that the manufacture of pornographic literature should be restricted. On Rawls's later account, there have to be good "public reasons" grounded in democratic "political values" to overcome the presumption of liberty. But it does imply that the production of pornographic literature, or (another example) recreational drug use, might be restricted for reasons other than protecting "a fully adequate scheme" of basic liberties. The change Rawls makes from *Theory*'s standard of "the most extensive scheme" of basic liberties, to *Political Liberalism*'s "fully adequate scheme" is then substantial. Whereas the first principle in *Theory* seems to imply something akin to the "harm principle" implicit in Mill's principle of liberty — that a liberty may be restricted only if it interferes with or "harms" others in exercising their liberty — Rawls's later work endorses greater restrictions on individuals' liberties, when they are not within the "central range of application" of the basic liberties.

SUMMARY

Rawls's final views regarding liberty and its priority are more complicated than is suggested by the phrase "liberty may be restricted only for the sake of liberty" in *A Theory of Justice*. It is difficult to gain a sense of the full complexity of his position by looking at the explication of the first principle of justice in *Theory* or even in "The Basic Liberties and Their Priority" (lecture VIII of *Political Liberalism*) and without taking into account his final works on public reason (especially "The Idea of Public Reason Revisited," which is discussed here in Chapter 9). With regard to freedom of expression, clearly some forms of speech and expression deserve greater protection than others (political, literary, scientific, and religious/philosophical expression more than advertising and other forms of commercial speech); some speech (product warnings and disclosure of ingredients and nutritional information, for example) may be legally required for health, safety, and other reasons; and other forms of expression warrant no legal protection and can be prohibited (fraud, false advertising, libel, bribery, threats, socially wasteful ads, and perhaps "obscenity" at law). The same complex standard applies to conduct, even conduct that J.S. Mill would call "purely self-regarding." Rawls is not averse to a limited kind of paternalism that would restrict purely self-destructive conduct that is motivated by no legitimate reason (for example, self-destructive use of narcotics, or insufficiently motivated suicides). Rawls's position is, then, difficult to summarize in a sentence but, roughly, his position is that liberty of thought and action can only be restricted or regulated for (what he later calls) sufficient *public* reasons. What public reasons are sufficient for limiting liberties? In the case of basic liberties essential to the exercise of the moral powers of free and equal persons, they can be limited only for the sake of maintaining a "fully adequate scheme" of basic liberties for all. Certain non-basic liberties can only be limited for these and other reasons relating to the second principle, namely considerations of fair equal opportunity and economic justice. And as for non-basic liberties not protected by the principles of justice, there is still a presumption in their favor: They cannot be limited for the "wrong" reasons, such as purely religious reasons or reasons of perfectionist value; instead they may be limited only for "public reasons" that relate to "political values of justice." The "presumption of liberty" can then only be overcome and limited by "the political values of public reason."

But even this does not capture the full complexity of Rawls's account of basic and permissible liberties. For in the case of behavior that does not concern "constitutional essentials and matters of basic justice" (as he terms conduct in *Political Liberalism* not covered by the first and second principles of justice) it may well be that majority democratic decision by itself is sufficient "public reason" for restricting conduct. Suppose Congress decides to establish a national park for purely recreational and aesthetic purposes, or protect a dwindling and endangered species of moles that live in unspoiled prairie land that Old MacDonald plans to sow in wheat? This would be a legitimate restriction on property or use of eminent domain powers on Rawls's account, even though it is for what are arguably "non-public reasons" for Rawls (reasons of recreational and aesthetic enjoyment, and preservation of species with no economic value). The "presumption of liberty" can then be overcome for even non-public reasons when constitutional essentials and matters of basic justice are not at stake. Or rather, one might say that democratic deliberations followed by majority decision are by themselves sufficient public reasons for restricting conduct in cases not covered by Rawls's two principles of justice.

To sum up, Rawls's account of liberty is then governed by the following principles:

1 *The priority of basic liberties:* There is a set of liberties that are called *basic* in so far as they are essential social conditions for the adequate development and full exercise of the two powers of moral personality over a complete life as these liberties are exercised in the two fundamental cases (PL, 293). The exercise of basic liberties that are part of a scheme that is fully adequate to the exercise and development of the two moral powers has absolute priority over other social primary goods (including non-basic liberties), and the exercise of these basic liberties in the "two fundamental cases" can be limited only to protect the exercise of other basic liberties in the scheme. This is the priority of the first principle over the second, or "the priority of *basic* liberties." Some examples: Freedom of political speech can be limited to protect the fair value of the political liberties, but not to discourage anti-war activities or even advocacy of revolution during wartime unless imminent violence is likely. Freedom of (religious or moral) conscience can only be limited to protect others' persons or property; so clearly human sacrifices can be prohibited, even if consented to, but probably not the religious sacrifice of other animals if genuinely integral to a religion's beliefs, so long as there is not a public health risk.

2 *The priority of non-basic liberties protected by the second principle over other social values and political concerns:* The exercise of an abstract liberty

(such as freedom of speech) in a manner that does not fall within the central range of application of that liberty (in the two fundamental cases) is "non-basic," and can be restricted for reasons other than securing a fully adequate scheme of basic liberties. However: (a) If the exercise of these and other non-basic liberties falls within the central range of application of the fair equality of opportunity principle, they may be restricted only for reasons of justice allowed by that principle. Similarly, (b) if the exercise of these liberties is essential to economic justice as determined by the difference principle, they may be restricted only for reasons of justice allowed by the first and second principles. Rawls's example of (a) is freedom of expression in advertising positions. Such advertisements cannot be restricted and may even be required for certain open positions so far as ads are needed to secure fair equal opportunity. On the other hand, advertise-ments to positions that exclude applicants of ethnic, racial, or gender groups ("Non-whites, non-Protestants, and women need not apply") can be prohibited as a violation of fair equality of opportunity (see PL, 363–64). This is a direct restriction on the content of speech, but Rawls has no problem with it since some restrictions on content are needed to insure fair equality of opportunity. An example of (b), a non-basic liberty of speech that promotes the ends of the difference principle, is advertising of price and product infor-mation; it cannot be restricted, though it might be regulated as to time, place, and manner. Moreover, inaccurate or misleading product information can be restricted for the same reason (perhaps also for reasons related to the first principle's right to personal property). Also, Rawls strongly implies that the kind of misleading ads that fill a substantial portion of broadcasting time and which simply involve "puffing" or jockeying for market shares is socially wasteful, and that "reasonable ways to limit it" can be imposed to achieve the aims of the difference principle (PL, 364–65). This is for Rawls another permissible restriction on the content of commercial speech.

3   *The presumption of liberty in other cases*: The exercise of non-basic liberties that are not needed for purposes of the second principle can be restricted, but still there is a "general presumption against imposing legal and other restrictions on conduct without sufficient reason" (PL, 292; JF, 112). From Rawls's later writings it seems that to be a sufficient reason for restricting non-basic liberty a restriction must meet the requirements of *public reason*. This means, roughly, that non-basic liberty may not be restricted purely for religious reasons, or for reasons of perfectionist value, or simply because others find one's conduct offensive or do not like what a person aims to do. More generally liberty may not be restricted solely on grounds of comprehensive moral, religious, and political doctrines. Instead, the reason for restriction must relate to realizing some public *political value*. Already in *Theory* there is a suggestion of this approach to restrictions on liberty. Rawls says that certain kinds of sexual relationships considered "degrading and shameful" cannot be restricted simply because of "aesthetic preferences and personal feelings of propriety" (TJ, 331/291 rev.). So even if freedom of sexual relations were not protected by freedom of the person and freedom of association among the basic liberties (again, it's not clear), they should be protected due to the restrictions of public reason. Here Rawls suggests that monogamy or the prohibition of same-sex marriages cannot be enforced for non-public religious or moral reasons, but only for such public reasons as that monogamy is needed for the equality of women, and that same-sex marriages would be destructive to the raising and educating of children (not that he believes this last claim) (CP, 587). Later Rawls says recognition of full gay and lesbian marital and family rights and duties is in order so long as they are consistent with orderly family life and the education of children (CP, 596n.). On the other hand, I assume that Rawls would argue that public nudity – in the sense of walking the streets naked for all the world to view (as opposed to nudity for commercial purposes in a restricted private space) – is not among the liberties of

expression or freedoms of the person protected by the first principle, nor by reasons related to the second principle. There may be public reasons for regulating public nudity (e.g., the interests of children or avoiding public disruption); if it cannot be restricted entirely, at least it can be limited by time, place, and manner considerations (restricted to non-common areas such as nude beaches, for example). Here it may be that democratic decision itself, even if motivated for non-public reasons such as modesty, provides sufficient public reasons for restricting conduct that the vast majority of people find offensive. For it is hard to see how public nudity is among the liberties needed for the adequate exercise and full development of either moral power, or how it bears on equal opportunities and economic justice.

Finally, this three-part summary of the first principle is somewhat complicated by Rawls's discussion of abortion in *Political Liberalism* (PL, 243–44n., lv–lvin.). It can safely be assumed that the right to control one's own procreation is among the basic liberties of the person; neither the state nor any person or institution can force a person to have children or prohibit her (or him) from having children. This can be justified as among the liberties needed if a person is to be able to control her life so as to be in a position to fully develop and effectively exercise her moral powers. Accordingly it would seem that the right to procreate can only be limited for the sake of maintaining a fully adequate scheme of basic liberties. But Rawls says that among the political values of public reason to take into account in deciding whether women have a right to abortion include "due respect for human life," the "equality of women as equal citizens," and society's interest in its ordered reproduction over time (PL, 243n.). Rawls suggests then that, even if the fetus is not a person with rights of its own, it is still a form of human life that warrants respect; moreover, this *public reason*, along with society's interest in reproducing itself, can play a role in limiting women's right to abortion. But this implies that there are reasons *other than* maintaining the equal basic liberties themselves that can be taken into account in deciding whether to restrict women's basic liberty to control their own procreation. Accordingly, Rawls conjectures that "any reasonable balance of these three values will give a woman a duly qualified right to decide whether or not to end her pregnancy during the first trimester [since] at this early stage of pregnancy the political value of the equality of women is overriding" (PL, 243n.). But after the first trimester the question of a woman's right to abortion is less clear.

Perhaps Rawls's recognition of the potential restriction of the basic liberty of procreation for reasons other than the basic liberties is limited to the special features of abortion, due to the controversy about whether the fetus is or is not a person. But if this case were generalized to other basic liberties, it would suggest that there are few cases where the strict priority of liberty over all other social values is being maintained in Rawls's later account of the first principle.[29] This would suggest that the idea of the priority of liberty is, then, to a large degree replaced in Rawls's later account of the first principle by the idea that the basic liberties may at least sometimes be restricted on grounds of "a reasonable balance of public reasons." I do not for myself think Rawls, intentionally or unintentionally, gives up the priority of liberty in this way, but perhaps it will become clearer when the idea of public reason is taken up in Chapter 9.

FURTHER READING

Cohen, Joshua, "For a Democratic Society," *The Cambridge Companion to Rawls*, Samuel Freeman, ed., New York: Cambridge University Press, 2003, chap. 2. (Discusses how Rawls's account of democracy is grounded in the ideal of a democratic society of free and equal citizens.)

Hart, H.L.A., "Rawls on Liberty and Its Priority," *University of Chicago Law Review* 40 (1973): 534–55; also in *Reading Rawls*. (An important challenge to the first principle of justice, to which Rawls responds in "The Basic Liberties and Their Priority" (*Political Liberalism*, lect. VIII).)

Nagel, Thomas, "Rawls and Liberalism," in *The Cambridge Companion to Rawls*, chap. 1. (A very good account of Rawls's version of liberalism.)

Three

The Second Principle and Distributive Justice

The second principle of justice says:

> Social and economic inequalities are to be arranged so that they are both:
>
> (a) to the greatest benefit of the least advantaged, consistent with the just savings principle, and
> (b) attached to offices and positions open to all under conditions of fair equality of opportunity.
>
> (*TJ*, 302/266 rev.)

A duty to support the poor is endorsed by the major religions. It is an individual moral duty of charity, not a duty the benefits of which the poor can claim as a matter of right. The idea that the members of *society* collectively, through their agents the government, have a political duty to support the poor is different. In *Leviathan* Hobbes says that "men . . . unable to maintain themselves by their labour . . . ought not to be left to the Charity of private persons; but to be provided for, (as far-forth as the necessities of Nature require,) by the Lawes of the Commonwealth."[1] The major historical representatives of the liberal tradition (Locke, Adam Smith, Kant, Mill, and so on) also accepted that one of the roles of government is to provide for the poorest members of society when they are unable to provide for themselves. But only a few of them saw this as a duty of justice (not simply public charity), the benefits of which the poor can claim as a right.

Different still is the idea of *distributive justice*, in the modern sense of a just or fair distribution of income and wealth. Rawls suggests that, unlike society's duty of assistance, its duty of distributive justice has no "target" or "cut-off point."[2] A society has an ongoing duty to fairly distribute income and wealth among people engaged in social and economic cooperation, without regard to whether they are poor or not. (The duty of assistance presupposes distributive justice, in that allocation of productive resources must be settled before a duty of assistance can be satisfied.) This idea of distributive justice is relatively recent. It largely grew out of the socialist criticism of capitalism in the nineteenth century and the great disparities in wealth between workers and owners that accompanied capitalist industrialization. The French socialists reasoned that, since laborers were largely responsible for production, they should have a greater share of the product than the low wages the capitalists gave them – if not an equal distribution, at least a fair distribution. Marx himself ridiculed the French socialists' idea of "fair distribution" as "absolute verbal rubbish," for he thought that socialists' moralizing appeals to the bourgeoisie's sense of justice was ineffective and it was also the wrong sort of consideration to motivate the proletariat to act for their economic interests.[3] Non-Marxian socialists and left-liberal critics of laissez-faire capitalism mainly are responsible for the idea that there is some objective standard for assessing the distribution of income and wealth in society. Many classical liberals and libertarians (most notably Friedrich Hayek) still reject the idea of distributive justice, since it implies that there is some standard by which to assess the "natural distributions" that result from free markets and private ownership of productive resources. Others, such as Robert Nozick, reluctantly accept the idea of distributive justice, and try to neutralize its threat to market distributions by contending that distributive justice is satisfied by individuals' full ownership of whatever distribution results from free market exchanges of their entitlements and through other voluntary gifts or transactions (sales, gambling, etc.).

The difference principle, requiring society to maximize the share that goes to the least advantaged, is only a part, even if the most significant part, of Rawls's account of distributive justice. Rawls says that "We cannot possibly take the difference principle seriously so long as we think of it by itself, apart from its setting within prior principles" (JF, 46n.). For prior principles have important distributive effects; these include the requirements to provide for the fair value of the political liberties, and to set limits on concentrations of wealth to insure fair equality of opportunity (referred to as FEO hereafter) – Rawls's main justification for estate and inheritance taxes, designed to break up large holdings of property. Moreover, the just savings principle imposes duties to save for future generations. Rawls also says that FEO is necessary if justice as fairness is to achieve its aim of making distributive justice a matter of pure procedural justice. This will be explained in due course, but the general point is that for Rawls a just distribution is determined only once the requirements of all the principles of justice are met.

This chapter begins with a discussion of the principle of FEO. Then the difference principle is discussed, and the chapter concludes with a discussion of the relationship between these two principles.

FAIR EQUALITY OF OPPORTUNITY

The idea of equal opportunity is a fixed point in liberal thought. At a minimum it involves the absence of restrictions on entry into desired social and political positions. Positions are to be held open to everyone to compete for on grounds of qualifications relevant to performing the tasks of that position, regardless of people's racial, ethnic, or gender group, religious or philosophical views, or social or economic position. Equal opportunity developed out of the rejection of hereditary nobility, and the idea that people are to be assigned social positions by birth. As Kant said, "Every member of the commonwealth must be permitted to attain any degree of status . . . to which his talent, his industry, and his luck may bring him; and his fellow subjects may not block his way by [appealing to] hereditary prerogatives."[4] Open positions partly defines equality of opportunity. Equal opportunity is another way that liberals incorporate the value of equality (in addition to equality of basic rights and liberties).

Liberals have different understandings of equal opportunity. The idea of open positions was integral to classical liberalism. Adam Smith argued for "careers open to talents" mainly on grounds of economic efficiency. To allot positions solely on the basis of applicants' talents and abilities is presumed to be the best way to take advantage of people's diverse skills so as to lead to maximum productive output. (At the same time Edmund Burke and G.W.F. Hegel objected to equal opportunity on grounds that a class society supports a class of landowners better suited to political rule in the interests of all members of society; see TJ, 300/264 rev.).

To really achieve the classical liberal ideal of open positions it is not enough that there be no legal restrictions on groups entering into professions or taking advantage of educational opportunities. There also must be an absence of social or conventional restrictions; otherwise private employers can discriminate at will in hiring. Some classical liberals argue that market considerations alone are sufficient to achieve open positions and "careers open to talent"; those who discriminate for irrelevant reasons will succumb to competitors who hire solely on the basis of job qualifications. But if everyone conventionally discriminates against a group (as was the case with blacks and women for most of our history) then markets cannot address the problem of unequal opportunities. Achieving open positions, then, requires laws prohibiting private discrimination in hiring and educational decisions (for example, the Civil Rights Acts of 1964). For this reason libertarians such as Robert Nozick and Milton Friedman reject equal opportunity, since it imposes restrictions on people's abilities to use their property and employ whomever they please.[5]

Rawls distinguishes the classical liberal idea of open positions – or "formal equality of opportunity" – from a more substantive idea, "fair equality of opportunity." In addition to preventing discrimination and enforcing open positions, fair equal opportunity seeks to correct for social disadvantage. Few people would deny that upper- and middle-class children normally enjoy greater educational and job opportunities than those poorer, by virtue of the privileges that attend being born into a more advantaged social class. Rawls depicts FEO as correcting for these social class differences.

> Those with similar abilities and skills should have similar life
> chances. More specifically, assuming that there is a distribution

of natural assets, those who are at the same level of talent and ability, and have the same willingness to use them, should have the same prospects of success regardless of their initial place in the social system. In all sectors of society there should be roughly equal prospects of culture and achievement for everyone similarly motivated and endowed. The expectations of those with the same abilities and aspirations should not be affected by their social class.

(*TJ*, 73/63 rev.)

In *Theory* Rawls mentions only two institutional requirements imposed by FEO (though he implies there are more): "preventing excessive accumulations of property and wealth and . . . maintaining equal opportunities of education for all" (TJ, 73/63 rev.). Since the first is left quite vague, I focus for now on the latter requirement. FEO mainly imposes on society a positive duty to offer educational opportunities so that those with similar talents who are socially disadvantaged can compete on fair terms with those more advantaged by social class. Public funding of education is then a requirement of FEO. Rawls does not say this requires a public school system, as opposed to public funding of private schools. Indeed, his writings imply that a publicly funded and regulated but still entirely private educational system (for example, a voucher system) would be compatible with FEO.[6] Any grounds for mandatory public education in Rawls would need to derive from somewhere else, perhaps his emphasis on democracy in the first principle and on the conditions for the stability of a democratic society.[7]

In presenting FEO as mainly a corrective to formal equal opportunity's treatment of social class, Rawls assumes a competitive framework. Both forms of equal opportunity assume, then, a right to compete for open positions, and neither is designed to insure equal or proportionate success to salient social groups. So-called "affirmative action," or giving preferential treatment for socially disadvantaged minorities, is not part of FEO for Rawls, and is perhaps incompatible with it. This does not mean that Rawls never regarded preferential treatment in hiring and education as appropriate. In lectures he indicated that it may be a proper corrective for remedying the present effects of past discrimination. But this assumes it is temporary. Under the ideal conditions of a "well-ordered society," Rawls did not regard preferential treatment as compatible with fair equal opportunity. It does not fit with the emphasis on individuals and individual rights, rather than groups or group rights, that is central to liberalism.

Consider now the grounds for (fair) equality of opportunity. According to the utilitarianism of Adam Smith and the classical economists, opening careers to talents secures the most productive use of people's abilities and is economically efficient. Hobbesian contract views endorse equal opportunity for its economic efficiency too, but also because people want to achieve for themselves the external benefits (the income, reputation, and influence) that desirable positions bring and do not want to forgo these benefits for arbitrary reasons.[8] Rawls recognizes efficiency and the external rewards of office and reputation as among the reasons for the fair opportunity principle, but he does not see them as the primary reason for it. The main reasons for this principle are, first, it is *integral to the equal status of free and equal citizens.* Like equal basic liberties, FEO is one of the social bases of self-respect. To be excluded from social positions on grounds of race, gender, religion, and so on, is an affront to one's dignity as an equal person and citizen. Second, people deprived of fair opportunities are "debarred from experiencing the realization of self which comes from a skillful and devoted exercise of social duties [and as such] would be deprived of one of the main forms of the human good" (TJ, 84/73 rev.). Here Rawls seems to connect FEO with the Aristotelian Principle and the idea of a social union of social unions (discussed in Chapter 6). The main idea is that FEO is essential to the adequate exercise and development of our "higher capacities" (to use Mill's term), including our capacities for productive labor and for a sense of justice.[9] We will see (ch. 6) that Rawls's Aristotelian Principle implies that the development of our capacities is rationally desirable, a part of the human good.

A third main reason for fair opportunity is that it complements the difference principle. "The role of the principle of fair opportunity is to insure that the system of cooperation is one of pure procedural justice. Unless it is satisfied, distributive justice could not be left to take care of itself" (TJ, 87/76 rev.). The difference principle, then, works in tandem with FEO; both are needed to establish a just distribution of income and wealth. It is only in a society where FEO to compete for open positions is satisfied that distribution designed to maximize the share of the worst-off will satisfy the requirements of distributive justice. How this may be so is discussed in the following section.

Lexical Priority of FEO over the Difference Principle

As Rawls's first principle has lexical priority over the second, so too within the second principle Rawls gives the principle of FEO lexical priority over the difference principle. There are several ways this priority might express itself. First it may limit the degree of inequality of income, wealth, and other resources otherwise allowed by the difference principle. The difference principle allows inequalities in income and wealth so long as these differences maximally benefit the least advantaged members of society. But suppose there comes a point where greater inequality has the effect of concentrating economic power in those better off so that it limits opportunities for those less advantaged. Then the inequality is prohibited even if it works to the greater benefit of the worst-off in terms of greater income and wealth. The role of equal opportunity in maintaining the equal status of free and equal citizens is more important than is their having the marginal increase in income and wealth. These and other egalitarian effects of lexical priority are discussed later along with the difference principle.

Second, lexical priority implies that fair educational opportunities cannot be limited for the sake of greater income and wealth to the worst-off. For example, on the basis of Rawls's claim that FEO aims to establish similar life chances for those with similar talents, some have interpreted FEO mainly as a kind of compensation for those who are socially disadvantaged but naturally advantaged: it allows them to fully educate their capacities and compete on equal terms with those with similar natural talents who are born socially better off. But, as Thomas Nagel says, since FEO seeks to educate individuals to the limits of their capacities, "It is pretty clear that the good of education is unequally distributed by such a system."[10] It is unequally distributed in favor of the more talented since they require presumably more years of education to train their greater natural talents to the fullest, and have more interest in education than the less advantaged. On this reading, FEO corrects the inequalities of educational opportunity that result from social class, but does nothing to correct for natural inequalities. On the contrary, it may aggravate the effects of unequal natural talents by generating greater social inequality. Some object to this inegalitarian effect of FEO, contending that it provides little benefit to the naturally untalented, and may even harm them by exaggerating inequalities and undermining the difference principle.

Is this an accurate interpretation? Assuming FEO dictates unequal education benefits between the more and less talented, it is not clear that these must translate into greater inequality of income and wealth. Clearly by opening up job opportunities FEO promotes less inequality than formal equality of opportunity would, for more candidates are in a position to compete for desirable positions, thereby driving down the level of income the more advantaged receive. Moreover, while it may be true that greater inequalities may result from FEO under the system of liberal equality where distribution of income and wealth is decided by market distributions (TJ, sect. 12), this is no longer the case when FEO is combined with the difference principle, which allows only those inequalities of wealth that benefit the worst-off.

Finally, it is questionable whether in fact FEO does necessarily allow for inequalities of education benefits favoring the talented. Rawls does not conceive of the FEO principle as part of a meritocratic social system that rewards talent to promote economic efficiency over other social values (TJ, 84/73 rev.). His example of the fair opportunity principle's requirements is just the opposite: FEO requires that those with less (not more) natural talent be given greater educational benefits than normal, so that they are able to develop their capacities in order to effectively take advantage of the full range of opportunities available in society.

> We must when necessary take into account the primary good of self-respect ... The confident sense of their own self-worth should be sought for the least favored and this limits the forms of hierarchy and the degrees of inequality that justice permits. Thus, for example, resources for education are not to be allotted solely or necessarily mainly according to their return as estimated in productive trained abilities, but also according to their worth in enriching the personal and social lives of citizens, including here the least favored.
>
> (*TJ*, 107/91–92 rev.)

The primary justification for the FEO is not technological advancement or encouraging a meritocracy to the greater realization of productive efficiency or perfectionist values. It is rather the egalitarian aim of guaranteeing an important social basis of self-respect for all citizens without regard to their natural abilities. When citizens are unable to fully develop their capacities, no matter how modest, and positions are "not open on a basis fair to all," then those excluded are "debarred from experiencing the realization of self which comes from a skillful and devoted exercise of social duties. They would be deprived of one of the main forms of human good" (*TJ*, 84/73 rev.).

So while FEO may, if taken in isolation or as part of "liberal equality," allow for unequal educational benefits favoring the naturally talented, this is not its consequence within justice as fairness. Given both the importance of the primary good of self-respect and the difference principle, justice as fairness requires greater educational benefits for the worst-off. What this shows is that Rawls's three principles (equal basic liberties, FEO, and the difference principle) acquire their meaning only in relation to each other. What FEO means in the context of Liberal Equality is different from what it requires in Democratic Equality (see *TJ*, 106/91 rev.). As Rawls says, "The difference principle transforms the aims of society in fundamental respects" (*TJ*, 107/91 rev.).

Rawls may encourage the (mis)understanding in *TJ* sect. 12 that FEO is designed mainly to enable the socially disadvantaged to compete with the socially advantaged who are equally talented. But the problem with reading FEO this way – as if it were designed mainly to benefit the talented born into low social positions – is that it obscures the way in which this and other principles are to be construed in light of the ideal of persons as free and equal that informs justice as fairness. A broader reading of FEO becomes apparent in *Political Liberalism* and the *Restatement*. Here Rawls adds that rights to provision of health care are among the requirements of FEO.[11] For without the guarantee of health care a person is not in a position to take advantage of the opportunities generally available to people with his or her talents and abilities. Being in a position to develop one's capacities and talents, *whatever* they may be, is needed to maintain one's status and self-respect as a free and equal citizen capable of social cooperation over a complete life. The governing idea (brought out in Rawls's later works) is that all three principles of justice are to be construed in accordance with the ideal of free and equal persons and what is needed for them to achieve their fundamental interests. Unlike liberal equality, where FEO might be construed simply as a way of rectifying the effects on the naturally talented of their being born into a socially disadvantaged position (Nagel's reading), in justice as fairness, FEO is given a much broader reading, one that is tailored to the requirements of the liberal and democratic ideal of the person that underlies the view.

So it is not clear how, as some suggest, the lexical priority of FEO over the difference principle implies that opportunities or benefits for the poor are to be sacrificed for the sake of greater educational or economic opportunities for the naturally talented. Still, lexical priority of FEO must involve *some* restriction on resources going to the worst-off. To see how, suppose untalented children of unskilled workers have no desire to take advantage of the educational subsidies designed to expand their opportunities (to acquire technical skills within their capabilities, for example). They'd rather quit school as soon as legally permissible and take up unskilled labor positions like their parents, knowing full well that they are forgoing future gains and consigning themselves to the worst-off position. Clearly they would be better off if they took advantage of educational subsidies. Failing that, they would be better off if they were allowed to collect (either in a lump sum payment or over a term of years) the educational resources that otherwise would have been spent on them, and use them to buy whatever they please. (Cf. Milton Friedman's suggestions to replace in kind welfare measures with cash grants.) But arguably it would be unwise to give it to them, since this would act as an incentive to drop out of school and forgo training in labor skills for the sake of immediate financial gain. Assuming this is a reasonable policy then the lexical priority of FEO over the difference principle works to the disadvantage of unskilled workers in this case. Unskilled workers would be better off if they were allowed to collect the training subsidies set aside in their behalf, and spend them as they please. But in the interest of encouraging people to develop their capacities and maintaining FEO, this is not allowed. I believe this is not an unreasonable policy, though others may think differently, saying it is not only paternalistic but also results in less overall welfare.

There may be other objections to the lexical priority of FEO not dealt with here. It should be noted that in his lectures Rawls himself expressed uncertainty regarding the lexical priority of FEO, recognizing others' misgivings that it is too strong. "How to specify and weight the opportunity principle is a matter of great difficulty and some such alternative [either a weaker priority or a weaker form of the opportunity principle] may well be better" (JF, 163, n. 44). The general point, however, is that the main purpose of fair equal opportunity is to provide citizens generally, not simply the more naturally talented, with the means to develop and train their natural abilities so that they (a) can take full advantage of the range of opportunities open to people with similar abilities, and (b) attain self-respect in their status as equal citizens. It is not the role of fair equal opportunity to promote economic efficiency or establish a meritocracy by bringing to fruition the natural talents of those who are naturally gifted but socially disadvantaged in relation to others with equal natural talents.

FEO and the Family

Another problem in interpreting FEO arises in determining its scope. Suppose it is argued that genuinely equal opportunities are achieved only if all have the same likelihood of achieving any social position from birth. Call this 'perfect equality of opportunity.' The problem is that people are born with diverse talents and abilities, among other differences, and, assuming a fair competitive system designed to take advantage of people's diverse abilities, those with greater skills and motivation normally will win out over those with fewer talents. We might, of course, allocate social positions by a random process (a lottery perhaps), but few would want to live with that. Most believe society should take advantage of people's talents and skills, since in general most people benefit from them (at least potentially). The liberal idea of equal opportunity has always implicitly assumed that opportunities should be equal, not in a random sense, but for those who are similarly endowed and who are willing to work to develop their natural abilities and compete for positions.

But even then, one might object, it is hard to see how genuinely equal opportunities can be afforded, given the different circumstances in which people are raised and educated. As Rawls himself says, "The principle of fair opportunity can only be imperfectly carried out, at least as long as some form of the family exists" (TJ, 74/64 rev.). This suggests to some that the only way to really achieve FEO is to abolish the family, and some feminists have taken this as grounds for doing so.

The family a person is born into bestows enormous advantages on some – mainly those who are socially better situated – and disadvantages on others with regard to their future opportunities. Economic class differences parallel differences in how parents raise their children. For example, upper-middle-class parents devote far more attention and time to the education and extra-curricular activities of their children than do less advantaged parents. This has enormous consequences for children's life prospects, perhaps even more so than the kind of formal education they have.[12] But while abolishing the family might go some way towards resolving the problem of unequal opportunities it would not completely resolve it (not to mention that abolishing the family would also violate the first principle's freedom of association, plus be enormously detrimental to children's emotional development). There are all kinds of other contingencies that affect the opportunities of those similarly endowed – education, friendships, geographical location, brute fortune, among others. For this reason Rawls says, "It is impossible in practice to secure equal chances of achievement and culture for those similarly endowed" (ibid.). Does this mean that the idea of (fair) equal opportunity is an illusory aim? Libertarians, such as Robert Nozick, have suggested it is and think we should just give up on the idea. Rawls's position is to limit the understanding of what FEO involves. It does not require the practically impossible, namely equal chances for everyone, or even for those who are similarly endowed. Instead it requires much more modest measures, namely educational opportunities that enable all to fully develop their capacities, universal health-care provisions, and so on. By itself, FEO does not require that the family be abolished any more than it requires that friendships be abolished.[13] Both are protected by freedom of association. But even if they were not, Rawls does not understand FEO as requiring equal chances for the equally endowed. Perfect equality of opportunity to succeed in life and compete for desirable social positions is not worth achieving whatever its costs. For Rawls, equality of opportunity is not grounded in the "luck egalitarian" ambition to equalize life chances where possible and compensate for natural disadvantage and bad luck when it is not. Nor is it grounded, as we have seen, in the classical liberal ambition to promote economic efficiency and the aims of a meritocratic society. Instead, one of the main grounds of equal opportunity resides in promoting the independence and self-respect of equal citizens. What is important is that people, whatever their natural abilities and social circumstances, be given the means to fully develop and effectively exercise the talents and abilities that they are endowed with, so that they may engage in public life as equal citizens, and have a fair opportunity to compete with others of similar abilities for positions within the range of their developed skills. We turn next to a second major purpose of fair equal opportunity, namely its role in establishing distributive justice.

ECONOMIC JUSTICE AND THE DIFFERENCE PRINCIPLE

Rawls's difference principle does not simply add a duty of justice to assist the poor to the traditional list of duties a society owes to its members. It is not simply a duty to provide "welfare payments" or public assistance to those straitened by unfortunate circumstance. The difference principle goes deeper than that and functions on a different plane. Legal institutions specifying rights of property and contract, and economic institutions that make production, trade, and consumption possible are to be designed from the outset focusing on the prospects of the economically least advantaged. Rather than setting up the economic system so that it optimally promotes some other value (efficiency, aggregate utility, freedom to choose, etc.) and then allowing its benefits to "trickle down" to the poor – as if their well-being were an afterthought, the last thing to be taken care of by the social system – the difference principle focuses first on the prospects of the least advantaged in determining the system of ownership and control, production and exchange. One economic system is more just than another in the degree to which it better advances the economic interests of the least advantaged. Moreover, the economic system that is *most just* makes the least advantaged members of society better off than the least advantaged in any other feasible economic system (subject to the important condition that it is consistent with basic liberties and FEO).

The Application of the Difference Principle to the Basic Structure of Society

The difference principle is a principle for institutions, not for individuals. This is not to say that the difference principle does not imply duties for individuals – it creates innumerable duties for them. It means rather that the difference principle applies in the first instance to regulate economic conventions and legal institutions, such as the market mechanism, the system of property, contract, inheritance, securities, taxation, and so on. It is, you might say, a "rule for making the rules" individuals are to observe in daily life. It is then to be applied directly by legislators and regulators as they make decisions about the rules that govern the many complicated institutions within which economic production, trade, and consumption take place. Rawls envisions the difference principle as the primary principle to guide the deliberations of democratic citizens as they debate the common good, and the decisions of legislators as they enact laws to realize the common good of democratic citizens. Individuals' conduct is to be guided or regulated by these laws and norms made pursuant to the difference principle. In this way the difference principle *applies indirectly to individuals*. This means that the difference principle is not designed to be taken into consideration and directly applied by consumers or firms as they make specific economic choices. For example, in my buying decisions the difference principle does not impose a duty to "buy American" or to purchase more costly goods from a less efficient firm when this leads to greater benefits for the worst-off. Consumers do not have the kind of information needed to apply the difference principle in their individual economic choices. Rarely can any individual ever know whether his economic choice is more or less beneficial to the less advantaged. Rawls assumes that individuals normally will act like ordinary economic agents, seeking to obtain as much "bang for the buck" as they can and thereby maximize their economic utility. This does not mean Rawls assumes that only self-interested market motives are an ineluctable fact of human nature. Instead he thinks that taking advantage of markets in production results in the most rational (productive and least wasteful) use of economic resources – land, labor, and capital. Because of limitations on the information that any person or planning committee can have regarding supply, demand, and other relevant information, market allocations better utilize available resources to satisfy individuals' demands than any non-market allocation and distribution procedure. Now it is against a background of market allocations of factors of production that Rawls assumes that the difference principle will work best to advance the position of the worst-off within a market economy where people act in their own interests in making their economic choices. The difference principle applies directly to institutions and only indirectly to individuals, partly in order to take advantage of Adam Smith's "invisible hand."

The direct application of the difference principle to structure economic institutions and its indirect application to individual conduct, exhibits what Rawls means when he says that the "primary subject of justice is the basic structure of society" (TJ, 7/6 rev.). The *basic structure of society* consists of the arrangement of the political, social, and economic institutions that make social cooperation possible and productive. These institutions have a profound influence on individuals' everyday lives, their characters, desires, and ambitions, as well as their future prospects. The *basic institutions* that are part of the basic structure include, first, the political constitution and the resulting form of government and the legal system that it supports, including the system of trials and other legal procedures; second, the system of property, whether public or private, that must exist in any society to specify who has exclusive rights to and responsibilities for the use of goods and resources. The system of property specifies the rights, powers, and duties that individuals and groups have with respect to the use and enjoyment of resources and other things; third, the system of markets and other means of transfer and disposal of economic goods, and more generally the structure and norms of the economic system of production, transfer, and distribution of goods and resources among individuals; and, fourth, the family in some form, which from a political perspective is the primary mechanism any society must have for the raising and education of children, and thus the reproduction of society over time.

The distinguishing feature of each of these institutions, what makes them part of the basic structure of society, is not simply that they have such a profound influence on individuals' lives and future prospects. This might be said of other institutions in society, such as its religious institutions, its universities, or its mass communication networks. Nor is the distinguishing feature of these institutions that they all in some way involve coercive political enforcement of their rules, unlike the rules of voluntary associations. It is true that most if not all societies exercise some degree of coercive political enforcement of the constitutive rules of basic institutions. There is a large degree of voluntary cooperation within markets and the family, but still the constitutive rules that constitute markets, property, and the family are normally coercively enforced. (Children have no right to permanently leave home, and voluntary contracts are legally enforced.) But it's not the coercive enforcement of social rules themselves that distinguishes basic institutions from other institutions. After all, if everyone freely accepted the application of the rules all the time, coercion might never be needed. Rather it's the *reason* for coercion, namely that *basic institutions are essential to social life*. The distinctive feature of the basic social institutions that constitute the basic structure is that they are, in some form or another, *necessary for productive social cooperation*, and hence for the continued existence of any society, particularly any relatively modern one. As Hume recognized, any society must have rules of private and/or public property specifying which persons or groups have exclusive rights to use and control goods and resources and under what conditions. Likewise, if production and division of labor are to be possible, rules for the transfer of goods and resources are needed, whether by gifts, bequests, markets, or some other form of sale. And even in societies where there is no official state with coercive powers, there needs to be some system of commonly accepted second-order rules (i.e., a "constitution" whether written or unwritten) with offices and rules for identifying, applying, and revising the many first-order social rules and basic institutions that otherwise are needed to make cooperation possible. The need for some form of the family for the reproduction of society over time has been mentioned.

In many respects Rawls's account of basic institutions and the basic structure follows Hume's account of justice. Hume also saw norms specifying and governing property, transfers by markets and other allocative mechanisms, and promises, contracts and other modes of consent, to be necessary for the economic production, distribution, and consumption that sustain social life. Governments, or some mechanism for making, revising, applying, and enforcing these and other social rules, were also among the

necessary "conventions" of justice.[14] Rawls's idea of a social institution is in many regards patterned upon Hume's account of the
conventions of justice (though there are certain important differences we need not go into).[15] This resemblance in large part is
due to the mediating influence of H.L.A. Hart, whose own account
of the nature of law is influenced by Hume's account of justice.[16]

The basic social institutions that make up a society's basic structure can be designed in different ways, and can be combined with
other basic institutions to form potentially many different socially
cooperative schemes. The clearest example is the different kinds of
political constitutions that maintain feasible forms of government
(various forms of democracy or republican governments, as well
as monarchies, oligarchies, and so on). Moreover, any society
must allow for at least some degree of personal property – individuals have to control their own clothing and certain resources
they immediately need to function and be productive – and the
scope and limits of permissible forms of personal property are
numerous. For example, consider ownership of intangibles such
as patents, copyrights, securities, bonds, and so on, and the
different ways each of these can be structured. Also the institution
of property in the means of production and in transportation and
communications systems and "public utilities" can be either
privately or publicly held, or, as in many Western countries, held
mostly privately and but also partly publicly. (For example, in the
U.S. there is public ownership of the highway and postal systems,
airports, water and sewer systems, and in some cases still public
utilities such as natural gas and electricity; but the railroad system
and airlines, the telephone and cable system, and many natural gas
and electricity distributors are private.) The main point is that
there are many different ways to define the myriad rights, powers,
duties, and liabilities that constitute ownership or property in
something. A primary role of the difference principle is that it is
to be applied to specify appropriate forms of ownership and property rights and responsibilities, as well as permissible and
impermissible transactions in the economic system.

It is not only the difference principle that is to apply to the basic
structure, but the first principle and FEO too. The first principle of

justice is the primary principle to be used for designing the political constitution, while the second principle is the primary principle to apply to economic institutions and property. This is what Rawls means when he says that the basic structure of society is "the first subject of justice." The most basic principles of social justice are to apply in the first instance and most directly to the basic institutions that make social cooperation possible.

Earlier I said that it is against a background of market allocations of factors of production that Rawls assumes that the difference principle will work best to advance the position of the worst-off within a modern economy. It is now generally accepted by advocates of capitalism and socialism alike that markets are a more effective way to allocate factors of production than any planning system of the kind found in command economies (such as Soviet communism). But importantly the acceptance of market systems by no means implies that the distribution of income and wealth is to be decided by whatever people gain from the sale of their goods and services on the market. Rawls indicates that using market prices for purposes of allocation of productive resources is quite different from relying exclusively on markets for the distribution of income and wealth (TJ, sect. 42; 273–74/241–42 rev.). Indeed, the main point of the difference principle is to provide a non-market criterion for deciding the proper division of income and wealth resulting from market allocations of productive resources and the resulting social product. This is clear from Rawls's initial contrast of democratic equality and the difference principle with liberal equality and the system of natural liberty, both of which advocate the principle of efficiency (TJ, sects. 12–13). The principle of efficiency is a market criterion for distribution characteristic of classical liberalism. Taken by itself, the principle of efficiency implies that any distribution that results from market transactions is just (TJ, 72/62 rev.). As such, it seems to allow for most any distribution, even one where a small minority of people have most everything, and the great majority have next to nothing. (Here it should be noted that, though classical liberals such as Adam Smith and Friedrich Hayek normally regard market distributions as just, they also usually recognize society's duty to provide public goods and a social minimum for the poorest and the disabled. This distinguishes classical liberals from libertarians.)

By contrast with classical liberalism's efficiency criterion of distributive justice, the difference principle requires that economic institutions be designed so that the least advantaged class enjoys a greater share of income, wealth, and economic powers more generally, than it would under any other economic arrangement (with the important qualification that the final distribution is compatible with equal basic liberties and fair equal opportunities). For purposes of illustration, imagine the difference principle is applied by legislators to choose from among a range of economic systems.[17] To simplify, imagine a continuum of economic systems (see Table 3.1), starting from libertarian *laissez-faire* capitalism on the right (where all property is privately owned and all allocations and distributions are decided by unregulated market exchange, or by gift, bequest, gambling, or some other free choice), through classical liberalism, then a variety of mixed economies, all the way to Soviet-style command economy on the left (where allocation and distribution is decided according to a central plan).

The difference principle says the preferred economic system along this continuum is the one whose mix of economic and legal institutions makes the least advantaged class better off (in terms of its members' share of income and wealth and powers and positions of office) than all other systems along the continuum. Later we will discuss Rawls's conjecture that the preferred system will be either a property-owning democracy or market socialism (JF, 138–39). He believes that the least advantaged will fare better in terms of economic power and income and wealth in one or the other of these two economic systems, depending on cultural conditions, than under welfare-state capitalism or some other form of capitalism or socialism.

Command-economy communism	Market socialism	Property-owning democracy	Welfare-state capitalism	Liberal equality	Classical liberalism	Libertarian *laissez-faire*

Table 3.1

Who are the least advantaged members of society? Rawls means least advantaged in the sense of a group's share of primary goods. He says that, since one's share of income and wealth generally corresponds also with one's share of the primary goods of powers, positions of authority, and bases of self-respect, we can regard the least advantaged to be the economically least advantaged people in a society – i.e., the poorest people (though they may not in fact be poor in an absolute sense). So the least advantaged are not the people who are the unhappiest or the unluckiest, nor are they the most handicapped. Rawls deals with the problem of special needs, such as handicaps, separately from the difference principle. Nor are the least advantaged even the poorest among people, those who are unemployed because they are unable or unwilling to work; for example, the least advantaged are not beggars or homeless people, or people who just hate work and had rather surf all day off the California coast while making do as best they can. Again, Rawls deals with the homeless, beggars, and the unemployed under separate principles other than the difference principle. By "least advantaged," Rawls means the *least advantaged working person*, as measured by the income he/she obtains for gainful employment. So the least advantaged are, in effect, people who earn the least and whose skills are least in demand – in effect, the class of minimum-wage workers.

Rawls has been widely criticized for leaving the handicapped out of his account of distributive justice.[18] The objection is that surely people with severe mental and physical handicaps are worse off than the working poor; at least the poor have the potential to improve their situation. Why does Rawls define "least advantaged" this way? Basically he conceives of society in terms of social cooperation, which he regards as productive and mutually beneficial, and which involves an idea of reciprocity or fair terms. Since social cooperation is by nature productive and involves reciprocity, for a person to fully engage in social cooperation suggests that this person has the requisite capacities for cooperation (including the moral powers and capacities for productive labor), that he or she exercises these capacities, and is willing and able to do his or her fair share in contributing towards social cooperation and the resulting social product. (This is not to say that the handicapped do not engage in cooperation and contribute to production in a more limited sense, for clearly many, perhaps even most, have a capacity to, except the most severely handicapped.) More specifically Rawls is concerned with finding the most appropriate principles of justice that specify the fair terms of social cooperation among free and equal persons who cooperate with one another on grounds of reciprocity and mutual respect. He assumes the ideal case where people live a normal course of life, engage in gainful employment, and are capable of making contributions to the social product. The question he raises with regards to distributive justice is, then: What are the most appropriate principles for designing basic economic institutions and distributing the product among socially productive and freely associating equal citizens, each of whom is willing to contribute his/her fair share to social cooperation? This is the question that, Rawls assumes, underlies discussions of economic justice in a democratic society at least since Mill and Marx. It was the question that motivated the socialist criticism of *laissez-faire* capitalism in the nineteenth century. Since this question concerns how to design and structure basic economic and legal institutions that are necessary for society and social cooperation, it is a question that must be answered first, *before* a democratic society can address more specific questions of special needs of the handicapped, the unemployed, and so on.

This does not mean that Rawls "sidelines" the handicapped and fails to address their special claims. The needs of the handicapped are surely questions of justice. But for Rawls they are not questions of *distributive justice* in *his* sense of the principles that structure basic economic and legal institutions. These other problems should be addressed by principles and duties of *remedial justice*, such as the duty of mutual aid, duties of assistance and rescue, and the duty of mutual respect for persons. For Rawls it is the role of democratic legislators (or any government) to decide what kind and how much in the way of special benefits are to be extended to the mentally and physically handicapped, once they know the level of resources and wealth available in society. Surely there *is* some sort of social minimum that follows from the various duties of assistance society owes the handicapped. But it is separate from the question of how much society owes to its members who are fully engaged in productive social cooperation, and who must produce the resources that ultimately are needed to satisfy special needs. The handicapped who are socially productive, as many are, are due their fair share under both principles of distributive and remedial justice. But from Rawls's perspective, we cannot begin to address handicaps and other special needs without first settling the design of the basic structure of economic institutions and the legal background of property and other rights that make economic production, trade, and consumption possible. It misreads Rawls's project to just assume that he must begin answering this question of the appropriate shape of the basic structure by focusing its design and his account of distributive justice on the needs of the handicapped.

I suspect that much of the criticism leveled against Rawls for leaving special needs out of the difference principle stems from conceiving distributive justice along the lines of so-called "luck egalitarianism." This is the view that distributive justice is in the first instance a matter of equalizing or at least neutralizing undeserved inequalities, by compensating people for social disadvantages, natural disabilities, and other forms of "brute bad luck" they are not responsible for. Clearly the handicapped do not normally deserve their disabilities, and their needs should be addressed. Rawls is sometimes thought to have committed himself to some sort of luck egalitarianism early in TJ (sect. 12), and is said to be guilty of inconsistency for not drawing its implications. Later we will consider if this criticism of Rawls is justified.

Another point is that "least advantaged" refers to a relative position in society that people can move into or out of. It is not a name for a group of people who are known by name and who remain fixed members of this group (as Rawls has said, "least advantaged" is not a rigid designator). So when the difference principle says that economic institutions are to be designed to maximally benefit the least advantaged, the idea is not that we are to make the poorest people in society (A, B, C . . .) better off than some other group of people whose names we also know (T, U,

V . . .). This would just create a new group of least advantaged people whose needs would have to be addressed, ad infinitum. Instead, the idea is that in any society where income and wealth are unequally distributed, there is a least advantaged position (e.g., the minimum wage position), the occupants of which earn less and are less powerful than those in other social positions. We are to maximize the prospects of people occupying this social position while they are members of it, i.e., the prospects of minimum-wage workers whoever they might be.

Now consider Rawls's more abstract illustration of the difference principle, which gives a still better idea of how it works (see Figure 3.1; this is taken from Restatement, 62, which improves upon TJ, sect.13, figure 6, 76/66 rev.). First, what does the OP curve represent? Rawls says "the curve OP represent[s] the contribution to x2's [or LAG's = Least Advantaged Group's] expectations made by the greater expectation of x1 [MAG = More Advantaged Group]" (TJ, 76/66 rev.). Rawls also calls OP "the production curve." Any point on the curve is allocatively efficient; given the shares held by LAG and MAG productive output is optimized. Moreover, as we proceed further to the right along the OP curve, with increasing returns to the more advantaged, there are corresponding increases in productive output and hence in society's total income and wealth. Point O represents equal division, where "both groups receive the same remuneration" (JF, 63). O is not then a zero point where no one has anything; rather it refers to the origin point of equality where all have as much as can be expected given an equal distribution. (This may be a quite comfortable way of living, if leftists such as G.A. Cohen are right, assuming a large degree of solidarity felt among members of society.) The "P" in "OP curve" refers, again, to "production" (JF, 61). The OP curve itself captures Rawls's assumption that departures from equality under cooperative circumstances are productive and can result in a gain to both the least advantaged as well as the most advantaged up to a point. The OP curve represents the respective gains to each over equality under cooperative circumstances where production is assumed to be efficient. The expectations Rawls refers to are of primary goods – not welfare or utility – and particularly expectations of income and wealth (or "shares in output," Rawls says, JF, 63). So as MAG's share of income and wealth increases along the x-axis, LAG's share does too, until the point D is reached, at which point LAG's share declines as MAG's continues to rise. B (for Bentham) is the point at which overall wealth and income (and economic utility too) in society are maximized; it is then "efficient," in the Kaldor–Hicks sense idealized by utilitarian economists. The difference principle is not satisfied by point B, even though B represents a point of greater total income and wealth than at D. The difference principle is satisfied rather by point D, the (Pareto efficient) point on the OP curve that is closest to equality of income and wealth. At this point the share that goes to the worst-off is maximized.

A question frequently asked by my students is: "Why don't we allow for conditions that achieve point B, with maximal aggregate income and wealth, and then just redistribute from MAG to LAG, thereby giving LAG the maximal amount they would receive at point D, and giving MAG still more than they would otherwise

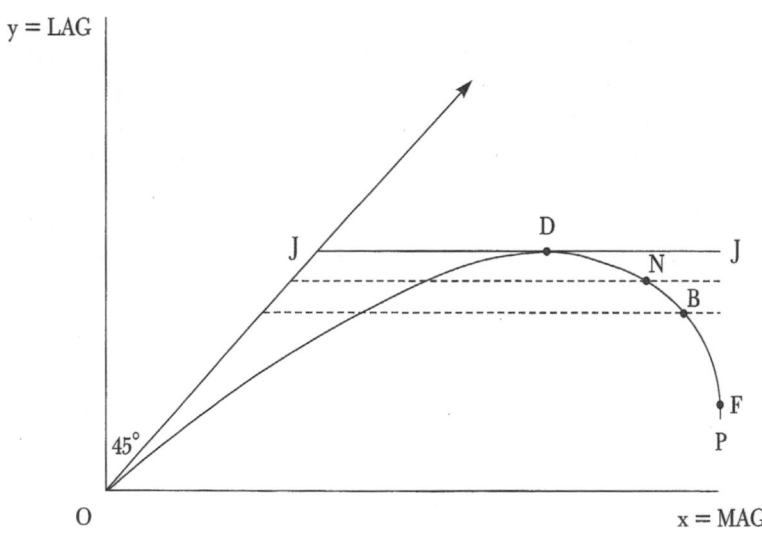

Figure 3.1
Source: Reprinted by permission of the publisher from *Justice as Fairness: A Restatement* by John Rawls, p. 62, Cambridge Mass.: The Belknap Press of Harvard University Press, Copyright © 2001 by the President and Fellows of Harvard College.

receive at D?" The answer is that this possibility has already been taken into account in Rawls's graphical depiction above (figure 6 in TJ, 76/66 rev. and figure 1 in JF, 62). The redistribution envisioned would change the expectations of both classes. If LAG expects the amount of income they would achieve at point D, then MAG could no longer expect the share that leads them to undertake the risks that will get them to point B, and they would end up with shares that put them back at D as well. What is envisioned by the question is in effect an ad hoc redrawing of the OP curve that allows for greater inequality, with a shifting of the D point further to the right on the x-axis while remaining at the same point on the y-axis. But this would just create a different B(entham) point than that in Rawls's text. Moreover, there is little reason to assume that the B point and the D point will ever be the same; it would be fortuitous if the worst-off were made as well off as they can be, right at the point at which overall wealth is maximized in society. Some classical liberals (e.g., Adam Smith) claim that the worst-off are made better off in a *laissez-faire* economy which maximizes wealth than in any other economic system. But comparisons of the circumstances of the worst-off in countries that rely more heavily on market distributions, such as the U.S., with social-democratic countries such as Sweden or Germany where the least advantaged have greater social dividends and are better situated, empirically disproves such claims.

Rawls says there are "different OP curves for different schemes of cooperation" (JF, 63). Imagine that for each of the economic systems listed in Table 3.1, we can draw an OP curve which represents the amount that goes to the least advantaged, given the expectations of the most advantaged under that economic system. (For example, in welfare-state capitalism, the shape of its OP curve would reflect the level of welfare payments going to the poorest. The D point then would be the optimal level of welfare payments to the poor, which is the point at which the poor receive the largest sustainable level of transfers without undermining incentives needed to create payments at that level.) Now the difference principle does not simply say that, given whatever economic system a society already has in existence, it should aim to maximize the position of the least advantaged within the existing institutions of that already established system. Instead, the difference principle requires that over time society seeks to institute the economic system that is "the most effectively designed" in so far as the least advantaged fare better than in any other alternative economic arrangement. Then, second, "Other things being equal, the difference principle directs that society aim at the highest point on the OP curve of the most effectively designed scheme of cooperation" (JF, 63); that is, it should aim to maximize the position of the worst-off within this most effective system.

This *seems* to suggest that a society is under a duty to put into place the economic system that maximally benefits the least advantaged, and then continually increase productive output within this system so long as it accrues to the benefit of the least advantaged. There appears to be nothing in *A Theory of Justice* that suggests otherwise. Taken by itself, this would rule out a society's democratic decision to avoid a high degree of industrial development and technological advantages, and pursue instead a more relaxed or even pastoral existence. What is puzzling about this is that in *Justice as Fairness: A Restatement* Rawls says (immediately following the last sentence in the preceding paragraph):

> A feature of the difference principle is that it does not require continual economic growth over generations to maximize upward indefinitely the expectations of the least advantaged measured in terms of income and wealth . . . That would not be a reasonable conception of justice. We certainly do not want to rule out Mill's idea of a society in a just stationary state where (real) capital accumulation may cease. A property-owning democracy should allow for this possibility.
>
> (*JF*, 159; see also *JF*, 63–64, which is almost verbatim)

How is this seeming incongruity – that society does, but then again it may not, have a duty to continually increase economic growth so long as it benefits the least advantaged – be explained? Rawls's *ceteris paribus* clause, in the penultimate quote above, may be important here. First, notice that Rawls says a society is not required to maximize the expectations of the least advantaged "measured in terms of income and wealth." While it is true that Rawls defines the least advantaged primarily in terms of the class with the least income and wealth, this is mainly a heuristic device to make for ease of application of the difference principle. But the fact is that the relative well-being of the least advantaged is determined by an index of primary goods, including not simply their share of income and wealth, but also their opportunities for powers and positions of office, non-basic rights and liberties, and the institutional bases of self-respect. The difference principle is the criterion for the just distribution of these primary goods as well. (The distribution of the other primary goods of basic liberties and opportunities to compete are already settled by the other principles of justice; that is they must be equally distributed.) Suppose a society democratically decides to afford all its members, including the least advantaged, a greater share of opportunities for powers and positions of office and bases of self-respect, by structuring its economy so as to give workers more control over their working conditions and the means of production, and ownership interests in real capital (e.g., by workers' cooperatives, or a "share economy" where workers have partial ownership of the firms they work in). This contrasts with the traditional capitalist economy with a welfare state, where there is a sharp division between owners of capital and workers who work for an hourly wage. In this economic system – one version of what Rawls calls a "property-owning democracy" – workers may well have less income and wealth than they might have achieved in a capitalist welfare state, where a separate class of owners make all economic decisions regarding production and investment, and wage workers and the unemployed are insured against misfortune but otherwise have no powers or positions of control within the productive process. But in a property-owning democracy, workers' share of economic powers and the bases of self-respect are greater than they are in a capitalist welfare state, since they have partial control over their working conditions and the management of production. In this regard, the index of primary goods of the least advantaged can exceed that of the least advantaged in the capitalist welfare state, even though the latter have greater income and wealth. As we will see in the next chapter when a property-owning democracy is discussed, this is one way to explain the seeming incongruity above in Rawls's claim, in effect, that the difference principle does not require ever-increasing economic growth, even if it benefits the least advantaged in terms of income and wealth. It is not, however, his suggestion, but my attempt to make sense of what he says.

What kind of economic system does the difference principle then imply? When *A Theory of Justice* was first published, it was widely thought that Rawls was offering a justification of the welfare state. But in the 1990 Preface to the Revised Edition, Rawls says that he should have made clearer in *Theory* that he was not arguing for the welfare state. Instead, when the difference principle is applied to institutions in light of knowledge of how economic and social systems function, Rawls sees it as requiring either a "property-owning democracy" or "liberal socialism." Which of these social and economic systems is more just depends upon historical and other circumstances, such as a society's culture and traditions, institutions, resources and level of development and technology (TJ, 280/248 rev.). Rawls does not, then, unlike many to his right or left, seek to settle once and for all the traditional question of "capitalism versus socialism" on grounds of philosophical argumentation alone. Clearly he rejects command-economy socialism (Soviet-style communism) since it allows violations of such basic liberties as freedom of occupation and choice of careers, and freedom of association (TJ, 274/242 rev.). But he also rejects capitalism as traditionally understood, since it gives excessive economic and political power to the class of owners, and thus violates the first principle's requirement of affording fair value to the political liberties, as well as fair equal opportunities and the fair distribution of economic powers and positions. Moreover, capitalism, because of its gross inequalities and resulting exploitation of wage laborers, does not optimally promote the economic interests of the worst-off, running afoul of the difference principle. But then neither does communism, because of its inherent inefficiencies. Rawls contends that market allocations of factors of production (labor, land, and capital) are required by justice as fairness for two reasons: mainly to guarantee freedom of occupation and association, and also because market allocations normally benefit the least advantaged under the difference principle (assuming markets' greater efficiency in allocating productive factors). But the use of markets for allocative purposes can be satisfied with public ownership of the means of production, where the public leases capital and the means of production to competing firms of worker cooperatives and gains the interest on their use. For this reason Rawls leaves open the possibility that liberal socialism might just as well satisfy the difference principle as would a property-owning democracy that allows for widespread private ownership of the means of production.[19] The significant point here is that the principles of justice taken in abstraction from historical conditions do not decide between a (private) property-owning democracy and liberal socialism. Moreover, it is on the basis of the historical tendencies of *laissez-faire* capitalism and welfare-state capitalism that Rawls conjectures that both property-owning democracy and liberal socialism would be preferred to them under the difference principle. Property-owning democracy is discussed in greater detail below and in the next chapter.

OBJECTIONS TO THE DIFFERENCE PRINCIPLE

In this section I discuss some objections to the difference principle, mainly in order to clarify it and address misunderstandings. Rawls himself discusses frequent objections to the difference principle in his *Restatement* (66–72), and his extensive discussion of the difference principle in that book provides a great deal of insight into how the principle is supposed to apply (see JF, Part II, sects. 14, 17–22; Part III, sects. 34, 36, 38–40; Part IV, sects. 41, 42, 49). Here I focus mainly on some objections Rawls does not mention in his discussion.

Is the difference principle redundant?

Consider the objection that, because of the priority of liberty, the difference principle may never have a chance to come into effect, since all questions of distributive justice are decided beforehand by what is needed to maintain the system of basic liberties. There are two versions of this argument. (1) Some have argued that the only way to maintain the fair value of the political liberties as required by the first principle is to institute an egalitarian distribution, or at least a more egalitarian distribution than is required by the difference principle. Rawls himself recognizes the corrupting influences of wealth on democracy, and says that the first principle requires that "property and wealth must be kept widely distributed" (TJ, 225/198 rev.). Suppose, then, that, in order to minimize the influence of wealth and maximize the effectiveness of citizens' equal political liberties, society must impose an egalitarian (or some other) distribution. Then the difference principle would have no substantial role. (2) Similarly, others have argued that in order to maximally secure the basic liberties and fair equal opportunities, all society's resources might need to be expended. More can always be spent on increased security measures (more policing, street lights, video cameras) that protect citizens' persons and property, thereby guaranteeing greater physical and psychological integrity and freedom of movement. Also, ever-greater outlays for education increasingly lessen the effects of family, gender, race, and social background on access to desirable social positions, guaranteeing greater equality of fair opportunities.[20] But these and other measures may diminish to insignificance the resources available for distribution by the difference principle.

In response to (1), Rawls does not see a particular distribution of income and wealth as needed to establish the fair value of the political liberties. So long as inequalities are not too disparate and are kept within certain limits he thinks the corrupting influence of wealth on the political process can be neutralized by such measures as public financing of political campaigns, bans on corporate contributions, regulation of political advertising to insure undistorted information and equitable opportunities for candidates to present their positions, and strict limits if not outright bans on individual contributions (PL, 327–29, 356–63). Whether these measures are sufficient to neutralize the inequitable influences of wealth on the democratic political process is still questioned by many; some believe that private ownership of capital inevitably will lead to the corruption of the democratic process. Whether this must be the case under the widespread ownership conditions Rawls envisions in a property-owning democracy seems less likely.

Regarding (2), the second objection, it should be emphasized that neither the principle of basic liberties nor fair equal opportunities are consequentialist principles directing that society *maximize* some state of affairs. The first principle does not say society is to maximize people's opportunities to exercise their basic liberties.[21] It says rather that a "fully adequate scheme" of basic liberties is to be equally provided for all citizens – fully adequate (again, not maximally effective) for the exercise and development of the moral powers in the "two fundamental cases." The objection confuses the formal provision of an equal basic liberty with the "worth" of a basic liberty. My basic rights to physical integrity and freedom of movement may be worth more to me if society spent much more on police protection, street lighting, and traffic safety. Then I'd never need fear going out at night or on the highways. But the first principle does not require that society maximize the worth of basic liberties to each person; nor does it require that society secure equal worth of the basic liberties for all people. As discussed in Chapter 2, the worth of a basic liberty to a person depends on her circumstances, things such as wealth, education, intelligence, interests, and so on, and individual circumstances inevitably will differ in these and other respects. In justice as fairness the measure for determining the fair worth of the basic liberties (aside from the political liberties) is not determined by the first principle, but is settled by the difference principle. Rawls says that justice as fairness, rather than aiming to secure equal worth of the basic liberties, aims to maximize the worth of the basic liberties of the worst-off. "This defines the end of social justice" (TJ, 205/179 rev.). The role of the difference principle in enabling citizens to effectively exercise their basic liberties suggests that, far from being made redundant by the first principle, the difference principle is crucial to its operation. It is needed to enable citizens to enjoy basic liberties that are fully adequate to the exercise and development of their moral powers to be reasonable and rational.

Does the difference principle have absurd implications?

Suppose there are two social systems to choose between, Society A and Society B. The alternative distributions between the worst-off and best-off are indicated by Tables 3.2 and 3.3. The difference principle prefers the distributions of Society B in both cases. But this means in Example 1 that enormous sacrifices must be made by everyone except the worst-off, in order to increase the position of the worst-off only minimally, by 1 unit. Why should nearly everyone be deprived of so much for such small gains to the poorest? In Example 2 many have egalitarian intuitions that incline them to ask: "Why should the poor gain so little given such enormous gains to everyone else? The least advantaged are being ruthlessly exploited for the sake of gains to everyone else, and this seems to be sanctioned by the difference principle."

Rawls's response to these sorts of examples reveals the degree to which he makes certain empirical assumptions in his argument for the principles of justice. He says the principles of justice are not supposed to apply to such abstract possibilities but presuppose a theory of social institutions (TJ, 157/136 rev.). Assuming this social theory is accurate, the purported counterexamples are not really counterexamples at all, for they ignore the empirical conditions under which the difference principle applies (JF, 70). If (1)

Society	Most Advantaged	Least Advantaged
A	10,000	1
B	3	2

Table 3.2

Society	Most Advantaged	Least Advantaged
A	1001	1000
B	100,000	1,001

Table 3.3

the difference principle is taken as intended, and not in isolation but together with the other principles that are part of justice as fairness, and (2) we consider how background social institutions and economic systems realistically work, then these examples will never arise. For there is a continuum of practicable basic structures with different distributions, and, if so, then these two sets of alternatives will never be the only alternatives we have to choose between. If in Example 1 Society A with its enormous wealth but enormous inequalities is a feasible alternative to impoverished Society B, then there must be many workable intermediate societies in between with distributions which allow for less inequality and much greater gains to the least advantaged without lowering the prospects of the more advantaged too substantially. One obvious way to achieve these intermediate distributions is by an institutional device that transfers via income taxation part of the large return to the more advantaged in Society A to the less advantaged. Suppose, then, that among these intermediate distributions there is one, Society C, in which the return to LAG is maximized at 4000, while MAG has 8000. This is the social system preferred by the difference principle, not Society B in the example above.

Rawls says that such gross disparities between income classes like those in the examples result when the more advantaged unite as a group and exploit their market power to force increases to their income (for example, as monopolists or oligopolists will do if left unregulated). This is made possible by an absence of fair opportunities to enter positions for all and effective competition among suppliers of goods and services. When the difference principle is taken together with fair equal opportunities, then again there are going to be many feasible alternative distributions to A and B. So the disparities in Example 2 are also unrealistic under conditions in which the difference principle is intended to apply. If Society B is a feasible alternative to A, then there must be many intermediate stages in between where the worst-off are much better off than under either alternative A or B.

The examples indicate how much Rawls's argument for the difference principle depends upon the way that social and economic systems work. General facts about the world, including tendencies of human psychology and the workings of economic systems, play a large role in the justification of the difference principle over other proposed principles of justice. Of course, it is *logically* possible that we might be confronted only with alternatives A and B in choosing economic policies (most anything is logically possible), but Rawls's contention is that it is not *realistically* possible given the way social and economic systems normally function; so we don't need to worry about these supposed counterexamples. From his point of view, they are not real counterexamples at all.

Do individual incentives really benefit the worst-off?

Some critics (most notably G.A. Cohen) raise the following objection: Rawls contends that the difference principle applies to the basic structure; it is a principle for institutions, and not a principle for individuals directly to apply in making economic choices. Rawls clearly favors a competitive market economy providing individuals economic incentives to promote their economic position. But competitive markets, because they rely on incentives that encourage people to take risks or work longer hours exercising special skills, generate self-seeking attitudes. The difference principle, when applied only directly to the basic structure is compatible with a capitalist economy where the worst-off are poorer than they would be in a different economic system (perhaps non-market socialism) where people are more directly concerned with equality and promoting the well-being of the less advantaged. In an economy where people are not encouraged to be self-seeking and materialistic but have an ethos of justice and are directly concerned with the effects of their preferences on the worst-off, surely the worst-off fare better than under market conditions allowed by the difference principle.

Cohen's argument is more complicated than this, and requires a fuller discussion than can be given here.[22] But a preliminary response to the objection is that, if the worst-off did not thrive best in a competitive market economy that engenders self-seeking attitudes, then it would not be "the most effectively designed scheme of cooperation" and would not satisfy the difference principle. The difference principle does not simply require that society maximize the position of the worst-off within the economic system that happens to be in place. Rather, it imposes a two-fold requirement (1) to institute that economy that consistently makes the poorest class better off than they would be in any other economy (compatible with basic liberties and fair equal opportunities), and then (2) to maximize the poor's position within that "most effective" system. If a non-competitive economy were more effective in instilling motives that lead people to act in ways that make the poor better off than they would be in a market economy, then the difference principle would require that non-market system (again, *so long as* it did not violate the priority of liberty and fair equal opportunity). Taken in abstraction from human nature and facts about how economic systems work, the difference principle does not decide whether market economies are preferable to non-market economies. It is only once the difference principle is applied to institutions, in light of knowledge about human nature and how economic systems work, that Rawls believes a market system of some form will be preferable to any non-market alternative.

But Cohen might still agree that a market system for setting prices for productive resources, including labor, is better than non-market alternatives (so long as income and wealth subsequently produced are justly distributed according to the correct egalitarian principle). His real criticism seems to be that, nonetheless, in a competitive market system people can still have an "ethos of justice" (as in Swedish social democracy, for example) and can be motivated to take into account the effects of their economic choices on the less advantaged; and when they do the less advantaged will fare still better than they do in a Rawlsian society where the difference principle applies directly only to the basic structure, and there is no requirement that the difference principle motivate individuals' particular choices. In this regard, Cohen's point is well taken. For it may well be true that the least advantaged would fare better in a society where the difference principle not only regulates basic institutions but also directly influences individuals' market decisions. Then those who are better off because of undeserved differences such as superior natural talents would not then demand whatever the market will bear as an incentive to work longer hours. Instead they will apply their talents in ways that directly benefit the least advantaged.

The objection then draws into question, not Rawls's application of the difference principle to the basic structure, but his failure to require that individuals also directly apply it in their economic choices. There is no duty of justice in Rawls that says that we must express concern for the well-being of the less advantaged in our daily economic choices. That attitude is not part of the sense of justice as Rawls conceives it. Instead, for Rawls the sense of justice is a settled disposition to act from the principles of justice and their requirements, and therefore respect and abide by laws and institutions that are designed to maximally benefit the least advantaged. Cohen, by contrast, claims that people's sense of justice should be informed by an "ethos" of justice that inspires them, not simply to observe and politically support laws and constraints that are designed to maximally benefit the least advantaged, but *also* to make everyday economic choices that *directly benefit* (if not maximally benefit) the poorest in society.[23] If the naturally talented had this disposition, then they would not demand such high premiums for the exercise of superior natural talents, and this would accrue to the greater benefit of the less advantaged. Framed in this way, Cohen's objection concerns how we are to conceive of the *sense of justice*: Rawls fails to define appropriately the sense of justice, for he does not require that it incorporate a concern for the poor in our individual economic choices.

Two general points in response: First, the point of Rawls's reliance on markets is not to unleash capitalist forces driven by self-seeking attitudes. Of course, Rawls recognizes that people will often make economic choices for self-interested reasons. But he assumes that in a well-ordered society of justice as fairness, where the principles of justice are effective and all are motivated by their sense of justice to comply, there will not be "high-flying" "buccaneer" capitalists who seek to exploit people or to game the system so that it maximally benefits people with acquisitive attitudes. For a sense of justice involves a desire to comply with the "natural duties" of justice, mutual respect, mutual aid, and so on (TJ, sects. 19, 51), as well as the principle of fairness (TJ, sects. 18, 52). A just person endorses the natural duties and wants his economic decisions to comply with rules that over time maximally benefit the least advantaged, not rules that maximally benefit the most advantaged or most acquisitive people.[24] Moreover, in accepting the duty of mutual respect, a just person does not try to exploit others' disadvantage or misfortune, or take advantage of weaknesses of others' bargaining position. Instead, just persons, being reasonable, "take into account the consequences of their actions on others' well-being" (PL, 49n.). One who has a sense of justice recognizes that "Mutual respect is shown . . . in our willingness to see the situation of others from their point of view . . . and in our being prepared to give reasons for our actions whenever the interests of others are materially affected," reasons that they can reasonably accept (TJ, 337/297 rev.). Finally, in acting on the duty of mutual aid, a just and reasonable person inspires "a sense of confidence and trust in other men's good intentions and the knowledge that they are there if we need them" (TJ, 339/298 rev.). These and other attributes of reasonable persons with a sense of justice should go a long way towards mitigating the kinds of acquisitive attitudes and lack of concern for others that Cohen suspects Rawls's difference principle will be prone to. There is an "ethos of justice" shared by members of a well-ordered society of justice as fairness, even if it is not exactly the same ethos advocated by Cohen.

Still, this does not mean that reasonable economic agents with a sense of justice will act for reasons of benevolence, or that in their economic choices they will consider the least advantaged and always seek to benefit or not further disadvantage them. For Rawls, it is not unreasonable for reasonable persons to act out of economic self-interest, even if they have exceptional natural talents that could otherwise be used to directly benefit the least advantaged. Even in a well-ordered society of justice as fairness, only occasionally will people's economic choices be predominantly motivated by concern for the poor. Instead, people normally will be motivated by a multiplicity of aims due to the pluralism resulting from basic liberties of conscience, thought, and association, and different religious, philosophical, and moral views. It would be unusual for everyone to uniformly converge on a *predominant concern* for the least advantaged in their economic choices, even though they *can* be relied on to give priority to the least advantaged in their political choices of laws and social policies. This is not an unreasonable position. Why should a person *always* be concerned with the least advantaged in economic transactions, such as salary negotiations with an employer, or in deciding whether to work an extra 5–10 hours per week, when he or she might otherwise devote the same 5–10 hours (or increased earnings) to helping autistic children or people with Alzheimer's or to other charitable aims, or to just spending the extra time and money at home with the family? Why should the economic position of the least advantaged take precedence in my *individual choices* over all other social and individual ends, especially when the difference principle *already* is designed to insure them a fully adequate share of income and wealth that enables them to effectively exercise their basic liberties and pursue many worthwhile plans of life? Rawls does not conceive of the least advantaged in a well-ordered society as poor in the traditional sense. They should have sufficient resources to take advantage of a wide array of opportunities, enjoy leisure time, and pursue many worthwhile ends. If so, what could be the point of requiring *everyone* in society, not just in their political choices, but also in their daily economic decisions to take into account the effects of their choices on the least advantaged, when the least advantaged are already sufficiently provided for, and when there are so many other worthy aims and activities to pursue in life? Cohen's criticism seems to underestimate the significance of "the fact of reasonable pluralism" and assign undue priority to the position of the least advantaged over all other aims. This "fact" says that people will have many different worthwhile aims and pursuits in a well-ordered democratic society, in addition to concern for the economic status of the least advantaged, and many of these aims may be equally worthy of pursuit. Providing a place for the *plurality of goods* and the *freedom* of individuals to make justifiable choices about which goods to pursue underlies Rawls's recognition of the appropriateness of economic incentives,[25] and also accounts, in part, for his definition of the sense of justice as a willingness to comply with just institutions.

In the next section, I discuss another reason for Rawls's direct application of the difference principle only to the basic structure. Again, it is not to unleash the forces of economic efficiency and self-interest in a market economy; quite the contrary, it is to rectify the tendency of fair market transactions to result in grossly unequal and unjust distributions of wealth.[26]

FAIR EQUALITY OF OPPORTUNITY AND THE DIFFERENCE PRINCIPLE

Rawls sees FEO as essential to the difference principle; without it and the first principle, he says, the difference principle cannot be taken seriously (JF, 46n.). This might seem a strange thing to say: What's so peculiar about setting up the economy to maximally benefit the least advantaged without qualification? Some have suggested that the difference principle's focus on the needs of the poor ought to have priority over FEO and the basic liberties; or that the difference principle should be detached from social cooperation entirely and used as a principle of global justice. These proposals make sense if one sees the difference principle and distributive justice more generally as a matter of what Rawls calls "allocative justice." [Allocative justice is where we take a given stock of wealth or commodities, whatever its origins, and divide it among individuals according to some division rule.] Utilitarianism conceives of distributive justice this way: [we are to distribute the aggregate social (or global) product, without regard to how it was produced or who produced it, so as to maximize overall utility or welfare.] One might regard the difference principle in a similar fashion: rather than distributing aggregate wealth to maximize utility, we distribute it to maximize the position (either resources or welfare) of the least advantaged. These might be regarded as

competing interpretations of the capitalist welfare state, along
with other alternatives, such as Ronald Dworkin's luck egalitarian
account, "Equality of Resources," which provides social insurance
for undeserved misfortune, and otherwise distributes income and
wealth according to people's market and other free choices.

Rawls does not have this allocative understanding of the difference principle. The problem with the allocative-difference principle
is that it takes for granted questions of how and by whom wealth
gets produced, the specification of property and other legal institutions relevant to the economy, rights and obligations in the
production process, and other issues crucial to economic justice.
For Rawls distributive justice involves more than just finding the
correct algorithm for allocating to consumers rights to income
and wealth that are the product of social cooperation. This is but
the final stage of a far more complicated process. Rather than
being an allocation principle, the difference principle is a principle for establishing "pure background procedural justice" (JF,
50). This means that the difference principle's primary application
is not to the division of a preexisting fund of wealth, but to the
basic institutions that make economic production, trade, and
consumption of wealth possible: the legal institution of property;
the structure of markets; the relations between capital and labor
including the role and powers of labor unions within firms; the
law of contracts, sales, securities, negotiable instruments, corporations, partnerships, and so on. All these background institutions
are to be designed so that, when their rules are complied with and
people's legitimate expectations are met, the final outcome is one
that maximally benefits the least advantaged. "Pure procedural
background justice" means, then, that once agents engage in
economic cooperation according to the terms of these background
rules and institutions and form their expectations accordingly,
then a just distribution of income, wealth, powers, and positions
of authority will be whatever distribution results from the full
compliance with the institutional requirements of these basic
background institutions. As opposed to a principle of allocative
justice such as the principle of utility or the "allocative-difference
principle" above, we cannot say what economic agents' legitimate

expectations and just entitlements are independent of our knowledge of a history of their actually satisfying the rules of the economic system. "There is no criterion for a just distribution apart from background institutions and the entitlements that arise from actually working through the procedure" (JF, 51; also TJ, 87/76 rev.). By contrast, to apply allocative principles of justice we do not need to have any such historical knowledge of economic agents' expectations and transactions in the production of the sum of wealth and commodities that are to be distributed, or of who produced what and in exchange for what contributions. To apply the utility principle, we only need to know people's existing preferences or welfare levels, or to apply the non-Rawlsian allocative-difference principle, we need to know people's current shares of primary goods, and then (in both cases) the projected consequences on future production of distributing various alternative sums of income and wealth.[27]

Here one might object to "pure procedural background justice" on the following grounds: "When we look at a society where wealth and income are grossly unequal and a minority is nearly destitute, we do not need to know anything about its procedures or the history of how this unequal distribution was actually arrived at in order to know it is unjust. We can see it is unjust because of its grossly unequal distribution." This is correct, but our judgment of distributive injustice need not depend upon some egalitarian allocative principle. Rather, we know that such gross inequalities could not have been arrived at had society observed a just procedural background principle, such as the difference principle. But with the difference principle still we cannot say, unlike an allocative principle, what the just distribution should be, nor who specifically has a right to what resources, independent of people actually pursuing their legitimate claims within the requirements of a just basic structure.

Offhand, one might think that Rawls's focus on pure procedural economic justice resembles the classical liberal and libertarian views which say that people should have a right to all that they gain by market procedures, or via gift and other voluntary transfers. But the difference principle's form of pure procedural justice differs in a crucial respect from these "non-patterned, historical" entitlement views (as Nozick terms his libertarian entitlement account). For Rawls, the market is but one among several institutions needed to achieve pure procedural justice in distributions of income, wealth, and other relevant primary goods. Rawls rejects the libertarian (and common-sense) view that a person has full rights and entitlements to possess all market and other consensual transfers of property he or she receives. How otherwise could the taxation necessary for maintaining institutions of justice, including the preservation of markets and the legal institution of property themselves, be possible if people had complete rights to market distributions with no moral or legal duty to pay taxes to maintain these institutions and other public goods?[28] Classical liberals such as Hume and Adam Smith recognized that maintaining these and other institutions of justice and providing for public goods are necessary functions of government. Like classical liberals, Rawls relies upon markets to allocate productive resources (land, labor, and capital) but unlike them he does not use markets as the standard for deciding just distributions. Even though markets play a functional role in distributing to people their just entitlements – a less-advantaged worker may be entitled to keep his entire paycheck, plus collect an income supplement from government – still they do not provide the *criterion* for just distributions. There is no moral presumption that a person has a right to consume whatever she receives by market activity. Rather, it is the combined rules and procedures of the entire complex of legal and economic institutions satisfying the difference principle that settle one's distributive shares and entitlements. Accordingly Rawls envisions a taxation system with a number of regulatory and distributive roles. The taxation system is one of the primary institutions and procedures, along with markets, income supplements, fair equal educational opportunities, and universal healthcare, that are necessary for pure procedural economic justice. The institutions needed for economic justice are taken up again in Chapter 5.

It is in the context of pure procedural background justice that we are to understand Rawls's assertion that we can only take the difference principle seriously in connection with FEO and the first principle. "The role of the principle of fair opportunity is to insure that the system of cooperation is one of pure procedural justice" (TJ, 87/76 rev.). (The centrality of FEO to distributive justice accounts for the otherwise peculiar fact that in *Theory*, sect. 17, on FEO, Rawls seems to hardly discuss FEO at all, but mainly discusses pure procedural justice and its differences from allocative justice.) To see his point, suppose there is in place an economic system satisfying the difference principle, but professional and trade positions are passed along according to one's family membership or are otherwise monopolized and distributed according to the rules and privileges of some closed group. The income these professionals receive and the price of their services is then excessive because of a lack of open positions. More familiarly, suppose there are no such legal constraints on entry into favorable positions, but still opportunities are largely determined by social connections, class membership, and class bias. Hence children of those better off largely monopolize desirable professional positions, and Caucasians are more successful than others in their applications to service and manufacturing jobs, while non-Caucasians fall behind due to subtle racial discrimination, as do all socially less-advantaged children due to a lack of fair educational opportunities and an absence of family and other social networks. Again, in the absence of fair educational opportunities, and because of class discrimination, there will be fewer qualified people able to compete for positions, and desirable positions will demand a premium, aggravating inequality between income groups, and limiting the relative and absolute wealth of the less advantaged.

The ways in which discrimination and an absence of formal equality of opportunity can unfairly affect the distribution of income and wealth, powers and positions of office, and the bases of self-respect are familiar: racial, ethnic, gender, religious, and other forms of discrimination have long prevented people from economic, educational, and professional advancement. There are at least three more ways that FEO complements the difference principle: (1) FEO limits the degree of inequality of income and wealth allowed by the difference principle; (2) FEO raises the absolute level of income and wealth going to the worst-off; (3) FEO can help limit the kind of control that capital exercises over labor, and perhaps tend towards greater worker-control of working conditions and even production itself.

To take these in order: (1) How FEO limits inequalities and advances the *relative position* of the least advantaged: One objection to the difference principle we discussed is that it puts no upper limit on the amount of wealth those better off may accumulate. Suppose, then, Society A where the worst-off have $45,000 per year and the best-off a yearly income of $1 million, compared with Society B where the worst-off have an income of $45,500 and the best-off $1 billion. Assuming these were the only two possibilities (which is highly unlikely), the difference principle taken by itself would prefer Society B, in spite of the enormous inequality it allows. Rawls's response is that the degree of excessive inequality in B could be generated only in a society where those better off exploit their rare skills and training, social networks, and resulting market power to monopolize preferred professional positions. In a society where FEO guarantees widespread educational opportunities for people regardless of social position, open competition between greater numbers of better educated and skillful citizens will reduce the enormous differences in income and social power between the worst-off and best-off to a more reasonable and acceptable level (see JF, 67).

(2) How FEO advances the *absolute position* of the worst-off in ways not provided by the difference principle: Compare two societies with the difference principle which differ in that the first "Democratic Equality" has FEO whereas the second, "Natural Aristocracy," has only formal equality of opportunity (see TJ sects. 12–13). Because of FEO, Democratic Equality provides universal education and health benefits not available under Natural Aristocracy. Not only do these benefits directly benefit members of the worst-off class (who otherwise cannot afford them), but they also allow society to call upon a larger pool of trained skills and abilities, thereby improving *overall productivity and output*. A society of Democratic Equality is then more prosperous in the aggregate than is Natural Aristocracy. Since the difference principle governs

distribution of this greater economic output, Democratic Equality must make the worst-off financially better off in absolute terms than they would be under Natural Aristocracy.

(3) How FEO regulates concentrations of wealth that might be allowed by the difference principle: Rawls says that an implication of FEO is that "A free market system must be set within a framework of political and legal institutions that adjust the long-run trend of economic forces so as to *prevent excessive concentrations of property and wealth*, especially those likely to lead to political domination" (JF, 44, emphasis added). It would seem that the role of FEO in preventing inequalities leading to political domination may be redundant. For Rawls's first principle already insures the fair value of the political liberties and prevents inequalities of wealth and power that undermine political democracy and citizens' equal rights of political participation. Since Rawls says so little about how FEO otherwise limits concentrations of wealth, we can only conjecture about additional ways it might mitigate inequalities. For example, if the inequalities in income and wealth allowable under the difference principle had the effect of undermining other bases of self-respect for the less advantaged, then that would be a reason for mitigating these economic inequalities, even though they might otherwise redound to the absolute economic benefit of the less advantaged. It may be, for example, that there comes a point at which the degree of inequality is so great that, even if it satisfies the difference principle by providing greater income and wealth to the least advantaged, it nonetheless causes them to feel diminished and less than civic equals of those who are more advantaged, leads them to see themselves as failures, and therewith neglect taking advantage of opportunities to educate and develop their capacities. If the degree of *relative inequality* in society were to have these psychological effects, then it would seem to be a breach of FEO, and could require diminishing the inequalities allowable under the difference principle.

This is directly relevant to the following puzzle: Why does Rawls think that the capitalist welfare state is inadequate to satisfy justice as fairness? One might think that, if the difference principle is simply a question of the social minimum and the absolute amount of income and wealth going to the least advantaged, then it is realistically possible that there could be a relatively stable capitalist welfare state that is able to maximize the social minimum in absolute terms more than any other economic system. For after all, capitalism is touted as maximizing aggregate wealth more effectively than other economic systems, and if so, then it would seem to be able to provide a social minimum above the income and wealth provided as a social minimum under the most successful, but still not as economically efficient, property-owning democracy. There are a number of potential sources for Rawls's rejection of the capitalist welfare state in favor of a property-owning democracy: (1) considerations of the priority of FEO and equal political liberty; (2) a different understanding of how the difference principle functions under conditions of property-owning democracy versus conditions of welfare state capitalism; and (3) a different understanding of the requirements of FEO under property-owning democracy versus under the welfare state.

(1) *The priority of the first principle and FEO over the difference principle*: Even if a capitalist welfare state were to provide greater income and wealth to the least advantaged, because of the priority of the first principle over the second and the priority of FEO over the difference principle, a property-owning democracy is preferable. For because of the greater inequalities of income, wealth, powers, and opportunities allowed by the capitalist welfare state, both the fair value of the equal political liberties and FEO are undermined; their demands cannot be met adequately under capitalist conditions. Under capitalism, even in the welfare state, a privileged class is in a position to control the means of production. As a result they have certain prerogatives which they often use to gain unequal political influence and to compromise fair equal opportunities for the less advantaged. (Consider the corrupting influence of wealth on democratic politics in the U.S. capitalist welfare state, and the weak, largely formal sense in which there are equal opportunities for the children of a WalMart employee compared with the children of President George Bush, Sr.) Because of the enormous inequalities of opportunities and unequal political influence that the capitalist welfare state allows, the less advantaged

tend to withdraw from political and civic participation, seeing it as pointless, and suffer therewith a loss of their self-respect. Even if the capitalist welfare state's economic inequalities were designed to maximize the income and wealth going to the least advantaged compared with all other economies (currently the U.S. comes nowhere near that goal), still, because there is no limit to the inequalities allowed, the equal citizenship and fair equal opportunities of all are not sustainable under welfare-state capitalism. Rawls's rejection of it in favor of a property-owning democracy is a good example of how the priorities of the first principle of justice and the principle of FEO over the difference principle work to realize the egalitarian ideal of citizens as free and equal. This exhibits forcefully the degree to which justice as fairness is based on an ideal of maintaining the freedom, independence, and self-respect of equal citizens, and not simply on an idea of promoting citizens' welfare, even the welfare of the worst-off.

The next two reasons (2 and 3) for Rawls's preferring a property-owning democracy to the welfare state seek to come to grips with the following claim. In *A Theory of Justice* Rawls says that, while a well-ordered society does not do away with the division of labor,

> The worst aspects of this division can be surmounted: no one need be servilely dependent on others and made to choose between monotonous and routine occupations which are deadening to human thought and sensibility. Each can be offered a variety of tasks so that the different elements of his nature find a suitable expression . . . work is meaningful for all.
>
> (*TJ*, 529/464 rev.)

How are we to make sense of this in terms of the second principle of justice?

(2) *Interpreting the difference principle*: Suppose that under conditions of welfare-state capitalism that maximize gross national product, increased profits going to the more advantaged indirectly increase the wage rate for unskilled workmen (the least advantaged) by 25 percent; nonetheless, the accompanying gains to capital are such

that managers are now in a position to demand still greater, even arbitrary, managerial control at work, longer working hours and less vacation, and fewer work amenities. If the long-term effects of further economic gains to the worst-off concentrated wealth and economic power in the most advantaged so much that they unfairly reduced the quality of working conditions and bargaining power of unskilled workers or their opportunities for advancement within and outside the firm, then the difference principle itself could restrict those economic gains, even though the least advantaged would have greater income and wealth under welfare-state capitalism. For "powers and prerogatives of office" and the bases of self-respect are among the primary goods distributed by the difference principle, along with income and wealth. Because of the nature of capitalist markets, increased income to the least advantaged in welfare-state capitalism is not accompanied by their having additional powers and prerogatives in the workplace; on the contrary, as the example above suggests, increased income might be accompanied by the opposite effect. If we factor in powers and prerogatives of office and the bases of self-respect into the index of primary goods, there might be little or no net gain to the worst-off under the difference principle even with substantially increased income; for the prerogatives and powers that accompany their position (degree of worker control, etc.) have been substantially diminished, or in any case not increased. In his *Restatement* Rawls speaks favorably of J.S. Mill's support for worker-owned and controlled firms as the preferred form of ownership that a private-property market economy might assume (JF, 176, 178). Such an organization of ownership (a form of Syndicalism) is compatible with the difference principle on Rawls's assumption that powers and prerogatives of office and the bases of self-respect are among the primary goods it is designed to distribute. Only in a property-owning democracy can the fair and adequate distribution of powers and prerogatives of office for the least advantaged be achieved. This argument is more conjectural than that in (1) above; while consistent with, it is not directly implied by what Rawls explicitly says. But it makes sense of his preference for a property-owning democracy over the capitalist welfare state.

(3) *Reinterpreting fair equality of opportunity*: (3) is even more conjectural than (2), and might be considered a friendly amendment: Let's assume now an index of primary goods combining income, wealth, and powers and prerogatives of office that satisfies the difference principle within the capitalist welfare state (CWS) and that in absolute terms even exceeds that achievable within a property-owning democracy (POD). Though workers in a POD have greater powers and prerogatives in the workplace, still the diminution of less-advantaged workers' prerogatives and powers in the welfare state is offset by large increases to their income and wealth. (Suppose they earn $30 an hour in the CWS versus $15 in the POD.) How then can Rawls contend that a property-owning democracy is superior to the welfare state? He can still rely on (1) above and the priority of FEO and the fair value of the political liberties over the difference principle. But we might also construe FEO in such a way that it puts a limit on the degree of inequalities not only in wealth and income but also in powers and prerogatives of office allowed by the difference principle. Suppose that some degree of worker control may even be required for fair equality of opportunity. Does FEO simply mean fair access to whatever opportunities happen to exist within an efficient economy that satisfies the difference principle? Or does FEO and its priority impose on society a positive duty beforehand to create for all citizens a *fair and adequate opportunity for control* over their means of production and working conditions, even though such opportunities may not now exist under conditions of the welfare state that satisfy the difference principle? The latter seems to take more seriously the priority of FEO over the difference principle. If we understand the aim of FEO to be, as Rawls says, not meritocracy but to maintain the self-respect of all citizens by providing opportunities to educate and exercise their capacities, then the latter interpretation seems more appropriate. FEO, then, is to be understood to require providing all citizens with FEO to exercise powers and prerogatives in the workplace in the exercise of their productive capacities. Arguably, this is a necessary basis for the self-respect of citizens, "perhaps the most important primary good" (TJ, 440/386 rev.). This requirement would then impose

fixed limitations upon the degree of inequality in powers and prerogatives of control between the most and least advantaged. Given the priority of FEO over the difference principle, these limits on inequalities could not be exceeded, no matter how large the income and wealth that might otherwise be that goes to the least advantaged in the capitalist welfare state. Rawls does not discuss this issue, and unfortunately has all too little to say about the institutional implications of FEO. But this interpretation is one way to lend force to his preference for a property-owning democracy over the capitalist welfare state. We return to this topic in Chapter 5 in discussing the institutions of a property-owning democracy.

THE JUST SAVINGS PRINCIPLE

We cannot conclude this discussion of economic justice without attention to Rawls's just savings principle. Utilitarianism requires that aggregate utility be maximized, not just among existing people but also across future generations. But this means that, just as it may not be wrong but may even be our duty to sacrifice the interests of the few in order to create greater overall utility for many, so too it may be our duty to sacrifice the happiness of present generations to create greater happiness for future generations. These considerations are sometimes invoked to justify the hardships that the working classes endured during industrialization and the rapid growth of capital in the nineteenth century. It is a convenient rationalization for the hardships endured by our forebears – they suffered, justifiably, so that we might benefit. Rawls thinks that, just as it is unfair for the less advantaged to sacrifice their well-being for the sake of a majority, so too it is unfair for earlier generations to forgo their good for the sake of later generations.

The difference principle of course encounters no such problem, but it might seem to be subject to a different problem. If society is to maximally benefit the least advantaged, understood as those currently existing, then the difference principle seems to have the opposite flaw that Rawls attributes to utilitarianism: it would seem to require that we sacrifice the well-being of future generations so that people in the present can benefit. This would feed into our current generations' willingness to consume more than we produce, creating large deficits for future generations to deal with. What is to prevent well-meaning legislators under the difference principle from exhausting existing natural and manufactured resources, and not only refusing to save *anything* for future generations, but put them into debt, all for the sake of maximizing the share that goes to the current generation of least advantaged?

This argument misreads the difference principle. It does not in fact allow current generations to exhaust resources and put future people in debt for the sake of present consumption. In applying the principles of justice we are to see ourselves as members of an ongoing society enduring from one generation to the next. We are not just to focus on the circumstances of those now existing, but the interests of future generations as well. "The appropriate expectation in applying the difference principle is that of the long-term prospects of the least favored *extending over future generations*" (TJ, 285/252 rev.). Each generation has a duty to *preserve just institutions* intact that it and its forebears have established, and pass on the gains of culture and civilization, in order to benefit future generations, including their least advantaged.

It is, then, somewhat misleading when Rawls himself says, "The principle of just savings holds between generations, while the difference principle holds within generations" (JF, 159). For this suggests that when legislators apply the difference principle, they are to focus *only* on the position of the least advantaged who are *currently* existing and ignore the interests of the least advantaged in future generations. But Rawls elsewhere is clear that the difference principle does not allow current generations to maximize the share that goes to those currently existing at the expense of future generations and their least advantaged. We have a duty to *maintain*, and not exploit to our advantage, just institutions.

What problem, then, is Rawls addressing with the just savings principle? It is that, while the difference principle may require us to focus on the least advantaged in the future as well as in the present, it does not require us to save anything by further building up the social wealth we inherited from our forebears.

Without a just savings principle, it would seem that the difference principle entails that we save nothing for the future, but simply maintain the status quo. For by saving for future generations, we take away from the less (and more) advantaged now existing, and thereby fail to maximize their index of primary goods.

Rawls's insistence on a just savings principle requiring current generations to save for future generations shows how seriously he regards a just society as a cooperative effort that endures from one generation to the next. We have benefited enormously from the efforts, investment, savings, and sacrifices of our forebears. A kind of reciprocity requires that we do the same for those who come after us – by passing on to those who follow us the just institutions we have inherited, and also some element of the progress we enjoy in benefiting from those institutions. Had previous generations not saved a portion of their product, we would still be at a rather primitive stage of civilization, unable to enjoy the benefits of liberal and democratic social institutions.

What, then, is the level of just savings? There is no specific uniform rate or percentage of savings that each generation owes the next. Instead, different rates of savings apply to different stages of development of a society. "When people are poor and saving is difficult, a lower rate of saving should be required; whereas in a wealthier society greater savings may reasonably be expected since the real burden of saving is less" (TJ, 287/255 rev.). How, then, are we to decide this rate of saving? Rawls says:

> In arriving at a just saving principle ... the parties are to ask themselves how much they would be willing to save at each stage of advance on the assumption that all other generations have saved, or will save, in accordance with the same criterion. They are to consider their willingness to save at any given phase of civilization with the understanding that the rates they propose are to regulate the whole span of accumulation.
>
> (*TJ*, 287/255 rev.)

The just savings principle constrains the difference principle; it must have priority since otherwise it would be ineffective (see TJ, 292/258 rev.). This means that in the course of applying the difference principle, legislators are to take into account the needs and interests of future generations. They are to save and invest for the future that percentage of wealth or social product that it would be rational for them to want their own forebears to have saved for them. While this is not a principle of reciprocity – after all, future generations are not able to reciprocate the benefits we bestow on them by bestowing benefits on us – it resembles a principle of reciprocity in that it says in effect: "Do unto future generations as you would have previous generations do unto you." It thereby requires current generations to set aside and save for the future as much as they would rationally want their predecessors to have saved for them knowing that they are obligated to provide the same amount for those who come after them.

Notice that the principle, of course, does not say that each generation is to save for following generations the amount that its predecessors *actually* saved, but what they rationally would want them to save. Perhaps the evidence of our current zero-savings rate and our borrowing against the future played some role in Rawls's subsequent revision of his initial criterion for savings in the first edition of *A Theory of Justice* (sect. 44). There he tried to deal with the just savings principle by assuming that the parties in the original position would know that they had emotional ties to their children and grandchildren, and therefore would care enough to set aside a reasonable amount of savings for them. Rawls later says, "While this is not an unreasonable stipulation, it has certain difficulties . . . " (JF, 160n.), perhaps reflecting here upon our current indifference regarding the costs of our consumption patterns on future generations. In the revised edition of *Theory* Rawls eliminates the argument that the rate of just savings is to depend on one generation's concern for the next.

CONCLUSION

Rawls's account of distributive justice is complex. The difference principle plays the central role, but other principles have important distributive effects. The difference principle requires society to structure its basic economic institutions so that, over time, they maximize the index of primary goods – income and wealth, and powers and positions – available to the least-advantaged members of society. But for Rawls the difference principle "cannot be taken seriously" independent of institutions guaranteeing FEO and the fair value of equal political liberties. Inequalities in income and wealth that might otherwise benefit the least advantaged under the difference principle are not allowed if they undermine fair equal opportunities or the fair value of the political liberties to others or to the less advantaged themselves. Moreover, greater educational and professional opportunities for the less advantaged cannot be exchanged for greater income and wealth for them. Finally, I understand Rawls's preference of a property-owning democracy over the capitalist welfare state to suggest that both the difference principle and the FEO principle are to be read to render the less advantaged economically independent, providing them fair opportunities to accede to powers and positions of office and own and control the means of production they professionally employ. These conditions are necessary bases of self-respect among equal citizens in a well-ordered society. In Chapter 5 the social and economic institutions that institutionalize this complex conception of distributive justice will be discussed.

FURTHER READING

Cohen G. A., *If You're an Egalitarian, How Come You're So Rich?*, Cambridge MA: Harvard, 2000, chs 8–9. (Critical treatment of difference principle from a more egalitarian perspective.)

Nozick, Robert, *Anarchy, State, and Utopia*, ch. 7, "Distributive Justice," esp. 183–231. (A sustained argument against Rawls's difference principle, juxtaposed with Nozick's libertarian entitlement theory.)

Parijs, Philippe van, "Difference Principles," in *The Cambridge Companion to Rawls*, ch. 5. (Thorough discussion of difference principle from a left perspective).

Four

The Original Position

There are three parts to Rawls's complex argument for the principles of justice. In this chapter I focus on the first, which comprises arguments made from the *original position* (set forth in chapter 3 of *A Theory of Justice*). In the next chapter I discuss the second part of Rawls's argument (set forth in *TJ*, Part II, "Institutions," and elsewhere), which applies the principles of justice to social institutions (*TJ*, chs. 4–5) and individual duties and obligations (*TJ*, ch. 6). Then the third part of Rawls's argument is discussed in the following chapter, regarding the "stability" of justice as fairness; this is designed to show that justice as fairness is compatible with human moral psychology, affirms the human good, and describes a feasible social world (all this in Part III of *TJ*, "Ends").

Rawls basically argues that the principles of justice would be chosen by rational representatives of free and equal persons in an impartial initial situation; there the parties know general facts about human nature and social institutions but have no knowledge of particular facts about themselves or their society and its history. Behind this "veil of ignorance" the principles of justice are regarded as preferable to utilitarian, perfectionist, libertarian, and pluralist conceptions of justice. While this basic idea is simply stated, the argument is in the details. Rawls's argument is controversial and many philosophers do not find it convincing. Some more common objections will be discussed as I proceed. Part I of this chapter discusses the structure of the original position and the requirements on the parties' choice. Then Part II discusses Rawls's arguments for the choice of the principles in the original position.

THE ORIGINAL POSITION: DESCRIPTION OF THE PARTIES AND THE CONDITIONS ON CHOICE

Background

The original position develops the basic idea underlying the liberal and democratic social contract traditions stemming from Locke, Rousseau, and Kant – namely that just laws, constitutions, or principles are those that *could* or *would* be agreed to among free persons from a position of equal right. Like his predecessors, Rawls's social contract is hypothetical: it is not an actual agreement made at some point in history; rather it is a kind of thought experiment (JF, 17) where hypothetical people, described as fairly situated and as free, equal, and rational, are given the task of coming to a unanimous agreement upon principles of justice that are to be applied within their ongoing society. What is distinctive about this agreement is that the parties do not know any particular facts about themselves or anyone else in society. The "veil of ignorance" has the effect of requiring the parties to make a strictly impartial choice, one that does not favor persons in their position. Rawls calls his conception of justice "justice as fairness" since it aims to discover the principle of justice that would be agreed to in a fair initial situation. His idea is that the fairness of the original position transfers to the principles agreed to within it, and thus the principles agreed to should also be fair (TJ, 12/11 rev.). This is what Rawls means in saying that the original position "incorporates pure procedural justice at the highest level" (CP, 310–11). He means there is no independent criterion for justice separate and apart from hypothetical agreement in the original position; "what is just is defined by the outcome of the [fair] procedure itself" (CP, 311).

Some critics contest Rawls's claim that the parties are fairly and impartially situated by the veil of ignorance and other conditions of Rawls's social contract. For example, libertarians like Robert Nozick object that there is nothing fair about a contract that forces people to choose redistributive principles that jeopardize their pre-existing property rights. Nozick assumes, like other libertarians, that property rights are pre-social and that distributive justice is established by non-cooperative principles; the idea of a social contract carries little, if any, weight in their thinking.[1] Rawls, by contrast, sees property as a social institution, and regards principles of justice as needed to decide how this and other basic institutions ought to specify and distribute rights and liberties, powers and opportunities, and income and wealth. Since principles of justice are to regulate the basic structure of a society of persons who are free and equal, then the appropriate way to derive principles, Rawls believes, is via a fair agreement among all the parties themselves, where each is given an opportunity to accept or reject the principles (cf. JF, 14–15, 17).[2] What makes an agreement *appropriate* is that the principles of justice behind coercive laws should be acceptable to a free and equal person whose conduct is regulated by them. This is a fundamental assumption of social contract views. But free and equal persons have different values and beliefs, and there is no commonly accepted moral, religious, or philosophical authority that otherwise could be consulted to decide rights or settle disagreements about justice and principles of justice. Thus the only way for principles of justice to be acceptable to everyone (if they are at all) is by a social agreement.

Rawls thinks that for this agreement to be *fair*, the parties must be represented all in the same way, solely *as* free and equal moral persons who abstract from the factual characteristics and circumstances that individuate them and set them at odds. The features of the original position are then closely connected with this conception of persons. Rawls says the original position "represents" or "models" free and equal moral persons, or "maps" their characteristics. Perhaps a more intuitive way to regard the original position is that it captures ("models") what we now regard as morally acceptable *restrictions on reasons* in arguments for principles of justice for the basic structure of society (JF, 17; TJ, 18/16 rev.). For example, assuming we care about justice, we presumably believe that like cases should be treated alike, and that people *are* equals in some basic sense. But this implies that some information is not morally relevant in arguments for principles of justice, for example, people's religion, race, gender, ethnic group, social class, and so on. Accordingly the veil of ignorance excludes this information; the veil and other conditions of the original position are designed to focus our attention upon the reasons that are morally relevant, and to exclude those that are not, to justifying principles of justice.

Why is the social contract hypothetical, and not real? Hypothetical agreements are characteristic of the social contract tradition. Hobbes's and Locke's social contracts take place in a hypothetical state of nature, whereas Rawls's takes place in a hypothetical original position. The social contract serves as a test or criterion for morally assessing currently existing constitutions, governments, and laws, and deciding our duties of justice. For these purposes, it is irrelevant to the justification of principles that they have been or ever will be actually agreed to by anyone in the real world. Here Ronald Dworkin and others object that hypothetical contracts cannot create moral obligations; only real contracts do.[3] For example, the fact that I would promise to give you my purse were you to save my life surely cannot mean that I have an obligation now to give you my purse, not having made any actual promise. Similarly, it would seem that the fact that people would agree to the principles of justice in the original position cannot commit us either, since we have not actually made any such agreement. In response, Rawls says that the original position is a "device of representation, or alternatively, a thought experiment for the purpose of public- and self-clarification" (JF, 17). This means that its purpose is not to impose an obligation on us that we do not already have. Its purpose rather is to elucidate the reasons behind our considered convictions of justice, in order to see what principles of justice our sincerest moral convictions, considered in light of the best reasons, already commit us to accept. We are committed to these principles by our considered convictions and the best reasons, and not by any actual agreement; and we are committed to them whether or not we ever want to accept and follow their demands. (Many people do not.) Moreover, the fact that an agreement or other event is hypothetical surely cannot imply that it has no probative value. Some of the most fundamental advances in inquiry are based on thought experiments regarding the behavior of individuals or objects in hypothetical situations that are not practically possible (for example, conditions of perfect competition in price theory, motion in a vacuum in Newtonian physics, and objects with mass traveling at the speed of light in special relativity). Just as hypothetical situations can be used to state fundamental laws of physics or economics, they should be helpful in philosophy in discovering or justifying basic moral principles.

The original position is not a free-floating philosophical discussion in which the parties reason *ab initio* and design the principles that are to regulate their social relations. Many objections have been raised to Rawls's original position argument that assume that the parties in the original position engage in extensive philosophical deliberation and argument, and thereby acquire beliefs that lead them to choose some other principles of justice (we see later that utilitarians contend the parties would choose the principle of utility, and cosmopolitans argue they would choose global principles of distributive justice). But Rawls sets up his original position to forestall such speculation. Of course, someone might set up an original position argument differently than Rawls, but it would not be the original position that Rawls uses. To this some have argued that Rawls "stacks the deck" in his favor, making assumptions in the original position that lead only to his principles of justice. But why should this be a defect and not a virtue of the theory, so long as these assumptions are not arbitrary and really do capture better than any alternatives our considered convictions about reasonable restrictions on arguments for principles of justice? Rawls says that for each traditional moral conception of justice, there is a way to structure the original position so that its principles are chosen. This suggests, he says, that the general idea of the original position can be applied as a useful theoretical device that uncovers the philosophical assumptions behind different theories of justice, enabling us to compare the reasonableness of the different assumptions and arguments. (TJ, 121–2/105 rev.)

Thus, the original position for Rawls is not a free-floating philosophical discussion of justice but a way to combine in a perspicuous manner the many reasonable assumptions that justify a conception of justice. Another way to see it is as a selection device where the parties are presented with a list of principles and moral conceptions they are to choose from, drawn up from the tradition of moral and political philosophy (see TJ, sect. 21 for this list). The parties' deliberations have to begin somewhere, and Rawls wants to make them as straightforward and clear-cut as possible and to present the parties with a definable and decidable problem. So Rawls has the parties consider the major political conceptions of justice that have been discussed among philosophers in the modern era (since Hobbes) – namely, various versions of utilitarianism, justice as fairness, perfectionism, intuitionism, and rational egoism (TJ, 124/107 rev.). He does not explicitly mention as among the alternatives certain popular conceptions, particularly the libertarianism that grew out of *laissez-faire* liberalism. Rawls does, however, take into account classical liberalism of Adam Smith, Friedrich Hayek, and others, which he calls, following Smith, the "system of natural liberty" (TJ, sect. 12). Subsequently, Rawls suggests that libertarianism and other omitted conceptions are easily incorporated into his argument, by comparing their desirability within the original position with his own and other principles of justice. One reason for not discussing libertarianism is that it did not have a well-known advocate among academic philosophers until Robert Nozick, Rawls's junior colleague, set forth the position in 1974, in *Anarchy, State, and Utopia*. There Nozick himself admits that his entitlement principles would be rejected in the original position.[4] He argues that a social contract is both inappropriate and unnecessary, since a limited government could arise via a series of private contracts starting from a state of nature.

For the most part, Rawls discusses utilitarianism as the main alternative to justice as fairness. He regards utilitarianism as the dominant systematic account of justice in the modern democratic era (TJ, viii/xviii rev.). His discussion and argument against utilitarianism provides a pattern of argument that can be applied to many other teleological conceptions, i.e., those which hold that it is right and just to always act to maximize the good. But as for what he calls "Intuitionism" (TJ, sect. 7), which includes a large class of moral conceptions that recognize a plurality of basic moral principles and/or primary ends, different arguments have to be made. It is characteristic of intuitionist views that no ranking of the relative importance of principles (such as the priority of liberty) can be set down once and for all; instead the plurality of principles has to be balanced on appropriate occasions "in intuition," and the balance struck may be different, depending on the circumstances. This is a common-sense view, and it may be the best we can do for many moral principles. Rawls argues, nonetheless, that in the case of principles of justice, we should try to do better.

Rationality of the Parties and the Concept of a Person's Good

In order for the parties in the original position to make a *rational choice*, they must have certain interests or ends they aim to promote, some idea of what is and what is not to their benefit. Rawls describes the parties as rational in a "thin" sense (TJ, sect. 25).[5] His "thin theory of the good" has both formal and substantive aspects. The formal aspects are principles of rational choice, the idea of deliberative rationality, and the idea of a rational plan of life. The substantive aspects are the account of the parties' higher-order interests, the primary goods, and the Aristotelian Principle (the latter to be taken up in ch. 6). (Here I'll mention only those aspects needed to understand the argument from the original position, and will take up others later in Chapter 6 when they become especially relevant to the argument for stability.) Formally, Rawls aims to set forth a conception of rationality that is "with the exception of one essential feature" compatible with "the standard one familiar in social theory" (TJ, 143/123–24 rev.), by which he means economics and other disciplines that apply a theory of rational choice.

Rational persons do not try to do the impossible: (1) they seek to make their ends *consistent* and then they take *effective means* to achieve their ends; (2) they also take into account the *probability* that alternative courses of action will meet with success; (3) and given their limited means, rational persons try to achieve as many of their important purposes as is feasible; they observe a principle of *inclusiveness*. These three features – which Rawls calls the "counting principles" – are relatively uncontroversial aspects of most accounts of practical rationality. More generally, rational persons have a *conception of their good*, or of their primary values and the best kind of life to live. This *"rational plan"* incorporates their primary aims, commitments, and ambitions, and is informed by the conscientious moral, religious, and philosophical convictions that give meaning to their lives. Rational persons have carefully thought about these things and their relative importance, and have coherently ordered their purposes and commitments into a *"rational plan of life,"* which extends over a person's lifetime. For Rawls, rational persons regard life as a whole, and do not give preference to any particular period of it. Rather, in drawing up their rational plans, they are equally concerned with their good at each part of their lives. In this regard, rational persons are *prudent* – they care for their future good, and while they may discount the importance of future purposes based on probability assessments of likelihood of achieving them, they do not discount the achievement of their future purposes simply because they are in the future (TJ, sect. 45).[6]

We might then imagine that each party in the original position has a good idea of what they want to accomplish in life (through a career or avocation), as well as an idea of the importance of personal relationships (friendships, families, children, and so on), of their identity as members of various groups (ethnic, religious, political, and so on), and more generally of the kinds of values and pursuits that give their lives meaning for them. These aims, convictions, ambitions, and commitments are among the primary motivations of the parties in the original position. They want to provide favorable and secure conditions for the pursuit of the various elements of the rational plan of life that defines a good life for them. This is ultimately what the parties are trying to accomplish in their choice of principles of justice. In this sense they are rational.

The parties in the original position are "mutually disinterested." What does this mean? It is sometimes said that the parties to Rawls's original position are entirely "self-interested." If true this would seem to misrepresent human nature. For all of us other people matter a great deal – our loved ones, friends, members of the groups we identify with, and so on. A similar view of "limited altruism" is also true of the rational parties to the original position. But the benevolence and affections they have towards particular persons and groups are not expressed directly towards *other parties* to the social contract. They are indifferent to each other *as contracting parties* in the sense that they "take no interest in each others' interests," at least for purposes of this particular agreement. This means that the parties are motivated neither by affection nor by rancor for each other. On the one hand the parties are presumed not to be motivated by envy for others' position. (The absence of envy is the one special assumption Rawls says his account of rationality makes that distinguishes it from the one used in social theory.) (TJ, 143/124 rev.) This implies that the parties do not strive to be wealthier or better off than others for its own sake, and thus do not sacrifice rewards to themselves to prevent others from having more than they do. Instead, each party in the original position is motivated to do as well as he/she can in absolute terms in promoting the optimal achievement of the many purposes that make up a conception of the good, without regard to how much or how little others may have. As the parties are not envious, so too they are not moved by affection for each other in their agreement. That is, they are not directly concerned with promoting other *parties'* aims and commitments – which is *not* to say that they are not concerned with promoting other *people's* aims and commitments, for as we have seen they surely are in so far as they have many affections and commitments to other people. Their commitments to others are indeed among the primary purposes they seek to further through their agreement. Thus it is misleading to say (as many do) that the parties to Rawls's social contract are egoists, or are purely self-interested (cf. TJ, 147–49/127–29 rev.). While they aim to promote their interests as parties to this particular agreement, they are no more self-interested as persons than you and I are.[7] Rawls believes this account of the parties' motivations promotes greater clarity, and that to attribute to the parties moral motivations or benevolence towards each other would not result in the definite choice of a conception of justice (TJ, 148–49/128–29 rev.; 584/512 rev.).

This relates to Rawls's assumption that the parties have a capacity for *reasonableness* and a *sense of justice* (TJ, 145/125 rev.). Rawls distinguishes the concept of rationality from that of reasonableness, and sees both as imposing requirements on practical reasoning about what we ought to do. The concept of "the Rational" concerns a person's *good* – hence Rawls refers to his account of value as "goodness as rationality." A person's good for Rawls is the rational plan of life he/she would choose under conditions of "deliberative rationality" (TJ, sect. 64). "The Reasonable" on the other hand has to do with the concept of *right* – including individual moral duties and moral requirements of right and justice applying to institutions and society. Both rationality and reasonableness are independent aspects of practical reason for Rawls. He does not claim that an immoral person is irrational, or that morality is necessarily required by rationality. However, a person who is perfectly rational still violates requirements of practical reason if he or she infringes upon reasonable moral demands. So being reasonable, even if not required by rationality, is still an independent aspect of practical reason. We have an intuitive idea of this distinction in ordinary speech when it is said of a person who unfairly takes advantage of others, "I can see why it might be rational for him to do that given his aims, but he's being wholly unreasonable." Intuitively we think of a reasonable person as one who is cooperative and fairminded, who respects others and their position and is sensitive to the reasons and purposes they have, and who is willing to moderate his demands and meet others halfway when conflicts arise.

For Rawls, essential to being reasonable is having a *sense of justice*. The sense of justice is a willingness and normally effective desire to comply with duties and obligations required by justice. Rawls sees a sense of justice as an attribute people normally have; it "would appear to be a condition for human sociability" (TJ, 495/433 rev.). He rejects the idea, popular in extensions of economic theory, that people are motivated *only* by self-interest in all that they do; he also rejects the Hobbesian assumption that a willingness to do justice must be grounded in self-interest. Later in Chapter 6 we will see how it is essential to Rawls's argument for the feasibility and stability of justice as fairness, that the parties upon entering society have an effective sense of justice

After *Theory*, in Kantian and political constructivism, Rawls says that the parties to the original position have a "higher-order interest" in the exercise and development of their capacity for a sense of justice (as well as in their capacity to be rational), and that this is one of the main aims behind their agreement on principles of justice. The parties' interest in developing these two "moral powers" is a substantive feature of Rawls's account of the rationality of free and equal persons. The idea behind the rationality of justice (among free and equal persons) is that, since reasonableness is a condition of human sociability, then it is in people's *rational interest* – part of their good – that they develop their capacities for a sense of justice under conditions of a well-ordered society. Otherwise they will not be in a position to cooperate with others and benefit from social life. For without great power to dominate others, a person who is wholly unreasonable will be eschewed by others, for he is not trustworthy or reliable or even safe to interact with. If others are not convinced that you are capable of understanding laws and other norms of justice, applying them, and complying with their demands, they will be unwilling to cooperate with you in any enduring relationship. Unreasonable people are often shunned. The parties to the original position know this, so they take a "higher-order interest" in establishing conditions for the exercise and development of their sense of justice, a condition of sociability. The parties' interest in developing their sense of justice is then a purely rational interest in being reasonable; in other words, justice is regarded by the parties as instrumental to their realizing their conception of the good. The parties themselves, in the original position, have no interest in justice for its own sake, but only as a means to their non-moral aims. In this regard, the parties reason about justice as Hobbes says that all rational people do.

Three factors are then fundamental in motivating the parties in the original position: (1) First, they aim to advance their determinate conception of the good, or rational plan of life. Then, they also seek conditions that enable them to exercise and develop their "moral powers," namely (2) their rational capacities to form, revise, and pursue a conception of their good, and (3) their capacity to be reasonable and to have a sense of justice. These are the three "higher-order interests" the parties to Rawls's original position aim to promote in their agreement on principles of justice. The higher-order interests in the moral powers might be seen as *fundamental interests* of the parties and of rational persons who regard themselves as free and equal; they are necessary to achieve the primary ends of utmost importance in a person's life.

Whereas the principles of rational choice provide formal structure, the three higher-order interests provide substantive content to Rawls's account of rationality and the good. Among persons who are or conceive of themselves as free and equal, one who cares nothing for any one of these three ends is simply irrational. Now the three higher-order interests provide the basis for Rawls's account of *primary social goods*. This is the second substantive aspect of Rawls's account of the Rational. The primary goods are the all-purpose social means that are necessary to the exercise and development of the moral powers and to pursue a wide variety of conceptions of the good.[8] Rawls describes them initially in *Theory* as goods that any rational person should want, whatever his or her rational plan of life. The primary social goods are: rights and liberties, powers and opportunities, income and wealth, and the bases of self-respect. These should be familiar from earlier discussions; rights and liberties have been discussed in Chapter 2, and powers and opportunities, income and wealth in Chapter 3. By "powers" Rawls does not mean the abstract ability to effect outcomes, nor does he mean power in the sense of a capacity to dominate or even have control over others. Rather he uses the term to refer to the legal and institutional abilities and prerogatives that attend offices and social positions. Hence, he sometimes refers to the primary goods of "powers and positions of office." Members of various professions and trades have institutional powers that are characteristic of their profession and which are necessary if they are to carry out their respective roles. Physicians, lawyers, teachers, electricians, plumbers, accountants, stock brokers, and so on, are all trained and authorized to carry out certain social and economic functions. To do so they need certain legal and institutional powers or capabilities. "The social bases of self-respect" are features of institutions that are needed to enable people to have the confidence that their position in society is respected and their conception of the good is worth pursuing. These features depend upon history and culture. Primary among these social bases in a democratic society are the conditions needed for equal citizenship, including equality of political rights and fair equal opportunity. Blacks and women were denied these bases of self-respect for most of U.S. history.

The parties to the original position are motivated to achieve an adequate share of primary goods so that they can achieve their higher-order interests in their rational plans of life and the moral powers. "They assume that they normally prefer more primary social goods rather than less" (TJ, 142/123 rev.). This too is part of being rational. Here again it has been objected that the parties' preference for more rather than fewer of the primary goods is not necessarily rational, but presupposes a particularly Western conception of the good, and wrongly implies that certain conceptions are irrational that are not (for example, a simple life eschewing wealth, or the life of a mendicant monk). Rawls uses the term "wealth" in a broad economic sense, to mean not simply money, but control or use of any concrete resources or services that have a market value and enable a person to pursue his ends. A mendicant monk with no visible income still has access to far more wealth than a poor person if the monk lives in a monastery with access to a library, a private room, an elaborate chapel, and tranquil cloisters or gardens in which to relax, stroll, and meditate. In this broad sense of the term, some degree of wealth is instrumental to any person's good. Moreover, those who might eschew wealth in the usual sense for themselves do not have to personally take advantage of it, but if they have it they still can donate their wealth to persons and causes they care for. Even the ascetic cares for others with needs. Finally, a rational person has to take into account that he or she might revise his or her conception of the good in the future; so even if one lives a life eschewing material objects and the uses of wealth, it would be prudent to have available some resources to make a revision of life-plans possible.

To sum up, the parties in the original position are formally rational in that they are assumed to have and to effectively pursue a rational plan of life with a schedule of coherent purposes and commitments that give their life meaning. As part of their rational plans, they have a substantive interest in the development and exercise of their capacities to be rational and to be reasonable. These "higher-order interests" provide them with reason to procure for themselves in their choice of principles of justice an adequate share of the primary social goods that enable them to achieve these higher-order ends and effectively pursue their plan of life. The third and final substantive feature of Rawls's account of "the Rational," the Aristotelian Principle, says that rational people normally should incorporate into their rational plans activities that call upon the exercise and development of developed skills and their distinctly human capacities. This will be discussed in Chapter 6, since it is especially relevant to Rawls's argument for the stability of justice as fairness.

The Veil of Ignorance

This strong impartiality condition is the most distinctive feature of Rawls's social contract; the parties are required to put aside reliance on knowledge of all particular facts about themselves and their social and historical circumstances, including their particular conceptions of the good, and even including their comprehensive religious, philosophical, and moral convictions. Rawls contends that particular facts about a person's situation – one's intelligence and skills, gender, religion, race, wealth, health, and so on – do not serve as good reasons in arguments to justify principles of justice. To insure that the parties do not rely upon these particular facts about themselves and their society, Rawls imagines them placed behind a *veil of ignorance*. As a result, no one knows any specific facts about himself or anyone else, or even about the historical situation they live in. They do not know the wealth or natural resources their society has, its population or level of development, and so on. The parties' decision is to be based entirely on their knowledge of *general facts* that they share in common with each other, which include general knowledge of psychology, economics, and other relevant social, biological, and physical sciences.

The veil of ignorance sharply distinguishes Rawls's social contract from state-of-nature views. In both Hobbes's interest-based and Locke's rights-based contract doctrines, the social contract transpires among individuals historically situated in a (hypothetical) state of nature. All the parties to the contract know as much about themselves and others as you and I know now about ourselves. In this regard, their social contracts are "historical" – not in the sense that they actually took place but rather in that they transpire under hypothetical historical conditions where the parties know their circumstances and personal characteristics and histories.

In the normal course of events contractors bargain with one another based on their knowledge of their attributes, circumstances, and relative positions. Each brings to the negotiations whatever knowledge about facts he or she has, and takes full advantage of these facts in reaching an agreement. In ordinary agreements people are normally constrained by laws and their moral convictions from entering into certain kinds of agreements. Thus, few people today would demand that their debtors submit to involuntary servitude in the event that they default on payments, however effective this remedy might be in encouraging people to make good on their debts. Slavery and forced servitude are regarded today as unconscionable in both law and morality. Locke's right-based contract is similarly constrained by moral demands. The parties recognize that their agreement is void if it violates the moral duties implicit in God's laws of nature. No one may agree to conditions that would require anyone to alienate his or her freedom of the person, and other inalienable moral rights.[9]

Nonetheless, for Locke natural rights of equal political authority are not among the *inalienable* rights that constrain the social contract. Even though all persons are born free and equal, with equal political jurisdiction, Locke imagines that the great majority of the population – including all women and most men (those who do not satisfy certain stringent property qualifications) – could rationally choose to give up their equal political rights in order to gain other benefits of political society. For this reason, Locke endorses a constitutional monarchy in which only the class of propertied males (none of whom could be atheists) could vote for members of parliament. Somewhere in this process the equal political liberties all citizens are born with have been jettisoned by Locke. How is it possible? Locke's contractarian argument for unequal political rights relies on the assumption that the social contract transpires in a state of nature where the parties know their own gender, level of wealth, religious beliefs, and so on. It's because the parties to Locke's social contract are historically situated and have knowledge of their situation that more advantaged parties are positioned to take advantage of their bargaining power, and require that others give up certain rights they otherwise might have, in exchange for other compensating benefits. Thus, even though Locke's social contract is constrained by moral demands, it still permits the parties to take advantage of, or suffer the disadvantages for, their unequal bargaining positions.

Reasonable people today find it unjust to deprive a large majority of the adult population of the political franchise simply because they are not white, wealthy males. It does not square with our considered moral convictions. But there seems to be no clear-cut way to avoid these and other unacceptable inequalities within a contractarian framework so long as the historical circumstances of a state of nature form the baseline for the social contract. People will always be prone to the self-righteous exercise of their "threat-advantage," whether it be their de facto political power, wealth, native endowments, or whatever. But these contingent facts about people are not morally relevant to agreement on principles of justice. Rawls's veil of ignorance is designed to respond to this problem. By rendering the parties ignorant of their social and historical circumstances, the veil in effect deprives them of knowledge of facts that otherwise can be used to unfairly advantage and disadvantage people. If the parties do not know any particular facts about themselves, then no one is in a position to exploit others' disadvantages for their personal benefit. The veil is intended to render the social contract a fair and strictly impartial agreement.

What sort of knowledge does the veil exclude? It excludes knowledge of all particular facts that people may have regarding both themselves and also everyone else in society, and even knowledge of the historical and cultural circumstances of society itself (its resources and level of wealth, its population, and so on). Rawls claims that none of this knowledge is relevant to an agreement on the principles of justice for the basic structure of society. It may be relevant for many other kinds of agreement – for example, a potential employer surely is entitled to knowledge of potential employees' level of training and skills. But knowledge of these and all other facts about individuals and society are "morally irrelevant" to this specific agreement on principles of justice. In this regard, Rawls's veil of ignorance is "thick" rather than "thin." Suppose the parties knew all kinds of particular facts about people in their society (people's race, gender, religion, wealth, etc.), but did not know their own identities – no one knows which person he or she is. That would be a "thin" veil of ignorance. A thin veil allows for a degree of impartiality. Not knowing whether I am rich or poor, male or female, I would certainly hesitate before agreeing to principles of justice that allow for an unequal franchise that excludes women and the non-propertied from voting rights. But suppose I know that only a small percentage of people in society – say 5 percent – are non-Christian. I might be inclined to play the odds, and agree to allow for principles that give political preference to the Christian religion in education and other institutions. After all, I have a 95 percent chance of benefiting from a principle that officially endorses my religion. But is it really fair to non-Christians? A thin veil of ignorance, though it provides for a "thin" degree of impartiality, still is not sufficient, Rawls believes, to rule out unfair discrimination against minorities of people on the basis of religion, race, and other characteristics that should be irrelevant to their political and civil rights.

The distinction between a thick and a thin veil captures the distinction between Rawls's original position and the point of view of an "impartial spectator" found in David Hume, Adam Smith, C.I. Lewis, Amaryta Sen, and later utilitarians such as John Harsanyi. The idea of a moral point of view from which moral judgments are made originates with Hume's "judicious spectator," which, Rawls says, is one of the most important ideas in the history of moral philosophy.[10] Hume applied the idea as part of his naturalistic moral psychology, to explain how people with such different interests can nonetheless agree in their moral judgments. The subsequent development of Hume's idea provides the basis for a powerful argument for the principle of utility. For, as Hume contends, the judgments of a judicious or impartial spectator are governed by his/her response to the sum of individual utilities. The stronger the sum of utilities, the stronger should be the approvals or disapprovals of a judicious spectator who sympathetically identifies with everyone's desires. It is as if the judicious spectator, given complete knowledge of each person's desires and circumstances, were applying in its impartial judgments the classical principle of utility.[11]

Complete knowledge of all particular facts about people's desires and circumstances is necessary for moral judgment from the point of view of the judicious spectator. Otherwise an impartial judge could not sympathetically identify with everyone's situation and their interests. By contrast in Rawls's original position sympathetic identification with others' desires is not possible because the thick veil of ignorance prevents the parties from knowing these and other particular facts about people. Rawls thinks that knowledge of particular facts, including people's desires, tends to distort the kind of judgment that is needed in the original position. Recall that the parties are to choose principles of justice for the basic structure of society, which are to be applied to assess the justice of existing societies and their basic institutions. To allow the parties knowledge of particular desires and interests, distributions of rights, and other historical facts would improperly skew their judgments. For whatever principles of justice were chosen would then improperly reflect the status quo, including the very desires, interests, and facts regarding distributions that these principles themselves are to be used to assess. Any existing injustices would then bias choice of the very principles that are to be used to assess these and other injustices. Rawls regards a thick veil of ignorance as necessary in order to abstract from the biasing conditions of the status quo. (Recall the example above, of the likely adverse effects on freedom of religion of knowledge that one's society is 95 percent Christian.)[12]

Another reason for a thick veil of ignorance is that it situates the parties equally in a very strong way. This relates to the Kantian interpretation and moral constructivism, where Rawls sets up the original position so that it represents a conception of persons as free, equal, reasonable, and rational. Since no one in the original position knows any particular facts about society, the parties all have the same knowledge available to them. They are then "situated symmetrically," purely as free and equal moral persons. They know only characteristics and interests of themselves in their capacity as moral persons – the moral powers, their higher-order interests, and so on. For the moral powers are the "basis of equality, the features of human beings in virtue of which they are to be treated in accordance with the principles of justice" (TJ, 504/441 rev.). This, along with knowledge of other general facts, is all the knowledge that is relevant, Rawls believes, to a decision on principles of justice that are to reflect people's status as free and equal moral persons. A thick veil of ignorance thus represents the equality of persons purely as moral persons, and not in any other contingent capacity or social role, thereby providing content to the Kantian notion of equal respect that moral persons are due. (The Kantian interpretation will be discussed in Chapter 6, and Kantian Constructivism in Chapter 7.)

A frequent objection to Rawls's original position is that the parties are deprived of so much information that they are incapable of making any choice at all. How can we make any rational choice without knowledge of our fundamental values? To begin with, the parties do know of their need for the primary goods and their higher-order interests in the moral powers. Moreover, it is important not to get too caught up in the fiction of the original position, as if it were some historical event that has to transpire among real people who are being asked to do something psychologically impossible. It may well be impracticable for you and me to bracket all our knowledge of our primary values and particular circumstances in making life choices. But the original position is a thought experiment, and like most thought experiments it depicts unrealistic if not physically impossible situations. Here once again it is important to emphasize just what the veil of ignorance and the original position are designed to do. The veil of ignorance is a vivid representation of the kinds of reasons and information that are relevant to a decision on principles of justice for the basic structure of a society in which moral persons regard themselves as free and equal. Many different kinds of reasons and facts are morally irrelevant to that kind of decision (e.g., people's race, gender, religious affiliation, wealth, and even, Rawls claims, more controversially, their conceptions of their good), just as many different kinds of reasons and facts are irrelevant to mathematicians' ability to work out a formal proof of a theorem. Do a group of mathematicians, all working on proving the same theorem, need to keep in mind particular facts about their personal lives in order to successfully do the proof? It would be both distracting and irrelevant to the task at hand. Whether or not it is psychologically possible for a person to enter into the original position is inconsequential to the validity of the argument (just as it is irrelevant to the soundness of price theory whether economic agents' complete knowledge of all options for choice under conditions of perfect competition is realistically possible). We can reason now (knowing all kinds of facts about ourselves) about what the appropriate decision would be if we were in that situation, given the general information about persons and societies provided to the parties.

Other Conditions on Choice in the Original Position

The circumstances of justice

Among the general facts the parties know are "the circumstances of justice." These are "conditions under which human cooperation is both possible and necessary" (TJ, 126/109 rev.). The general idea of the circumstances of justice is found in David Hume.[13] Rawls distinguishes two general kinds: the objective and subjective circumstances. The former include physical facts about human beings, such as their rough similarity in mental and physical faculties, and vulnerability to attack. It also includes conditions of moderate scarcity of resources: there are not enough resources to satisfy everyone's demands, but there are enough to provide all with adequate satisfaction of their basic needs; unlike conditions of extreme scarcity (e.g., famine) cooperation then seems productive and worthwhile for people. Among the subjective circumstances the parties' "limited altruism"[14] has been discussed above under the rationality of the parties. Hume says that if humans were impartially benevolent, equally concerned with everyone's welfare, then justice would be "superfluous." People then would almost always willingly sacrifice their interests for the sake of others and not be concerned about personal rights or possessions. But we are (naturally) more concerned with our own interests, including the interests of those nearer and dearer to us, than we are with the interests of strangers with whom we have no connections. This implies a potential conflict of human interests. The subjective circumstances of justice also include limited human knowledge, thought, and judgment, as well as differences in experiences. These lead to inevitable disagreements in factual and other judgments, as well as to people having different plans of life and religious, philosophical, and moral views. In *Political Liberalism*, Rawls highlights these subjective circumstances, calling them "the burdens of judgment." They imply, significantly, that regardless of how impartial and altruistic people are, they still will disagree in their religious, philosophical, and moral judgments. Disagreements in these matters are inevitable even among rational and reasonable people. This is "the fact of reasonable pluralism," which is another general fact known to the parties in the original position.

Publicity and other formal constraints of right

There are five "formal constraints" on the principles of justice the parties must meet in their choice: generality, universality in application, ordering of conflicting claims, publicity, and finality (see TJ, sect. 23). The ordering condition says that a conception of justice should aspire to completeness: it should be able to resolve conflicting claims and order their priority. Ordering implies a systematicity requirement: principles of justice should provide a determinate resolution to problems of justice that arise under them; and in so far as a conception of justice is not able to order conflicting claims and resolve problems of justice, that is a reason against choosing it in the original position. The ordering condition is important in Rawls's argument against pluralist moral doctrines he calls "intuitionism."

The publicity condition says that the parties are to assume that the principles of justice they choose will be publicly known and recognized as governing among the people whose relations they regulate. This implies that people will not be falsely indoctrinated or have false beliefs about the bases of their social and political relations. There are no "noble lies" obscuring principles of justice. Their publicity is required to respect persons as free and equal. People should know the bases of their social and political relations, or at least not have to be deceived about them in order to cooperate and live together in peace. Rawls regards publicity as implicit in the social contract tradition – if parties are thought of as agreeing to principles of justice, then presumably they have knowledge of them in their day-to-day relations and activities. This condition plays an important role in Rawls's arguments against utilitarianism and other consequentialist conceptions.

Related to publicity is that principles should be universal in application. This implies not simply that "they hold for everyone in virtue of their being moral persons" (TJ, 132/114 rev.). It also means (Rawls does not say why) that everyone can understand the principles of justice and use them in deliberations. Universality in application then imposes a limit on how complex principles of justice can be – they must be understandable to common moral sense.

Both publicity and universality in application (as Rawls defines it) are controversial conditions. Utilitarians, for example, have argued that the truth about morality and justice is so complicated and controversial that it might be necessary to keep it hidden from most people's awareness. After all, morality often requires a good deal of people that is contrary to their personal interests. Also sometimes it's just too complicated for people to understand why their moral duties require of them what they do. So long as they understand their duties, it may be better if they do not understand the principles and reasons behind them. So Sidgwick argues that the aims of utilitarianism might better be achieved if it remains an "esoteric morality," knowledge of which is confined to "an enlightened few." The reason Rawls sees these conditions as necessary relates to the conception of the person implicit in justice as fairness. If we conceive of persons as free and equal moral persons, then they should not be under any illusions about the nature and bases of their social relations. For people to act under such illusions is, in an important way, a limitation on their freedom as rational and responsible moral agents.

A further reason for the publicity condition (though not explicitly cited by Rawls) connects with the Kantian interpretation of justice as fairness, which attempts to work out Kant's idea that principles of justice are "constructed" on the basis of our practical reason, and that we are morally autonomous beings. In order for moral autonomy to be possible, moral principles of justice must be capable of serving moral agents as *principles of practical reasoning*; and for this to be possible principles must be publicly knowable by moral agents, without causing undue social instability. Finally, in *Political Liberalism* the publicity condition is important since democratic citizens' public knowledge of the political bases of their social relations is a condition of their political autonomy (which is different from moral autonomy). (These matters will be discussed in Chapters 7–9.)

The requirement of stability

Another controversial feature of Rawls's argument for the principles of justice is the requirement that principles of justice and the just system of social cooperation they enjoin should be "stable." The stability of a just society does not mean that it is unchanging.

It means, rather, that in the face of social change, which is always inevitable, the society should be able to maintain its allegiance to the principles of justice in regulating social cooperation and the evolution of society. Moreover, when disruptions to society do occur (via economic crises, war, natural catastrophes, etc.) and/or society departs from justice, citizens' commitments to principles of justice are sufficiently robust that justice is eventually restored. Normally in game theory to say that a situation is "stable" implies that it is difficult to change, and if the situation is disturbed, internal forces tend to restore it to its initial equilibrium. Rawls uses the concept of stability in a more special sense. The role of the stability requirement for Rawls is to test whether potential principles of justice for the basic structure of society are compatible with human nature, our moral psychology, and general facts about social and economic institutions, and also to determine whether principles are conducive to realizing the human good. To be stable, principles of justice should be realizable in a *feasible and enduring social world*. They need to be practicably possible, given the limitations of human nature. Moreover, this feasible social world must be one that can endure over time, not by just any means, but by gaining the *willing support* of people who live in it. For Rawls, this means that it must be a social world that people knowingly want to uphold and maintain, and which they can affirm and support with their *sense of justice*.[15]

In choosing principles of justice, the parties in the original position must take into account their "relative stability." They have to consider the degree to which a conception describes an achievable and sustainable system of social cooperation given the circumstances of justice – the normal conditions of human life; whether the norms of such a society will attract people's willing compliance; whether society can withstand normal cultural changes, and if justice is disrupted (for example, by economic depression) whether it can restore itself to a just condition.

It is tempting to regard the stability requirement as nothing more than the requirement that "ought implies can": namely, if principles of justice impose duties and requirements that we simply cannot live up to then they should be rejected. For example, suppose principles of justice were to impose a duty to practice impartial benevolence among all people, and thus a duty to show no greater concern for the welfare of ourselves and loved ones than we do towards billions of others. This principle demands too much of human nature, and would not be feasible – people simply would reject its onerous demands. But Rawls's stability requirement implies more than just "ought implies can." It says that principles of justice and the scheme of social cooperation they describe should evince "stability for the right reasons" (PL, xliii). A just society should be able to endure not simply as a *modus vivendi*, by coercive enforcement of its provisions and its promoting the majority of people's interests. Stability "for the right reasons" requires that people support society for *moral reasons*; society's basic principles must respond to reasonable people's capacities for justice and engage their sense of justice. Rawls regards our moral capacities for justice as an integral part of our nature as sociable beings. He believes that one role of a conception of justice is to accommodate human capacities for sociability, the capacities for justice that enable us to be cooperative social beings. So not only should a conception of justice advance human interests, but it should also answer to our moral psychology by enabling us to knowingly and willingly exercise our moral capacities and sensibilities. This is one way that Rawls's conception of justice is "ideal-based"[16] – it is based on an ideal of human beings as free and equal moral persons and an ideal of their social relations as acceptable and justifiable to them (the ideal of a well-ordered society). Principles of justice are designed to enable us to realize these moral ideals of persons and society.

One objection to stability is that principles of justice should not be subject to the vagaries of human nature and the human condition. Rawls himself makes much of the fact that people's capacities for knowledge are limited and people will always have different religious, philosophical, and moral convictions. But this means that many people, perhaps even the vast majority, will *always* have many false beliefs. Why should moral principles of justice and their justification be designed to accommodate the willing acceptance by people with many false beliefs about fundamental issues? Of course, we should take into account the foibles of human nature in the *application* of principles of justice and not impose duties that require more than people can do. But we should not allow the foibles of human nature and sociability to affect the most basic moral principles or their justification.[17]

This is a serious objection and demands more attention than I can give here. One reply is that a conception of justice that does not directly address the limits of human nature in its first principles is utopian, so long as it aspires to establish a feasible social world in which conscientious people generally can affirm and accept the principles that regulate their social relations. Social-contract doctrine proceeds from an assumption that not just gods or other perfect beings, but human beings, with all their limitations, should be able to live together on terms of mutual respect that every reasonable and rational person can freely accept.[18] Rawls's stringent stability condition is set forth to accommodate this ideal.

Moreover, another reason for the stability condition is that principles of justice should be compatible with, and even conducive to, the *human good*. Because of the "priority of right over the good," Rawls does not define justice as those moral principles that maximally promote the good. Justice is derived independently of a determinate conception of the human good, primarily on the basis of an ideal of the person as free and equal and moral constraints that follow from the concept of Right (the veil of ignorance, the five formal constraints of right, etc.). Still, it speaks strongly in favor of a conception of justice that it nonetheless is compatible with and promotes the human good. If a conception of justice requires of many reasonable people that they give up their pursuit of their good, then this is a serious reason against it (as Rawls argues against utilitarianism). We will be in a better position to understand these ideas and respond to the objection to the stability condition more fully later, in addressing the argument for the congruence of the right and the good in Chapter 6. Now it is time to turn to the arguments for the principles of justice in the original position.

ARGUMENTS FROM THE ORIGINAL POSITION

Rawls makes four arguments in *Theory*, Part I, for the principles of justice. These are later reinforced when Rawls discusses institutions that conform to the principles (*TJ*, Part II) and the stability of justice as fairness (*TJ*, Part III). The main argument for the difference principle is not found until section 49 and is easy to miss. In *Justice as Fairness: A Restatement* Rawls amends his initial arguments and adds further considerations to support the parties' agreement on justice as fairness. Here I discuss each of the four initial arguments in sections 26–29, and then the argument for the difference principle. Rawls seems to think that the justification of justice as fairness is forged through the combined force of these arguments plus later arguments in Part III showing justice as fairness is compatible with human nature and the human good.

The common thread throughout the original position arguments is that it is more rational for the parties therein, given their fundamental interests in adequate provision of the primary goods, to choose the principles of justice over any other alternative. For the sake of presentation, Rawls imagines the parties being presented with conceptions of justice in pairs and making pairwise comparisons between them. This simplifies the argument and allows him to focus upon each alternative to the principles of justice. He devotes most of his attention to utilitarianism, with briefer discussions of perfectionism (*TJ*, sect. 50) and intuitionism. I focus mainly on Rawls's arguments against utilitarianism.

The Argument from Maximin

The basic idea of the original position is to devise a choice situation where rational decision is subject to reasonable constraints (the veil of ignorance, the formal constraints of right, etc.). The parties to the original position are rational in a "thin" sense in that they choose principles that effectively promote their interests, particularly in obtaining primary social goods needed to pursue their conception of the good. Though the parties have a capacity for justice and a higher-order interest in its development, this is a purely rational consideration relating to their own good. They need to be able to understand, apply, and obey just laws and other moral requirements to get along and pursue their aims in a well-ordered society. In the original position they are not moved by moral considerations (e.g., to do what is just or fair, or make a morally right decision) or by benevolence toward other parties; nor are they directly concerned with others' developing their capacities for justice except in so far as it benefits themselves. They are "disinterested" in that they are *indifferent to one another* under these extraordinary circumstances of choice in the original position.

Describing the parties' choice as strictly rational and disinterested while subject to moral constraints allows Rawls to invoke the theory of rational choice and decision under conditions of uncertainty. In rational choice theory there are a number of potential "strategies" or rules of choice that are more or less reliably used depending on the circumstances. One rule of choice – called "maximin" – directs that we play it as safe as possible by choosing the alternative whose worst outcome leaves us better off than the worst outcome of all other alternatives. The aim is to "maximize the minimum" regret or loss to well-being. To follow this strategy, Rawls says you should choose as if your enemy were to assign your social position in whatever kind of society you end up in. By contrast, another strategy leads us to focus on the most advantaged position, saying that we should "maximize the maximum" potential gain – "maximax" – and choose the alternative whose best outcome leaves us better off than all other alternatives. Which of these strategies (if either) is more sensible to use depends on the circumstances and many other factors. For example, suppose you are relatively prosperous, and you have a chance to invest $100 in two different real-estate ventures. The first promises a one in three chance of making $5000 if all goes well, with risk of loss of only $5 of your $100 if it does not pan out. The second provides a one in ten chance of making $50,000, with a loss of your entire $100 if you do not succeed. If you are averse to risk and uncertainty then you would likely follow maximin and choose the first venture, thereby protecting your $100 investment. If you are more willing to take a chance, then you might follow maximax and choose the second venture. It is difficult to say which of these strategies is more rational without knowing more about your situation. For example, if you would not miss the $100 if the venture turns out badly, then the second venture makes more sense. If, on the other hand, you are poor and you owe the Mafia $95, to be collected very soon, then prudence suggests choosing the first venture (if you must choose at all) where there is little to lose.

Many decision theorists believe that a different strategy than either of these is suitable for *all* choices no matter what the circumstances. In orthodox Bayesian decision theory there is in effect but one rule of choice; it says basically *directly maximize expected utility*.[19] For any choice made under conditions of uncertainty (and most choices are) the degree of uncertainty of outcomes should be factored into one's utility function, with probability estimates assigned to alternatives based on the limited knowledge that one has. Given these subjective estimates of probability incorporated into one's utility function, one can always choose the alternative that maximizes *expected* utility. The virtue of Bayesian decision theory is that it provides a way to make theoretical sense of the influential idea that a rational choice always is one that maximizes an individual's (or society's) utility. This is a highly attractive idea, *so long as* one can accept that rationality always demands the maximization of *expected* utility (not actual utility).

What about those extremely rare instances, however, where there is absolutely *no* basis upon which to make probability estimates? Suppose you don't even have a hunch regarding the greater likelihood of one alternative over another. According to orthodox Bayesian decision theory, the "principle of insufficient reason" then should be observed; it says that an *equal probability* is to be assigned to each possible outcome. This makes sense on the assumption that if you have no more premonition of the likelihood of one option rather than another, they are *for all you know equally likely* to occur. By observing this rule of choice consistently over time along with the general Bayesian strategy, a rational chooser should maximize his or her individual expected utility, and perhaps even actual utility as well.

Now consider these decision rules when applied to choice of principles of justice under conditions of extreme uncertainty in Rawls's original position. Rawls argues that, given the importance of choice in the original position, it is rational for the parties to follow the maximin strategy when choosing between the principles of justice and principles of average or aggregate utility. Not surprisingly, maximin results in choice of the principles of justice over the principles of utility (average or aggregate). Here it is important to recall what is at stake in choice from the original position. The decision is not an ordinary choice. It is rather a unique and irrevocable choice – a kind of choice where the parties decide the basic structure of their society, or the kind of social world they should live in and the background conditions against which they will develop new aims and make all future choices. Rawls argues that, because of the unique importance of the choice in the original position – including the gravity of the choice, the fact that it is not renegotiable or repeatable, and the fact that it determines one's future prospects and conditions for future choices – it is rational to follow the maximin rule and choose the principles of justice. For should the worst transpire, the principles of justice provide an adequate share of primary goods enabling one to maintain one's conscientious convictions and sincerest affections and pursue a wide range of permissible ends, by protecting equal basic liberties and fair equal opportunities, and guaranteeing a social minimum. The principles of utility, by contrast, provide no such guarantee of any of these goods.

We will go into the details of the maximin argument momentarily. But first, contrast an argument by the economist John Harsanyi, who argues on strictly Bayesian grounds that a rational chooser in an original position would assign an *equal likelihood* to being each person in society, and in effect choose the principle of (average) utility. In Harsanyi's original position, a lone rational chooser is confronted with a thin veil of ignorance allowing complete knowledge of everyone's preferences in society, but complete uncertainty regarding her own identity (or which person she is) within that society. How could a rational person choose to maximize *her own* utility if she does not know *her own preferences?* First, she should imagine that she has an equal likelihood of having the preferences of any person in society. Then, to maximize her *own* utility, she sympathetically identifies with the preferences of each person in society, and asks herself, "How much utility would I experience if I had the preferences of *this* individual *i* under conditions C?" (Rawls questions whether this exercise makes sense, but that need not detain us; see *TJ*, 173–75/150–52 rev.). By multiplying the utility that the lone rational chooser would experience under C if she were i_1, i_2, i_3 ... i_n, by $1/n$ (according to the equiprobability assumption), and adding up the results, the rational chooser achieves a measure of her expected utility when she chooses outcome X or Y under C. That is:

$$\Sigma U_{\text{rational chooser}} = 1/nUi_1 + 1/nUi_2 + 1/nUi_3 \ldots + 1/nUi_n$$

In maximizing her *individual* utility behind a thin veil of ignorance it is as if the single rational chooser were applying the principle of *average* utility, which directs that we are to maximize the average happiness of members of society, summed across all individuals.

What now about the maximin rule of choice that Rawls applies in his original position? Harsanyi contends that the absurdity of maximin is easy to demonstrate. For example, suppose you have the opportunity to choose between two bets, (1) and (2), each of which has two outcomes, A and B. You have no knowledge of the likelihood of outcomes A and B, but you do know the bets' respective payoffs. It is clear by looking at these examples (see Table 4.1) that a rational person (absent extraordinary circumstances) would not hesitate to choose alternative (2). Following the equiprobability rule suggests this too.[20] The maximin strategy, however, since it requires that we focus on the worst-off position, requires choice of (1) (since if circumstance A prevails, you avoid the worst outcome, namely ten cents). But by choosing (1) you give up the chance of enormous gains for the sake of assuring yourself an additional 90 cents. This seems clearly irrational. So Harsanyi says, "Rawls makes the technical mistake of basing his

	Outcome A	Outcome B
Bet(1)	$1	$2
Bet(2)	10¢	$1,000,000

Table 4.1

analysis on a highly irrational decision rule, the maximin principle, which [has] absurd practical implications."[21]

There are certain basic differences between Rawls's and Harsanyi's original positions: Harsanyi's involves the rational choice of one person, while Rawls's involves a social agreement among members of society; and Harsanyi's chooser has complete knowledge of everyone's desires and characteristics and is only ignorant of her identity while Rawls's parties are in complete ignorance of any of these facts. But setting these differences aside, no doubt maximin is an irrational strategy under most circumstances of choice uncertainty. Rawls admits this.[22] But simply because it is most often or almost always irrational does not mean that it is *never* rational to follow maximin. Suppose, by parallel with the example above, you need a small sum of money *immediately* to save your child's life? For example, imagine you are an optimistic foreigner traveling the Nevada desert who has come to the U.S. with hopes of striking it rich. Your car overheats, so you stop at an isolated rest stop, where your woes are multiplied when your 3-year-old is bitten by a rattlesnake. Fortunately, there is a phone which charges a quarter for any call, and you have exactly one quarter. This being Nevada, there is also a quarter slot machine, saying "Take a chance and win a billion dollars!"[23] Being a foreigner and incredibly naive, you know absolutely nothing about the likelihood of a payoff. But you are clearly tempted, reasoning that if you win, you could both call in emergency rescue assistance, and also be an instant billionaire. Would it be rational to assume an equiprobable payoff in the absence of any information whatsoever? Would it be rational to base your decision on the assumption of *any* probability? To do so seems to foolishly and recklessly risk losing the person dearest to you. Given the potential grave loss involved, it is rational to do whatever you can to avoid the worst outcome (your child's death) and immediately call for the ambulance.[24]

Now consider a decision problem more akin to the one Rawls envisions (though still involving knowledge of factual information his original position does not allow). You are confronted with the choices and schedule of payoffs shown in Table 4.2. (1) and (2) are two potential choices and A and B represent two states of the world you might end up in. The numbers represent potential payoffs, what you receive if you choose alternative (1) or (2) and state of the world A or B transpires. These payoffs may be winnings (in $) from bets, or the average utilities experienced (over a lifetime) by individuals in different social classes (A = the least fortunate) and (B = the most fortunate) in societies (1) and (2) respectively.

Now assume that you have no knowledge whatsoever regarding the likelihood of either alternative, A or B. Bayesians say that, ignorant of probabilities of A or B we are to apply the principle of insufficient reason: We are to calculate the expected utilities of choices (1) and (2) as if the probability of A and B were each .5, then pick the course of action whose expected utility is maximal. Therefore we should choose (1) over (2) (since the expected utility of (1) [-100 (.5) + 500 (.5) = 200) exceeds the expected utility of (2) [100 (.5) + 200 (.5) = 150].

But now assume that, unbeknownst to you the chooser, 98 percent of choosers end up in Class A, and 2 percent in Class B.

Choices	States of the world		Sum of expected utility assuming equal probability
	(A)	(B)	
(1)	-100	500	= 200
(2)	100	200	= 150

Table 4.2

Given accurate information we can say then that the real likelihood or risk of A is .98 and of B is .02. Then the expected utility of choosing (1) is -88, that is [-100 (.98) + 500 (.02) = -88], while the expected utility of choosing (2) is 102, that is [100 (.98) + 200 (.02) = 102]. The result is shown in Table 4.3.

Depending on what is at stake, to form expectations according to the principle of insufficient reason in the absence of *any* information whatsoever about probabilities can result in a minor setback, or complete ruin. If all that is involved in choosing between (1) and (2) is a choice between bets on horses or voting on some ordinary piece of legislation, insufficient reason might be the rational strategy if you are ignorant of relevant information, for these are recurring situations and you will have the opportunity to choose again and recoup your losses. Then one might legitimately think, "You win some and you lose some." But you cannot think this way in the original position, for it is a decision where all one's future prospects and choices are at stake and there is no second chance allowing you to recoup previous losses. Suppose then you are choosing which society to enter, and (1) is winner-take-all, while (2) protects individuals' freedoms and provides a social minimum. There are two classes in each society, A and B, which represent (A) the downtrodden-unfortunates and (B) the dominant class in each society. Given that the risk of being (A) an unfortunate is .98, it would be most unfortunate indeed to assume otherwise, choose according to the principle of insufficient reason, and end up in (A), the worst-off class, in the winner-take-all society.

Choices	States of world (A&B)		Sum of expected utility given accurate information
(1)	-100 (x .98)	500 (x .02)	= -88
(2)	100 (x .98)	200 (x .02)	= 102

Table 4.3

Strictly orthodox Bayesians like Harsanyi contend that the principle of insufficient reason is the rational strategy to adopt under complete uncertainty no matter what is at stake and regardless of the gravity of the choice. But in what sense can it be rational to risk (if one can avoid it) one's deepest held conscientious convictions and moral and personal commitments, all future prospects, and life itself, in complete ignorance of the likelihood of outcomes and relying on a strategy of choice that lacks any basis in evidence whatsoever? The choice seems completely reckless. The principle of insufficient reason says that if there is no reason for assigning one set of probabilities rather than another, then we ought to assign equal probability to each outcome.[25] But if there is insufficient reason for one set of probabilities rather than another, it should follow that there is no reason to assign equal probability either. If every probability assignment is groundless, then perhaps the rational thing to do is to assign no probability at all,[26] at least under life and death circumstances or when one's life prospects and all one lives for are at stake and there is an acceptable alternative that guarantees them.

Since there is no reason arising from knowledge of the circumstances of choice that justifies assigning equiprobability, the reasons must come from somewhere else. One argument appeals to the recurring nature of choice situations under complete uncertainty: one's utility is more likely to be maximized over time when equiprobability is always assumed whenever completely uncertain outcomes arise. Perhaps this strategy makes sense with ordinary choices when the dangers of loss are not grave, and one has the opportunity to recoup one's losses and choose again and again. But the choice made in the original position is extraordinary; it is a kind of super-choice of the background conditions in which all future choices will be made. Moreover, it is permanent and there is no way to renegotiate the principles determining one's life prospects once the decision is made.

Another reason for the equiprobability assumption is more theoretical, grounded in a view of practical reason and its systemic demands. Some assumption regarding probabilities is necessary if we are to be able to compare any two alternatives and construct a utility function for a person. Given that with complete uncertainty there is no more reason to make one probability assignment rather than another, probability assignments themselves are all equally arbitrary. While equal arbitrariness of probability assignments does not imply equal likelihood of outcomes,[27] still equiprobability of outcomes seems to be the least arbitrary assumption given the theoretical requirement that *some* probability assignment has to be made to construct a utility function.

This argument illustrates that it is theoretical reasons of systematicity and completeness of practical reason, and not the normative demands of practical reason itself, that speak in favor of the principle of insufficient reason. The theoretical assumption is that practical reason must be complete in the sense there must be a rational choice for all possible alternatives; and that it is only by making *some* probability assumption that a utility function can be constructed for a person and a rational choice made. Even if there is no independent practical reason for assuming equal probability, it is the least arbitrary assumption (purportedly) to carry through the theoretical idea of the complete systematicity of practical reason, that there is a rational choice between any alternatives with no indeterminacy of choice.

On behalf of Rawls, one can say: Surely it is not *practically* rational to assume equal chances of ending up in any position *simply* for theoretical reasons of preserving system, when you are deciding in complete ignorance of the facts what kind of society to live in, all your future prospects are at stake, and there is no second chance to recoup losses in the event the worst transpires. It is then entirely questionable whether equal likelihood is indeed "the least arbitrary assumption." If a probability assumption *must* be made, why not assume a high probability of ending up in the worst-off position when the consequences are as grave as in the original position? (Here it is noteworthy that Rawls himself, 20 years later when working on political liberalism, constructs an argument indicating how a utilitarian who seeks to maximize average utility might rationally follow the maximin rule in the original position and choose the two principles of justice (JF, 108–09)). Moreover, why should we accept to begin with the conception of the theoretical requirements of practical reason that underlies utilitarian arguments relying on the equiprobability assumption: the idea that there is a completely rational morality and a rational choice for all possible decisions, moral or otherwise, with no indeterminacy of choice; and that rational choice can only be made by assuming the principle of insufficient reason under conditions of complete uncertainty? This is a highly complicated issue that depends upon competing views of practical reason. Further discussion of these issues would take us too far afield.[28]

This roughly represents, I believe, the reasoning behind Rawls's argument against adopting the principle of insufficient reason in the original position.[29] But by itself the rejection of the equiprobability assumption under conditions of complete uncertainty does not speak in favor of adopting the maximin strategy. Two further conditions are needed to make maximin a rational choice rule. These conditions are (2) that the choice singled out by observing the maximin rule is an acceptable alternative we can live with. There's little point in choosing conservatively if it results in an unacceptable worst outcome that is only marginally better than some other possible worst outcome. When this condition is satisfied, then no matter what position one eventually ends up in, it is at least acceptable since one's most important aims are secured. The third condition for applying the maximin criterion of choice is (3) that all the other alternatives have (worse) outcomes that we could not accept and live with. This means that if there is some other alternative with a worst outcome that you could live with and accept, then maximin is not an appropriate or rational strategy.[30]

Rawls contends all three conditions for the maximin strategy are satisfied in the original position when choice is made between the principles of justice and the principle of utility (average and aggregate). Because all one's values, commitments, and future prospects are at stake in the original position, and there is no hope of renegotiating the outcome, a rational person would agree to the principles of justice instead of the principle of utility (average or aggregate). For the principles of justice imply that no matter what position you occupy in society, you will have the rights and resources needed to maintain your valued commitments, to enable you to exercise your rational capacities to pursue a wide range of conceptions of the good, and to exercise and develop the moral powers. With the principle of utility there is no such guarantee; everything is up for grabs and subject to loss if required by the greater sum of utilities. Conditions (2) and (3) for applying maximin are then satisfied in the comparison of justice as fairness with the principle of (average or aggregate) utility.

It is often claimed that Rawls's parties are "risk-averse." Rawls denies that the parties have a psychological aversion to risk or uncertainty (JF, 88, 106–07). He argues, however, that it is rational to choose *as if* one were risk-averse under the exceptional circumstances of choice in the original position. This is not as confusing as it seems. The point is simply that, while there is nothing rational about a fixed disposition to risk-aversion, it is nonetheless rational in some circumstances to choose conservatively and protect certain interests one has against loss or compromise. It is not being risk-averse, but rational, to purchase, when given the opportunity, auto liability, health, home, and life insurance against accident or calamity. The original position is such a situation writ large. One who relies on the principle of insufficient reason in the original position is foolishly reckless given the gravity of choice at stake. It is not being risk-averse, but rather entirely rational, to be unwilling to gamble, in the face of no information whatsoever about probabilities, with the liberties, opportunities, and resources needed to pursue one's most cherished ends and commitments, all for the sake of gaining the marginally greater income and wealth that may be available in a society governed by the principle of utility.[31]

Rawls exhibits the force of the maximin argument in his discussion of liberty of conscience. He says (TJ, sect. 33) that a person who is willing to jeopardize the right to hold and practice his conscientious religious, philosophical, and moral convictions, all for the sake of gaining uncertain added benefits via the principle of utility, does not know what it means to have conscientious beliefs, or at least does not take such beliefs seriously.[32] A rational person with convictions about what gives life meaning is not willing to negotiate with and gamble away the right to those convictions. After all, what could be the basis for negotiation, for what could matter more? Of course, some people (perhaps genuine hedonists or nihilists) may not have any conscientious convictions, and are simply willing to act to maximize satisfaction of whatever desires they happen to have at the moment. But behind the veil of ignorance no one knows he or she is such a person, and there are no grounds for making this assumption. The parties must take into the account that they might have convictions and values they are unwilling to compromise. (Besides, even hedonists find meaning in unadulterated pleasure-seeking or dissolute living. What if they were to choose the principle of utility and end up in a puritanical society?) Thus it remains irrational to jeopardize basic liberties by choosing the principle of utility instead of the principles of justice.

To close out this discussion of the maximin argument, consider a different objection frequently made in defense of utilitarianism. It is argued that parties in the original position should understand, without knowing any specific facts, that in a utilitarian society the great majority of people will be fairly well-off, with only a small portion in unacceptable circumstances. For if too many people were dissatisfied overall utility would not be maximized. Moreover, it is entirely likely that the great majority of people in a society that follows the difference principle will be only marginally better off than the worst-off, and that everyone will be moderately poor. Knowing these facts, the parties to the original position would be foolish to choose justice as fairness.[33]

Let's stipulate that the parties know that the best-off in a utilitarian society are much more likely to be richer than the best-off under justice as fairness – after all, utilitarianism allows for greater inequalities in wealth than justice as fairness. It can even be stipulated that if the parties choose the principle of utility, they are more likely to end up economically better off than worse off. (This is more doubtful, however, since history shows that, with the help of religion, the poor learn readily to accept and be content with their subservient state.) The problem with the objection is that, first, choosing the principle of utility does nothing to allay the parties' fundamental concern that their basic liberties (to practice their religion, or vote, or freely associate with others) be protected from trade-offs in the name of greater economic prosperity for society as a whole. Second, given how economic systems work, it is most unlikely – indeed practicably impossible – that the difference principle will result in an economy where the worst-off do best when everyone else is only marginally better off than they are and *everyone* is poor. To hold otherwise seems to make the (false) conservative assumption that serious efforts to do the best to extract the poorest from their poverty are likely to end up impoverishing everyone else, and that poverty is an inescapable fact of human existence. But choice of the difference principle rests on an assumption that poverty is not endemic to societies, that we can raise the position of the worst-off without sacrificing general prosperity, and indeed that general prosperity, economic efficiency, and taking advantage of organization and technology are conditions of raising the income and wealth of the worst-off (see TJ, 150/130 rev.).

The Strains of Commitment

Critics' focus upon Rawls's maximin argument have obscured three other arguments Rawls makes to support justice as fairness (all in TJ, sect. 29). Each of these depends on the concept of a "well-ordered society"; two of them also rely on the idea of stability. The first of Rawls's three arguments highlights the idea that choice in the original position is an *agreement*, and involves certain "*strains of commitment*."[34]

It is often objected that there is no genuine agreement in the original position, for the thick veil of ignorance deprives the parties of all bases for bargaining (see TJ, 139–40/120–21 rev.). But in the absence of bargaining, it is said, there can be no contract. For contracts must involve bargaining and *quid pro quo* – something given for something received (called "consideration" in the common law). How can one bargain without knowing what he or she has to offer or to gain in exchange? So (the objection concludes) Rawls's original position does not involve a real contract, but rather, since the parties are all "described in the same way," it is really the rational choice of one person. It is a mistake then for Rawls to contend that his argument involves a social contract.[35]

To respond to this objection: First, at common law an exchange of promises or commitments is considered *quid pro quo* and sufficient "consideration" to make a valid contract. The parties exchange promises in the original position since they mutually commit themselves to be bound by the terms of their agreement, to the degree that they will not permit its renegotiation should circumstances turn out to be different than some hoped for. "Still, there's no basis for bargaining," the objection says. But not all contracts or agreements must involve anything resembling economic bargaining between parties with conflicting interests: marriage contracts, for example, or agreements by members of a church, union or other association to shared goals and pursuits. Compacts among members of a group who share the same basic purposes are not like economic bargains – the Mayflower Compact, for example, was a mutual understanding and shared commitment to pursue common aims. By their compact, parties made clear to themselves and others what they were about to do, and tied themselves into the pursuit of their shared ambitions. It is by a similar shared understanding and mutual precommitment that the parties to Rawls's original position enter into a social compact. By their agreement, they set up the conditions for social and political institutions and commit themselves to general terms of cooperation in perpetuity. Each agrees only on condition others do too, and all tie themselves into social and political relations permanently, to achieve certain common purposes as well as their individual interests.

This is typical of the social-contract tradition. For each of Rawls's major historical predecessors, the social contract did not resemble an economic bargain, but was a kind of mutual precommitment designed to achieve common purposes as well as each individual's interests. For Hobbes the social contract is a mutual authorization compact where each person agrees to authorize a sovereign to exercise nearly absolute powers needed to enforce the rules of justice Hobbes calls "the Laws of Nature." In Locke the social contract is an agreement to form and join a legal body, the "body politic" or "the People," which is given the responsibility to create a political constitution and a government that exercises political power in trust for the People's benefit. Rousseau's social contract is an agreement from the point of view of free and equal citizens where each deliberates on the common good and tries to express the "general will" of free and equal citizens. This suggests that the "no-contract" objection directed against Rawls is based on a misunderstanding of social contract doctrine.

To understand the original position as a mutual precommitment indicates why it can rightly be said to involve a contract or agreement. By mutual accord and on condition that others do too, all the parties commit themselves in advance to principles of justice in perpetuity. Their precommitment to justice is reflected by the fact that once these principles become embodied in institutions there are no legal means that permit anyone to depart from the terms of their commitment. As a result, the parties have to take seriously the legal obligations and social sanctions they will incur as a result of their agreement, for there is no going back to the initial situation. So if they do not sincerely believe that they can accept the requirements of a conception of justice and conform their actions and life plans to it, then these are strong reasons to avoid choosing those principles. It would not be rational for a party to take risks, falsely assuming that if he ends up badly, he can violate at will the terms of agreement and later regain his initial situation.

Rawls gives special poignancy to this commitment by making it a condition that the parties cannot choose and agree to principles in bad faith; they have to be able, not just to live with, but also to endorse the principles of justice once in society. Essential to Rawls's argument for stability is the assumption of willing compliance with requirements of justice. This is what he means by "the strains of commitment." The parties are choosing principles for a well-ordered society, where everyone is assumed to have a sense of justice: they accept the principles of justice, and want to act as these principles demand. Given this restriction, the parties can only choose principles they believe they will be able to accept and comply with, come what may. A party then cannot take risks with principles he knows he will have difficulty voluntarily complying with. He would be making an agreement in bad faith, and this is ruled out by the conditions of the original position.

Rawls contends that these "strains of commitment" created by the parties' agreement strongly favor the principles of justice over the principles of utility and other teleological views. For everyone's freedom and basic needs are met by the principles of justice because of their egalitarian nature. Given the lack of these guarantees by the principle of utility, it is much more difficult for those who end up worse off in a utilitarian society to willingly accept their situation and commit themselves to the utility principle. The person is rare who can freely and without resentment sacrifice his life prospects so that those who are better off than he can have even greater comforts, honors, and enjoyments. This is too much to demand of our capacities for human benevolence. It requires a kind of commitment that people cannot make in good faith, for who can willingly support laws that are detrimental to oneself and the people one cares about most? Besides, why should we encourage such subservient dispositions and the accompanying lack of self-respect? The principles of justice, by contrast, conform better with everyone's interests, their desire for self-respect and their natural moral capabilities to reciprocally recognize and respect others' legitimate interests while freely promoting their own good. The strains of commitment incurred by agreement in the original position provide strong reasons for the parties to choose the principles of justice and reject the risks involved in choosing the principles of average or aggregate utility.

Stability, publicity, and self-respect

Rawls's strains of commitment argument explicitly relies upon a rarely noted feature of his argument: it involves in effect two social contracts. First, hypothetical agents situated equally in the original position unanimously agree to principles of justice. This agreement has attracted the most attention from Rawls's critics. But hypothetical agreement in the original position is patterned on the general acceptability of a conception of justice by free and equal persons with a sense of justice in a well-ordered society. "The reason for invoking the concept of a contract in the original position lies in its correspondence with the features of a well-ordered society [which] require . . . that everyone accepts, and knows that the others accept, the same principles of justice."[36] In order for the hypothetical parties in the original position to agree on principles of justice, there must be a high likelihood that real persons, given human nature and general facts about societies, can also agree and act on the same principles, and that a society structured by these principles is feasible and can endure. This is the *stability* requirement. Rawls's argument for the stability of justice as fairness has attracted little commentary. But it is crucial to understanding Rawls's argument.

Rawls expresses this second contractarian requirement via the condition that principles of justice are to be agreed to among the parties in the original position only if they could be generally accepted within and remain stable under conditions of a "well-ordered society" arranged according to those same principles. A *well-ordered society* is a central idea in Rawls's theory. He says, "The comparative study of well-ordered societies is, I believe, the central theoretical endeavor of moral theory."[37] The idea of a well-ordered society provides a way for testing whether moral conceptions of justice are both consistent with psychological and social theory, and with a reasonable conception of the human good. If a conception of justice is neither feasible, given human nature and the possibilities of social cooperation, nor compatible with the human good, then that is a compelling reason for the parties rejecting that conception in the original position.

Rawls describes a *well-ordered society* as one whose main features are: (1) everyone accepts the same public conception of justice, and their general acceptance is public knowledge; (2) society's laws and institutions conform to this conception; and (3) everyone has an effective sense of justice, leading them to want to comply with the conception of justice. These formal features of a well-ordered society specify a kind of ideal social world.³⁸ For it is desirable that people know and freely accept the principles of justice that regulate basic social institutions and shape their characters and interests.

The *stability* requirement says that the parties in the original position are to choose principles that will be feasible and enduring within a well-ordered society. It bears emphasizing that Rawls is not concerned with stability in the sense of peace and tranquillity for its own sake. The stability of a grossly unjust or oppressive society is worth little if its destabilization will result in a substantially more just society without great loss of life. Rawls's requirement refers to the stability of a presumptively just (or "well-ordered") society. Moreover, stability depends upon society's members having certain moral motives; it is not the result of a *modus vivendi* among self-interested people with no regard for justice. A conception of justice then is *stable* for Rawls when "those taking part in [just] arrangements acquire the corresponding sense of justice and desire to do their part in maintaining them" (*TJ*, 454/398 rev.). Later in *Political Liberalism* Rawls uses the term "stable for the right reasons" to distinguish stability based in people's sense of justice from stability as a *modus vivendi* as found in Hobbesian contract doctrines (*PL*, 392; *CP*, 589). One conception of justice is relatively more stable than another, the more willing that people are to observe its requirements under conditions of a well-ordered society. The stability question raised in *Theory* is: Which conception of justice is more likely to engage our moral sensibilities and our sense of justice as well as affirm our good? This requires an inquiry into moral psychology and the human good.

Though Rawls does not discuss stability at length until Part III of *Theory*, he initially appeals to the idea in the remaining arguments from the original position (in Part I, sect. 29) to argue against utilitarianism and perfectionism. These are the arguments (1) from publicity and stability, and (2) from self-respect and stability. (1) Rawls contends that utilitarianism, perfectionism, and other "teleological" conceptions are not likely to be freely acceptable to many citizens when made *public* under the conditions of a well-ordered society.[39] Recall the publicity condition discussed earlier: A feature of a well-ordered society is that its regulative principles of justice are publicly known and appealed to as a basis for deciding laws and justifying basic institutions. A conception of justice that cannot satisfy this condition is to be rejected by the parties. Rawls contends that under the publicity condition justice as fairness remains more stable than utilitarianism.[40] For public knowledge that reasons of maximum average (or aggregate) utility are to determine the distribution of benefits and burdens understandably would lead those worse-off to object to and resent their situation. After all, their well-being and interests are being sacrificed for the greater good of those who are more fortunate and have more; it is too much to expect of human nature that people should freely acquiesce in and embrace such terms of cooperation.[41] By contrast, the principles of justice are designed to advance reciprocally everyone's position; those who are better off do not achieve their gains at the expense of the less advantaged. "Since everyone's good is affirmed, all acquire inclinations to uphold the scheme" (TJ, 177/155 rev.). It is a feature of our moral psychology that we normally come to form attachments to people and institutions that are concerned with our good; moreover, we tend to resent those persons and institutions that act contrary to our good. As Rawls argues at length in chapter VIII of *Theory*, justice as fairness accords with the reciprocity principles of moral psychology that are characteristic of human beings' moral development.

(2) The publicity condition is also crucial to Rawls's final argument for the principles of justice in §29 of *Theory*, from self-respect (TJ, 178–82/155–59 rev.). These principles, when publicly known, give greater support to citizens' *sense of self-respect* than do utilitarian and perfectionist principles. Rawls says self-respect is "perhaps the most important primary good" (TJ, 440/386 rev.) since few things seem worth doing if a person has little sense of his or her own worth or no confidence in his or her abilities to execute a worthwhile life plan. The parties in the original position will then aim to choose principles that best secure their sense of self-respect. Now justice as fairness, by protecting

the priority of equal basic liberties and fair opportunities, secures the status of each as *free and equal citizens*: because of equal political liberties, there are no "passive citizens" who must depend on others to protect politically their interests; and with fair opportunities there is no danger that desirable social positions will be closed to them or those with whom they identify. Moreover, the second principle secures adequate powers and resources for all to make everyone's equal basic liberties worthwhile. It has the effect of making citizens socially and economically independent, so that no one need be subservient to the will of another. Citizens then can regard and respect one another as equals, and not as masters or subordinates. Equal basic liberties, fair equal opportunities, and political and economic independence are primary among the bases of self-respect in a democratic society. For in the absence of a generally accepted religion or other shared system of comprehensive values, people confront one another mainly as citizens. The parties in the original position should then choose the principles of justice over utilitarianism and other teleological views both to secure their sense of self-respect, and to procure the same for others, thereby guaranteeing greater overall stability.[42]

Rawls substantially relies on the publicity condition to argue against utilitarianism and perfectionism. He says publicity "arises naturally from a contractarian standpoint" (TJ, 133/115 rev.). In *Theory* he puts great weight on publicity ultimately because he thinks that giving people knowledge of the moral bases of coercive laws is a condition of fully acknowledging and respecting them as responsible moral and rational agents. With publicity of first principles, people have knowledge of the real reasons for their social and political relations and the formative influences of the basic structure on their characters, plans, and prospects.[43] In a well-ordered society with a public conception of justice, there is no need for an "esoteric morality" that must be (as Sidgwick says of utilitarianism) confined "to an enlightened few." Moreover, public principles of justice can serve agents in their practical reasoning and provide democratic citizens a common basis for political argument and justification. These considerations underlie Rawls's later contention that having knowledge of the principles that determine the bases of social relations is a precondition of individuals' freedom.[44] Rawls means not simply the absence of external constraints ("negative" freedom), but the exercise of the powers and abilities that enable individuals to take full responsibility for their lives. Full publicity is a condition of the moral and rational autonomy of persons, which are significant values or intrinsic goods made possible by justice as fairness. (More on autonomy in Chapter 6.)

The Argument for the Difference Principle

The maximin rule of choice criterion requires the parties in the original position to focus on the worst-off position, and similarly the difference principle says that society is to strive to make the worst-off as well off as is feasible. One might think then that the maximin choice rule leads directly to the choice of the difference principle. Rawls in *Theory* encourages this impression in discussing the difference principle at length in section 26, immediately after the maximin argument for justice as fairness over average utility (see TJ, 156–61/135–39 rev.). Rawls even called the difference principle "the maximin criterion of distributive equity" at one point.[45] But ultimately, the maximin rule of choice cannot be used to justify the difference principle (JF, 43n.). For when justice as fairness is compared with "mixed conceptions" of economic justice that provide for basic liberties and a social minimum, the conditions for applying maximin are not fully satisfied. The third condition says that there can be but *one* acceptable alternative for choice. If there is a second alternative whose least advantaged position is one that rational persons can accept and live with, then the maximin rule is not a rational rule of decision. For in that case, grave risks to one's future prospects are no longer involved.

A mixed conception combines the principle of equal basic liberties together with a principle of distributive justice other than Rawls's second principle. (See TJ 124/107 rev. and sect. 49.) For example, instead of deciding the social minimum by the differ-ence principle, one mixed conception allows it to be democratically determined according to citizens' moral intuitions of an adequate standard of living; above and beyond this social minimum, society applies the principle of average utility to decide the distribution of income and wealth. Rawls calls this the "principle of restricted utility," since the pursuit of social utility is restricted by the basic liberties, fair opportunities, and a fixed social minimum. This is one of several possible "mixed conceptions" that combine the first principle of justice with a principle of distributive justice other than the difference principle (*TJ*, 124/107 rev.). Another example of a mixed conception, which might be called "restricted perfectionism," joins a perfectionist principle with a social minimum, basic liberties, and equal opportunities. From the point of view of the original position, these and other mixed conceptions providing a social minimum are, unlike unrestricted utility or perfectionism, not unacceptable. For no matter what one's social position is in a society governed by these mixed conceptions, basic needs along with basic rights and liberties are guaranteed.

Rawls concedes that "mixed conceptions are much more difficult to argue against than the principle of utility," since "the strong arguments from liberty cannot be used as before" (*TJ*, 316/278 rev.). He discusses mixed conceptions in *Theory*, section 49, and devotes more attention to them later in *Justice as Fairness: A Restatement* (sect. 36ff.). Rawls makes one main argument in favor of the difference principle and several specific arguments against the principle of restricted utility. The main argument in favor of the difference principle depends on the idea of *reciprocity*: in a society structured by the difference principle, gains are not made at others' expense; by contrast, restricted utility, even if it provides a social minimum, still permits losses to the worst-off so that those better off may prosper. Such a situation, Rawls contends, would be unacceptable to free and equal persons in a well-ordered society.

Robert Nozick complains that Rawls begs the question when he says that, under the difference principle, gains to some are not made at others' expense. For compared to the *laissez-faire* capitalist distribution that results from Nozick's entitlement principle, the worse-off under the difference principle *do* gain at the expense of the well-to-do, who must be taxed to benefit them. This suggests that the question "Who gains at whose expense?" cannot be answered without assuming a baseline for comparison. Clearly if we use anything other than the status quo (which few think is wholly just) as a baseline for comparison, then on any standard other than Pareto efficiency, some must lose in order that others may prosper if distributive justice is to be done. This is true even of Nozick's libertarian entitlement principles, which if enacted would require massive transfers from the less advantaged to the more advantaged (by eliminating the social entitlements the less advantaged now receive). Why does the difference principle not then also violate Rawls's maxim of distributive injustice, namely that some are being required to suffer so that others may prosper? It does not since Rawls assumes neither the status quo nor a libertarian entitlement distribution, but a *baseline of equality* as the relevant position for comparisons to determine whether people are made better or worse off. Under the difference principle, departures from equality are justified only if everyone's prospects are improved. But this is not sufficient, since other standards can satisfy this condition too (including Pareto efficiency TJ, §12), and Rawls would still say that some (the least advantaged) are made to sacrifice so that others may prosper. To fully satisfy Rawls's criterion of distributive reciprocity, gains to those better off are justified only if and when they also benefit the least advantaged, and benefit them maximally.

Again, the best way to understand the idea of reciprocity Rawls incorporates into the difference principle is by referring to figure 6 in *Theory* (sect. 13) and figure 1 in *Justice as Fairness* (62). The difference principle requires that distribution of powers, prerogatives, and economic resources put the least advantaged on the highest point on the efficient production curve, D, the point that is closest to an equal distribution. At D and all prior points on the curve, improvements to the most advantaged are always accompanied by improvements to the least advantaged and vice versa. Hence with all increments to social output, no one gains at any point at the expense of the others.

Here it's important to distinguish the reciprocity of the difference principle from a principle of Pareto efficiency which also uses equality as a baseline. Assuming externalities are eliminated, Nozick's entitlement principles, though they need not, nonetheless could satisfy Pareto efficiency from a baseline of equality (presuming that under ideal conditions of perfect competition of exchange and gift no transfers are made unless someone benefits and no one is disadvantaged). But of course *laissez-faire* entitlement principles are compatible with enormous gains to the most advantaged while the least advantaged gain only minimally, if at all. This is "trickle-down," which is very different from the difference principle. For the difference principle requires that the rich may not gain unless it benefits the least advantaged, but not vice versa; moreover, it is to benefit the least advantaged maximally, or better than any other alternative arrangement. By contrast, trickle-down *laissez-faire* has the opposite tendency: in effect the poor cannot gain unless the rich greatly if not maximally benefit, and also gains to the rich need not benefit the poor at all. (Indeed, given current conditions of declining real wage levels, unemployment, and other real-world market phenomena, gains to those better off often disadvantage the poor, and thus do not even satisfy the Pareto criterion.) There are, then, several ways to satisfy some idea of reciprocity, and reciprocity under the difference principle is quite strict. Strict reciprocity under the difference principle requires that the degree to which everyone benefits is conditioned by maximal gains to the least advantaged: the requirement is not simply that incremental changes to laws and policies within existing economic systems (such as the U.S.) be designed to benefit them more than alternative laws and policies; also the economic system as a whole must be designed so that they fare better than the least advantaged would in any other economic system (consistent with basic liberties and fair equal opportunities). The reciprocity of *laissez-faire* trickle-down by contrast is lax; while all may benefit from the economic system (compared to no economic system), the rich maximally benefit, potentially up to the point at which the least advantaged are made only marginally better off than they would be with no economic system at all.

The kind of reciprocity provided by the principle of restricted utility is also more robust than libertarian entitlement principles, for it insures a social minimum. In Chapter 3 we saw that Rawls identifies restricted utility with the capitalist welfare state that prevails in most Western democracies. In the capitalist welfare state everyone is insured a social minimum, but beyond this point wealth and income are generated and distributed (in theory at least) so as to maximize overall wealth and, therewith, presumably, overall utility. Everyone benefits from this system in so far as all are better off than they would be presumably under perfect equality. But still, gains to those better off need not advance the position of the least advantaged, and indeed sometimes come at the expense of the least advantaged so long as these gains increase overall utility. The mixed conception of restricted utility that is implicit in the capitalist welfare state may be represented by the B = Bentham point in Figure 4.1, and in *Justice as Fairness*, 62.

What does the argument from reciprocity have to do with the original position? Rawls's argument from reciprocity for the difference principle and against restricted utility cannot be simply an appeal to our intuitions of fairness. For in the original position itself, considerations of fairness technically do not motivate the parties. They are moved to agree on the difference principle for rational considerations alone, in this case mainly due to concern

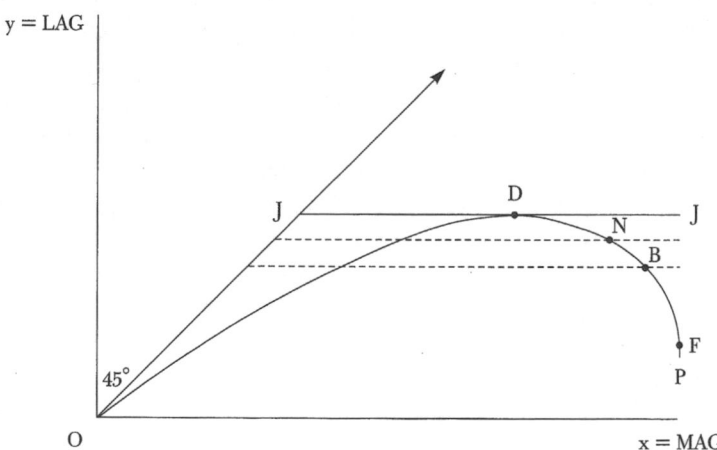

Figure 4.1
Source: Reprinted by permission of the publisher from *Justice as Fairness: A Restatement* by John Rawls, p.62, Cambridge Mass.: The Belknap Press of Harvard University Press, Copyright © by the President and Fellows of Harvard College.

for their own self-respect, for reasons of stability, and upon considering the strains of commitment. So why should the parties in the original position care about the strict reciprocity of the kind implicit in the difference principle? Compare the difference principle with the principle of restricted utility: Once the social minimum is met, there is nothing about the principle of restricted utility that insures that the worse-off will benefit in any regard from gains to those better off. Indeed, restricted utility allows for gains to those better off even if they disadvantage the least advantaged – for example, a falling wage rate or unemployment for unskilled workers in the face of increased supply of labor or decreased demand for labor often benefits owners and consumers but not the least-advantaged workers. It is true that under restricted utility the least advantaged may be better off than under conditions of equality – a weak sense of reciprocity is realized in this sense – but there is then no consistent tendency toward reciprocity, for once the social minimum is satisfied the less advantaged are as likely to gain nothing as to benefit from further gains to those better off. (Compare this situation with the extraordinary rises in national wealth and median income in the U.S. since the 1990s, at the same time that the rate of poverty has increased and the living standards of the least advantaged have declined.)

Rawls's conjecture (based on sound empirical evidence judging from contemporary circumstances) is that in the capitalist welfare state structured by restricted utility, the less advantaged are likely to become dispirited and frustrated with their situation, for they know that their well-being is ignored and often sacrificed so that the majority of citizens may prosper. While stability as a *modus vivendi* is maintained among the less advantaged (subject to periodic disruptions in the event of excessive unemployment perhaps), still the less advantaged are likely to withdraw from active participation in politics and public life; for they justifiably feel left behind by society and as if they no longer have a stake in improvements in social prosperity and in public life. This is an all-too-familiar phenomenon in modern capitalist welfare states such as our own, observable from the striking lack of political participation by the poorest members of society. It may be that

welfare-state capitalism is stable, but it is the stability of indifference or hopelessness among the less advantaged, not *stability for the
right reasons* grounded in equal citizens' affirmation of social institutions out of a sense of justice. Due to their lack of self-respect in
the capitalist welfare state, and the excessive demands it places on
their moral sensibilities, the least advantaged are unable to willingly affirm the organizing principle of society out of their sense
of justice. The principle of restricted utility then places excessive
strains of commitment on the worse-off, and undermines their
sense of self-respect and causes them to resent their situation.
Because of these problems, the parties in the original position
cannot in good faith rationally affirm restricted utility and the
capitalist welfare state when they have the alternative of the difference principle (see JF, 128–29). This reconstructs what seems to
be Rawls's main argument for the difference principle.

To bolster this argument Rawls discusses several other shortcomings of the principle of restricted utility (see JF, sect. 38).
Among these are: (1) the indeterminacy and uncertainty of the
principle of utility and the problems this occasions when it is
applied as a public conception of justice. In so far as there is no
agreed public measure to decide when or if utility is maximized,
this will occasion lasting and irresolvable public disputes and
therewith mistrust among income classes. Moreover, (2) with
restricted utility there is no clear way to decide the social
minimum itself and it too is left indeterminate. No standard for
judgment is provided, and hence the level of the social minimum
must be decided by the majority's diverse intuitions about what is
needed for the poor to lead a decent life; once again inevitable
disagreements about this can lead to dissatisfaction and mistrust.

Here the (restricted) utilitarian might reformulate earlier objections to Rawls's original position argument: "Even if it be
conceded that it is irrational for the parties to gamble with their
basic liberties and an assured social minimum, is it so clearly irrational for them to risk the unlikelihood of being among the least
advantaged in a capitalist welfare state regulated by restricted
utility? At least they have the basic rights to pursue their conscientious convictions and chosen conceptions of the good, as well as

sufficient all-purpose means to lead a decent (if not a thriving) life. So they are no longer risking their right to freely lead the life plan they choose. All they are really gambling by choosing restricted utility, it seems, is the amount of the social minimum."

To this Rawls might reply that, on the contrary, they gamble their self-respect as equal citizens and the full development of their moral sensibilities. Admittedly, it is difficult to make the argument that there is something clearly irrational about choice of restricted utility instead of the difference principle from the original position. For Rawls's argument for the difference principle to succeed, it would seem to have to depend on arguments from the strains of commitment, maintaining the bases of self-respect for all citizens, and stability "for the right reasons." And here, many philosophers (particularly utilitarians) will respond that these are inappropriate conditions to impose on the parties' choice in the original position: "Even if it be conceded that social stability is an important consideration for principles of justice to meet, why should it be so important that people be able to willingly affirm the principles of society 'for the right reasons,' that is, on the basis of their sense of justice? What is so bad about some people accepting their fate just as a *modus vivendi*? So what if they are sullen and resentful against those better off, so long as they are decently treated by society, generally observe the laws, and do not constantly seek to disrupt society? After all, mixed conceptions like restricted utility already go far beyond Rawls's own standards of decency that he later develops in *The Law of Peoples*."

Let's grant (for the sake of argument) that there is no clear decision in the original position between the difference principle and restricted utility when the parties take into account their interest in achieving their particular conceptions of the good. (Perhaps an argument from the parties' interest in their self-respect as equals can be developed here in favor of the difference principle, but leave that aside.) The response Rawls would then need to make to these sorts of objections redirects attention to the ideal of the person and of society underlying justice as fairness. Because of the parties' higher-order interests in development of their capacity for a sense of justice they are concerned with the strains of commitment and stability for the right reasons. A conception of justice that does not engage and affirm people's sense of justice undermines the ideal of the person and society that Rawls assumes that we (as reasonable and rational people) all share. Moreover, it stunts human nature in Rawls's view if a governing moral conception (like utilitarianism or even restricted utilitarianism) cannot be willingly affirmed by people, for justice then does not engage their moral sentiments. Only a conception of justice that achieves reciprocity in a strict sense fully satisfies these conditions. These are the kinds of considerations that must be developed to show that the difference principle would be preferred over mixed conceptions in the original position. Though perhaps not as explicit as they should be in Rawls, the ultimate force of the argument for the difference principle would seem to have to rely on the conception of free and equal moral persons and on the idea of a well-ordered society. This indicates once again the crucial role these ideals play in Rawls's argument for justice as fairness.[46]

Finally, regarding stability for the right reasons, the objection has been raised that, if the poor cannot fully affirm restricted utility, what's to say that the rich can wholeheartedly affirm the difference principle? A reasonable person might well think: "The least advantaged already benefit enormously from our savings, investments, and skills, and a social minimum, and that is fair enough. But why should they *maximally* benefit, gaining a greater social minimum than they would under any other distributive principle?" Why doesn't this objection raise the same "strains of commitment" problem with the difference principle as with any other principle, only this time focused on the doubtful commitments of the more advantaged?[47]

This is a serious objection; it reflects the way that most of the middle class, even liberals, now think. Two things can be said on Rawls's behalf in reply. First, as Figure 4.1 indicates, up to point D under the difference principle gains to the less advantaged always involve gains to the more advantaged too. This is not true of restricted utility, where the Bentham point B (or any point to the right of D) involves sacrifices by the less advantaged so the more advantaged may prosper. The situation is then *not symmetrical*. So the more advantaged cannot rightfully say that, when the economy is functioning well at point D, they are required to "sacrifice" anything so that those less advantaged may prosper. It is true, they could gain more if the economy were at B or any point to the right of D, but this does not mean they unfairly sacrifice anything at D. What is it that they are sacrificing at D, except gains that must come at the expense of the least advantaged? If they are unable to commit themselves to the difference principle, it can justly be said they are being unreasonable.

Second, unlike the adverse effects that restricted utility has on the self-respect of the least advantaged, the difference principle, though it may not obtain the wholehearted commitment of many more advantaged citizens, at least does not undermine their sense of self-respect and cause resentment for that reason. So instability due to loss of self-respect among the more advantaged will be absent in a well-ordered society that applies the difference principle; but instability due to loss of self-respect among the less advantaged will be a feature of a society that applies restricted utility. There are at least two reasons, then, why the objection is misguided. Otherwise, it is left to the reader to assess the force of this and other objections to the difference principle.

CONCLUSION

Justice as fairness interprets the democratic values of freedom and equality. Freedom is protected by the priority of the basic liberties, and equality is guaranteed by equality of basic liberties and fair equality of opportunity. The difference principle is also egalitarian in many respects, as suggested by the title "Democratic equality" Rawls assigns to it (*TJ*, sect. 13).[48] But there is a third democratic value that was lauded by Rousseau, and that was part of the catchphrase of the French Revolution − "*Liberté, Egalité, Fraternité*." "Fraternity" is not a value that receives much attention in democratic capitalist societies; it plays a more substantial role (like the cognate idea of "solidarity") in European social-democratic thought. There are several connotations of the idea of fraternity; it involves a sense of civic friendship and some degree of social solidarity, as well as equality of social respect and a lack of deference and civility. These attitudes are important, but by themselves do not impose any definite requirements of justice on institutions or citizens. One way to understand the difference principles is as an institutional expression of the value of fraternity; for it requires that no one gain at others' expense, that departures from equality of income and wealth as well as powers and positions of office must benefit everyone, and that citizens enjoy greater advantages only if they are to the benefit of others who are less well off. In these respects justice as fairness incorporates all of the fundamental democratic values (TJ, 105–6/90–91 rev.).

FURTHER READING

Hampton, Jean, "Contracts and Choices: Does Rawls Have a Social Contract Theory?," The Journal of Philosophy, 77, 6 (June 1980), 315–38. (Argues that Rawls's position is not contractarian but Kantian. See Freeman, Justice and the Social Contract, ch. 1, for a reply and defense of Rawls's contractarianism.)

Harsanyi, John, "Can the Maximin Principle Serve as the Basis for Morality? A Critique of John Rawls's Theory," American Political Science Review, 69, 1975, 694–706. (Argues that maximin is wrong choice rule and that principle of average utility would be chosen in original position.)

Nussbaum, Martha, Frontiers of Justice, Cambridge, MA: Harvard University Press, 2006. (Extensive critique of Rawls's contractarianism in favor of her capabilities approach to justice. See Freeman, Samuel, "Frontiers of Justice: Contractarianism vs. the Capabilities Approach," Texas Law Review, 85, no. 2, 2006, 385–430, for a reply and defense of Rawls.)

Scheffler, Samuel, "Rawls and Utilitarianism," in The Cambridge Companion to Rawls, ch. 12. (A very good account of Rawls's complicated positions regarding utilitarianism, including its influences on his views.)

Five

Just Institutions

Rawls envisions two roles for the principles of justice as fairness. First, the principles of justice embody abstract ideals that provide the basis for social unity in a well-ordered society. In a liberal society, where there is no shared religious or philosophical doctrine, a shared conception of justice is needed to unify people so that they are able to live together harmoniously in the same society. In later work Rawls emphasizes how the principles of justice foster social unity by serving as a kind of public charter for a well-ordered society, providing a "basis for public justification" among people with different values and religious, philosophical, and moral views. The public role of a conception of justice is explored in Chapter 9 when public reason is discussed.

A second role for principles of justice is to enable the assessment of the justice of policies and to give practical guidance in formulating laws. What laws and political and social institutions are needed to realize Rawls's principles of justice? What is the conception of democracy implicit in his view? What kinds of economic policies and institutions do the principles of justice support? And what bearing do they have on the institution of the family? This chapter addresses these questions, to convey an idea of how Rawls thinks his principles apply to the basic structure of society. It discusses material in both Part II of Theory, on "Institutions," as well as Rawls's later views on democracy, the economy, and the family.

In the first section of this chapter the four-stage sequence is explained which is Rawls's ideal procedure for applying the principles of justice. The second and third sections discuss the institutions of a constitutional democracy, taking up the application of the first principle to specify constitutional rights and liberties, and discussing deliberative democracy and the justification of judicial review, respectively. The fourth section discusses the institutions of distributive justice, and compares property-owning democracy with welfare-state capitalism. In the final section the role of the family in perpetuating and maintaining a just society is discussed.

APPLYING THE PRINCIPLES OF JUSTICE: THE FOUR-STAGE SEQUENCE

The capacity of the principles of justice to order and resolve conflicting claims provides one of the main arguments Rawls uses to argue for justice as fairness over the pluralist conceptions he calls 'intuitionism.' By assigning priority to the basic liberties over the second principle p. 86, and the second principle over efficiency and the general welfare, Rawls tries to avoid many of the problems intuitionists face in deciding the relative importance of basic liberties compared with other values. Still, the problem remains for Rawls of providing some way to apply the first principle and decide how to resolve conflicts among the basic liberties themselves. The initial problem in *Theory* of finding a criterion to resolve people's disagreements about legitimate restrictions on, for example, such basic liberties as freedom of expression and freedom of the person is to be resolved by, first, deciding what is a "fully adequate scheme" of basic liberties, and then, second, the "significance" of basic liberties to the exercise and development of the moral powers in the two "fundamental cases" (discussed in Chapter 2). Though Rawls provides examples of how these problems are to be addressed, it is not a straightforward exercise (to say the least) to decide when one basic liberty is more "significant" than another to the exercise and development of one or the other moral power. There is also the problem of deciding what measures are needed to provide fair equality of opportunities. Again, Rawls would have us look to the ideal of free and equal citizens, but here he has even less to say about what this might involve. And there remains the question of how to construct the complete index of primary goods (including powers and positions of office as well as income and wealth), and whether Rawls's expedient of using income and wealth alone to determine who is least advantaged accurately reflects this index.

Rawls did not presume, even at his most optimistic, that problems of vagueness, ambiguity, and indeterminacy of these and other standards for applying the principles of justice could be completely resolved. He recognizes in *Theory* that there may be a degree of indeterminacy in each of the principles of justice and the institutions they require, and that in some cases a range of institutions, rather than a particular one, may satisfy the principles of justice. In this case a "political settlement" upon one permissible alternative within the range is to be reached by democratic decision and majority rule (TJ, 200–201, 362/176, 318 rev.). This might seem a weakness in Rawls's theory, but indeterminacy and vagueness cannot be avoided within any conception of justice. Utilitarianism is often held out as a model for systematizing alternatives and ordering conflicting claims. But in spite of the apparent attractions of its maximizing idiom, Rawls says that indeterminacy, vagueness, and ambiguity are built into the principle of utility, hidden within its elusive concept of aggregate utility. He argues that one reason for preferring the two principles is that they are less vague and indeterminate than are interpersonal comparisons required to reach estimates of aggregate utility (TJ, 320–21/281–82 rev.). In any case, Rawls held that sometimes the best that principles of justice can do is to help narrow the range of our disagreements, or at most help clarify in what regards we disagree: "This indeterminacy in the theory of justice is not a defect. Indeed it is what we should expect" (TJ, 201/176 rev.). Rawls thought that the ordering potential of any principles of justice and their capacity to resolve conflicting claims is more limited than philosophers might presume who are drawn to utilitarianism's presumed systematic ordering capabilities.

Still, Rawls seeks to provide a reasonable "decision procedure" (of sorts) for applying the principles of justice. The main way he does this is by extending the basic idea of the original position via a series of hypothetical deliberative procedures – rational agreements subject to reasonable constraints. This is "the four-stage sequence" (TJ, sect. 31). Like the initial choice in the original position, there are constraints upon the reasons that can be relied upon in applying the principles of justice to a constitution and to legislative and judicial decisions. The principles of justice apply directly to the basic structure of society. There are at least three kinds of judgments that need to be made before the principles of justice can be applied to influence or direct individuals' actions. First, a just constitution with procedures for making and applying laws must be put into place. Second, laws and social policies satisfying constitutional procedures must be justly legislated. Third, laws must be justly interpreted and executed, and applied to particular circumstances and individual actions, which are tasks for the judiciary, the executive, and for citizens themselves.

Needed, then, is a method to apply the principles of justice to decide what political constitutions are just, when laws are just according to a just constitution, and when laws apply and what actions are required or permitted by them. This is the role of the "four-stage sequence," which extends the hypothetical thought-experiment in the original position (the first stage) to three further stages of hypothetical deliberation and decision applying the principles of justice. These are the constitutional, legislative, and "last" stages of the four-stage sequence. Each stage represents an appropriate point of view from which different kinds of questions are to be decided.

Rawls's four-stage sequence is the framework for deliberating about and applying principles of justice. It is not a procedure that our political representatives have to use in order for our own constitution or laws to be just or legitimate. In an ideal world it might be a procedure that constitutional or legislative representatives reflect upon and even emulate; but in the world as we know it this is perhaps too much to ask of our representatives, who are often short on philosophical skills. A constitution or laws can be relatively just without anyone trying to emulate or even reflect on Rawls's hypothetical procedures. The four-stage sequence is a kind of hypothetical inquiry which you and I can reflect on now, individually or jointly, to judge and assess the justice of existing constitutions, laws, and judicial decisions.[1] It is a way of discovering the degree to which our existing constitution and laws are compatible with the principles of justice, and provides a basis for justification, argument, and criticism in a democratic society.

The Constitutional Stage

How, then, do we decide on a just constitution? It is a constitution that could be agreed to among rational representatives of free and equal persons, who are ignorant of particular facts about their circumstances, and whose judgment is now guided and constrained by the principles of justice. Since the principles of justice now apply directly to constrain the decision of the representatives, their choice of a constitution is no longer purely a rational choice based on instrumental reasoning about what measures best achieve the fundamental interests of those they represent. The reasonable constraints the principles of justice impose on constitutional choice allow for "lifting" of the veil of ignorance somewhat, in order to give representatives to a hypothetical constitutional convention relevant information about their social and historical circumstances, level of economic development, and political culture. This information is relevant since societies with different histories, cultures, resources, and levels of development might require different kinds of constitutions to enable them to best realize the requirements of justice.[2] The parties still do not have information about particular persons and they do not know their own or anyone else's personal characteristics or their conception of the good.

The constitutional stage for applying the principles of justice resembles somewhat John Locke's social contract criterion for a legitimate constitution. For Locke, a political constitution is legitimate only if it could have been contracted into from a position of equal right among hypothetical free persons (each of whom has joined together into a political society one with another by an initial social contract), without violating any of their natural duties (owed to God and mankind), without surrendering any of their inalienable natural rights, and without making themselves worse off than they would be in a state of nature.[3] Locke envisions, however, that free persons, equally situated in a state of nature, can agree to a number of different constitutions that do not violate any natural rights or duties. For this reason he relaxed the unanimity condition of the original social contract (which itself is an agreement to form and join the body politic), and held that the decision upon a just constitution is to be decided by a majority of hypothetical representatives.[4] This implies that a number of political constitutions of different forms will likely pass Locke's social contract test for a legitimate constitution. Democracy presumably would satisfy Locke's moral constraints on the range of just constitutions. But so too would a constitutional monarchy which denies the great majority of people any rights of political participation. It is in response to this problem that Rawls sees a need for a veil of ignorance, for Locke's social contract allows for inequalities of basic rights among people who are born free and equal. For Rawls, no constitution can be just unless it embodies some form of democratic rule and provides all its citizens with equal basic liberties including equal rights of political participation.

The Legislative Stage and Imperfect Procedural Justice

Rawls sometimes speaks as if, given its history and political culture, there is a uniquely appropriate democratic constitution for each society that would be agreed to by its constitutional representatives (TJ, 197, 198/173, 174 rev.). At other times Rawls seems to concede that sometimes the justice of alternative laws, and even the justice of alternative democratic constitutions, can be hard to decide and perhaps even indeterminate even from the objective perspective of the four-stage sequence. "It is not always clear which of several constitutions, or economic and social arrangements, would be chosen" (TJ, 201/176 rev.). But though the four-stage sequence sometimes may be unable to theoretically decide between two or more alternatives, this means simply that there are equally just alternative constitutions, not that there is no "fact of the matter" regarding justice.

Rawls says that there is a "division of labor" between the constitutional and legislative stages of the four-stage sequence that corresponds to the two parts of the basic structure regulated by the principles of justice. The primary purpose of constitutional deliberation is to put into place constitutional rights and procedures that specify and protect the equal basic liberties: "The first principle of equal liberty is the primary standard for the constitutional convention. Its main requirements are the fundamental liberties of the person . . . [and other "constitutional essentials."[5]] The second principle comes into play at the stage of the legislature" (TJ, 199/174–75 rev.). This means that the difference principle and fair equal opportunities are the primary focus for deliberation at the third, "legislative stage" of the four-stage sequence. Rawls envisions the second principle to function ideally as a guide for the deliberations by democratic legislators, regarding laws and social and economic policies that regulate opportunities and economic production and consumption. At the legislative stage, "the full range of economic and social facts are brought to bear" in deciding on laws that best satisfy the difference principle (TJ, 199/175 rev.). In order to apply the difference principle to a particular society, all kinds of factual information is needed regarding society's circumstances and resources. Legislative decisions on the justice of economic and legal measures affecting the distribution of income and wealth depend upon knowing these sorts of contingencies. Still, Rawls maintains, information about particular people's particular characteristics is not relevant to a decision on laws; there remains a "thin" veil of ignorance even at the legislative stage. Rawls's hypothetical legislators not only do not know their own personal characteristics, but also they should not know many of the particular characteristics of their constituents. For example, of what relevance is it that a suburban legislator have information regarding the wealth, race, and religious orientations of his well-to-do constituents, in deciding economic or social legislation (such as affirmative-action measures)? Since this sort of factual information regarding particular groups of people is morally irrelevant to deciding on just legislation, it is not available to the representatives of equal citizens in the legislative stage.

The division of labor between the constitutional and legislative stages implies that the difference principle is not to be made part of the constitution. Rawls gives several reasons for saying that the difference principle is not a constitutional essential.[6] Among these is that complicated questions of economic policy require a great deal of information, more than we often have, and because of the resulting disagreement, questions whether the difference principle is satisfied are better left up to the legislative branch, and not made a matter for constitutional resolution. In *A Theory of Justice* the main reason for this restriction appears to be Rawls's argument for judicial review of democratic legislation. He seems to assume that, if the difference principle is included in a (written) political constitution, then the courts will be in a position to review and reverse democratic decisions on economic policy, which Rawls wants to avoid.[7] For judicial review is a kind of limitation on equal political liberties, which can be justified, on Rawls's account, only for the sake of protecting a fully adequate scheme of basic liberties. The priority of liberty implies that a fully adequate scheme of the basic liberties cannot be limited for the sake of the difference principle or fair equality of opportunity. Therefore, according to *Theory*, it would be a violation of the priority of the basic liberties to allow courts the powers to second-guess and reverse legislative decisions regarding economic policies and questions of distributive justice.

But what if a democratically elected legislature decides not to provide for the basic needs of the least advantaged at all? Or what if it decides not to provide for fair equal opportunities? These would seem to be gross violations of the second principle of justice, but Rawls in *Theory* seems to have no explicit institutional means to correct them. In his later works Rawls distinguishes the requirements of the difference principle, which is not a constitutional essential, from a basic minimum of income and wealth adequate to the effective exercise of the basic liberties. A basic *social minimum* is, Rawls contends, a constitutional essential which cannot be infringed by democratically enacted legislation. This implies that democratic legislatures have a constitutional duty to provide an adequate social minimum, and that the adequacy of the social minimum is reviewable by courts under the power of judicial review (assuming egregious inadequacy, for example).

Return now to the question of indeterminacy of justice. Rawls says that when alternative democratic constitutions, or economic or social arrangements, would be chosen within the four-stage sequence, "justice is to that extent likewise indeterminate" (TJ, 201/176 rev.). "On many questions of social and economic policy we must fall back upon a notion of quasi-pure procedural justice: laws and policies are just provided they lie within the allowed range" (ibid.). It is peculiar that Rawls suggests that this indeterminacy applies to social and economic policy rather than to questions regarding basic liberties. In applying the first principle to decide disputes about constitutional rights and the greater significance of one liberty over another, there seems to be far more room for indeterminacy than in applying the difference principle. It may be, as Rawls says, that there is more agreement about the question whether a constitutional right or liberty has been violated than about whether the difference principle is satisfied (this is one of the reasons he gives for not making the difference principle a constitutional essential). But this is not a theoretical question of greater indeterminacy of the difference principle than the first principle. It is rather a pragmatic question about whether people in a constitutional democracy organized by justice as fairness are more likely to agree when the basic liberties are violated than when the difference principle is satisfied. Perhaps this is true, but of the two principles it still seems the criterion provided by the difference principle is theoretically more determinate than is the criterion of "significance of a basic liberty in the two fundamental cases" that Rawls provides for applying the first principle of justice.

The last stage of the four-stage sequence

Since the final stage involves the application of laws and policies to decide particular cases, it is tempting to call it "the judicial stage." But that would occlude the very important fact that the "last stage" (as Rawls calls it) also involves citizens and their decisions about what just laws require of them. At the last stage of the four-stage sequence the abstract principles of justice, mediated by a democratic constitution and laws, touch down and result in specific prescriptions and permissions regarding what individuals or institutions are to do in particular cases. It is the stage at which we finally learn the specific actions we are obligated to perform under the principles of justice and the constitutions and laws that satisfy them. According to "the principles of natural duty," each person has a duty to observe the constraints of justice and do what the principles of justice require, and once these constraints are satisfied, a further duty to promote and maintain just institutions. We also have duties of mutual respect and duties of mutual aid, among other positive duties (TJ, sects. 19, 51). (Unfortunately Rawls has little to say about what these natural duties require of us beyond the obvious.) Then there are duties of fairness which require us to keep our promises and commitments and to do our fair share in upholding just institutions, and which impose on government officials political obligations to uphold the responsibilities of their office under a just constitution (TJ, sects. 18, 52). The natural duties and principle of fairness are the "*principles for individuals*" that are needed to put into effect the two principles of justice, which are themselves the "*principles for institutions*" that apply to the basic structure of society.

In order to accurately decide what is our duty of justice according to just laws in particular circumstances, or in order for judges to decide how to apply just laws decided at the legislative stage, all relevant information about factual circumstances is needed. Accordingly, Rawls says, at the last stage of the four-stage sequence, the veil of ignorance is completely lifted, and "everyone has complete access to all the facts" (TJ, 199/175 rev.). This is the standard for the correct application of the principles of justice to particular circumstances: impartial hypothetical citizens, with full knowledge of relevant facts, and guided by their sense of justice and the fundamental interest of free and equal citizens, are to judge what requirements on action are imposed by laws that issue from just institutions conforming to the principles of justice. This is the standard that judges and citizens are to emulate in deciding what just laws require of them: they are to act in a manner that conforms to the way that a sincere and conscientious moral agent, guided by his or her sense of justice, and with full information, would act after deliberating upon the application of relevant laws to their particular circumstances. This formal characterization of *just actions* does not tell us much specifically, but it provides an idea of how Rawls conceives of our duties and obligations of justice as they apply to order our individual actions.

THE FIRST PRINCIPLE OF JUSTICE: SPECIFICATION OF CONSTITUTIONAL RIGHTS

Rawls says, "The first principle of equal liberty is the primary standard for the constitutional convention" (TJ 199/174 rev.). Hence:

> The liberties of equal citizenship must be incorporated into and protected by the constitution. These liberties include those of liberty of conscience and freedom of thought, liberty of the person, and equal political rights. The political system, which I assume to be some form of constitutional democracy, would not be a just procedure if it did not embody these liberties.
>
> (*TJ*, 197–98/173 rev.)

Rawls regards the constitutional stage primarily as an attempt to (1) create political institutions with the normal powers of governments (legislative, executive, judicial, and so on), each with their respective procedures; and then (2) "specify" the basic liberties in greater detail, in a bill of rights, which in turn acts not simply as a constraint on political procedures, but which, together with the conception of persons as free and equal, informs officials of the ideal that is to guide their actions. What is involved in the "specification" of the basic liberties at the constitutional stage? We have already seen in Chapter 2 how Rawls regards this stage as the standpoint from which to "specify," by reference to the conception of free and equal persons and their fundamental interests, the constitutional liberties needed for the full development and adequate exercise of the moral powers. The political liberties will be discussed in the next section. Here I briefly focus on the specification of basic liberties as constitutional rights.

By the "specification" of the basic liberties at the constitutional stage, Rawls means that the highly abstract basic liberties are to be more particularly defined in terms of constitutional liberties. For example, freedom of thought is further specified into such liberties as freedom of speech and expression, freedom of discussion and inquiry, the right to engage in scientific investigation, and literary and artistic endeavors of all kinds. The rights and liberties of the person are to be specified as freedom from involuntary servitude, freedom of movement, freedom from assaults and threats to one's person, freedom of occupation and choice of careers, the right to personal property, and the right to personal privacy. Then each of these constitutional liberties may be further specified at legislative and judicial stages. For example, the right of privacy implies freedom of procreation and the right to use birth control, freedom of choice in one's intimate relations including same-sex relations, and perhaps the right of abortion; a right to assisted suicide, and perhaps even a right to others' assistance in dying under conditions of terminal illness (cf., CP, 596 n.60/605 n.80).

Regarding freedom of speech and expression, Rawls does not regard all forms of speech and expression as on a par and deserving equal protection. As discussed in Chapter 2 above, some forms of expression are more "significant" than others, depending on the degree that they are needed for the adequate exercise of the moral powers. Rawls argues, in "The Basic Liberties and Their Priority" (PL, VIII), that political expression is to receive the utmost constitutional protection, given its essential bond with the development of the capacity for justice. Freedom of political expression may be limited only if a person's speech threatens an imminent breakdown of social order. By contrast, most "commercial speech," or advertising of products is not needed for the exercise and development of the moral powers. Rawls suggests that commercial speech is not protected by the first principle of justice but rather by the second principle when it is protected at all. Ads for employment and education positions are essential to fair equality of opportunity, and ads for consumer products, that provide product information needed for informed choice, are protected by the difference principle. But ads designed purely for market strategic reasons, to entice consumers to purchase products, should receive no constitutional protection, Rawls says, since they are "socially wasteful" (PL, 365). A democratic legislature, then, should be free to regulate such ads whenever needed to promote the ends of the principles of justice or the public good.

There is nothing unusual about Rawls's assignment of greater protection to political, scientific, literary, and artistic expression than to commercial speech. It is accepted in American constitutional law that political speech, even if very offensive, cannot be restricted in ways that commercial speech can. For example, U.S. federal courts have held that the neo-Nazi party cannot be denied a parade permit to stage a demonstration in a largely Jewish town with the largest concentration of Holocaust survivors.[8] But courts would also hold that municipalities can deny merchandisers of products the right to "demonstrate" their wares on the same public streets, or deny on purely aesthetic grounds the right to put up billboards. In many regards Rawls's account of freedom of speech and expression is built upon U.S. Supreme Court jurisprudence. Indeed, his position is more restrictive in some ways of free speech than the current Supreme Court's, which in the interest of business has relaxed the distinction between political and commercial speech, and thus prohibited many former state restrictions on advertising (by physicians and drug companies, for example) than Rawls would find warranted.

Two things are new and distinctive about Rawls's account. First, he seeks to provide a relatively definite standard for interpreting such constitutional rights as freedom of expression, to decide the occasions when the exercise of these rights can be regulated, or restricted, as the case may be. This is one of the more significant roles played by the conception of the person as free and equal citizen: the "significance" of a particular liberty is to be decided by its bearing on the full development and adequate exercise of the moral powers of citizens. Rawls regards a conception of persons and their fundamental interests as citizens as necessary to constitutional law and interpretation of constitutional liberties. He thinks the conception of free and equal moral persons is implicit in the public culture of a democratic society, and is part of the self-conception of its citizens. The second major contribution that Rawls's account makes to constitutional interpretation is his idea of public reason. Public reasons basically are considerations and values that we can reasonably accept in our capacity as democratic citizens and which answer to our interests as citizens. Only "public reasons" can be relied upon to interpret the nature, scope, and extent of "constitutional essentials." This rules out appeal to religious, philosophical, and moral considerations that cannot be appropriately related to the needs and interests of the ideal of free and equal democratic citizens. The implications of this restriction will be discussed in connection with the abortion controversy in Chapter 9.

CONSTITUTIONAL DEMOCRACY AND ITS PROCEDURAL REQUIREMENTS

There are different ways to conceive of a democracy. One popular way is to regard democracy simply as a *form of government*, where laws are decided by majority rule by representatives who are elected by citizens with equal rights to vote, hold office, and express their political views. We might also regard democracy not simply as a form of government but as a kind of *political constitution*, wherein a legal body known as "the People" is deemed sovereign and has ultimate political authority. The People, or their constitutional representatives, make and amend the constitution and thereby set up (democratic) government as agent for the People with the responsibility to make and enforce laws that promote the common good of citizens. (Rousseau says the good of "the whole and all of its parts.") This is the conception of political democracy developed within the social-contract tradition most prominently by Rousseau, and which Rawls seeks to revive and bring to fruition in *A Theory of Justice*. A third way to think about democracy is socially rather than (or in addition to) politically: a democratic society is one in which inherited privilege is rejected and people are widely regarded as equals and as free; they are judged, not according to their lineage, but according to their accomplishments (or lack thereof); moreover, people are allowed equal opportunities and are treated as civilly free (in some sense). This is the social sense of democracy that de Tocqueville discusses in *Democracy in America*.[9]

Rawls intends to provide an ideal of a just society that incorporates all three senses of democracy. We've seen how he sets forth as one of his primary aims to provide a conception of justice that "constitutes the most appropriate moral basis for a democratic society" (TJ, viii/xviii rev.). In a democratic society people regard themselves as free and equal. Starting from citizens' self-conception and an ideal of social cooperation (a well-ordered society) he works out a conception of justice that mandates a democratic constitution and government, and an egalitarian account of social and economic institutions. The form of the democratic constitution that he sets forth is that of a "constitutional democracy," which is different from a purely majoritarian democracy. In the latter, there are no constitutional restrictions upon the will of a majority, and no judicial review of legislation. A constitutional democracy, by contrast, requires a democratic government with restricted majority rule; legislative majorities are enjoined from laws that infringe constitutional essentials and basic justice. Finally, Rawls's account of a democratic society suggests a social and economic system where productive assets are widely dispersed and controlled, economic entrepreneurship is largely free except when needed to maintain all citizens' economic power, and citizens are rendered economically independent, not subservient to any person for their economic well-being. In the remainder of this section I focus on Rawls's account of a constitutional democracy and the limits on democratic government that it implies; then in the next section I discuss the economic institutions of a property-owning democracy.

Suppose that a democratic constitution provides or implies that the body of citizens is sovereign, that this body delegates its sovereignty occasionally to representatives elected by citizens, and that this delegation is complete, at least during the time that these representatives are assembled into a parliament or similar deliberative assembly. Exercising sovereignty when in session, this parliament has complete authorization to make laws and is subject to no constitutional or other legal limits (except perhaps those it imposes on itself). Since unanimity is almost never to be had, decisions are made according to a majority rule. Finally, it is assumed that representatives conscientiously strive to determine what is for the good of their constituents, whether this be satisfying the desires of as many as is feasible, or acting for their rational interests and needs. Such a constitution is strictly *majoritarian* since it embodies at both the constitutional and governmental levels the principle that a (bare) majority always rules (whether of citizens or representatives).

One traditional argument for a majoritarian constitution is utilitarian. Bentham accepted majoritarian democracy on utilitarian grounds. He believed that the most reliable way to promote overall happiness in society is to set up a government where representatives are given incentives to satisfy the desires and interests of the greatest majority of their constituents. Since all persons are purely self-interested in Bentham's view, the problem is to find a way to motivate self-seeking legislators to promote the happiness of the greatest number of people. A desire to be re-elected, presumably, normally should induce democratically elected legislators to seek to satisfy the interests of a majority (at least a bare majority, if not the greatest number). A rational legislator, by the "artificial identification of interests," would therefore ascertain and sympathetically identify with the wishes and desires of his or her constituents, and then vote for measures that best advantage a majority of them. Voting according to majority rule does not always guarantee that greater overall happiness in the aggregate will be realized; for the one person/one vote rule does not take into account the intensity and duration of people's satisfactions. So on occasions, when the desires of a passionate minority are outvoted by a largely indifferent majority, greater overall utility may not be realized. But all things considered, government by bare majority rule is as good a procedure as we are likely to find for ascertaining and maximizing aggregate social utility.

There are other ways to argue for majoritarianism, and one does not have to be a utilitarian by any means to endorse the view.[10] What is important for our purposes is that majoritarianism often is responsive to people's different and often conflicting individual interests and seeks to satisfy a majority of them. As such majoritarianism is a kind of welfarism; it regards morality and justice as the promotion of individual happiness.

Rawls regards majoritarian democracy as an inappropriate forum within which to realize the principles of justice. For, other than providing for equal rights of political participation, it lacks any institutional means for protecting and maintaining the basic rights and liberties of equal citizens. Under normal conditions of social life, Rawls assumes, purely majoritarian decisions will sometimes result in the limitation of certain basic liberties, and unfair discrimination against the basic rights and interests of minority groups. One reason for this is that there is no institutional recognition of basic rights and liberties other than equal political rights.

Among such institutional mechanisms for recognizing and maintaining basic liberties are a written constitution with a bill of rights, the separation of powers, bicameral legislatures, and judicial review (see TJ, sects. 36–37). A bill of rights provides a standing reminder for legislators of the reasons that should be of utmost priority in democratic legislation; when joined with judicial review a bill of rights directly limits the kinds of decisions that majorities can make. Other "checks and balances" on majoritarian legislative power operate to slow the pace of legislative change, and therewith encourage public discussion and serious legislative deliberation regarding all aspects of issues. Deliberation is important not just to insure that basic rights are not infringed, that all sides are heard, and that legislators take into account the effects of proposed legislation upon the fundamental interests of minorities. Public and legislative deliberation is also of fundamental importance to the discernment and achievement of the public interest and the common good of all citizens.

Majoritarian democracy's lack of institutional mechanisms for protecting basic liberties is an indirect result of its normal focus on promoting individual welfare. From a welfarist perspective there can be no restraints upon the satisfaction of individual desires or preferences (assuming they are rational in a thin sense) if the happiness of the greater number is to be achieved. For constitutional restraints on majority rule operate as an impediment to enacting the wishes of legislative majorities. They constrain what majorities can do in pursuit of their individual interests, and thereby put a check upon majorities' pursuits of individual happiness.

The primary aim of democratic legislation for Rawls is not to promote individuals' happiness, whatever it may be. It is rather to promote individuals' freedom and the common good for all citizens. Rawls says that it is a convention of democracy that laws are to promote the common good. "Government is assumed to aim at the common good, that is at maintaining conditions and achieving objectives that are similarly to everyone's advantage" (TJ, 233/205 rev.). There is a long tradition of thought (shared by utilitarians, contractarians, natural law theorists, among others) that says that certain institutions benefit everyone's rational interests. Hobbes says, "Peace is good, and so too are all the means of peace." Political institutions and a system of laws are among the means of peace. (Imagine what things would be like with no government or system of property or trials or punishment at all.) Since all (rational) persons desire peace, it follows for Hobbes that everyone, in some manner, benefits from political and legal institutions – in the minimal sense that all are better off with them than without.

Still, there is nothing particularly democratic about Hobbes's thin conception of the common good. Hobbes's sense of the common good does not even turn out to be always true, since many people persecuted by repressive governments would be better off, or at least no worse off, if there were no government at all. So Hobbes's claim should be that everyone benefits from non-repressive institutions. But there's still nothing particularly democratic about the common good in this sense either, since non-democratic governments (of the kind Locke argues for) could also achieve it.

Rousseau says that the common good is justice, and he specifies justice in terms of measures that promote the freedom and equality of citizens. Rawls follows Rousseau in this regard. Just social conditions and institutions (a just political constitution, legal procedures, economic norms, a just property system, and so on) benefit all reasonable and rational citizens.[11] Different conceptions have competing views about the common good of justice and about how institutions and laws can be designed to be just. Rawls's democratic conception of justice is built around an ideal of free and equal moral persons. This is an ideal of free and equal citizens cooperating on a basis of reciprocity and mutual respect. The primary role of just institutions is to provide the conditions for realizing this ideal of citizens as free, equal, and independent. Of course each citizen is concerned that his or her happiness not be undermined by legislation and that laws generally prove favorable to his or her pursuit of their good. But Rawls assigns to democratic citizens fundamental objective interests in maintaining the conditions for their freedom and equality, which in turn are elaborated in terms of realizing their higher-order interest in the development and exercise of the moral powers. Given their sense of justice, free and equal citizens normally want to pursue their personal aims in a way that is consistent with just institutions and the common good of justice.

If it is a convention of democracy to promote the common good, and if justice is the common good, then the primary purpose and role of a democratic government is to promote justice. Within the context of justice as fairness this means that the role of legislators in enacting laws is to reflect upon and ascertain the requirements of the principles of justice. In the ideal world of a well-ordered society of justice as fairness, democratic legislators deliberate on the measures that are most needed to achieve the principles of justice. They do not, then, seek in the first instance to promote individuals' particular interests. Nor do they exercise their powers by voting to satisfy a majority of individual interests to the exclusion of others, as dictated by a majoritarian conception of democracy. In so far as democratic legislators seek to promote the individual interests of democratic citizens, they do so indirectly by voting first to satisfy the demands of the common good of justice as fairness.

Rawls later, in *Political Liberalism*, fills out his conception of a constitutional democracy via the idea of public reason. The idea of public reason enables him to specify the kinds of reasons that are relevant for democratic officials to rely upon and vote for in reaching their decisions. It allows him to give content to the idea of a constitutional democracy as being also a *deliberative democracy*. Sometimes these two ideas are depicted as distinct and separate views about the nature of democracy.[12] But Rawls joins the two conceptions of democracy via the idea of public reason. This later elaboration of Rawls's account of constitutional democracy as deliberative is discussed in Chapter 9, along with the idea of public reason.

Finally, Rawls regards the institution of *judicial review* of the constitutionality of democratically enacted legislation as compatible with a constitutional democracy and a democratic society. This is true so long as judicial review is exercised to uphold the basic liberties of citizens and other essentials of a democratic constitution. It is often argued that judicial review is anti-democratic. This is of course trivially true if by "democracy" all that is meant is democracy as a form of government by majority rule; for it is the nature of judicial review in a democracy to overturn the will of legislative majorities. But we've seen that Rawls has a much more expansive idea of democracy as a special kind of constitution and society of equal citizens. Within a democratic society judicial review can play a vital role in upholding a democratic constitution against the anti-democratic decisions of a bare majority. Rawls regards the institution of judicial review as justifiable within a democratic society when it is needed to uphold the basic liberties and other constitutional essentials of a democratic constitution. This does not mean that judicial review is always needed. It is an empirical question whether it is appropriate within a particular constitution. In some democracies, such as the United Kingdom, it may not be needed, since there are cultural forces that satisfactorily maintain the basic liberties of citizens. But in other democracies, such as the United States, judicial review may be for historical reasons necessary to protect citizens' equal basic liberties. Because of ethnic and religious diversity and its federal system of fifty separate state legal systems, judicial review may be needed in the U.S. to coordinate state laws and above all prevent majorities from limiting the basic liberties of racial, religious, and other minorities. Our Supreme Court has often acted to uphold basic liberties against the racial, religious, and class-based biases of legislative majorities. Whether this is adequate to justify its power of judicial review and offset its history of promoting the interests of capital and the property-owning classes is a historical issue of great moment, but not one that can be settled here.

ECONOMIC INSTITUTIONS: A PROPERTY-OWNING DEMOCRACY

An interesting feature of Rawls's account of distributive justice is that it leaves open the question whether a private-property market system or some form of socialism is the more just social system. Here it is important to understand how Rawls uses these terms. The former suggests a market economy that allows for private ownership of means of production. So-called "*capitalism*" is but one kind of private property market system. Ironically, the term "capitalism" was invented by nineteenth-century socialists and put into general usage by Marx. Rawls uses the term "capitalism" much as Marx did. In capitalism, regarded as an abstract model which economic systems more or less approximate, real and liquid capital is largely owned and controlled by the class of capitalists, who are largely distinct from the class of workers, the vast majority of whom own little or no capital but rather labor for a market wage.[13] Rawls distinguishes two forms of capitalism. In the "System of Natural Liberty," often called *laissez-faire capitalism*, markets are unregulated while government maintains the background institutions (property, contract law, etc.) necessary for markets to function; but other than providing for public goods that are in each person's self-interest (highways, public-health measures, etc.), government makes no public transfers for the less advantaged and generally allows distributions to be determined by market transactions. *Welfare-state capitalism*, by contrast, is the prevailing form of capitalism in most Western economies; therein government evens out the contingencies of markets by making social provisions for unemployment, social security during retirement, and public assistance for the handicapped and those unable to support themselves. *Syndicalism*, by contrast, is a private property market system where unions of workers both labor on and own and control capital, or at least own the firms they work for. What Rawls calls a *property-owning democracy* might be regarded as somewhere in between syndicalism and welfare-state capitalism: it involves widespread ownership of capital and other means of production, whether by individual workers, unions, corporations, and so on, with perhaps varying degrees of worker participation and democratization of management. Presumably these might include anything from traditional owner-controlled firms to obligatory consultation with employees where owners make final decisions, co-determination by management and workers (as in Germany and other West European social democracies), and fully fledged workers' ownership and management.[14] A private property market economy implies nothing specific about how much of society's wealth is to be devoted to public goods or to social security and other forms of public assistance. A capitalist economy, such as welfare-state capitalism, might be quite lavish in providing public-funded benefits.

Rawls uses the term *"socialism"* to indicate, not distributive egalitarianism, but instead economic systems with primarily public ownership of the means of production (land, natural resources, and real capital). Use of the term also says nothing about how much of society's output is devoted to public goods or to transfer payments for social security, public assistance payments, and so on. In this regard, socialism has no particular implications about the distribution of income and wealth. A socialist system might spend lavishly on public goods and public assistance, and even seek to equalize income and wealth. Then again, a socialist system might be rather stingy in these regards, saving and reinvesting most of its social product for future generations. Importantly, when regarded simply as public ownership of the means of production, socialism is compatible with the use of market prices to allocate factors of production, so long as capital and the means of production remain publicly owned (see *TJ*, 271–74/239–42 rev.). This is called *liberal socialism*, or *market socialism*.[15] By contrast, *Marxian communism* is a form of socialism which rejects markets and instead relies upon a (presumedly) rational plan of production (ideally to be determined democratically) to allocate factors of production.[16]

To show how socialism can be compatible with markets, Rawls invokes John Stuart Mill's distinction between the *allocative function* and the *distributive function of market prices* (TJ, 273/241 rev.). Markets may be used to allocate factors of production regardless of who owns them (whether private individuals or the state). If a state owns the means of production, it can lease real capital to groups of entrepreneurs and workers at a market rate, or charge an interest rate for the use of liquid capital. This enables land, labor, and capital to be used in production in the industries where there is greatest demand, leading to their efficient allocation. The same is true when there is private ownership of all means of production and market prices are used to allocate them. The important point is that, in order to take advantage of market prices for allocative purposes in order to enable production to be efficient, there is no need to rely upon markets alone to distribute the income and wealth that is produced for consumption purposes. The exclusive use of market prices – of others' willingness and ability to pay – to distribute income and wealth is a position advocated by libertarians and other proponents of unrestrained capitalism as traditionally understood. But most accounts of distributive justice require the use of the tax system to determine distributions of income and wealth and what distributive shares people have rights to, or property interests in. Even classical liberals such as Adam Smith recognized the need for taxation to provide for public goods, and supported "Poor Laws" designed, however stingily, to alleviate economic destitution. Only if one believes that a person has complete rights to all the market gains – or the marginal product – that result from ownership of land, capital resources, and labor does it follow that distributive justice is completely satisfied by markets and other forms of consensual transfer. Rawls's difference principle implicitly denies that a person has complete rights to the marginal product of his or her productive resources. For Rawls, property rights as specified under a regime governed by the difference principle are not absolute nor among basic liberties, and so do not include complete rights to income and wealth generated by uses of property.

One way Rawls's position is liberal is that it regards market allocations of productive resources to be required by the principles of justice. Free markets in labor are needed to guarantee basic freedoms of occupation and choice of careers and other freedoms of the person (e.g., freedom of movement), as well as fair equality of opportunity. A fully planned economy (such as Marxist communism) jeopardizes these and other rights and liberties (TJ, 272/240–41 rev.). Rawls's thought here seems to be that since command economies determine production by a supposedly rational plan, they must to some degree also allocate labor according to the plan to meet production quotas; therefore some workers must be assigned their occupation and work position, which infringes individuals' freedom of occupation and choice of careers. (Here one might reply that even in a command economy the plan itself can allow for a degree of market allocation of positions, so that less desirable positions are paid at a higher rate.)

Rawls recognizes that markets allow for more efficient allocation of factors of production than do planned economies; therewith markets more effectively use resources and reduce economic waste. The efficient allocation of factors of production normally (though of course not always) benefits everyone, including the least advantaged, so markets in labor are normally required by the difference principle too. We might say, then, that for Rawls, allocative justice relies mainly on markets and considerations of economic efficiency. But significantly, distributive justice is not market-determined. The share of the economic product that workers and owners respectively have a right to is decided, not by considerations of economic efficiency – in order to maximize productive output for example. Rather it is to be decided mainly by the difference principle, by putting into place and actually carrying out the system of economic practices that maximally promote the share of income, wealth, and economic powers and positions of office going to the least advantaged. Rawls therefore accepts that economic gains to the more advantaged also benefit the less advantaged, up to a point. But this is not "trickle-down"; rather it is just the way that economic systems that rely on incentives have to work. "Trickle-down" relies primarily, if not exclusively, upon market distributions of income and wealth; and as the term suggests, it focuses on the most advantaged first, maximizing the return they receive, then allowing to "trickle down" to less advantaged classes the economic effects of whatever is not immediately consumed by those more advantaged. The difference principle implies exactly the opposite. Inequalities are allowed *only* if they benefit the less advantaged, and indeed benefit the least advantaged optimally. At some point, inequalities and further economic gains to the better-off begin to work to the detriment of the worse-off. It is just prior to that point – where any further gains work to the disadvantage of the worse-off – that the optimal distribution is reached under the difference principle.

This comparison suggests that libertarianism and traditional *laissez-faire* capitalism cannot satisfy the difference principle; for they prohibit public transfers of wealth to the less advantaged and do not guarantee a social minimum. Like everyone else, any gains to the least advantaged depend entirely upon others' willingness to make private transfers to them. "From each as he chooses, to each as he is chosen" is Robert Nozick's shibboleth for his libertarian entitlement system.[17] Nothing in this principle guarantees that a person will be chosen to benefit from transfers by other individuals. Still, advocates of *laissez-faire* capitalism often contend that the poorest unskilled laborer working at a minimal market wage is better off than are most people in non-capitalist economies (other than the elites perhaps).[18] If we compare nineteenth-century *laissez-faire* capitalism with command economies such as the Soviet Union or Cuba, then this claim is probably false, since the least advantaged under Soviet and Cuban communism had life's basic necessities taken care of in a way that stock Dickensian street characters from nineteenth-century London did not. Still, the claim may well be true in the case of more developed modern capitalist economies, particularly those that provide unemployment insurance and other means of social security. No doubt over the past 250 years the economic gains in advanced capitalist economies have raised the living standards of everyone, including those worse off, many times over. But capitalism, even welfare-state capitalism such as in the U.S., results in enormous inequalities of wealth which are normally accompanied by gross inequalities of political power and educational and professional opportunities. Moreover, were non-market transfer mechanisms of the welfare state not in place to alleviate unemployment and disability, then the circumstances of the least advantaged and disabled under capitalism would be as bad as the conditions of the destitute in undeveloped countries.

Rawls clearly rejects capitalism when traditionally understood as the doctrine of *laissez-faire*. This is implicit in his rejection of the "System of Natural Liberty" and "Liberal Equality" too, both of which are governed by the principle of efficiency and market distributions of income and wealth (TJ, sect. 12). What is surprising is that he also rejects capitalism even when it is moderated by the modern welfare state. This is surprising since *A Theory of Justice* is often described as the major philosophical justification for the welfare state.[19] But for Rawls, even though welfare-state capitalism provides a social minimum, it does not recognize a principle of reciprocity to regulate social and economic inequalities. As a result, and because of the concentration of property ownership, "the control of the economy and much of political life rests in a few hands" (JF, 138).

Rawls sees welfare-state capitalism as having three major institutional flaws. First, welfare-state capitalism's social minimum is inadequate to the demands of the difference principle and to maintaining the fair value of the basic liberties of the less advantaged. Rawls sees welfare-state capitalism as having its philosophical justification in a kind of restricted utilitarianism. (Indeed, the term "welfare state" has its origin in the 1930s in welfare economics, a branch of utilitarianism.) The general idea of the "welfare state," as originally conceived, is that the overall level of utility or "welfare" in society could be increased by alleviating poverty caused by unemployment, disability, and old age. This is true up to a point, so long as welfare payments themselves do not create such disincentives to work that they considerably undermine the level of output and the efficiency of labor markets. Presumably there is an optimal level of public assistance to the poorest which pays them just enough to alleviate some dissatisfaction, without improving their position so much that they are unwilling to take on work (normally at the minimum market wage) when it becomes available.

The guiding rule in determining the social minimum in the welfare state is then to be decided by utilitarian calculations regarding the comparison of a projected social minimum with a minimum wage level that does not create disincentives to work, taking into account their relationship to the level of overall social welfare in society. Unlike the difference principle, the welfare state's social minimum is not determined by focusing on the needs of the least advantaged themselves or by considerations of equality or reciprocity.

Welfare-state capitalism's second institutional flaw for Rawls is that no effort is made to limit the inequalities of wealth and economic influence that undermine the fair value of the political liberties. Rawls thinks the social and political inequalities allowed by welfare-state capitalism are incompatible with the political equality of citizens since welfare-state capitalism compromises the fair value of political liberties of the less advantaged. Due to gross inequalities and the concentration of wealth, powers, and positions of office, as well as lack of campaign regulation and restrictions on spending, the wealthy and corporate interests effectively lobby and influence politicians and other government officials to enact legislation primarily benefiting the more advantaged. They largely control the political agenda and use it to further their economic interests.

Finally, the third shortcoming of welfare-state capitalism is that, because of the concentration and gross inequality of wealth and most citizens' lack of effective political influence, there is an absence of fair equal opportunities, and most citizens exercise no effective power and lack positions with any authority in social and economic life. Effective control over capital and industry is concentrated in the hands of a small class, and the great majority of people have no control over their working conditions. There is not widespread ownership and control of productive assets (even if workers' pension funds do largely consist of corporate stocks, they have no effective voting power in companies). Managerial control is decided by privileged members of the owning classes, those who control by far the greater share of wealth in society.[20] Equal opportunity in the welfare state is largely formal, providing that careers are open to talents, which fits with the overall emphasis on economic efficiency that guides the utilitarian welfare state. But no effort is made to regulate or to expand the positions of authority open to competition to insure that they include widespread availability of positions or any sort of worker control or participation in management, which is altogether owner-controlled. To the contrary, worker control or participation is seen as economically inefficient. Labor is regarded as but another resource that must be expendable on short notice and under complete owner-controlled management.

The alternative private property market system that remedies the defects of welfare-state capitalism is property-owning democracy. Unfortunately, Rawls does not say enough about the institutions of either a property-owning democracy or market socialism (though he says a good deal more about the former than the latter). We can infer that a property-owning democracy (POD) differs from welfare- state capitalism (WSC) in the following respects:

(1) Unlike capitalism, a POD seeks widespread ownership of the means of production, so that workers normally can control real capital and their work conditions, whether as private owners or as members of unions or worker cooperatives (see JF, 139). Rawls does not suggest, however, that ownership by non-workers of capital, land, and resources is excluded, and he would perhaps contend that partial ownership of this kind should be allowed for reasons of economic efficiency. Still he would say that nothing about the first principle of equal basic liberties requires private ownership of the means of production. The advisability of private ownership of the means of production is decided rather by what bests satisfies the difference principle.

(2) In a POD, as contrasted with WSC, there are not such huge disparities of income and wealth between the most and the least advantaged, since (in addition to the effects of the difference principle) gross inequalities are curtailed in order to protect the fair value of equal political liberties and fair equal opportunities. One way that great disparities of wealth are discouraged is by estate, inheritance, and gift taxes on transfer by the more advantaged to succeeding generations.

(3) A POD, unlike WSC, provides for the fair value of the political liberties. It then limits the effects of private wealth on political campaigns by providing for public financing of campaigns, restricting private contributions and private campaigning, making available public forums for political debate among alternative political programs, and so on.

(4) There is greater fair equality of opportunity in a POD than WSC. Workers are not consigned to work for wages with no interest in their product. They have at least the opportunity to own and control the capital they use in the day-to-day exercise of their working capacities. Moreover, workers have increased control and protections in their workplaces.

(5) The social minimum normally is larger in a POD than in WSC, at least when the latter is governed by the principle of restricted utility, since the POD aims not to maximize the sum total of (national) wealth like WSC, or the average level of income and wealth, but the economic and social position of the least advantaged.

(6) Inheritances (and gifts) are limited in a POD so that large concentrations of wealth are not passed down from one generation to the next. This is needed to provide for fair equal opportunity, which is severely undermined by concentrations of wealth being perpetuated across generations. This requires that bequests (and other gifts) be taxed at the receiver's, rather than the bequeather's, end. (In legal terminology, Rawls envisions a progressive "inheritance tax" rather than an "estate tax.") Those who already are wealthy would be taxed at a much higher rate than are inheritances by the less advantaged, which may involve little or no tax at all. One who makes gifts and bequests in a POD might then even avoid the inheritance tax entirely by widely dispersing his or her estate to the less advantaged. This is no longer a problem since wealth is no longer concentrated due to the widespread dispersion of wealth encouraged by the tax system.

(7) Rather than an income tax – which can discourage work due to income effects – a *proportional expenditure tax* is to be used to tax consumption in a well-ordered property-owning democracy, with the tax applying only after a minimum level of expenditures has been reached. (In this way a proportional expenditure tax differs

from the familiar sales tax, which applies to people regardless of their income and wealth.) An expenditure tax means that people are not taxed on how much they contribute to social product through work and investments, but rather on how much they take from the social product via consumption. The idea is not so much to discourage people from consuming (after all, if they did not consume, there would not be demand for further production); but it is rather to prevent the tax system from directly discouraging work and productive efforts and contributions (JF, 161; TJ 278–79/246 rev.).

Rawls seems to say that a proportional (consumption) tax is preferable to more familiar progressive taxes because a proportional tax (a) is more efficient, for it does not discourage incentives, and (b) "treats everyone in a uniform way (assuming . . . income is fairly earned)" (TJ, 278/246 rev.). Proportionate (consumption) taxes are advocated by many economists and by conservatives alike, on grounds of both fairness and efficiency. Reasons of efficiency aside, it might be inferred from (b) that Rawls indeed accepts the conservative argument that there is something intrinsically fairer about proportionate (or "flat") tax than progressive taxes. He has been criticized for this, and rightly so if it is his assumption.[21] But it seems that there is no basis for such an argument by Rawls, for in his account of distributive justice, there is no presumption that a person is entitled to all that he/she earns by market activity. On the contrary, the presumption must be that each person is obligated to pay his/her fair share in taxation, where "fair share" is clearly not to be decided by some proportionate taxation rule, but by the difference principle and other requirements of distributive justice. So if Rawls gives the appearance of condoning for reasons of fairness a "flat tax" on income or consumption, then he is indeed mistaken given the implications of his view. I think that he can be exonerated of this charge, for he says (immediately after his claims that a proportionate tax may be justifiable because it is "uniform" and "more efficient") that "these are questions of political judgment and not part of a theory of justice." This suggests that a proportionate rather than a progressive tax is to be decided, not by the principles of justice or considerations of fairness alone, but by the application of these principles to the particular circumstances of a well-ordered society. In any case, Rawls says that "given the injustice of existing institutions, even steeply progressive income taxes [may be] justified when all things are considered" (TJ, 279/246–47 rev.).

(8) Rawls affirms the idea that all able-bodied persons should be encouraged to work in a well-ordered democracy. He does not regard it as appropriate to provide people with full "welfare" payments if they are able but unwilling to work. By providing a social minimum for all whether they work or not, the welfare state can encourage dependency among the worst-off, and a feeling of being left out of society. Rawls thinks that part of being an independent person with a sense of self-respect is to be in a position to provide for oneself while working in a job that itself is not demeaning and does not undermine self-respect. He also suggests that if people are engaged in just and fair cooperation, then each has an obligation to do his or her part, and not take unfair advantage of others' efforts. This might be seen as one application of Rawls's principle of fairness (TJ, 18/16 rev., 60/52 rev.). "We are not to gain from the cooperative efforts of others without doing our fair share" (TJ, 343/301 rev.). (But see the reservations below.)

Thus, Rawls rejects Philippe van Parijs's claim that a just society should provide a social minimum to those who decide not to work but instead choose (for example) to loaf or surf all day off Malibu. Even if they are driven to unemployment due to their education and beliefs that labor is repugnant or beneath them, Rawls maintains that individuals are to be held responsible for their ends and their conceptions of the good and cannot impose the costs of their choices of lifestyle upon others. This does not mean that Rawls believes that those who freely choose not to work should be required to fend for themselves by begging for their livelihood or foraging through others' garbage. Rather his suggestion is that leisure time itself ought to be treated as a primary social good. His thought seems to be that those who choose not to work should have the monetary value of a normal work day (eight hours) subtracted from the social minimum that the least advantaged normally receive. (For example, if the social minimum is

$100 per day per adult person – not an unrealistic figure since it adds up to only $36,500 per year, which is still nearly double the current official poverty level for a family of four – and we subtract eight hours at a minimum wage, let's say $6 per hour, then the surfer will receive $52 per day – a sum still adequate to provide for him in his chosen existence.) So in a sense, the surfer is provided with what many may call "welfare," but the monetary sum he receives is less than he would receive if he chose to work.

The social minimum under the difference principle is then set at a level that assumes that people will work, since it is assumed that people will do their fair share in contributing to maintaining social cooperation. But here one might object, "But why is the surfer provided with anything at all since he refuses to work?" The answer is that it is not "welfare" in the traditional sense of public assistance offered to raise the level of individual or total welfare or utility in society. It is rather a payment that democratic citizens are due, as a matter of right, for their taking part in and complying with just terms of social cooperation. Simply because a citizen refuses to work does not mean that he is not otherwise doing his fair share to maintain social cooperation. He obeys the laws, respects others' expectations, and performs his civic duties (e.g., jury service, voting, national service, and conscription during wartime). Citizens contribute to social cooperation through more than just productive labor. The leisurely well-to-do do not engage in productive labor or actually produce any more than the leisurely or unemployed lesser advantaged; whatever "contribution" they make via their property is a legal construct (a "fiction" as Bentham would say). Perhaps this is the reason Rawls refuses to say that the refusal to work violates the principle of fairness. He does not want to say that able-bodied non-workers are acting unfairly or unjustly – their way of life is just as worthy of respect as the lives of the equally unproductive leisurely well-to-do who pay their fair share of taxes under the difference principle. But if people – whether more advantaged or less advantaged – choose not to work, then they cannot reasonably complain when they are not provided with income supplements designed for those who do work but are still least advantaged.

(9) As for the laboring least-advantaged, Rawls evidently opposes

(under conditions of a well-ordered society) a fixed minimum wage that employers must provide, for it discourages creating new employment positions.[22] But a worker's market income is not all he/she is entitled to, for again, market prices (of labor and capital) have no role as a criterion for a person's legitimate expectations or entitlements under the difference principle. Those with low market income are to be subsidized by government-funded income supplements (or "wage subsidies"), which are designed to bring the less advantaged up to the reasonable social minimum required by the difference principle (*TJ*, 285/252 rev.). (A so-called "negative income tax" or the current Earned Income Tax Credit are examples of public income supplements.)

(10) If government is to expect all able-bodied citizens to be productive, then it must take on the role of serving as an *employer of last resort*. It is not fair to condition the amount of the social minimum on work, and then do nothing in the face of a "natural unemployment" rate of 5 or 6 percent. So if the economic system cannot provide genuinely full employment – in the sense of a position to all who seek it – it is the government's job to do so, via public works (on national parks, for example), national service (working in veterans and other public hospitals for example), or some other means.

(11) *Universal health care* is essential to a property-owning democracy. Rawls sees it, along with universal education, as required by fair equality of opportunity. For people who suffer from chronic illness or handicaps are not in a position to take advantage of the opportunities available to people with their level of skills and talents.[23] (Later we see that Rawls regards universal health care as required by any liberal society.) Accordingly justice requires public funding of adequate health care for all citizens.

These are just some of the features of a property-owning democracy. Again, one wishes that Rawls had said more to explicate the idea and respond to obvious criticisms. For example, how is a property-owning democracy to guarantee an opportunity for workers to control their means of production? To do so, must government put restrictions on the amount of capital that non-workers control, or on the rights of workers to transfer their ownership in the firms they work for without giving up their position? Would such measures be so economically inefficient that they seriously undermined the social minimum that goes to the worst-off? If wage subsidies are to be provided by government, by what measures are employers to be prevented from offering minimal wages ($1 per hour), knowing that the government will subsidize the rest so as to enable a worker to achieve the social minimum? How would Rawls respond to the criticism that government-provided jobs are unnecessary "make-work," unlikely to encourage anyone's sense of self-respect? To at least some of these questions, Rawls might respond that these are not questions for a theory of justice but rather are policy questions of implementation of the principles of justice (cf. TJ, 279/246–47 rev.). No doubt in non-ideal circumstances, such as our own society with its unjust economic institutions, it would be difficult to undertake some of these measures without business and other interests trying to exploit if not undermine them. The many questions of non-ideal theory and "partial compliance" that would need to be confronted to apply justice as fairness to our own condition are not questions Rawls thought that he, or any other philosopher, was in a position to adequately respond to. They require knowledge of historical, social, and cultural facts that are more appropriately addressed by social scientists and historians.

There are several interesting developments over the years in Rawls's thoughts about how the difference principle should be applied. In *Theory* he seems to have held the following:

(A) The difference principle is to be applied at the legislative stage to assess the effects of legislation on the prospects of the least advantaged. Moreover, the difference principle is consciously to be applied to each and every act of legislation, at least when laws have any tangible effects on the prospects of the worst-off. If proposed legislation is likely to make the least advantaged worse off than some feasible alternative, then legislators are required to reject it in favor of that alternative. According to *Theory*, then, the difference principle provides a supremely regulative condition, if not a positive aim, of all legislation, unless the basic liberties and fair equal opportunities take precedence.

(B) Unless the least advantaged benefit, the difference principle prohibits the use of public resources to fund perfectionist values of culture, such as public art museums, orchestras, operas, theaters (and the same would apply to public funding of sports stadiums). Universities may be funded for ordinary purposes of educating people so that they may earn a living and live a worthwhile life. All kinds of subjects may be taught for these purposes. But this is different from maintaining cultural institutions for perfectionist values of culture. The use of public funds to further perfectionist values comes at the expense of the least advantaged. This does not mean that public funding of cultural institutions is altogether prohibited. But they must be voluntarily funded by people who use or are willing to support them, so that "no one is taxed without his consent" (TJ, 331/291 rev.).[24] Rawls would then support public administration of cultural institutions that are self-supporting.

(C) Subsequent to Theory Rawls says that the difference principle should not be made part of a political constitution, particularly in a democracy with judicial review (JF, 162). Given the difficult empirical judgments needed to apply the difference principle, the legislative branch should make these decisions and not the judiciary. Rather than being required by a written constitution as a matter of right and made a "constitutional essential" (as Rawls later says), the difference principle should be part of public understanding. It might be made part of a preamble to a written constitution so long as it is not given legal force within the constitution (ibid.).

Twenty years later, when Rawls comes to Political Liberalism, he holds the following:

Regarding (A) above, Rawls says it may not be necessary that the difference principle be consciously applied by legislators to tailor or even assess every act of legislation or policy matter. Recognizing others' objections to the "drag" on deliberations that would be caused by constantly taking into account the prospects of the worst-off in legislation, Rawls says that the difference principle need not

require such constant vigilance. For once the economic consequences of providing for equal basic liberties, the fair value of the
political liberties, and measures for fair equal opportunity are realized, "perhaps the difference principle can be roughly satisfied by
adjusting upward or downward the level of income exempt from
the proportional income tax ... Doing this frees us from having
to consider the difference principle on every question of policy"
(JF, 162). Again this shows how the difference principle is part of
a larger system of principles that do a large part of the work of
distributive justice, even before the difference principle becomes
relevant. Regulation and taxation of large concentrations of wealth
is independently required to maintain equal political liberties and
fair equality of opportunities. Given that fair equal opportunities
genuinely exist, and there is full employment, Rawls thinks society
will not need to be concerned in a property-owning democracy
about alleviating poverty – normally a primary concern of
welfare-state capitalism. Assuming full employment and widespread
availability of education, training, skills, and access to real capital,
even the least advantaged should be fairly well off.[25] If so, then
the major way the difference principle is to come into play legisla-
tively is in determining the level of income or spending exempt
from taxation (though here income supplements still will be
required to correct for the minimum market wage).

Regarding (B) above: Rawls seems to relax his earlier strictures on
using public funds to pay for art museums and other cultural
institutions. Whereas in Theory it must be shown that such institutions indirectly are needed to either maintain basic liberties and
fair opportunities or advance the position of the least advantaged,
in Political Liberalism Rawls implies that there is no problem with
advancing perfectionist values of culture for their own sake, so
long as "constitutional essentials and matters of basic justice" are not
at stake. The difference principle is not a constitutional essential,
and Rawls seems to suggest it is not a requirement of "basic justice,"
so long as an adequate social minimum (i.e., adequate to citizens'
exercising their capacities and taking advantage of opportunities)
is provided. Thus, though taxation to maintain art museums and
operas may not benefit the least advantaged and may even deny

them monetary benefits they otherwise would have, this appears permissible within political liberalism so long as a reasonable social minimum (see below) is not jeopardized. This is a significant change in the position argued for in *Theory*.

Finally, regarding (C): Suppose a right-wing Congress tries to repeal all social-security measures designed to redress the poverty of the poorest (food stamps, AFDC, Medicaid, and so on). While it is not the role of the judiciary to enforce the difference principle and review complex legislative decisions regarding economic policies and regulations, still in a democracy with judicial review Rawls thinks it is appropriate for the judiciary to enforce an adequate social minimum in the event that the legislative branch repeals or refuses to provide measures to meet the basic needs of the worst-off. A social minimum — one that goes well beyond what is needed to meet basic human needs — is a requirement of "basic justice." For in the absence of all-purpose means that enable a person to effectively exercise his or her liberties, the basic liberties are merely formal and of little value to the worst-off. As a matter of basic justice, the social minimum is appropriately enforced through judicial review. Unlike the difference principle, there are no complicated economic policy questions involved that need be decided to determine if a social minimum is adequate. Of course reasonable people may disagree about what is required to meet the social minimum, and courts should normally defer to conscientious legislative judgments. But in the face of a recalcitrant legislature's failure to provide anything at all or clearly too little, Rawls invokes the power of the judiciary to enjoin the provision and enforcement of a social minimum.

THE INSTITUTION OF THE FAMILY

Rawls's identification of the family as among the institutions constituting the basic structure of society has led to much misunderstanding among his critics. Much of this was due to the initial absence, in *Theory*, of much discussion about how the principles of justice bore on the family. He mainly discussed the family's importance in moral education and inculcating the bases in character for a sense of justice (TJ, sect. 70). It is only much later, in "Public Reason Revisited" (1999), that Rawls first published a discussion of the family as a basic institution (CP, 595–601). As a result some mistakenly assumed that the principles of justice were designed to apply within the family itself – and that, for example, parents were committing an injustice when they failed to distribute family resources in a way that conformed to the difference principle. But the principles of justice no more apply internally within the family than they do within any other association, such as churches, universities, military units, or sports teams. Instead they impose external constraints upon these and other institutions. Others argued that Rawls presupposed the traditional male/female marriage bond as part of family life, with the male ascendant and in charge.[26] This claim seems to result from Rawls's suggestion that one way to deal with the problem of justice between generations is to assume that the parties in the original position are "heads of families" (TJ, 128/111 rev.), which insures that the interests of children and future generations are represented (TJ, sect. 44). Critics may have assumed that, if the parties knew they were heads of families, they would also know they were males. But such social and historical knowledge is explicitly denied the parties in the original position. In any case, the "heads of families" assumption makes no more difference to the argument for the principles of justice themselves than if Rawls instead assumes one representative for each person in the original position, for the veil of ignorance prevents anyone from having information about their age or gender, just like any other fact.

Much of the criticism of Rawls on the family seems to presuppose that Rawls has a traditional view of it. Traditionally, the family has been thought of as built around a husband and wife, who nurture and educate their natural children. But with half of all marriages ending in divorce, with a large number of children born "out of wedlock," and with many same-sex couples raising their own children, the traditional idea of the family is rapidly changing. While still regarded by many as an ideal, marriage between male and female is increasingly coming to have less relevance to the essential features of family life. Rawls has a similarly inclusive conception of the family. He regards it, not as a natural grouping, but as a *social* institution; it is therefore conventional, and it can be constructed in several different ways and still perform its primary function. The *primary function of the family* for Rawls – what makes it a basic social institution – has nothing to do with romantic love or even marriage between the natural or adoptive parents or caretakers of children. The family rather is regarded as a basic social institution since any society has to have some social structure for nurturing and raising its children. Without some kind of family formation, a society cannot *reproduce itself over time*. "The family is part of the basic structure, since one of its main roles is to be the basis of orderly production and reproduction of society and its culture from one generation to the next" (CP, 595).

A democratic society has an interest in regulating family life to insure that the fundamental interests of potential citizens are protected, and that children are raised so that their capacities develop and they are able to take advantage of the rights and fair opportunities available to citizens: "Citizens must have a sense of justice and the political virtues that support political and social institutions." For this reason, Rawls suggests, "The family must ensure the nurturing and development of such citizens in appropriate numbers to maintain an enduring society" (CP, 596). Rawls's basic claim, then, is that the family, however it is organized, has the role of reproducing a just society across generations by providing for children's basic needs and enabling them to develop their capacities for justice and for a rational conception of the good. Because of this fundamental role of the family Rawls says "reproductive labor is socially necessary labor" (CP, 595–96), implying that it ought to be recognized and respected as such.

Still, some of Rawls's critics argue that he leaves parents with too much control over their children. Some contend that Rawls should include among the principles of justice additional principles specifically designed to protect the interests of children against their parents' anti-egalitarian views. The concern here is that parents often indoctrinate their children with illiberal and superstitious views that undermine their interests as free and equal persons. Rawls says that parents' legal powers over their children cannot extend to denying them the education needed to fully develop and, upon maturity, adequately exercise the moral powers. But he sees this as consistent with parents raising their children within their own religion, and even with teaching them anti-liberal moral and religious views (at least he does not specifically deny parents that right). The reasons for this seem to be that Rawls, for reasons of freedom of religion, association, and other basic liberties, did not want to give to governments the powers to intervene within family life and impose a positive duty upon parents to bring up their children as morally autonomous beings. Governments can impose a positive duty upon parents to care for the physical health, safety, and nutrition of the child, to school the child in a publicly approved curriculum until maturity, and satisfy other familiar requirements (vaccinations, etc.). Moreover, governments can require that children be educated outside the home about their rights and privileges as citizens, and also be educated in liberal and democratic political values, so that they develop their sense of justice and become politically autonomous citizens. These are the primary ways that a liberal society regulates the institution of the family – through its roles protecting the vital interests of children and overseeing their health and education, to enable them to develop their capacities so that they will be able to effectively exercise their basic liberties and take advantage of the fair opportunities available to them in a liberal society.

Hence, parents cannot prevent their children from being exposed, in public or private school, to awareness of their basic rights and liberties as free and equal citizens or from developing their capacities so they can take advantage of a wide range of fair opportunities. This follows from the higher-order interests of free and equal citizens in the exercise of their moral capacities – that interest cannot be overridden by the claims of parents to exercise control over their offspring. Still, parents do not have to affirm the moral autonomy or individuality of their children; they can teach them traditional views (that women should not take part in public life, for example, and that women's place is in the home tending to children and family life) without fear of public censure. Some feminists and egalitarian liberals object to this consequence of Rawls's view. They contend that it perpetuates the social inequality of women and is inconsistent with Rawls's commitment to an egalitarian liberalism. Rawls's response to this objection seems to be twofold: First, even though *A Theory of Justice* endorses the values of moral autonomy and individuality, it implies that it would unduly interfere with freedom of the person, freedom of association and freedom of choice within the family, to legally prohibit parents from teaching their children traditional religious or other inegalitarian ideas about the role of women. It is not reasonable to allow government to supervise the amount of time each parent devotes to childcare and household chores, or to monitor their conversations with their children to insure they are not trying to indoctrinate them to reject liberal values. Nor would it be rational for free and equal persons to grant such enormous coercive power to monitor family life.

Second, starting with *Political Liberalism*, Rawls argues that it is not the role of a liberal government to enforce a comprehensive liberal doctrine which affirms the moral autonomy and individuality of persons and denies other permissible more traditional conceptions of the good and of family life. From the point of view of public political reason, there is nothing wrong with parents teaching their children religious and other doctrines that affirm traditional family roles and division of labor among the sexes, so long as they do not teach them illiberal political views. While this may seem inconsistent with (or for many, unfortunate because of) the emphasis on moral autonomy in Rawls's argument for the congruence of the right and the good in *Theory*, it reveals the degree to which Rawls's liberalism changed in *Political Liberalism*. As will be seen later, according to political liberalism it is not the role of government to publicly advocate any particular religious, philosophical, or moral "comprehensive" scheme of values beyond the values of liberal political justice. It would be undue interference with family life for government to tell children that their parents are mistaken to teach them that justice originates in God's commands (as many religions believe) rather than within our practical reason, or that their parents should both work and equally divide up household and childcare duties.

Now turn to the institution of marriage, and consider a qualification of the foregoing. Rawls sees the family as independent of marriage, for the family has a social role – the reproduction of a just society from one generation to the next – that can be and increasingly is effectively realized in the absence of married life. With regard to marriage itself, Rawls seems to endorse same-sex marriage as required by justice, so long as it is the case that it does not undermine the interests of children in developing their cognitive and emotional capacities (CP, 596n.). Some feminist philosophers, however, have suggested more than this, namely that a liberal government has no business anyway in recognizing marriage as a civic institution. Governments should not officially recognize marriages that take place within various religions, and governments should not civilly perform marriages, since marriage only perpetuates the inequality of women. To the degree that this argument is driven by a comprehensive liberal view of the good of individuality and self-realization, and denies religious accounts of the role of women at home and within the family, it could not be endorsed by Rawls. If it is democratically decided that society should give civic recognition to the institution of marriage, and bestow certain benefits upon that union, then justice does not prohibit it, other things being equal. Only if there were empirical evidence which showed that the civil recognition of marriage has an inevitable tendency to undermine women's *political* autonomy and status as free and equal citizens, then this would seem to be an argument Rawls would have to take seriously. In response to Mill's claim that the Victorian era family is a "school for despotism" that inculcates habits of thought and conduct incompatible with democracy, Rawls says: "If so, the principles of justice enjoining a reasonable constitutional democratic society can plainly be invoked to reform the family" (CP, 598).

This statement may have far-reaching implications. It suggests that if parents inculcate in their children comprehensive doctrines that lead them over time to advocate and act on unjust positions – denying the equal civic status of women, Blacks, and other minorities, for example – then it would be within the authority of a liberal society to prohibit such instruction or influence. For to teach children the ways of injustice would be a kind of abuse of children, akin to their violent physical abuse and injury which any reasonable person can admit should be prohibited by the state. Consider, for example, racist parents who raise their children to hate others. Like violent abuse, if indoctrination in injustice were ongoing and there were no sign of its ceasing, it would seem to be entirely appropriate to deprive parents custody of their children and put them in an environment with kinfolk or someone else who will not distort their moral sensibilities and sense of justice. This seems to follow from Rawls's view of the family's institutional role of educating young citizens so that a just society may reproduce itself across generations. The consequence, then, is that, while parents may inculcate in their children a religion that teaches them they are not morally autonomous, self-realizing individuals but rather are miserable sinful creatures subject to God's commands, they may not undermine their children's capacities for political autonomy by teaching them gross injustice and refusing to allow them to develop the moral powers necessary for free and equal citizens. This may seem paradoxical but I believe it is not. The crucial distinction between moral and political autonomy relied upon will be clarified in Chapters 8–9.

What now about the effects of family life on fair equality of opportunity? Rawls says, "The family imposes constraints on ways in which [equality of opportunity] can be achieved" (CP, 596). His thought here is not that the family, by its nature, necessarily influences women to adopt motherhood as the centerpoint of their lives, thereby giving up their careers and other opportunities of public life. Even once these cultural influences are overcome and the civic equality of women is fully recognized, still parents, depending on their own education, background, and interests, influence their children differently, instilling in them many of their own habits and predilections. This results in some children having advantages – of education, environment, developed talents, social abilities, and so on – not enjoyed by others, which in turn puts them in a more favorable position to take advantage of available opportunities.

"Even when fair opportunity (as it has been defined) is satisfied, the family will lead to unequal chances between individuals. Is the family to be abolished then?" (TJ, 511/448 rev.). Rawls obviously thinks it should not, given its role as a basic social institution. The reason is that, to give up *any* form of the family in order to overcome its unequalizing effects on people having equal chances in life – suppose we raised all children in orphanages – would not only be contrary to freedom of association with one's own offspring, but it would be of great detriment to children and their moral and social development to be deprived of the individualized nurture and affectionate concern that normally attends family life. As a result it would undermine the development of children's sense of justice and other virtues of citizens, thereby jeopardizing the reproduction of a just and stable society. For Rawls, to eliminate the institution of the family in order to achieve as closely as possible perfect equality of opportunities would be like abolishing the institution of property in order to prevent theft and inequalities of wealth. Both the family and property are institutions that are necessary to the justice and feasibility of a well-ordered society, even if they do bring with them problems of their own.

FURTHER READING

Cohen, Joshua, "Deliberation and Democratic Legitimacy," and "Procedure and Substance in Deliberative Democracy," in *Deliberative Democracy*, James Bohman, ed., Cambridge MA: MIT Press, 1997, chs. 3, 13. (Develops a Rawlsian account of deliberative democracy.)

Krouse, Richard and Michael MacPherson, "Property-Owning Democracy and the Welfare State," in Amy Gutmann, ed., *Democracy and the Welfare State*, Princeton, NJ: Princeton University Press, 1989. (Discusses the two economic and property systems in connection with Rawls.)

Michelman, Frank, "Rawls on Constitutionalism and Constitutional Law," in *The Cambridge Companion to Rawls*, ch. 11. (A discussion of how Rawls's account applies to the political constitution.)

Nussbaum, Martha, "Rawls and Feminism," in *The Cambridge Companion to Rawls*, ch. 14. (Thorough account of Rawls on feminism and the family.)

Six

The Stability of Justice as Fairness

The parties in the original position have to decide whether a conception of justice is "stable" under conditions of a well-ordered society. This decision is integral to the arguments from the strains of commitment, publicity, and self-respect, discussed earlier in Chapter 4. Recall that in *Theory* a society is "well-ordered" in the following respects: (1) its political, economic, and social institutions meet the requirements of a particular conception of justice; (2) this is publicly known by its inhabitants; (3) in this society people generally accept its regulative conception of justice and observe the laws of justice; and (4) they generally believe their society to be just and want to act accordingly. Rawls regards these conditions as desiderata for any conception of justice; they express the contractarian ideal of a society in which all agree on and endorse basic terms of cooperation. For any conception of justice we might conjecture whether it is capable of being realized in a well-ordered society and what such a society would be like if it were governed by that conception. The importance of this to Rawls is evident from his claim, "The comparative study of well-ordered societies is, I believe, the central theoretical endeavor of moral theory."[1]

What needs to transpire for a conception of justice to be stable – that is, for it to be realistically possible and endure as a well-ordered society as circumstances change, institutions evolve, and society confronts various pressures (economic recessions or depressions, natural disasters, conflicts with other societies, etc.)? Philosophers respond differently to these questions, depending on their assessment of human nature, the human good, the conditions of social cooperation, the human potential for moral motivation, and how these factors relate to the demands a conception of justice makes on people. A conception of justice might place such stringent demands that, even if people want to accept it, many cannot because their natural propensities will not allow them regularly to do what is required of them. Or, a society, even if it seems just, may influence people to care little for justice except when it furthers their own wants and personal interests. Finally, even if people care about justice, they may not have confidence that others do; or, they cannot see how justice advances their good, and are often forced to choose between the two. Any of these eventualities tend to destabilize and eventually undermine a social system.

Rawls says that a conception of justice is *stable* when, once realized in political, economic, and social institutions, it generates forces that lead to its own support. A well-ordered society is "inherently stable," or "*stable for the right reasons*" when the forces that support it are primarily its members' moral motivations and sense of justice. A just and stable well-ordered society is one regulated according to the correct conception of justice, which its citizens accept, and also where they are motivated to conform to its requirements and are motivated for good reasons (as defined by that moral conception of justice). When internal or external influences disrupt just institutions, forces are called into play that tend to restore the just arrangement (TJ, 457/400–01 rev.). The stability of a conception of justice, and of a well-ordered society that embodies it, would then seem to be of great importance to their feasibility. If a conception of justice is not stable, then for Rawls this raises serious questions, and doubts, regarding its justification. For a society that seeks to realize an unstable conception of justice is utopian in the sense that it cannot long endure and can never be well-ordered; it is not, then, humanly possible for all reasonable and rational members of society to willingly accept and act upon society's norms of justice.

The problem of stability for Rawls turns on the question whether a conception of justice is compatible with both human nature and with the human good. There are two main parts to Rawls's argument for the stability of justice as fairness in *A Theory* of Justice. In chapter 8, "The Sense of Justice," he tries to show how the development and exercise of a sense of justice is a normal part of individual development in a well-ordered society of justice as fairness. This means that, in such a well-ordered society, individuals should normally have a desire to support and maintain just institutions that conform to the principles of justice. This shows that there is nothing in human nature that renders individuals incapable of complying with and supporting the norms of a society defined by justice as fairness. Then, in chapter 9, "The Good of Justice," Rawls argues that the development and exercise of a sense of justice, and complying with justice's requirements for their own sake, are part of the human good. If justice is both consistent with human nature and good for persons, then it is *rational* for people to do what justice demands of them. This means that a just society, once in place, should be stable and capable of enduring, since rational people should regard it as worthy of their support.

In the first section of this chapter, I discuss the problem of stability in Hobbes and how it contrasts with the problem Rawls addresses. I then take up in the second section the role of the sense of justice in Rawls's account, and discuss the first stage of his stability argument. The remaining three sections of this chapter treat the second stage of Rawls's argument for stability, the argument that justice as fairness is congruent with the human good.[2]

STABILITY AND THE SENSE OF JUSTICE

There are different ways for a society to be stable, and thus it is important to understand what "stability" means for Rawls. No significant political philosopher, not even Hobbes, argues that social order is valuable for its own sake, no matter what its conditions. (Prisons and concentration camps are stable in some sense, and even Hell has its peculiar stability, but none are stable schemes of social cooperation.) Throughout social contract doctrine the concern has been with the stability of a *just* social order, one that embodies correct norms and principles of justice. For Hobbes a just social order is one characterized by the "Laws of

Nature." These are the "means of Peace," or "Articles of Peace," since, taking human nature into account, they are designed to procure peaceable and prosperous social cooperation. Without the Laws of Nature, social cooperation is not possible. The problem of stability for Hobbes is to show how everyone can come to have good and sufficient reason to observe the Laws of Nature. The primary role of political institutions, or "the Sovereign," is to provide stability for these conditions of social cooperation. The Sovereign's role is then to enforce the Laws of Nature, by positing laws and administering sanctions when they are breached. In coercively enforcing the Laws of Nature, the Sovereign provides everyone with the assurance that everyone else will normally observe these laws of justice. Having this assurance, all have good and sufficient reason to obey the Laws of Nature themselves. In this way, the Sovereign stabilizes the Laws of Nature, and social cooperation along with it.[3]

One part of the stability problem – of showing that everyone has good and sufficient reasons to comply with laws of justice – is to resolve this assurance problem. Another part of the problem is to show that when disruptions to social cooperation occur, there are forces in society that tend to return society to general compliance with the norms of justice. Social cooperation on just terms should then be (as game theorists say) a "stable equilibrium." Hobbes argued that nearly absolute political power was necessary to resolve these problems. To provide all with the assurance that others will comply with justice, and to insure that society can withstand internal conflicts and disturbances, the Sovereign required de facto powers unlimited by legal restrictions and regulations.

Hobbes's conditions for stability are decidedly non-liberal and anti-democratic. While an absolute sovereign might provide us with sufficient reason – or sufficient motivation – to comply with justice, it does not provide good reasons to comply. In Rawls's terms, absolute sovereignty does not provide "stability for the right reasons." To begin with, unrestricted sovereignty conflicts with the basic liberties protected by any liberal and democratic conception of justice. Moreover, the primary motivations reasonable and rational individuals have for abiding by laws of justice should not be external coercion; rather justice should in some way be compatible with human nature and conducive to individuals' interests independent of its coercive background. Rawls does not deny that coercive enforcement is needed even in a well-ordered society, to provide all with the assurance that others are not normally tempted to deviate from the laws. But coercion should not be the main source of motivation to comply if a conception of justice is to be "stable for the right reasons" (PL, xlii, 392).

Contemporary Hobbesians might say that a purely interest-based conception of justice need not rely on coercive force for it to be rational for individuals to comply with cooperative requirements. Assuming that norms of justice promote each person's interests, the problem of assuring people that their cooperation will not be exploited by defectors or "free riders" can be non-coercively resolved. For non-cooperators and others who fail to comply whenever they believe non-compliance is advantageous will eventually become known and will acquire a reputation as untrustworthy. People will then refuse to cooperate with them. Knowing this, rational individuals will not start down the path of defection or occasional non-compliance. As a result assurance and stability are achieved even in the absence of fear of coercive sanctions among fully rational people.

This sort of argument, while it might account for non-coercive cooperation within relatively small groups, does not fare so well in explaining social cooperation among large numbers of people. Dishonest and untrustworthy people in modern societies often do quite well before they encounter infamy and opprobrium from others, and by then they have moved on to other exploits and innocent victims. Moreover, the argument from reputation does not address the problem of how a conception of justice can survive disruptions in the balance of power, wealth, and influence among members of society. Why should the "haves" cooperate any longer on fair terms with the "have-nots" if circumstances develop so that the "haves" no longer need to fear infringing the civil rights of the "have-nots" or worry about withholding their fair share? Stability on Hobbesian terms is a *modus vivendi*, a practical compromise among different parties and their competing interests, which is subject to disruption whenever circumstances substantially change. Such a balance of powers may prove stable for a while, but it does not inspire confidence or trust in those who are less advantaged or in a precarious situation. It does not then lead them to develop emotional attachments to society or a willingness to maintain and defend it when subject to destabilizing forces. Like coercion, neither the desire to maintain reputation nor a *modus vivendi* provides "stability for the right reasons." For this, cooperation must be anchored in people's sense of justice.

Rawls defines a scheme of social cooperation as stable when it is "more or less regularly complied with and its basic rules willingly acted upon; and when infractions occur, stabilizing forces should exist that prevent further violations and tend to restore the arrangement" (TJ, 6/6 rev.). With Hobbes, Rawls maintains that for any social scheme to be stable, people need the assurance that everyone else has sufficient reason to comply with the rules; and coercive political power is necessary for this assurance.[4] But unlike Hobbes, it is not sufficient for Rawls. "To insure stability men must have a sense of justice or a concern for those who would be disadvantaged by their defection, preferably both. When these sentiments are sufficiently strong to overrule the temptations to violate the rules, just schemes are stable" (TJ, 497/435 rev.).

Rawls regards the sense of justice and other moral sentiments as psychological dispositions that are part of normal social development (TJ, 489/428–29 rev.). A person who lacks a sense of justice not only is without ties of friendship, affection, and mutual trust, but is incapable of experiencing resentment and indignation. Put another way, one who lacks a sense of justice lacks certain fundamental attitudes and capacities included under the notion of humanity (TJ, 488/427 rev.).

At the simplest level, the sense of justice is an acceptance of and willingness to comply with the rules of justice in one's society, and to do so at least partially independent of one's tendency to promote one's own particular interests. Most people believe they have a duty to keep their commitments and respect the laws even when it is not to their advantage, and normally they are inclined to act on this conviction. This propensity exhibits their sense of justice.

There is some ambiguity in Rawls's use of the concept of a sense of justice. On the one hand he defines the sense of justice broadly, as a complex moral capacity to judge matters just and unjust, and to support these judgments by reasons, as well as a desire to act in accord with judgments of justice (TJ, 46/41 rev.).[5] For Rawls a theory of justice might be regarded as an attempt to characterize our sense of justice, by eliciting the principles that account for its considered judgments.[6] But more often (and especially in Part III), Rawls uses "sense of justice" narrowly, to refer to a moral motivation to do what rules of justice require. When defined in relation to justice as fairness, the sense of justice is "a normally effective desire to apply and to act upon the principles of justice" (TJ, 505/442 rev.).[7]

Regarded as a moral motivation, Rawls sees the sense of justice as but one motivation among others we have; it often conflicts with them, and is sometimes outweighed or qualified in our deliberations and actions (e.g., by self-interest, altruism toward individuals or groups, even by other moral motives). Like Rousseau, Rawls sees the sense of justice as a social motivation; it is the primary condition of human sociability (TJ, 495/433 rev.). It is not to be confused with altruism or benevolence, which are desires for the well-being of particular persons or groups. Many altruistic actions, even those stemming from general benevolence, are unjust; injustice often has its source, not in egoism, but in misplaced altruism. Also, the sense of justice, unlike altruism, is an "artificial" motive or an "artifice of reason" (as Hume says). It is not a desire for any particular object or natural state of affairs, but is a desire to act according to norms or conventions (laws, rules, or principles of justice) that are the product of human reasoning and reflection upon the conditions of social cooperation.[8]

In Political Liberalism, Rawls contrasts the sense of justice with "object-dependent" desires, such as desires for physical satisfaction, or particular ends or states of affairs that are describable in terms of the natural or social sciences. Most desires are object-dependent. Rawls depicts the sense of justice, however, as a "principle-dependent," or even a "conception-dependent" desire (PL, 82–86; cf. TJ, sect. 75). It is a desire that cannot be described without invoking normative principles, which it has for its content. As a desire to act on principles of justice, the sense of justice resembles the desire to be rational, also a desire to act on normative principles (e.g., to take effective means or to have consistent ends). Like the desire to be rational, the sense of justice is a higher-order or regulative desire: it presupposes desires for other objects or states of affairs, and is a desire to regulate actions in pursuit of these ends according to certain norms. As one can pursue a career, a pastime, or a relationship more or less rationally, one also pursues them more or less justly or fairly. To say a desire is of a higher order does not imply it is more important than object-dependent desires, or desires for final ends. Wanting to act politely (or rudely for that matter) is higher order, but it is often outweighed by other desires for more important ends we have. What is distinctive about higher-order desires or ends is that they regulate the pursuit of the objects of other desires or ends. The degree of importance of these regulative desires and ends in deliberation has to be settled by other considerations.

Return now to Rawls's stability problem: According to Theory, the primary basis for the stability of a well-ordered society of justice as fairness is that its members normally have an effective sense of justice, a settled disposition to act according to the principles of justice and their institutional requirements. All members of a well-ordered society of justice as fairness agree on the principles of justice as the basis for laws and social conventions. The problem of stability is motivational: Given their agreement, can individuals be brought to regularly will justice and act according to its principles?

There are two general problems here. First, given natural human propensities, how do people come to care about justice? The answer depends on what justice requires of people. Utilitarian justice makes quite different demands than perfectionism or justice as fairness. Since Rawls is concerned primarily with the stability of justice as fairness, the question for him is whether the desire to act on the principles of justice can become a normal disposition in a well-ordered society. Or does Rawls's conception order society so that its inhabitants, though not encouraged to be egoists, nonetheless are led to frequently compromise justice for the sake of their attachment to particular persons, groups, or projects?

Second, assume that people are reasonable in that they do normally develop a sense of justice. Still, do they care about justice *sufficiently* so that they have *good* reason to regularly subordinate pursuit of their ends to requirements of justice? People have multiple ends, which are assigned a position in an order of priority; they normally have more than one final end, and they effectively pursue these according to some plan that provides a place for each. What position rationally is to be assigned to the desire for justice in a reasonable person's priorities and plans? Is it rational to give justice any sort of priority over other ends? Or should the sense of justice be treated like other desires, and weighed off against them in ordinary ways in deciding what is rational to do? Again, this question depends on what a conception of justice demands of us. Its answer depends upon whether citizens in a well-ordered society can be *rationally* motivated by their sense of justice to act *consistently* as just institutions demand. Any social system can tolerate occasional lapses from justice. But if many people believe they have no good reason to give their sense of justice regular priority, then this tends to undermine everyone's assurance in the faithfulness of others and renders the social order defined by justice as fairness unstable, making it effectively unrealistic if not utopian.[9]

These two problems form the two parts of Rawls's stability argument. They are addressed respectively in chapter 8 ("The Sense of Justice") and chapter 9 ("The Good of Justice") of *A Theory of Justice*. In chapter 8, Rawls sets forth a moral psychology designed to show how people in a well-ordered society of justice as fairness normally can be expected to acquire a sense of justice. (I turn to this momentarily.) Then, in chapter 9, Rawls argues how the sense of justice is rational: how it is compatible with, and can even constitute part of, a person's good. This is the congruence argument, the subject of the third section of this chapter.

Before we turn to these sections, note should be taken of an important objection to Rawls's stability argument. Jürgen Habermas and G.A. Cohen object to Rawls's appeal to facts about human beings and social cooperation to justify his principles of justice. Their claim (roughly) is that fundamental moral principles are not to be grounded in the factual contingencies of the world. Rather, fundamental moral principles should apply, as it were, to all possible worlds. This criticism resembles Kant's contention that the Moral Law has its basis in "pure practical reason" and applies to rational beings as such, regardless of their empirical nature or factual circumstances. Rawls himself notes that he rejects this aspect of Kant's position, along with rejecting his many dualisms (LP, 86–7; CP, 304). Habermas and Cohen claim that, since the arguments for stability rest on factual considerations about human nature and conditions of social cooperation, Rawls is mistaken to regard the stability of a conception of justice as a condition of its justification. For factual truths, however general, ultimately have to do, not with the justification of moral principles, but with their application to real-world empirical conditions. It is of course necessary to take into account facts about human moral psychology and economic production and exchange in applying principles of justice, but these contingent matters should not play a role in the justification of the most fundamental moral principles.

This is an important objection. A full response is beyond the confines of this book, for the objection ultimately addresses the nature and possibilities of moral (if not philosophical) reasoning. A more modest response will be made at the end of this chapter, once we have considered Rawls's congruence argument. The argument I will make is that facts about human nature and social cooperation are relevant to the justification of principles of justice in so far as we are to conceive of justice as achievable by us, and as compatible with, if not part of, the human good. There is a tradition that goes back to Plato that contends that justice is among the greatest of human goods. Rawls accepts at least this much of the Platonic tradition.

MORAL MOTIVATION AND THE DEVELOPMENT OF A
SENSE OF JUSTICE

The problem addressed in chapter 8 of *Theory* is the conditions for developing moral motives of justice: Assume individuals are not egoists; that is, the objects of human desire include not just states of the self (one's own security, comfort, reputation, appearance, etc.). Humans normally have other ends that do not specifically relate to states of themselves (cultural, political, and social ends). Moreover, we often desire the good of others for its own sake (as in love, friendship, solidarity, etc.). Humans are then normally altruistic. But we are "limited altruists," and not "pure" altruists – that is, we are not impartially benevolent, equally concerned for everyone's good. These are among the subjective circumstances that make justice necessary.[10] For evolutionary reasons perhaps, we normally care more about our own good and those near and dear to us than we care about the good of strangers. Now given this fact about human nature – our lack of impartial benevolence – the question is whether individuals nonetheless can normally develop and exercise moral motivations to act on impartial rules of justice. If so, what is the psychological mechanism that leads individuals in a well-ordered society of justice as fairness to develop the moral motive of the sense of justice?

By 'moral motivations' is meant certain desires to conform to moral rules and principles by which people regulate their (largely object-dependent) desires for their own and others' good. Benevolence by itself is not a moral motive if unregulated by moral principles. Unregulated benevolence towards a particular person or group often results in immoral actions against others. Impartial benevolence, however, is a moral motive: it is a desire to act for the good of others according to an impartiality principle which requires that equal consideration is to be given to everyone's interests. The stability of a well-ordered utilitarian society might well depend on this moral motive. If so, then the question of stability for a utilitarian conception is whether impartial benevolence is likely to be a normal and effective disposition among the inhabitants of a well-ordered utilitarian society. The stability of a well-ordered society of justice as fairness, on the other hand, depends upon the likelihood that citizens will normally develop their sense of justice into a willingness to support and maintain institutions conforming to the principles of justice.

Rawls's account of the development of the sense of justice is informed by the following claims:

(1) The sense of justice is the primary motivational basis of human sociability. To be without a sense of justice is to have a flawed humanity (TJ, 488/428 rev.).
(2) The sense of justice is normally developed in the course of maturation under favorable conditions, as a result of familial influence and the effects of friends and other social bonds and institutions.
(3) The sense of justice is an extension of our natural social sentiments, such as love and affection, and friendship and camaraderie (TJ, sect. 74).
(4) Once developed, the sense of justice has as its object, not simply laws and other social norms, but more abstract principles and potentially a philosophical conception of justice. Consequently,
(5) The acquisition of this motive depends on reasoning, and not simply habituation. It is acquired only once persons' capacities for reason, understanding, and judgment are developed, and they are capable of identifying with others and understanding and applying abstract principles.
(6) Being an extension of natural social sentiments, the constraints of the sense of justice are not injurious to but are compatible with the agent's rational interests, or his or her good.

A primary feature of Rawls's account of moral development is the idea of reciprocity: it is a "deep psychological fact" that we form attachments to persons and institutions according to how we perceive our good to be affected by them (TJ, 494/433 rev.).[11] This tendency to reciprocity is the most significant psychological assumption in Rawls's theory of justice. On the basis of it Rawls formulates three psychological "laws" of moral development, the "reciprocity principles."[12] He applies these laws to argue that normally people come to want to do justice in response to justice, and that under the special circumstances of a well-ordered society of justice as fairness, people eventually will acquire a desire to support just institutions because they benefit them and those they care about.

It is easy to find counterexamples to Rawls's reciprocity principles, along with others that Rawls relies on (e.g., the "Aristotelian Principle," to be discussed later). Because of this, many summarily dismiss Rawls's psychological generalizations.[13] This seems to be the wrong response. Humans act from a number of motives and for complicated reasons. It is overly simplistic to think that there is some dominant motivation, like the desire for comfort and security, that determines our actions in all that we do. Rawls's reciprocity principles, like any credible psychological generalization, are not aimed at capturing permanent patterns of behavior, or dominant impulses that direct our behavior in whatever we do. Rather, they characterize diverse human tendencies that exhibit themselves under certain conditions. There are numerous tendencies that combine and often vie with one another in influencing what we do. One has to consider the combined effect of these human tendencies, and the circumstances under which they are operative, before assessing the soundness of a psychological account. In this respect, Rawls's moral psychology does not differ from others'. The point is simply that counterexamples alone do not undermine a psychological account, so long as the counterexamples can be accounted for in terms of competing tendencies and special circumstances.

Rawls's reciprocity principles cover three stages of moral development.[14] The first law says that, at the first stage of moral development, when the institution of the family is itself just, children gradually develop a loving attachment to their parents once they are lovingly cared for and nurtured by them, and the parents affirm the child's sense of self-worth.[15] The basic idea here comes down from Rousseau, who contends that the child, starting from

self-love or *amour de soi*, instinctively becomes attached to what
contributes to its preservation. Eventually others' "evident intention of helping us" transforms this instinctive affection into trust,
and love of parents or caregivers for their own sake.[16] The child
acquires then a new emotion which, though it develops out of
self-love, gradually acquires a life of its own. Love and trust of
parents lead the child, over time, to adhere to parental injunctions, not out of fear of sanction, but due to love and respect for
the parents and a desire to emulate and not disappoint them. The
child is not yet in a position to understand the reasons for his
parents' precepts, not having developed the capacities for reasoning
or moral understanding; but he obeys them because he trusts
them and their evident intention for his good. It follows in the
natural course of events that, when disobedient, the child comes
to experience a kind of guilt (which Rawls calls "authority guilt")
for violating parental injunctions, once he becomes inclined to
share their attitude toward transgressions (TJ, 465/407 rev.). As
guilt, this feeling is distinct from whatever fears of sanction he
might also have.

Rawls calls this stage of moral development (following Piaget)
the "morality of authority." It is important not to confuse this
morality with a punitive morality that is based in coercive threats
and fear of reprisals (by parents, God, etc.). Essential to the
morality of authority is love, mutual trust, and developing the
child's sense of self-respect (where all this transpires within the
framework of family institutions that are just as specified by the
principles of justice). Out of these sentiments the child acquires
respect for its guardians, who are manifestly concerned for the
child's good. It is this specific kind of respect for authority, not
fear of reprisal, that is the primary motivation leading the child to
act in conformity with moral precepts.

The other side of Rawls's reciprocity principle implies that a
person's sense of justice and other moral sentiments can be, indeed
often are, distorted by a punitive moral education, especially if it
is joined with uncaring parents or guardians, and unjust family
institutions (e.g., gross inequality and lack of respect between
parents, favoritism towards selected children, and a domineering

parent). For example, children brought up under an oppressive religious education, who are taught that violations of God's commandments result in divine retribution, and are corporeally punished for misbehavior, are often afflicted by an oppressive conscience in adulthood, and may themselves develop punitive moral sentiments (desire for vengeance, etc.). Another implication of Rawls's account is that the sense of justice is distorted when joined with unreasonable moral rules and principles – such as principles which require us to sacrifice our well-being simply because of others' displeasure, or simply because actions are not approved of by those in arbitrary authority situations. Under these circumstances there is an absence of reciprocity in the content of moral principles that are taught, and the moral feelings that develop around them are liable to be unreasonable and capricious. In some cases, moral development can be wholly retarded. The extreme case is children who are neglected and abused, and subjected to arbitrary parental injunctions; as a result they may never develop the feelings of trust or self-worth that are essential for development of moral sentiments.

The second stage of moral development Rawls calls "the morality of association" (TJ, sect. 71). It is marked by learning and becoming emotionally attached to moral standards that are appropriate to one's role (friend, classmate, neighbor, teammate, etc.) in various associations to which one belongs. Guiding the child are a number of ideals appropriate to the status or role occupied in various associations. From these ideals one learns the virtues of character proper to one's role in the association. One of the most important features of this stage is that, as the child comes to understand the different roles and positions that make up associative schemes, he or she acquires a conception of the system of cooperation that defines the association and the purposes that it promotes. Seeing the different roles and the division of functions and duties within the cooperative scheme, the child gradually learns to put himself or herself into others' positions, and to see things from their perspective and the perspective of their place within the association. The *second reciprocity principle* says that, assuming that the division of roles and their respective duties are seen as fair, and that associates live up to their duties and obligations, a person develops friendly feelings towards associates, along with feelings of trust and confidence. These lead to the acquisition of a desire to do one's part within the association, by abiding by one's duties and living up to the ideal of one's role.

Here it is noteworthy that Hegel and his communitarian followers see something very much like the morality of association as the ideal for political morality. What prevents Rawls from adopting this position is that he does not conceive of society as an association, voluntary or non-voluntary, which is guided by a definite purpose that is separate and apart from the norms that regulate it. Society is rather a kind of association of associations (or better, a union of associations), wherein the role of each is not defined by their particular ends and associations, but by their position as equal citizens.

Finally, the third stage of moral development is "the morality of principles." Assume that a person has experienced attitudes of love and trust within the family, and of friendly feeling and mutual confidence within other associations in accordance with the two preceding psychological laws. Rawls argues that we develop a desire to support just institutions, therewith the sense of justice, once (1) we recognize that we and those we care about benefit from these institutions, *and* (2) these institutions are publicly recognized to be just. This moral motivation shows itself by our willingness to comply with our duties and obligations and do our part in just institutions; and by a desire to contribute to the reform of institutions when they are unjust.

What is noteworthy about the sense of justice, and what distinguishes it from the moral motives acquired at earlier stages, is that Rawls sees it (in its purest form) as not dependent on an attachment to specific persons, or even on fellow-feeling or sympathy; it is an independent acceptance of and attachment to public moral principles of justice. Here the contrast with Hume's account of the sense of justice is illuminating. Hume maintained that the sense of justice is not a self-sufficient sentiment, but has its grounding in sympathy for others and a regard for the public good.[17] It is by enlarged fellow-feeling, extended to all the members of society, that we approve of justice and acquire a disposition to act according to conventions of justice. Without this grounding in (impartial) fellow-feeling, Hume can see no point to the sense of justice – why, after all, should we care about the enforcement of general rules if they do not benefit people we care about? Justice has its origin in utility, so a desire to do justice that is not subordinate to a concern for others' utility makes no sense (to him); it is perhaps even irrational (so far as Hume was able to concede irrational desires).

Rawls does not deny extended fellow-feeling; indeed he relies on it in his account of the morality of association to account for the origins of the sense of justice. He even says, in explaining how "moral principles can engage our affections," that they define agreed ways of advancing human interests, and that "the sense of justice is continuous with the love of mankind" (TJ, 476/417 rev.). But ultimately Rawls divorces the sense of justice, once acquired, from fellow-feeling, and says it is an independent "principle-dependent" moral sentiment. His reason seems to be that enlarged fellow-feeling, and especially impartial benevolence towards everyone, is not sufficiently common or even if common, is still not sufficiently reliable or vigorous enough to bind together the body of citizens in a democratic society. Impartial benevolence, as a moral sentiment, is too prone to the contingencies of circumstance to provide a reliable motivational basis for social stability.

This raises the question why the sense of justice is any less subject to circumstance, and this question just compounds the difficulty of answering the Humean challenge of how to make sense of an independent desire to act on principles. These questions cannot be fully addressed or answered until we take up the problem of congruence in the next chapter. But part of Rawls's answer can now be given. It is that, independent of our fellow-feeling and desires to advance human interests, we have a desire for fairness, that is, a desire to see that human interests are advanced in ways that are fair, or (what comes to the same thing in Rawls's account) in ways that are acceptable to all from a position that is reasonable and fair between them. As Rawls says:

[F]or one who understands and accepts the contract doctrine, the
sentiment of justice is not a different desire from that to act on
principles that rational individuals would consent to in an initial situation which gives everyone equal representation as a moral
person. . . . Being governed by these principles means that we
want to live with others on terms that everyone would recognize
as fair from a perspective that all would accept as reasonable.
The ideal of persons cooperating on this basis exercises a natural
attraction upon our affections.

(*TJ*, 478/418–19 rev.)

The sense of justice is not, then, an arbitrary attachment to rules or
principles ("rule worship") as critics of Kant and Kantian views
often claim. It has an explanation in terms of Rawls's version of the
social contract. In Rawls's account, the desire to to be just and act on
principles of justice is the same as the desire be reasonable and fair
in one's actions, to cooperate with others and pursue one's interests on terms all can accept and agree to from an equal position.
Why we have this desire is another question. On its face, it would
appear (to many) that it needs no further explanation. It is as
understandable, and perhaps just as basic, as the natural sympathetic concern for human interests that Hume and Mill rely upon.
Certainly it is at least as credible, and I believe far more realistic,
than the impartial sympathy or universal benevolence Hume, Mill,
and other utilitarians invoke to account for the sense of justice.[18]

Rawls then, like Hume, regards having a sense of justice as a
normal part of psychological development, one that in large part
accounts for the stability of societies existing under favorable non-
oppressive conditions. He sees this motivation, once fully
developed, as self-sufficient and independent of other motivations; it is normally a desire to see justice done for its own sake
and a motivation to act accordingly. The question remains,
however, whether the sense of justice, as a desire to be reasonable,
is itself *rational*, and "congruent" with a person's good. Here we
come to the second part of Rawls's argument for stability, the
argument from congruence. As will be seen in the next section, it
is important to distinguish the question whether the sense of

justice is a rational motivation from the question we have just considered, whether it is an arbitrary motive. Whether the sense of justice is arbitrary is ultimately a question of what justice is about, its nature or subject matter. Whether justice is rational, on the other hand, raises a different question, about the relation of justice to the human good. If one thinks that the nature of justice is simply to promote the human good, then these two questions are easily confused. Finally, it is important to distinguish both of these questions just mentioned from a third, viz., whether the sense of justice has its basis in reason. These are, as we shall eventually see, three distinct issues for Rawls.

In chapter 8 of *A Theory of Justice* Rawls argues that the principles of justice are compatible with the three reciprocity principles, and therefore that the members of a well-ordered society of justice as fairness will normally come to acquire the sense of justice to act upon these principles. "The Problem of Relative Stability" (the title of sect. 76) is to show that justice as fairness is more stable than alternative conceptions of justice considered in the original position. This involves arguing that the principles of justice fit better with the three reciprocity principles than do any of the other traditional conceptions of justice Rawls considers. But as usual, Rawls mainly compares justice as fairness with utilitarianism.

As a preliminary to his argument for the greater stability of justice as fairness relative to other alternatives, Rawls says: "The most stable conception of justice, therefore, is one that is perspicuous to our reason, congruent with our good, and rooted not in abnegation but in affirmation of the self" (TJ, 499/436 rev.). One of the elements of the operation of the three psychological laws, Rawls says, is "an unconditional caring for our good," first by our parents, then by friends and other close associates, and finally by members of our society. The principles of justice, by insuring equal basic liberties, fair opportunities, and an economic system whose rules are designed so that gains to one group do not come at others' expense, guarantee that the interests of each citizen are advanced. Because reciprocity conditions are built into the principles of justice themselves, the various aspects of justice as fairness "heighten the operation of the reciprocity principle," that are part of our moral psychology, and thereby "strengthen our self-esteem" and "lead to a closer affiliation with persons and institutions" (TJ, 499/437 rev.). By contrast,

> Why should the acceptance of the principle of utility (in either form) by the more fortunate inspire the less advantaged to have friendly feelings toward them? This response would seem in fact to be rather surprising, especially if those in a better situation have pressed their claims by maintaining that a greater sum (or average) of well-being would result from their satisfaction.
>
> (*TJ*, 500/437 rev.)

Rawls's argument for the greater relative stability of justice as fairness over utilitarianism is that general endorsement of the principle of utility is incompatible with human nature, since it demands that the less advantaged in society willingly support institutions that disadvantage them for the sake of those better off. As such, the institutions of a utilitarian society do not aim for reciprocity among persons nor achieve an "unconditional caring for our good," but rather unconditionally promote the aggregate good at the expense of those less advantaged. As a result, "Some groups may acquire little if any desire to act justly (now defined by the utilitarian principle) with a corresponding loss of stability" (TJ, 500/437 rev.).

The claim, then, is that justice as fairness is *more compatible with human nature* as characterized by normal moral psychology and the three reciprocity principles. To argue that justice as fairness is more compatible with human nature than utilitarianism, Rawls does not need to argue that sympathy for the public good or feelings of impartial benevolence are beyond our capacities. Indeed, he concedes "such altruistic inclinations no doubt exist" (TJ, 500/438 rev.).[19] But they are not anywhere near as likely to be as strong, widespread, or as reliable as the inclinations that stem from the reciprocity principles, which depend upon affirmation of each person's good. Rawls contends that J.S. Mill, though a utilitarian, even tends to agree that reciprocity is a condition of society and an effective sense of justice, and that sympathy is not sufficient.[20]

As final confirmation of the greater relative stability of justice as fairness, Rawls appeals to evolutionary biology (TJ, 502–4/ 440–1 rev.). A species in which social groups act upon moral principles that do not demand supererogatory conduct and self-sacrifice in the way the principle of utility does, but which instead incorporate reciprocal beneficence, is more likely to survive evolutionary pressures. Here Rawls cites works by ethnologists which show the selective advantages of "reciprocal altruism" over unconditioned altruism. Rawls is not arguing, as some naturalists (particularly utilitarians) do, that certain moral principles are themselves implicit in human nature.[21] But facts about our psychological tendencies and our evolutionary development may help to confirm that the principles of justice are more compatible with human nature than the demands placed upon it by utilitarianism.

Here, of course, it is open to the utilitarian and others to argue that, even if it is true that justice as fairness is more stable in these regards, that does not count against utilitarianism. For considerations of stability, while they are relevant to the application of moral principles, are not relevant to their justification. The fact that human beings are naturally more concerned with themselves and their good than with others should not be an impediment to morality's demands, for after all morality is designed just to take the focus off of the self and extend our consideration to the good of other people.

This is an important criticism of Rawls. To see why Rawls sees facts about human nature as important to the justification of a conception of justice, we need to complete the discussion of Rawls's argument for stability. I now turn to the argument from congruence.

GOODNESS AS RATIONALITY, THE CONGRUENCE PROBLEM, AND THE ARISTOTELIAN PRINCIPLE

The question addressed by Rawls's congruence argument is the following. Assume that people in a well-ordered society of justice as fairness have an independent sense of justice, and want to do what is right and just for its own sake. Still, this does not mean that justice is always a good thing for them to do. Not only may its demands frequently conflict with their rational plans and achieving their most important purposes. It may also stunt the development of higher human capacities and impede our achievement of excellences of culture. Rawls assumes that people can be expected to consistently act on and from moral motives of justice only if justice is compatible with their good. What assurance do we have that it is realistically possible for people to affirm justice as fairness as part of their good, and that they will then consistently affirm and act upon their sense of justice and regularly observe requirements of justice?

Of course a good deal rides on how we are to conceive of the human good. What does Rawls mean by a person's good? His account was briefly discussed in Chapter 4. He formally defines a person's good in terms of what is rational for a person to want under certain ideal deliberative conditions. Hence he calls his account "Goodness as Rationality." Rationality is specified in terms of certain principles of rational choice. Some of these are standard in most any account of practical rationality: taking effective means to one's ends, ranking one's ends in order of priority and making one's final ends consistent, taking the most probable course of action to realize one's ends, and choosing the course of action that realizes the greater number of one's ends. These "counting principles," as Rawls calls them, are not controversial, so there is no need to dwell on them.[22] More controversial is Rawls's assumption of the rationality of prudence, or no-time preference – to give equal concern to all the (future) times of one's life. This assumption, taken from Sidgwick, enables Rawls to incorporate the idea of a "plan of life" into the account of rationality, making it part of the formal definition of a person's good. If it is rational to be equally concerned with all the parts of one's life, then a rational person presumably has some conception of and plan for his life as a whole. A plan of life consists of a schedule of the primary ends and pursuits a person values, and activities that are needed to realize them, over a lifetime. Each of us can imagine more than one such plan we might be satisfied with even if all of them might include some of the same things (e.g., having children, having a mate). The most rational plan of life for a person satisfies the counting principles, and is the plan the person would choose under conditions of "deliberative rationality." These are hypothetical conditions of choice where a person is assumed to have full knowledge of what it is like to live a life pursuing chosen ends, critically reflects upon this plan, imagines what it would be like to live that way, and appreciates the consequences.[23] The account of the plan of life a person would choose in deliberative rationality provides Rawls's formal definition of a person's good.

In order to say what is good for a person to do, or whether a course of action is rational for him or her to take, we often need to refer to his or her rational plan of life. Of course, because of human nature and similarities, there are many things we can say it is rational for anyone to do. Staying in good health, learning a language, developing one's skills and educating one's capacities are rational for anyone since, among other reasons, they are either necessary to forming and pursuing a plan of life, or they make one's life more interesting and seem more worthwhile. Later, Rawls's "Aristotelian Principle" will be discussed, which provides grounds for saying what kinds of activities are rational for individuals to choose and pursue as part of a rational plan.

The idea of a rational plan of life supplies the basis for Rawls's formal or "thin theory of the good." It is presupposed in the argument from the original position; the parties are rational in this sense. With this formal outline of the thin theory in place, we can get a better idea of the congruence problem. There are two ideal perspectives in Rawls's conception of justice: the original position and deliberative rationality. The former provides the foundation for judgments of justice; the latter provides the basis for judgments regarding a person's good. The original position abstracts from all information particular to our situations, including the specific ends and activities constituting an individual's good. In deliberative rationality all this information is restored: judgments of value, unlike judgments of right, are explained relative to individuals' particular ends and situations, so Rawls assumes they require full knowledge of one's circumstances. The original position is a collective public perspective[24] – we occupy this position jointly, and judgment is common since we must all observe the same standards of justice. So Rawls characterizes it as a unanimous social agreement. Deliberative rationality, by contrast, is an individual perspective – the "point of view of the individual," to use Sidgwick's terms. Judgments there are made singly, by each individual; because our ends and circumstances differ, Rawls assumes our individual good must differ. There can be no thoroughgoing agreement on the human good, even under ideal conditions; pluralism of values is a fundamental feature of Rawls's view. Both perspectives are idealizations; neither takes individuals just as they are. Instead both artificially control the information available and constrain the judgments of those occupying these positions by normative principles: by rational principles in judgments of one's good, and by reasonable principles constraining rational judgment in case of judgments of justice. Finally, both perspectives purportedly specify objective points of view, providing a basis for true moral judgments of justice and true valuative judgments of any individual's good.

The *congruence argument* purports to show that under the ideal conditions of a well-ordered society, the judgments that would be made from these two ideal perspectives coincide: reasonable principles judged and willed as rational from the common perspective of justice are also judged and willed as rational from each individual's point of view. The basic question of congruence is: Is it rational in a well-ordered society of justice as fairness for persons to affirm individually, from the point of view of deliberative rationality, the principles of justice they would rationally agree to when they take up the public perspective of justice? If so, then it is rational for the members of a well-ordered society to make their sense of justice a regulative disposition within their rational plans, and justice becomes an essential part of each person's good. If Rawls can show this, then he has gone a long way towards resolving Sidgwick's "dualism of practical reason."[25] For then he will have shown that the point of view of the individual, defined by rational principles, and the impartial public perspective of justice, defined by reasonable principles, are not fundamentally at odds, as Sidgwick feared, but are "congruent."

The congruence problem is not to be confused with the traditional question whether it is rational to be just, *whatever* one's desires and situation. Many philosophers have argued, following Hume, that there is no necessary connection between rationality and justice. Given their supposition that rationality is simply taking effective means to whatever ends a person has, these arguments seem correct. For if it is assumed that people can want most anything, and that there may be people with absolutely no moral sentiments, then it is a truism that rationality does not require the pursuit of justice. Rawls seems to agree (TJ, 575/503–4 rev.). But this has little bearing on his argument. For Rawls has no interest in showing the rationality of justice whatever people's preferences.[26] His argument applies only to the favorable situation of a well-ordered society. And even then, it assumes that everyone in these circumstances already has an effective sense of justice, and so has prima facie reason to act on it.[27]

But if congruence already assumes so much, why is it relevant to the stability problem? If members of a well-ordered society normally have a sense of justice, why is that not already enough to prove stability? It is the very fact that a sense of justice is "a normal part of human life" (TJ, 489/428 rev.) that poses the problem addressed by the congruence argument. For nothing has been said yet which would show that our moral sense of justice is not "in many respects irrational and injurious to our good" (ibid.).

Several distinct problems arise once it is assumed that people have a desire to do what is just for its own sake:

(1) First, what is to assure us that our sense of justice is not entirely conventional, a peculiar product of our circumstances with no deeper basis in human tendencies? Or what is worse, the sense of justice may be illusional, grounded in false beliefs covertly instilled in us, either by those in power, or by our circumstances and social relations? People's suspicion that their sense of justice is arbitrary or manipulated in these ways can cause it to waver and subside, giving rise to social instability. The most forceful criticism of this kind is the Marxian argument that justice

is ideological, even incoherent, based on our affirming false values and living under distorting conditions.

(2) Second, Rawls says (*TJ*, ch. 8) that justice developmentally has its origins in a "morality of authority" which is acquired from our parents and upbringing. What guarantees that our sense of justice does not remain anchored in submission to authority and is simply an infantile abnegation of responsibility? Freud argues, for example, that our existing moral feelings may be in many ways punitive, based in self-hatred, and that they incorporate many of the harsher aspects of the authority situation in which these feelings were first acquired (cf. *TJ*, 489/428 rev.).

(3) Conservatives contend that the tendency to equality in modern social movements and democratic demands for redistribution are expressions of envy directed against those who are more gifted and successful at managing life and its contingencies. Envy masks a lack of self-worth and a sense of failure and weakness. Here Freud was more evenhanded. The sense of justice, he argued, has its origins in both the envy of the poor and in the jealousy of the rich to protect their advantages. As a compromise, the rich and the poor settle on the rule of equal treatment, and by a reaction-formation envy and jealousy are transformed into a sense of justice. If so, why does the sense of justice not have its source in these undesirable characteristics?

(4) Similarly Nietzsche argues that justice and morality are self-destructive sentiments, a kind of psychological catastrophe for us, requiring abnegation of the self and its higher capacities and a renunciation of important human purposes.

(5) Finally, most people reflectively affirm the value of sociability and of community. The things that are worth pursuing are not simply private ends purely for oneself. Many common ends can be shared, ends which people not only hold in common and achieve jointly, but where each person takes enjoyment in the participation of others in the same activity. (Family life, at its best, might achieve these shared ends, as can many other joint activities.)[28] Now, achieving justice requires a common effort. But acting for the sake of justice, while an end we might hold in common, is not on its face a *shared* end. Can justice also be shared as an end

where each recognizes the good of others and enjoys participating in and accomplishing this joint activity? Is there any value in being a *participating* member of a just society? How, in other words, can a theory of justice account for the values of community?

These are problems that any theory of justice needs to address. It may be that we want to do our duty of justice for its own sake; still, if these moral sentiments are grounded in illusions, defeat our primary purposes, prevent us from realizing important human goods, or require ways of acting that are inconsistent with human nature, then surely this is relevant to the justification of a conception of justice. These problems explain the peculiar array of arguments in chapter 9 of *Theory*. One role of the argument (in sect. 78) that justice as fairness allows for the *objectivity* of judgments of justice is to defuse the instability that would result if people thought their moral judgments of justice purely conventional, arbitrary, or grounded in illusion. The argument for autonomy (in sect. 78) shows that justice as fairness is not grounded in a self-debasing submission to authority. The argument (sects. 80–81) that feelings of excusable envy will not arise sufficient to undermine a well-ordered society indicates how justice as fairness does not encourage propensities and hopes that it is bound to repress and disappoint. And the account of social union (sect. 79) shows how justice as fairness can account for the good of community. What I will focus on here is a further argument for the congruence of justice with people's good, which responds to the Nietzschean objection, mentioned above, that justice is a self-destructive moral sentiment.

To do so, consider another important psychological principle Rawls uses to provide specific content to the concept of a person's good. By itself the "purely formal" (*TJ*, 424/372 rev.) or "thin theory of the good" in *Theory* says little about the kind of ends that people ought to pursue to make their lives worthwhile to them.[29] Rawls does not want to affirm the position that the object of just any desire can be part of a person's good. There are certain facts about human nature that make it irrational to have certain desires and ends, and rational to have others.

Rawls suggests a psychological law in chapter 7 of *Theory*, the "Aristotelian Principle." This principle involves a rather substantial claim about human nature. It says basically that we desire to exercise our higher human capacities and want to engage in complex and demanding activities for their own sake so long as they are within our reach.

> Other things equal, human beings enjoy the exercise of their realized capacities (their innate or trained abilities), and this enjoyment increases the more the capacity is realized, or the greater its complexity. The intuitive idea here is that human beings take more pleasure in doing something as they become more proficient at it, and of two activities they do equally well, they prefer the one calling on a larger repertoire of more intricate and subtle discriminations. For example, chess is a more complicated and subtle game than checkers, and algebra is more intricate than elementary arithmetic. Thus the principle says that someone who can do both generally prefers playing chess to playing checkers, and that he would rather study algebra than arithmetic.
>
> (*TJ*, 426/374 rev.)

The Aristotelian Principle does not imply an invariable pattern of choice. It states a natural tendency that may be overcome by countervailing inclinations, such as the desire for comfort and satisfying bodily needs. But it does imply, first, that once a certain threshold is met in satisfying these "lower pleasures" (to use Mill's term), a disposition to engage in activities that call for the exercise of our higher capacities takes over; and second, that individuals prefer higher activities of a kind, the more inclusive they are in engaging their educated abilities.

While this principle, like any psychological law, seems of limited use in explaining people's choices on particular occasions, it may be useful in explaining the more general aims and activities about which people structure their lives. Rawls's main contention is that, assuming the Aristotelian Principle characterizes human nature, then a plan of life is *rational* for a person *only* if it takes this principle into account. It is thus rational to train and realize our mature capacities, given the opportunity to do so. In conjunction with Rawls's account of a rational plan, this means that the plan of life rational persons would choose under deliberative rationality is one that allows a central place for the exercise and development of their higher abilities. As such, the Aristotelian Principle "accounts for our considered judgments of value. The things that are commonly thought of as human goods should turn out to be the ends and activities that have a major place in rational plans" (TJ, 432/379 rev.). This means that certain valued activities (Rawls mentions knowledge, creation and contemplation of beautiful objects, meaningful work; TJ, 425/373 rev.) are valued and thought of as human goods largely because they engage and call for the development of aspects of our nature that permit of complex development. We enjoy such activities for their own sake; that is what the Aristotelian Principle asserts. If so, then the exercise and development of at least some of one's higher capacities will be a part of most anyone's good.

Interestingly, the Aristotelian Principle introduces an element of perfectionism into Rawls's formal account of the good via a claim regarding human nature. The implication of this principle is that a person's good is not simply what he or she happens to desire and make part of a rational life plan. Rather, assuming a person has functioning human capacities that are not too far impaired, an important part of a person's good is engaging in activities that exercise and develop distinctly human capacities. It is a normal fact about human nature that we will not be satisfied, or will not "flourish," with a life plan that does not take into account the Aristotelian Principle.

This demand belies the objection that Rawls's account of the good is "subjectivist" or "desire-based" and that he puts no restrictions on the objects of desire that can be part of a person's good. This objection is sometimes based on Rawls's claim that it is at least possible that a person might rationally choose a life plan largely devoted to counting blades of grass, rather than engaging in any constructive activities exercising developed capacities (TJ, 432/379 rev.). Of course, we would want to know a lot about this person's psychological and physiological history before we could say it is part of his good. Perhaps he is autistic and is comforted by obsessional behavior that has a predictable course. In that case, it may well be good for that person, an appropriate way to exercise his capacities. Many philosophers, however, argue that part of the meaning of the concept of the good disqualifies such a life plan as a good life for any person. With Rawls, I think claims about the meaning of concepts are of little help in deriving substantive principles and values. It makes perfectly good sense (to me, being the father of an autistic child) to say that counting blades of grass can be a rational activity that is part of a person's good. For some people, this may just be all they can tolerate and the best they can do. For a perfectionist to say, on the basis of some supposed necessary truth, that such a life is not worth living is presumptuous (to say the least).

THE GOOD OF JUSTICE AND THE KANTIAN CONGRUENCE ARGUMENT

Now to consider Rawls's main argument for the good of justice.[30] A just person has the virtue of justice, which Rawls defines as a normally "regulative desire" to abide by reasons of justice in all of one's actions. Rawls's main argument for the rationality of this virtue aims to show that it is an intrinsic good. For the virtue of justice to be an intrinsic good means that exercise of the capacities for justice in appropriate settings is an activity worth doing for its own sake. The primary basis for making such an argument within Rawls's theory derives from the account of rational plans in conjunction with the Aristotelian Principle.

How then does the Aristotelian Principle fit into Rawls's congruence argument? In *Political Liberalism* Rawls says that in a well-ordered society, justice as fairness is a good for persons individually, because "the exercise of the two moral powers is experienced as a good. This is a consequence of the moral psychology used in justice as fairness. . . . In *Theory* this psychology uses the so-called Aristotelian Principle."[31]

This suggests that the congruence argument involves a straightforward appeal to the Aristotelian Principle. The idea here would be that the capacity for a sense of justice is among our higher capacities. It involves an ability to understand, apply, and act on and from requirements of justice (see TJ, 505/443 rev.). This capacity admits of complex development and refinement. Since all have a sense of justice in a well-ordered society, it is rational for each to develop it as part of his or her plan of life.

Consider now two objections. First, though all may have the same natural capacities, we have them to varying degrees. None of us can develop any capacity well without neglecting others. The capacities that are rational for people to develop depends on their natural endowments, their circumstances, their interests, and other factors. All that follows from the Aristotelian Principle is that it is rational for each to develop *some* higher capacities. If so, then the range of abilities individuals ought to develop will differ. How, then, can it be inferred that the capacity for justice should occupy a place in everyone's rational plan?[32] In what way does this higher capacity differ from the capacity for dance or sport, or other highly coordinated physical activity? Some of us might aim to develop these capacities, but others understandably do not.

A second objection: What warrants making the capacity for justice supremely regulative of *all* our pursuits? Suppose that, consistent with the Aristotelian Principle, I decide, like Kierkegaard's aesthete "A," to perfect my capacities for elegance and aesthetic appreciation.[33] I resolve to act in ways that are aesthetically appropriate, according to received rules of style and etiquette. Is there anything intrinsic to my sense of justice that would make it regulative of this disposition? Why could I not, consistent with the Aristotelian Principle, just as well make my sense of elegance supremely regulative, sacrificing justice when it conflicts with aesthetic norms? More generally, what is to prevent my giving weight to my sense of justice only according to its relative intensity, and subordinating it to stronger dispositions, weighing off my concern for justice against other final ends in ordinary ways?

The simplified argument from the Aristotelian Principle is not Rawls's argument for congruence. But it is extremely difficult to piece together what his argument is. One way to uncover his argument is to conjecture how he would respond to the two objections above. The answers he gives depend on the Kantian conception of the person built into Rawls's view.

According to the "Kantian Interpretation" of justice as fairness (TJ, sect. 40), and what Rawls later calls "Kantian Constructivism,"[34] justice is construed as those principles that would be justified to and accepted by everyone under conditions that characterize them as "free and equal moral persons" (or "free and equal rational beings," in TJ, 252/222 rev.). The original position specifies these conditions; it is a "procedural interpretation" of our nature as free and equal rational beings (TJ, 256/226 rev.).[35] Rawls says that by acting from the principles that would be chosen from this standpoint,

> persons express their nature as free and equal rational beings subject to the general conditions of human life. For to express one's nature as a being of a particular kind is to act on the principles that would be chosen if this nature were the decisive determining element. . . . One *reason* for [acting from the principles of justice], for persons who can do so and want to, is to *give expression to one's nature.*
>
> (*TJ*, 252–53/222 rev., emphases added)

Conjoining this conception of the person with the formal account of rationality and the Aristotelian Principle, the focal points of Rawls's Kantian argument for congruence are apparently as follows:[36]

(1) On the Kantian interpretation, persons, regarded as moral agents, are by their nature free and equal rational beings (TJ, 252/222 rev.); or, the same idea in Theory, "free and equal moral persons" (TJ, 565/495 rev.).[37] Rational agents in a well-ordered society (WOS) conceive of themselves in this way "as primarily moral persons" (TJ, 563/493 rev.).[38]

(2) Rational members of a WOS "desire to express their nature as free and equal moral persons" (TJ, 528/462–63 rev., 572/501 rev.). (Rawls evidently sees this as a non-arbitrary rational desire.) Combined with the formal account of a person's good under the thin theory, this implies,

(3) Members of a WOS desire to have a rational plan of life consistent with their nature; which implies, in turn, a "fundamental preference . . . for conditions that enable [them] to frame a

mode of life that expresses [their] nature as free and equal rational beings" (TJ, 561/491 rev.).

(4) Having a plan of life compatible with the desire to express their nature as free and equal rational beings requires that persons act from principles that "would be chosen if this nature were the decisive determining element" (TJ, 253/222 rev.). This is the original position: it specifies conditions that characterize or "represent" individuals as free and equal moral persons on the Kantian Interpretation (TJ, 252, 515, 528/221, 452, 462–63 rev.).[39]

(5) On its standard interpretation, the original position is designed to "make vivid to ourselves the restrictions that it seems reasonable to impose on arguments for principles of justice" (TJ, 18/16 rev.). It embodies fair conditions of equality that you and I (presumably) find appropriate for an agreement on principles to regulate the basic structure of society.

(6) The normally effective desire to apply and act upon principles that would be agreed to from an original position of equality is the sense of justice (TJ, 312/275 rev.; 478/418 rev.).

(7) Taken together, 4–6 suggest that the desire to act in ways that "express one's nature" as a free and equal rational being is "practically speaking" the same desire as the desire to act upon principles of justice acceptable from an original position of equality (TJ, 572/501 rev.).[40]

(8) So, for individuals in a WOS to achieve their rational desire to realize their nature as free and equal rational beings requires that they act on and from their sense of justice (TJ, 574/503 rev.).

(9) By the Aristotelian Principle, it is rational to realize one's nature by affirming the sense of justice. "From the Aristotelian Principle it follows that this expression of their nature is a fundamental element of [the] good" of individuals in a well-ordered society (TJ, 445/390 rev.).[41]

(10) The sense of justice is, by virtue of its content (what it is a desire for) a supremely regulative disposition: it requires giving strict priority to the principles of right and justice in reasoning and action (TJ, 574/503 rev.).

(11) To affirm the sense of justice is to recognize and accept it as supreme by adopting it as a highest-order regulative desire in one's rational plan.[42]

(12) To have justice as a highest-order end is the most adequate expression of our nature as free and equal rational beings, and is to be morally autonomous (cf. TJ, 515/452 rev.). Autonomy is then an intrinsic good for free and equal moral persons.

In (9) the role of the Aristotelian Principle here is to suggest that it is intrinsic to persons' good to realize their nature as free and equal rational beings. Just as crucial, however, are (7), identifying the sense of justice with the desire to realize one's nature, and (10) and (11), establishing the priority of the sense of justice in rational plans. (7) is important since by connecting the sense of justice with our "nature" (I will discuss what this means), (7) establishes that the desire to act justly is not psychologically degenerate.[43] If it were, the sense of justice clearly would not warrant affirming as an intrinsic good. It might even be better not to have this desire, assuming we could get along in society without it. But if the sense of justice can be shown to belong to our nature, then Rawls can contend that by affirming it we exercise a capacity that is fundamental to our being. Since (by the Aristotelian Principle) persons' expressing their nature as free and equal rational beings "belongs to their good, the sense of justice aims at their well-being" (TJ, 476/417 rev.).

The sense of justice "belongs to our nature" in the following sense: In Theory Rawls endorses Kant's position that persons are free, equal, and rational, and that in a well-ordered society they publicly regard themselves as such. The "nature" of free, equal, and rational beings is their "moral personality" (TJ, sects. 77, 85). Moral personality is defined by the moral powers; these are the capacities for practical reasoning as applied to matters of justice. They include (a) a capacity for a sense of justice: to understand, to apply, and to act on and from requirements and principles of justice, as well as (b) a capacity for a conception of the good: to form, to revise, and to pursue a rational plan of life.[44]

These capacities are central to human agency. Rawls's idea is that from a practical point of view, when acting as rational and moral agents, we regard ourselves and others as free agents, capable of determining our actions, adjusting our wants, and shaping our ends, all according to the demands of rational and moral principles: "Since we view persons as capable of mastering and adjusting their wants and desires, they are held responsible for doing so."[45] The bases for persons' conception of themselves as free and responsible moral agents and as equals are the moral powers.[46] A person without these capacities is not recognized by others as answerable for his or her acts or ends (morally or legally), or deemed capable of taking an active part in social cooperation.[47] Moreover, we do not see our lives as a matter of happenstance, simply imposed on us by our situations. Instead, within the limits of the circumstances we confront, we normally see our actions and lives as under our control. It is by virtue of the capacities for moral personality that we are able to decide what ends and activities we should pursue, and can fashion these ends into a coherent and cooperative life-plan that accords with principles of rational choice and principles of justice. So it is by virtue of the moral powers, as capacities to act upon rational and moral principles, we are able to give "unity" to our lives, and so to our selves, by adopting and pursuing a rational plan of life.[48]

It is because of their central role in making possible our agency that Rawls says that the moral powers "constitute our nature" as moral persons. "Moral person" and "moral personality" (terms used by Locke and Kant) are to be understood broadly in that they refer to agents and their capacities for both moral and rational agency. To say these powers "constitute our nature" does not carry any metaphysical overtones for Rawls. It means simply that, when regarded in our capacity as agents who are engaged in planning our pursuits in social contexts, most important to our being an agent for these purposes are the moral powers. Contrast thinking of oneself purely naturalistically, as a physical organism or object whose behavior is determined by a combination of forces. This is not how we see ourselves in practical contexts when engaged in deliberation and action, even if some of us might in other contexts think of ourselves purely naturalistically. That persons are free and responsible agents, capable of controlling their wants and answering for their actions, is something we just assume from a practical standpoint. It provides our orientation in the realm of human activity. And it is hard to see how it could be any other way. For otherwise we must see ourselves and one another as natural objects, beyond the realm of responsibility.

The centrality of the capacity for a sense of justice to the self-conception of moral and rational agents underlies Rawls's claim (in (7)) that the sense of justice and the desire to express one's nature are "practically speaking the same desire." This supports (8), the conclusion that to realize one's "nature" (or practical self-conception) requires acting on and from the sense of justice. This addresses the first objection (raised above), namely, how can everyone have sufficient reason, even assuming the Aristotelian Principle, to develop and exercise their capacity for justice? What distinguishes it from other capacities (like the capacity for dance, poetry, or higher math) which we may not have reason to develop depending on our choice and circumstances? The answer is that development of the sense of justice (along with the capacity for a conception of the good) is a condition of persons being rational moral agents who are capable of assuming responsibility for their actions and taking part in and benefiting from social life. People who do not develop their capacities for dance, poetry, or higher math, while they may miss out on worthwhile activities, can nonetheless lead equally good lives engaged in other pursuits. But those whose moral capacities for justice and the capacity to be rational remain undeveloped are not capable of social life. They are not, then, in a position to achieve the benefits of society and will be hard pressed to learn and pursue most any worthwhile way of life.

FINALITY AND THE PRIORITY OF JUSTICE

The second objection above was: Even if we assume justice is a good, why should it be regulative of all other values and pursuits? Acting according to the demands of justice expresses our practical nature as free and equal rational beings on Rawls's Kantian interpretation (TJ, 252/222 rev.). This goes some way towards responding to this objection. Still, people have ends and commitments which they believe are equally if not more important than justice or expressing their nature, and often they have more pressing desires to act for these ends. Rawls says, "A perfectly just society should be part of an ideal that rational human beings could *desire more than anything else* once they had full knowledge and experience of what it was" (*TJ*, 477/418 rev., emphasis added). But given the multiple aims and commitments that people care about, how is it realistically possible for this to be true?

The problem here is assigning the appropriate position to developing the sense of justice within rational plans of life of people who are morally motivated and want to be just persons. How should their sense of justice be situated in relation to other final ends and within their "hierarchy of desires"? Rawls says that, in drawing up a rational plan, final ends and fundamental desires need to be organized and combined into one scheme of conduct (see *TJ*, 410–11/360–61 rev.). Sometimes, after taking into account all relevant reasons and considerations (including the Aristotelian Principle), critical deliberation upon reasons might run out, at which point the rational choice may just be to decide according to the intensity of desire (*TJ*, 416/435 rev.): "The real problem of congruence is what happens if we imagine someone to give weight to his sense of justice only to the extent that it satisfies other descriptions which connect it with reasons specified by the thin theory of the good" (*TJ*, 569/499 rev.). I interpret this passage as follows: Suppose a person is morally motivated by a sense of justice and is trying to decide how to fit considerations of justice into her life-plan. She wants to be a just person, yet she also aims to be loyal to her family and friends, successful in her career, devoted to her religion, and an accomplished amateur musician. These are the primary ends that provide structure to her life. What happens if, after full deliberation, she assigns the sense of justice a position of importance alongside other final ends, and weighs it off against them in ordinary ways, sometimes even relying on the relative felt intensity of desires to resolve conflicts among her final ends? If people generally reasoned this way and it were publicly known, then people could not have the kind of assurance regarding others' actions that is needed for a well-ordered society to be stable in Rawls's sense. Ultimately, the congruence argument, to succeed, must show that it is contrary to reason to weigh the sense of justice off against other ends "in ordinary ways." It needs to be shown that it is rational to give the sense of justice a *highest-order* position in rational plans. It should have "regulative priority" over all other ultimate ends and activities that make up rational plans.

One way to argue for assigning priority to a disposition is to establish that it is a desire to be a certain kind of person. Part of the content of this desire is that a person's first-order desires (desires for particular objects) conform to an ideal that a person aspires to. Given the content of the desire to live up to this ideal, one cannot achieve the ideal if the desire is balanced off against other desires. Rawls conceives of the sense of justice in a similar way: "[A]n effective sense of justice . . . is not a desire on the same footing with natural inclinations; it is an executive and regulative highest-order desire to act from certain principles of justice in view of their connection with a conception of the person as free and equal" ("Kantian Constructivism," in CP, 320). As a higher-order regulative desire, the sense of justice cannot be weighed off against first-order desires "in ordinary ways." Still, Rawls needs to say more than this. For people have other regulative desires too, such as the desire to be courteous or elegant. What gives the sense of justice priority over these higher-order desires? (This is the question raised by Kierkegaard's aesthete, who chooses to be elegant above all other ideals.) Rawls contends that, unlike all other desires, there is something special about the desire to be a just person that makes it *supremely regulative* of all other desires, *independent* of a person's desires or choices:

> This is a consequence of the condition of finality: since these principles [of justice] are regulative, the desire to act upon them is satisfied only to the extent that it is likewise regulative with respect to other desires. . . . This sentiment cannot be fulfilled if it is compromised and balanced against other ends as but one desire among the rest. It is a desire to conduct oneself in a cer-

tain way above all else, a striving that contains within itself its own priority. Other aims can be achieved by a plan that allows a place for each, since their satisfaction is possible independent of

their place in the ordering. But this is not the case with the sense of right and justice.

(*TJ*, 574/503 rev.)

As a desire to act on the principles of justice, the sense of justice is subject to the condition of finality implicit within these principles. Finality requires that considerations of justice have absolute priority over all other reasons in practical deliberation (reasons of prudence, self-interest, private benevolence, etiquette, and so on) (TJ, 135/116–17 rev.). Given this condition, persons cannot fulfill their desire for justice if they balance it off against other desired ends, even other final ends, according to their relative intensity or in other ways. To do that would compromise what this desire is a desire for. The sense of justice in effect is a desire that *all* one's desires and their aims conform to the regulative requirements of justice. On its face the sense of justice reveals itself as a supremely governing disposition. We can satisfy what this desire is a desire for only if we assign justice highest priority in our activities. Moreover, given the practical identity of the sense of justice with the desire to express our nature (see (6) above), we cannot "express our nature by following a plan that views the sense of justice as but one desire to be weighed off against others" (TJ, 575/503 rev.). "Therefore in order to realize our nature we have no alternative but to plan to preserve our sense of justice as governing our other aims" (TJ, 574/503 rev.).

One final claim ((12) above) and the congruence argument is complete: What does it mean to realize the conception of the person as a free and equal rational being within one's rational plan? Rawls says, "Kant held, I believe, that a person is acting autonomously when the principles of his action are chosen by him as the most adequate possible expression of his nature as a free and equal rational being" (TJ, 252/222 rev.; cf. TJ, 584/511 rev.). On the Kantian interpretation of justice as fairness, Rawls assumes that citizens in a well-ordered society "regard moral personality . . . as the fundamental aspect of the self" (*TJ*, 563/493 rev.); as a result they desire to be fully autonomous agents. Autonomy, on Rawls's Kantian account, requires acting for the sake of principles that we accept, not because of our particular circumstances, talents, or ends, or due to allegiance to tradition, authority, or the opinion of others, but because these principles give expression to our common nature as free and equal rational beings (*TJ*, 252/222 rev.; 515–16/452 rev.). By affirming their sense of justice, members of a well-ordered society accomplish their conception of themselves as free, i.e., as moral agents who are free from the eventualities of their circumstances, their upbringing, and their social position. "Acting from this precedence [of the sense of justice] expresses our freedom from contingency and happenstance" (*TJ*, 574/503 rev.). And this in part is to be autonomous. So, "When the principles of justice . . . are *affirmed* and acted upon by equal citizens in society, citizens then act with full autonomy."[49] Full autonomy (as opposed to simply "rational autonomy," or acting from a freely chosen rational life plan that is one's own) is, then, the ultimate consequence of persons realizing their nature when they assign the sense of justice highest-order priority in their rational plans. This means, given the rest of Rawls's argument, that autonomy is an intrinsic good. So Rawls concludes: "[T]his sentiment [of justice] reveals what the person is, and to compromise it is not to achieve for the self free rein but to give way to the contingencies and accidents of the world" (*TJ*, 575/503 rev.). It reveals "what the person is" practically, *as* a moral agent, and so to compromise it is to compromise one's free agency.

CONCLUSION

Rawls regards justice as a distinctly human activity that renders society and political, economic, and other relations within society possible. He then aims to work out a conception of justice that is compatible with human nature and affirms individuals' pursuit of their good. The role of the argument for the stability of justice as fairness is to "confirm" that the choice of the principles of justice in the original position meets these conditions. The argument does so by showing how a well-ordered society of justice as fairness – a society in which all reasonable persons affirm and act on and from the principles of justice – is realistically possible. First, assuming that the reciprocity principles express psychological tendencies implicit in human nature, people appropriately raised to be citizens in a just society by people who care for them will normally acquire a sense of justice and willingness to support just institutions. Then, given this settled disposition, it is rational for citizens to exercise their sense of justice, not simply to avoid sanctions and maintain good reputations, but for its own sake. For in acting for the sake of justice they realize their nature as free and equal rational and autonomous beings. Justice is, then, congruent with the human good in a well-ordered society. Since doing justice is everyone's best response to these circumstances, justice as fairness is inherently stable. This is an important conclusion. It means that the contractarian ideal of a well-ordered society in which free and equal citizens all agree upon and affirm the same conception of justice is within human reach.

FURTHER READING

Hill, Thomas, E., Jr., "The Stability Problem in *Political Liberalism*," *Pacific Philosophical Quarterly*, 75 (1994), 332–52. (Stability argument in Rawls's later work.)

McClennen, Edward F., "Justice and the Problem of Stability," *Philosophy and Public Affairs*, 19 (1990), 122–57. (General account of the idea of stability in Rawls and in game theory.)

Sachs, David, "How to Distinguish Self-Respect from Self-Esteem," *Philosophy and Public Affairs*, 10 (1981), 346–60. (Well-known account which led Rawls to clarify his position.)

Seven

Kantian Constructivism and the Transition to Political Liberalism

This chapter discusses Rawls's main new works between the publication of *A Theory of Justice* in 1971 and 1985, when Rawls began a series of papers (CP, chs. 18, 20–22) that are incorporated into *Political Liberalism* (1993). During the 1970s much work was devoted to clarifying and defending TJ (see CP, chs. 11–14). But Rawls also further developed the Kantian interpretation of justice as fairness in three lectures entitled "Kantian Constructivism in Moral Theory" (1980; CP ch. 16). These lectures, discussed in the first section below, are a transition stage in Rawls's work; he brings to full fruition the Kantian and contractarian aspects of his theory of justice, and at the same time begins the transition to *Political Liberalism* (1993).[1] Rawls's paper "The Independence of Moral Theory," discussed in the second section below, also is an important transition piece; he argues that moral philosophy is largely independent of epistemology and metaphysics. As seen in the next chapter, *Political Liberalism* takes this idea a step further, and argues for the independence of political philosophy from comprehensive philosophical, moral, and religious views. The third section below discusses the problems Rawls finds in his Kantian interpretation of justice as fairness. These are the problems he seeks to rectify in *Political Liberalism* to sustain his contractarian ideal of a well-ordered society whose citizens agree on the same conception of justice.

KANTIAN CONSTRUCTIVISM

In section 40 of *A Theory of Justice*, Rawls cryptically says that acting on and from the principles of justice might be regarded as an "expression" of the nature of free and equal rational beings. "For to express one's nature as a being of a particular kind is to act on the principles that would be chosen if this nature were the decisive determining element" (TJ, 253/222 rev., emphasis added). What is missing from Kant, Rawls continues, is an identifiable way in which acting from the moral law can be an "expression" of our nature (TJ, 255/224 rev.).

> This defect is made good, I believe, by the conception of the original position. . . . The description of the original position resembles the point of view of noumenal selves, of what it means to be a free and equal rational being. Our nature as such beings is *displayed* when we act from the principles we would choose *when this nature is reflected in the conditions determining the choice.* Thus men exhibit their freedom, their independence from the contingencies of nature and society, by acting in ways they would acknowledge in the original position.
> (*TJ*, 255–56/224–25 rev., emphasis added)

This suggestion, then, is that the original position might be construed as a reflection of fundamental features of free and equal rational moral beings. Because the original position "resembles . . . what it means to be a free and equal rational being," the principles chosen therein "display" or "express" their nature. Kantian Constructivism incorporates this basic idea and seeks to translate and explicate it in a more perspicuous idiom.

Moral Personality and the Basis of Equality

In *A Theory of Justice* Rawls first appeals to the idea of free and equal rational beings to establish the basis for equality. On what grounds do persons as such warrant respect as equals and equal justice? A utilitarian or welfarist might say that it is people's equal capacities for happiness or well-being that entitle them to equal justice. For Kant it is the capacity for "humanity," which is our practical reason, including the rational capacity to "set ends" for ourselves and act upon them. Similarly, Rawls contends (TJ, sect.

77) that the basis of equal justice is "the capacity for moral personality," which includes the two moral powers: first, a capacity for a conception of the good expressed by a rational plan of life; and second, a capacity for a sense of justice, "a normally effective desire to apply and to act upon the principles of justice, at least to a certain minimum degree" (TJ, 505/442 rev.). These are purely natural characteristics, Rawls says, which people develop to some degree in the normal course of social life. In *Political Liberalism* Rawls says that having these characteristics to some degree is essential to taking part in, and gaining the full benefits of, social cooperation.

Rawls in *Political Liberalism* does not seem to regard the centrality of the moral powers to social cooperation as a controversial claim, for he does not argue for it. His assumption appears to be that a person who is without a developed capacity for a conception of the good cannot make effective judgments regarding what is in his or her interest. Such persons are normally judged legally incompetent, incapable of taking care of themselves and their interests. Children are legally regarded this way, as are the mentally handicapped – they are without the capacity to be rational to the degree necessary to take care of their own affairs. Limitations upon their freedom and other paternalistic measures are thought to be entirely appropriate. Similarly with respect to a capacity for a sense of justice, a lack of the capacity to distinguish between right and wrong has long been regarded as the primary mark of legal insanity in the Anglo-American legal system. Under contemporary standards one who can distinguish between right and wrong but is still unable to exercise self-control and conform to moral or legal standards might also be considered immune from legal responsibility and legal sanction.

Rawls contends that having the moral powers *to a minimum degree* is sufficient to warrant respect as a person and equal justice. "The minimal requirements defining moral personality refer to a capacity and not to the realization of it. A being that has this capacity, whether or not it is yet developed, is to receive the full protection of the principles of justice" (TJ, 509/445–46 rev.). Importantly, Rawls says that having to a minimal degree the moral powers is *sufficient* to warrant equal justice (*TJ*, 505/442 rev.). He does not say that it is also *necessary* to have these powers to warrant respect or moral consideration. Rawls does not want to foreclose affording justice to the incapacitated and incompetent, but it would have to be for other reasons than their moral personality. He says, "Whether moral personality is a necessary condition is a question I shall leave aside . . . Even if the capacity were necessary, it would be unwise in practice to withhold justice on this ground. The risk to just institutions would be too great" (*TJ*, 505–06/442–43 rev.). This is purely a pragmatic reason for affording justice to the mentally impaired. Here one might object that they deserve moral consideration for their own sake, simply because they are human beings and even if they are without the moral powers to the requisite degree. While this is, I believe, compatible with Rawls's view, Rawls evidently feels he does not need to address fully this question in his theory of *social* justice, given its more limited aims. Rawls has been criticized on grounds that he does not adequately account for the respect and duties of justice we owe to the mentally and physically impaired.[2]

Later, in *The Law of Peoples*, we'll see that Rawls indirectly addresses these issues, when he distinguishes social justice from humanitarian justice, and distinguishes the liberal rights protected by his principles of justice from human rights. Among human rights are the right to life and to means of subsistence, freedom from involuntary servitude, the right to own property, a degree of freedom of speech and of conscience, etc. Human rights apply to humans *as such* without regard to their capacities for moral personality. An incompetent person without the moral powers clearly enjoys the protection of human rights for Rawls. What is the difference between humanitarian justice and social justice? One difference is that Rawls regards *social justice* as focused primarily upon discovering terms of *social cooperation* among people who are capable of taking part in cooperation and doing their fair share to sustain it. Having the moral powers is necessary to taking part in social cooperation; this I believe explains Rawls's focus on the conception of moral personality, both early and late. Principles of humanitarian justice, on the other hand, extend to human beings generally, without regard to whether one stands in cooperative relations with them. They set forth the necessary minimum (Rawls does not say sufficient) degree of respect that we owe to members of the human species as such. There are other duties of justice and duties of benevolence or charity we owe them as well.

Moral Personality and Autonomy as Basis for Construction

On the Kantian interpretation, we've seen, Rawls makes a more substantial claim – namely, that the moral powers constitute "our nature as free and equal rational persons" (TJ, 256/226 rev.). This is clearly more controversial than is the empirical claim that the moral powers are necessary for social cooperation and part of our social and legal practices of holding people responsible. It is a philosophical claim based in a (Kantian) conception of the foundations of rational moral agency. This philosophical claim regarding rational moral agency underlies Rawls's congruence argument and his effort to show that, by acting on and from the principles of justice, we act upon principles that are an "expression of our nature as free and equal rational persons." To completely realize the capacity for a sense of justice is to be morally autonomous; to completely realize the capacity for a rational conception of the good is to be rationally autonomous. A person who is both, has "full autonomy" (CP, 315).

In Kantian Constructivism, Rawls seeks to show in detail how justice as fairness can be interpreted as grounded in moral personality and the capacities for rational moral agency. Kant's idea of autonomy is developed from Rousseau's idea of moral freedom (la liberté morale)[3] or "acting on a law that one gives to oneself," to which Kant adds "out of one's reason" (cf. TJ, 256/225 rev.). How should we understand Kant's enigmatic notion of reason legislating a law for itself? This in effect is what Rawls is trying to exhibit in Kantian Constructivism; he aims to provide, as he says in Theory, a "procedural interpretation of Kant's conception of autonomy" (TJ, 256/226 rev.). The moral powers – the capacities to be reasonable and rational – are the capacities for practical reason applied to justice. In Kantian Constructivism, Rawls seeks to show how the principles of justice are "constructed," via a "procedure of construction" (CP, 305), from these capacities and other relevant principles and ideas of reason. This is the main point of Kantian Constructivism, construed as an attempt to work out, in the context of justice as fairness, Kant's notion of moral and rational autonomy, conceived broadly as reason giving principles to itself out of its own resources.

This is a distinct idea of autonomy. In liberal thought, "autonomy" usually suggests freedom of choice and/or freedom from external control, but in philosophy the idea is given different meanings. One sense of autonomy involves a person's freely deciding, upon critical reflection, his or her aims and pursuits, and enacting the courses of action and ways of life needed to achieve them. This resembles J.S. Mill's idea of "individuality," an ideal of "self-government" and "self-development," and making our beliefs, desires, and plans of life "our own." An autonomous person in this sense does not take her conception of a good life from others. She actively creates her own "life plan" based upon her own desires and interests, after critical reflection upon them and their consequences.

Mill's idea of individuality resembles in many respects Rawls's account of rational autonomy in shaping a rational plan of life, discussed in the preceding chapter. To live a "rational plan of life" that takes into account the Aristotelian Principle and that would be chosen in "deliberative rationality" is an ideal of a rational person for Rawls. Rawls does not mean to stipulate, as a matter of the thin theory of the good, Mill's ideal of individuality, or say that engaging in critical deliberation and living a rational life plan one has freely chosen is an intrinsic good that is essential to living a good life. This is a highly controversial claim. Even if rational autonomy is an intrinsic good – any life plan is better if freely chosen upon critical reflection – to say it is *essential* to a good life, as Mill suggests, seems to imply that J.S. Bach's life as a composer was not a good life. (For generations male members of the Bach family were expected and raised to become church or town musicians.)

While not making this controversial claim, Rawls, I believe, at least intimates that whatever a person's good otherwise might be, it is rational, or better for that person to arrive at it by engaging in critical reflection upon ends and freely exercising the rational powers. For the implicit suggestion in A Theory of Justice is that both rational and moral autonomy – the full development and exercise and engagement of the two moral powers – are intrinsic goods, necessary to fully realizing our nature as free rational moral agents.

Rawls, following Kant, has in another respect an even fuller conception of autonomy than Mill. Mill's account of individuality requires "self-government" according to rules of justice. But unlike Rawls he does not endorse Kant's idea that reason provides its own principles to itself, out of its own resources. "Full autonomy" for Rawls involves moral as well as rational autonomy – the exercise and development for its own sake of our capacity for justice according to moral principles of justice that have their origin in practical reason. In Kantian Constructivism, Rawls rejects "rational intuitionism" and other forms of moral realism, which say that moral principles are read off from the world as facts independent of human reasoning. Nor are moral principles given to us by God, or by our emotions or our culture (as divine command theory, moral sense theory, and cultural relativism respectively maintain). Instead, Rawls endeavors to show in Kantian Constructivism how reasonable moral principles of justice are principles of practical reason itself; they can be construed as "constructed" out of practical reason with their "origins" in the moral powers. Full autonomy means for Rawls, in its complete sense, that rational moral agents (1) act according to a rational plan of life they have individually created as their own in the free exercise of their critical capacities for deliberative rationality; (2) that this rational plan is subordinated to and regulated by principles of justice that are affirmed for their own sake, (3) where these principles would be chosen in the original position, a "procedure of construction" that incorporates "all the relevant requirements of practical reason," (4) among the requirements of which are "representations" of the ideas (also products of practical reason) of persons as free and equal, reasonable and rational beings, and of a well-ordered society of such persons, all of whom freely accept the same principles of justice. This ideal of full autonomy supplies the general background to Rawls's Kantian Constructivism, which aims to exhibit how moral principles of justice originate in the exercise of practical reason itself.

Moral Constructivism and Objectivity

There are different kinds of constructivist positions in ethics; Rawls's Kantian Constructivism and his later political constructivism are but two possibilities. Generally speaking constructivism in ethics addresses what is traditionally regarded as a "metaethical" (or metaphysical) question regarding the possibility and nature of moral truth or similar standards of correctness ("reasonableness" for Rawls, or "universal validity" in Kant). As opposed to moral realism, constructivism denies that moral statements correspond to antecedent moral facts or to a realm of values that are prior to and independent of practical reasoning. Rawls's examples of realist positions are the Platonism of the logical atomists such as G.E. Moore and Bertrand Russell, and Sidgwick's Philosophical Intuitionism (CP, 344–45). As opposed to moral skepticism, which denies moral truths or objective standards of correctness (e.g., "expressivism" says that moral statements are expressions of feelings), constructivism affirms that there are truth conditions for moral statements. Finally, as opposed to relativistic conceptions which say that moral judgments only apply to a particular society's members and are relative to its norms and conventions,[4] moral constructivism affirms a universal conception of moral objectivity and applies fundamental moral principles to all persons capable of understanding moral requirements, no matter how culturally situated. The fact that justice as fairness relies upon our considered convictions of justice as members of a democratic society does not mean that Rawls endorses cultural relativism. He is not saying, as a cultural relativist might, that the appropriate morality for any society is the principles that are in reflective equilibrium with its members' considered convictions of justice. Rawls thinks in Theory that justice as fairness applies to ascertain the degree of justice or injustice in any society, regardless of how people there think of themselves.

While there are different kinds of moral constructivism, they share in common the idea that moral principles are correct (true or reasonable) when they are the outcome of a deliberative procedure that incorporates all relevant criteria of correct reasoning.[5] In this regard, constructivism affords priority to the *objectivity of judgment* in determining moral truth: true moral judgments are those made by correctly reasoning from an *objective point of view*, which incorporates "all the relevant requirements of practical reasoning" (PL, 90). It is because the constructivist deliberative procedure incorporates the formal and substantive requirements of practical reasoning that the procedure has its "truth-bestowing" status. Unlike moral realism or rational intuitionism, there is no standard for correctness, independent of reasoning correctly from this objective point of view and the principles it implies. Rawls expresses this point by saying that justice as fairness regards principles of justice as a product of pure procedural justice at the highest level. In effect, objectivity of judgment sets the standards for moral truth. By contrast, realism reverses this priority and explains the objectivity of judgments in terms of their satisfying the conditions needed for ascertaining prior moral truths. In this regard moral constructivism rejects moral realism's claim that morally true or correct judgments in some manner represent moral facts or moral principles or values that are prior to practical reasoning. Apart from reasoning in terms of the deliberative procedure for constructing moral principles "there are no moral facts," Rawls says.[6] Objectivity is, as it were, prior to the universe of moral "objects."[7]

Constructivist accounts differ primarily in their accounts of practical reason's requirements that are to be incorporated into the procedure for "constructing" moral principles. Most, but not all, contractarian conceptions are constructivist.[8] Hobbesians rely upon a conception of practical reason as individual utility maximization along with a conception of human nature as largely self-focused and indifferent to others. John Harsanyi's utilitarian choice procedure (discussed earlier in Chapter 3) relies upon a similar utility-maximizing account of practical rationality, conjoined with a thin veil of ignorance and a Bayesian assumption of equiprobability insuring equal consideration of everyone's interests. T.M. Scanlon's contractualism eschews altogether the idea of rationality as utility maximization; his co-deliberators have interests and ends they aim to protect, but they are morally motivated to justify themselves to others on terms no one could reasonably reject. In his Lectures on the History of Moral Philosophy, Rawls demonstrates how Kant's categorical imperative is a non-contractarian constructivist procedure that tests individuals' rules of action ("maxims") by asking whether they could be consistently willed as universal laws. Finally, for Rawls, among the "relevant requirements of practical reason" (PL, 90) to be incorporated into his "procedure of construction" – the original position – are ideal conceptions of persons as free, equal, and reasonable and rational, and of society as well-ordered by a public conception of justice that all accept. The aim of moral constructivism for Rawls is to show how moral principles of justice are "constructed" from these and other relevant ideas of reason and principles of practical reason. On the assumption that all relevant requirements of practical reasoning have been incorporated into the original position, the moral principles of justice agreed to there can be said to be among the requirements of practical reason.

It is by incorporating an ideal of moral persons and a well-ordered society that Rawls integrates features of Kant's view into Kantian Constructivism. He refers to these conceptions of the person and society as "model-conceptions," and says they are analogous to "Ideas of Reason" in Kant, in so far as they are moral ideals that are not given to us by nature, rational intuition, or divination, but are the product of our human reasoning. In Kantian Constructivism Rawls depicts the various features of the original position (the veil of ignorance, for example) as a "representation" of the Kantian conceptions of free and equal moral persons and of a well-ordered society. To do so, Rawls first sets forth the relevant features of the ideal of moral persons. Moral persons are persons who have the two moral powers and who consequently regard themselves as free and as equal. Having the moral powers means that moral persons are rational since they have a capacity to form, revise, and pursue a conception of the good; and also they are reasonable since they have a capacity for a sense of justice, including the abilities to understand, apply, and follow requirements of principles of justice.

Freedom and Equality of Moral Persons

In what regards are moral persons free and equal? Rawls says that moral persons are *equal* in that they regard one another as having an *equal right* to determine the first principles of justice (CP, 309). This resembles Locke's idea of natural political equality, the idea that persons are born with a right of equal political jurisdiction and are not politically subordinate.[9] For this reason Locke says political power can only be based in consent. Moral persons are also equal in that their moral powers are effective: they are capable of understanding and complying with the public conception of justice in their society, as well as forming and revising a conception of the good, and in general being full participants in social cooperation throughout their lives.

Moral persons are *free* in three ways; first, they have the moral power to have a conception of the good, and they have final ends to pursue. One might ask, "What makes them free in this regard, for their conception of the good might be imposed upon them by the force of convention?" Rawls says what makes them free is that they are "independent": they do not think of themselves as inevitably tied to a particular conception of the good, but see themselves as capable of revising and changing their final ends and pursuits. (Communitarians question this condition.) Second, moral persons are free in that they believe themselves entitled to make claims on social and political institutions in the name of their fundamental aims and interests – they are "self-originating sources of claims," with respect to social and political institutions (CP, 309, 330–33). This means in part that they do not see their conception of the good as imposed upon them by, or its worth contingent upon, the State or other coercive authority. Third, moral persons are free in that they assume responsibility for their ends. They do not see their ends as foisted upon them by nature or by desires and impulses beyond their control. They are capable of adjusting and revising their aims and ambitions in light of what they can reasonably expect as their fair share of society's resources, and they do not believe the weight of their claims on others is given by the strength and intensity of their desires (CP, 332). So the fact that a person has expensive tastes is not regarded as a reason for making a claim against the rest of society to meet those expensive tastes. People are held responsible for regulating the demands they impose on others.

Notice that none of the three ways in which moral persons are free suggests that they are independent of natural causes or conditioning – that they have a "free will" in the metaphysical sense of that term. Persons are responsible agents so long as their moral powers are developed to the requisite minimum degree. This is the ordinary idea of responsibility that is employed in legal contexts and in everyday moral contexts. The question of responsibility is a factual one depending upon the capacity for a person to act rationally in his or her own interests, and understand, apply, and conform to moral and legal rules. In so far as a person has these capacities, he or she is regarded as free in the requisite sense, and responsible for ends and actions. Rawls's account of freedom of the person builds upon this common-sense notion of freedom and responsibility. He takes no explicit position on the metaphysical question of free will and determinism – he endorses neither metaphysical libertarianism nor compatibilism. But as a result he must take a position by default on the moral question whether moral responsibility is compatible with determinism – clearly he thinks it is, since he regards the metaphysical question as irrelevant to moral responsibility. This is all part of Rawls's idea of "the independence of moral theory" from metaphysics and epistemology (discussed further below).

The Reasonable and the Rational

Another feature of moral persons is that they have the capacities to be reasonable and rational. By this Rawls means that they have the moral powers, the capacities for a sense of justice and a conception of the good. There is a good deal built into Rawls's use of the idea of reasonableness (also into his idea of rationality). In *Theory* Rawls frequently says that certain considerations and assumptions are "reasonable" but he does not explicitly say how he uses this notion. Rawls uses the term "reasonable" in a general sense from early on; his first publication aims to discover a "reasonable decision procedure" to adjudicate between competing interests.[10] Here he also refers to "reasonable man," "reasonable principles," "reasonable acceptance," and sets forth a number of "tests of reasonable- ness." In *Theory* and the 1980 Dewey Lectures, he speaks of "reasonable claims," "reasonable conditions on agreement," "reasonable agreement," "reasonable persons," and "reasonable terms of social cooperation." Eventually, in *Political Liberalism*, he will use ideas of "reasonable pluralism," "reasonable political conceptions," "reasonable comprehensive doctrines," "reasonable moral psychology," and "politically reasonable." The general sense of reasonableness Rawls uses in these instances has to do with moral reasoning and the concept of Right. Rawls thinks that moral reasoning is a distinct sphere of practical reasoning, not reducible to considerations of the good or what is rational to do. The idea of reasonableness is used in connection with reasons and principles that appeal to our distinct capacity for moral reasoning and our sense of justice.

Beginning with "Kantian Constructivism" Rawls refers to "the Reasonable" and "the Rational" as nouns (CP, 316), to draw attention to these two distinct aspects of practical reason as they relate to social cooperation. Rawls says the Reasonable refers to the fair terms of social cooperation, and involves a notion of reciprocity and mutuality among people. Most people understand what it means to say that a person might be acting rationally but is nonetheless being unreasonable. Such a person takes advantage of every opportunity to get what benefits him, but in doing so is insensitive to the interests of others and does not care about the adverse effects of his demands upon them. In this regard he is acting unfairly and is being "unreasonable." A reasonable person does not take advantage of others whenever the opportunity arises but rather takes their interests into account and is attuned to the reasons they have for acting. He or she wants to act only in ways that can be justified to others (assuming they too are reasonable), and thus is willing to abide by fair terms of social cooperation for their own sake.

By contrast, the Rational refers to each person's rational advantage or good, what he or she is trying to advance by engaging in social cooperation. In its more general sense the Rational parallels Rawls's idea of a person's rational conception of the good, or their rational plan of life (TJ, ch. VII). The Rational then involves the principles of practical reason that provide structure to the concept of the good. These include the "counting principles" as well as the framework of practical deliberation he calls "deliberative ratio nality" which applies to determine a person's rational good (discussed in the previous chapter).

In 'Kantian Constructivism' Rawls introduces the idea of "rational autonomy." He says the parties in the original position are rationally autonomous in that they have a "highest-order interest" in the exercise and development of these moral powers, and are motivated in their decision on principles of justice by these highest-order interests and by their determinate (albeit unknown) rational conception of the good. (Rational autonomy of the parties also appears to mean that the parties are not constrained by any prior considerations of right and justice (CP, 308, 315).) Their highest-order interests in the moral powers is an aspect of the Rational, and not the Reasonable, for these capacities are needed to gain the benefits of social cooperation – it is rational to be reasonable for this reason. From the parties' interests in the exercise and development of their moral powers, Rawls justifies the list of primary social goods. The primary social goods, recall, are the all-purpose resources that the principles of justice are designed to distribute: rights and liberties, powers and opportunities, income and wealth, and the bases of self-respect. What makes these resources so important is that they are not only needed by free and equal persons to pursue permissible conceptions of the good, but they are also necessary means for exercise and development of the moral powers. They therefore answer to the parties' highest-order interests.

The significant point here is that having the highest-order interests in the moral powers is part of being a *rational person* for one who regards himself as free and as equal with others. This is a substantial philosophical claim. Rawls says in his *Lectures on the History of Political Philosophy* that one feature of social contract doctrines is that they attribute certain "fundamental interests" to persons and to the parties who enter into the social agreement. Thus Hobbes's rational contractors have fundamental interests they seek to protect and further by their social contract, in their self-preservation, "conjugal affections," and acquiring "riches and the means for commodious living" (*Leviathan*, ch. 30). Rousseau's social contractors, Rawls says, are motivated by their fundamental interests in their freedom, proper *amour propre*, and the perfectibility of their faculties. For Rawls the fundamental interests that motivate the parties to his social contract, and which explain their desire to obtain maximal or at least adequate primary goods, are the two moral powers and their determinate conception of their good. This is the main revision Rawls makes to the conception of the Rational as presented in *A Theory of Justice*.

In saying that the parties are "rationally autonomous" with a "highest-order interest" in their capacity to be rational (and reasonable), Rawls does not mean that they aim to be autonomous in Mill's sense of individuality. Rawls then does not assume that the parties all have a rational plan that they have freely articulated and designed after due deliberation in the informed exercise of their capacities for practical reasoning, and that this plan is authentic and not the product of others' influence. To build such a strong conception of the autonomy into the original position would bias its outcome by insuring principles designed to promote individuality at the expense of the pursuit of other goods. By the "rational autonomy" of the parties in the original position, he means that they are rational in the thin sense discussed in *Theory*, and that they regard themselves as free in the two ways mentioned above: they have the developed capacities to form, revise, and rationally pursue a conception of the good, and they have a highest-order interest in the moral powers, and therefore in acquiring adequate primary goods. This does not mean that the parties, or free and equal moral persons, regard the exercise of their rational capacities and moral capacities as worth doing or perfecting for their own sake. In *A Theory of Justice* Rawls insists that principles of justice must be based on a "thin" conception of the good. He intends to retain the thin conception of the good in the original position, even though, given the highest-order interests in the moral powers, it is now "thicker" than originally. But to do that, he cannot presuppose the good of individuality or any other "comprehensive conception."

But if so, how can Rawls call the parties', and moral persons', interest in development and exercise of their moral powers a "highest-order interest?" Rawls says, "By calling these interests 'highest-order' interests I mean . . . these interests are supremely regulative as well as effective. This implies that, whenever circumstances are relevant to their fulfillment, these interests govern deliberation and conduct" (CP, 312). As Rawls uses these terms, interests can be "supremely regulative" or "fundamental" and of a "highest order" without being final ends, pursued for their own sake. For example, our interest in self-preservation is of the "highest order," according to Hobbes, but that does not mean self-preservation is one of the final ends we pursue and which give our lives meaning. It means rather that it is an essential interest that must be fulfilled if *any* of our final ends and pursuits are to be realized. In this sense it is an essential good. Free and equal moral persons' development and exercise of the moral powers are "essential goods" in this sense. They are necessary if free and equal persons are to engage in and gain the benefits of social cooperation, and thereby achieve their final ends, whatever they might be. Likewise, to say that the moral powers are "supremely regulative" means that, for any number of reasons, moral persons effectively regulate their thinking and judgments about justice and the good by principles of justice and principles of rationality. This may be purely for instrumental reasons, namely, because rational people realize that, whatever their final purposes, they cannot achieve them unless they do so rationally (by taking effective means to their ends, etc.), and reasonably (by abiding by the laws and requirements of justice society imposes upon its members).

The highest-order interests of moral persons and of the parties in the original position are then consistent with the "thin theory of the good" presupposed in the original position. The theory is still "thin" in that it makes no assumptions regarding final ends or ultimate goods humans ought to pursue. There can be no assumption at the outset that justice and morality are intrinsically rational or worthy of pursuit for their own sake. To make such a strong assumption would defeat one purpose of constructivism, which is to show how both moral principles and also the full account of a person's good are "constructed" on the basis of a conception of practical reason and of the person as reasonable and rational.[11] Rawls's full theory of the good must avoid presupposing any account of intrinsic goods in its justification of principles of justice, for these principles are themselves to regulate a person's good and constitute the supreme good reasonable individuals ought to realize.

The Representation of Moral Personality in the Original Position

Before proceeding, let's recall why the conception of free and equal moral persons deserves attention. In *Theory* Rawls assumes that the account of moral personality depicts our "nature" as moral and rational agents. The moral powers are characteristics which enable us to engage in rational and moral deliberation and actions; for this reason any rational person should be concerned about living under conditions under which these characteristics are fully realized or at least are not stymied. After *Theory* Rawls tries to avoid importing any metaphysical assumptions into justice as fairness in order to show that moral theory is "independent" of metaphysics and epistemology. For this reason apparently, he no longer refers to our "nature," but rather to our "self-conception" as free and equal moral persons. The suggestion is that it is simply a social fact that in practical contexts we regard ourselves as free agents who can be held equally responsible for our actions; and that in matters of justice we regard one another as equals. Since these facts are central to our self-conceptions as agents, and to how we think about morality and holding others responsible, the conception of free and equal moral persons provides an appro- priate focal point for "constructing" a conception of justice. This less ambitious account of persons does not make any metaphysical claim regarding our nature. But notice that it also does not rule one out either. For one can always ask, "Why do we conceive of ourselves as free and equal persons?" And the answer may well be that our self-conception stems from our "nature" as such beings. So Rawls really gives up nothing in Kantian Constructivism by the change in terminology. It is only in *Political Liberalism* that he even- tually will have to forswear any reliance upon a Kantian conception of agency.

Now, what does this conception of the person mean in terms of the original position, and how is it used in the argument for principles of justice? Rawls says that Kantian Constructivism seeks to "represent" relevant features of free and equal moral persons in the "procedure of construction" of principles of justice. Adopting terms from logic and mathematics, he says the original position "maps" the primary features of the "model-conception" of persons into the original position. In what way then is the conception of free and equal moral persons, and of a well-ordered society, represented in the original position? Rawls's discussion here may seem rather tedious, but the general point to keep in mind is that, by exhibiting how the conception of the person and of society is modeled in the original position, Rawls is incorporating the rele- vant principles and ideas of practical reason into his "procedure of construction." This is a crucial step in achieving Kantian Constructivism's aim of showing how objective moral principles can be "constructed" out of practical reason's own resources, and thus are "given" to us by reason.

Starting with the representation of the Reasonable and the Rational, this part of Kantian Constructivism is relatively straight- forward with only a few significant additions since *Theory*. Rawls says the original position is set up so that "the reasonable constrains the rational"; certain moral conditions frame and constrain the rational deliberations of the parties in the original position. These *reasonable conditions* include, again, the veil of

ignorance, the five formal conditions of right (generality, universality, ordering of principles, publicity, and finality), and finally
the condition that principles of justice are to apply to regulate the
basic structure of society. It is not altogether clear how the basic
structure condition is a requirement of reasonableness. What
Rawls seems to mean is that applying principles of justice to the
basic structure is necessary to maintain "background justice." It is
not sufficient for justice that people simply respect others' rights
and abide by local norms of justice (by respecting property,
honoring contracts, etc.). Sometimes everyone can respect each
others' rights and local norms of fairness in economic exchange,
but still the accumulated outcome of a series of fair transactions
may itself be unfair when it results in inequalities in wealth of
such magnitude that they disadvantage the worst-off (for
example). For this reason, Rawls contends, principles of justice
must first apply to basic social institutions, to define standards
of background justice, which regulate and correct when necessary the outcomes of fair and just procedures that citizens
observe in everyday transactions. The basic structure condition
establishes a kind of "division of moral labor" between institutions and individuals in bringing about a just and well-ordered
society.[12]

The *Rational* is represented in the original position rather
straightforwardly as well: the parties are described as rational in
that they reason according to the principles of rational choice and
deliberative rationality, have a rational plan of life, and desire an
adequate share of the primary social goods as all-purpose means
for promoting their plan of life. There is no change from *Theory* in
this regard. What is added to the rationality of the parties since
Theory, as we've seen, is the stipulation that the parties are also
deemed to have two "highest-order interests" that they aim to
further in choosing principles of justice. These are their interests
in the exercise and development of the two moral powers. Here
again one might ask: "How can a desire and interest in exercising
and developing the sense of justice be part of the Rational, if the
parties are described as not being motivated by moral concerns?
Why isn't this a moral motivation attributed to the parties that

belies Rawls's claims that the parties are disinterested?" The answer again is that in seeking to develop their sense of justice, there is no assumption that the parties want to do what is just for its own sake or for other moral reasons (for example, because they are impartially concerned with others' well-being). Rather, they are presumed to want to develop their sense of justice to promote their own good since it is necessary to social cooperation with others, which in turn is necessary if they are to achieve their rational plan of life. Rawls has to avoid ascribing moral motivations to the parties if he is to maintain the basic idea that the original position involves rational choice constrained by reasonable conditions.

Regarding the *equality of moral persons*, the most prominent way it is represented is by the veil of ignorance. First, by rendering the parties ignorant of all particular facts about themselves and others, the veil of ignorance represents moral persons as such, as equally endowed with the moral powers of practical reason. No one knows any particular aims, interests, or exceptional capacities he or she has. The parties do know, however, that they all have a conception of the good, and they know they have a "highest-order interest" in the development and exercise of their moral powers. This is regarded as their essential good – essential, again, in that it is necessary if they are to engage in social cooperation and act freely to achieve their rational plans. Second, the veil of ignorance represents equality in that it situates the parties symmetrically, purely *as* free and equal moral persons and without any distinguishing characteristics. Since persons are moral equals by virtue of the moral powers, "similar cases should be treated similarly" in their joint decision upon principles of justice. Hence no one knows anything more about himself than another, and all know only those general facts needed to come to a decision upon principles of justice that reflect or express their nature as free and equal moral persons. The parties are also equals in that they have the same rights and powers in the original position, including equal rights to participate in discussion and to "vote" (one per person) for the final determination of principles of justice.

How is the *freedom of moral persons* represented in the original position? Rawls says that the freedom of the parties as "self-originating sources of claims" is represented by not requiring the parties to justify their ends or the claims they make (CP, 334). Part of their rational autonomy is that they do not have to account for their aims in terms of some prior moral standard. The second kind of freedom of moral persons, freedom as independence, "is represented in how the parties are moved to give priority to guaranteeing the social conditions for realizing their highest-order interests, and in their having grounds for agreement despite . . . the veil of ignorance . . . Rational deliberation is still possible even when the final ends of this conception [of the good] are unknown" (CP, 335). What Rawls means here (though it is not entirely clear) is that the parties, because of their moral powers, do not regard themselves as inescapably tied to any particular conception of the good. They see themselves as capable of rationally changing their final ends, and this is central to how they conceive of themselves as persons. Hence, just as their decision is rationally autonomous in not being governed by prior moral constraints, it is also rationally autonomous in not being governed by any substantive final ends or rational conception of the good. "In a Kantian constructivist view, then, it is a feature attributed to persons . . . that they can stand above and critically survey their own final ends by reference to a notion of the Reasonable and the Rational. In this sense, they are independent from and moved by considerations other than those given by their particular conception of the good" (CP, 335).

Communitarians criticize Rawls regarding this point. Michael Sandel has argued that Rawls conceives of persons as detached from the basic aims, commitments, and relationships that define their "identity" and give life meaning.[13] He contends that, in characterizing people as able to "stand above and critically survey" their ends, it is as if Rawls thinks of people as though they were detached and asocial choosing mechanisms that are ultimately committed to no one and value nothing except their freedom to choose. But this (Sandel says) is a false picture of the nature and moral identity of persons. For communitarians our moral identity is given by the final ends and commitments we affirm, and these are provided to us by social contexts and the community with which we identify or within which we thrive. It makes no sense, communitarians claim, to regard people as detached from their aims and social relations; moreover, to do so results in a false account of our duties and obligations to one another and to society as a whole, one that is typical of liberalism. This criticism is patterned upon Hegel's criticism of Kant's categorical imperative and ideal of autonomy. The intuitive idea is that, when Kantians (such as Rawls) define persons as (rationally) autonomous, they regard the self as a being without any character or identity and absent all the aims and commitments that give life its meaning. As Rawls himself says in TJ (560/491 rev.), "the self is prior to the ends affirmed by it." But surely, communitarians say, this is a false conception of the kinds of beings we are.

Many people regard political liberalism as Rawls's attempt to come to terms with the communitarian criticism. I do not think this is an accurate view of political liberalism (Rawls denies it too). Still, in Political Liberalism and elsewhere Rawls rejects Sandel's charge that he presupposes a bare, detached conception of the self (PL, 27; CP, 403n.). Rawls says that justice as fairness does not presuppose any metaphysical conception of persons, but rather relies upon a normative conception (an ideal we ought to realize) of citizens as free and equal moral persons. Rawls also suggests that Sandel's criticism mistakes the description of the parties in the original position – who are rationally autonomous and take no interests in each others' interests – for his account of the person that underlies justice as fairness (see PL, 28). Indeed, a careful reading of Theory shows that Rawls does regard a person's ends and commitments as central to a person's self-conception or "identity" (in the communitarian sense). For he says in chapter VII that he follows Royce in regarding a person as "a human life lived according to a plan [of life]. . . . [A]n individual says who he is by describing his purposes and causes, what he intends to do with his life" (TJ, 408/358 rev., emphasis added). Moreover, "Royce uses the notion of a plan to characterize the coherent, systematic purposes of the individual, what makes him a conscious, unified moral person. . . . And I shall do the same" (TJ, 408n./358n. rev.). This suggests that Sandel's criticisms are off the mark.

Still, communitarianism presents an important challenge for Rawls which cannot be fully assessed here. For the more general criticism is that Rawls cannot justify principles of justice without relying upon a social conception of the human good. Contemporary Aristotelians, some of whom are communitarians, endorse this position. Now in a sense Rawls argues for, though he does not presuppose, a social component to the human good; for one point of the congruence argument is to show that justice and social union are rational features of any person's plan of life in a well-ordered society. But communitarians claim that the centrality to the good of participation in community is undermined by the Kantian deontological framework of Rawls's view. The good of community must be presupposed in the first instance as the basis for any argument for ethical principles (of justice or otherwise), and not be treated, as Rawls does, as a coincidental consequence of them. This suggests a kind of perfectionism that regards the promotion of certain social virtues and "excellences" – love, friendship, political participation, and other forms of community – as ultimate goods about which social principles of justice ought to be constructed. Rawls himself regarded communitarianism, at its best, as a kind of perfectionism.[14] As such he rejects it for the same reasons he rejects other perfectionist positions (see TJ, sect. 50). He also sees it as implying a conception of political community at odds with liberalism in so far as communitarianism sees participation in a particular community – whether it be political or religious – as a final end that is necessary to everyone's good. This is incompatible with the good of the freedom to determine one's good from among a wide range of intrinsically valuable activities.

The Full Publicity Condition

The final feature of Kantian Constructivism to be discussed is Rawls's further development of the idea of publicity (discussed earlier in Chapter 4). Rawls says, "Publicity . . . has an important place in a

Kantian theory. Roughly publicity requires that in assessing moral conceptions we take into account the consequences of their being publicly recognized. Everyone is presumed to know that others hold the corresponding principles . . . it is just as if these principles were the outcome of an agreement" (CP, 292–93).[15] In *A Theory of Justice* Rawls often refers to the publicity of the *principles* of justice, but also sometimes he refers more broadly to the "public conception of justice" (TJ, 453–54/397–98 rev., where both terms are used). The idea of a public *conception* of justice suggests that members of a well-ordered society are to be aware not only of the principles of justice but also of their justification from the original position. In Kantian Constructivism, this would include public awareness of the conception of the person as free and equal and reasonable and rational (CP, 294).

Rawls distinguishes three levels of publicity in Kantian Constructivism. First, there is public knowledge of the principles of justice themselves and their role as the basis for social and political relations. Second, there is public knowledge of the general beliefs in light of which the principles of justice can be accepted by members of society, "that is, the theory of human nature and of social institutions generally" (CP, 324). Third, there is public knowledge of "the complete justification of the public conception of justice as it would be presented in its own terms," everything that might be said in setting up a moral conception and defending its principles of justice. Rawls says, "A well-ordered society satisfies . . . the full publicity condition when all three levels are exemplified" (CP, 325). This means that, in deciding on principles of justice, the parties must take into account that members of society will not only know and be expected to accept principles of justice themselves, but also know and accept the full justification of those principles, just as a philosopher, such as Rawls, might give one. People, then, have to be able not only to live with, but to accept and affirm, principles of justice and the complete justification of these principles in the terms Rawls provides in *Theory* and elsewhere (or, assuming there is a better justification of principles of justice, in the terms provided by it).

We will later see why this is a very strong condition on the justification of principles of justice. But first, why does Rawls think full publicity is needed? One of the main reasons for publicity beginning with Kantian Constructivism is its *educative role* in instilling in citizens knowledge of the ideal of free and equal persons and their relations, therewith encouraging citizens to acquire the *moral motivation* to be those sorts of persons and to foster those relations. For a conception of justice to fulfill this role, publicity has to be "full" – that is, citizens need to know not simply the principles of justice that they are expected to comply with, but also their "full justification" in terms of the original position and the conception of the person and society that it articulates. Rawls says after *Theory* that political philosophy has a *"practical task"* in a democratic society, which is to reconcile the apparently conflicting values of freedom and equality and citizens' conflicting understandings of these values (CP, 305–06, 325). The conception of free and equal moral persons and their relations is to be the main basis for this reconciliation. To achieve a reconciliation so that the practical task of political philosophy is fulfilled, the full justification of principles of justice must be publicly available to all citizens.

Two other reasons Rawls gives for the full publicity of a conception of justice are: (2) that the political institutions to which principles of justice apply are *coercive*, unlike other moral principles, and the use of coercive force against free and equal persons always requires justification to them; and (3) the basic social institutions to which principles of justice apply have profound effects upon the kinds of persons we are and want to be (CP, 325–26). For these reasons, Rawls says, the grounds and tendencies of social and political institutions should stand up to public scrutiny among people who regard themselves as free and equal. On the face of it, this seems to be an appeal to the moral intuition that if society forces us to do something, and also shapes us into being certain kinds of persons, then in all fairness and decency it owes us an explanation of why it imposes these requirements and influences upon us. But there seems to be more to it than this. For Rawls says:

When political principles satisfy the full publicity condition . . . then citizens can fully account for their beliefs and conduct to everyone else with assurance that this avowed reckoning itself will strengthen and not weaken the public understanding. The maintenance of the social order does not depend on historically accidental or institutionalized delusions, or other mistaken beliefs about how its institutions work. Publicity ensures . . . that free and equal persons are in a position to know and to accept the background social influences that shape their conceptions of themselves as persons, as well as their character and conception of their good . . .

(CP, 326)

Why is it so important that people not be under delusions or illusions about their social and political relations? One answer is the intrinsic value of knowing the truth. But this is a perfectionist ideal which Rawls would have a hard time squaring with the Kantian basis of his conception. After all, if knowing the truth is so important, why allow freedom of conscience and of thought and expression to get in the way, since these liberties permit people to spread all kinds of falsehoods and cause multiple false religious and moral beliefs? (Consider the fact that 76 percent of people in the U.S. say they believe in the biblical account of creation, and only 15 percent believe in Darwinian evolution. A religious skeptic will say that this unfortunate fact can only be due to freedom of religion.)[16]

Rawls says that the reason it is important that people know the truth about their social relations and their influences upon their characters, is that: "*Being in this position is a precondition of freedom;* it means that nothing is or need be hidden" (CP, 326, emphasis added). The appeal here is to an idea of *positive freedom,* i.e., the ideal of *moral and rational autonomy* that informs the Kantian interpretation and Kantian Constructivism. The ultimate reason for the full publicity of a conception of justice, down to its full justification, is that full autonomy requires that people know not only the bases of their social relations and why they are the kinds of persons they are (a requirement of rational autonomy); in addition, to be fully autonomous people must also know that they are, as reasonable and rational and free and equal persons, the origin of justice itself and the source of the very moral principles that regulate their conduct and their social relations. The restrictions and requirements of justice in a just and well-ordered society have been imposed by free and equal citizens upon themselves out of their own practical reason. For them to know this, to accept it, and to be motivated to act for the sake of justice for this very reason, realizes their full autonomy. The full publicity condition is necessary to the value of full autonomy that is implicit in the congruence argument in Theory.

THE INDEPENDENCE OF MORAL THEORY

Another important feature of Rawls's work, early and late, is the idea of the independence of moral theory from metaphysics and epistemology. Philosophers have traditionally believed, as Michael Smith affirms, "that we should do normative ethics only after we have given satisfactory answers to certain questions in meta-ethics,"[17] including questions regarding the possibility of moral truth, the nature of moral facts, and so on. From early on Rawls in effect denies this claim. In his first writings, Rawls takes morality and moral discourse to be a social practice that is necessary to social life, and he assumes that moral reasoning has its own standards of correctness independent of other practices and areas of inquiry.[18] Later, due to Kant's influence, Rawls maintains a position opposite to the traditional philosophical view expressed above: he argues that the traditional questions of meta-ethics can only be addressed once we have made advances in normative moral theory.

Kant distinguishes between reason in its theoretical use and its practical use, and between a "theoretical point of view" and "practical point of view." The former basically concerns the uses of reason in our judgments about what is the case – judgments of matters of fact about what exists and its causes – and our knowledge of them. Judgments of fact involve theoretical reasoning, including the application of standards of evidence to determine what is the case. More generally, scientific inquiry of all kinds involves theoretical reasoning, as do philosophical investigations into metaphysics, epistemology, and logic.[19] Practical reason and the practical point of view, by contrast, concern the uses of reason in deciding what *ought to be* the case, including both judgments about how we ought to act, and the ends that we ought to pursue in action. While practical reasoning must rely upon theoretical reasoning (upon its factual and logical judgments, etc.) in coming to decisions about what to do, it is also guided by its own independent "principles of practical reasoning." These tell us, in most general terms, how we ought to act and the ends we ought to pursue. For Kant, "hypothetical imperatives" tell us what kinds of actions to take in order to achieve our desired ends; these resemble Rawls's account of the Rational: namely the rational principles of choice and deliberation (the "counting principles" (e.g. to take effective means to ends) and the principles of deliberative rationality). Kant's "categorical imperative" on the other hand provides the foundation for moral reasoning; it is the "Moral Law" applied to the human condition. This parallels Rawls's idea of the Reasonable and reasonable principles of justice.

Rawls's thesis in 'The Independence of Moral Theory' resembles Kant's claim of the "priority of practical reason." By this Kant did not mean that practical reason was more important than theoretical reason or that the latter was dispensable in favor of the former; without theoretical reasoning, including standards of evidence to determine the relevant empirical facts underlying decisions, practical reasoning could not get started. He meant rather that we are entitled to assume that judgments made from a practical point of view can be objective, that moral and rational principles can be "universally valid," and that when applied the conclusions of these principles are sound (reasonable or true), even though they do not meet the same standards that apply to theoretical reason (empirical verifiability, correspondence to antecedent facts, etc.). Practical reason has a distinct subject matter and functions according to its own principles; thus it has its own standards of objectivity and "validity" (correctness) that apply uniquely to it. We have already seen an example of this in Rawls's Kantian Constructivism, which says that the soundness of moral judgments of justice does not depend upon their accurately corresponding to moral facts that are prior to and independent of our reasoning and judgments about them. Rather, moral judgments are sound when they follow from the correct application of a procedure of practical reason that incorporates all the relevant standards of practical reason.

By the "independence of moral theory" Rawls means basically that moral theory is not derivative from but is independent of other traditional areas of philosophy, including metaphysics, epistemology, and philosophy of language. Metaphysical conceptions of the nature of the self or personal identity, epistemological standards regarding the conditions of scientific or other theoretical knowledge, and linguistic conceptions regarding the meaning of moral terms do not determine the correct moral theory or the principles of moral reasoning that apply in deciding what we ought to do. This is not to say that they are wholly irrelevant, but rather that, by themselves, metaphysical, epistemological and linguistic conclusions do not determine any particular moral theory or conception of justice, but rather are compatible with a wide range of views. For example, there are different theories of the meaning of moral terms, or statements, or concepts. The philosopher R.M. Hare argued that moral statements are universalizable prescriptions; they command everyone in similar circumstances to act in specified ways. He also claimed that these formal features of moral concepts spoke in favor of utilitarianism.[20] Rawls agrees that generality of terms and universality of application are conditions of moral principles. But these formal conditions at most can set necessary conditions and limit the range of admissible moral principles. Examination of the meanings of moral terms cannot by themselves yield moral principles or speak in favor of utilitarianism or any particular moral conception of justice. There is no avoiding the need to appeal to considered moral judgments to justify the superiority of one moral conception over another.

Another example Rawls gives is the Humean account of personal identity. This is the metaphysical theory that persons are not enduring substances, but are merely "bundles of perceptions" (to use Hume's terms), i.e., psychologically connected and continuous states of consciousness and experience that endure over time. The person I am at any time is only more or less psychologically connected and continuous with the person whose psychological states were caused by this body twenty, thirty, and forty years ago. This account of personal identity has substantial consequences for our conceptions of the nature of personhood and our personal identity. It implies that there is something misleading about our using the terms "same person" (as in "I am the same person I was 30 years ago"), as if sameness of person-hood were all-or-nothing, as opposed to being a matter of degree. Derek Parfit contends that the Humean account of personal iden-tity also speaks in favor of utilitarianism, since it shows that boundaries between persons and their experiences are not as distinct as traditional morality has assumed.[21]

To Parfit's arguments Rawls responds that the metaphysical conception of the person and personal identity can reveal very little at all about the correct moral conception, for Parfit's account of personal identity is compatible with most traditional moral concep-tions of justice. A Kantian moral conception such as justice as fairness does not assume that persons are simple enduring substances, just as it does not assume that persons are metaphysically undetermined by external causal forces and act wholly of their own free will. It presupposes rather only that persons be able to exercise the moral powers to take responsibility for their ends and life plans, and thereby have the capacity to forge strong connections between the various parts of their lives. Since "there is no degree of connected-ness that is natural or fixed, the actual continuities and sense of purpose in people's lives" depends upon a large number of social and environmental factors, including to a great degree "the socially achieved moral conception" that a society embodies in its norms and institutions (CP, 300–01). In this regard, the degree to which we are psychologically connected and continuous beings is to a large degree up to us, dependent upon the conception of justice that we endorse as regulative of the basic structure of our society. It may be that in a well-ordered utilitarian society people's lives and purposes will be more disconnected and discontinuous than in a well-ordered society of justice as fairness. But this is by no means determined by the metaphysics of the person, but rather by the conception of justice that governs these societies.

There is a second aspect to Rawls's claim of the independence of moral theory from theoretical philosophy: Rather than moral theory being dependent upon other areas of philosophy, many of the traditional philosophical problems about morality are themselves not resolvable without first working through problems in normative moral theory. "Answers to such questions as the analysis of moral concepts, the existence of objective moral truths, and the nature of persons and personal identity, depend upon an understanding of these structures" of substantive moral conceptions. "Thus the problems of moral philosophy that tie in with the theory of meaning and epistemology, metaphysics and the philosophy of mind, must call upon moral theory" (CP, 287). In effect, Rawls seeks to reverse the traditional methodological ordering of philosophical inquiry into morality. It has long been assumed that the correct moral theory depends upon metaphysics and epistemology, and that we could not address substantive issues, such as the correct principles of justice, without first resolving some of the most intransigent problems of metaphysics and epistemology. Moral philosophy on this traditional view is seen as secondary and supervenient upon other areas of philosophy. But this way of thinking has stymied the development of moral theory, Rawls believes. And this in turn has prevented philosophers from gaining insight into the very metaphysical and epistemological problems that they feel they need to resolve before addressing substantive moral issues. But on the contrary, "further advance of [these problems of] moral philosophy depends upon a deeper understanding of the structure of moral conceptions and their connections with human sensibility" (CP, 287). Rawls's thesis of the independence of moral theory then calls for a methodological reordering of inquiry into the traditional problems of moral philosophy. Not only is substantive moral theory independent of metaphysics and epistemology, but moral epistemology (e.g., problems of moral objectivity and moral truth) and moral metaphysics (e.g., the problems of personal identity and free will) are themselves dependent to some degree upon advances in substantive moral theory.

This thesis has not been willingly embraced by the great majority of meta-ethicists. It requires that they immerse themselves in the substantive moral theories of Aristotle, Hobbes, Kant, Sidgwick and the utilitarians, and others, as a condition of further advance in their metaphysical and epistemological inquiries. Rawls, however, sees the idea of the independence of moral theory in other moral philosophers. As he remarks, it is one of the distinctive contributions of Sidgwick to have seen that further advance in moral philosophy, including the discovery of moral truth, depends upon the systematic comparisons of the different "Methods of Ethics." "Sidgwick felt that progress in moral philosophy is held up by the desire to edify; it is also impeded by giving way to the impulse to answer questions one is not yet equipped to examine. In this case at least [resolving the problem of moral truth] it seems that, if there is any relation of priority, it runs the other way, from moral theory to moral epistemology" (CP, 291).

The idea of the independence of moral theory plays a major role in Rawls's political liberalism. For the idea of "the domain of the political" and a "freestanding conception of justice" assume that there is a domain of practical reasoning about "the political" that is not only independent of theoretical philosophy – of metaphysics, epistemology, etc. – but that is also independent of "comprehensive" moral theory itself. The idea of political liberalism is a further extension of Rawls's idea of the independence of moral reasoning. Political reasoning in a democratic society has, Rawls will argue, standards of reasonableness and correctness that set it apart from other kinds of reasoning, including even non-political moral reasoning.

THE SOCIAL ROLE OF A CONCEPTION OF JUSTICE AND PROBLEMS WITH THE KANTIAN INTERPRETATION

In Kantian Constructivism Rawls brings to fruition the Kantian interpretation of justice as fairness in *A Theory of Justice*. But there is more to it than this. In "Kantian Constructivism in Moral Theory"

Rawls introduces, for the first time, the idea of the "practical task of political philosophy," which is the "social role" (or "public role") that a conception of justice must play in providing a basis for public justification among members of society.

> The social role of a conception of justice is to enable all members of society to make mutually acceptable to one another their shared institutions and basic arrangements, by citing what are publicly recognized as sufficient reasons, as identified by that conception. To succeed in doing this, a conception must specify admissible social institutions . . . so that they can be *justified to all citizens*, whatever their social position or more particular interests.
>
> (*CP*, 305, emphasis added)

For a conception of justice to fulfill this social role, it not only has to meet the basic contractarian aim of framing principles of justice that are generally acceptable to free and equal citizens; in addition these principles must be "justified to all citizens" in terms of reasons they can also accept. To do this, the conception of justice must take into account the fact that democratic citizens will inevitably have opposing religious, philosophical, and moral convictions. Rawls says that diversity of these kinds of views is inevitable due to our "limited powers and distinct perspectives" (CP, 329). "Many conceptions of the world can plausibly be constructed from different standpoints" (ibid.). This diversity of religious, philosophical and moral beliefs and doctrines (which Rawls later terms "the fact of reasonable pluralism" (PL, 36)) is a further consequence of the subjective circumstances of justice in *Theory* (CP, 323). The subjective circumstances of justice, recall, are the inevitable differences in values, beliefs, and commitments that people have, which are a source of disagreement among them. Because of these circumstances of justice, Rawls suggests that the full publicity condition can only apply to principles of political and social justice and not to all moral principles or conceptions of the good.

> Justice as fairness assumes that deep and pervasive differences of religious, philosophical, and ethical doctrine remain. For many

philosophical and moral notions public agreement cannot be reached; the consensus to which publicity applies is limited in scope to the public moral constitution and the fundamental terms of social cooperation.

(*CP*, 326)

For this reason, Rawls says, "Justice as fairness tries to construct a conception of justice that takes deep and irresolvable differences on matters of fundamental significance as a permanent condition of human life" (CP, 329). To do this justice as fairness "needs to be appropriately impartial among those differences." This means that the justification of a conception of justice suitable for a democratic society must rely "on but a part of the truth, and not the whole, or, more specifically, on our present commonly based and shared beliefs" (ibid.). By invoking our commonly based and shared beliefs, it may seem that here Rawls is simply reiterating the account of justification in Theory, as bringing our shared considered moral and other convictions into reflective equilibrium. But nowhere in Theory did Rawls say that such justifications involve relying upon but "a part of the truth" and not the whole truth. This means that certain kinds of reasons and arguments must be put off-limits, so to speak, in public life, even though people sincerely believe them to be true, and even though some of them *are* true. These include reasons and arguments that rely exclusively on people's different religious, philosophical, and ethical views; for these are all matters about which even reasonable and rational people cannot agree. In order for citizens in a well-ordered society to reach agreement on public principles of justice they must accept that:

For certain parts of their common life, considerations of justice are to have a special place. Other reasons are taken not to be appropriate, although elsewhere they may have a governing role, say within the life of associations. In public questions, ways of reasoning and rules of evidence for reaching true general beliefs that help settle whether institutions are just should be of a kind that everyone can recognize.

(*CP*, 326)

This claim is the basis for a very important idea that is essential to Rawls's later political liberalism, the idea of public reason. Rawls plants the seeds in "Kantian Constructivism" for subsequent major revisions to his argument for justice as fairness, including revisions to Kantian Constructivism itself. Now let's turn to the problem that the ideas of full publicity and the social role of a conception of justice raise for Rawls's view.

The purpose of the Kantian congruence argument in *A Theory of Justice* is to complete the argument for the stability of justice as fairness by showing how a well-ordered society is realistically possible. If it can be shown that a well-ordered society of justice as fairness describes conditions under which justice is an intrinsic good, then it has been shown how justice can be rational for each person. Being rational for each, stability has been demonstrated in the strongest possible way, for justice is everyone's best response to their circumstances. Does this ambitious argument succeed?

The congruence argument contains many controversial philosophical claims. It presupposes a philosophical conception of the nature of human agency, as having its ground in the moral powers (as opposed to the intensity of human desires, for example). It assumes the capacity for our practical reason to control and structure our desires into a rational plan of life that guides our actions. Also, the congruence argument implies the distinctly Kantian claim that moral autonomy is an intrinsic good. Kantian Constructivism implies a controversial thesis about the nature of value and morality, and about standards for the correctness and objectivity of moral claims: Moral principles and the realm of value are not given to us by God, nature or an independent domain, but are "constructed" from the activities of practical reason and its own principles and ideas.[22] Moreover, the correctness of moral statements ultimately derives, not from a prior moral order or antecedent moral or natural facts, but from an objective procedure of construction which incorporates all the requirements of practical reason.

My concern here is limited to the question whether the congruence argument, and more generally Kantian Constructivism, succeed on their own terms. Assume that congruence successfully shows that justice is an intrinsic and supremely regulative good for reasonable and rational persons in a well-ordered society. Still, this does not show that each (reasonable and rational) person in a well-ordered society will in fact *recognize and accept* justice as an intrinsic good; or even if many do, it does not show they do so for the reasons Rawls sets forth in the congruence argument (namely, because justice expresses their nature as free and equal rational beings who are morally autonomous). Perhaps they are incapable of doing so because of some impediment to their beliefs stemming from lack of knowledge, or false information or mistakes of reason. Or perhaps people might have philosophical or religious beliefs that prevent them from recognizing that the practical reason of humankind is the original source of morality and value. As Rawls says, "deep and irresolvable differences on matters of fundamental significance [are] a permanent condition of human life" (CP, 329). The problem is that, unless the great majority of inhabitants of a well-ordered society recognize and respect justice as an end worthy of pursuit "for the right reasons," the Kantian congruence argument does not succeed. What is needed in order to establish the stability of a well-ordered society is not, then, just an argument that justice is a supremely regulative good for each reasonable and rational person; in addition, these persons also have to *believe and accept* this argument, if they are to reliably do what justice requires of them.

In *Political Liberalism* Rawls says that there is a "serious problem internal to justice as fairness [arising] from the fact that the account of stability in Part III of *Theory* is not consistent with the view as a whole" (PL, xv–xvi). "[T]he serious problem I have in mind concerns the unrealistic idea of a well-ordered society as it appears in *Theory*" (PL, xvi). What is primarily unrealistic about the account in *Theory*, I believe, is the Kantian congruence argument, and perhaps also the argument for the good of social union. They fail to appreciate the extent of the "subjective circumstances of justice," or what Rawls later calls "the fact of reasonable pluralism" that characterizes a well-ordered society. These circumstances imply that, even if all reasonable and rational individuals might agree on the same principles of justice (as the idea of a well-ordered society assumes), still under conditions of freedom of thought, conscience, and association, it is unrealistic to expect that people will all agree in their religious, philosophical, or ethical beliefs.[23] But if so, then it is unrealistic to expect that all citizens in a well-ordered society will agree on the intrinsic good of moral autonomy, or the good of community regarded as participation in a social union of social unions, or even that justice ought to be pursued for its own sake.

For example, because of the basic liberties of conscience and association there will be many people in a well-ordered society who accept the principles of justice but who endorse them mainly for religious reasons. Rawls has little to say about religion in *A Theory of Justice*, but he clearly does not presuppose its absence in a well-ordered society. Consider then the liberal Catholic who accepts the principles of justice as fairness, the natural duties, and the principle of fairness, but who sees them as natural laws, part of the divine law willed by God in creating the universe. According to the liberal Thomist's view of morality, natural laws of justice are divinely ordained and are knowable, some as self-evident truths, by the natural light of reason. This denies a basic position of the Kantian interpretation, that moral principles have their origins in and are constructed from principles of practical reason. Rejecting the constructivist view of justification and objectivity, the liberal Thomist also rejects the Kantian conception of agency and of the intrinsic good of moral autonomy that underpins the congruence argument. This argument depends on showing that the sense of justice is the same as the desire to realize our nature as free and equal rational beings and thereby become morally autonomous. But the liberal Thomist denies this identification; the sense of justice is to be regarded instead as a desire to conform to God's natural laws, not a desire to express our nature as the author of these laws. Not only is autonomy not an intrinsic good; to think so is a profane conceit of human reason that comes from rejecting the divine origins of moral laws. Similar problems may beset Rawls's argument in *A Theory of Justice* for the good of community regarded as participation in a well-ordered society as a social union of social unions. The liberal Catholic may reply that the only community that is worthy of participation in for its own sake is the community of believers, the Church.

A comprehensive religious and ethical view such as liberal Thomism is not incompatible with the principles of justice.[24] It is then a permissible conception of the good in a well-ordered society, and presumably could gain many adherents. But if so, then the content of this (and other) permissible conceptions of the good conflict with the Kantian conception of the good that is a part of public culture and education in a well-ordered society. This could have the consequence of undermining many people's sense of self-respect, and cause resentment since their most basic values are implicitly recognized as false values by the public culture. The problem here is that there is a rejection of non-Kantian conceptions of the good built into the political culture of a well-ordered society of justice as fairness. Even if many religious and ethical views are false they are nonetheless permissible doctrines and conceptions of the good. Their public rejection can only have the effect of undermining many people's self-respect and allegiance and support for just institutions.

The problem with the Kantian interpretation may be even more significant. Perhaps it cannot be said of non-Kantians that they are mistaken about their good, and that the congruence argument fails on its own terms. This depends upon features of Rawls's account of deliberative rationality he does not discuss in *Theory*. According to this account a person's good is the plan of life that person would choose if he or she had full information of "all relevant facts," reasoned correctly, and imaginatively appreciated the consequences of choosing alternative rational plans of life (*TJ*, sect. 64). If the full information condition means that a person's good is what he or she would hypothetically choose in the absence of false beliefs, then we encounter the same problem mentioned previously; namely, that many misinformed persons in a well-ordered society will have mistaken beliefs (about God's creation of the universe, for example, including the realm of value), and so will not recognize that autonomy is an intrinsic good they would choose given accurate information in deliberative rationality. In this case, the congruence argument does not insure the stability of a well-ordered society, since many persons' subjectively perceived good is at odds with their objective good. On the other hand, if the full information condition for deliberative rationality expresses a weaker condition, and means simply that everyone has access to all relevant evidentiary information, this suggests that objectively rational plans on Rawls's account may indeed be informed by false beliefs (such as, presumedly, belief in God's creation of the realm of value). This interpretation is suggested by the "burdens of judgment" (PL, 54–58), which imply that reasonable and rational persons with the same accurate information still will have different philosophical, moral, and religious beliefs. But if this is the case even under conditions of deliberative rationality, then Rawls's Kantian congruence argument fails on its own terms for large numbers of people. For it imputes to all a conception of the good (the good of moral autonomy) which many would not rationally endorse even under conditions of full information and deliberative rationality.

Whether or not moral autonomy is an intrinsic good for reasonable and rational persons as such, the general point is that insufficient numbers of people in a well-ordered society will be motivated to comply with justice for the Kantian reason that they realize their nature as free and equal rational moral beings and are thereby morally autonomous. This is what the congruence argument seeks to prove in order to show how a well-ordered society is stable "for the right reasons." The only way around this problem is to abandon the Kantian congruence argument (as well as the social union argument, which has similar problems). But this still leaves the problem the congruence argument was designed to redress, namely to show the rationality of justice for reasonable and rational persons in a well-ordered society. Stability then has to be satisfied by some other means. As we shall see, this problem accounts in large part for Rawls's turn to political liberalism.

FURTHER READING

Hill, Thomas E., Jr., "Kantian Constructivism in Ethics," *Ethics*, 99, 1989, 752–70. (Sympathetic development of Kantian position along lines suggested by Rawls.)

O'Neill, Onora, "Constructivism in Rawls and Kant," The Cambridge Companion to Rawls, ch. 9. (Compares Rawls's constructivism with Kant's, and argues for the latter approach.)

Rawls, John, Lectures on the History of Moral Philosophy, "Moral Constructivism," 235–52. (Ch. 6 of Rawls's Kant lectures shows how constructivism is developed by Kant.)

Eight

Political Liberalism I – the Domain of the Political

THE PROBLEM OF *POLITICAL LIBERALISM*

There are two ways to understand *Political Liberalism*. It might be seen as a remedy to the problem (discussed in the final section of Chapter 7) that Rawls encounters with the argument for the stability of a well-ordered society of justice as fairness. Rawls discusses the remedial task of *Political Liberalism* in the first Introduction:

> To understand the nature and extent of the differences [between *Political Liberalism* and *A Theory of Justice*] one must see them as arising from trying to resolve a serious problem internal to justice as fairness, namely from the fact that the account of stability in Part III of *Theory* is not consistent with the view as a whole. I believe all differences are consequences of removing that inconsistency.
>
> (*PL*, xvii–xviii, see also xlii, 388n.)

I will discuss how the main ideas of *Political Liberalism* remedy the problems Rawls encounters in Part III of *A Theory of Justice*. But *Political Liberalism* also can be understood independently of *Theory* and as responding to different problems. Taken on its own terms, *Political Liberalism* responds to two main questions, one regarding the practical *possibility* of a well-ordered liberal society, and the other the conditions of the *legitimacy* of the exercise of political power in a liberal society. Legitimacy is not a concept that Rawls uses in *A Theory of Justice*. It is a different concept than justice, and it becomes especially important under non-ideal conditions in societies where justice as fairness is not uniformly applied.

This is how Rawls describes the relationship between the two books in his final writings. He says the primary ambition of *Theory* was to develop the social contract doctrines of Locke, Rousseau, and Kant, in order to provide an account of social justice that would serve as an alternative to the predominant utilitarian tradition in moral and political philosophy, one more consistent with our considered convictions of justice and a democratic society (cf. LP, 179). Like his predecessors, Rawls's social contract doctrine is presented as a "partially comprehensive" philosophical account of social and political justice. It is "comprehensive" in that, first, it appeals to moral values in addition to justice (full autonomy, the good of community); and second, it invokes philosophical accounts of the nature of agency and of practical reason, of moral objectivity, moral justification, and moral truth. Rawls never wavers in his conviction that these philosophical and moral positions set forth in *A Theory of Justice* are all correct and philosophically justifiable (even if his defense of them was partially defective), just as he never wavers in his conviction that justice as fairness is also true (or "most reasonable" in his parlance). But to say these positions are *philosophically* justifiable and true does not mean they are *publicly* justifiable to the members of a democratic society. Rawls's accounts in *Theory* of value, agency, objectivity, moral justification, etc. are all controversial philosophical positions, and reasonable people can disagree about them. It is the nature of philosophy to be controversial and subject to reasonable disagreement, even though (as Rawls continued to believe of *A Theory of Justice*) one philosophical position may be *most* reasonable and/or true. The inevitability of reasonable disagreement upon philosophical, moral, and religious issues is due to what Rawls calls "the burdens of judgment." The primary problem with the argument in *Theory* is that, because of the burdens of judgment, the members of a well-ordered society of justice as fairness could not themselves reasonably agree upon the philosophical justification of the principles of justice that they all endorse. This is the problem that gives rise to and which is addressed in *Political Liberalism*.

This brings us to the second, more positive statement of the problem that *Political Liberalism* is designed to address. Forget about the philosophical dispute between justice as fairness and utilitarianism, and between liberal democracy and other forms of government that *A Theory of Justice* responds to. The general problem that *Political Liberalism* addresses is the more general *practical* question: How is it possible for there to exist over time a just *democratic* society that is stable for the right reasons, of free and equal citizens, all of whom agree on a *liberal* conception of justice, but who nonetheless remain profoundly divided by reasonable philosophical, religious, and moral doctrines (cf. PL, xxvii, xxxix, 4)?

This in effect is a more general statement of the same question that motivates Rawls's inquiry in Part III of *Theory* regarding the stability of justice as fairness. But rather than being tied specifically to justice as fairness, the question now asks how enduring agreement on *any* reasonably just liberal and democratic conception of justice is realistically possible, *given* the fact that reasonable people in liberal societies will inevitably hold different "reasonable comprehensive doctrines." *Political Liberalism* thus has a different focus than *Theory*. It does not ask what conception of justice is true or most reasonable and best fits with our considered convictions of justice. Rather, it presupposes the justice of a liberal and democratic society where people regard themselves as free and equal citizens, and then asks, "How is it possible for reasonable people living under these liberal and democratic conditions, given all their religious, philosophical and moral differences, to come to agree upon a conception of justice that will enable their society to endure?"[1]

Here many philosophers object that Rawls's inquiry in *Political Liberalism* is too limited. They say in effect: "Rawls just presupposes what many people think needs to be proved, namely the justification of a liberal and democratic society. How is he going to convince people who reject freedom and equality to accept liberalism and democracy?" It is true that *Political Liberalism* starts out with the assumption that a liberal democratic society is more just than the alternatives, and addresses itself to people who accept the fundamental political importance of freedom and equality. But this does not beg any questions against non-democratic societies, for

Political Liberalism is not addressed to them. If people do not regard themselves as free and equal citizens, nor believe that freedom and equality are fundamental political values, then *Political Liberalism* may not be of much interest to them. But why is this an objection to Rawls's project? Analogously, surely it is not an objection to treatises on the U.S. Constitution that they are not addressed to people in other nations, but only to U.S. citizens who recognize the Constitution as higher law. Here Rawls's critics might say that this refusal to address in universal terms people with different values who do not think of themselves as free and equal citizens renders Rawls's argument relativistic, relevant to the political preferences of people in a democracy. But clearly Rawls thinks freedom and equality are universal values of justice and that every society in the world ought to strive to become a liberal democratic society. This is the clear implication of the argument in *A Theory of Justice*, and neither *Political Liberalism* nor Rawls's later *The Law of Peoples* suggests that Rawls has given up on the "comprehensive doctrine" expressed in that volume. *A Theory of Justice* responds to critics' concern for an argument for universal justice that addresses reasonable people in all the world. It mistakes *Political Liberalism*'s purpose to think that it must duplicate the ambitions of that earlier book. *Political Liberalism*, unlike *Theory*, addresses a problem within democratic and liberal theory; namely, how is it possible that there exists a stable and enduring liberal and democratic society that tolerates different views and ways of life when reasonable citizens disagree about fundamental moral and religious values?

To appreciate the scope of the problem Rawls confronts in *Political Liberalism*, consider the following objections:

(1) *Of course* a liberal society where all reasonable people agree on the same conception of justice is not realistically possible. For given freedom of thought and expression, freedom of conscience and of religion, and freedom of association, many different *false* comprehensive religious, philosophical, and moral doctrines will be advocated and will gain adherents. And these will lead many people to have false beliefs about justice and the grounds of justice. Just look at the United States, the freest country in the world in protecting basic

liberties, where over half of American citizens believe the biblical account of creation, that the miracles in the Bible actually took place, and that angels and the devil, or at least immaterial souls, actually exist, while less than 15 percent believe the Darwinian account of evolution![2] Given these unreasonable beliefs, why should we expect people's beliefs about the grounds of justice to be any more reasonable? Rawls has unrealistic if not utopian aspirations.

(2) Moreover, Rawls's utopian aspirations are not of that much moral or political importance. Why should it matter whether people have similar beliefs about the justification of their liberal constitution? So long as people obey the laws of a liberal society and most of them accept the terms of a liberal and democratic constitution, then a democratic society is stable enough.

This skeptical response to Rawls's aspirations in *Political Liberalism* is indicative of the kinds of problems he confronts. The first problem is that since even reasonable people will never agree upon religious, philosophical, and moral doctrines, why should they be expected to agree upon a conception of justice down to its justification? Phrased in this way the problem of *Political Liberalism* seems virtually insurmountable. For clearly people's views about justice will be largely determined by the particular comprehensive doctrine that they hold. And if they differ in comprehensive doctrines, then surely they will also differ in their conceptions of justice. But this seems to suggest that a well-ordered liberal and democratic society is not possible. The second problem might be called the "sour grapes" challenge: It says that a liberal society in which all reasonable citizens agree on a liberal conception of justice is not that important after all. Why should we even aspire to it?

Rawls's response to the first problem, in brief outline, consists of three parts:

(1) Even if disagreements and false beliefs about religion, philosophy, and ethics are inevitable among reasonable and rational democratic citizens, the *political conception* of justice that is publicly endorsed in a liberal well-ordered society need not depend upon or be influenced by these disagreements and false beliefs. A public

political conception of justice is *freestanding* (or "self-standing") of the comprehensive doctrines and false beliefs of citizens. What makes a political conception of justice freestanding is that it has a *political justification*, one that is framed in terms of democratic values and ideals that are part of public culture and that are independent of the values and reasons peculiar to any comprehensive moral, religious, or philosophical doctrine.

(2) In a well-ordered democratic society reasonable and rational citizens should be able to endorse the liberal political conception of justice that governs society. For this to be realistically possible all the *reasonable* comprehensive doctrines affirmed by citizens must accept and endorse its political conception of justice in an *overlapping consensus*. When such an overlapping consensus exists, then all free and equal citizens endorsing reasonable comprehensive doctrines agree on the political conception of justice, on the basis of their own particular comprehensive reasons and views.

(3) The final requirement for the possibility and enduring stability of a well-ordered society concerns the application of the political conception of justice: decisions regarding *constitutional essentials and matters of basic justice* should be decided by political authorities on the basis of *political values*, and these decisions must be justifiable to citizens in terms of *public reason*. When laws affecting constitutional essentials and matters of basic justice are justifiable on the basis of the political values of public reason, then they are justifiable for reasons that all can accept in their capacity as free and equal democratic citizens. Laws are thereby rendered *politically legitimate*.

When these three conditions are all met – in short, where (1) there is a freestanding political conception of justice (2) that is acceptable to reasonable persons and endorsed by all reasonable comprehensive doctrines in an overlapping consensus, and (3) that provides content to public reasoning about constitutional essentials and basic justice – then a liberal and democratic well-ordered society is *stable for the right reasons*: its conception of justice is generally acceptable to and guides the actions of free and equal citizens on the basis of moral reasons implicit in their *sense of justice* and also in their reasonable comprehensive views.

The ideas in (1)–(3) are new in Rawls's work and are in need of clarification. In this chapter and the next I will explain each of these conditions and the related concepts needed to understand *Political Liberalism*.

But first, consider the second objection set forth above. This returns us to a question raised earlier, in connection with Rawls's social contract doctrine, namely, why Rawls thinks agreement on justice to be such an important moral and political value. If we regard ourselves as free persons who warrant equal respect as citizens, and freedom and equality are regarded as fundamental political values, then it is a desirable feature of our relations that the political constraints of justice that regulate our conduct should be freely acceptable to us as equal citizens from a fair position. Otherwise, we are being required to live according to terms of cooperation that we cannot freely accept or endorse. The contractarian focus on consent and general agreement within a well-ordered society stems from the fundamental significance Rawls assigns to equal freedom and independence, and fair cooperation on a basis of mutual respect. But in *Political Liberalism* that focus must change to a degree. Rawls can no longer affirm, as in *Theory*, freedom and equality as fundamental moral values that are part of a comprehensive Kantian moral doctrine. Because of the fact of reasonable pluralism, for a conception of justice to be generally accepted in a well-ordered society, it must "bracket" disputed issues such as the most basic moral values. Rawls, however, assumes that, in a modern democratic society, our conception of ourselves as free and equal citizens is of great importance to any reasonable person's self-image and self-respect; it also occupies a significant position within any reasonable comprehensive moral, philosophical, or religious views, whatever they might be. All of us, then, assuming we are reasonable and rational, should have sufficient reason to want to live according to a conception of justice that affirms our self respect and status as equal citizens, and that also enables us to pursue our conception of the good and the fundamental values of our comprehensive views. We should have, then, Rawls contends, a "higher-order interest" in preserving our equal status and self-respect as free citizens, and in maintaining the moral powers that enable us to take part in social cooperation. The crucial point here is that a condition of our realizing this higher-order interest is that we be able to *freely accept and endorse* this conception of justice in our capacity as free and equal citizens. Rawls sees the realistic possibility of general acceptance and agreement by all reasonable citizens of a democratic society's conception of justice as implicit in liberal and democratic values of freedom and equality and the ideal of citizens. It is a condition of what he calls "political autonomy," a basic political value of public reason that undergirds *Political Liberalism* similar to the way Kantian moral autonomy in *Theory* sustained justice as fairness as a partially comprehensive view.

A FREESTANDING POLITICAL CONCEPTION OF JUSTICE

The first three chapters of *Political Liberalism* are devoted to clarifying the idea of a political conception of justice. These chapters are substantially revised versions of the three 1980 Dewey Lectures discussed in the preceding chapter. Rawls pours new wine into old wineskins. He retains the ideal conception of free and equal persons and their moral personality that undergirds Kantian Constructivism; but rather than regarding them as aspects of our "nature" as moral agents (as he did clearly in *Theory* and somewhat less clearly in the Dewey Lectures), he now depicts the conception of free and equal, reasonable, and rational persons as a *political ideal of democratic citizens* that is implicit in the political culture of a democratic society. In other words Rawls assumes that, as a matter of fact, citizens in a modern democratic society conceive of themselves as free and equal in political contexts. He sets forth idealizations of this self-conception – the ideal of free and equal moral persons – and then sets about "constructing" a conception of justice that best fits with and realizes this ideal of citizens. His hope is that this conception of justice best captures the democratic values and ideas about justice we commonly use, and at the same time is compatible with the philosophical, moral, and religious doctrines we affirm. The project of justification in *Political Liberalism* is similar to *Theory*, only this time Rawls has to meticulously avoid relying on controversial philosophical and moral positions, and rely instead on ideas and reasons that are widely shared in democratic culture.

Now to examine what Rawls means by a "political conception of justice." Rawls says a political conception has three features: First, it is drawn up to apply to the basic structure of society (nothing new here). Second, it is independent or "freestanding" of the concepts, values, and principles of comprehensive moral, philosophical, and religious doctrines held by members of a democratic society. Rawls defines a "comprehensive doctrine" as one that includes conceptions of what is of value in life and gives life its meaning. Metaphysical doctrines regarding the nature of reality, and epistemological doctrines regarding the possibility and conditions of human knowledge are also comprehensive doctrines, as are all religions. Natural, social, and mathematical sciences, however, are not comprehensive doctrines for Rawls, at least not in so far as they incorporate generalities, laws, theorems, hypotheses, and theories that are generally accepted by experts in the field, and the science itself is generally accepted by reasonable people.[3] As we saw in his argument for justice as fairness, it is important to Rawls that non-controversial findings among experts in the social sciences be permissible bases for arguing for a political conception of justice, and also within the public reason of a democratic society. Third, rather than comprehensive doctrines, a political conception of justice is worked up from certain "fundamental intuitive ideas" that are implicit in the public culture of a democratic society. Rawls regards these fundamental ideas, along with our "fixed considered convictions of justice," as the building blocks and argumentative means of support for the political conception of justice. Fundamental intuitive ideas are themselves fixed considered convictions, in the sense that Rawls presumes they are presupposed by public debate and deliberation in a democratic society, and as part of common-sense public reasoning. He mentions three fundamental intuitive ideas: the idea of society as a fair system of social cooperation, the idea of free and equal citizens, and the idea of a well-ordered society. Rawls also discusses three more "fundamental ideas" which are theoretical "companions" to the intuitive ideas: the ideas of the basic structure of society, the original position, and public justification.

We have encountered most, if not all, of these ideas in different guises in Kantian Constructivism and *A Theory of Justice*. Here, then, I mainly emphasize some of the differences from those earlier works in their presentation of these ideas.

The Political Conception of the Person

Rawls says that it is a part of democratic culture that citizens are regarded as free and as equal. This is a social and institutional fact. Of course, people disagree about the ways in which citizens should be free and treated as equals, but still these fundamental political values are generally shared by reasonable persons in a democratic society. Now the ideal conception of free and equal citizens with the two moral powers is, of course, a variation on the account of free and equal moral persons that Rawls relied upon in the Kantian interpretation and Kantian Constructivism. But now he claims that this is a *political conception of the person*, and is not intended as a statement regarding the nature of human agency or as any sort of metaphysical view (PL, 29–35). What is a "political conception of the person"?

A prime example of a metaphysical conception of the person is the Humean account of personal identity, which says that persons are simply continuous and interconnected bundles of experiences. Recall also Michael Sandel's criticism that Rawls's original position presupposes an account of the self as detached from any fundamental ends or commitments, a kind of "bare" agent of pure willing that chooses its ends, relations, and commitments and is not regarded as having any prior personal or social commitments. Whether or not such a conception of the self makes sense or was ever implicit in *Theory*, it is an example of the kind of metaphysical or at least normative conception of the self that Rawls wants to avoid. Rawls says that the political conception of the person goes with the idea of *society as a fair system of social cooperation*, which is the fundamental intuitive idea that Rawls uses to organize other fundamental ideas and considered convictions (PL, 15). Rawls suggests that when we think of social cooperation, we think of something other than efficiently coordinated behavior, where people might have an assigned role in some joint activity from which they may or may not benefit. In the case of prisoners working on a chain gang, for example, or other forms of enforced servitude, a great deal might be accomplished depending upon how effectively participants' behavior is coordinated, but it is mistaken to say they are engaged in *social cooperation* with their captors or even with one another. By contrast, social cooperation involves people more or less voluntarily engaging in activities and social relations according to terms of cooperation that they accept and regard as more or less fair, and from which everyone benefits in some manner. If they do not all benefit optimally, however that is to be understood, still they benefit in the minimal sense that all are better off than if there were no cooperation at all. Social cooperation involves, then, an idea of fair or reasonable terms of cooperation – an element of "the Reasonable" – and also an idea of the good of each person who participates – which Rawls calls "the Rational" (PL, 48–54).

The intuitive idea of the person Rawls uses in *Political Liberalism* is adapted to this idea of social cooperation (PL, 18). Rawls says that since ancient times (in Roman civil law) a *person* is one who takes part, or has a role, in social life and can exercise and respect its various rights and duties. In order to take part in social cooperation, people need to have developed *capacities* to observe the fair terms of cooperation, and they also need to have some conception of what benefits them, of their interests or their good. This means that they have to have the *moral powers*, a capacity for a sense of justice and a rational capacity for a conception of the good. It is an empirical fact about people that they need these developed capacities if they are to take part in and enjoy the benefits of social cooperation.

This fact about the capacities needed for social cooperation, conjoined with the fact that democratic citizens conceive of themselves as free and equal, provides a kind of empirical basis for our accepting an ideal of citizens as free and equal persons with two moral powers. But Rawls does not think that facts about democratic citizens engaged in social cooperation commit us to any such ideal. Rather, he suggests that the ideal conception of citizens as free and equal moral persons is the most suitable way to represent, theoretically, how we actually conceive of ourselves in our capacity as democratic citizens. We may not think of ourselves in this way in all that we do – as members of a religion or university, for example, or when we regard ourselves as purely biological beings subject to natural and environmental forces. But for purposes of social cooperation as members of a democratic society the ideal conception of free and equal moral persons captures (Rawls conjectures) how we think of ourselves and one another in our capacity as democratic citizens.

Thus in Political Liberalism Rawls resourcefully converts the Kantian conceptions of the person and the nature of agency into what he regards as non-controversial claims about how citizens in fact conceive of themselves in a democratic society, and the natural capacities they need to effectively participate in society. This is partly what Rawls means by a "political conception of the person." It is not a metaphysical conception of the self, or a controversial normative conception of the person of the kind presupposed by comprehensive moral doctrines (as in Theory). Rather, it is a conception of the person that is based in empirical facts about social cooperation and how we actually conceive of ourselves in one important area of our lives, in our capacity as citizens.

Here again we might compare this conception with the legal conception of persons that is predominant in Western legal systems. Legal personality is the capacity of persons to have and to exercise legal rights and to comply with legal duties. When a legal hearing is held to assess individuals' mental competency, the main inquiry is into whether they have the capacity to take care of themselves and protect and pursue their own interests. A senile person, or a young child, does not have this capacity – they lack the capacity to be rational – and for this reason they are assigned legal guardians to protect their interests (normally parents or other relatives). Another example is the traditional common-law test for insanity in criminal law, the M'Naghten Rule, which is whether a defendant has the capacity to distinguish right from wrong. A person who does not have it is deemed legally insane in common law and is not held responsible for his or her actions. Modern insanity tests are more liberal, excusing people from culpability even if they have the capacity to distinguish right from wrong, but are still unable to control their impulses or actions – they have a "diminished capacity." In this case, the criminally insane lack, in effect, the capacity to be reasonable, or a sense of justice. They are unable to do what is morally and legally required.

As the legal conception of the person is based in common-sense psychology familiar to our ordinary assessments of people in holding them responsible, so too does Rawls intend that the political conception of the person that undergirds a political conception of justice have a similar basis in common-sense psychology and our ordinary practices of holding people responsible. In this regard, the conception of the person is "political, not metaphysical" (CP, ch. 18).

The Freedom of Citizens

One of Rawls's aims in *Political Liberalism* is to reconcile the Lockean and Rousseauian understandings of the fundamental democratic values of freedom and equality (PL, 4–5). There are three senses of *freedom* that Rawls associates with the idea of free and equal citizens. First, citizens are free in that they *have a conception of the good*; if they have not freely formed it for themselves, they nonetheless have the capacity to revise and reform it as they pursue their good (PL, 30–32). Second, citizens see themselves as *"self-authenticating sources of valid claims,"*[4] in that they can make claims on social institutions to advance their conception of the good that are not derived from duties and obligations owed to society (PL, 32–33). Third, citizens are free in that they see themselves as *responsible for their ends*, and capable of adjusting their wants to what they can legitimately expect as a result of social cooperation. The first and third of these kinds of freedom are "positive" freedoms; they concern capacities or powers that people have. The second appears to be freedom as a kind of status that stems from others' recognition of the legitimacy of one's claims on them, independent of others' and society's own purposes. Rawls contrasts freedom of the second kind with its opposite, the status of slaves and their inability to make recognizable claims on society and others.

Here again, the focus on these three aspects of citizens' freedom has to be different than earlier, to comply with the limits of *Political Liberalism*. Rawls cannot mean in *Political Liberalism* that these three kinds of freedom are valuable for their own sake, or that they stem from a more general conception of freedom as full autonomy that is intrinsically good. No such appeal to comprehensive values can be made within *Political Liberalism*. For many, the freedoms they enjoy as citizens might be nothing more than a means to other ends. For example, a liberal Catholic may so identify with his faith and the pursuit of the Vision of God that exercising his freedom in the first sense (having the rational capacity to form and revise his conception of the good) is of little intrinsic value to him. For changing this conception of the good may be the last thing he wants. Nonetheless, that he has the capacity to deliberate and rationally pursue the good that he already endorses, and therewith revise and adjust ends subordinate to his final end, must still be of great importance to him. He might need to change his career or "calling," for example, and develop new skills and interests, if he is to fulfill his religious duties to God. For this reason, maintaining the freedom that goes with having the capacities for a rational conception of the good should be of great political and even religious importance to him, even though rational autonomy and individuality are not themselves of intrinsic value in his conception of the good.

Well-ordered society

Rawls says in his exposition of the fundamental intuitive ideas:

> We must keep in mind that we are trying to show *how the idea of society as a fair system of social cooperation can be unfolded*, so as to find principles specifying the basic rights and liberties and

the forms of equality most appropriate to those cooperating, once
they are regarded as citizens, as free and equal persons.

(*PL*, 27, emphasis added)

This sentence is an important comment on Rawls's method in
Political Liberalism. In the first two chapters of *Political Liberalism* Rawls
is "unfolding" (he does not say "analyzing") the idea of society as
a fair system of social cooperation. In doing so, he arrives at the
conception of the persons engaged in social cooperation and the
powers and capacities they must have to successfully do so. Then,
he "unfolds" or develops this conception of moral persons and
arrives at the idea that these persons regard one another as free
and as equals in part because they have these moral powers. Then
he reviews the various respects in which these persons are free.
None of this is conceptual analysis. Rather Rawls is engaged in
exposition, laying out the various aspects of his position. But it is
not simply arbitrary stipulation either, for all these ideas are interconnected and also are a reasonable way (he does not say the only
way) to see what is involved in the fundamental intuitive ideas
Rawls thinks we all share as members of a democratic society. The
eventual aim is to set up the argument for a liberal conception of
justice, which Rawls sees as best fitting with this exposition. His
method is to put into place a number of key ideas that bring into
focus the idea of fair social cooperation among free and equal citizens, discuss what each of them involves, and then to "construct"
from these fundamental ideas and their corollaries (an argument
for) liberal principles of justice. This is part of Rawls's constructivism – in this case *political constructivism* – which (recall from
Chapter 1, pp. 38–9) is all "within" and an aspect of reflective
equilibrium. Constructivism provides meaning to the idea of "best
fit," or what is involved for our considered convictions at all
levels of generality and principles of justice to "fit . . . into one
coherent scheme" in "general and wide reflective equilibrium"
(CP, 289, 321). The activity of bringing into reflective equilibrium with principles of justice both our more and less general
considered convictions takes place largely within and is structured
by "the procedure of construction," the original position.

The point of this methodological interlude is to emphasize how the entire conception centers on and develops from the idea of society as a fair system of social cooperation. The idea of free and equal persons is a "companion idea" to fair social cooperation; it is needed to tell us who are the parties to cooperation, which in turn is needed to decide what are the appropriate terms for cooperation. This brings us to the next "model conception": the "companion idea" of a well-ordered society (PL, 35). Here we revisit a familiar idea set forth in *A Theory of Justice*. A well-ordered society is an ideal of social cooperation – Rawls says, "This is a highly idealized concept" (PL, 35) – and it is one Rawls presumes we aspire to. In the Kantian interpretation in *Theory* Rawls might have explained this aspiration in terms of an idea (of practical reason) implicit in the moral consciousness of free and equal moral persons with a capacity for moral autonomy (remember that a well-ordered society is an analogue to Kant's idea of a Realm of Ends). Here, however, the ideal of a well-ordered society emerges as an ideal of social cooperation among citizens of a democratic society. Rawls says, "Any conception of justice that cannot well order a constitutional democracy is inadequate as a democratic conception" (PL, 35). Why is it inadequate? Presumably Rawls says this since he thinks the ideal of a well-ordered society goes with the freedom and equality of democratic citizens. A well-ordered society embodies the contractarian ideal of a society in which everyone freely accepts society's regulative principles of justice. Since justice normally involves the social and often coercive enforcement of social and legal norms, free and equal persons ought to be able to accept and endorse the principles of justice regulating their society, even if they do not agree with all its laws. It is practicably impossible for free citizens to agree on all the laws, or even on all provisions of the constitution. But it is not practicably impossible for all to accept and agree upon the principles of justice that underlie the constitution and the laws. Such a society would be well ordered by its conception of justice.

One reason a society of free persons might be prevented from being well ordered is that its conception of justice puts such great burdens on some people that they cannot endorse that conception once it is publicly known. This was the primary focus in *A Theory of*

Justice in the comparison of justice as fairness with utilitarianism and other conceptions of justice. Rawls argued there that only justice as fairness could serve the role of a public conception of justice acceptable to all members of a well-ordered society. But after *Theory*, because of "the fact of reasonable pluralism," Rawls comes to see that even justice as fairness, regarded as a partially comprehensive Kantian moral conception, also could not gain unanimous allegiance and provide the moral constitution of a well-ordered society. The "serious problem" with the argument in *Theory* is that it relies upon an "unrealistic idea of a well-ordered society [wherein] all its citizens endorse [justice as fairness] on the basis of what I now call a comprehensive philosophical doctrine" (PL, xviii). But rather than giving up the idea of a well-ordered society, and therewith his contractarianism, Rawls redefines the conditions of a well-ordered society's stability. A question in the background of *Political Liberalism*, then, is whether justice as fairness (or any liberal view), when reinterpreted as a freestanding political conception, can gain unanimous consent among reasonable persons, once the conditions of its justification are altered to take into account the fact of reasonable pluralism.

The main point, then, is that Rawls's idea of the conditions for the stability of a well-ordered society must change, once he takes into account the "*fact of reasonable pluralism*." Little has been said about this idea thus far or about the related idea of "reasonable comprehensive doctrine." The fact of reasonable pluralism is not simply the fact that in a liberal society where people enjoy basic liberal liberties of conscience, thought, expression, association, and other basic liberties, there will be many different and conflicting ethical, philosophical, and religious positions or "comprehensive doctrines." Rawls thinks that, given the propensities of human nature and people's personal circumstances, such pluralism is inevitable. Moreover, some people are always going to entertain fantastic, or intolerant, or downright malevolent, religious, philosophical, and moral views. But pluralism per se and the inevitability of uncivil doctrines is not the main problem Rawls is concerned with, though he recognizes that the numbers of people holding them cannot be too great in a well-ordered society (PL, 39). The main problem is the plurality of *reasonable doctrines* – different moral, philosophical, and religious doctrines – reasonable and rational people themselves will affirm, even when presented with the same arguments and the same evidence. (Here it is important to stress that Rawls means "reasonable" and "rational" in a definite sense from within *Political Liberalism*, which is discussed below.) This is because of the *burdens of judgment*. It is in the nature of morality, philosophy, and religion that they result in disagreement, even among similarly informed reasonable and rational persons; *reasonable disagreement* mainly distinguishes these doctrines from mathematics and the genuine sciences.

In *Political Liberalism*, unlike *Theory*, a well-ordered society is marked by reasonable pluralism and reasonable disagreement about the foundations of justice, even among reasonable and rational citizens. As a result, agreement on principles of justice becomes all the more unlikely and a well-ordered society much more difficult to achieve. Rawls can no longer rely upon agreement on a Kantian conception of morality and the good to guarantee agreement on a conception of justice and its application. Instead, given reasonable disagreement about morality, what is needed to make agreement on justice as fairness, or liberal justice more generally, possible is an "overlapping consensus" among reasonable comprehensive doctrines on society's freestanding political conception of justice. This is the primary distinction between the way the idea of a well-ordered society is used in *Political Liberalism* from its use in *Theory*. It marks an important difference in Rawls's social contract doctrine from that of his predecessors, Locke, Rousseau, and Kant, and makes his position resemble Hobbes's at least in this respect: like Hobbes, Rawls appreciates the importance of the inevitability of disagreement in philosophical and moral as well as religious doctrines. But unlike Hobbes, and in line with these earlier advocates of natural rights social contract views, Rawls still believes that agreement on liberal justice is possible among reasonable people, not because of a compromise or *modus vivendi* backed by coercive sanctions, but on the basis of citizens' moral sense of justice as grounded in their different reasonable comprehensive views. This is the significance of the idea of *overlapping consensus*. It locates a basis for reasonable agreement within the sources of reasonable disagreement themselves, in the different and conflicting moral, philosophical, and religious views affirmed by reasonable citizens.

The original position

Before explaining the idea of overlapping consensus, we should finish the exposition of the main ideas that clarify a freestanding political conception. Starting with the idea of society as a fair system of social cooperation, we have discussed Rawls's accounts of the agents of cooperation, the capacities that enable them to take part in cooperation, and their self-conception and higher-order interests as free and equal citizens. We also reviewed the ideal of social cooperation to which free and equal citizens aspire to maintain their status as free and equal, a well-ordered society. Now the question is, how would free and equal persons go about deciding upon a conception of justice for a well-ordered society? What supplies the bases for their agreement on principles of justice? Since they differ in their conceptions of the good and do not endorse the same comprehensive doctrine, there is no particular doctrine or conception of the good they can all refer to that would provide a well-ordered society's principles of justice. Moreover, to appeal to any religious or otherwise authoritative figure to decide upon a conception of justice for them would be inappropriate in view of their conception of themselves as free and equal. The only way for free and equal persons to arrive at a conception of justice they all accept is by an agreement among themselves; a general agreement is needed to supply the bases for agreement and public justification among free and equal persons. Thus we arrive at the idea of a social contract.

Following the model set forth in Kantian Constructivism, Rawls explains the various features of this social contract by reference to the conception of persons as free and equal moral persons coming to a fair agreement. This should be familiar territory. A fair agreement to terms of social cooperation among free and equal persons requires that they be equally situated. This requires the elimination of bargaining advantages, including citizens' reliance upon facts about their relative wealth, professional and social standing, talents and abilities, gender, race and ethnicity, and so on. More controversially, it requires that they not even rely upon their particular conceptions of the good and the comprehensive philosophical, moral, and religious doctrines that might supply life's meaning. For these are primary among the facts that underlie their most fundamental disagreements, and would impede agreement on principles of justice. But how are people to come to an agreement on anything as important as principles of justice if they do not have access to the philosophical, moral, and religious doctrines that provide them with guideposts in everyday moral decision making? Here Rawls appeals to the exercise of the moral powers as an *essential good* of free and equal citizens. Even though citizens have fundamental differences in their conceptions of the good, including their reasonable comprehensive doctrines, still they all have an interest in social cooperation. This provides them with grounds for taking a *"higher-order interest"* in the development and exercise of the capacities that are necessary for successful social cooperation. For Rawls, a person's interests are not what a person desires. Rather, a person's interests concern what is *rational* for a person to desire; and as we've seen, rational desire is more or less synonymous with a person's good on Rawls's account of "goodness as rationality." To say free and equal persons have a higher-order interest in the development and exercise of their moral powers means it is rational for them to desire to develop and exercise these capacities, since they are so crucial to their taking part in and gaining the benefits from social cooperation; they are in this respect essential to everyone's good. Importantly, this does not mean that the development and exercise of the moral powers are worth doing for their own sake. This claim would saddle Rawls with the very difficulties that led to *Political Liberalism*. For to claim that some activity is good for its own sake at this stage of argument is to assume a comprehensive doctrine, and this is what the original position must avoid. Rawls has to be careful not to build too much into his claim regarding the interests of free and equal moral persons. The claim that they have a higher-order interest in their moral powers is only meant to supply a mutual basis for agreement on principles of justice among people who fundamentally disagree about comprehensive doctrines and what is good for its own sake.

Finally, what does the original position, along with the elaborate account of free and equal persons and their essential interests, and a well-ordered society, have to do with you and me? "We introduce . . . the original position because there seems to be no better way to elaborate a political conception of justice for the basic structure from the fundamental idea of society as an ongoing and fair system of cooperation between citizens regarded as free and equal" (PL, 26). But this, you might say, just warrants the same question: What does this "elaboration" of ideas have to do with you and me? This objection to Rawls takes many forms. As we saw in Chapter 4, Ronald Dworkin objects to the original position on grounds that it is a hypothetical contract.[5] He says that the fact that we would agree to something under hypothetical conditions cannot be binding upon us; to be bound by a contract requires an actual promise or agreement. But the original position (like social contract doctrine generally) is not intended to bind us to any promise we might make. Rather its purpose is to clarify *what we now think and are committed to believe,* assuming that we conceive of ourselves as free and equal citizens and have a willingness to cooperate with others as equals on grounds of mutual respect.[6] The conception of justice the parties would adopt identifies, Rawls believes, the conception of justice that we regard – here and now – as fair and supported by the best reasons (PL, 26). Rawls presumes that as members of a democratic society we in fact think of ourselves as free and equal citizens, and that we are drawn to affirm the idea of a well-ordered society as an ideal of fair social cooperation among free and equal people like ourselves. These are "ideas of practical reason" implicit in the political consciousness of members of a democratic society (see PL, 107, 110). The point of a social contract in the original position is to clarify the implications of these ideas and democratic ideals we endorse. Assuming that the original position is set up so as to incorporate "all the relevant requirements of practical reason," (PL, 90) then the conception of justice that would be chosen there is one that we also should endorse to remain consistent with our political self-conception. In this regard it might be said (in response to Dworkin's objection) that indeed we are committed or "bound" to this political conception of justice. It is not an actual or hypothetical promise in the original position that binds us; rather, it is the combined force of our political self-conception and the ideals and considered judgments of justice that we have as democratic citizens.

Reasonableness, Reasonable Persons, and Reasonable Comprehensive Doctrines

The idea of reasonableness is a crucial concept in Rawls's work, beginning with his first article.[7] But in *Political Liberalism* the concept receives its most extensive use and its most thorough explication. We saw in the previous chapter how Rawls contrasts the Reasonable with the Rational in Kantian Constructivism. In *Theory* these distinct ideas parallel Rawls's distinction between the Right and the Good. Rawls's social contract position differs from Hobbesian positions primarily in its claim that reasonable moral principles cannot be derived simply from the concept of rationality, or a person's good. Rather, the Reasonable forms a distinct and independent domain of practical reasoning with its own independent moral principles. Rawls says "the reasonable and the rational are complementary ideas," and that "neither the reasonable nor the rational can stand without the other" (PL, 52). He does not mean that we cannot understand rational action without moral principles. Rather, he seems to mean that reasonable and rational agents are the basic units of responsibility in social and political life (PL, 50). A person who is rational but wholly unreasonable is not fit for social life, and a person who is reasonable but wholly irrational is incapable of concerted action.

There is an epistemic sense of reasonableness which should not be confused with the way that Rawls normally uses the term. The "burdens of judgment" imply that there will be *reasonable disagreement among reasonable and rational persons* about philosophical issues. Rawls says: "In philosophy questions at the most fundamental level are not usually settled by conclusive argument. What is obvious to some persons and accepted as a basic idea is unintelligible to others" (PL, 53). Some have understood Rawls to mean here that philosophical questions are unanswerable;[8] for if fully reasonable and rational people, presented with the same reasons, arguments, and evidence, cannot agree on their answers, then this must mean that the answer is not open to reason and is indeterminate. The problem with this interpretation of *Political Liberalism* is that it commits Rawls to a controversial philosophical position – a kind of skepticism regarding metaphysics, epistemology, and other philosophical fields – and this position is incompatible with the idea of public reason.[9] The suggestion seems to be that Rawls uses "reasonable person" epistemically, in the sense of a person who reasons correctly, assesses all the available reasons and evidence and assigns them the appropriate weight, and whose judgments are not swayed by emotions or interests. There is an element in Rawls's account of "reasonable persons" that relies to some degree on these epistemic elements. Also, Rawls defines "reasonable comprehensive doctrines" epistemically, as doctrines that are responsive to evidence and possess certain other theoretical features.[10] But the main sense of Rawls's many uses of the concept of reasonableness is *moral*. "Being reasonable is not an epistemological idea (though it has epistemological elements). Rather, it is part of a political ideal of democratic citizenship that includes the idea of public reason . . . [T]he reasonable, rather than the rational, addresses the public world of others" (PL, 62).

Reasonable citizens and *reasonable persons* are seminal concepts in *Political Liberalism*. They provide the focal point for other uses of the idea of reasonableness; normally Rawls explicates this idea in connection with the concept of reasonable persons. For example, reasonable disagreement is characterized as disagreement between reasonable persons (PL, 55); and reasonable comprehensive doctrines initially are characterized as "doctrines that reasonable citizens affirm" (PL, 36). In general Rawls characterizes reasonable persons via a list of characteristics, with the first two receiving the most emphasis:

(1) Reasonable persons desire to cooperate with other reasonable persons on terms that they can accept, and have a willingness to

propose such terms when the question arises. This is part of their sense of justice, which they all have. Thus, reasonable persons do not want to coerce or manipulate other reasonable people to accept terms of cooperation – a constitution, or an economic system for example – that they might otherwise reject. This implies that they respect others' freedom and equality.

(2) Reasonable persons also recognize and appreciate the consequences of the burdens of judgment (PL, 54–58). They understand that agreement on moral, philosophical, and religious issues is difficult for reasons other than simply ignorance, self-interest, and emotional differences. There are factors that lead people to make different judgments, even when they seek to be impartial and are presented with similar reasons and evidence. These include differences in education and experiences; vagueness of concepts, especially moral concepts; complexity of factual evidence; differences in the weight that people assign to the same considerations and evidence; and the complexity of normative considerations on both sides of a controversial issue (PL, 56–57).

(3) Reasonable persons want to be seen as reasonable and as having a sense of justice. Being reasonable is part of their self-image, a basis of their self-respect, and they want others to recognize them as reasonable persons. This is a familiar characteristic. As T.M. Scanlon has noted, people will go to great lengths to convince others that their actions are reasonable and justifiable. No reasonable person wants to be regarded as malevolent or even unreasonable by others.

(4) Finally, reasonable persons not only want to be seen as reasonable, but they also have a "reasonable moral psychology." This means that they have a "moral nature," including a sense of justice, which enables them to do what is right and just for its own sake, and not simply because it benefits them or someone else. It also means that they have "principle-dependent desires," or desires to act for the sake of reasonable and rational principles which regulate their "object-dependent desires" to pursue specific ends or states of affairs. Rawls here challenges welfarism and other positions which hold that interests of persons (in oneself and others) provide the only rational end of all conduct.

Other features of reasonable persons follow from these primary characteristics. For example, reasonable people are not egoists; they are not concerned only with promoting their own interests. Rather they recognize the independent validity of others' claims (PL, 52). Also they "take into account the consequences of their actions on others' well-being" (PL, 49n.). They are willing to govern their conduct by a principle from which they and others can reason in common (PL, 49n.). In addition, reasonable persons are sensitive to the reasons that others have that stem from their conceptions of the good. They do not just act on what is rational from their own individual perspective, but take into account others' points of view in deliberating on their own actions and deciding what is rational for themselves to do. This does not mean they are altruistic, in the sense of always acting impartially for the interests of others (PL, 54). Rather, reasonable people have their own rational ends and plans of life to which they assign primary importance; but they are willing to rationally pursue their ends according to fair terms of reciprocity that respect others as equals. Rawls says reasonable persons "insist that reciprocity should hold . . . so that each benefits along with others" (PL, 50). He distinguishes reciprocity from both altruism and mutual advantage (PL, 16–17). The altruistic person is impartially concerned with the general good whereas the reasonable person is impartially concerned with justice. Unlike the purely altruistic person, the reasonable person is not willing to sacrifice the good of the few for the greater good of the many. A person who is rational but not reasonable may be willing to comply with terms of cooperation that are mutually advantageous. But unlike the reasonable person he has no idea of fair terms of cooperation independent of the bargains and compromises that can be negotiated with others on the basis of competing interests.

Finally, since reasonable persons want to cooperate with others on terms they can accept, they address others who hold comprehensive doctrines contrary to their own exclusively in terms of *public reasons* within the "public political forum." As discussed in the next chapter, public reasons are shared by democratic citizens and address citizens in their capacity as democratic citizens. The idea of public reason is connected with the moral motive of reasonable persons to justify themselves to others in terms of principles that other reasonable persons could not reasonably reject.[11] This and other "principle-dependent desires" – or desires to act from moral principles – are part of reasonable persons' "reasonable moral psychology."

Turn now to Rawls's other uses of the concept of reasonableness. The main problem *Political Liberalism* addresses is that reasonable and rational persons, because of different reasonable comprehensive doctrines, cannot agree upon the ultimate justification of a conception of justice; this raises the question how a well-ordered democratic society is possible, one in which reasonable persons all agree upon a liberal conception of justice. The ideas of "reasonable comprehensive doctrine," or "reasonable religious, philosophical, and moral doctrines," are crucial here. What do they mean? Rawls initially says, "These are the doctrines that reasonable people affirm and that *Political Liberalism* must address" (PL, 36). He repeats this several times in the book. The question is whether this is intended as a necessary feature of reasonable comprehensive doctrines, or whether it is a contingent feature that results from an "overlapping consensus" of reasonable comprehensive doctrines. Now if Rawls intends it as a definition and defines reasonable comprehensive doctrines simply in terms of the comprehensive doctrines that reasonable persons affirm, this would seem to suggest that reasonable comprehensive doctrines all must incorporate features consistent with the defining features of reasonable persons. Since reasonable persons appreciate the burdens of judgment and want to cooperate with others on terms they accept, we might then expect that reasonable doctrines also affirm these features, and thus would necessarily avow toleration of other reasonable comprehensive doctrines, as well as freedom of expression and association, and other liberal basic liberties. The problem with this understanding of reasonable doctrines (as some of Rawls's critics have recognized) is that it seems to render trivial the problem of stability that Rawls confronts in *Political Liberalism*. For if the problem of stability is simply whether the reasonable and hence tolerant doctrines that reasonable and hence tolerant people affirm will also all affirm a tolerant and liberal political conception of justice, then the answer is obvious: "Of course they will, for reasonable doctrines are virtually defined as affirming liberal values of justice from the outset." Because this trivializes the stability problem, I believe we must attend to Rawls's other account of reasonable comprehensive doctrines in order to understand what the crucial problem is that he confronts.

Rawls uses the term "reasonable" in "reasonable comprehensive doctrines" largely in an epistemological sense. In what Rawls terms the "definition of such doctrines" he assigns them three main features (PL, 59). First, "a reasonable doctrine is an exercise of theoretical reason: it covers the major religious, philosophical, and moral aspects of human life in a more or less consistent and coherent manner . . . and [its values] express an intelligible view of the world." The emphasis here is placed on the completeness and coherence of a comprehensive doctrine and its ability to address a wide range of philosophical, religious, and moral issues. Second, "a reasonable comprehensive doctrine is also an exercise of practical reason," in that it singles out which values are especially significant and how to balance important values when they conflict. It provides, then, an account of the human good as well as the values and ends that give life meaning. Finally, third, "a comprehensive doctrine is not necessarily fixed and unchanging . . . it tends to evolve slowly in the light of what, from its point of view, it sees as good and sufficient reasons" (PL, 65). This suggests that a comprehensive doctrine has standards of evidence and of falsifiability that would allow it to admit mistakes and revise itself in light of new or changing information. Rawls's inclusion of this last condition excludes what he calls "fundamentalist doctrines," which do not admit of change, in spite of changed conditions and evidence that contravenes their major doctrines. Rawls suggests that Catholicism has shown itself to be a reasonable comprehensive doctrine, since in Vatican II, and at other times in its history, it adjusted its doctrine to accommodate many of the scientific and political realities of the modern world. On the other hand, fundamentalist Christians who insist upon the literalness of the Bible and the historical accuracy of the account of creation set forth in Genesis are not reasonable. Nothing can be said to fundamentalists to persuade them that the earth was created billions of years ago; they explain away scientific evidence of ancient dinosaur and other fossils as fabricated by God to test our faith. In being closed-minded to any and all evidence that would disprove factual or historical statements in the Bible, fundamentalist doctrines are unreasonable.

Rawls's definition of reasonable comprehensive doctrines leaves many questions to be answered. Rawls concedes that it is "deliberately loose" (PL, 59). Most any philosopher would provide a more strenuous account that would count as clearly unreasonable, and untrue, many doctrines Rawls's criterion regards as reasonable. For example, most philosophers would contend that most any religious doctrine is unreasonable in so far as it believes in miracles, an afterlife, spiritual beings, and so on. But Rawls regards religious doctrines as reasonable so long as they satisfy his three criteria. The looseness and flexibility of Rawls's criteria must be considered in light of his limited purposes. He needs to avoid controversial epistemological claims in order to achieve agreement upon a liberal political conception of justice among reasonable persons. The main role the idea reasonable comprehensive doctrines plays is in Rawls's overlapping consensus argument for stability. Rawls's argument, briefly, is that the stability of a well-ordered society primarily depends upon the convergence upon a freestanding political conception of justice by all the reasonable comprehensive doctrines affirmed by reasonable persons. All the reasonable doctrines, in the limited sense outlined above, should endorse a politically reasonable liberal political political conception, each for its own comprehensive reasons. This is not a trivial conclusion but an empirical hypothesis that Rawls contends is supported by what we know about human nature and social cooperation. This argument is examined after a discussion of how *Political Liberalism* is a constructivist conception.

POLITICAL CONSTRUCTIVISM

A. Political vs. Kantian Constructivism

Regarding political constructivism, Rawls says:

> Political constructivism is a view about the structure and content of a political conception. It says that once, if ever, reflective equilibrium

is attained, the principles of political justice (content) *may be represented* as the outcome of a certain procedure of construction (structure). . . . This procedure [the original position], we conjecture, embodies all the relevant requirements of practical reason and shows how the principles of justice follow from the principles of practical reason in union with conceptions of society and person, themselves ideas of practical reason.

(*PL*, 89–90, emphasis added)

Recall from the preceding chapter that constructivism in ethics is a view about the conditions of the objectivity of moral judgments and the nature of standards of moral correctness. Against moral realism, constructivism says that the correctness of moral judgments depends, not upon their being true of a prior moral order of facts or principles, but on their basis in principles that are the product of an objective procedure of construction that embodies all the requirements of practical reasoning. In Kantian Constructivism the original position is said to "model" the conception of free and equal moral persons and their capacities for practical reason, along with other formal and substantive ideas and principles of practical reasoning. On the assumption that this procedure incorporates "all the relevant requirements of practical reason," it might be said that principles uniformly derived therein are "given" to us by our own practical reason. To act for the sake of these principles is to be morally autonomous. Constructivism so construed is a highly controversial thesis about morality, objectivity, and moral truth; it cannot provide a basis for public justification in a pluralist society. How, then, can Rawls incorporate *any* form of constructivism into *Political Liberalism*? Indeed, why should he even want to retain constructivism given its provenance as the methodological expression of autonomy?

One reason Rawls incorporates a form of constructivism is that his political contractarianism requires that he retain a full publicity condition, including a generally acceptable *public political justification of* society's political conception of justice. A public political justification acceptable to citizens generally is needed for pragmatic reasons, in order that government officials may consistently apply liberal principles of justice in making and applying the political constitution and the laws, and in deciding legislative and judicial disputes. Officials need something other than their own moral, religious, and philosophical views in order to interpret laws, a liberal constitution, and its principles of justice. How otherwise could there be a shared basis for deciding how basic liberties are to be specified at constitutional, legislative, and judicial stages? Do the basic liberties imply a constitutional "right of privacy" or constitutional rights to birth control, abortion, same-sex relations, assisted suicide, euthanasia, and so on? Also, without a public justification of its conception of justice, how can a liberal society politically decide how to set the social minimum so that it is adequate to citizens' fair and effective exercise of their basic liberties and opportunities?

But even if a well-ordered democratic society needs *some* basis for deciding how its principles of justice are to be justified and applied to its constitution, why should this public justification be a constructivist one? There are two related reasons. First, a constructivist justification of a circumscribed kind is needed in order to make "political autonomy" possible. While moral autonomy is the moral value driving Kant's and Kantian Constructivism, political autonomy undergirds political constructivism. Second, a constructivist justification of the political conception of justice is needed to make the political conception "freestanding" of all comprehensive views. But how can this be, since constructivism is itself a comprehensive thesis about practical reason's autonomy in giving principles to itself? This is where Rawls crucially alters the sense in which constructivism implies practical reason's autonomy. He distinguishes "constitutive autonomy" from "doctrinal autonomy" (PL, 98–99). Kant's, and also Kantian, constructivism aim for the constitutive autonomy of a moral conception of justice – reason giving moral principles to itself – in order to make the moral autonomy of persons possible. *Political Liberalism* by contrast embodies the *doctrinal autonomy* of a political conception of justice – its basis in democratic political ideas independent of all comprehensive doctrines – which is needed to make the *political autonomy of citizens* possible. "In affirming the [doctrinally autonomous] political doctrine as a whole we, as citizens, are ourselves autonomous, politically speaking. An autonomous political conception provides then an appropriate basis and ordering of political values for a constitutional regime characterized by reasonable pluralism" (ibid.).

Rawls's shift from the constitutive to doctrinal autonomy is suggested when he says that in political constructivism, political principles may be *"represented"* as the outcome of a procedure of construction itself based on principles of practical reason and ideas of persons and society (PL, 98–99). This is a significant qualification of the Kantian claim that principles of justice *are* the outcome of a constructive reasoning procedure, for it does not commit Rawls to any particular position regarding the *origins* of principles of justice in principles of practical reason (PL, 99). Principles of justice may indeed have their origins in practical reason, as Kant's and perhaps Rawls's Kantian Constructivism claim. Then again they may not, originating instead in an independent moral order, God's will, or in mere expressions of our emotions. *Political Liberalism* tries to "bracket" these and other philosophical issues, and take no stand either way. To *represent* principles as originating in political ideas of practical reason is not to rely upon or commit oneself to any of these comprehensive philosophical positions. It is simply a way to depict the bases of political principles of justice for political purposes only. If this maneuver succeeds, political constructivism preserves the freestanding nature of a political conception of justice, while allowing it to serve its role as a shared basis for public justification among citizens with different comprehensive doctrines. *Doctrinal autonomy*, then, fills out the sense in which a political conception is a freestanding view. Political constructivism makes doctrinal autonomy possible: by relying on political ideas and the political values of public reason, a political conception of justice need not appeal to any reasons or values beyond the domain of the political in the public justification and application of society's principles of justice.

Constitutive autonomy, by contrast, is the kind of autonomy involved in Kant's constructivism and in Rawls's Kantian Constructivism (when construed as an extension of the Kantian interpretation). It is a substantive epistemological thesis about the philosophical origins of morality: it says moral principles are *constituted* out of the activity of practical reason, and do not have their origins in an independent moral order (such as God's will). Constitutive autonomy denies that moral principles have their origins prior to and independent of the exercise of practical reason. It denies, then, rational intuitionism and other forms of moral realism, natural law, divine command theories, moral sense doctrines, and all forms of moral skepticism and moral relativism. Doctrinal autonomy rejects none of these things. It is simply the methodological claim that a "freestanding" conception of justice can be arranged starting with certain fundamental intuitive ideas and considered convictions of justice shared by citizens holding different comprehensive doctrines in a democratic society. Doctrinal autonomy assumes only that free and equal citizens share certain reasonable moral/political beliefs, in spite of their many differences. It starts from these shared reasonable beliefs, without inquiring into their truth value (they may have none if moral skepticism is true), or into their philosophical, psychological, or social origins. The shared moral/political beliefs or convictions are arranged into a "procedure of construction." If principles on the basis of this procedure are agreeable to reasonable persons regardless of their comprehensive view, they can be said, for *political purposes*, to have their origins in the *public political reason* of democratic citizens. It is compatible with this, Rawls contends, that these principles have their *ultimate foundation* in one or more reasonable comprehensive views. If overlapping consensus is true, the political principles of justice have a "full justification" within the terms of all reasonable comprehensive views that gain credence in a well-ordered democratic society.

Rawls suggests the doctrinal autonomy of political constructivism should, then, be a non-controversial idea among different and conflicting philosophical positions regarding the nature of morality and the possibility of knowledge of it. This is Rawls's intention. (Later, in Chapter 9, we examine some objections in discussing the related idea of public reason.) It is perhaps in order to remain non-controversial, or "neutral," among different philosophical doctrines that Rawls refrains from contending that political principles of justice are "true" (PL, 126–27). This does not mean that he entirely eschews the public political use of the idea of truth. How could he? The concept of truth is clearly necessary when matters of fact are politically at issue (in trials or legislative hearings, for example). Moreover, Rawls recognizes that there are "natural uses for the notion of truth in moral reasoning," when we are talking about ordinary moral rules (e.g., "it is true that we normally ought to keep our promises"), or making particular moral judgments that "follow from, or are sound applications of, reasonable first principles" (CP, 355). But he wants to avoid the use of "true" within Political Liberalism when applied to basic political principles of justice and a liberal political conception itself. Why?[12] Apparently, it is because the concept of truth applied to moral principles is a metaphysical concept, notoriously contested within philosophy, and comprehensive doctrines have different accounts of the nature and possibility of moral truth, with some of them denying its possibility altogether. Political Liberalism must avoid these controversies, Rawls believes, if agreement among free and equal citizens on principles of justice is to be possible. But if reasonable people all agree the principles of justice are true, why should their disagreements about the nature of truth pose a problem? Rawls may well think that there will be many moral skeptics – those who deny the possibility of moral truth and who believe (for example) that political principles of justice are only expressions of our emotions – who can accept that liberal political principles are nonetheless more or less "reasonable," and can accept and reason within the political justification of society's conception of justice. Moral reasoning by reasonable moral skeptics is not paradoxical; though moral skeptics reject moral truth, they still accept (unless they are nihilists) that moral judgments are more or less reasonable.[13] Being a moral skeptic does not then disqualify one from being reasonable, or from engaging in political reasoning about justice. Of course, if a person is a skeptic about the idea of reasonableness altogether, or about the validity of political, legal, and other forms of practical reasoning, then this person cannot sincerely reason about political justice. But such a person is, by his or her own confession, not reasonable – he or she does not want to cooperate with reasonable persons on terms they can reasonably accept. There is probably nothing short of threats of sanction that can be said to such persons about why they ought to accept or comply with requirements of justice.

Objectivity of Political Judgments

But if Rawls really aims to avoid controversial claims regarding the truth of a political conception of justice, what are we to make of his claim that political principles of justice possess objectivity as a result of their derivation from a procedure of construction? This seems especially troublesome in light of Rawls's earlier claim that Kantian Constructivism's account of objectivity offers a better standard of the correctness of moral principles than rational intuitionism. Rawls's constructivist standard is that moral principles that derive from an objective procedure of construction that expresses all the relevant requirements of practical reason are "most reasonable" and provide the grounds for claims of moral truth of more particular judgments.

Political constructivism has to have some criterion of correctness of principles and political judgments of justice, if not "truth" or "universal validity" then "reasonableness," "political objectivity," or some other standard of correctness understood in an appropriate way. Otherwise we could not make valid political arguments within a political conception of justice, and contend or agree with people who have different comprehensive views about reasons for or against political positions. The problem is to come up with a characterization of the kind of correctness that principles and political judgments can have, without running afoul of the restrictions against invoking ideas that are incompatible with reasonable comprehensive doctrines. How can a claim of "political objectivity" avoid conflicting with non-constructivist comprehensive doctrines? A bit of reflection indicates that this is perhaps not as big a problem as it might seem. Consider legal objectivity and an analogy with legal reasoning, where appellate lawyers argue over the correct outcome of a case within common law, constitutional law, or statutory interpretation. While these questions may often be indeterminate, it is also often quite clear what legal principles apply and what the correct outcome should be. Of course, legal positivists might contend that it is only because of prior legislative or judicial fiat that it is clear when a given case comes under a statute or prior precedent and one outcome as opposed to another is correct. But even if legal positivism is true, prior legislative or judicial fiat does not deprive a subsequent judicial ruling of its correctness or legal validity within the constraints provided. Another analogy based on a different kind of reasoning is formal systems. Here certain axioms are stipulated and rules of inference set forth, so that the axioms, when combined according to the rules of inference, yield theorems. These theorems are regarded as objective or valid inferences and can even be said to be true within the terms set forth by the axioms and the rules of inference. They are not objective or true "in all possible worlds"; perhaps they are true only relative to the particular domain within which they are set forth. The point, however, is that objectivity, validity, and truth claims can be made within the formal system, even though nothing is said about the truth of the axioms or the correctness of the rules of inference in themselves or for purposes outside this particular system. Someone (a Platonist, for example) might contend that the axioms indeed are true in the great scheme of things. But this does not alter their status within the formal system, and the internal validity and objectivity of inferences correctly drawn from them according to appropriate rules of inference.

These analogies, while not exact, are still of some use in helping to understand Rawls's claim regarding the objectivity of political principles without committing us to accepting their moral truth or validity within a comprehensive doctrine. Suppose once again a sincere moral skeptic. As a citizen he conceives of himself as free and equal, and is reasonable and rational in Rawls's sense of exercising the moral and rational capacities for practical reasoning. But he regards his moral judgments as possessing no truth value and his political self-conception as a cultural contingency, not based in any kind of moral reality or in practical reason. Still, the moral skeptic should be able to accept his democratic self-conception as an appropriate basis for a political conception of justice. For it fits with his considered convictions of justice and the way that people think about justice in his society. This is so even though he regards his democratic self-conception and his considered convictions of justice in the scheme of things as possessing no more truth or validity than do arbitrarily stipulated axioms in a formal system. But as with a formal system, he can readily accept the objectivity and correctness of conclusions from those axioms, once stipulated, when validly drawn according to the appropriate decision procedure. It's just that, unlike others, he thinks the conclusions of political justice that are *politically objective* have no objectivity, truth, or universal validity, outside the framework of "the domain of the political." Others will have different reasonable comprehensive doctrines according to which the principles of justice and political conclusions derived from them are universally objective or true.[14] Then there would be an overlapping consensus between us and the moral skeptic on the political conception of justice.

The criteria for political objectivity that Rawls sets forth in *Political Liberalism* might be regarded in a similar way. They do not presuppose a comprehensive epistemological view (at least Rawls does not think so) but rather should be compatible with a wide range of epistemological conceptions of objectivity. Since these criteria are rather straightforward and uncontroversial, I just list them here, with little discussion; Rawls's discussion is clear and succinct enough (PL, 110–12). Rawls sets forth "five essential elements" for a conception of objectivity (adding later a sixth). Some of these conditions would seem to apply to any conception of objectivity, while others, since they presuppose agency, apply only to judgments of practical reason. Rawls's essential conditions are: (1) First, a conception of objectivity must establish a public framework of thought sufficient to apply the concept of judgment and for conclusions to be reached on the basis of *evidence and reasons*, after discussion and/or due reflection. (2) It must specify a concept of *correct judgment* made from its point of view, such as the truth or reasonableness of its conclusions. (3) It must specify an *order of reasons* as given by its principles and criteria, which provide agents with reasons that are to be weighed and acted from, and which can *override* the reasons agents think they have from their own point of view. (4) A conception of objectivity must distinguish the *objective point of view* from the point of view of any particular agent or group. (5) There is an account of *agreement in judgment* among reasonable agents, that can be reached (when it is to be had) by correctly applying concepts, principles, and standards and relevant rules of inference; given accurate and adequate information, reasonable persons with the same information who correctly apply these standards normally should reach the *same conclusion*. Finally, Rawls adds a sixth essential element later, (6) a conception of objectivity must be able to explain disagreement in an appropriate way, consistent with its criteria (PL, 121).

Rawls claims that the account of agreement from the original position meets these criteria of objectivity, and therefore that political liberalism is capable of resulting in objective judgments within the domain of the political. Rational intuitionism and Kant's moral constructivism also meet these conditions of objectivity, though they differ from *Political Liberalism* in how they satisfy some conditions. For example, rational intuitionism contends that the criterion of correctness required by (2) is whether a moral statement is true of an independent order of moral principles and values. By contrast, *Political Liberalism*'s criterion of correctness is whether political judgments of justice are *reasonable*, in the sense that they conform to principles of justice that would be chosen by free and equal citizens from an appropriately designed objective procedure of construction that expresses all relevant requirements of practical (political) reason. But here it seems there are two conflicting accounts of objectivity (at least), one grounded in the idea of truth, the other in the idea of reasonableness. How are these to be reconciled? As discussed in the next chapter, it is the role of Rawls's argument from overlapping consensus to suggest a way in which rational intuitionism and other reasonable comprehensive views can accept *Political Liberalism*'s criterion of correctness and account of objectivity as sufficient for *political purposes* alone, even though they may not find it sufficient for non-political purposes of providing a true philosophical view.

Remarks on Political Autonomy

Earlier I gave reasons why Rawls needs a political conception of objectivity and political justification for a well-ordered society's political conception of justice. First, it is needed for pragmatic purposes, in order to have shared standards by which to apply society's conception of justice. Second, it is needed for moral/political purposes, namely, it is a requirement of public reason (discussed in the next chapter). Then I asked why the conception of justification had to be a constructivist conception, and again I mentioned two reasons. First, if it is to remain free-standing, the political conception must be constructed solely on the basis of political ideas implicit within the political culture of a democratic society and this political construction must be doctrinally autonomous from ideas peculiar to any comprehensive doctrine. Second, the doctrinal autonomy of the public political conception and its public justification is necessary for citizens' *political autonomy*. We have not discussed yet this key idea. What is political autonomy? Again, this question depends in part upon the idea of public reason, and must await the discussion of public reason in the next chapter. But something should be said about how political autonomy is distinct from moral autonomy.

A morally autonomous person is one who acts on and for the sake of principles of justice that are the product of the constitutive autonomy of practical reason. In this regard he or she acts from moral principles self-legislated out of the resources of practical reason. The morally autonomous person's actions are not governed therefore by laws, influences, and forces that are externally imposed, whether by God, an independent moral order, or social convention. Even if her actions conform to God's will or social convention, this is not the motivating or justifying *reason* for her actions; the reasons for her actions rather are justice and principles of justice themselves, which are principles implicit in her own practical reasoning.

None of these things can be said to be (necessarily) true of a politically autonomous person (though they *may* be true if he or she seeks to be morally autonomous also, *and* if a Kantian account of morality is true). Rawls initially supplies a very minimal description of political autonomy: it is "the legal independence and assured political integrity of citizens and their sharing with other citizens equally in the exercise of political power" (PL, xliv). But since he says (PL, Lecture III) that doctrinal autonomy, and political constructivism itself, are necessary if political autonomy is to be possible, he clearly envisions further conditions. Accordingly, we might say, provisionally, the following (by rough parallel with moral autonomy): A person is *politically autonomous* when he or she (1) acts upon democratically or otherwise duly enacted laws; (2) where these laws are justified by liberal principles of justice, (3) and these principles *can be represented* as part of a freestanding (doctrinally autonomous) political conception, (4) that has a constructivist political justification based in citizens' considered judgments and ideas implicit in democratic culture, including the self-conception of democratic citizens as reasonable and rational. One major difference between moral and political autonomy, so defined, is motivational; it is that political autonomy does not require that a person act for the sake of principles of justice themselves. He or she may act for the sake of the primary purposes that are part of one's comprehensive moral, religious, and philosophical doctrine. Thus liberal Catholics can be politically autonomous even though they act ultimately on principles of justice only *because* they believe they are part of God's natural law.

Second, is it a condition of political autonomy of citizens that a person actually participate in some way in the enactment of the laws she acts upon? This is a condition for what Rousseau calls "political freedom." For Rousseau both political freedom and moral freedom require that citizens actively participate in the making of laws that themselves are an expression, not of the combination of the majority of their particular wills, but of the general will. Is active political participation similarly a condition of Rawls's political autonomy? Rawls of course does not require a direct democracy for political autonomy as Rousseau did. Arguably, according to the definition above (PL, xliv), Rawls uses "political autonomy" simply in an institutional sense, denoting the "political freedom" that a well-ordered democratic society realizes so long as it provides equal basic liberties and protects their fair value. But in saying that doctrinal autonomy is a condition of political autonomy, he must mean more than political freedom in an institutional sense. When we discuss the idea of public reason, we will see why Rawls thinks a deliberative democracy is necessary for political autonomy. For Rawls, unlike Rousseau, political autonomy does not require acting upon laws that one has participated in legislating. But it does involve citizenship within the strenuous institutional requirements of a well-ordered deliberative democracy that is itself regulated by a freestanding liberal political conception, and whose laws are justifiable according to public reasons.

Finally, it should be noted that in his final work, *The Law of Peoples*, Rawls says that his claims in *Political Liberalism* – that a procedure of construction should be designed to "express the principles of practical reason" (PL, 114), or "embodies all the relevant requirements of practical reason" (PL, 90) – were misleading. (LP, 86n.). They should not be taken as implying a philosophical account of the nature of practical reason of the kind that Kant or anyone else advocates, or that principles of justice are deduced from practical reason in any sense. "Practical reasoning as such is simply reasoning about what to do, or reasoning about what institutions and policies are reasonable, decent, or rational and why. There is no list of necessary and sufficient conditions for each of these three ideas, and differences of opinion are to be expected" (LP, 87). Instead, Rawls suggests, once we lay out the content of these ideas "properly," by which he seems to mean in a way mutually acceptable to us, "the resulting principles and standards of right and justice will hang together and will be affirmed by us on due reflection" (ibid.). It is only in this relatively weak sense – namely of principles standing in reflective equilibrium with our considered political convictions – that principles of right and justice can be said to be an "expression" of our practical reason. Rawls in the end completely deflates Kant's idealism within political constructivism.

FURTHER READING

Cohen, Joshua, "A More Democratic Liberalism," Michigan Law Review, 92: 6, May 1994. (An excellent review of Political Liberalism, emphasizing its basis in democratic thought and ideals.)

Habermas, Jürgen, "Reconciliation Through the Public Use of Reason: Remarks on John Rawls's Political Liberalism," Journal of Philosophy, 92, 1995, 109–31. (Combined with Rawls's response "Reply to Habermas" (reprinted as Lecture IX of Political Liberalism, paperback and expanded editions) these articles are an exciting exchange between two major political philosophers.)

Waldron, Jeremy, "Disagreements about Justice," Pacific Philosophical Quarterly, 75, 1994, 372–87. (Questions whether reasonable agreement upon a liberal conception of justice is attainable, since reasonable disagreement is as prevalent about justice as about religious, philosophical, and moral comprehensive doctrines.)

Nine

Political Liberalism II – Overlapping Consensus and Public Reason

Now that the basic concept of a reasonable person has been defined, we can better understand the problem *Political Liberalism* addresses. The overarching aim of *Political Liberalism* is to show how it is realistically possible for reasonable democratic citizens to agree upon and endorse for moral reasons a liberal conception of justice that assigns priority to the basic liberties of free and equal citizens and provides a reasonable social minimum. This may not seem to be a difficult problem since Rawls defines "reasonable persons" as those who want to cooperate with other reasonable persons on terms acceptable to them; it may seem that toleration of others' ways of life required by the basic liberties is built into this definition. But Rawls's definition of "reasonable persons" does not necessarily imply their acceptance of equal political liberties nor of fair equal opportunities or a social minimum. Moreover, even tolerance of others' alternative beliefs and ways of life can be a challenge, since free and equal persons have conflicting moral, philosophical, and religious views. We often tolerate others for self-interested reasons, simply to avoid unnecessary conflict and strife. But why tolerate for *moral reasons* – because we believe it is morally right – someone who rejects our most deeply held moral and religious beliefs? Even if we want to cooperate on terms others can accept, toleration for moral reasons of others' speech and ways of life we find morally and religiously repugnant can seem to be a peculiar position.[1]

Defining the idea of a political conception of justice that is free-standing of comprehensive doctrines is the first step of Rawls's solution to this problem. There are at least two further essential ingredients: first, an *overlapping consensus* of reasonable comprehensive doctrines on a liberal political conception; second *the idea of public reason*, which provides the terms of deliberation and debate citizens are to use for politically applying the political conception and justifying laws under it. These and related ideas are addressed in this chapter.

OVERLAPPING CONSENSUS

The primary role of the idea of overlapping consensus is to solve the stability problem. The argument for the congruence of the Right and the Good in *Theory* presupposes an unrealistic view of a well-ordered society of justice as fairness. Stability was prefaced on the argument that reasonable persons would find it rational to affirm their sense of justice as supremely regulative in order to realize their capacities for agency and therewith their status as autonomous moral agents. But given the fact of reasonable pluralism, many people will not want to affirm their status as autonomous moral agents even in a society where justice as fairness is generally accepted. Thus the stability problem remains: How is it possible that reasonable and rational citizens find it not just *reasonable to agree* upon justice as fairness (or any liberal conception of justice), but *also* find it *rational to endorse* this conception of justice as supremely regulative of their pursuit of their good?

Overlapping consensus on a political conception of justice is the main idea Rawls develops to address the problem of stability. Overlapping consensus at its simplest means that people in a well-ordered society will normally act in conformity with reasonably just laws and will endorse a liberal conception of justice for the many different reasons that stem from their conceptions of the good, including their comprehensive moral views. Given reasonable pluralism, what primarily motivates most citizens in a well-ordered society to comply with public principles of justice are the many different values and reasons implicit in the various reasonable comprehensive doctrines people subscribe to in a well-ordered society. Overlapping consensus is essentially a hypothesis about the kinds of conceptions of the good that predominantly will be fostered by a well-ordered society. It extends the reasoning behind the psychological principles of reciprocity underlying development of the sense of justice from *Theory* (see above, ch. 6) to reasonable comprehensive doctrines.[2] The crucial assumption behind the reciprocity principles is that, as individuals tend to develop a desire to support just institutions that benefit them and those they care for, so too will they incorporate this desire into their conception of the good and will come to have a regulative desire to do justice as defined by a well-ordered society's just institutions and laws. Similarly, overlapping consensus assumes that the reasonable comprehensive religious, philosophical, and moral doctrines that gain adherents in a well-ordered society will evolve doctrinally so as to endorse liberal political values and liberal principles of justice as part of their comprehensive accounts of morality and the good. Taken together, these two tendencies suggest that, from among the many possible religious, philosophical, and ethical doctrines, those that will predominantly gain adherents among reasonable people and that will thrive in a well-ordered society will explicitly endorse – each for their own specific moral, religious, and philosophical reasons – the public principles of justice and society's liberal constitution. Secondly, unreasonable, irrational, or "mad" doctrines will not muster sufficient support to gain sizable adherence; for (assuming the psychological principles of reciprocity are effective) reasonable persons will not endorse these views, and the unreasonable persons in a well-ordered society who do endorse them will not be of sufficient number to destabilize society. There should, then, be no widely accepted set of unreasonable comprehensive doctrines that rejects liberal principles of justice, or that assigns an insignificant position to considerations of liberal justice in its scheme of beliefs, values, and moral principles.

Assuming that these conjectures hold true in a well-ordered society, all reasonable and rational citizens will have *sufficient reason* to comply with liberal principles of justice for the *comprehensive reasons* that are specific to their comprehensive doctrines. Kantians, utilitarians, pluralists, Catholics, Protestants, Jews, Muslims, cultural relativists, moral skeptics, and so on will all accept and endorse a liberal conception of justice for reasons peculiar to each of their comprehensive doctrines (if they have one); and if not, then simply because they find a liberal political conception of justice intrinsically reasonable. Justice will then be *rational* for each – instrumentally or intrinsically, depending on their particular conception of the good – and society will evince *stability for the right reasons*. Society is stable *for the right reasons* since reasonable citizens endorse society's liberal conception for *moral reasons* of justice and the comprehensive moral values specified by their particular views. This is what makes the consensus overlapping and not a *modus vivendi*. Stability is not then simply everyone's second-best choice, growing out of a rational compromise of each person's fundamental moral, religious, and philosophical values. It is the best choice for everyone given the moral, religious, and philosophical principles implicit in their reasonable comprehensive views.

Here notice the dissimilarity with the congruence argument in *Theory*. Both overlapping consensus and congruence aim to show that it is rational, an essential aspect of their good, for reasonable and rational persons in a well-ordered society to endorse and abide by society's regulative principles of justice. But overlapping consensus does not address all of the issues the original congruence argument responds to. It does not claim, for example, that justice as fairness is true or objective according to epistemological criteria, or that it will be publicly recognized as such. Given different philosophical views about these issues – the nature and possibility of moral truth, moral knowledge, free agency, and so on – such issues cannot be argued on the basis of public reasons or resolved as part of the public conception of justice. These and other issues are part of ongoing non-public moral and political debate in the "background culture" among conflicting comprehensive philosophical views. Assuming an overlapping consensus exists, such disputes should have little effect on the stability of a liberal conception of justice. For whether or not all reasonable citizens see liberal principles of justice as objective or true, all of them (even moral skeptics) should find liberal principles to be reasonable principles of justice for persons who conceive of themselves as free and equal moral persons. Moral skepticism and relativism are, then, effectively neutralized as threats to stability.

Unlike Rawls's congruence argument, overlapping consensus also does not imply that justice is an intrinsic good or supremely regulative end for all. So far as overlapping consensus goes, justice, though important, may be regarded by many reasonable persons as instrumental to achieving more final ends implicit in their comprehensive doctrines (e.g., the Vision of God, or maximal global utility). Rawls's thought here seems to be that, since justice nonetheless occupies a significant position in each person's view and psychological disposition, conflicts with their final ends will be rare, or at least not so frequent as to undermine the stability of a well-ordered society. Moreover, the secondary status of justice for many reasonable and rational citizens does not deprive justice of its finality. Recall that the finality condition (TJ, sect. 23) means that considerations of justice are the final reasons of appeal within practical reason – they have ultimate reason-giving force and "trump" all other reasons. Rawls can no longer say this within public reason and political liberalism, since many reasonable persons may think differently, holding (for example) that aggregate utility or God's will is the ultimate source and arbiter of all practical reasons. But given an overlapping consensus, Rawls can still affirm the finality of principles of justice within a more restricted domain, namely, for political purposes. Even if reasons of justice do not override all other reasons within everyone's conception of the good, they do override all other considerations within public reason and the public political domain.[3] For if all reasonable religious, philosophical, and moral doctrines accept a liberal political conception, then they will also accept that in public political deliberation and decisions, the ultimate reasons to appeal to in order to decide questions of justice are society's liberal principles of justice and their accompanying public reasons. This *political finality* of principles of justice is part of the idea of public reason (discussed below).

Overlapping consensus is a rather simple idea, but it is easily misunderstood. One misunderstanding is the idea that an overlapping consensus is a kind of compromise among different and conflicting reasonable comprehensive doctrines, the outcome of some sort of bargain where each position sacrifices something for the sake of achieving agreement and social stability. This is the way that democracy often works – different and conflicting doctrines and interests all negotiate and come to a consensus which no one is entirely satisfied with, but which is adequate so far as all are concerned. This sort of consensus is known as a *modus vivendi*. Rawls insists that an overlapping consensus is not a *modus vivendi*, a kind of second-best solution for everyone to controversial political issues. Rather, overlapping consensus involves agreement on liberal principles that are from the perspective of everyone's reasonable comprehensive doctrine the best solution to the problem of finding the most appropriate conception of justice for a democratic society. What makes an overlapping consensus "stable for the right reasons" is that, from the standpoint of all the reasonable comprehensive conceptions, there is no better conception of justice. They all agree on the same liberal conception (or at least on a liberal conception affirming the priority of basic liberties and a social minimum) on the basis of their own different comprehensive doctrines. In this way, the idea of an overlapping consensus reformulates but sustains for Rawls the kind of social agreement that underlies social contract doctrine. Rather than all agreeing on justice for the same reasons (as we find in Locke, Kant, Rousseau, and Rawls in *Theory*), when an overlapping consensus prevails different comprehensive doctrines can agree on the same conception of justice in a well-ordered society, each for its own particular comprehensive reasons.

The idea of overlapping consensus represents an extraordinary development within traditional social contract theory. It suggests that the kind of general agreement on society's principles of justice need not be a *modus vivendi* among conflicting interests or comprehensive doctrines, as Hobbes and contemporary Hobbesians maintain. Nor does the social contract require that all reasonable citizens in a well-ordered society agree on principles of justice for the same comprehensive reasons or because they endorse the same (partially) comprehensive doctrine. In Locke, the social contract was grounded in everyone's recognition and acceptance of God's natural laws and the self-evidence of the fundamental law of nature; whereas Rousseau, Kant, and Rawls in *Theory* held that the social contract is to be grounded in everyone's recognition of their moral autonomy that stems from their "general will" or their joint authorship of moral laws as reasonable and rational citizens. The kind of social agreement that is assumed by overlapping consensus is more optimistic than Hobbesian views about the human capacity for reasonable agreement. At the same time it is more realistic about the feasible bases for reasonable agreement among free and equal persons than are natural rights theories of the social contract.

Finally, Rawls does not seek to incorporate into society's overlapping consensus on justice either unreasonable people or unreasonable doctrines. In so far as such persons and doctrines reject principles of liberal justice, they are to be "contained," Rawls says, and not compromised with. This refusal to compromise should not affect stability for the right reasons, unless there are so many unreasonable people in a well-ordered society unwilling to comply with reasonably just laws that they undermine a just society's stability. Some critics find Rawls's refusal to address unreasonable persons or doctrines objectionable, as if Rawls is being unfair by not trying to accommodate them. But unreasonable persons, by definition, either do not want to cooperate with others on terms they can reasonably accept, or they refuse to accept the inevitability of pluralism in a democratic society. As a result, they are either intolerant of other persons (e.g., racists) or doctrines (e.g., religious fundamentalists), or they do not accept the role of society to meet the basic needs of all citizens (e.g., libertarians). Hence, any accommodation reached with unreasonable persons or unreasonable doctrines will be unacceptable to reasonable citizens, and results in an injustice to them (e.g., respectively, to the despised racial groups, religious non-fundamentalists, and nonbelievers, and the less advantaged whose rights and interests have been compromised.) Any overlapping consensus with unreasonable persons or doctrines is itself unreasonable.

THE LIBERAL PRINCIPLE OF LEGITIMACY

Rawls initially introduces the idea of public reason as part of justice as fairness. He distinguishes two kinds of liberal political values: first, "the values of political justice – fall under the principles of justice for the basic structure"; and second, "the values of public reason – fall under the guidelines for public inquiry, which make that inquiry free and public" (PL, 224). The "values of public reason" are initially described rather narrowly, as among the guidelines for applying the principles of justice that presumably all reasonable persons accept in a well-ordered society. Assuming that there are different comprehensive conceptions in a well-ordered society, then even though everyone accepts the same principles of justice (justice as fairness), they will apply these principles differently. For along with differences in basic values and beliefs, standards of evidence, inference, good reasons, and judgment also differ among comprehensive views. As a result there is a need in a well-ordered society for standards of inquiry and reasoning that will allow people holding different comprehensive views to come to the same conclusions in applying the public conception of justice. So Rawls depicts the parties in the original position as agreeing, in addition to principles of justice, to "guidelines of public reason" for applying these principles.[4]

But Rawls has an alternative route to the idea of public reason, one not tied specifically to justice as fairness, and which leads to a broader characterization of public reason. Here Rawls introduces the idea of public reason by way of a requirement of political legitimacy. The *liberal principle of legitimacy* applies in any liberal society, not just one regulated by justice as fairness. It says: "Our exercise of political power is proper and hence justifiable only when it is exercised in accordance with a constitution the essentials of which all citizens may reasonably be expected to endorse in the light of principles and ideals acceptable to them as reasonable and rational."[5] The requirement is that citizens must be reasonably expected to endorse, not each and every exercise of political power (legislative, judicial, or executive action), but the "*essentials*" of a *constitution* that regulates the exercise of political power. A requirement that all citizens must reasonably be expected to endorse each and every government action is too strenuous; for most any reasonable political action has alternatives that may also be reasonable for a citizen to endorse, and it is unreasonable to expect all citizens to endorse only one of these reasonable alternatives. Recall also that "reasonable acceptance" and "reasonable expectation" are to be understood in terms of the measures that reasonable citizens could accept or endorse in their capacity as free and equal persons with higher-order interests in developing and exercising their moral powers. The standard of reasonable acceptance is not, then, to be defined by reference to persons in some other capacity (e.g., reasonable person of faith, reasonable perfectionist, reasonable skeptic, and so on). One cannot import from outside political liberalism an account of reasonableness (or reasonable acceptance, reasonable belief, etc.) as it is defined within some comprehensive philosophical, religious, or moral doctrine. Clearly, Catholic natural law doctrine, or Kantian moral theory, or strict Bayesian decision theory, etc., have competing conceptions of what is reasonable to accept that involve far more than the idea of political reasonableness that informs political liberalism. (We return to this crucial point in the next section's discussion of public reason.)

Rawls says that liberal legitimacy imposes a moral duty of civility on citizens: a duty "to be able to explain to one another on those fundamental questions [regarding constitutional essentials and matters of basic justice] how the principles and policies they advocate and vote for can be supported by the political values of public reason."[6] This does not mean that we must actually explain to others in terms of public reasons the political measures we support. That would be an extraordinarily burdensome and time-consuming duty, leaving us time for little else. It might even be overly burdensome to expect (if indeed Rawls does) that people themselves be prepared to explain all their political decisions. Some people might have intellectual or other limitations that prevent them from doing that. For example, I may just not know enough about its economic consequences to justify my belief that a progressive tax on wealth is more just than a "flat" (same percentage) tax. ("It just seems fairer to me that the rich should pay a greater percentage than the poor. Why should I have to be able to explain or justify that conviction in voting for a candidate who supports it?") But then, if the duty is simply meant to imply that our decisions be explainable in terms of public reason whether we know that they are or not, then it might seem too weak a requirement. Rawls does not do much to clarify these questions. Perhaps the best way to understand the duty of civility is that citizens must *sincerely believe* that their political decisions are justifiable in terms of public reason, and that, if they are not able to explain this justification, then there should be *someone* whose judgment citizens trust who is in a position to explain their political decisions in terms of public reasons.[7]

Now to introduce a third idea relevant to public reason: In later works Rawls indicates how liberal legitimacy and public reason are both based on a *criterion of reciprocity*. It requires that in proposing terms of cooperation "those proposing them must also think it at least reasonable for others to accept them, as free and equal citizens, and not as dominated or manipulated, or under the pressure of an inferior political or social position."[8] Rawls says, "the criterion of reciprocity is normally violated whenever basic liberties are denied" (CP, 579). Let's focus momentarily on the ideas of legitimacy and reciprocity that Rawls uses here, starting with the criterion of reciprocity since Rawls says the principle of legitimacy is based upon it.

The Criterion of Reciprocity: Rawls uses the term "reciprocity" in different ways throughout his works. At least three important uses can be distinguished. (1) In *Theory* the *principles of reciprocity* refer to the three psychological laws of moral development discussed earlier, in Chapter 6 of this volume. Rawls used these principles to account for the development of a sense of justice and citizens' willingness to abide by the principles of justice. As we saw earlier in this chapter, these psychological laws later play an implicit role in *Political Liberalism* in Rawls's explanation of how an overlapping consensus on liberal principles of justice might come about in a well-ordered liberal society. (2) Rawls also uses the term "reciprocity" in *Theory* and later works in connection with the idea of social cooperation and the principles of justice, to suggest terms of social cooperation that fairly benefit everyone. We might call this "reciprocity of advantage."[9] He contrasts reciprocity of advantage with the idea of mutual advantage to be found in Hobbesian contract views, as well as the idea of impartiality, understood in an altruistic sense. (For the sake of symmetry we might call this third view "impartial advantage.") Reciprocity, Rawls says, lies between mutual advantage and altruistic impartiality (PL, 16–17). Mutual advantage suggests that all persons benefit from cooperation, where their added advantage is measured from a baseline of a status quo where they know their interests, and they take advantage of whatever bargaining resources they have to do the best for themselves. By contrast reciprocity (of advantage), as Rawls understands it, involves a notion of fairness independent of the idea of (mutual) advantage and what promotes everyone's good; it implies rather that all benefit from cooperation where added advantages are measured from a baseline of equality. Thus, the difference principle embodies reciprocity of advantage since it allows for inequalities in income and wealth not simply when (a) they benefit everyone (which mutual advantage also achieves), but also only if (b) those who are least advantaged by the inequality are maximally benefited, and (c) assuming an efficient production process, the least advantaged are at the closest point to an equal distribution on the efficient production curve as they can be.

To be distinguished from reciprocity of advantage is (3) the criterion of reciprocity, which requires that citizens believe in good faith that the fair terms of social cooperation that they propose and expect all to abide by are reasonably acceptable to everyone in their capacity as free and equal citizens, without their being dominated or manipulated, or under pressure because of an inferior social or political position (PL, 136–37). We might call this kind of reciprocity "reciprocity of justification," since it requires that all reasonable persons be prepared to accept as good reasons the public justification of the use of coercive political power according to the terms of its political constitution. Reciprocity of justification implies citizens' general acceptance of the reasons that publicly justify the principles of justice that determine reciprocity of advantage. The criterion of reciprocity is in this way connected with the ideas of public justification and public reason, and therewith the liberal principle of legitimacy. This sense of reciprocity of justification is a natural extension of the idea of a social contract, since it builds on the contractarian idea that principles of justice are to be reasonably acceptable to free persons from a position of equal right (see PL, 135n., 136–37). Now I'll turn to focus on the principle of political legitimacy, which embodies the criterion of reciprocity.

Political Legitimacy: In general, the idea of legitimacy in law and politics relates to the proper enactment and application of laws and the bestowal of authority upon officials, all according to generally accepted and respected procedures. "Being legitimate says something about [laws' or governments'] pedigree" (PL, 427). When political officials are legitimate, they are regarded as having legal authority to act according to recognized procedures, and the laws, legal judgments, or executive regulations and decrees they issue are generally accepted as legally valid and binding by other political and legal officials and much of a nation's population. This fits with the positivist or Weberian account of legitimacy typically used in the social sciences – according to which general acceptance *de facto* by the majority of people of social and political institutions and officials' actions is sufficient for the legitimate exercise of political power (see PL, 429n.).

By contrast, Rawls's liberal principle of legitimacy is a moral/political standard for the recognition of laws' and governments' authority in a liberal and democratic society. Implicit in it is a requirement of basic justice. It says that even generally accepted or democratically enacted laws are not legitimate if they do not accord with a constitution that is reasonably acceptable to democratic citizens. Laws that clearly violate the basic liberties are then neither just nor legitimate, and should have no legal or political authority, for no constitution is reasonably acceptable if it violates these liberties. Rawls then departs from a purely legalistic or Weberian account of legitimacy; he rejects the view that compliance with recognized procedures and general acceptance by a people of laws and political institutions – no matter how unjust they are – are sufficient for the legitimate exercise of political power (see PL, 429n.). "Laws cannot be too unjust if they are to be legitimate" (PL, 429). Certain injustices deprive even democratically enacted laws of their authority. Nonetheless, Rawls clearly sees legitimacy as a different concept than justice, even though essentially related to it. "Democratic decisions and laws are legitimate, not because they are just but because they are legitimately enacted in accordance with an accepted legitimate democratic procedure" (PL, 428).

This suggests why there is a need for the concept of political legitimacy. First, as Rawls already indicates in Theory, "There is no feasible political process which guarantees that the laws enacted in accordance with it will be just" (TJ, 353/311 rev.). Even a just constitution cannot always insure a just outcome, and therefore embodies "imperfect procedural justice." Conscientious democratic legislators following the dictates of a just constitution will sometimes make laws that are to some degree unjust. Rawls suggests that these laws are still legitimate and have legal authority in so far as they meet the liberal principle of legitimacy. What this means for Rawls is significant: Provided duly enacted laws do not exceed certain limits of injustice (by violating the basic liberties and basic justice) and meet the legitimacy principle, democratic citizens normally have a duty to obey them even though they may be (moderately) unjust.[10] That we can have a duty to obey unjust laws is controversial. There are traditions of political and moral theory which deny this. But Rawls seems to think that recognition of a moral duty to obey (moderately) unjust laws is needed if a just constitution is to be feasible and stable. For imagine the consequences of a publicly recognized right to disobey laws which people believe unjust. Most citizens and representatives in a democracy believe that they vote as justice requires (or at least permits); so those voting in a minority often believe that justice has not been done when a law or judgment they oppose is duly enacted. Is it reasonable to say that democratic citizens always have a moral right or duty to ignore or violate laws they do not regard as just? How could a democratic system withstand such a blanket permission of disobedience? Of course, one could say that people have a right to disobey only those laws that are actually unjust, and not laws they simply believe unjust; but from an aggrieved or disgruntled citizen's point of view there is no difference: the consequences would be the same as a right or duty to disobey laws we believe to be unjust – namely, political turmoil if not bedlam.

Another need for an idea of legitimacy concerns the need to assess the status of potential laws and other measures that are just in their content, but which are not duly enacted; examples are when measures are arbitrarily enforced by executive or judicial fiat, or where legislative bodies violate just democratic procedures. For example, universal health care is for Rawls a requirement of liberal justice (PL, lix). Still, it would not be legitimate for an executive officer (such as then President Clinton) to seek to put such a system into effect by decree once it had been democratically rejected and in the absence of any other authorization. Or suppose the judiciary goes beyond the clear terms of a just constitution to review economic legislation, and declares certain laws unconstitutional since they do not wholly accord with the difference principle.[11] While the content of such decisions is not unjust and indeed may be required by justice, the manner in which they were put into effect is not legitimate.[12]

A third way the idea of liberal legitimacy is needed is to guide the deliberations of government officials and citizens in a society where different comprehensive conceptions of liberal justice may be endorsed by citizens holding different comprehensive views. A constraint upon citizens and officials proposing or supporting any law is that they sincerely believe that it meets the criterion of reciprocity, and that it is justifiable according to the requirements of public reason. Otherwise a law is not politically legitimate. This appears to be true, even if the law is a just law. For example, assume justice as fairness is, as Rawls contends, the *most* reasonable political conception of justice; still it would not be legitimate to make, enforce, and seek to publicly justify laws under it for reasons of moral autonomy, since these reasons cannot be endorsed by other reasonable comprehensive views. Rawls indicates that this conception of legitimacy, like public reason, is necessary "if each citizen is to have an equal share in political power" (JF, 90).[13] Apparently, it deprives citizens of equal political power to enact even substantively just laws for non-public reasons. For Rawls there is no genuine difference between government officials deciding on and enforcing a law or decree that is purely for reasons of autonomy, or aggregate social utility, and their deciding on and enforcing the same law or decree purely for religious reasons. Both cases are not *legitimate* exercises of political authority, even though the laws enacted may be substantively just.

The principle of legitimacy suggests that political liberalism itself is an exercise in non-ideal *partial compliance* theory. The main focus of *A Theory of Justice* is to describe the principles that regulate a well-ordered society that is wholly just. But *Theory* is an ideal theory in that it assumes general compliance by citizens with the correct principles of justice; thereby it provides the ultimate ideal of a society that all societies should aspire to emulate, even if none of them will ever actually achieve it. What is needed to supplement and apply this ideal theory are several non-ideal theories that assume conditions of "partial compliance" with the ideal. We might see *Political Liberalism* as the most fundamental part of non-ideal, partial compliance theory. It proceeds from the assumption that, because of the fact of reasonable pluralism, the normal conditions of liberal societies, even under the best of feasible conditions, are not going to be those wherein all reasonable citizens accept and comply with requirements of justice as fairness for the sake of justice itself and to achieve moral autonomy. Moreover, as becomes clear in Rawls's late article "Public Reason Revisited," political liberalism drops the assumption that reasonable citizens all can affirm the same liberal conception of justice, justice as fairness. Not only is reasonable pluralism of comprehensive doctrines inevitable; *reasonable disagreements about demands of liberal justice are also inevitable* even under the best of feasible circumstances. Under these circumstances the principle of legitimacy and the idea of public reason acquire great significance. Even if reasonable and rational democratic citizens cannot agree on the *same* conception of liberal justice – not to mention the *most reasonable* conception for Rawls, justice as fairness – all are under a duty to propose and support laws that they reasonably expect other citizens can reasonably endorse in their capacity as free and equal citizens. Such laws may not be justifiable according to the most reasonable conception – they will not then be wholly just; but they will be justifiable according to some reasonable liberal conception (as Rawls defines them) – therefore they will be nearly just. Moreover, they will also be legitimate, and hence will morally demand compliance, even if not wholly just. In this regard, Rawls's principle of legitimacy – a principle designed to apply mainly under less than ideal conditions – is an essential feature of justice as fairness and of any liberal conception of justice.

Let us return now to the duty of civility, citizens' duty to be able to explain to one another on fundamental questions how the principles and policies they advocate and vote for can be supported by the political values of public reason (PL, 217). Rawls says that the duty of civility also involves (1) a willingness to listen to others and (2) fair-mindedness in deciding when it is reasonable to make accommodations to their views. The duty of civility applies to citizens but it especially applies to political officials responsible for enacting and applying laws. Not only are officials under a moral duty to enact laws that others can reasonably be expected to accept and endorse as democratic citizens, but they have a further duty to publicly justify political enactments, explaining to citizens how their laws and decisions conform to "the political values of public reason." (CP, 584).

The duty of civility also implies that citizens have a moral duty to vote for and support laws only if they are also justifiable on the basis of public reasons, and citizens sincerely believe this. This does not mean that citizens cannot vote for candidates and support legislation on the basis of their comprehensive views – their religious, philosophical, and moral beliefs. It would be unreasonable to impose a requirement that religious people, for example, not be allowed to vote for candidates or laws on the basis of their religious and religiously informed moral views. How can it reasonably be expected of people that they leave their most conscientiously held moral and other beliefs behind when they discuss and reason about political issues? This cannot be part of the often-voiced liberal requirement that "religion should be kept out of politics." This requirement is satisfied mainly by the separation of church and state, freedom of conscience, and the prohibition against legally enacting religious doctrines. But it is unreasonable to think that religious (or non-religious) people should not refer to their conscientiously held convictions at all when voting and discussing political issues. What the duty of civility requires is that, when citizens do rely on reasons provided by their comprehensive religious, philosophical, and moral doctrines, they conscientiously believe their actions are justified on grounds of *public reasons also*, and that they, or someone on their behalf, be able to provide this justification to other democratic citizens.

What citizens are not allowed to do is to vote for candidates and laws on the basis of religious and other comprehensive doctrines that are incompatible with the political values of public reason. This violates the duty of civility. For example, the Catholic Church has long supported the use of public funds to support parochial schools. Part of the reason that Catholics support vouchers is surely religious: they want their children to be educated in an environment that is not hostile to their religion, and that instills moral values supported by the Catholic Church. This position is compatible with the duty of civility (1) so long as the use of vouchers to pay for private school tuition is also consistent with the political values of public reason, and also (2) the Church and its members fulfill the duty of civility to explain how religious school vouchers can be publicly justified in terms of the political values of public reason. For the Church not to seek to give a public justification arouses not just opposition but hostility among others who might think that they are being required to support a religion which they reject. Such a failure violates the duty of civility, even if there is an unstated justification of vouchers for religious schools in terms of public reasons. Now let's turn to the seminal idea of public reason itself.

THE IDEA OF PUBLIC REASON

The idea of public reason was introduced in Chapter 2. There we saw that by the time of *Political Liberalism* Rawls's account of the specification of basic liberties at the constitutional stage had evolved so that it came to depend upon the idea of public reason. Public reasons, not comprehensive reasons from religious, philosophical, and moral doctrines, are the kinds of considerations that should be invoked to decide the nature and limits of constitutional liberties. In this section the idea of public reason is discussed in more detail. It is one of the main ideas Rawls develops in the latter part of his life's work, and it is crucial to understanding political liberalism and many of its main features, including the domain of the political, political justification, the principle of liberal legitimacy, the specification of the basic liberties, and Rawls's idea of a deliberative democracy.

The Nature of Public Reason

In a constitutional democracy, citizens and officials normally have a sense of the kinds of reasons that are and are not appropriately invoked in legislative and judicial forums and when arguing about laws and constitutional issues with people holding conflicting religious or philosophical views. We often see in public contexts, in newspaper editorials for example, that people make an effort to appeal only to certain reasons shared with other citizens. There are of course strategic considerations for these limitations on the arguments we make in trying to convince others with different philosophies and religions; in order to persuade them appeal must be made to reasons held in common. But there are also moral/political reasons for limiting arguments to shared reasons in public political contexts; reasonable persons normally should not be legally compelled to act in ways that are justifiable only via ideas that conflict with their most fundamental convictions. To compel others to act according to your personal religious beliefs is in effect a violation of their liberty of conscience and more generally of democratic freedom.

It is, however, very hard to give a general characterization of what permissible political reasons ought to be. It is not enough to say that, because citizens have different faiths and their differences are unresolvable, religious doctrine ought to be kept out of political life. For citizens have unresolvably conflicting philosophical and ethical beliefs too; shouldn't the same "exclusionary rule" apply to these beliefs as much as to religious beliefs? A classical utilitarian's insistence that maximizing aggregate pleasures should be the aim of all legislation seems no less unreasonable to many than is the insistence that religious aims should serve this role. Moreover, sometimes it may be proper within public political life for people to declare the religious (or philosophical and moral) beliefs that lead them to support or oppose measures involving fundamental questions of justice. Martin Luther King's religious declarations in support of civil rights are a good example of the public appeal to religious considerations in order to address effectively many people's sense of justice. How, then, are we to make sense of the idea of "public reasons"?

The idea of public reason is easily misunderstood. If all that is meant by "public reason" is the reasons that people in a society share in common, then any society has a conception of public reason. In this sense the basis for public reasoning in a theocracy might be the Bible, the Koran, or some other religious text. But for Rawls the idea of public reason is essentially a feature of a *democratic society*. Rawls says "Public reason is characteristic of a democratic people; it is the reason of its citizens [as such], of those sharing the status of equal citizenship."[14] This implies that simply because people in a society commonly accept and reason in terms of a common religion does not make that doctrine part of public reason. Even assuming that all the members of an Islamic state, such as Saudi Arabia, accept the Muslim religion and appeal to religious reasons in deliberating and discussing laws, this does not make Islam part of public reason. Saudi Arabia has no public reason in Rawls's sense, only shared comprehensive reasons which rule out the possibility of a public reason. Differences among comprehensive views supply the background for Rawls's idea of public reason.

Public reason is a complicated idea for Rawls. He says:

– Public reason is characteristic of a democratic people; it is the reason of equal citizens. (*PL*, 213)

– Public reason's subject is the good of the public; its content is a political conception of justice. (*PL*, liii)

- Public reason's constraints apply in the "public political forum," not in the "background culture." (*CP*, 575)

- Public reason is "complete": it is capable of providing reasonable answers to all questions regarding constitutional essentials and matters of basic justice. (*CP*, 585)

- Public reason aims for public justification and as such is reasoning addressed to others in their capacity as reasonable democratic citizens. (*CP*, 593)

- Public reason and public justification meet the "criterion of reciprocity"; they proceed from reasons and premises we reasonably think others could reasonably accept, to conclusions they also could reasonably accept. (*CP*, 578–9)

- When government officials act from public reason, legal enactments by a majority are politically legitimate even when they are not fully just. (*PL*, 427–8)

- Finally, "in a constitutional democracy with judicial review, public reason is the reason of its supreme court. . . . the supreme court is the branch of government that serves as the exemplar of public reason." (*PL*, 231)

In saying that public reason is the reason of the supreme court we can infer that, though public reason is democratic, it cannot be simply the will of the majority. Rather, like a supreme court, it serves as a kind of limit on majority will. Here Rawls is talking about the office of a supreme court with power of judicial review. He is not talking specifically about the U.S. Supreme Court, which does not always fulfill its office and conform to public reason. But still the Supreme Court does often enough provide examples of what Rawls means (an example is the Court's refusal in *Roe v. Wade* to enter into the dispute over whether the fetus has a soul or is metaphysically or morally a person). When the Supreme Court decides a case under the U.S. Constitution, its judges are expected to set aside, not only their personal interests and moral views, but any religious, philosophical, and moral values that are irresolvably contested among democratic citizens. They are expected to rely upon reasons, values, and procedures embedded in the U.S. Constitution, which (for the most part) are public reasons.

Rawls contrasts public reasons with "non-public" and "comprehensive reasons." Comprehensive reasons are reasons that are peculiar to one or more comprehensive doctrines. Non-public reasons include comprehensive reasons, plus other considerations which, even if shared among citizens, it would not be legitimate to appeal to in public political deliberation. Also, Rawls speaks of both "public reason," and "public reasons." Formally speaking, public reasons are the kinds of considerations and values that legitimately may be invoked in democratic public political life. Public reason is more than the sum of public reasons; it includes also the norms of reasoning and standards of evidence that are appropriate to officials and citizens as they engage in democratic deliberation and judgment. Public reason for Rawls involves then two general kinds of consideration, to be addressed momentarily. But first, it is important to note the *scope* of public reason. Rawls says "its limits do not apply to our personal deliberations and reflections about political questions, or to reasoning about them by members of associations such as churches and associations" (PL, 215). The implication of reasonable pluralism of comprehensive doctrines is that it is unrealistic if not unreasonable to expect that democratic citizens should not appeal to their reasonable comprehensive doctrines to decide issues of justice and to vote their convictions about justice. The idea of public reason is not designed to in any way restrict liberty of conscience and freedom of thought on all issues, political as well as non-political. But if there is an overlapping consensus of reasonable comprehensive doctrines, then citizens' thinking about justice within the terms of their reasonable doctrines more or less should match the decisions they would reach if they reasoned purely within the confines of a political conception of justice and public reason. (Of course, the match will not always be precise since they may be referring to non-political values, such as religious values, to ultimately decide issues.) What kind of requirement, then, does public reason impose? The easy case is that of public officials, who normally are only to reason in terms of public reason in the appropriate circumstances (defined below) when they are fulfilling the duties of their office. Public reason "applies in official forums and so to legislators . . . and to the executive in its public acts and pronouncement." Most especially, public reason applies "in a special way to the judiciary and above all to a supreme court" (PL, 216). When Rawls says that "public reason is the reason of a supreme court," he means that a court is to reason only in terms of public reason on all issues that come before it. Legislators and the executive may sometimes apply non-public reasons, when "constitutional essentials and questions of basic justice" (PL, 214) are not at stake. But a supreme court entrusted with the power of judicial review under the constitution is only to appeal to public reason.

What now about citizens? Public reason requires that when citizens vote in elections when matters of constitutional justice and basic justice are at stake, then, if they vote according to their comprehensive views, their vote must at least be compatible with the political values of public reason. There must be reasons of justice and political values of public reason that support their decision if they are to vote fairly and legitimately. Otherwise citizens violate the duty of civility. Also, Rawls says, "the ideal of public reason does hold for citizens when they engage in political advocacy in the public forum" (PL, 215). This suggests that when citizens are addressing other citizens who have different comprehensive views, they are to appeal to the political values of public reason to argue for or against political issues or candidates. Obviously, it is not appropriate then to invoke a candidate's religion as a reason to vote against them, in an effort to stir up religious bigotry. But less obviously, Rawls here suggests that it is also not appropriate to argue in the public political forum that abortion should be legally prohibited on the basis of religious or philosophical reasons incompatible with public reason (for example, because it involves murder, which assumes that the fetus is a person, a claim not sustainable by public reason).

Now to turn to the two general kinds of public reasons: First, there are "the guidelines of public reason" (PL, 225). These "fall under the guidelines for public inquiry, which make that inquiry free and public" (PL, 224). Standards of evidence, inference, good reasons, and judgment differ among comprehensive views even though they agree on the same conception of justice. As a result there is a need in a democratic society for standards of inquiry and reasoning that allow people holding different comprehensive views to come to the same conclusions in applying the public conception of justice. These are formal and procedural rules of argumentation and justification, including shared standards of evidence and reasoning (rules and standards of inference in deductive, inductive, and probabilistic reasoning, for example). A good example of standards for public reasoning would be the rules of evidence used in trials, which exclude certain kinds of evidence in order to increase not only reliability (e.g., the rule against hearsay evidence), but also fairness (e.g., the *Miranda* rule excluding confessions made without being apprised of one's constitutional right to remain silent and right to counsel). In this connection, Rawls says that it is against public reason for political officials to rely on complicated and disputed theories of probability, such as Bayesian assumptions, particularly in addressing constitutional issues and matters of basic justice. For they involve complicated epistemological assumptions about which reasonable persons disagree. But settled scientific theories with standards of evidence generally accepted by experts in their fields are admissible within public reason. When they are relevant, Rawls would then accept as admissible within public reason (for example) genetic theory, the theory of relativity, and neo-classical price theory in economics, and even neo-Darwinian theory of natural selection. The latter suggests that being shared by a majority of citizens generally is *not* a necessary feature of public reason (since Darwinism is not accepted by a majority in the U.S.); public reason thus can include some reasons that are *not shared* among democratic citizens on the basis of their comprehensive views. The criterion for what is (and is not) a guideline of or value of public reason, like what is (and is not) politically reasonable, is not whatever reasons people in our society actually accept, but the democratic ideal of citizens as reasonable and rational, free and equal moral persons and their interests.

The second kind of public reasons is a subset of substantive moral values that Rawls calls the "*political values of public reason.*" "These values provide public reasons for all citizens" (CP, 601). They count as good reasons in public deliberation and argument about laws and their interpretation, among reasonable and rational democratic citizens who endorse different fundamental values and conceptions of their good. The assumption underlying public reason is that, since citizens in a democracy, despite their differences, also normally endorse democratic values, ideals, and principles, then there should be shared values, considerations, and standards that are not peculiar to any comprehensive view, but which can be accepted by all reasonable views in so far as they accommodate democratic ideals. These political values of public reason are a complex array of considerations that are especially relevant to citizens' achieving their status as free and equal democratic citizens and pursuing reasonable conceptions of their good.

Among the liberal political values of public reason that Rawls specifically mentions are such values of justice as equal political and civil liberty, equality of opportunity, social equality and economic reciprocity, the common good, the social bases of self-respect, and the necessary conditions for these values (PL, 139). There are also, he says, political virtues such as reasonableness, fair-mindedness, and a readiness to honor the duty of civility, all of which make reasoned public discussion possible (PL, 224). Later Rawls says that the values mentioned in the Preamble to the U.S. Constitution are examples of political values: a more perfect union, justice, domestic tranquility the common defense, the general welfare, and the blessings of liberty for ourselves and our posterity, all of which include more specific values under them, such as the fair distribution of income and wealth (CP, 584). Efficiency and effectiveness are political values, which would include economic productivity and maintaining free and efficient markets, and controlling economic, environmental, and other kinds of social loss or waste (ibid.). Political values that relate to human health, the environment, etc., that Rawls mentions are: preserving the natural order to further the good of ourselves and future generations; promoting biological and medical knowledge by fostering species of animals and plants; and protecting the beauties of nature for purposes of public recreation and "the pleasures of a deeper understanding of the world" (PL, 245). From Rawls's discussion of abortion we learn that among the political values are: appropriate respect for human life, the full equality of women, the reproduction of liberal society over time, and respect for requirements of public reason itself in political discussion of controversial issues, such as abortion (JF, 117). Political values relating to the family are: the freedom and equality of women, the equality of children as future citizens, the freedom of religion, and the value of the family in securing the orderly production and reproduction of society and its culture from one generation to the next (CP, 601). Rawls's listing of the substantive political values of public reason should not be taken as exhaustive. There are others, some of which may not even be apparent to us just yet.

Where does Rawls's list of political values, and more generally a complete listing of political values, originate? He does not tell us. It is not drawn up by a survey of shared values in any existing society; if that were all it were, then religious values might be among public reasons, since close to 90 percent of people in the U.S. say they believe in a god. Instead, Rawls's idea seems to be that in a liberal and democratic society certain kinds of values are of political interest (and others are not) to people in their capacity as democratic citizens. Many of these liberal and democratic values exclude from the public political domain other substantive values that a majority of citizens might find of fundamental importance. If freedom of conscience, freedom of association, and freedom of the person with a right of privacy are all political values, then it follows that the salvation of souls, religious truth, preserving the "sanctity" of traditional marriage bonds, and exclusively promoting male–female relationships of intimacy should not be among political values that a liberal society should impose on its citizens or pursue in its policies. More generally, the political values of public reason are the values that are of interest and significance to free and equal citizens *in their capacity as democratic citizens*, judging in light of their shared higher-order interests in developing and exercising their moral powers, and in maintaining their civic equality, their freedom to pursue a rational good, and their individual and economic independence. It is, then, the democratic conception of citizens as free and equal moral persons that Rawls seemingly refers to in order to ground and explicate the idea of public reason, its political values, and the idea of political reasonableness. The goal here is that, once the democratic ideal of the person and its features are fully clarified, then the political values of public reason can all be explained in terms of their connection with the status and higher-order interests of citizens regarded as free and equal moral persons.

We saw a good example of the connection between political values and the ideal of citizens in Rawls's specification of the basic liberties by reference to the moral powers (discussed in Chapter 2). The political values of freedom of thought and expression and individuals' political liberty with equal political rights are all necessary conditions for the realization of the capacity for a sense of justice whereas liberty of conscience and freedom of association are necessary to the adequate exercise and full development of our rational capacity to form, revise, and pursue a conception of the good. Other political values can be explicated in a similar way. For example, the political values of public health and public safety are clearly necessary to maintaining for citizens their freedom of movement and the conditions for the physical and psychological integrity of persons which are among the basic liberties. Economic efficiency is among the measures needed for economic reciprocity and the fair distribution of income and wealth, which in turn are clarified by referring to equal citizens' higher-order interests in justice and maintaining their freedom and equality. And so on.

Rawls includes among the values of public reason "the pleasures of a deeper understanding of the world" (PL, 245). How is this to be understood? If understood as a perfectionist value, then it may well seem that there is little restriction upon what may be regarded as among "political values of public reason." What then is to prevent "spirituality" from being a political value, which might open the door to equitable government support of each person's religion (e.g., public salaries for clergy of all faiths)? This seems to conflict with Rawls's account of liberalism and undermines the purpose of the idea of public reason, which is to restrict the kinds of reasons and considerations that are proper to take into account in public political argument and governmental decisions. We have already seen how the basic liberties play a role among political values in restricting the range of non-political moral and religious values (such as the values of spirituality) from public reason. But why should not the basic liberties also restrict "the pleasures of a deeper understanding of the world" from inclusion in the political values of public reason as well? Two things can be said here in Rawls's defense. First, an argument can be made that public support for "a deeper understanding of the world" (in public education clearly and via support for cultural institutions) is conducive to the realization of the moral powers, particularly to the development and exercise of our capacity to form, revise, and rationally pursue a conception of the good. The same cannot be said of "spirituality," I believe (though the argument would have to be made). If this is what Rawls had in mind, then it is not the case that government is supporting perfectionist values for their own sake. Rather, the pursuit of scientific and other fields of knowledge is done for public political reasons of enabling citizens to further their legitimate higher-order interests in developing their capacities for rationality. Moreover, public funding for scientific knowledge and research has beneficial consequences for such political values as public health, public defense and safety, and the improvement of living standards. Again, these are not perfectionist values, and thus the public pursuit of the values of "a deeper understanding of the world" is not for its own sake, but for the sake of other public political values.

Second, Rawls is not saying that it is necessary for a democratic society to pursue this seemingly perfectionist value (assuming it is that), or that a society that did not publicly provide for it would be unjust (as a society would be unjust if it did not provide for such political values as equal opportunity, public safety, and public health). Rather, achieving a deeper understanding of the world might be regarded as a sort of *public good* that it is *permissible* for a democratic society to pursue, so long as it is democratically endorsed and done so in a way that does not undermine "constitutional essentials" or "matters of basic justice" (about which more will be said momentarily). Granted, this may conflict with Rawls's seeming refusal in *Theory* to support compulsory taxation for purposes of pursuing perfectionist values of culture (art museums, civic symphonies, etc.). Rawls did recognize in *Theory* a mechanism, the "exchange branch," which would coordinate (what appears to be) a kind of voluntary taxation scheme for public goods that are not required by justice (*TJ*, 282–84/249–51 rev.). But if in fact the exchange branch exacts only voluntary contributions, it would be unfair for a democratic society to require people to pay the tax to support perfectionist values of culture if they did not want to participate in this scheme, since the supposed public good is not a good for them (e.g., the pleasures of a deeper understanding of the world). This, at any rate, is suggested by Rawls's claim regarding public goods covered by the exchange branch that "no public expenditures are voted upon unless at the same time the means of covering their costs are agreed upon, if not unanimously, then approximately so" (*TJ*, 282/249–50 rev.). (It is not clear here whether he means unanimous support among citizens who enjoy the good, or simply among their representatives.)

Whether or not this is a correct reading of *Theory* is open to question.[15] But it does raise an interesting question, not only within Rawls's account but in democratic theory more generally. Assume that all the requirements and public expenditures for achieving distributive justice and equal opportunities are met. If a democratic society can permissibly impose compulsory taxes (in addition to charging user fees) on its citizens for the sake of such perfectionist values as maintaining public art museums and symphonies, may it also impose taxes to pay for sports stadiums for privately owned franchises? The usual argument made in support of such public support (for multi-millionaire franchise owners) is that public funding of stadiums pays for itself by bringing in business and contributing to the tax base. (Much evidence shows the contrary.) Either way, is it politically legitimate? Is it just? Imagine a California referendum where a majority of citizens vote to approve Governor Schwarzenegger's plan to use public funds to support the American Bodybuilders Association and to underwrite a series of *Terminator* movies starring the Governor himself. Is this a permissible use of public funds? Is it just or legitimate for democratic majorities to tax others who think this is a misuse of public funds and who oppose the glorification of violence in such films? When compared with these examples, the question whether it is legitimate, or just, for a democratic society to publicly maintain cultural institutions by charging citizens taxes (in addition to user fees) to sustain them is not such an easy question for liberal theory after all, especially given a broad view of "cultural institutions" that includes the foregoing examples (sports arenas, bodybuilding, and action movies).

In any case, by the time of *Political Liberalism* it becomes clearer that Rawls does *not* deny the legitimacy or authority or justice of democratic decisions to impose taxes to support perfectionist values of culture. And while democratic funding of sports stadiums might not be just under the difference principle, still it appears *legitimate* under the liberal principle of legitimacy since a political justification in terms of public reasons (however flimsy the argument) can be given to support this practice (e.g., bringing in new jobs, increasing the tax base). Two reasons support this interpretation of Rawls.

First, as discussed previously, he includes the seemingly perfectionist value of "the pleasures of a deeper understanding of the world" among the political values of public reason. I've contended that public support of this value seems to be instrumentally justifiable in terms of the development and exercise of the moral powers and enabling citizens to educate their capacities and pursue a wide range of conceptions of the good.

Second, in an apparent departure from *Theory*, Rawls limits the *domain of public reason* so that it applies mainly to "constitutional essentials and matters of basic justice" (PL, 214, 227). *Constitutional essentials* are mainly the basic liberties and their priority and the democratic political institutions needed for making, applying, and administering laws. *Matters of basic justice* include mainly matters relating to social and economic inequalities, and concern measures bearing upon equal opportunities, economic justice, and setting the social minimum. Rawls's first principle of justice provides a basis for determining constitutional essentials and the second principle provides a basis for deciding matters of basic justice. Rawls says that since questions of social and economic inequality are "open to wide differences of reasonable opinion" (PL, 229) and it is often difficult to determine if social and economic institutions meet requirements of distributive justice, it is advisable that principles of justice regulating economic justice not be included among constitutional essentials and made part of the political constitution. Questions of social and economic inequality, including taxation policies, specification of property rights, and regulation of commerce, are best left to ordinary democratic legislative determination and should not rise to the level of a constitutional dispute subject to judicial review. By contrast a question whether the basic liberties are being denied "is more or less visible on the face of constitutional arrangements and how these can be seen to work in practice" (PL, 229); it is therefore appropriate that disputes over the denial of basic liberties be constitutional issues which may be subject to judicial review. Moreover, while deciding the social minimum is best left to legislative determination, still for Rawls a democratic society which refuses to provide *any* adequate social minimum to the less advantaged is violating a constitutional essential; such a legislative refusal can also be subject to judicial review in democratic societies where this institution is appropriate.

One basis for Rawls's distinction between constitutional essentials and matters of basic justice is that Rawls thinks that it is much easier to gain agreement among free and equal reasonable and rational persons about what the basic liberties should be in broad outline, even if not in every detail of their specification or application (PL, 230). By contrast, reasonable people can disagree about the correct principle for regulating social and economic inequalities and setting the level of the social minimum. The difference principle and fair equality of opportunity are not the only reasonable principles of justice to use to decide these matters of basic justice. This does not mean (as some critics have mistakenly supposed) that Rawls is abandoning his argument in *Theory* that the difference principle and fair equality of opportunity are the *most* reasonable principles for regulating permissible social and economic inequalities. There is no suggestion at all in Rawls's later works that he questions his earlier arguments for or commitments to the difference principle. On the contrary, he restates and elaborates on them in great detail in *Justice as Fairness: A Restatement* (2001). Critics' claims that Rawls diluted the egalitarian requirements of economic justice and abandoned the difference principle in *Political Liberalism* confuse that book's arguments for the requirements of *political legitimacy* with Rawls's account (in *Theory* and the *Restatement*) of the more stringent requirements of social and political *justice*. The fact that one principle of distributive justice is most reasonable does not mean that reasonable and rational people cannot still reasonably disagree and reasonably believe that some other way to decide the social minimum is more appropriate to justice. There can be *reasonable disagreements about distributive justice* and how to set the social minimum within the terms of public reason in a well-ordered democratic society. Views such as libertarianism, or those classical liberal views which entirely deny a social minimum, *are* unreasonable, Rawls contends, since a social minimum is necessary to the adequate development and full exercise of the moral powers, and to pursue a rational conception of the good. For this reason, Rawls does not regard libertarianism as a *liberal* political conception; it cannot attain democratic legitimacy under the principle of political legitimacy. But a "mixed conception" that provides a social minimum adequate to the development of the moral powers, but which allows income and wealth generally to be distributed according to the principle of average utility, is a reasonable conception, or at least is "not unreasonable." Such a principle underlies, Rawls believes, the capitalist welfare state, which is not wholly just by Rawls's lights, but which is nonetheless politically legitimate.

By contrast, Rawls seems to suggest that the first principle of justice and its priority is a reasonable requirement for *any* legitimate political conception. It is *unreasonable* for any political conception to deny the equal basic liberties and their priority; laws which do so are not legitimate under the principle of legitimacy. Moreover, Rawls seems to suggest that the list of basic liberties that are necessary to the first principle is basically the same list that he argues is necessary to the exercise and development of the moral powers. All these basic liberties are among "the political values of public reason" which no reasonable liberal political constitution can deny and still remain legitimate.

This implies that the *range of reasonable disagreement within public reason is rather narrow* in Rawls's view. There can be reasonable disagreements about justice among free and equal citizens, but these reasonable disagreements cannot extend to the list of equal basic liberties of the first principle and maintaining their priority over equal opportunity and distributive justice, and other political values of public reason. The equal basic liberties and their priority are not up for reasonable disagreement among reasonable democratic citizens regarded as free and equal moral persons. Anyone who rejects some or all of the list of basic liberties and their priority rejects the idea of a democratic society of free and equal, reasonable and rational citizens upon which the idea of reasonable agreement itself is based. This means that traditional utilitarianism is unreasonable as a political conception since it rejects the equality and priority of basic liberties. Libertarianism is too, since it rejects the inalienability of basic liberties (because libertarians sees all rights as alienable), and any social minimum needed to guarantee their effective exercise.

Return now briefly to the question of the domain of public reason and whether perfectionist values can be legislated legitimately by democratic decisions. If the constraints of public reason only apply to constitutional essentials and matters of basic justice, and non-public reasons may be invoked to argue for and justify laws not within these areas, this implies that a democratic society can legitimately pursue perfectionist values – taxing people to fund art museums, opera houses, and the preservation of the natural environment for purely aesthetic reasons, for example – so long as such measures do not undermine constitutional essentials and basic justice. Indeed, while Rawls does not say so, if the restrictions of public reason are limited in scope, it may be that a democratic society can pursue legitimately many non-public values a majority chooses – perhaps even funding sports arenas – so long as all the requirements of political legitimacy are met. Rawls would probably say that it is foolish, inefficient, a waste of public funds, and perhaps even unjust (under the difference principle) for democratic assemblies or citizens to vote to fund football stadiums for multi-millionaire franchise owners, but it is not politically illegitimate. Perhaps the only restriction on such legislation would be that it be justifiable as a kind of quasi-public good. ("Quasi" since, strictly speaking, a public good should advance the good of, if not directly benefit, each citizen, and here we are considering goods that are not acceptable to a sizable minority of citizens.) Thus, while there is at least an argument that public funding of sports arenas can be a public good (purportedly they bring in new business and new employment and increase the tax base), it is hard to see how majority decisions to tax people to support the public funding of bodybuilding competitions and action movies starring the "Governator" could be justified as any kind of public good, especially given that these economic goods are already adequately provided by markets.

Critics object here that Rawls should extend the requirement of public reason to apply to justification of legislation that goes beyond constitutional essentials and matters of basic justice. In *Political Liberalism* Rawls provides some support to this stronger position; he says, "Still, I grant that it is usually highly desirable to settle political questions by invoking the values of public reason. Yet this may not always be so" (PL, 215). Perhaps Rawls's misgiving about appeals to public reasons in all political decisions are that they put too many restrictions on democratic citizens' exercise of the equal rights of political participation to prevent them from enacting any laws except those pursuant to the political values of public reason. For example, is it really undemocratic or democratically illegitimate for a democratic assembly to vote to preserve wetlands, or approve a national park to preserve the beauty of the environment or to pay for a civic orchestra, even though many citizens have no interest in or actively oppose these things? Issues of the quality of civic life go beyond issues of justice, and it is often hard to see how the political values of public reasons can be invoked to respond to people's comprehensive aesthetic and moral views: for example, many environmental issues, preserving wilderness areas and animal and plant species, and public support for cultural institutions – museums, concert halls, civic symphonies and operas, public radio and television – that have traditionally been funded publicly. It should not be beyond the capacity of a democratic people to put their own stamp (if they have one) on the aesthetic or cultural quality of life in their society, without having to worry about whether all publicly supported institutions further political values of public reason. If this opens the way to such non-perfectionist purposes as publicly funded sports arenas, speedways, and stock car races, then that may be the price of democracy. Having laws enacted by reasonable citizens motivated by their sense of justice does not guarantee the absence of foolishness or misspending of public funds. Justice is but one virtue among others, and while necessary to, its realization does not insure, the achievement of a good society.

Finally, it is worth emphasizing once again that in *Political Liberalism* Rawls is concerned with *political legitimacy* and not with strict justice. The various requirements of basic liberal justice and the political values of public reason are requirements of political legitimacy, but strict justice is not required for laws to be politically legitimate. Rawls is saying that laws that are enacted for purely non-public reasons can still be politically legitimate, so long as they do not involve constitutional essentials and basic justice. He is not saying that legitimate laws are wholly or strictly just; they may rise even to a level of being *unjust*. Rawls thinks the capitalist welfare state is unjust, but it is still politically legitimate since it provides an adequate social minimum. The standard for the full justice of laws for Rawls is, as always, supplied by justice as fairness. But justice as fairness is but one member of a family of liberal political conceptions that can satisfy the liberal principle of legitimacy, provide content to public reason and a basis for political justification in a well-ordered democratic society.

The Need for Public Reason – Public Justification and Political Autonomy

Now to consider in more detail why there is a *need* for an idea of public reason in a democracy. Rawls designed his idea of public reason initially to deal with the gap which arose after he discerned problems with the account of the stability of a well-ordered society in *A Theory of Justice*. According to Rawls's congruence argument, reasonable and rational citizens would regard the development and exercise of the moral powers as supremely regulative and worthwhile for their own sake; therewith they should affirm full autonomy as an intrinsic good. The consequence of the general affirmation of autonomy is that reasons of moral and rational (individual) autonomy and related Kantian ideas would serve a role in legislative and judicial deliberations, and more generally in public justification in a well-ordered society. For example, what kinds of considerations are relevant in *Theory* to deciding the scope and limits of the basic liberties in Rawls's first principle, such as freedom of the person and freedom of association? What kinds of constitutional rights do these abstract liberties require? Do they imply a general right of privacy that protects a right of abortion and a right to same-sex relations? People with different religious and philosophical views disagree about this. But in *A Theory of Justice* Rawls envisioned political recourse to the values of moral and rational autonomy to decide these questions.

We have seen the problems Rawls subsequently discovered with political appeals to autonomy. The value of autonomy is part of one or more comprehensive doctrines which cannot be generally endorsed by all conscientious citizens, even in a well-ordered society. Consequently, moral and rational autonomy cannot have a role in public justification in a well-ordered society. To give the contested value of moral autonomy a central role in interpreting the political constitution is inconsistent with the *political autonomy* of free and equal citizens. Even if *Theory*'s partially comprehensive doctrine of Kantian autonomy were true, still to enforce it politically differs little from the point of view of citizens who reject that value from political enforcement of a religious faith.

The idea of public reason remedies these and other defects: There are at least four reasons the idea of public reason is needed: (1) First, it provides considerations that all reasonable democratic citizens can accept for applying the principles of justice they also all accept, in order to specify the constitution and the laws. In this regard, the idea of public reason is a natural development of Rawls's *contractarianism*; it is needed to explicate and carry through the contractarian ideal that social cooperation should be based upon a general agreement. For citizens to act on laws enacted for reasons that all can reasonably accept in their capacity as democratic citizens meets the requirements of the criterion of reciprocity. (2) Public reason, then, enables justice as fairness to serve its "practical role" in providing a basis for *public political justification* among democratic citizens who have different and conflicting comprehensive views. The standards and values used to justify the interpretation of the political constitution are reasons all can accept in their capacity as democratic citizens. The idea of public justification is integral to Rawls's idea of respect for persons *as* equal citizens. Where there is a public justification of the laws, no one is forced to act for the sake of values (e.g., moral autonomy, or individuality, or public utility, or the Vision of God) which fundamentally conflict with his or her comprehensive view. (3) This means that no citizen's liberty of conscience or freedom of their person is undermined in the application of the political constitution. Religious citizens and others who reject moral autonomy and individuality as fundamental values are not required to act according to laws justifiable only on the basis of comprehensive reasons they reject. Likewise, agnostics and atheists who reject religious and spiritual doctrines are not forced to observe laws designed to accord with those kinds of reasons. In this way, enacting laws on the basis of public reasons is integral to maintaining both democratic citizens' fundamental *liberties and individual freedom* to pursue their conception of the good, as well as their *higher-order interest* in the capacity to form, revise, and pursue a rational conception of their good. (4) Finally, political reliance upon public reason enables all citizens to achieve their *political autonomy*, or "the legal independence and integrity of citizens and their sharing equally with others in the exercise of political power" (CP, 586). As discussed in the previous chapter, political autonomy is a *political value* that replaces moral autonomy as an essential good for citizens in *Political Liberalism*; it is achievable even if citizens reject moral autonomy and endorse other values (see PL, xliv–xlv). Political autonomy is only achievable when citizens act upon laws fairly and legitimately enacted on the basis of public reasons under conditions of equal political power. Political autonomy does not require that citizens actually endorse all the laws, so long as they can reasonably endorse in their capacity as equal citizens the reasons for which laws are enacted. They may disagree with the political justification provided for laws in terms of public reason, because, for example, they believe too much significance is being attached to one political value at the expense of another they deem more significant in this instance. But so long as a political justification in terms of the values and standards of public reason is made in good faith and is itself not unreasonable, citizens at least are being required to act for reasons that they themselves can endorse in their capacity as democratic citizens, even if they oppose a particular law and do not accept the balance of reasons struck by democratic deliberation and decision. In this regard, the idea of public reason resembles Rousseau's idea of the general will. Rousseau would say that we are "morally free" or autonomous when we act on the general will; by analogy, Rawls would say that *we are politically autonomous when we act on laws enacted through democratic deliberation on the common good on the basis of public reasons under conditions of equal political rights of participation* (so long as the fair value of the political liberties has been guaranteed). The idea of political autonomy is then explicated in part by the idea of public reason.[16] This brings us to the next question: What kind of democracy does Rawls see associated with the idea of public reason?

Public Reason and Deliberative Democracy

Rawls distinguishes between the *idea* and the *ideal* of public reason (PL, l–lvii). The idea of public reason is the requirement in any democratic society that political power be exercised only pursuant to the political values of public reason when constitutional essentials and basic justice are at stake. The *ideal* of public reason is that of a well-ordered democratic society whose citizens generally accept a reasonable political conception of justice, which is regularly referred to in order to provide *content* to public reason and construe political values and their relative significance. (We return to the role of a political conception in providing "content" to public reason later.) In his later works Rawls envisions a background of institutions required by public reason if its ideal is to be realized. The political conceptions that provide content to public reason are all *liberal conceptions* in so far as: (1) they guarantee the basic rights, liberties, and opportunities of free and equal citizens; (2) they assign priority to these basic rights, liberties, and opportunities over other social and political values; and (3) they insure measures providing all citizens, whatever their social position, adequate all-purpose means to make effective use of their basic liberties and opportunities.[17] By (3), Rawls means more than simply the provision of a social minimum, or income supports for the less advantaged. Rather, in order for a liberal political conception to satisfy the third condition it must (as a matter of common sense political sociology) provide for five kinds of institutions: (i) public financing of political campaigns and ways of assuring the availability of information on matters of public policy, to prevent the distortion or manipulation of public reasoning; (ii) "[a] certain fair equality of opportunity" especially in education and training; (iii) a decent distribution of income and wealth; (iv) society as an employer of last resort, needed in order to provide security and meaningful work, so citizens can maintain their self-respect; and (v) "[b]asic health care assured all citizens."[18]

A political conception is unreasonable for Rawls unless it meets these conditions. It is unreasonable since, without these conditions, a political conception cannot meet the criterion of reciprocity. It cannot reasonably or sincerely be thought that other democratic citizens could reasonably accept as a basis for cooperation the absence of effective means to exercise the basic liberties. Thus

Rawls says libertarianism is unreasonable since it does not try to meet these conditions, but explicitly rejects them.[19]

Significantly, Rawls also suggests that these same institutions are required by the ideal of public reason. These institutions are, he says,

> essential prerequisites for a basic structure within which the ideal of public reason, when conscientiously followed by citizens, may protect the basic liberties and prevent social and economic inequalities from being excessive. *Since the ideal of public reason contains a form of public political deliberation, these institutions, most clearly the first three, are necessary for this deliberation to be possible and fruitful.* A belief in the importance of public deliberation is essential for a reasonable constitutional regime, and specific institutions and arrangements need to be laid down to support and encourage it. The idea of public reason proposes how to characterize the structure and content of society's fundamental bases for political deliberations.
>
> (*PL*, lix–lx, emphasis added)

Rawls suggests here that the ideal of public reason requires as background conditions also the institutions of a deliberative democracy. Earlier I mentioned the connection between public reason and political autonomy and drew a comparison with Rousseau (cf. *PL*, 219). Rousseau held that in voting, democratic citizens are not to express their private interests or interests of some group (religious, economic, or otherwise). Rather, citizens are to reflect upon measures that advance the common good of all citizens, understood primarily as achieving justice among free and equal persons. Parallel with his distinction between private good and the common good of citizens, Rousseau distinguishes "private reasons" from "public reasons." What Rousseau says of the magistrate applies equally to any citizen in voting: "His own reason ought to be suspect to him, and the only reason he should follow is the public reason, which is law."[21] Likewise, for Rawls public reason is integral to the ideal of citizenship and democracy as deliberation upon justice and the common good. "A belief in the importance of public deliberation is vital for a reasonable constitutional regime" (LP, 51).

The distinction between the idea and the ideal of public reason is important here. Rawls is not saying that a democracy cannot be governed by public reasons to any degree unless it guarantees all the background institutions (i)–(v) listed above. (The United States, for example, is to some degree governed by public reason; or at least legislators often try to justify their actions in terms of public political values, however inadequately they might succeed.) But clearly Rawls thinks something essential to public reasoning is missing in the absence of a deliberative democracy and these background conditions. Public reason is the mode of discourse in a deliberative democracy and one of its most essential features.[22] Moreover, deliberative democracy is the primary forum within which public reasoning takes place. Citizens in a democracy cannot effectively engage in public reasoning (i) if they or some of their members' basic needs are not adequately provided for, to the degree that they can take effective and intelligent advantage of their basic freedoms; (ii) if the political forum and the free flow of public information are corrupted by monied interests or by other concentrations of power; and (iii) if there are not widespread fair opportunities for education, job training, and participation in public life. "Otherwise all parts of society cannot take part in the debates of public reason or contribute to social and economic policies."[23]

The Content and Completeness of Public Reason and the Right of Abortion

Rawls says that the criterion of reciprocity is "expressed in public reason" (PL, li). This means that public reason must consist of reasons (values, moral principles, factual and scientific claims, etc.) and ways of reasoning that citizens can reasonably expect that others can reasonably accept in their capacity as free and equal citizens. What Rawls calls the *content of public reason* is to be ultimately specified by a political conception of justice that meets the criterion of reciprocity in the way that it orders and interprets the political values of public reason (PL, 453, 467). It might seem peculiar to say that a political conception of justice is needed to provide "content" to public reason. For the political values of public reason listed earlier already are recognized as good reasons in public debate in democratic societies, and yet no current democratic society has a political conception of justice that is publicly recognized and regularly appealed to. Why, then, does Rawls say that a political conception of justice is needed to give "content" to public reason? Or that "A feature of public reasoning is that it proceeds entirely within a political conception of justice?" (PL, 453). This suggests that public reason is not possible without reliance on a political conception, yet it seems that government officials now engage in such reasoning without explicitly recognizing a political conception.

The reason he says this seems to be that a political conception of justice is necessary if public reason is to be "complete." (Perhaps, then, Rawls should have simply said that a political conception is needed to *complete* the content of public reason.) The *completeness* of public reason is its capacity to fully interpret public political values and determine their relative significance, in order to resolve all significant political questions regarding constitutional essentials and matters of basic justice in terms of public reason. Public reason must be complete in some manner if society is to avoid appealing to comprehensive religious, philosophical, and moral doctrines to decide these crucial issues. If appeal to comprehensive doctrines is needed to interpret and decide conflicts among political values, then to that degree the criterion of reciprocity and principle of political legitimacy are violated; citizens are being subject to laws that they cannot reasonably be expected to accept in their capacity as democratic citizens.

In his later work Rawls concedes that "It is crucial that public reason is not specified by any one political conception of justice, certainly not by justice as fairness alone. Rather, its content – the principles, ideals, and standards that may be appealed to – are those of a family of reasonable political conceptions of justice and this family changes over time" (PL, lii–liii; see also PL, 451, 453). Rawls, then, does not conceive of the content of public reason as tied to justice as fairness specifically. A number of liberal political conceptions can provide content to public reason, and these conceptions can even change over generations as different political problems arise. Here again it is important to keep in mind that Rawls is addressing the question of political legitimacy in *Political Liberalism*. He is not saying that the content of justice can change from one generation to the next, but rather the content of public reason can and laws can still remain politically legitimate. As far as justice is concerned, justice as fairness remains for Rawls the most reasonable political *and* moral conception of justice. But different liberal political conceptions can bestow legitimacy on laws in a well-ordered democratic society, and laws can remain legitimate across generations, hence authoritative and worthy of citizens' support, even though the political conceptions relied upon to publicly justify them may develop and change.[24]

The implication is that public reason should not be regarded as anything like a single method of reasoning that settles questions in advance. Rather it specifies the reasons in terms of which questions are to be argued in the public political forum and then democratically decided (PL, liii). "Public reason is not a view about specific institutions or policies, but a view about how they are to be argued for and justified to the citizen body that must decide the question" (PL, liv, n. 28). But if so, then how can Rawls presume that public reason is "complete," or capable of deciding all political questions without appeal to comprehensive reasons? In fact, he does not presume completeness but rather advances the hypothesis that public reason is complete. "Whether public reason can settle all, or almost all, political questions by a reasonable ordering of political values cannot be decided in the abstract independent of actual cases" (PL, liii).

A frequent criticism of Rawls's idea of public reason is indeed that it cannot decide all constitutional essentials and matters of basic justice. The example most frequently raised in this connection is the question whether women should have a right of abortion. What motivates the objection of the incompleteness of public reason in the case of abortion appears to be the question whether the fetus is or is not a person. If the fetus is a person, then abortion is either murder or some kind of homicidal act. This is a question about which comprehensive doctrines vigorously conflict. But it is not within the purview of public reason to decide the metaphysical/moral question whether the fetus is a person; it is beyond public reason's capabilities. Still, Rawls's critics say, this question must be publicly decided, preferably democratically, for how otherwise can society come to a decision regarding women's rights to choose an abortion?

Rawls sets forth a number of political values which bear on the question of a woman's right of abortion, including due respect for human life, the equality of women, and society's interest in repro-ducing itself across generations (PL, 243n.). He conjectures that due reflection upon the relative importance of these values suggests that a right of abortion is justifiable, at least within the first trimester of pregnancy. Here it might be asked how respect for human life can be rendered a purely political value, especially since so many comprehensive doctrines have conflicting views on the nature and conditions of human life and what it is to respect human life. Something like this seems to underlie the objection that appeals to non-public reason are needed to decide the abortion issue. But I believe Rawls means 'human life' in a straightforward sense, as it is understood in empirical sciences such as biology and psychology. He clearly cannot mean 'human life' as conceived by many reli-gions, as life that is endowed with or animated by a soul. That is a metaphysical/religious account of human life, and it cannot be called upon to assess the political value of respect for human life.

I believe the best way to understand Rawls's position on the right to an abortion is as follows. Questions regarding the meta-physical personhood of the fetus or its moral status as a being with interests are not questions resolvable by public reason or about which free and equal citizens can reasonably agree. But it is not necessary to resolve them to address the constitutional ques-tion of abortion and whether women have constitutional rights of choice at some stage of pregnancy. On political grounds of public reason reasonable citizens can agree that no abortion rights at all are a severe restriction on women's freedom and their ability to function as equals in social and civic life. Moreover, there is no compelling case that the fetus is a person, under the political constitution. For, applying standards of evidence consistent with public reason, the fetus, certainly in its early stages, does not have the capacities of political personhood (the moral powers) even in an undeveloped state. This does not necessarily imply that constitutionally speaking the fetus is not a person; for while having these capacities is clearly sufficient for constitutional personhood, it may not be necessary.[25] Still there has to be *some* compelling case for the constitutional personality of the fetus if we are to limit altogether women's freedom to choose, and it has not been – and it is not clear how it could be – established in terms satisfactory to public reason.

Therefore, the reason that women should have rights of choice is that there are substantial political values and interests – regarding women's privacy, their social and civic equality, equality of opportunity, and their freedom – that would be greatly burdened by an absence of rights of choice. Moreover, there is no indication or agreement that any undisputed constitutional person would be burdened by women exercising rights of choice. Given these substantial political values, the burden of proof should reside on the side of opponents to choice, to make the case that there are sufficiently compelling public political reasons that justify burdening those political values and women's vital interests. That there are such burdens on women's interests should not be a point of dispute between pro-choice and anti-choice views, for these are political values of public reason acceptable to reasonable citizens. The disagreement rather is (or should be) over whether there are sufficient public reasons for entirely overriding those political values and prohibiting all abortions for the sake of the political value of due respect for human life. The pro-choice argument is that there is no acceptable case within public reason for the constitutional personhood of the fetus, and that the political value of due respect for a form of human life is not sufficiently compelling, for public political reasons, during its gestation to *completely* outweigh the political values regarding women's political interests; therefore there is no acceptable case for burdening women's privacy, equality, and liberty so completely as to deny altogether a right of choice.[26]

Now it is important to emphasize that, just because public reason can provide an answer based on political values to the abortion issue that is acceptable to people in their capacity as citizens, this does not mean that all reasonable persons will accept this political solution. That will depend on their reasonable comprehensive views and the priority they give to political values of justice. It may well be that many reasonable orthodox Catholics and Jews, and theologically conservative Protestants will never be able to morally accept the political right to abortion that is (presumably) justified on the basis of public reason. But this does not mean that they must reject public reason or even the political legitimacy of abortion rights. (In this connection, Rawls cites former Governor Cuomo of New York, a Catholic who is morally opposed to abortion, but recognized his moral and political duty, as a Catholic, a governor, and a citizen, to respect and enforce that right [CP, 607n.].) Moreover, even if they do reject the moral and political legitimacy of abortion rights, it still does not mean they must reject the requirements of public reason in all other constitutional essentials and matters of basic justice. They are in the same position as Quakers who reject the politically liberal account of just war: Even though they dissent from the conclusions of public reason on that issue and see all or nearly all wars as unjust or not morally legitimate, this does not mean that they must reject the political legitimacy of the law or of the constitution. This of course will be decided by their reasonable comprehensive doctrine. But there are few if any reasonable opponents of abortion who are prepared to abandon democracy, or who, aware of the burdens of judgment, are prepared to abandon public reason and use whatever political means are available to legally enforce the demands of their comprehensive views. To do so would mean they are unreasonable.

The point, then, is that a politically reasonable resolution of a constitutional essential or matter of basic justice in terms of public reason does not imply that reasonable citizens will agree or that the issue will be resolved to everyone's satisfaction. It has never been a feature of Rawls's, or any other, contractarian view to maintain that all reasonable and rational people should be able to agree on all, or even most, laws. (The failure of agreement on ordinary laws is Rousseau's justification for majority rule.) The burdens of judgment apply to political disputes too, and render practicably impossible unanimous agreement in the vast majority of cases. People can then reasonably disagree about what is a politically reasonable outcome of disputes within public reason just as they disagree about what is morally reasonable on the basis of their comprehensive views. But, unlike their moral disagreements, citizens' political disagreements are based in political values that they all accept in their capacity as free and equal democratic citizens. This is the *crucial distinction between reasonable political disagreement and reasonable moral disagreement*. Agreement on political values of public reason is crucial for the political autonomy of free and equal citizens; it is not essential that citizens always agree on laws and the appropriate resolution of disputes within public reason. General agreement among all reasonable citizens is only to be had on a few fundamental matters. Among these are most (if not all) of the political values that count as public reasons, the guidelines for public reason, and the basic requirements of a liberal political conception of justice (the basic liberties, their priority, and a social minimum). For much of his career, Rawls hoped that he could show how it is possible that reasonable free and equal moral persons could come to generally agree upon justice as fairness as a regulative conception of justice. But he finally gave up on this ideal of a well-ordered society, once he fully realized the implications of the burdens of judgment.

Finally, it is important to emphasize once again that Rawls's main concern in political liberalism is to show how a well-ordered constitutional democracy governed by a liberal political conception is practicably possible ("stable for the right reasons") and politically legitimate. For these purposes he does not need to argue that all reasonable persons morally will agree on all the politically reasonable decisions reached by deliberations based on public reason. As we have seen, clearly some will not (Quakers and liberal orthodox Catholics); they may even reject *any* politically reasonable resolution based on political values of public reason in the case of some moral issues (e.g., the right of abortion).

When they do, they are being unreasonable, but this does not make them unreasonable persons, for they normally accept the sufficiency of public reasons to resolve most other constitutional issues and questions of basic justice. Serious problems arise for Rawls's account only if many reasonable comprehensive doctrines in a well-ordered constitutional democracy cannot endorse a liberal political conception in an overlapping consensus, and accept as politically legitimate, if not as wholly just, most (not necessarily all) of the deliberations and conclusions of public reason based on the family of liberal political conceptions. For in that event a well-ordered democratic society would not be stable for the right reasons, and justice, indeed even political legitimacy, would be beyond the reach of human capacities.

The Proviso

I opened this section on public reason by saying that sometimes it may be proper within public political life for people to declare the non-public religious (philosophical or moral) reasons that lead them to support or oppose measures involving fundamental questions of justice. Rawls's example here is Martin Luther King's religious invocation of God's will in support of civil rights. King invoked religious reason in order to address many people's sense of justice. Among those he addressed were some who might only have been reachable via religious reasons. Now it may seem that such people would pose a problem for the idea of public reason. If there are reasonable people whose reasons for accepting liberal principles are purely religiously-based, then it may seem that public reason is not up to the task, at least in this instance, of providing a justification that all reasonable persons can accept.

There may well be such people who do not accept or even understand a public justification of laws in terms of public reasons, but they are not "reasonable" in Rawls's sense. An implication of Rawls's account of reasonable citizens is that they do understand themselves as free and equal citizens and want to justify themselves to others in terms of public reasons. This follows from the account of reasonable persons as those who appreciate the consequences of the burdens of judgment – hence they appreciate that other reasonable persons do not accept their religious or otherwise non-public reasons – and also who aim to cooperate with others on terms they can reasonably accept, namely, on terms specified by public reasons. People who do not understand or who reject public reason and the idea of a public justification are a problem for partial compliance theory. There may be many such people around today in the U.S.A. and other democracies, but they do not show that a well-ordered democratic society governed by public reason and a liberal political conception is not possible. They pose a problem for Rawls's account of the feasibility of a well-ordered democratic society only if an overlapping consensus on a political conception of justice among reasonable persons is not realistically possible.

Is it unfair to prevent such unreasonable people from arguing, and voting according to their religious and other non-public beliefs in the political forum? Many have suggested that it is. The duty of civility, to rely in public argument on public reason, is not a legal restriction on freedom of speech or the right to vote, but rather a purely non-coercive moral requirement. No one is being legally prevented from doing anything by the duty to justify the use of coercive force by citing public reasons. The question rather is whether people who argue and vote for their views only on the basis of their religious and other comprehensive doctrines, without regard to the requirements of public reason, are being unreasonable and violating a moral/political duty. The answer to that question is, "Yes, clearly they are, especially if their vote is not justifiable in accordance with public reason." What is unfair about requiring people, when advocating or voting for the coercive use of state power according to the demands of their comprehensive doctrines, to justify themselves to other reasonable persons on terms they can reasonably accept? The unfairness seems to lie on the side of those who suggest that there is no duty of civility upon people, who are religiously or otherwise motivated, to be able to justify or explain themselves to other reasonable persons who reject their comprehensive doctrines. The suggestion that there is something "unfair" about the duty of civility is an ironic claim; for what is at issue here is the political unfairness of coercion according to the dictates of one's religion or philosophy that cannot be justified according to the political values of public reason.

But what about appeals, not by unreasonable but by reasonable persons themselves to religious and other comprehensive reasons within the public political forum? Are such appeals ever justifiable and, if so, on what grounds? Here the concern is not arguments among people of the same religious, philosophical, or moral view, regarding the political implications of their comprehensive doctrine. Clearly, given the basic liberties and their priority, arguments within and among comprehensive doctrines are permissible and entirely appropriate within the "background culture" of a democratic society. The question rather is whether citizens or government officials may properly enter the public political forum – in political campaigns, and legislative and other political assemblies, for example – and appeal to comprehensive reasons in defense of their judgments and decisions on laws and policies. Does this not violate the duty of civility? Not necessarily; in *Political Liberalism* Rawls allows such appeals (albeit somewhat grudgingly at first). He says they are permissible if (1) they are *needed* to convince other citizens of the appropriateness of some measure, (2) the measure is itself *defensible* in terms of public political values, *and* (3) a public justification is eventually forthcoming that sets forth the argument for the measure in terms of public reason. This is the "proviso" on the public use of religious and other comprehensive reasons in the public political forum (PL, lii). In "Public Reason Revisited," Rawls loosens the requirements of the duty of civility still further, deleting condition (1). He suggests that religious and other comprehensive reasons may be used in the public political forum, even when they are not designed or needed to reach people who might otherwise not be reachable by arguments based purely on public reason. "Reasonable comprehensive doctrines, religious or non-religious, may be introduced in public political discussion at any time, provided that in due course proper political reasons . . . are presented that are sufficient to support whatever the comprehensive doctrines introduced are said to support" (PL, 462). So long as this proviso is met, then, the duty of civility can be satisfied, even if one beforehand has invoked religious and other non-public reasons in the public political forum purely for reasons of "declaration" or "witnessing" of one's comprehensive view. By letting other citizens know the doctrinal basis in support of one's political convictions regarding a controversial issue, "Citizens' allegiance to the democratic ideal of public reason is strengthened for the right reasons" (PL, 463). It demonstrates to others one's good faith commitment to constitutional and political values in terms of one's comprehensive view. This is the *"wide view of public political culture."*

Notice here that the proviso does not sanction the use of religious and other non-public reasons in the political forum to support measures not supportable by public reason; an example might be the prohibition against all abortions at any period of gestation and no matter what the reason. The frequently heard argument in today's political forum (e.g., in legislative debate) that "Human life is sacred and begins at conception," and therefore, "All (or almost all) abortion should be prohibited since it is the taking of an innocent human life" is not rendered permissible by the proviso, since it implies restrictions that are not defensible in terms of public reasons (violating both conditions (2) and (3) above). On the other hand, so long as the proviso is later satisfied, the non-public argument that "The fetus is a person from the 23d week because its nervous system is functional and it is capable of feeling pleasure and pain" would seem to be a permissible comprehensive reason to invoke in the public forum for restricting abortion during the third trimester; for there are other public political reasons for restricting abortion at some stage of gestation (viz. due respect for human life) that might be later cited to fulfill the proviso's requirement.

Concluding Remarks

The role of public reason is to provide the terms of political debate and justification for the use of coercive political power among free and equal citizens. Public reason, like the original position, is supposed to achieve a kind of impartiality among free and equal citizens in our political judgments of justice and in the reasons for laws. It requires us as citizens or political officials, when making arguments and decisions in political contexts about constitutional essentials and basic justice, to abstract from many different kinds of considerations and "bracket" what we regard as the "whole truth." We are instead to rely upon political values and a liberal political conception of justice. As such, the idea of public reason aims to carry through to completion the contractarian ideal of democratic citizens cooperating on terms that all can accept, which Rawls believes is necessary if citizens are to be genuinely equals and politically free.

FURTHER READING

Greenawalt, Kent, "On Public Reason," *Chicago-Kent Law Review*, 69, 1994, 669–89. (Presents a more constrained account of public reason which contrasts with Rawls's.)

Larmore, Charles, "Public Reason," in *The Cambridge Companion to Rawls*, ch. 10. (Generally sympathetic account of the idea of public reason.)

Raz, Joseph, "Disagreement in Politics," *American Journal of Jurisprudence*, 1998, 25–52. (Challenges Rawls's ideas of public justification and public reason.)

Ten

The Law of Peoples

THE LAW OF NATIONS

The principles of justice are a conception of *social* justice; they regulate the relations among people living in the *same society*, specifying their duties to one another and society's duties to them. They are not a conception of human rights, and do not specify duties that societies owe to other societies or their members; nor does the difference principle require that societies globally distribute their social product to the world's less advantaged.

In the opening sections of *A Theory of Justice* Rawls says:

> I am concerned with a special case of the problem of justice . . . There is no reason to suppose ahead of time that the principles satisfactory for the basic structure hold for all cases. These principles may not work for the rules and practices of private associations or for those of less comprehensive social groups . . . [Also] The conditions for the law of nations may require different principles . . . I shall be satisfied if it is possible to formulate a reasonable conception of justice for the basic structure of society conceived for the time being as a closed system isolated from other societies.
>
> (*TJ*, 7–8/7 rev.)

Rawls's assumption of a "closed system isolated from other societies" has been widely criticized, for no modern society can remain closed and isolated from the influences of other societies for long. But unrealistic hypothetical assumptions of closed isolated systems are common in the natural and social sciences.

Their purpose is to bracket outside influences that are not regarded as central to the understanding of the phenomena to be explained. For example, to determine how prices are set in market systems, economists assume unrealistic conditions of perfect competition among rational self-interested economic agents and therewith the absence of many normal motivations (altruism, patriotism, envy, religious fervor, a sense of justice, etc.) and political and economic facts (government fiscal policy, tariff restrictions, oligopolies, etc.) that influence people's choices. Once the basic economic laws and tendencies are ascertained based on these and other hypothetical assumptions, relevant information can be restored and its complex influences ascertained.

In *A Theory of Justice* and *Political Liberalism* Rawls also focuses on a "special case" (ibid.); he seeks to discover the most appropriate conception of justice to regulate social cooperation among the members of a well-ordered democratic society. Once this ideal conception of *social and political justice* has been ascertained, Rawls thinks that the hypothetical assumption of a closed society can be relaxed, and that other "special cases" of justice can be addressed, including principles of international justice that regulate the relationships between societies and their governments. This is the "law of nations," later called the "law of peoples." Social principles of justice regulate domestic policies and social relations domestically, within society. But a society's relations with other societies is unavoidable, and a foreign policy is needed to regulate them. Where is this foreign policy to come from? Rawls's idea is not to start anew, but rather "to extend the theory of justice to the law of nations. . . . Our problem then is to relate the just political principles regulating the conduct of states to the contract doctrine and to explain the moral basis of the law of nations from this point of view" (TJ, 377/331 rev.).

Already in *Theory* Rawls envisions a method for extending the contractarian framework to cover international justice and relations among different nations. The law of nations is to be determined by a hypothetical contract, not among all people in the world but among the representatives of different nations. They too are to be put behind a veil of ignorance regarding facts about themselves and their societies, and come to an agreement upon principles of justice to regulate relations among different societies. As in the domestic original position, the parties in the international original position are motivated only by individual interests, in this case the interests of their individual nation. But their national interest is primarily a moral one – not aggrandizement of power or economic gain, but maintaining the justice of their own basic structure. "The national interest of a just state is defined by the principles of justice that have already been acknowledged. Therefore such a nation will aim above all to maintain and to preserve its just institutions and the conditions that make them possible" (TJ, 379/333 rev.).

The parties in the international original position then differ from those in the domestic case in that they are morally motivated to preserve and maintain justice, as applied among their own people. Still, they are rational in that they are indifferent to the justice and interests of other nations, except in so far as it bears upon their own interests in achieving justice in their own society.

Here it is important that the representatives in the international original position do not directly represent individual persons but rather separate nations, or "peoples." Why is this? Rawls is mainly concerned with principles for institutions needed to establish moral relations of justice *among nations*. His question is: How should separate nations or peoples, regarded as independent agents, conduct themselves towards one another? He is not directly addressing individuals' rights or duties, or the problem: What are the relations and duties among individuals in the world, no matter what their affiliation as members of particular societies? To some degree this problem has already been addressed within justice as fairness, for the *natural duties* – of justice, mutual respect, and mutual aid – agreed to in the domestic original position are duties that individuals owe to all persons in the world, not just to members of their own societies. One way to look at the law of nations in *Theory* is that it extends the natural duties for individuals to relations among nations (TJ, 115/99 rev.). Nations too have duties of justice, mutual respect, and mutual aid towards each other. The problem of the law of nations (and the law of peoples) is to define the nature and scope of these duties.

Here cosmopolitans object: Why doesn't Rawls have a "global original position" among all the world's individual inhabitants instead of an international one among representatives of nations? After all, Rawls proceeds from the Kantian idea of mutual respect for persons regarded as free and equal persons. If equal respect for persons is the basis for social justice, why should it not also provide the basis for relations among everyone in the world? Rawls's "state-centric" view of global justice belies his commitment to equal respect for persons.

This is the challenge raised by cosmopolitan critics of Rawls's proposed law of nations and its subsequent development in *The Law of Peoples*.[1] To fully assess this objection we must look at the details of Rawls's Law of Peoples. But something in general should be said at the outset about why Rawls rejects cosmopolitanism. There are different ways to understand cosmopolitanism, and Rawls's own Law of Peoples has cosmopolitan features (such as human rights as limits on autonomy of governments and a duty of assistance to burdened peoples). Cosmopolitans do not necessarily endorse a world-state, but they do regard national boundaries and social affiliations as secondary, if not incidental, from a moral point of view. "Liberal cosmopolitanism" is defined by its main proponents as a moral ideal grounded in the equal moral status of all persons and the justifiability of social arrangements to everyone in the world.[2] These moral values are said to imply the recognition of equal basic rights and liberties for all persons in the world and a global egalitarian principle of distributive justice. The liberal cosmopolitan objection to Rawls is that his Kantian commitment to equal respect for persons conflicts with his primary focus on social justice; for *equal* respect requires that we ignore social affiliations and give equal consideration to all people in the world in deriving principles of justice.

"Equal respect and concern" is a key idea in Ronald Dworkin's liberal philosophy.[3] I am not aware that Rawls uses the term "equal respect," except to make the narrow claim that free and equal persons have "a right to equal respect and consideration in determining the principles by which the basic structure of *their society* is to be governed" (TJ, 475 rev.).[4] The terms he uses instead are "respect for persons," "respect for equal persons," "respect for free and equal persons," or "mutual respect." It's a minor point, perhaps, but relevant to the cosmopolitan claim that the priority Rawls assigns to social justice is inconsistent with a commitment to equal respect and concern for persons – for Rawls makes no such specific commitment in those terms.

The liberal cosmopolitan objection challenges Rawls's initial focus on social cooperation and the basic structure of society. Recall that Rawls opens *A Theory of Justice*, and later *Political Liberalism*, with the general question: What is the most appropriate conception of social and political justice for a *democratic society*, wherein citizens regard themselves as free and equal? Cosmopolitans, in effect, say that this question has no answer, for there is no conception of justice peculiarly appropriate for a democratic society that is any different from the correct cosmopolitan account that applies to all the world; or they say that the appropriate conception of justice for a democratic society can be, at most, an application of the correct cosmopolitan theory, and thus is not ascertainable until we first address cosmopolitan justice.

Why does Rawls start with the problem of social and political justice and regard it as the foundation for both international justice and "local justice" (justice within the family and other associations)? One reason Rawls gives for the basic structure of society as the "first subject" of justice is the profound effects of social cooperation and its basic institutions on people's present and future prospects, their characters, relationships, plans, and self-conceptions – the kinds of persons they are and can aspire to be. Cosmopolitans meet this with the rejoinder that there may be more frequent interaction among the members of a society but it's just a matter of degree, for global relations also have profound effects on people's future prospects, characters, etc.; moreover, societies benefit from one another and are becoming increasingly interdependent due to globalization. Now it is true that all sorts of real and potential benefits stem from cooperation among members of different societies, including economic benefits, technology and cultural exchanges, etc. In the absence of cooperation with other societies the living standards of (prosperous) people would be lower, and they would have to become economically self-sufficient. Still, for Rawls, there is a fundamental qualitative difference, not simply one of degree, between the effects of social cooperation and cooperation with people from other societies.

To begin with, social relations, unlike global relations, are coercively enforced. Social cooperation for Rawls invariably involves political cooperation, and with it the political enforcement of basic social rules and institutions necessary to society. People have no choice but to engage in social cooperation and comply with the demands of society's basic structure. For this reason Rawls sees it as essential that terms of social cooperation be reasonably acceptable to everyone, and justifiable by (public) reasons that all can accept. By contrast, economic and cultural relations between societies are normally voluntary and are based in treaties; they extend no further than the terms of their agreements. When coercive relations between peoples exist they signify duress or an absence of cooperation instead of being a precondition to cooperative relations as in the case of members of the same society.

But much more significant is social cooperation's centrality to who and what we are. While the absence of cooperative relations with other societies means the absence of many potential benefits, if we deprive people of society altogether then *everything* changes. Social cooperation is necessary to our development as persons, the realization of our reasoning and moral powers, the development of our social capacities, and our having a conception of the good. An individual may be able to survive without having ever experienced the benefits of social cooperation, alone in the wild or in herds not governed by social norms. But their lives would be primitive – as Rousseau says, the lives of "stupid limited animals." There would be no system of property and contracts, and no economic system with division of labor, cooperative productive activity, and trade. Production, if any, would be primitive, and without the recognition of property it is questionable whether agriculture would be possible. People would be without culture, scientific knowledge, technology, and formal and most informal associations (including the social institution of the family).

Morality and justice would be absent, as would even language itself. Social cooperation is the most profound and influential relationship that humans can have; it is the fundamental precondition for our developing our distinctly human capacities and achieving a status as free agents with a capacity for practical reason and a conception of our good. It is even a condition for our having a conception of ourselves as persons with a past and a future.[5]

By contrast, global cooperation is not a precondition of our survival or flourishing as developed persons, or to the development of our rational, social, and moral powers. In fact, global cooperation among *all* or even most of the world's peoples has never really existed in any significant measure. Instead, peoples normally enter into cooperative relations individually with other societies to one degree or another.[6] Clearly, cooperation with other societies, particularly trade between peoples, is beneficial to a society, but it is not a precondition to the existence of its social and political institutions, or to reasoning and language, moral personality, or the development of humans as social beings. It is optional and voluntary in a way that social cooperation is not. Without cooperation with *other societies*, we lose the economic and cultural benefits of commerce with other peoples. Without social cooperation with *other persons*, we lose civilization and all its essential benefits and are without reason itself. All other forms of cooperation are dependent upon social cooperation, while societies can endure and even flourish in many respects in the absence of most other forms of cooperation. Of course, some form of the family is needed during our formative years; but the family itself is a social institution, and familial cooperation, unlike social cooperation, is not needed to survive and flourish for all of one's life. The basic point is that it is primarily because of the all-encompassing and pervasive significance of social relations to our development as moral and rational beings that Rawls regards social justice as the primary foundation of our moral relations with others. For purposes of justice, we are fundamentally social beings, not natural or cosmopolitan beings.

Some cosmopolitans may dismiss these considerations and minimize the significance of social cooperation to justice altogether.[7]

Like libertarians, they see cooperation as irrelevant to justice. Other cosmopolitans regard social cooperation as important but see global cooperation as one form of social cooperation. ("After all, it is a social relationship and it is cooperative, so what else could it be?") But for Rawls social cooperation presupposes a shared basic structure of basic social institutions, including political institutions, and these do not exist at the global level or between peoples. Social justice for Rawls has to do with the principles that regulate basic social and political institutions and the relations of people living within them, and not the relations among different societies or among all people in the world.

While cosmopolitans usually recognize that relations within the family have their own distinctive moral norms and special rights and obligations and that we have good reason to have a special concern for family members, they do not recognize that there are distinct and independent principles of social and political justice that apply within societies to structure and regulate social cooperation among its members. Social principles of justice, if they exist at all, are derivative from allegedly more basic principles of cosmopolitan justice; if there are any distinct social duties and special obligations owed to a society's members, they are largely instrumental to promoting the primary end of cosmopolitan justice.[8]

Cosmopolitanism in this regard resembles libertarianism; both are in their own distinctive way asocial, apolitical views. Both deny a basic assumption of the social contract tradition, the fundamental moral significance of social and political relations to justice. But social and political cooperation among members of a society are not simply arbitrary facts; they are not just one-way, rather they are the *only realistically possible way* that individuals' basic rights are recognized and protected, that property exists as an institution, that production of goods and services takes place, and that economic value is created. In this and other regards, cooperation with other peoples, and clearly global cooperation with all peoples, are secondary; they may be conducive to but are not necessary for respect for basic rights and liberties, and the production, use, and consumption and enjoyment of income and wealth.

These facts are for Rawls of fundamental significance to any account of political and distributive justice.

THE LAW OF PEOPLES AND POLITICAL LIBERALISM

The Law of Peoples (1999) is Rawls's final work. It delivers on the promise of a contractarian account of the Law of Nations made in A Theory of Justice, suitably modified to comply with the limitations and requirements of Political Liberalism. Rawls now refers to "peoples" instead of "nations." He has little to say about what constitutes a people, but clearly it is an idealization. Apparently, "peoples" is meant to convey that it is distinct societies of persons, cooperating within one basic structure of institutions, that are the primary actors in relations between societies – not "states" or the governments that represent a people, or even nations in the traditional sense. A people is responsible for the kind of government it creates, at least under the ideal conditions of well-ordered societies that Rawls regards as the appropriate condition from which to ascertain principles of justice. A precondition for the existence of a people is political cooperation, which for Rawls is part of social cooperation. A people may constitute more than one ethnic group or "nation" as traditionally understood. Rawls is not then a "nationalist," certainly not in the sense which says that each nation of people, whether ethnically, culturally, or linguistically constituted, has a right to political self-determination. Of basic importance to being a people are not shared ethnic, communal, or even linguistic bonds, any more than shared religious bonds. While all these might be present to some degree, they are not necessary. Rather, social cooperation and sharing the same basic structure are all that are absolutely necessary to being a people. There are many different kinds of associational bonds – ethnic, linguistic, political, historical, and so on – that might account for social unity among a people. As in the United States, social unity among a people might rest simply on individuals of different ethnic, linguistic, religious and other groups all recognizing and being committed to the same political constitution, having a sense of its history, and valuing their membership in the same political culture. The main distinguishing feature of a people, then, is that they "share a common central government and political culture, and the moral learning of political concepts and principles . . . in the context of society-wide political and social institutions that are part of their shared daily life" (LP, 112).

Rawls's account of the Law of Peoples is an essential part of *Political Liberalism*. For this reason it is easily misunderstood. Rawls is not addressing the question, "What is the ideal constitution of the cosmopolitan order?" Kant, Rawls's model in many respects, did address this question. Kant rejected a world-state since he thought it would degenerate into either global despotism or a fragile empire torn by civil wars where regions and peoples seek to gain their political autonomy. He held that an ideal cosmopolitan order consists of an international society of politically independent and autonomous peoples, each of whom has a republican constitution. A republican constitution, Kant says, affirms the democratic sovereignty of the people as that legal person which "possesses the highest political authority." It guarantees each member the status of free and equal citizen, and gives them the "civil rights" of citizens.[9] Rawls follows Kant in rejecting a world government as utopian.[10] Rawls's Law of Peoples also endorses the independence and autonomy of different peoples. But Rawls does not incorporate Kant's requirement that every government should be republican and guarantee all the civil rights of free and equal citizens. What underlies this surprising conclusion? It may seem as if Rawls no longer endorses the position advocated in *A Theory of Justice* – namely, that a well-ordered democratic society is a universal ideal of justice, and that equal rights of political participation are morally required once a society achieves the requisite social and economic conditions for democracy.

The Law of Peoples addresses a different question than Kant and others who are concerned with the questions of cosmopolitan justice raised above. Within his own partially comprehensive doctrine presented in *A Theory of Justice*, Rawls always believed that every society in the world has a duty to develop its institutions so that it realizes the moral requirements of justice as fairness. Any society that does not conform to justice as fairness is not just, and societies, both liberal and non-liberal, are unjust to the degree that they depart from the principles of justice. Rawls says nothing within *Political Liberalism* or *The Law of Peoples* that changes this position. *The Law of Peoples* is not intended to endorse relativism or multiculturalism; it does not imply that it is morally appropriate for non-liberal or non-democratic societies to continue in their ways without reforming their institutions. Instead, in *The Law of Peoples* Rawls assumes the realistic conditions of a less than perfect international order consisting of both liberal and non-liberal governments and peoples. He does not question the possibility of a world of liberal societies (however unlikely it may be), for there is no character flaw in human nature (like original sin) that prevents such a world from coming about. Indeed, *The Law of Peoples* contains an account of the principles of justice that should apply in that most ideal world of exclusively liberal societies (for it deals first, in Part 1, exclusively with relations among liberal societies). But the Law of Peoples also is designed to address a more likely scenario of a world with both liberal and non-liberal peoples. One of the main questions it raises then is: How are liberal peoples to relate to non-liberal peoples, and in particular to non-liberal peoples who are "decent," even if not just by the standards of a well-ordered constitutional democracy?

Rawls's Law of Peoples is then developed within political liberalism; it is an extension and hence part of a liberal political conception of justice. A liberal political conception, such as justice as fairness, mainly pertains to domestic justice and the basic structure of society. But social and political justice is not the only kind of justice a liberal political conception must address. Also needed are principles of foreign policy to regulate a constitutional democracy's interaction with other societies, both liberal and non-liberal (LP, 10, 83). "The Law of Peoples proceeds from the international political world as we see it, and concerns what the foreign policy of a reasonably just liberal people should be. . . . It allows us to examine in a reasonably realistic way what should be the aim of the foreign policy of a liberal democratic people" (LP, 83).

The eight principles that constitute the Law of Peoples are straightforward and unsurprising, though Rawls says that they require much interpretation and explanation. He also says they are incomplete and that others need to be added (LP, 37). The principles require that all peoples (1) respect the freedom and independence of other peoples; (2) observe treaties and undertakings; (3) respect the equality of peoples in agreements and relations; (4) observe a duty of non-intervention; (5) wage war only in self-defense or in defense of other peoples unjustly attacked; (6) honor human rights; (7) observe just restrictions in waging war, such as not attacking non-combatants; and (8) come to the assistance of burdened or other peoples living under unfavorable conditions that prevent their having a just or decent political and social regime. In saying this list is incomplete, Rawls leaves leeway for additional principles. But he excludes any role for a principle of global distributive justice or a resource distribution principle that would be in addition to (8) the duty of assistance.

Rawls's argument for these principles relies upon a "second original position." He imagines the representatives of well-ordered liberal peoples coming together to work out the terms of their cooperation. Not knowing which society they represent, they would all agree to the principles of the Law of Peoples behind a (thick) veil of ignorance that brackets all factual information about their own and other societies. The parties then do not know the size of any society, their resources or wealth, their ethnic, religious, cultural makeup, and so on. They do know the same general facts as parties know in the first original position regarding principles of domestic justice. They also know that they are well-ordered liberal and democratic societies whose social unity depends upon citizens' affirmation of a liberal and democratic conception of justice. The primary interest of the parties to the second original position is not to maximize their wealth, power, or any other advantage, but rather to provide appropriate conditions for maintaining just social institutions in their own society. This moral aim is the rational motivation of the parties who are representatives of liberal peoples. They are concerned with promoting the demands of domestic justice among their own people. Importantly, as in the domestic original position, they are indifferent towards other peoples, and are not concerned with their well-being. While liberal citizens are directly concerned with the domestic justice of other peoples, their legal representatives in the second original position are not; it concerns them only in so far as it is relevant to liberal justice in their own society. Representatives of peoples are like trustees or legal guardians; they are instructed to ignore their personal interests and all other interests except those of the persons or society they are assigned to represent.

The representatives of liberal peoples, so defined, would all agree to the eight principles listed above, as "the basic charter of the Law of Peoples." Unlike the first original position, Rawls does not give them a choice of alternative principles or the opportunity to choose a global resource principle or principle of global distributive justice. He says (rather mysteriously), "Rather, the representatives of well-ordered peoples simply reflect on the advantages of these principles of equality among peoples and see no reason to depart from them or to propose alternatives" (LP, 41). Rawls's critics see this as an arbitrary limitation, even as question-begging.[11] In effect, Rawls prevents representatives from raising the issue of a global distribution principle or resource tax, or at least supposes that they do not have reason to upon reflection. (Later we will discuss why.) Instead, these eight principles provide the primary regulative norms of cooperation for the Society of Peoples. The *basic structure of the Society of Peoples* consists of the institutions that are needed to maintain the Law of Peoples. It does not include a world-state, or a comprehensive global legal system with original jurisdiction to specify global property, contract rights and other laws. *Original* political and legal jurisdiction to specify property and other rights within their own territories resides with independent peoples. Relations among peoples and any institutions and laws that result from their relations are to be based in treaties and agreements among them. On the basis of treaties the Society of Peoples is to include international political federations with *derivative jurisdiction* (such as a U.N.-like body) as well as federations that provide for fairness and efficiency in trade relations (resembling the WTO, though unlike it, focused mainly on fairness and not controlled by more advantaged nations), and other cooperative institutions, with judicial powers where appropriate to resolve disputes and enforce agreements and other measures (cf. LP, 38).

TOLERATION OF DECENT SOCIETIES

Rawls maintains that well-ordered liberal societies all would reasonably accept the principles of the Law of Peoples as fair principles of cooperation with other liberal societies, agreeing thereby not to interfere with their domestic affairs, and to recognize their independence and respect them as equals. But should liberal societies also tolerate and cooperate with non-liberal societies that are not just or legitimate according to (political) liberalism; and if so, how far should their toleration and cooperation extend? Or should liberal societies seek to shape in their own image all societies not yet liberal or democratic, intervening in their internal affairs and applying sanctions whenever they might be effective?

To address these questions Rawls distinguishes a *just society*, which is a well-ordered liberal society, from a *decent society*; then he distinguishes both from indecent or "outlaw" societies, which violate in some way the requirements of decency. Respect for human decency is a condition of justice, but not all decent societies are just in a liberal democratic sense. A *decent hierarchical society* Rawls defines as one that (a) is peaceful and non-expansionist; (b) is guided by a *common-good conception of justice* that affirms the good of all of its members; (c) has a *"decent consultation hierarchy,"* which represents each major segment of society, and which is seen as legitimate in the eyes of its people (LP, sect. 9); and (d) honors the basic *human rights* that respect the humanity of its members (LP, sect. 10). The basic human rights that are a condition of a decent society are, Rawls says: (1) the rights protecting the life and integrity of the person, which include the right to life and security of the person, and also minimum rights to the means of subsistence (a decent people does not let its members starve); (2) rights to liberty of the person (including freedom of movement, freedom from forced work and forced occupation, and the right to hold personal property); (3) rights of formal equality and to protections of the rule of law (rights to due process, fair trials, against self-incrimination, and so on); and (4) some degree of liberty of conscience, freedom of thought and expression, and freedom of association (LP, 65, 78–81). It is not a condition of a decent society that it affirm the equality of its members or give them equal political rights (it may afford them no political rights at all), or even that it provide for equality of all basic human rights. For example, a decent society may have a state religion and politically enforce a religious morality, as long as it provides an appropriate degree of freedom to practice dissenting religions. Also a decent society must respect the human rights of women, and represent their interests in its just consultation hierarchy (LP, 75, 110).[12]

It is essential to keep in mind that Rawls's Law of Peoples is (like his principles of social justice) specified for the ideal case, among "well-ordered societies." How the Law of Peoples is to be applied in our world, "with all its injustices," is a separate issue. All reasonable members of a well-ordered society generally accept the public conception of justice that regulates society and have a willingness to comply with it. In well-ordered liberal societies all citizens conceive of themselves as free and equal and they publicly endorse one or another liberal conception (all guaranteeing the basic liberties and their priority, equal opportunities, and a social minimum). In well-ordered decent hierarchical societies all endorse the non-liberal, common-good conception of justice that regulates society, including respect for everyone's human rights and other requirements of decency. Common-good conceptions, by definition, promote a conception of the good of each member of society. This does not mean that the common good promoted is the freedom and equality of society's members; nor does it mean that everybody in a well-ordered decent society accepts all laws designed to promote their common good. But still all do accept the common-good conception used to justify those laws, even if they do not agree with all its interpretations and applications. This parallels the account of well-ordered liberal societies, all of whose reasonable members accept a liberal political conception, but disagree about its interpretation and application.

Since decent hierarchical societies accept the requirements of decency and their members have a (non-liberal) sense of justice, they have a "moral nature" and are therefore reasonable to a degree. They seek to do what is right, comply with moral demands, and respect others' rights all for their own sake, not simply to avoid international sanctions or for other self-interested reasons. Apparently for Rawls, both a people and individual persons can be reasonable in a limited sense, even if they do not conceive of themselves as free and equal, as we liberals do, and do not accept liberalism. Having moral dispositions, including a sense of justice, and endorsing human rights, a common good, and other requirements of decency seem to be sufficient for non-democratic people to be reasonable, or at least not unreasonable. Interestingly, the same does not seem to be true of non-liberal members of democratic societies with the same beliefs; they are unreasonable for not endorsing the liberal terms of cooperation that regulate relations among free and equal persons in the society they are members of. This is not inconsistent; reasonableness for Rawls seems to depend in the first instance upon having moral motives and a sense of justice, and is made relative to the moral terms of cooperation that govern a liberal or decent society. ("When in Rome . . . " – though here I doubt Rawls would say that liberal dissidents in a decent society are being unreasonable for not accepting the non-liberal components of its common-good conception of justice.)

No existing societies seem to satisfy Rawls's description of a decent hierarchical society. Then again, no existing societies satisfy his account of a well-ordered liberal society either (LP, 75). So what is his point? One of Rawls's primary aims in the Law of Peoples is to define the limits of liberal peoples' toleration of non-liberal peoples. The idea of a decent hierarchical society is a theoretical construct developed for this purpose. Rawls contends that liberal societies should not tolerate dictatorial, tyrannical, and other "outlaw" regimes that violate human rights and do not act for the good of all their members. But what about non-liberal societies that are not just but are nonetheless decent? Is it reasonable to expect well-ordered decent societies to conform to all the liberal egalitarian norms of a constitutional democracy as a condition of peaceable co-existence and cooperation with them, even though liberal and egalitarian ideals are not part of their culture and are not generally endorsed by their members? Rawls contends that, so long as decent peoples respect the Law of Peoples, it is unreasonable for free and equal peoples to require them to be liberal and democratic or refuse to cooperate with them. To insist, as cosmopolitan liberals often do, that the *only* bases for cooperation with a non-liberal but decent and peaceable people are that they provide their members with the full rights and benefits of liberal-democratic citizens is an unreasonable position. A liberal society is to respect other societies organized by non-liberal, non-democratic comprehensive doctrines, *provided* that their political and social institutions meet conditions of decency and they respect the Law of Peoples.

Rawls's position does not imply that political liberalism endorses decent hierarchical societies as just and beyond criticism. Liberal citizens and associations have full rights (perhaps even duties according to their comprehensive views) to publicly criticize the illiberal or undemocratic character of other societies, and can boycott them if they choose. But critical assessment by liberal citizens is different from their government's hostile criticisms, sanctions, and other forms of coercive intervention. The Law of Peoples says that liberal peoples, *as peoples represented by their governments*, have a duty to cooperate with and not seek to undermine decent non-liberal societies. This means that liberal peoples have certain moral duties to decent non-liberal peoples, and their relations are not defined in purely strategic terms. Among the duties they have is a duty to respect the territorial integrity of decent peoples, as well as their political independence and autonomy (within the limits of decency).

Some object to Rawls's duty of non-interference since it seems to imply a duty not to come to the assistance of democratic liberation movements. But the duty of non-interference only prohibits assisting democratic resistance to decent hierarchical regimes, not to tyrannical and other "outlaw" regimes. This leaves room for assisting democratic rebellions against outlaw regimes, so long as internal resistance is likely to prove effective. This is very different from a decent non-liberal society, which is to be deemed capable of the self-imposition of democracy; otherwise, Rawls implies, its members are not likely to sustain democratic rule. More trouble-some perhaps is Rawls's suggestion that it is not reasonable for liberal governments to even provide incentives, such as subsidies, to decent regimes to reform their societies. Rawls says it is "more important" that subsidies be used to assist peoples burdened by unfavorable conditions (LP, 85). Here it helps to keep in mind that Rawls is engaged in ideal theory and so is referring to decent well-ordered societies, members of which have a non-liberal self-conception and generally accept the hierarchical system as legitimate and endorse its common-good conception. Under these conditions foreign incentives to become liberal are likely to be ineffective and cause resentment within the Society of Peoples and also can compromise the effective self-determination of non-liberal societies.

Rawls's account depends heavily upon the institutional division of labor in establishing justice. A just society is a liberal society, and non-liberal but decent societies are unjust (LP, 83). Rawls clearly is not a multi-culturalist or a relativist who thinks that once requirements of decency are satisfied, justice is relative to the culture and practices of a society. But he believes that non-liberal societies often are not yet ready to sustain liberal and democratic institutions. A cosmopolitan can accept this without accepting Rawls's strong view of political autonomy, which says that each liberal or decent society alone has the duty to establish and maintain liberal justice domestically on its own by guaranteeing liberal rights to free and equal citizens and just distributions for all its members. For Rawls, it is not the role of a liberal society's government to establish liberal justice non-domestically in decent societies. That is to be achieved by their own political self-determination as members of the same society. The political autonomy of decent peoples is, Rawls seems to suggest, a condition for the secure establishment of social justice. One society rarely is able to establish just liberal social institutions within another non-liberal society that will be stable and endure; its political culture is not yet ready to sustain them. The stability of just liberal and democratic institutions depends upon citizens conceiving of themselves as free and equal and developing a liberal sense of justice. But this duty of non-interference is not simply strategic. Rawls also seems to think it is *unreasonable* for a liberal society to sanction well-ordered decent peoples or interfere with relations among their members in order to coerce or intimidate them to liberalize their institutions. Later we need to consider why Rawls puts such great moral weight on a non-liberal but decent people's political autonomy.

Rawls's theoretical argument for the toleration of non-liberal, decent hierarchical peoples is straightforward. First, he envisions a third original position agreement exclusively among decent peoples' representatives. There, decent peoples would agree to the same Law of Peoples that liberal peoples agree to. Importantly, Rawls does not arrange for an agreement between liberal and non-liberal peoples on these principles. His reason perhaps is to avoid the objection that agreement on the principles of the Law of Peoples is simply a bargain or *modus vivendi* among liberal and non-liberal peoples, where liberal peoples compromise on globally enforcing liberal basic liberties on condition that decent peoples do not insist on a redistribution principle requiring liberal peoples to redistribute their wealth.[13] This objection is mistaken. For in the original position agreement among liberal peoples, all agree not to interfere with one another but to instead allow each liberal people to enforce liberal justice domestically. Since the eight principles of the Law of Peoples would hold in an ideal world of exclusively well-ordered liberal societies, these principles hold in the *most ideal case*. They cannot, then, result from a compromise among liberal and non-liberal decent peoples. Instead, Rawls's argument for tolerating non-liberal decent hierarchical peoples is that, since they also all accept the same eight principles of the Law of Peoples, liberal peoples have nothing to fear in their relations with them. They pose no threat to the domestic justice of a liberal society, which is the fundamental interest of the liberal parties in the second original position. For decent hierarchical peoples are reasonable in their foreign relations in that they respect the Law of Peoples and are committed to human rights and a (non-liberal) conception of justice that promotes a good common to all their members. Moreover, Rawls thinks that it would be unreasonable for liberal societies to refuse to tolerate decent societies who have a moral nature and a sense of justice; even though their members do not conceive of themselves as free and equal persons they are nonetheless reasonable within the confines of their members' non-liberal self-conception. This is sufficient grounds, Rawls contends, for liberal peoples to (agree to) tolerate well-ordered decent peoples and respect the Law of Peoples in their relations with them.

HUMAN RIGHTS AS THE PRIMARY CONDITION OF SOCIAL COOPERATION

Now to address Rawls's list of human rights. A people's respect for human rights is a condition of their rights to non-interference and political autonomy. The human rights are, again: (1) the rights protecting the life and integrity of the person, including to the means of subsistence; (2) rights to liberty of the person (including freedom of movement, freedom from servitude and forced employment, and the right to hold personal property); (3) rights of formal equality and guaranteed protections of the rule of law (due process, fair trials, right against self-incrimination, and so on); and (4) some degree of liberty of conscience, freedom of thought and expression, and freedom of association, though these rights need not be equal (LP, 65, 78–81). Where does Rawls's list of human rights derive from? Why does it not include democratic rights of political participation, or full and equal rights of free expression, freedom of occupation, and other liberal liberties? Rawls distinguishes human rights from the liberal basic liberties of the first principle of justice which are required by *Political Liberalism*. Human rights are conceived as a special class of rights that specify the minimum standards of decent political institutions. To deny people the right to vote or broad freedom of artistic expression seriously infringes liberal justice; they are not then enabled to fully develop and adequately exercise the moral powers that make social cooperation possible. But these offenses against the equal basic liberties of Rawls's first principle of social justice are not as egregious as denying people the right to life or property, or torturing or enslaving them, letting them starve, or persecuting them for their religion, all of which render people altogether incapable of social cooperation and pursuing their rational good. Rawls says human rights are the rights that are necessary for *any* system of social cooperation, whether liberal or non-liberal (LP, 68). People who are denied human rights are not cooperating in any sense, but (like slaves) are compelled or manipulated and treated as expendable when convenient. Without respect for their human rights, people are not seen as independent agents worthy of respect and moral consideration with a good of their own.

The centrality of social cooperation to Rawls's account of justice is once again manifested in his definition of human rights in terms of the conditions that are necessary to engage in social cooperation of any kind. Human rights are regarded as the *minimal* freedoms, powers, and protections that any person needs for the most basic development and exercise of the moral powers that enable him or her to engage in social cooperation in any society. Liberal rights, by contrast, are the freedoms, powers, and protections that are necessary for the *full* development and adequate exercise of the moral powers in a liberal and democratic society. Liberal rights depend on an ideal of persons and of citizens – as free, self-reflective, and self-governing agents with a good of their own that they have freely accepted. However important and inspiring this liberal ideal of the person, for a person to be denied specifically liberal rights and freedoms is not as egregious as the failure, implied by a denial of human rights, to recognize that one is a person who is due moral respect and consideration for the essential conditions of existence.

The idea of human rights has two primary roles within the Law of Peoples. The first role is to set limits to a government's internal autonomy: No government can claim sovereignty as a defense against its violation of the human rights of those subject to it. When a government consistently violates the human rights of some of its own people – the very persons whose interests government is entrusted to protect – then it forfeits its right to rule and to represent them as a people. A government then is to be regarded as an "outlaw" and no longer has immunity under the Law of Peoples from non-interference by other peoples; moreover, if its violations of human rights are egregious enough, other peoples are entitled to depose and replace an outlaw regime with a government that respects the human rights and common interests of its people.

This suggests the second primary role of the idea of human rights in the Law of Peoples: it restricts the reasons for war and its conduct. War can only be waged against another government in self-defense, or to protect the human rights of other peoples when violated by their own or another government. Wars cannot then be justly waged for the sake of maintaining military superiority or a balance of power, or access to economic resources, or to gain additional territory, which have been the usual reasons for warfare historically. All these involve unjust violations of a people's political autonomy. Also, within war the human rights of enemy non-combatants are to be respected; non-combatants are not to be targeted for attack and measures should be taken to protect them and their property from injury (LP, 95).

Because of the special role Rawls assigns to human rights in enabling social cooperation within the Law of Peoples, he does not include among them all the moral rights of persons as such. Peoples and governments which afford only human rights but not all liberal rights meet a threshold of decency; they are not just from the point of view of liberal conceptions. But for Rawls decency is an important political category in the Law of Peoples since it is sufficient for a people's enjoying rights to non-interference and self-determination that they respect everyone's human rights, pursue a common good and meet the other conditions of decency, and respect the Law of Peoples. The implication is that an international order of independent peoples can be just and even well-ordered without all of its members being just (in the liberal-democratic sense) towards their own people. It is the business of all peoples, as corporate bodies represented by their governments, to insure basic human rights of all peoples and to assist them in meeting basic human needs. But it is not the task of governments or the Society of Peoples to enforce liberal rights of democratic citizens among all peoples. Achieving democratic justice is to be left up to the self-determination of each independent liberal or decent people. This implies that for Rawls the duties of justice that governments and citizens owe to their own people are more extensive than the duties of justice they owe to other peoples. Many find this peculiar, since it appears to rest on nothing more than the arbitrariness of national boundaries. The puzzle for them is, "Why should we have duties to promote the political rights and economic interests of people within our own territory and not owe similar duties to those in worse positions just across the border?"

There are two separate but related questions here. First, what justifies a people having duties of justice to one another that they do not have to other peoples in the world? Second, what justifies a people having exclusive control over a territory and the right to exclude others from it? In response to the second, Rawls argues that a people having political control over a territory serves the important function of ascribing to identifiable peoples responsibility to care for that territory and its resources, and thus mitigates deterioration of the environment and waste of its resources, which is in the interest of all peoples and all their members (LP, 38–39). (This functional argument does not justify now existing boundaries, nor is it intended to. That is a separate issue Rawls does not address.) Moreover, residing in and politically controlling a territory is normally needed for a people and a society to exist. Without control over a territory and its boundaries the political autonomy of a people is not possible and political cooperation becomes extremely difficult. This renders effective productive social cooperation also very difficult if not impossible.

This relates to the first question above, of why we owe special duties to members of our own society not owed to other peoples. The answer is that special duties to members of one's society are a condition of the possibility of social cooperation. Just as families or friendships could not exist and thrive without recognizing and observing special duties and obligations among the members of their association, societies could not exist or flourish in the absence of mutual duties and obligations not owed to other societies and their members. We've seen that, for Rawls, what makes social cooperation such an essential good is that, among other things, it is necessary to realize our human capacities and our practical nature as free and equal moral persons. Special duties to the members of one's society and a people's exclusive control over a territory are both conditions for the existence of democratic government and a democratic society. Without both, the fundamental interests of free and equal persons in their political autonomy, in the realization of their moral powers, and in the free pursuit of their rational conception of their good, all would be undermined. This reiterates my earlier emphasis on social cooperation and the necessity of *social justice* to realizing the essential good of free and equal moral persons.

THE DUTY OF ASSISTANCE

Rawls contends that independent peoples have a duty to assist "burdened societies" in meeting their members' basic needs and in becoming independent members in the Society of well-ordered Peoples (LP, 106–13). Burdened societies exist under unfavorable conditions; they lack the political and cultural institutions, human capital and know-how, and often material and technological resources that are needed to be well-ordered societies. Unlike "outlaw" societies they are non-aggressive but they often are plagued by political corruption. Rawls's recognition of the duty to assist burdened peoples (LP, sect. 15), the 8th principle of the Law of Peoples, renders his Law of Peoples a so-called "weak" cosmopolitan position, which differs from the "strong" positions requiring a principle of global distributive justice.[14] The duty to assist burdened peoples differs from a principle of distributive justice, Rawls says, in that it has a "target" which, once achieved, serves as a "cut-off point" for further assistance. By contrast, a principle of distributive justice normally has no cut-off point but continues to apply to the distribution of income and wealth even once the minimum required by a duty of assistance has been reached. Rawls sees little justification for a global distribution principle (like the difference principle) (LP, 117) under ideal conditions in view of the independence and self-determination of a people who take responsibility for their political culture and for their rate of savings and investment (LP, sect. 16). Citing Japan (LP 108), largely devoid of natural resources, Rawls says once unjust political causes are removed and a people achieves independence, its wealth is largely determined by its political culture and industriousness, not its level of natural resources.

The duty of assistance requires more than providing assistance sufficient to enable burdened people to meet subsistence needs of all their members, and seemingly even more than is required for their effective exercise of all human rights. It requires in addition "provisions for ensuring that . . . people's basic needs be met" (LP, 38), where "basic needs" are regarded as the means that are necessary for people to take part in the life of their society and culture. "By basic needs I mean roughly those that must be met if citizens are to be in a position to take advantage of the rights, liberties, and opportunities of their society. These needs include economic means as well as institutional rights and freedoms" (LP, 38, n. 47). By defining basic needs, not in absolute terms, but in relation to what is needed to function in one's own society, Rawls emphasizes once again the societal bases of his conception of international justice.

The long-term goal of the duty of assistance is to help a burdened society to manage its own affairs both reasonably and rationally, and to achieve its capacity to become an independent member in the Society of well-ordered Peoples (LP, 106, 111). "This defines the target of assistance" (LP, 111). This requires more than just adequate economic wealth. A well-ordered society need not be wealthy by any means. But for a people to be independent members in the Society of Peoples they must have, in addition to adequate economic resources and capacity to utilize them, also the capacity for establishing and maintaining just or decent institutions. "The aim is to realize and preserve just (or decent) institutions, and not simply to increase . . . the average level of wealth, or the wealth of any society or any particular class in society" (LP, 107). Simply lifting people out of destitute conditions while leaving them economically or culturally impoverished is not sufficient. This suggests that the duty of assistance can be rather stringent. It may require a great deal more ongoing developmental assistance from advantaged peoples for education, infrastructure, agriculture, technology, cultural development, etc., until a burdened people is capable of political, economic, and social independence.

This is reinforced when Rawls says, "A second guideline for thinking about how to carry out the duty of assistance is to realize that the political culture of a burdened society is all-important" (LP, 108). (Recall that Rawls conceives of a people largely in terms of their having a shared constitution and political culture.) The crucial point is to "assure the essentials of political autonomy," and "to assist burdened societies . . . to be able to determine the path of their own future for themselves" (LP, 118). The duty of assistance then extends to helping burdened peoples establish a political culture that is capable of realizing and sustaining just or decent political institutions, and pursuing a common good for all members. This involves at a minimum measures that require or encourage burdened peoples to respect human rights, eliminate political corruption and institute the rule of law, relieve population pressures, and establish equal justice for women (see LP, 109–10).

Rawls's duty of assistance is not (as critics contend) a charitable duty. Rather it is a duty of justice that well-ordered peoples owe to burdened peoples existing under unfavorable circumstances. The duty of assistance is as much a duty of justice as is the domestic duty to save for future generations. Rawls discusses "the similarity" between these two duties; "[they] express the same underlying idea" (LP, 106–07). Like the just savings principle, the duty of assistance too should aim "to secure a social world that makes possible a worthwhile life for all" (LP, 107). The duty of assistance also resembles individuals' natural duty of mutual aid (TJ, sect. 19); it extends this duty of individuals to peoples.[15] Given the parallel Rawls draws with the just savings principle, it appears that the duty of assistance to burdened peoples to meet basic needs must be satisfied (like the just savings principle) prior to determination of the distributive shares under the difference principle.[16] The duty of assistance to burdened peoples then should have priority over the difference principle and duties of distributive justice to the members of one's own society. Rawls thus seems to afford a kind of importance to meeting basic human needs worldwide that moderates claims of distributive justice within society. In this regard, and also given the potentially exacting demands that the duty of assistance can place on advantaged peoples, Rawls's "weak" cosmopolitanism would seem to be stronger than his cosmopolitan critics allow.

DISTRIBUTIVE JUSTICE AND RAWLS'S REJECTION OF A GLOBAL DISTRIBUTION PRINCIPLE

Strong cosmopolitan positions hold that distributive justice is global in reach; that is, principles of distributive justice should encompass all people in the world regardless of their society, and not be applied individually to each society. Many have argued the difference principle should serve as a global distribution principle in this manner, and that global resources and economic activity in all societies should be directed towards benefiting the least advantaged people in the world.[17] Rawls rejects the global application of the difference principle; while it applies worldwide to every society in the world, within a society its reach is limited, extending only to the members of that society. One reason for this (I argue below) is that, in the absence of a world state and global legal system, the global application of the difference principle makes little sense. Moreover, to apply the difference principle at the global level is to misunderstand its function in specifying the special cooperative relations of reciprocity that define a democratic people. Critics may respond that, if not the difference principle, then some other global distribution principle should apply to fairly distribute natural resources and the products of industry. Rawls's rejection of any global distribution principle is harder to defend. On its face it seems to rely on considerations of fairness, but also it ultimately relates to his conception of the background conditions needed for a democratic society, democratic autonomy, and the essential good of democratic citizens.

The Problem with a Global Difference Principle

It is often claimed that for the sake of consistency Rawls himself must accept the global application of the difference principle. The reason most often cited is that Rawls's initial argument in favor of the difference principle and against the principle of efficiency (in TJ, sect. 12) requires it; for there he argues that in the distribution of income and wealth people should not benefit from, or be held responsible for, the natural or social advantages or disadvantages they are born with. But if so, cosmopolitans argue, people should not be advantaged or disadvantaged by the accidental fact of their birth in a rich or poor country. The social, rather than global, application of the difference principle works an injustice. The world's income and wealth should be distributed to maximally benefit the least advantaged people in the world, not the least advantaged in each particular society.[18]

Like (strong) cosmopolitanism generally, this objection discounts the centrality of social cooperation to social, political, and economic justice. It is in the context of socially cooperative relations on a basis of reciprocity and mutual respect that Rawls contends that accidental social and natural facts of birth should not by themselves determine distributive shares within a democratic society. It does not follow from this that the contingent fact of membership within a particular (democratic) society is also not relevant to determining distributive shares. In the determination of distributive shares membership is highly relevant. Analogously, the fact that a person is not born as naturally talented or as handsome as his siblings should not be relevant to the care and concern he receives within his family, whereas the contingent fact that another child was not born a member of that particular family is highly relevant to his standing and entitlements within that family (for he has none). As we saw in Chapter 2, the difference principle is designed to apply to the special cooperative relations existing by virtue of the shared political, legal, and economic institutions that constitute the basic structure of a democratic society. It is not designed to apply on a global level, to the more fluid and inchoate collaborative relations among world inhabitants.

What is usually envisioned by proponents of a global difference principle is a *reallocation* of wealth from wealthier to poorer societies, periodically and perhaps in lump sum payments. The problem with this reallocation model is that it is not Rawls's difference principle. We saw in Chapter 3 that the difference principle does not apply simply to allocating existing sums of wealth without regard to how or by whom they are produced and their legitimate expectations (cf. TJ, 64, 86/56, 77 rev.). This is not its proper role. Rather it applies directly to structure basic legal and economic institutions that enable individuals to exercise control over wealth and other economic resources. The crucial point is that the *difference principle* is a *political principle*: it requires legislative, judicial, and executive agency and judgment for its application, interpretation, and enforcement. There is no invisible hand that gives rise to the myriad complexities of the basic social institutions of property, contract law, commercial instruments, and so on. If *political* design of these and other basic economic and legal institutions is essential to applying the difference principle, and if distributions to particular individuals is to be left up to pure procedural justice once this design of the basic economic structure is in place, then there must exist political authority with legal jurisdiction, and political agents to fill these functions and positions. So in addition to complex economic practices and a legal system of property, contracts, commercial instruments, securities, etc., the difference principle requires for its application political authority with the normal powers of governments.

There is no global political authority to apply the difference principle; nor is there a global legal system or global system of property to apply it to. So a global difference principle is doubly infirm, without both agency and object – *no legal person* to implement it, and *no legal system* to which it is applicable. In this regard, one can see why advocates of a global difference principle might regard it as a simple allocation principle. But their global allocation principle is not a political principle that political agents can apply to design basic institutions or a basic structure. Such a principle is not the difference principle but is something quite different.

One way to think of global application of the difference principle which might preserve its political role is for the governments of many different peoples individually to apply the principle to their own basic institutions, with an eye towards advancing the position of the least advantaged group in the world (not in their own societies). The practical problem with this suggestion is that a people only has the power to shape the basic structure of their own society, and not the power to shape other peoples' basic institutions. How can a people effectively structure their own institutions to maximize the life prospects of the world's least advantaged persons when they have no political control over other peoples' policies or the life prospects of the world's least advantaged? There are enormous coordination problems with the world's governments individually applying the difference principle in this way, especially given each society's inability to directly influence the practices and laws of countries where the world's least advantaged reside. To apply the difference principle individually to the world at large is very unlikely to make the world's poorest better off than if governments were to follow some other policy.

A third alternative is to seek to apply the difference principle, not to all peoples' economic institutions worldwide or to the total product of all world economies, but to global institutions alone (lending policies, trade agreements, etc.) and the marginal product that results from economic cooperation among peoples. For example, (for all the talk of globalization) the U.S. currently exports 11 percent of its product and imports 13–14 percent of what it consumes in goods and services (hence our current trade deficit).[19] The difference principle might then be applied to structure trade policies, with appropriate taxes levied on imports and exports to benefit the world's least advantaged. This is not Rawls's difference principle either, for it applies only to a limited number of institutions and does not extend it broadly to structure all economic institutions and property relations. Moreover, it is questionable whether or how much this restricted difference principle will actually improve the situation of the worst-off in the world. It seems to impose an enormous deterrent on global trade and imports and exports of goods and labor if resulting wealth had to be subjected first to a global and then to a domestic difference principle. Whatever the case, this piecemeal difference principle, since it applies to but a marginal portion of the world's wealth, abandons the basic cosmopolitan position that distributive justice should be globally, not domestically, determined.

There are even more formidable dissimilarities between Rawls's domestic difference principle and a global difference principle. To begin with, Rawls's arguments for the difference principle rely upon a robust idea of social cooperation and of reciprocity among the members of a *democratic* society. "Democratic equality" and "property-owning democracy"[20] are the terms he uses for the economic system structured by the difference principle and fair equality of opportunity. Democratic social and political cooperation does not exist at the global level and most likely never will. Even if we agree that there should be some kind of global distribution principle, why should it be the difference principle? Outside the confines of a democratic society Rawls's reciprocity arguments for the difference principle (see Chapter 3) do not travel well when considered from the perspective of a global original position. If the argument from democratic reciprocity cannot be relied on, what then could be the argument for a global difference principle?

Even more to the point, Rawls envisions the difference principle to structure property and other economic institutions so as to encourage (when conjoined with fair equality of opportunities) widespread ownership and control of the means of production, either in a "property-owning democracy" or a liberal socialist economy:

> The intent is not simply to assist those who lose out through accident or misfortune (although that must be done), but rather to put all citizens in a position to manage their own affairs on a footing of a suitable degree of social and political cooperation. . . . The least advantaged are not, if all goes well, the unfortunate and unlucky – objects of our charity and compassion, much less our pity – but those to whom reciprocity is owed as a matter of political justice

among those who are free and equal citizens along with everyone else.

(*JF*, 139)

Like J.S. Mill, Rawls believed that for workers to have as their only real option a wage relationship with capitalist employers undermines individuals' freedom and independence, blunts their characters and imaginations, diminishes mutual respect among income classes, and leads to the eventual loss of self-respect among working people. For this and other reasons Rawls was attracted to such ideas as a "share economy" (where workers have part ownership of private capital), workers' cooperatives, public provision of capital to encourage workers in becoming independent economic agents or to start up their own businesses, and other measures for the widespread distribution of control of means of production.[21]

Since it does not apply to any substantial basic structure to shape property and other economic relations, and is not conjoined with a principle of fair equal opportunities, cosmopolitans' allocation model of the global difference principle can do little to further these aims. This is not to deny that the difference principle, when applied domestically, does have an allocative role (primarily in the form of supplementary income payments for workers who earn too little in the labor market for economic independence) (TJ, 285/252 rev.). But the difference principle (1) is not an instrument for alleviating poverty or misfortune (though it incidentally does that); nor (2) is its purpose to assist those with special needs or handicaps, or (3) compensate the unfortunate for bad luck, natural inequalities, and other accidents of fortune. Any number of principles, domestic and global, can provide a decent social or global minimum and serve the role of (1) poverty alleviation. Rawls's duty of assistance to meet basic needs is already sufficient to serve that role.

As for (2) assisting those with handicaps or special needs, in the domestic case Rawls envisions other principles to be decided at the legislative stage to serve this role. They are based in considerations of assistance and mutual aid similar to those behind the global duty of assistance, (cf., the natural duties of mutual aid and of mutual respect (*TJ*, sects.19, 51)). Here the frequent objection – that Rawls misdefines the least advantaged and does not take into account the needs of the handicapped in his account of distributive justice – misconceives the role of the difference principle in structuring production relations and property systems among free and equal democratic citizens. To oversimplify somewhat, the difference principle focuses initially on the side of production, not consumption. It is because of Rawls's focus on social cooperation in the production of wealth among members of a democratic society that he is able to insist upon reciprocity in its final distribution, as specified by the difference principle. As a principle of reciprocity the difference principle is not suited to deal with problems of meeting people's special needs. We could always spend more upon those who are especially handicapped, and to apply the difference principle to their circumstances would severely limit if not eliminate the share that goes to the economically least advantaged (currently, unskilled workers at the minimum wage) who contribute to production.

Finally, regarding (3), Rawls says, "the difference principle is not of course the principle of redress. It does not require society to try to even out handicaps as if all were expected to compete on a fair basis in the same race" (*TJ*, 101/86 rev.). Rawls suggests that "luck egalitarianism" by itself, taken as a conception of distributive justice, is implausible, for it does not take into account production relations, measures needed to advance the common good, or to improve standards of living on average or for the less advantaged. "It is plausible as most such principles are as a prima facie principle" (ibid.).

The general point then is that Rawls does not regard distributive justice in an alleviatory manner; rather he transforms the issue from a narrow question of allocation of a fixed product of wealth for alleviatory purposes in order to address a larger set of issues. "The main problem of distributive justice is the choice of a social system" (*TJ*, 274/242 rev.). Accordingly, "We reject the idea of allocative justice as incompatible with the fundamental idea by which justice as fairness is organized: the idea of society as a fair system of social cooperation over time. *Citizens are seen as cooperating to* produce the social resources on which their claims are made" (JF, 50). Distributive justice is then made part of the larger question about how to fairly structure economic and property relations among socially cooperative productive agents who regard themselves as free and equal, where each does his or her fair share in creating the social product. Rawls therewith incorporates the question of distributive justice into the tradition of Mill and Marx, wherein the primary focus is on how to fairly structure production and property relations in a way that affirms the freedom, equality, dignity, and self-respect of socially productive agents. "What men want is meaningful work in free association with others, these associations regulating their relations to one another within a framework of just basic institutions" (TJ, 290/257 rev.). The robust conception of democratic reciprocity implicit in the difference principle responds to this general issue. The difference principle is not a proper response to the problem of global poverty or to other alleviatory issues mentioned (meeting handicaps and special needs, redressing misfortune, etc.). These are specific problems to address in non-ideal theory, by reference to moral duties of assistance, mutual aid, and so on, and are to be determined by citizens' democratic deliberations, on the basis of their knowledge of available resources. These alleviatory problems of non-ideal theory raise issues separate and apart from the question of ideal theory of determining appropriate standards for just distributions among socially productive democratic citizens who are cooperative members of a well-ordered society.

Rawls's Rejection of a Global Principle of Distributive Justice

Many of the reasons just discussed for not globalizing the difference principle are also relevant to explaining why Rawls rejects any global distribution principle. Rawls argues that we have duties of humanitarian assistance to burdened peoples, but that distributive justice presupposes social cooperation. Distributive justice for Rawls is mainly about the design of basic social institutions, including the legal system of property, contract, and other legal conditions for economic production, transfers and exchanges, and use and consumption. The basic social institutions and legal norms that make production, exchange, and use and consumption possible are *political products*, one of the primary subjects of political governance. It is not just fiscal policies, taxation, public goods, and welfare policies that are politically determined; more basically it is decisions about the many property rules and economic institutions, including control of the means of production, that make these policies and economic and social cooperation more generally possible. A primary role for a principle of distributive justice is to provide standards for designing, assessing, and publicly justifying the many legal and economic institutions that structure daily life. Since these basic institutions are social and political it follows for Rawls that distributive justice also should be social and political. If so, then in the absence of a world state, there can be no global basic structure on a par with the basic structure of society. Indeed, there is nothing in global relations anywhere near to being comparable to a society's basic structure of political, legal, property, and other economic institutions. This parallels the fundamental significance of society and social cooperation to our nature and conceptions of ourselves as persons. There is global cooperation and there are global institutions,[22] but these are not *basic* institutions. Rather, global political, legal, and economic arrangements are *secondary* institutions and practices: they are largely the product of agreements and treaties among peoples and are supervenient upon the multiplicity of basic social institutions constituting the basic structures of many different societies. Consequently the only feasible global basic structure that can exist is also secondary and supervenient: In the ideal case it is nothing more than "the basic structure of the Society of Peoples," and its governing principles are the Law of Peoples.

Rawls's critics often rely upon the fact of gross inequality and world poverty to argue for a global distribution principle.[23] World poverty is certainly a problem of justice, for it is largely due to the great injustice that currently exists in many people's governments and in world economic relations, including the exploitation of resources of less advantaged peoples. But on Rawls's account it is an injustice that is to be addressed by the duty of assistance, by preventing the unfair exploitation of a people and their resources by other nations and international business, and by requiring corrupt governments to respect human rights and satisfy the basic needs and promote the good of their members. A global distribution principle is not needed to address the problem of severe global poverty, and indeed is an inappropriate remedy.[24] For distributive justice applies among peoples whether or not they are poor. Even if all the peoples of the world had adequate income and wealth to enable their members to pursue their chosen way of life, global principles of distributive justice would still apply. This suggests that there must be some other foundation than poverty for global principles of distributive justice.

Many assertions of a global distribution principle appear to be based in a kind of egalitarianism that Rawls rejects. This is the kind of egalitarianism which says that equality (of resources, or of welfare, or perhaps of capabilities) is good for its own sake. Taken strictly, the idea that equality of resources is good for its own sake implies that, even if people equally endowed voluntarily decide to use their resources in ways that create great inequalities – suppose you save your earnings and I spend mine drinking expensive wines – there are considerations that speak in favor of restoring equal distribution – hence transferring part of your savings to me so I can buy still more expensive wine. Most egalitarians, understandably, do not endorse this position. They claim, not that equal distributions per se are intrinsically good, but rather equal distributions that are not the product of people's free and informed choices (under appropriate conditions). The egalitarian position here is then one that seeks to equalize the products of fortune – "luck egalitarianism" so called. So long as the relevant products of fortune have been equalized or neutralized (e.g., people have been compensated for misfortune), then inequalities in resources, welfare, capabilities – whatever the relevant good – are warranted, assuming they are based in people's free and informed choices.

Luck egalitarianism drives many (though not all) cosmopolitan calls for a global distribution principle. We saw in Chapter 3 that

Rawls rejects luck egalitarianism. Justice does not require that we equalize or neutralize the products of brute fortune (whether the products of social or natural endowments or just brute bad luck). Instead, social justice requires that society use these inevitable inequalities of fortune to benefit everyone, starting with maximally benefiting the least advantaged members of society.

It has been objected that nothing in Rawls's Law of Peoples prevents the current practice by "affluent and powerful societies" of imposing "a skewed global economic order that hampers the economic growth of poor societies and further weakens their bargaining power."[25] This is mistaken. Trade practices and other economic relations among existing societies are to be tested against the principles that would be agreed to in the original position among the representatives of members of a Society of well-ordered Peoples. Since representatives behind a veil of ignorance do not know the relative wealth, resources, power, and other facts about their societies, these principles will not be biased against less wealthy and less powerful peoples, as the objection assumes. Moreover, Rawls clearly recognizes the injustice of existing international economic relations. While he does not directly say so, presumably he would recognize that transition principles should apply to rectify current and past injustices, as in the case of existing social injustices, in order to bring about a well-ordered Society of Peoples. For example, just as Rawls, in order to remedy generations of pernicious racial discrimination, might support as a provisional measure preferential treatment of minorities, though strictly speaking it would infringe fair equality of opportunity as practiced in a well-ordered society, so too he could have supported as a temporary measure a global distribution principle to rectify the history of exploitation, expropriation, and gross violation of human rights endured by burdened peoples around the world.

But, importantly, such a global principle would be remedial, not permanent. For, as Rawls contends, the problem with a permanent global distribution principle is that in a well-ordered Society of Peoples there would be no cut-off point for transfers from more advantaged to less advantaged nations, even when the less advantaged are well-to-do. Since a global distribution principle continuously applies to all wealth without a cut-off point, it would be unfair, Rawls maintains, to politically independent peoples. He gives two examples, both of which assume the ideal case of well-ordered societies whose reasonable members all accept its common-good conception of justice. The first example is two societies, A and B, that begin with the same wealth. Society A saves and invests its resources in industrialization and over time becomes wealthier, while Society B prefers to remain "a more pastoral and leisurely society" of modest means. It would be "unacceptable," Rawls says, to tax the incremental wealth of the richer society and redistribute it to the poorer nation. For Society B and its members freely eschewed the benefits of industrialization in order to gain those of a pastoral society. The second example is parallel but assumes a rather high rate of population growth. Society A undertakes population control measures to restrain the high rate of growth and achieves zero growth, while Society B, for religious and cultural reasons "freely held by its women," does not. (Rawls's example here presupposes "the elements of equal justice for women as required by a well-ordered society," LP, 118.) Over time the per capita income of Society A practicing population control is higher. Again, it "seems unacceptable" to tax the wealth of the richer nation A and redistribute it to the poorer nation B whose members freely chose to maintain its population at higher levels for religious reasons (LP, 117–18).

Underlying each of these examples is the assumption that each reasonable person in Society B freely endorses the economic and population policies leading to a lesser standard of living. To contend that, nonetheless, there still should be a redistribution of wealth from Society A to B goes far beyond luck egalitarianism to a position that says that people are not to be held responsible for the consequences of their choices. This seems to be a difficult if not untenable position.

Finally, Rawls claims that cosmopolitans' argument for a global distribution principle is grounded in concern for "the well-being of individuals and not the justice of societies." Rawls's rejection of welfarism is integral to his rejection of a global distribution principle. In the domestic case, the end of social justice is not individual welfare, but the freedom and equality of citizens. Similarly, in the international case, the end of the Law of Peoples is not the total welfare of a people or of all peoples. It is not even the welfare of least advantaged individuals. The ultimate end or "target" of the Law of Peoples is rather *political autonomy* – or "the freedom and equality of a people as members of the Society of well-ordered Peoples." Essential to this is that a society should meet the basic needs of all members so that they can participate in the social and political life of their culture. This, recall, is the basis for the duty of assistance. Here again, however, cosmopolitans may object that, if not welfare, then at least the freedom and equality of *individuals*, and not of peoples, should be the aim of an account of international justice. But Rawls focuses on peoples rather than individuals in the international case because of the priority he assigns to social cooperation, the basic structure of society, and the central role that political cooperation, political culture, and political autonomy all play in his account of social justice.[26] And this focus is precisely because of his concern for the freedom and equality of individuals, which is in the background throughout *The Law of Peoples*. (Recall again that its purpose is to "work out the ideals and principles of *foreign policy* of a just *liberal* people" (LP, 10).) For a condition of the freedom and equality of individuals, as Rawls conceives these basic democratic values, is *politically autonomous citizenship* within the basic structure of a democratic society that itself exercises political autonomy ("able to make their own decisions," and "able to determine the path of their own future for themselves") (LP, 118). In the end, Rawls's rejection of a global distribution principle rests not simply upon the assumption that political autonomy of a people is a good, or that a people should be economically self-sufficient (relatively speaking) and not subject to manipulation by external forces beyond their control, or that they can control their level of wealth by savings, investment, population control, and other measures. It also rests upon his ideal conception of the freedom and equality of democratic citizens, and the social and political conditions that must hold if that ideal of the person is to be realized. Rawls's thinking seems to be that a global distribution principle would (in fact, if not in theory) jeopardize these fundamental bases for social and political justice among free and equal, reasonable and rational persons.

CONCLUSION

Many cosmopolitans are rightly bothered that global capitalism has created ways to elude political control by the world's governments. Multinational corporations are in a position to require foreign governments to extract onerous demands on their citizens (for example, requiring them to pay for their own tools and production facilities) as a condition of creating employment in a foreign nation. There is a problem of justice here – the corporate exploitation of disadvantaged peoples – and part of the problem may be that there is no global basic structure to deal with it. If these kinds of problems cannot be taken care of by individual governments regulating their corporations' foreign dealings, and by treaties and international trade organizations (and it is not clear why they cannot), then perhaps some additions need to be made to Rawls's Law of Peoples to deal with this and other problems. Rawls clearly makes room for this. It is implicit in the duty to enable burdened peoples to become politically autonomous and independent peoples. He also says that the eight principles of the Law of Peoples are not a complete list, and some additions need to be made (LP, 37). But cosmopolitans seek the wrong solution to this and other problems of economic exploitation of less advantaged peoples. It is not a problem that can be addressed, much less resolved, by a global distribution principle that simply reallocates wealth from richer nations to poorer people in developing and underdeveloped nations. What are needed are measures enabling these peoples to become politically autonomous and economically independent, putting them in control of their own fate.

Finally, though Rawls doubted the feasibility of a world state, he did not deny that global economic cooperation could evolve its own institutions (such as the World Trade Organization), and that these might eventually multiply into an intricate and complex network of relatively independent institutions, with widespread effects upon peoples' future prospects. I do not think anything he says rules out the appropriateness of standards of justice in addition to the Law of Peoples that apply to these institutions, were they to become extensive and pervasive enough. It might even be a partial distribution principle like that discussed above, which reallocates a portion of the proceeds from international trade, or a principle that recognizes a kind of "global minimum" analogous to the liberal social minimum.[27] In the absence of an outline of what this global institutional framework would be like and the degree of cooperation it envisions, it is fruitless to conjecture what principles might be appropriate to it. The point is that Rawls does not have to rule out the possibility of some sort of global distribution principle that supplements the domestic difference principle in the event of the eventual evolution of a complex global web of economic institutions. It is not a situation Rawls addressed, but would conform to his view of the institutional bases of distributive justice.[28]

FURTHER READINGS

Beitz, Charles, "Rawls's Law of Peoples," *Ethics*, 110, July 2000, 669–96. (Critical review of The Law of Peoples by one of the main cosmopolitan critics of Rawls.)

Nagel, Thomas, "The Problem of Global Justice," *Philosophy and Public Affairs*, 33: 2, 2005, 113–47. (Argues, like Rawls, for the priority of social justice over claims of global justice.)

Pogge, Thomas, "An Egalitarian Law of Peoples," *Philosophy and Public Affairs*, 23: 3, Summer 1994. (Argues that representatives of peoples in Rawls's original position would choose a global resource tax to benefit poorer peoples.)

Eleven

Conclusion

RAWLS'S LEGACY AND INFLUENCE

Unlike other philosophers in this series, Rawls's legacy and influence have been short-lived for he died fairly recently, in late 2002, and his main works were all written in the past 40 years. His legacy is still a work in progress. Clearly he was one of the most significant, if not the most significant, moral and political philosophers of the twentieth century, and will be recognized as such for centuries to come. Of course, the twentieth century was not a century marked by great moral and political philosophers, and in this way is unlike the seventeenth (Hobbes, Leibniz, and Locke), eighteenth (Hume, Smith, Rousseau, and Kant), and the nineteenth centuries (Hegel, Bentham, Mill, Marx, Sidgwick, Nietzsche). But Rawls is a formidable philosopher by anyone's account,[1] and must be reckoned with by anyone who addresses philosophical issues of justice in the indefinite future.

As for Rawls's influence on contemporary thinking, outside academia, it is nil, but this is to be expected given the nature of his work and the present political atmosphere. Political events since the publication of *Theory* have flowed in a current that runs opposite to the direction pointed to by that book. In the political arena, the legacy of Adam Smith and the classical utilitarian economists, and to a degree Robert Nozick and libertarianism, are once again ascendant. The Republican Party in the U.S. is guided by nineteenth-century classical liberalism, and is in league with a conservative religious populism fed by a politicized evangelism reacting against the increasing secularism and liberalization in the wider culture.

But whatever the times, Rawls's or any other philosophers' lack of influence on contemporary events is normal. Judging from the list in the preceding paragraph, it appears that the work of philosophers in one century does not filter into people's moral and political consciousness (if it does at all) until at least a century later. (Witness Locke's indirect influence on the revolutions of the eighteenth century, Adam Smith's and Rousseau's indirect influence on (respectively) the classical liberalism and democratic upheavals and social reforms of the nineteenth century, and Marx's direct influence on twentieth-century communism.) It is fruitless to conjecture whether Rawls will have a similar political legacy at the end of the present century.

Rawls's influence in contemporary academic thinking about the issues he addresses is, of course, another matter. His work is still very much a preponderant influence in current debates on social, political, and international justice, and a major influence in moral philosophy as well. This is particularly true of current discussions of global justice. His position is regarded as the main contemporary defense of the traditional liberal position regarding relations among nations. It is easy to see why, since of his eight principles of the Law of Peoples, the only one that is not generally endorsed is the duty of assistance towards burdened peoples, and even that duty would receive lip-service from the representatives of many contemporary peoples. It is because his principles for the Law of Peoples are not very original that many find his last book to be a disappointment. But as Rawls frequently said, in liberally paraphrasing Hume's criticism of Locke's social contract doctrine, "There is little that is new in philosophy, and that which is new is almost always wrong." (Or as Hume put it: "New discoveries in these matters are not to be expected.")

What is genuinely new in Rawls's *The Law of Peoples*, and in his work as a whole, is not so much the principles of social and international justice he puts forth (the difference principle being a major exception here). It is that he frames traditional principles and positions within a new setting, helping us to better understand these positions and what they are about, appreciate how powerful they are, and how they conjoin with other moral and political positions we endorse or feel drawn to (or for some, perhaps not). It is not so much the role of moral and political philosophy to tell us how to live our lives or arrange social and political institutions (just as it is not the role of epistemology and philosophy of science to tell scientists how to do science or what counts as scientific knowledge). Rather its role is to provide new ways to understand longstanding moral and political traditions and principles, and new ways to argue for (or against) and justify these positions in terms that are amenable to contemporary moral and political consciousness. This is Rawls's major contribution, and it will be his major legacy. From the beginning, inquiry into the nature of practical reasoning and the possibility of moral justification were among the guiding themes of his moral and political philosophy. He sought to preserve an idea of moral justification within philosophy, and defend an idea of the objectivity of moral judgments once the traditional dualisms that had sustained moral philosophy for many centuries (analytic/synthetic, necessary vs. contingent truth, *a priori* vs. *a posteriori* knowledge, etc.) had come under attack by twentieth-century philosophers. His accounts of contractarianism, reflective equilibrium of considered moral convictions, public reason and public justification, moral and political constructivism, political liberalism, and reasonableness vs. rationality, were all an integral part of his sustained effort to provide an account of moral justification and objectivity in the face of contemporary naturalism, scientism, and skepticism about the validity of practical and moral reasoning and the soundness of their conclusions.

But more than this, Rawls provides the major explication and justification of the liberal tradition of democratic thought. Politically, he saw himself as arguing within the high liberal tradition that stems from Kant and John Stuart Mill, which is decidedly democratic in a way that the classical liberal tradition of Adam Smith, Jeremy Bentham, and the classical economists is not. Unlike Mill, he did not think that substantially revising utilitarianism could provide adequate defense for the basic principles of a constitutional democracy. This is where he turns to Kant for inspiration. One of Rawls's main legacies will be his revival and development of Kantian moral and political philosophy. His lectures on Kant's moral philosophy are among the most insightful ever written, and he inspired a new generation of Kant scholars. He explicitly aimed, in the Kantian interpretation and Kantian Constructivism, to provide philosophical content to Kant's ideas of moral autonomy and of reason giving principles to itself. He relied upon constructivism to provide structure to the idea of reflective equilibrium. And he showed how a conception of the person as a free and equal moral agent can be made integral to moral and political philosophy and the derivation of moral principles, by incorporating this conception of the person into the justification of liberal and democratic principles of justice.

CONCLUDING REMARKS

A recurring theme in Rawls's work from *A Theory of Justice* onward is the possibility of a "perfectly just" well-ordered society. A well-ordered society is central to Rawls's contractarianism, even more so than the original position. For a well-ordered society is one in which reasonable and rational free and equal citizens all agree on a conception of justice, and each has an effective sense of justice that provides adequate motivation to regularly comply with justice's requirements and regulate one's pursuits accordingly. Unanimity of agreement on justice by free and equal persons with a commitment to justice is the core ideal of the liberal and democratic social contract tradition that stems from Locke, Rousseau, and Kant. By seeking to show how a well-ordered society is realistically possible, and, in the course of doing so, revising and refining his theory and positing a plethora of ideas that are necessary for that purpose, Rawls maintains his contractarianism to the very end. The ideas of public reason, overlapping consensus, a freestanding political conception, public justification, and so on – all these ideas that are part of political liberalism are as much a part of Rawls's contractarianism as is the original position.

Rawls's account of a well-ordered society changed over the years, due more to the force and requirements of his own ideas than others' criticisms. By the end of his career, he had come to see that even among fully reasonable and rational free and equal persons, general agreement on justice as fairness was not realistically possible. One of the main reasons is the difficulty of convincing reasonable persons that the difference principle is clearly the most reasonable conception of distributive justice. There are other, if not equally reasonable then reasonable enough, accounts of how to set the social minimum in a democratic society that reasonable persons might adopt. This likelihood did not diminish Rawls's confidence that the difference principle is the most reasonable, but it did diminish his confidence in the realistic possibility of a well-ordered society of justice as fairness. Far more likely, he came to believe, is a society in which free and equal persons all agree on the basic outlines of a politically liberal conception of justice that guarantees the first principle of justice and its priority and an adequate social minimum decided in several different ways (in addition to the difference principle).

Finally, why was it so important to Rawls that he show the realistic possibility of a just and well-ordered society? I think there are two reasons. First there is his attachment to an ideal of a democratic society that started perhaps with Rousseau, and which was developed by Kant, and which then was influenced by the German Idealists, including Marx. It is the ideal of a society in which reasonable and rational persons know and fully endorse the bases for their social and political relations and are not under any illusions about them (CP, 326). Moreover, the principles and ideas, and the laws they inform, that structure and regulate their relations are not imposed by natural or circumstantial forces beyond citizens' control, but can be represented as a product of the free use of their reason when exercised in ways that best express their nature as free and equal and reasonable and rational persons. This is the ideal of moral and political autonomy Rawls had to give up in *Political Liberalism*, since he realized such a society is not feasible given the burdens of judgment and the fact of reasonable pluralism. The ideal of a democratic society then gets redefined in terms of the political autonomy of free and equal citizens who agree for a number of different reasons to a liberal conception of justice in an overlapping consensus, each on the basis of their comprehensive views.

This suggests a second reason Rawls continued to focus on the possibility of a well-ordered society. The concluding paragraph of Rawls's final written work, The Law of Peoples, indicates the continued importance of the idea of a well-ordered society, both domestically and among the world's many societies and peoples:

> If a reasonably just Society of Peoples [and well-ordered society] whose members subordinate their power to reasonable aims is not possible, and human beings are largely amoral, if not incurably cynical and self-centered, one might ask, with Kant, whether it is worthwhile for human beings to live on the earth.
>
> (*LP*, 128)

Even if a society of morally autonomous persons is not possible, still it is important to show that justice is consistent with human nature, and that a reasonably just, if not "perfectly just," society is within human reach. This is perhaps the main philosophical legacy of Rawls's lifework.

Aristotelian Principle (TJ, sect. 65) a "psychological law" or tendency that, other things being equal, people enjoy the exercise of their developed faculties, and their enjoyment increases the more developed their faculties and the more complex the activities engaged in. Rawls contends that the principle accounts for many of our considered judgments of value, and that choice of a rational life plan must take this principle into account. Therewith he incorporates perfectionist elements into his account of a person's good. It plays a significant role in Rawls's argument for the congruence of the right and the good.

autonomy (TJ, sect. 78) idea used initially in the Kantian interpretation in *Theory*; it implies acting from moral principles that reason gives to itself via the original position, when these principles are regarded as constructed from and expressing the moral powers of agency that constitute our nature as free and equal rational moral beings. In *Political Liberalism* Rawls uses the term "full autonomy" to signify acting reasonably and rationally from political principles of justice citizens would give to themselves when fairly represented as free and equal persons (PL, 77). Then citizens' judgments and actions (regarding laws, public policies, etc.) are determined by (or at least are compatible with) public reasons, consistent with their status and interests as free and equal citizens. See **political autonomy**.

background justice (PL, VII, sect. 4) the justice of laws and social and political institutions that provide background conditions and constraints upon people's decisions and actions.

Rawls contends that in the absence of background justice, a series of fair transactions among people can nonetheless result in unfairness or injustice (e.g., in the formation of monopolies, or gross inequalities in the distribution of income and wealth). The purpose of applying the principles of justice first to the basic structure is to maintain the background justice of basic institutions. See **basic structure of society**

basic liberties (PL, VIII)   the equal freedoms protected by the first principle of justice: liberty of conscience and freedom of thought; freedom of association; the political liberties; the rights and liberties constituting freedom of the person (including a right to hold personal property); and the rights and liberties of the rule of law. Rawls justifies this list by arguing that these liberties are especially needed to exercise and develop the moral powers and pursue a wide range of reasonable conceptions of the good. For this reason individuals' rights to own and control the means of production are not basic liberties but are made conditional on the second principle of justice, and libertarian rights to unlimited accumulation and unconstrained use of property and absolute freedom of economic contract are not protected liberties at all.

basic structure of society (TJ, sect. 2)   the design of the basic social and political institutions that structure daily life and individuals' decisions and actions, and which distribute fundamental rights and duties and determine the division of advantages of social cooperation. Rawls says that, because it has such a profound influence upon who we are and our life prospects, and is necessary for bachground justice, the basic structure of society is the "first subject" of justice: principles of justice apply directly to structure its basic institutions. The social institutions that make up the basic structure are the political constitution; the legal system of trials, property, and contracts; the system of markets and the regulation of economic relations; and the family. See **background justice**

burdened societies (LP, sect. 15)   societies that are incapable of economic independence and self-sufficiency, and hence unable to meet their members' basic needs and maintain conditions of decency. Peoples have a duty of assistance to burdened societies, with the goal of enabling them to establish the political culture sufficient to meet their members' basic needs and become well-ordered members of the Society of Peoples.

burdens of judgment (PL, II, sect. 2)   the main cause of reasonable pluralism. These are the facts other than conflicts of interest that lead even reasonable and rational persons to have different judgments regarding philosophical, moral, and religious issues. They include (among other things) complexity of evidence; assigning different weights to considerations agreed to be relevant; vagueness of concepts and differing interpretations of them; different ways of assessing evidence due to different experiences; complexity of normative considerations of differing forces on both sides of issues; pluralism of values and the fact that many hard decisions may seem to have no answer.

circumstances of justice (TJ, sect. 22)   the normal conditions under which human cooperation is both possible and necessary. The idea derives from Hume. Society involves cooperation and common interests but is also marked by a conflict of interests due to two general facts. First, its members have different aims and attachments, and often different religious and philosophical views, that constitute their conceptions of the good (the subjective circumstances of justice). Second, individuals of roughly similar powers live on the same territory, and there is moderate scarcity of natural and other resources; while resources are adequate for everyone's basic needs, they are not sufficient to satisfy everyone's wants (the objective circumstances of justice). Principles of justice are needed for dividing the benefits and burdens of social cooperation.

common good conception of justice   In *The Law of Peoples*, a feature of decent hierarchical societies is that they are governed by this, and therewith seek to promote a conception of the good of all members of society. Since these societies are non-liberal, their conceptions of justice do not incorporate freedom and equality into the common good.

comprehensive liberalism   liberalism as a moral (vs. political) doctrine that includes a conception of justice, and which affirms autonomy (or individuality) as an intrinsic human good that is to be promoted by institutions of justice. It cannot serve as a political conception reasonably acceptable to free and equal citizens. Illustrated by the liberalisms of Kant, Mill, Rawls in TJ, Dworkin, Raz, and others.

congruence of the right and the good Rawls's argument in TJ for stability of justice as fairness. It aims to show that it is rational for persons to exercise their sense of justice for its own sake and make justice supremely regulative of their rational plans of life in a well-ordered society of justice as fairness. Hence, under those circumstances doing what justice requires is part of each person's good. The two main arguments for congruence are from the idea of social union (TJ, sect. 79) and the Kantian interpretation (TJ, sects. 40, 86).

constitutional essentials and matters of basic justice (PL, VI, sect. 5) defines the kinds of political issues which are to be decided according to the political values of public reason. Constitutional essentials include questions of basic rights and liberties as well as constitutional powers and procedures of government. Basic justice includes matters relating to equality of opportunity, the social minimum, and other all-purpose means for effectively exercising basic liberties and fair opportunities.

constitutive autonomy the Kantian thesis that moral principles are constituted out of practical reason itself, and do not have their origins independent of it. Kant's and Kantian Constructivism affirm the constitutive autonomy of practical reason. Contrast **political constructivism** and **doctrinal autonomy** (see below).

constructivism in ethics (CP, ch. 17; PL, III) a meta-ethical position regarding the correctness or truth of moral and other ethical judgments. Moral and other ethical judgments are correct or true when they conform to principles that are "constructed" from an objective procedure of deliberation that itself incorporates all the relevant requirements of practical reason. Objectivity of judgment ultimately provides the criterion for moral truth. Contrast moral realism, which says that true moral principles exist prior to and independent of practical reasoning, and that objective judgments are those that represent relevant moral facts. For constructivism, there are no moral facts independent of correct reasoning.

counting principles of rational choice (TJ, sect. 61) integral to Rawls's account of rationality and a rational plan of life. The counting principles are the principle of taking effective means to ends, taking the more likely course of action, and a principle of inclusiveness, to act so as to realize a larger number of our ends.

decent consultation hierarchy (LP, sect. 9) the lawmaking and governing body of a decent hierarchical society. It must consult with representatives of all groups in a society whose every member belongs to a represented group; and any significant political decision is to be publicly justified according to a decent people's common-good conception of justice. Rawls borrows the idea from the non-democratic governing body depicted in part III of Hegel's *Philosophy of Right*.

decent hierarchical people (or society) (LP, sect. 8) In *The Law of Peoples*, a people or society that does not have aggressive aims and respects other peoples and the Law of Peoples, and which (1) is governed according to a common-good conception of justice; (2) respects human rights of all persons; and (3) is governed by a decent consultation hierarchy with representatives from all groups in society. Rawls contends that liberal peoples should tolerate and cooperate with decent hierarchical peoples, even though they are not liberal or democratic.

deliberative rationality (TJ, sect. 64) Part of Rawls's criterion of a person's good. A person's good is objectively defined as the rational plan of life he or she *would* choose under hypothetical conditions of deliberative rationality, which are marked by critical reflection upon all relevant facts, with correct and full information, and imaginative appreciation of the consequences of living alternative plans of life.

difference principle the first part of Rawls's second principle of justice, which regulates *differences* (inequalities) in primary social goods. It requires that social and economic institutions be arranged so as to distribute income and wealth, and powers and positions of office so as to maximize the share that goes to the least advantaged members of society (defined as the lowest paid, least skilled workers). The implication is that members of the least advantaged class are made better off in a society conforming to the difference principle than members of the least advantaged class would be in any other feasible economic system for that society. Rawls appeals to reciprocity among free and equal citizens to argue for the difference principle. He contends that the principle justifies either a property-owning democracy or liberal socialism, but not the capitalist welfare state.

doctrinal autonomy (PL, III, sect. 1)   A political conception of justice is doctrinally autonomous when it can be represented as constructed on the basis of democratic values and ideas and political values of public reason. It can then be regarded as independent from comprehensive moral, philosophical, and religious doctrines. Doctrinal autonomy is nonetheless compatible with a conception of justice having its real foundations (if any) in one or more comprehensive doctrines. Contrast **constitutive autonomy**; see **political constructivism**.

domain of the political   a basic idea of political liberalism; it is the relationship of persons within the basic structure of society and always involves coercive power, which in a constitutional democracy is always a public power, the power of free and equal citizens as a collective body. The political domain is distinct from the associational, which is voluntary, and from the personal and the familial, which are affectional in ways the political is not. A political conception of justice is drawn up for and is limited in its application to the political domain.

duty of assistance (PL, sect. 15)   a duty of justice owed to burdened societies who lack the political culture to be well-ordered and politically autonomous. Other peoples have a duty to provide resources that enable burdened societies to meet their members' basic needs and become well-ordered. It is not a duty of distributive justice, since it has a cut-off point once its target of political autonomy is achieved.

duty of civility   a moral (not a legal) duty of citizens and political officials to be able to justify to other citizens laws and policies they advocate in terms of the political values of public reason

(PL, 217). Rawls says the duty only applies when constitutional essentials and matters of basic justice are at stake.

efficiency, principle of (*Pareto*) (*TJ*, sect. 12) a principle of distributive justice Rawls contrasts with the difference principle. He associates it with classical liberalism and "liberal equality"; it is one interpretation of the contractarian requirement that institutions are to be to everyone's advantage. An efficient distribution is one in which it is not possible to find further profitable exchanges; hence no one can be made better off without making someone worse off. An arrangement of rights and duties in the basic structure is efficient when it is impossible to change the rules to raise the expectations of any representative person without lowering the expectations of someone else. Free market distributions of income and wealth are thought to approximate this principle better than any other economic system. Rawls argues that the demands of efficiency must be subordinate to the requirements of the second principle of justice.

equal political participation, principle of (*TJ*, sects. 36–37) a requirement of the first principle of justice, that citizens have equal political liberties, including rights to vote and hold office, form and join political parties, politically express their views, and fair opportunities to take part in public life. The principle also requires that the *fair value* of the political liberties be maintained by governments' taking measures to equalize individuals' political standing and influence, and by not allowing concentrations of wealth and power to distort the democratic process.

equality, basis of (*TJ*, sect. 77) the grounds for treating persons as equals, and giving them due moral consideration, equal justice, and mutual respect. Rawls contends that the basis for equality is having the powers of moral personality – a capacity for a sense of justice, and for a rational conception of the good. The moral powers are sufficient – Rawls does not say necessary – for equal justice.

fair equality of opportunity (*TJ*, sects. 12, 14) the second part of the second principle of justice. It requires that any inequalities

in primary social goods permitted under the difference
principle should be open to all under conditions of fair equality
of opportunity. Rawls sees it as crucial to distributive justice
and the difference principle that persons with similar natural
talents and similar motivations have the fair opportunity to
compete for powers, positions of office, and other social benefits. It mainly requires (in addition to formal equality of
opportunity or non-discrimination on grounds of race, gender,
religion, etc.) equal educational opportunities, a right to basic
health care for all citizens, and governments' limitations of
concentrations of wealth when they tend to undermine fair
equal opportunities.

fair value of political liberties (PL, VIII, sect. 12)   a requirement
of the first principle of justice, that the value of equal political
rights of participation be fairly secured for all citizens by
measures that neutralize the effects of wealth and social position and influence on the political process; including publicly
financed political campaigns, prohibitions on private contributions to candidates, etc. A condition of political equality.

fairness, principle of (TJ, sect. 18, 52)   a principle of conduct for
individuals agreed to in the original position. It provides the basis
for individuals' obligations to keep their promises and commitments, and in general to do their fair share in maintaining just
social institutions. Rawls appealed to a similar idea earlier, called
"the duty of fair play," to argue for political obligations to obey
the law and bear allegiance to a political constitution one benefits
from. It comes to occupy a position of lesser importance in later
works, starting with TJ where Rawls grounds most political
obligations directly in the natural duty of justice.

family, institution of (LP, 156–64, JF, sect. 50)   a basic social
institution that is part of the basic structure of society. Some
form of the family is needed to maintain social cooperation so
that children are nurtured and educated and society may
perpetuate itself from one generation to the next. The principles of justice apply to the family but not within it; they constrain
permissible forms of family life, but they are not principles of
local justice parents must observe in raising children.

first principle of justice (TJ, ch. 4, PL, VIII)   the principle of equal basic liberties: each person has an equal right to a fully adequate scheme of equal basic liberties which is compatible with a similar scheme of liberties for all. See **basic liberties**.

formal equality of opportunity (TJ, sect. 12)   the requirement that there should be an absence of legal impediments to persons entering into any career or occupying any educational position or office, without regard to their race, gender, religion, or other irrelevant disqualifying characteristics. Called "Careers open to Talents" by Adam Smith and the classical liberals. Contrasts with fair equality of opportunity, which requires more.

four-stage sequence (TJ, sect. 31)   the hypothetical deliberation procedures for deriving and applying the principles of justice to institutions and particular cases. The four stages of reasoning are: the original position, the constitutional stage, the legislative stage, and the judicial or "last" stage. At each stage after the original position, the veil of ignorance is gradually relaxed, and the principles or rules agreed to in the previous stage(s) are to constrain what is rational to choose.

free and equal (moral) persons   the ideal of persons that underlies justice as fairness and political liberalism. Rawls contends in Political Liberalism that citizens in a democratic society conceive of themselves as free and equal persons. He sets out to construct a conception of justice that best fits with this democratic self-conception and our considered convictions of justice. See **moral person**.

good, full theory   the account of a person's good Rawls constructs (TJ, part III) after deriving the principles of justice; unlike the thin theory, it incorporates the idea of the final ends that are worth pursuing for their own sake. The arguments for congruence (sect. 86) and social union (sect. 79) are part of the full theory: they show how justice and community (as defined by justice as fairness) can be intrinsic goods for each person in a well-ordered society. The full theory also includes an account of the moral virtues and of moral worth that comprise the concept of a good person (TJ, sect. 66).

good, thin theory   the account of goodness as rationality that is presupposed in the original position and the argument for the stability of justice as fairness. A person's good is formally (thinly) defined as the rational plan of life he or she would choose under conditions of deliberative rationality, after taking into account the Aristotelian Principle and (Rawls adds subsequent to *TJ*) the moral powers. The account of primary social goods is based upon the thin theory. It is called "thin" since, though complicated, it does not set forth any specific ends as rational to pursue for their own sake.

human rights (LP, sect. 10)   rights owed to humans as such, and which impose duties upon all peoples, their governments, and all individuals. They include a right to life (including security and means of subsistence); to liberty (freedom from forced servitude and liberty of conscience); to hold personal property; and to formal equality (LP, 65). One role of the idea of human rights within the Law of Peoples is that they restrict the justifying reasons for war and its conduct (wars can only be waged to protect human rights), and they specify the limits to a government's internal autonomy (no government can violate human rights and claim authority to rule).

ideal theory (**vs. non-ideal**)   Rawls's assumption of the ideal conditions of a perfectly just, or "well-ordered," society, in which everyone accepts and complies with principles of justice. The problem of *Theory* is to discover the principles of justice most suitable for these ideal conditions of "strict compliance" with principles of justice. Once principles for ideal circumstances are derived, questions of partial compliance in *non-ideal theory* can be addressed. These include a theory of punishment, the doctrine of just war, civil disobedience, revolution, preferential treatment, assistance to burdened societies and many other questions about how to deal with and remedy injustice or departures from the ideal.

the independence of moral theory (CP, ch. 15)   Rawls's thesis that moral theory is not derivative from but is independent of other areas of philosophy, including metaphysics, epistemology, and philosophy of language. The idea resembles Kant's thesis of the "priority of practical reason."

institutions (TJ, sect. 10)   Rawls's term for systems of rules that constitute social and political practices, including "games and rituals, trials and parliaments, markets and systems of property" (TJ, 55/48 rev.). Principles of justice apply to basic social institutions. See **basic structure**.

intuitionism (TJ, sect. 7)   a large class of moral theories that consist, first, of a plurality of first principles which may conflict and give contrary directives; and second, that include no priority rules for principles or other explicit method for weighing principles when they conflict. Then a balance is to be struck by intuition, by doing what seems most nearly right.

just savings principle (TJ, sect. 44)   a qualification of the difference principle, requiring that society's resources not be depleted, and that just savings of real capital accumulation be set aside by each generation. Each generation has a duty to save for its successors the same proportion of capital that it can reasonably expect previous generations to have saved.

just war doctrine (LP, sects. 13–14)   six principles that are part of non-ideal theory in the Law of Peoples. A just war is waged in self-defense, or in defense of other peoples, against aggression by outlaw states. Its aim is a just and lasting peace among well-ordered peoples. In the conduct of war, human rights of civilians and soldiers are to be respected, enemy non-combatants are not to be targeted, and precautions are to be taken to protect them from harm. For this reason Rawls condemns the targeted bombing of Japanese and German civilian populations in World War II as grave wrongs.

justice as fairness   the name Rawls gives to his conception of justice, including the two principles of justice, the natural duties, principle of fairness, and just savings principle, and the justification for them from the original position. The name derives from the idea that fair principles of justice should result from a fair initial choice situation that incorporates all the relevant moral and practical reasons – the fairness of the initial situation is presumed to transfer to the principles chosen therein.

Kantian Constructivism (CP, ch. 17)   the development of the Kantian interpretation, it aims to show how principles of justice can be "constructed" on the basis of a conception of moral persons as free and equal and reasonable and rational, and a "procedure of construction" that represents these and other fundamental features of moral persons and a well-ordered society. Kantian Constructivism is Rawls's attempt to give content to Kant's idea of moral autonomy as reason giving principles to itself out of its own resources. A transition stage in the development of political liberalism and political constructivism.

Kantian interpretation of justice as fairness (TJ, sect. 40) an interpretation of justice as fairness that relies upon the Kantian conception of moral personality, and which interprets the principles of justice as an expression of the moral powers of agency and practical reasoning. It plays a central role in the congruence argument, and later provides the basis for Kantian Constructivism.

Law of Peoples The Rawls's account of international justice, presented in his final book of the same name. Regarded as part of political liberalism, its role is to guide the foreign policy of liberal societies. Eight fundamental principles constitute the ideal theory of the Law of Peoples (PL, sect. 4). Just war doctrine (PL, sects. 13–14) and duty to assist burdened peoples (PL, sect. 15) are part of its non-ideal theory.

legitimacy, liberal principle of the requirement in Political Liberalism that citizens and government officials exercise political power only in accordance with a constitution, the essentials of which all citizens may reasonably be expected to endorse in light of principles and ideals acceptable to them as reasonable and rational citizens. It provides the basis for a duty of civility, to be able to justify laws affecting fundamental matters of justice in terms of the political values of public reason (PL, 137, 217, 427–9).

maximin rule (TJ, sect. 26) a conservative decision rule in decision theory that instructs one to choose the alternative whose worst outcome is better than the worst outcome of all other alternatives for choice. Rawls contends that the conditions for applying the maximin rule are present in the original position, and applies the rule to argue that justice as fairness would be chosen rather than the principle of (average) utility. Not to be confused with the "Maximin criterion," a term Rawls rarely applies to the difference principle. The maximin rule is not relied upon to argue for the difference principle (JF, 94–5).

mixed conceptions of justice (TJ, sect. 49) liberal conceptions that accept the first principle of justice and priority of equal basic liberties, but which substitute for the second principle a number of alternative accounts of distributive justice, including the principle of average utility, or average utility constrained by a social minimum, or some other consequentialist or intuitionist position regarding distributive justice. Rawls argues, on grounds of reciprocity, that justice as fairness and the difference principle would be chosen in the original position over mixed conceptions on grounds that it best meets conditions of reciprocity.

moral person (moral personality) a seventeenth–eighteenth-century term relied upon by Rawls to refer to a conception of agents (in TJ) or citizens (in PL) as being both rational and reasonable by virtue of having the two moral powers. Moral persons are said to conceive of themselves as free and equal, and as capable of taking responsibility for their actions and complying with moral requirements. See **moral powers**.

moral powers These are the capacities of moral personality. They include the moral capacity for a sense of justice and the rational capacity for a conception of the good. The development and exercise of these capacities are "higher-order interests" of free and equal moral persons and guide the choices of the parties in Rawls's original position. They also provide the basis for equality in that a person's having these capacities to a minimal degree requires that we treat that person with equal justice and according to the two principles of justice. See **moral person**.

moral psychology, principles of (TJ, sects. 70–75) the three reciprocity principles relied upon to show how a sense of justice can be a normal part of development and social life in a well-ordered society.

moral worth (of persons) (TJ, sect. 66) the third main concept of ethics, Rawls says, and part of the full theory of the good. A person's moral worth depends upon the degree to which he or she complies with the principles of justice and has the virtues of justice. Not to be confused with the concept of dignity, which in Rawls's Kantian framework all persons have regardless of their actions or moral worth, simply by virtue of being persons.

natural duties (TJ, sects. 19, 51) in justice as fairness, duties of individuals owed to persons as such, without regard to social or legal relationships to them. Among the natural duties agreed to in the original position are positive duties of mutual respect and mutual aid, the duty to comply with and promote justice, and negative duties not to injure or harm the innocent.

original position the initial situation from which transpires Rawls's version of the social contract. Rather than putting contracting parties in a state of nature where they know their historical situation, Rawls situates parties behind a veil of ignorance where they have no knowledge of facts about themselves or their circumstances. In later works it is a "procedure of construction" that represents features of free and equal moral persons.

overlapping consensus (PL, IV) the consensus of reasonable comprehensive doctrines in a well-ordered society on a liberal conception of justice. It holds when all reasonable doctrines endorse a liberal political conception of justice, each from its own point of view and for its own comprehensive reasons. The main reason for the stability of a well-ordered society.

peoples (LP, sect. 2) an idealization Rawls uses instead of 'nations' or 'states' in his account of international justice, the Law of Peoples. Peoples are united into a society by "common sympathies" that can have a number of grounds – ethnic, linguistic, religious, historical, etc. A necessary condition for the existence of a "people" is their having (or aspiring to have) a government and living under the same political constitution. Unlike states, a people has a moral nature and a conception of justice which it tries to observe in its internal and external relations.

perfectionism (TJ, sect. 50) ethical positions which incorporate the principle of perfection, and maintain that the achievement of human excellences in art, science, and culture constitutes the human good. The *principle of perfection* is a moral principle of right which defines duties in terms of conduct and institutions needed to effectively promote perfections and achievements of culture. Strict perfectionism is a teleological doctrine which says that right conduct and just institutions are those that tend to maximize perfections of culture or religion, etc. (a doctrine Rawls says can be found sometimes in Nietzsche, Aristotle, and Loyola). Moderate perfectionism is an intuitionist theory that balances the principle of perfection against other (non-teleological) principles to determine questions of right and justice.

political autonomy the legal independence and assured integrity of citizens (or of peoples), and their sharing equally with other citizens in the exercise of political power. See also **autonomy, doctrinal autonomy, political conception, political constructivism, public reason.**

political conception of justice (*Political Liberalism*) a conception that is "freestanding" of comprehensive religious, philosophical, and moral doctrines, and which is framed to provide a basis for public justification among democratic citizens. Only a political conception, Rawls contends, is reasonably acceptable and can gain an overlapping consensus among free and equal persons who have different moral conceptions implicit in their comprehensive doctrines.

political constructivism aspect of a freestanding political conception; it is the justification of political principles of justice in terms of political ideas and convictions implicit in a democratic culture and shared by free and equal democratic citizens with different comprehensive doctrines. Principles are "constructed" on the basis of a "procedure of construction" (e.g., the original position) that embodies or represents political ideas and public reasons shared by democratic citizens. It is necessary to the doctrinal autonomy and political objectivity of a liberal political conception of justice, and therewith, Rawls contends, to the political autonomy of citizens. Then principles of justice are justified only for reasons all accept in their capacity as citizens. See **doctrinal autonomy, political autonomy, political conception.**

political legitimacy see **legitimacy, liberal principle of.**

political liberalism a form of liberalism that assumes (reasonable) pluralism of moral, philosophical and religious views, and which seeks general agreement among citizens on a liberal political conception of justice that can serve as a public basis of justification among them. It is Rawls's attempt in his later works to show that a just society is realistically possible in which reasonable citizens all accept a liberal conception of justice on the basis of moral values implicit in democratic culture, even though they affirm many different "comprehensive" doctrines.

political values (**of public reason**)   values that are responsive to the higher-order interests of democratic citizens, in their capacity as free and equal citizens. Political values provide the core considerations that serve as legitimate public reasons upon which to base laws and other government measures. Among political values Rawls lists: liberty and equality of citizens; fair opportunities and other primary social goods; justice and the general welfare; the common defense; public health and other public goods; the security of persons and their property; fair distribution of income, wealth, and taxation; effectiveness and economic efficiency; respect for human life; the role of the family in achieving the reproduction of a just society over time, etc. Contrast nonpolitical values and "comprehensive reasons" that stem from religious, philosophical, and moral doctrines. See **public reason**.

primary social goods (TJ, sect. 15; CP, ch. 17)   the goods that principles of justice are designed to distribute and which serve as a basis of comparison and measure of individuals' level of well-being for purposes of justice. They include rights and liberties, powers, opportunities, and positions of office, income, and wealth, and the bases of self-respect. By "powers" Rawls means the institutional abilities and prerogatives attending offices and positions in society. Rawls contends these are all-purpose means that it is rational for persons who regard themselves as free and equal to want, whatever their conceptions of the good. In later work he argues they are necessary to realizing citizens' fundamental interests in exercising their moral powers and pursuing their rational life-plans.

priority of justice   the requirements that the principles of justice are to be met and take priority over the promotion of social welfare, efficiency, perfectionist values of culture, and other legitimate social ends.

priority of liberty   In justice as fairness, the requirements of the first principle protecting equal basic liberties are prior to and take precedence over the second principle. Hence, equal basic liberties may not be infringed for the sake of the difference principle or other requirements of justice.

priority of right (over the good)   a characteristic of Kantian and other deontological positions, including justice as fairness. Moral principles of right (including justice) have priority over, and hence constrain and regulate, the rational (maximizing) pursuit of all goods or values. It is not the idea that a conception of right or justice can be justified independent of a conception of the good (which Rawls does not attempt to do).

public basis of justification   (PL, 9–10, 100–1)   a role of a political conception of justice in a democratic society is to provide a public basis for deliberation, argument, justification, and agreement on the constitution and its laws. That laws be publicly justifiable to citizens is a condition of mutual respect and of their political and full autonomy.

public reason   (PL, vi)   reasons that are responsive to the fundamental interests of democratic citizens, in their capacity as free and equal moral persons. Rawls says that a political conception of justice provides content to the idea of public reason. Only a political conception and political values of public reason should be relied upon and cited in legislative, judicial, and administrative forums as legitimate reasons for laws and other government rulings. Reasons that stem from religious, philosophical, and moral doctrines should not be appealed to, unless a "Proviso" is satisfied, requiring that a justification in terms of public reasons also subsequently be given. See **political values of public reasons**.

publicity (of principles)   (PL, II, sect. 4)   the contractarian requirement that principles of justice or basic terms of social cooperation should be publicly known among persons whose conduct they regulate. Rawls argues that a precondition of freedom and equality is that publicity be "full," in that the evidence for and justification of principles of justice should also be publicly known.

pure procedural justice   the idea that the outcomes of certain fair procedures, when fully complied with, are necessarily just. An example is a fair lottery. There is no independent criterion to measure the fairness of its outcomes, independent of satisfying the procedure itself. Compare with *imperfect procedural justice*, where there exists an independent criterion and the outcome of fair procedures (e.g., fair jury trials) is likely to be just in so far as procedures satisfy or approximate that independent criterion. Rawls says an economic system whose rules fully satisfy justice as fairness exhibits pure procedural justice; once the rules of the system are satisfied, individuals is entitled to whatever they receive and the resulting distributions of income and wealth are just.

rational, the (PL, II, sect. 1; TJ, ch. 7)   The principles and considerations that are used to determine a person's or society's good. Among these are the "counting principles" (principle of effective means, etc.), deliberative rationality, and a rational plan of life. Rawls contrasts "rational" with "reasonable," and calls his account of the good "goodness as rationality." The primary social goods are said to be rational for persons generally.

rational plan of life (TJ, sect. 64)   Rawls's account of a person's good, which is the schedule of primary ends and activities that a person would choose with full knowledge of all relevant facts in deliberative rationality.

realistic utopia   an idea introduced in *The Law of Peoples* to suggest that the Society of Peoples is a feasible world where all peoples agree on and observe the constraints of the Law of Peoples, respect human rights, and provide for the common good of all their members. The idea parallels the idea of a well-ordered society, which also is regarded as an achievable ideal given the permanent conditions of human nature, including the burdens of judgment.

reasonable, the (**reasonableness**) (PL, II, sect. 1)   a term Rawls uses widely which contrasts with "rational," and which normally refers to moral characteristics related to fairness or justice of persons, principles, and conceptions of the good. Most uses of "reasonable" depend upon the idea of a reasonable person (see below). In some uses, such as "reasonable comprehensive doctrine," and in works up through TJ, Rawls often uses the word epistemically to mean "in conformity with reason." This is its meaning when Rawls refers to the "most reasonable" (instead of "true") conception of justice.

reasonable comprehensive doctrines (PL, II, sect. 3) doctrines which (1) cover the major philosophical, moral, and religious aspects of human life in a consistent and coherent manner; (2) single out which values are especially significant and how to balance them when they conflict; (3) belong to a tradition of thought that evolves slowly in light of what it sees as good and sufficient reasons. Reasonable persons can affirm different reasonable doctrines; in a well-ordered society with overlapping consensus reasonable doctrines all affirm a liberal conception of justice.

reasonable persons (PL, II, sect. 2) persons who (1) want to cooperate with others who are reasonable on terms they can accept; (2) appreciate the consequences of the burdens of judgment; (3) have a reasonable moral psychology, including a sense of justice; and (4) want to be seen as reasonable, or fair and just. A key concept Rawls uses to clarify other uses of 'reasonable.'

reasonable pluralism, fact of the diversity of reasonable comprehensive doctrines affirmed by reasonable persons in liberal societies, even when well-ordered. It is the long-run outcome of the work of human reason under free conditions, and a permanent feature of a democratic society due to the burdens of judgment. As a result, even fully reasonable and rational persons often cannot agree on philosophical, moral, and religious principles.

reciprocity, requirement of a general requirement that each person engaged in cooperation should not simply benefit (mutual advantage), but should benefit on terms that are fair. Rawls construes it to require terms of cooperation where gains to those more advantaged must benefit those least advantaged more than any other alternatives do. The main argument for the difference principle relies on reciprocity.

reciprocity, criterion of (political liberalism) a moral requirement on citizens and officials; they should reasonably believe that the terms of cooperation (laws, etc.) they propose be reasonably acceptable to others as free and equal citizens, and not as manipulated, dominated, or under pressure of being socially or politically inferior. A basis for the liberal principle of legitimacy.

right, concept of   one of the main concepts of ethics, along with the good and moral worth. Rawls follows Kant in arguing that principles of right, including justice, are not defined or specified as instrumental to good, but are independently specifiable in contractarian terms of agreement among reasonable and rational persons who are fairly situated; he calls this "Rightness as Fairness."

second principle of justice   the difference principle combined with the principle of fair equality of opportunities (for which, see above).

self-respect (TJ, sect. 67)   a psychological attitude grounded in (1) the sense of one's own value and conviction that one's conception of the good, or rational plan of life, is worth pursuing, and (2) confidence that one has the abilities to successfully fulfill one's intentions. It depends in large part on finding our person and deeds appreciated and confirmed by others, and having a rational plan of life that satisfies the Aristotelian Principle. Self-respect is "perhaps the most important primary good" (TJ, 440/386 rev.). Rawls relies on it to argue for equal political liberties and other features of equal citizenship. In a democratic society, not to be recognized as an equal person severely undermines one's self-respect.

sense of justice (TJ, ch. VIII)   the disposition to act on and from principles and rules of justice. Rawls contends this moral motivation is a normal part of social life and development, and is the main cause of stability of societies that are just or not too unjust. The *capacity for a sense of justice* is more broadly defined as a complex capacity to understand, apply, and act from principles of justice; it is the moral power that enables persons to be reasonable. Rawls regards this capacity as a fundamental or "higher-order" interest of free and equal moral persons in the original position. He relies upon it to justify many of the primary social goods, the basic liberties, and ultimately agreement on the two principles of justice.

social cooperation (PL, I, sect. 3) Rawls regards society as a fair system of social cooperation. As distinguished from efficiently coordinated activity, social cooperation involves an account of each person's rational advantage, and an account of fair or reasonable terms of cooperation. The role of principles of justice is to determine the fair terms of social cooperation.

social role of a moral conception (CP, ch. 17) In addition to its practical role in guiding the conduct of persons and institutions, a moral conception has a social role of providing a basis for public justification, including moral argument and criticism, among free and equal persons expected to comply with its terms. This puts a constraint on the moral conceptions that can govern people's conduct, since to serve a social role, a moral conception must be generally acceptable to them. See **publicity**.

social union (TJ, sect. 79) Rawls's account of how a just and well-ordered society realizes the value of community. A social union involves (1) a shared final end among its participants, and (2) common institutions and activities valued as good in themselves; moreover, (3) when common activities are collectively engaged in, the success and enjoyment of other participants are necessary for and complementary to each participant's good. Many common activities can be social unions; Rawls mentions orchestras, sports teams, families, friendships, and common endeavors in sciences and arts. He argues, as part of the congruence argument for stability, that participation in the common institutions of a well-ordered society of justice as fairness is a "social union of social unions," and therewith an intrinsic good for all reasonable and rational citizens.

society of peoples an ideal of just cooperation among all those well-ordered liberal and decent peoples who observe the Law of Peoples in their relations. Rawls uses the term 'peoples' rather than 'states.'

stability (of social cooperation and of a conception of justice) Social cooperation is stable when its rules are regularly complied with and willingly acted upon; and when infractions occur, stabilizing forces exist that prevent further violations and tend to restore the arrangement. Rawls is concerned in TJ part

III with the stability of a conception of justice and a just and well-ordered society that incorporates it, which depends on members having an effective *sense of justice*. One conception of justice is more stable relative to another if the sense of justice it generates is stronger and more likely to override disruptive inclinations and temptations to injustice.

veil of ignorance a strict impartiality condition on choice in Rawls's original position. The parties to the agreement are ignorant of particular facts about themselves and their society. They do not know their social class, race, religion, ethnic membership, nationality, or conception of the good, nor their society's resources or its history. They do know general facts about human nature, and social and economic institutions.

well-ordered society a formal ideal of a perfectly just society implicit in Rawls's contractarianism. It is a society where (a) all citizens agree on the same conception of justice and this is public knowledge; moreover, (b) society enacts this conception in its laws and institutions; and (c) citizens have a sense of justice and willingness to comply with these terms. The parties in the original position seek a conception of justice that will be stable under conditions of a well-ordered society, hence a conception that is generally acceptable to all reasonable and rational persons.

Notes

PREFACE

1 Philippe van Parijs's article "Difference Principles" in effect makes this charge in its opening section. See *The Cambridge Companion to Rawls*, Samuel Freeman, ed., Cambridge: Cambridge University Press, 2003, 201–02.

2 Among other things, Judge Hoffman bound and gagged the defendants to keep them quiet in the courtroom.

ONE INTRODUCTION

1 "A Brief Inquiry into the Meaning of Sin and Faith: An Interpretation Based on the Concept of Community," Senior Thesis submitted to the Department of Philosophy of Princeton University, December 1942. Publication forthcoming, Harvard University Press.

2 For example, The Thirty-nine Articles, the principal confession of the Church of England (and of the Episcopal Church Rawls belonged to) affirm the orthodox Christian doctrines of the Trinity, the Person of Christ, and human sinfulness, and are Protestant in character in their emphasis on justification by faith, the centrality of the Scriptures, and two holy sacraments (baptism and the eucharist). See *The Study of Anglicanism*, Stephen Sykes and John Booty, eds., New York: Fortress Press, 1988, 134–37.

3 Here Rawls adds the footnote quoting Kant: " 'If justice perishes, then it is no longer worthwhile for men to live upon the earth.' *Rechtslehre*, in Remark E following §49, Ak: VI: 332," LP, 128n.

4 See John Rawls, *Collected Papers*, Samuel Freeman, ed., Cambridge, MA: Harvard University Press, 1999, ch. 1.

5 "John Rawls: For the Record," an interview with *The Harvard Review of Philosophy*, 1, 1999, 38–47.

6 See Locke, *Second Treatise on Government*, sects 54, 6, 59 Kant, *The Metaphysical Elements of Justice* (*Rechtslehre*), VI: 237–38 of the standard Akademie edition.

7 See Rawls's lectures on Locke, in his *Lectures on the History of Political Philosophy*, Samuel Freeman, ed., Cambridge, MA: Harvard University Press, 2007.

8 See Rawls's lectures on Hobbes in *Lectures on the History of Political Philosophy*, Samuel Freeman, ed., Cambridge, MA: Harvard University Press, 2007.

9 David Hume, *An Enquiry Concerning the Principles of Morals*, J.B. Schneewind, ed., Indianapolis, IN: Hackett, 1983, 28 (Section III, Part II).

10 Joseph Raz, among others, contends that the justification of authority or principles of justice cannot be that people agree to them; rather, justification must reside in people's *reasons* for agreeing to authority or principles. The mere fact of agreement, like the mere fact of wanting or willing something, cannot justify anything. Only objective reasons can justify, and agreements by themselves, like desires, cannot serve this role. Raz, *Ethics in the Public Domain*, Oxford, UK: Oxford University Press, 1994, chs 4, 16.

11 See the first lecture on Rousseau in Rawls's *Lectures on the History of Political Philosophy* for Rawls's discussion of Rousseau's *Discourse on Inequality* and the doctrine of natural goodness.

12 See works by Joshua Cohen cited in the bibliography. Also Amy Gutmann and Dennis Thompson, *Democracy and Disagreement*, Cambridge, MA: Harvard University Press, 1998. Jürgen Habermas's work also has had a major influence in discussions of deliberative democracy.

13 In *Discourse on Political Economy* (1755), Rousseau says: "Even his own reason ought to be suspect to him, and the only reason he ought to follow is the public reason, which is the law." Then later: "It is to law alone that men owe justice and liberty. It . . . reestablishes as a civil right the natural equality among men. This . . . dictates to each citizen the precepts of public reason." In Rousseau, *The Basic Political Writings*, Indianapolis, IN: Hackett, 1987, 113, 117.

14 Rawls says Hegel misreads Kant's categorical imperative as a purely formal criterion with few substantive implications (*TJ*, 251n./221n. rev.); that he misreads equality of opportunity (*TJ*, 300–01/265 rev.); and that Hegel's depiction of civil society is based on Adam Smith and is a "private society" that denies the possibility of social union (*TJ*, 521n./457n. rev.).

15 Rawls's Hegel lectures are in his *Lectures on the History of Moral Philosophy*, Barbara Herman, ed., Cambridge MA: Harvard University Press, 2000. They were first written in the 1970s, and later were revised.

16 Rawls did, however, retain Kant's sharp distinction between theoretical and practical reason – it underlies his idea of the independence of moral theory and also political liberalism.

17 Rawls, *Lectures on the History of Moral Philosophy*, 336.

18 Ibid., 332

19 See "Outline for a Decision Procedure in Ethics" (1951), in Rawls, *Collected Papers*, ch. 1.

20 Rawls says that he benefited from Quine's work on justification, but that the initial idea of reflective equilibrium was worked out prior to Quine's work, in Rawls's own "Outline for a Decision Procedure in Ethics" (1951), where he sets forth a method of justification specifically applicable to moral principles. See TJ, 579n./507n. rev.

21 See Rawls's Lectures on the History of Political Philosophy, 384–85 on Sidgwick's criteria for justification.

22 The contrast of Sidgwick's rational intuitionism with constructivism in moral philosophy begins with Rawls's 1980 Dewey Lectures, "Kantian Constructivism in Moral Philosophy." See Collected Papers, ch. 16, Lecture III: "Construction and Objectivity," 340–59.

23 See TJ, 48–49. This sentence and the entire paragraph surrounding it were deleted in the revised edition. Cf. TJ, 578/507 rev., where Rawls also refers to the "Socratic aspects" of moral theory.

24 See Ronald Dworkin, "Objectivity and Truth: You'd Better Believe It," Philosophy and Public Affairs, 1996, 25, 117–18; see also Thomas Nagel, The Last Word, New York: Oxford University Press, 1997, ch. 6.

25 David Gauthier argues that economics and decision and game theory provide greater support for a Hobbesian contractarian view, of the sort he defends in Morals by Agreement, Oxford: Oxford University Press, 1986. Kin Binmore argues in Natural Justice, Cambridge, MA: Harvard University Press, 2005, that utilitarianism is supported by evolutionary theory and decision theory. Allan Gibbard made a similar argument in his Tanner Lectures at Berkeley in 2006.

26 Compare this with Kant's claim: "A moral principle is really nothing but a dimly conceived metaphysics, which is inherent in every man's rational constitution – as the teacher will easily find out who tries to catechize his pupil in the Socratic method concerning the imperative to duty and its application to the moral judgment of his actions." The Metaphysical Principles of Virtue, trans. James Ellington, Indianapolis: Bobbs-Merrill, 1963, 32 (Ak. VI, 376). See also Kant's Introduction to Part I of the Metaphysics of Morals: "Every man has such a metaphysics within himself, although commonly only in an obscure way: for without a priori principles, how could he believe that he has within himself a power of universal legislation?" (Ibid., 15 (Ak. VI, 216)). Rawls called these passages to my attention in the early 1980s when working on Kantian Constructivism and his lectures on Kant in LHMP, and said that by "metaphysics within himself" Kant simply means "moral conception."

27 This is the title of Rawls's 1980 Dewey Lectures, in CP, ch. 16. Rawls differs from Kant (as he has emphasized) in rejecting the idea that moral principles are a priori, and that they have a basis simply in "pure practical reasoning". As we see in Rawls's discussion of stability (see Chapter 6 below), it is very important for the justification of principles of justice that they be compatible with human nature and general facts about social cooperation (see TJ, 51/44 rev.).

28 See Norman Daniels's helpful discussions in his Justice and Justification, Cambridge, UK: Cambridge University Press, 1996, chs. 1–8, where

he seems to read reflective equilibrium as a more general method of justification.
29 See Rawls, "Reply to Habermas," in *Political Liberalism*, New York: Columbia University Press (1995 paperback edition, 2004 expanded edition), 385–95.

TWO LIBERALISM, DEMOCRACY, AND THE PRINCIPLES OF JUSTICE

1 See the Introduction to John Rawls, *Political Liberalism*, New York: Columbia University Press, 1993, xxiv.
2 Over time, Rawls formulated the first principle differently. The statement in the text is his final formulation from *Political Liberalism* (1993). In the *Restatement*, written in the early 1990s, the first principle begins: "Each person is to have *the same indefeasible claim to a fully adequate scheme* of equal basic liberties" (see John Rawls, *Justice as Fairness: A Restatement*, ed. Erin Kelly, Cambridge, MA: Harvard University Press, 2001, 42). The main difference between the formulation in the text (taken from PL) and that found in *Theory* is that in *TJ* it says "Each person is to have an equal right *to the most extensive basic liberty*," (*TJ*, 60) or "*most extensive scheme* of equal basic liberties" (*TJ*, 53 rev.; cf. 250/220 rev.) instead of "to a fully adequate scheme" (as in PL). I discuss the reasons for this and other changes later in the final section of this chapter. Since the formulation in the text of the first principle was arrived at ten years before *Political Liberalism* was published (in "The Basic Liberties and Their Priority," published as Lecture VIII of PL) it can be assessed for the most part independently of political liberalism.
3 See John Rawls, *Lectures on the History of Moral Philosophy*, ed. Barbara Herman, Cambridge, MA: Harvard University Press, 2000, 366.
4 See John Stuart Mill's *On Liberty*, chapter I, Introduction, where Mill in the closing paragraphs says that the principle of liberty protects primarily liberty of conscience and freedom of thought, freedom of association, and "freedom of tastes and pursuits," including the freedom to pursue a "plan of life" that fits one's character.
5 PL, 228, 232, 335.
6 PL, 298; see also TJ, 61/53 rev., where Rawls refers to the right to hold personal property independent of the more abstract liberty it is later subsumed under.
7 John Stuart Mill, *On Liberty*, ed. Elizabeth Rapaport, Indianapolis: Hackett, 1978, 12.
8 See Peter de Marneffe, "Contractualism, Liberty and Democracy," *Ethics*, 104, July 1994, 764–83, who argues that Rawls's account of basic liberties is not as expansive as Mill's principle of liberty.
9 This is not a problem that is distinctive to libertarianism, though it is more pronounced. For example, on any liberal account a publisher might use a newspaper to criticize someone, thereby harming their

prospects for succeeding. But this is considered a permissible harm since people do not have a right not to be criticized so long as it is not done in a libelous manner. The reference ASU in the text is to Nozick's *Anarchy, State, and Utopia*, New York: Basic Books, 1974.

10 I said "primarily" but not exclusively, for in *The Law of Peoples*, 69, Rawls says that among the human rights that all persons have is a right to subsistence.

11 On this subject see Samuel Freeman, "Illiberal Libertarians: Why Libertarianism is not a Liberal View," in *Philosophy and Public Affairs*, 2001, vol. 30, 105–51.

12 See H.L.A. Hart, "Rawls on Liberty and Its Priority," in *Reading Rawls*, Norman Daniels, ed., New York: Basic Books, 1975, 230–52 at 249–52. See Rawls, PL, 290 for this statement of the two problems Hart discerns.

13 Beginning with "Kantian Constructivism in Moral Theory" in 1980 (CP, ch. 16).

14 *Political Liberalism*, "The Basic Liberties and their Priorities" (1982), Lecture VIII, see 310–24.

15 See Mill, *On Liberty*, ch. 5.

16 See Robert Nozick's *Anarchy, State, and Utopia* (New York: Basic Books, 1974).

17 See Norman Daniels, *Reading Rawls*, 279.

18 In TJ, 250/220 rev., Rawls states the "Priority Rule" agreed to in the original position as: "The principles of justice are to be ranked in lexical order and therefore liberty can be restricted only for the sake of liberty. There are two cases: (a) a less extensive liberty must strengthen the total system of liberty shared by all, and (b) a less than equal liberty must be acceptable to those citizens with the lesser liberty."

19 It is unclear whether for Rawls freedom of the person includes what is called a "right of privacy" in U.S. constitutional law. Clearly Rawls wants to argue for such a liberty; if not on grounds of basic liberty, then on grounds that restrictions on liberty must meet requirements of public reason (discussed below and in Chapter 9).

20 Robert Taylor points out in "Rawls's Defense of the Priority of Liberty," *Philosophy and Public Affairs*, 2003, vol 31, 246–71, that Rawls, in discussing J.S. Mill's proposal that those with greater knowledge and education be given extra voting rights, leaves open the possibility that "plural voting may be perfectly just" if it can be shown that such an arrangement promotes the common good and would be acceptable to rational representatives of those with less than equal political liberties (TJ, 233/205 rev.). But in saying that "Mill's argument does not go beyond the general conception of justice as fairness" (TJ, 233/204 rev.), Rawls indicates that this arrangement would be allowable only under less than favorable conditions where the special conception does not apply, and clearly not in a well-ordered society. Of equal political liberties and fair equal opportunities, Rawls later says, "Their full achievement

is . . . the inherent long-run tendency of a just system" (TJ, 218 rev.).

21 See TJ, 244/215 rev.: "Even in a well-ordered society under favorable circumstances, liberty of thought and conscience is subject to reasonable regulation." In PL, 295–96 Rawls discusses the restriction vs. the regulation of a basic liberty.

22 Rawls once said in conversation with me that he did not see why the neo-Nazis should be allowed to march in Skokie, Ill. (then a community with the largest number of Jewish Holocaust survivors), since the Nazis could express their message in a neighboring municipality. He could not see any legitimate point in subjecting Jewish survivors to the Nazi message. His views on the issue were more conservative than the state or federal courts, which enjoined the town of Skokie to issue the Nazis a parade permit.

23 See especially Harry Kalven, *A Worthy Tradition: Freedom of Speech in America*, New York: Harper and Row, 1987, frequently cited by Rawls in PL, Lecture VIII. See also Cass Sunstein, *Democracy and the Problem of Free Speech*, New York: The Free Press, 1993, for a defense of a multi-tiered approach to freedom of expression similar to that advocated by Rawls.

24 H.L.A. Hart, "Rawls on Liberty and Its Priority," in Norman Daniels, ed., *Reading Rawls*, 252; Brian Barry, "John Rawls and the Priority of Liberty," *Philosophy and Public Affairs*, 2, 1974, 274–90.

25 Hart makes a similar point (ibid., 248).

26 For a similar reading of Rawls, see Robert Taylor, "Rawls's Defense of the Priority of Liberty: A Kantian Reconstruction," *Philosophy and Public Affairs*, 31, 2003, 246–71.

27 See Mill, *On Liberty*, ch. III, where he says that individuality is the greater part of well-being.

28 In "Liberalism, Inalienability, and Rights of Drug Use," in *Drugs and the Limits of Liberalism*, ed. Pablo DeGreiff, Ithaca, NY: Cornell University Press, 1999, 110–30, I argue on Rawlsian grounds that liberals may endorse restricting the use of self-destructive recreational drugs on grounds that they undermine a person's adequate exercise of his/her own moral powers.

29 This is suggested I believe by Robert Taylor's work, cited above.

THREE THE SECOND PRINCIPLE AND DISTRIBUTIVE JUSTICE

1 Thomas Hobbes, *Leviathan*, New York: Viking Penguin, 1986, ch. 30, 239.

2 See Rawls, *The Law of Peoples*, 113–20.

3 Marx believed that changes in the workers' conditions depended, not on appeals to justice, but on workers' immiseration and the eventual collapse of capitalism as a social and economic system, to be followed by a transition to a socialist society, and eventually "full communist society." See Rawls, LHPP, Lectures on Marx.

4 Immanuel Kant, "On the Proverb: That May be True in Theory But is of No Practical Use," in *Perpetual Peace and Other Essays*, Ted Humphrey, trans., Indianapolis: Hachett, 1983, 74.

5 See Robert Nozick, *Anarchy, State, and Utopia*, New York: Basic Books, 1974, 235–39; Milton Friedman, *Capitalism and Freedom*, Chicago: University of Chicago Press, 1962.

6 "Chances to acquire cultural knowledge and skills should not depend upon one's class position, and so the school system, whether public or private, should be designed to even out class barriers" (TJ, 73/63 rev.).

7 See Amy Gutmann, *Democratic Education*, Princeton, NJ: Princeton University Press, 1987, for such an argument influenced by Rawls.

8 For a contemporary Hobbesian contract conception, see David Gauthier's *Morals by Agreement*, Oxford: Oxford University Press, 1986.

9 For a fine discussion of how such goods as maintaining equal status and engaging in socially cooperative labor and respectful social relations all are connected with fair equal opportunity, see Seana Schiffrin, "Race, Labor, and Opportunity," in *Fordham Law Review*, 72, 2004, 1643–75 at 1666–70. Schiffrin contends, not unreasonably, that the importance of these goods to self-respect, social cooperation, and the equality of citizens warrants eliminating the priority Rawls assigns to the first principle over FEO. But see Rawls, JF, 163 n. 44.

10 See "Justice and Nature," in Nagel's *Concealment and Exposure*, New York: Oxford University Press, 2002, 127.

11 JF, 174; PL, 184n., where Rawls endorses Norman Daniels's reading of FEO as requiring rights to health care. In the *Restatement* Rawls indicates that provision of health care has multiple sources, including not only FEO, but the equal liberties and difference principle too. "Such care falls under the general means necessary to underwrite FEO and our capacity to take advantage of our basic rights and liberties, and thus to be normal and fully cooperating members of society over a complete life" (JF, 174).

12 On the effects of differences in informal education according to family background, see Annette Lareau, *Unequal Childhoods*, Berkeley, CA: University of California Press, 2003.

13 That the existence of the family and unequal chances are consistent with FEO seems clear from Rawls's claim: "It seems that even when fair opportunity (as it has been defined) is satisfied, the family will lead to unequal chances between individuals" (TJ, 511/448 rev.). See also TJ, 301/265 rev., where he distinguishes FEO from perfect equality of opportunity.

14 See David Hume, *Treatise of Human Nature*, Bk III, Pt. I.

15 For a discussion of Hume's account of justice that is influenced by Rawls, see my "Property as an Institutional Convention in Hume's Account of Justice," in *Archiv für Geschichte der Philosophie* 73, 1991, 20–49.

16 See Hart's *The Concept of Law*, Oxford, UK: Oxford University Press, 1960, widely recognized as a twentieth-century classic in jurisprudence and legal and political philosophy.

17 Rawls says, "The main problem of distributive justice is the choice of a social system" (TJ, 274/242 rev.). This is one way he sees the difference principle as applying holistically.

18 See, for example, Ronald Dworkin, Sovereign Virtue, Cambridge, MA: Harvard University Press, 2000, 113, for this and other criticisms of the difference principle. Also Will Kymlicka, Contemporary Political Philosophy, New York: Oxford University Press, 1990, 70–73; Martha Nussbaum, Frontiers of Justice: Disabilities, Nationality, Species Membership, Cambridge, MA: Harvard University Press, 2006, chs 1, 4. For a response to Nussbaum, see my article "Frontiers of Justice: Contractarianism vs. the Capabilities Approach," in Texas Law Review, 85, 2006, 385–430.

19 See John Roemer, A Future for Socialism, Cambridge, MA: Harvard University Press, 1994, on market socialism.

20 See Philippe van Parijs, "Difference Principles," The Cambridge Companion to Rawls, 224–26.

21 It is true that in TJ, prior to 1982 when Lecture VIII of PL was written, the first principle said in part, "Each person is to have an equal right to the most extensive basic liberty" (TJ, 60), and "Each person is to have an equal right to the most extensive total system of equal basic liberties" (TJ, 250/220 rev.). But Rawls never intended this language to mean that society is to maximize people's opportunities to exercise their basic liberties, as is evident from his distinction between a liberty and the worth of that liberty, discussed above.

22 For Cohen's criticism, see his If You're an Egalitarian, How Come You're So Rich?, Boston, MA: Harvard University Press, 2000. For discussions that defend Rawls, see articles cited in the bibliography by Samuel Scheffler, Joshua Cohen, K.C. Tan, David Estlund, and Andrew Williams, under the heading Egalitarianism, Distributive Justice, and the Difference Principle (pp. 526–27).

23 As G.A. Cohen says, "An ethos which informs choice within just rules is necessary in a society committed to the difference principle" (If You're an Egalitarian, How Come You're So Rich?, 132).

24 I owe this point to K.C. Tan.

25 On the role of moral pluralism in explaining Rawls's reliance on incentives, see Samuel Scheffler, in "What is Egalitarianism?" Philosophy and Public Affairs 31, 2003, 5–39; on the role of maintaining individuals' freedom to make personal choices about what goods to pursue in life, see K.C. Tan, "Justice and Personal Pursuits," Journal of Philosophy, 101, 2004, 331–62.

26 Samuel Scheffler emphasizes this account of why Rawls's account of distributive justice focuses mainly on the basic structure, in "What is Egalitarianism?"

27 For Rawls's discussion of pure procedural justice and the distinction between allocative justice and background justice, see TJ, sect. 17.

28 This point is well made by Liam Murphy and Thomas Nagel, The Myth of Ownership: Taxes and Justice, Oxford: Oxford University Press, 2004.

FOUR THE ORIGINAL POSITION

1 For Nozick's rejection of (a) social contract doctrine, see Robert Nozick, *Anarchy, State, and Utopia*, New York: Basic Books, 1974, 132–33; (b) of the original position, 198–204; and (c) the basic structure, 204–10. See *Political Liberalism*, 262–65 on libertarianism's rejection of the basic structure and Rawls's reply.

2 Since the parties are free, principles of justice should be acceptable to them, and for principles to be acceptable to everyone requires a social agreement.

3 See Dworkin, "Justice and Rights," in *Taking Rights Seriously*, Cambridge, MA: Harvard University Press, 1977, ch. 6, sect. 1.

4 *Anarchy, State, and Utopia*, 199. Nozick says that the original position is set up so that only "end-state" principles will be agreed to, not "historical" principles that distribute income and wealth according to a procedure. This is a mistaken understanding of the difference principle that stems from Nozick's regarding it as an allocative principle that divides up income and wealth after it has been produced. But Rawls says the difference principle incorporates pure procedural justice, since we cannot say what a just distribution should be independent of people complying with the rules of a just system designed according to the difference principle. The pure procedural justice of the difference principle is virtually indistinguishable from Nozick's definition of an "historical" principle. The problem is he does not consider that there are historical principles in addition to his libertarian entitlement principles.

5 There is a more detailed account of the features of a rational person later in the book (see *TJ*, ch. 7).

6 Rawls's claim of the rationality of prudence, or zero-time preference, which he shares with Sidgwick, is more controversial than he lets on. The account of rationality used in decision theory and the social sciences does not assume that it is necessarily irrational to have less concern for one's future. In this regard, they accord with Hume's view that whether it is rational to be concerned with one's future depends wholly on one's desires. As discussed in Chapter 6, Rawls's assumption of the rationality of prudence seems to be based in the conception of free and equal moral persons that he builds into the original position.

7 Rawls's distinction between being motivated by *one's own interests* and being motivated by *interests in oneself* is important (see *TJ*, 129/111 rev.). A purely self-interested or egoistic person is motivated solely by interests in *states of himself* – his power, his wealth and pleasure, his reputation, and so on. A person who is motivated by "his own interests," on the other hand, can just as well have the happiness and well-being of others as the object of his desires as he can desire to further states of himself or his own well-being. It is a father's interest that his children be happy; more generally it is the interest of benevolent people that others fare well or succeed in life. Acting from

one's own interests is unavoidable; it is not selfish or egotistical unless one's interests are predominantly selfish or egotistical. The parties are motivated ultimately by their own interests, not simply by interests in themselves. So they are not in this regard self-interested.

8 Rawls sets forth this argument in "Social Unity and the Primary Goods," in his *Collected Papers*, ch. 17.

9 On Locke's social contract, see Rawls's *Lectures on the History of Political Philosophy*.

10 See Rawls's lectures on Hume in his *Lectures on the History of Moral Philosophy*.

11 Rawls discusses the judicious spectator in *Theory*, sect. 5, and in more detail in his lectures on Hume in *Lectures on the History of Moral Philosophy*.

12 These remarks reflect the first two reasons Rawls mentions for a thick veil in "Fairness to Goodness," *Collected Papers*, 269: "There are, then, at least three different reasons for excluding information from the original position: it would permit self- and group-interest to distort the parties' deliberations; it refers to contingencies and accidents that should not influence the choice of moral principles; or it represents the very moral conceptions (or aspects thereof) that we seek to understand in the light of other and more basic notions." Rawls's most extended discussion of the reasons for a thick veil are in "Kantian Constructivism in Moral Theory," in *Collected Papers*, 335–36. See also *Political Liberalism*, 24n., 273, where Rawls justifies a thick veil by appealing to reasonable pluralism and the need for an overlapping consensus of comprehensive doctrines.

13 See Hume's *Enquiry Concerning the Principles of Morals*, Section III, part 1. Rawls's account of the circumstances of justice is also influenced by H.L.A. Hart.

14 Rawls takes this term from Hume, using it only once, in his chart summarizing the original position (*TJ*, 146/127 rev.).

15 "An important feature of a conception of justice is that it should generate its own support. Its principles should be such that when they are embodied in the basic structure of society men tend to acquire the corresponding sense of justice and develop a desire to act in accordance with its principles. In this case a conception of justice is stable" (*TJ*, 138/119 rev.).

16 See "Justice as Fairness: Political, not Metaphysical," in *Collected Papers*, 400–01n.

17 Joseph Raz has expressed this sort of objection most trenchantly in two papers: "Facing Diversity: The Case of Epistemic Abstinence," *Philosophy and Public Affairs*, 19, 1990, 3–46; "Disagreement in Politics," *American Journal of Jurisprudence*, 1998, 25–52. For a reply to the latter article, see Samuel Freeman, "Public Reason and Political Justification," *Fordham Law Review*, 72, 2004, 101–48.

18 As William Frankena is purported to have said, "Morality is made for man, and not man for morality."

19 My comments here apply only to strictly orthodox Bayesian decision theory, and are not intended to be a criticism of all those who argue

for other variations of Bayesian decision theory. The strictly orthodox theory requires that a rational agent harbor, for every hypothesis, a precise degree of confidence as to whether the hypothesis is true. This original variant of Bayesian decision theory faces the challenge of saying what degree of confidence an agent should have in a hypothesis when she hasn't even the slightest hunch as to whether it is true. Many Bayesians reject the propriety of Harsanyi's analysis of how decisions are to be made in the face of complete ignorance. I am grateful to Mark Kaplan for this clarification.

20 Since the expected utility of (2) is $500,000 [= ($.10 x .5) + ($1,000,000 x .5)], and the expected utility of (1) is only $1.50 [= $1 x .5) + ($2 x .5)].

21 See Harsanyi, "Morality and the Theory of Rational Behavior," in Amartya Sen and Bernard Williams, eds., Utilitarianism and Beyond, Cambridge, UK: Cambridge University Press, 1982, 39–62, at 47.

22 For Rawls's own example of the irrationality of maximin under most circumstances, see TJ, 157/136 rev.

23 If this sum is not sufficient to tempt you, imagine a larger sum that is. Orthodox Bayesians contend that all preferences are connected, and thus all of us have our price; rationally, we should be willing to trade off any end or commitment if the sum of utilities for which we exchange is high enough. An agent's preferences are connected when, for any two outcomes or options A and B, the agent either prefers one to the other or is impartial. Indecision is not rationally allowed. See Mark Kaplan, Decision Theory as Philosophy, New York: Cambridge University Press, 1996, 5, 24.

24 Decision theorists will say that we risk our loved ones' lives whenever we drive them to the store or anywhere else. Of course, this is unavoidable risk, assuming that we want our children to live a normal life with experiences of what they need to know to be sociable beings who live a flourishing life. Moreover, you know there is only a very small likelihood of harm. Betting your child's life upon the outcome of one try at a slot machine is not an unavoidable risk.

25 As quoted and helpfully discussed in Kaplan, Decision Theory as Philosophy, 26n., Harold Jeffreys writes (emphasis in original): "To say that the probabilities are equal is a precise way of saying that we have no good grounds for choosing between the alternatives. . . . The rule that we should take them as equal is not a statement of any belief about the actual composition of the world, nor is it an inference from previous experience; it is merely the formal way of expressing ignorance."

26 See Rawls, TJ, sect. 28; see also Michael Resnick, Choices, Minneapolis: University of Minnesota Press, 1987, 37; and Kaplan, 27.

27 This parallels Susan Hurley's argument against luck egalitarianism, that arbitrariness in the distribution of natural endowments does not imply their effects should be equally distributed. See her Justice, Luck, and Knowledge, Cambridge, MA: Harvard University Press, 2004, ch. 6.

28 Rawls's argument implies that it is not rational for the parties in the original position to make certain trade-offs, given complete uncertainty

of outcomes and the gravity of their decision. The parties to the original position have three "higher-order" interests (in the two moral powers and in pursuing their rational life plan) that they are not willing to trade off for the sake of other interests (such as the chance for greater income and wealth). They have what decision theorists term a "lexigraphical ordering" of these goods. This accounts in large part for the priority they assign to the basic liberties in the first principle. Orthodox Bayesian decision theory, by contrast, is committed to the connectedness of preferences, implying that all options and outcomes are comparable from the point of view of how desirable/preferable they are for an agent. There is always some rate of exchange at which a rational person is willing to accept a lesser fulfillment of one aim (equal liberties, for example) for the sake of greater fulfillment of another; hence we can never be rationally undecided (as opposed to indifferent) in comparing alternatives. Rawls contends, by contrast, that people have many aims for which there is no method or standard of comparison to decide between them when they conflict. Some decisions are indeterminate; "sooner or later we will reach incomparable aims between which we must choose with deliberative rationality" (TJ, 552/483 rev.). See Kaplan's discussion in *Decision Theory as Philosophy*, 23–31, on the assumption of "immodest connectedness" and complete determinacy of choice made by orthodox Bayesians, which he also rejects as requiring "false precision" (25).

29 Here it should be kept in mind that, unlike the examples in the text, in Rawls's original position the parties do not even know potential payoffs resulting from choice between alternatives.

30 Rawls's argument is that maximin is a rational strategy given three conditions: first, "the situation is one where knowledge of probabilities is impossible, or at best extremely insecure"; second, "the person choosing has a conception of the good such that he cares very little, if anything, for what he might gain above the minimum stipend that he can, in fact, be sure of by following the maximin rule"; and third, "the rejected alternatives have outcomes that one can hardly accept" (TJ, 154–55/134 rev.; JF, 98). Rawls argues that the original position exhibits all three of these features. Rawls's critics normally focus on the first condition alone and usually ignore the other conditions Rawls imposes on the rationality of using maximin. In *Justice as Fairness: A Restatement* Rawls says that in fact the first condition – no basis for making probability assessments – "has a relatively minor role.[W]hat is crucial is that the second and third conditions should obtain to a high degree" (JF, 99).

31 Critics (e.g., Harsanyi, op. cit.) of Rawls's maximin strategy contend that Rawls assumes the parties in the original position are too conservative, as if Rawls imagines the parties to have a psychological aversion to risk and that they follow maximin or some other conservative rule of choice in all circumstances. But the parties have no such psychological aversion: rather they have all different kinds of

attitudes towards risk, but are ignorant of these particular facts about themselves just as they are ignorant of all other particular facts. Rawls is claiming instead that it is rational for *anyone*, even people who enjoy taking risks, to follow the maximin strategy in the original position. This implies that, in the original position behind the veil of ignorance, even those who strongly value a lifestyle of gambling or risking their lives in dangerous pursuits would not jeopardize their rights to engage in their life plans of precarious pursuits.

32 See TJ, 207–08/181–82 rev.; JF, 102, 105.

33 Anthony Appiah makes a version of this argument in his Thinking It Through, Oxford, UK: Oxford University Press, 2003, 255–56. The argument is frequently made that Rawls's difference principle is compatible with a society where everyone is moderately poor. But Rawls makes persuasive empirical assumptions about how economic systems work (e.g., the chain-connectedness and close-knittedness of economic distributions, TJ, sect. 13) that show that this will not occur in a society where the position of the least advantaged is maximized.

34 See TJ, 176–77/153–54 rev.; see also Rawls, Collected Papers, 250–52 for further discussion of the strains of commitment.

35 David Gauthier and Jean Hampton, among others, raise this objection. (See bibliography references under subheading "Rawls and Social Contract Doctrine.") Actually the parties are not described the same way. They have different conceptions of the good, for example. The fact that they do not know the specifics of their conceptions of the good, or any other distinguishing facts about themselves, does not imply they are the same person, any more than the fact that a group of mathematicians, all intently focused on proving the same theorem while abstracting from their personal features and differences, are the same person.

36 See Rawls, Collected Papers, 250.

37 "The Independence of Moral Theory," in Rawls, Collected Papers, 294. See also, "Reply to Alexander and Musgrave," Collected Papers, 232–36 for an extended discussion.

38 See TJ, sect. 69; CP, 232–36. The idea of a well-ordered society occupies a position akin to Kant's Realm of Ends, as Rawls says, CP, 264. Cf. Rawls's remarks on Kant's Realm of Ends in his Collected Papers, 505–06, 508, 526; also Rawls, Lectures on the History of Moral Philosophy, 203–11, 311–13, 321–22.

39 A teleological moral conception, as Rawls defines it (TJ, 24/21–22 rev.), includes most, but not all, the conceptions more commonly known as "consequentialist." See Samuel Freeman, "Utilitarianism, Deontology, and the Priority of Right," Philosophy and Public Affairs, 23, 1994, 313–16 on this topic.

40 See TJ, 177–78/154–55 rev. The publicity condition is introduced at TJ, 133/115 rev.

41 For this and other reasons, Henry Sidgwick said that the principle of utility may be better satisfied when it is a non-public or "esoteric

morality." The implication is that people should be misled to believe that some other principle provides standards for right and justice. See Sidgwick, *Methods of Ethics* (7th ed.), Indianapolis, Hachett, 1981, 489–90.

42 For a thorough discussion of Rawls's argument from self-respect, see Joshua Cohen, "Democratic Equality," *Ethics*, 99, 1989, 727–51.

43 See "The Independence of Moral Theory," in Rawls, *Collected Papers*, 293.

44 See "Kantian Constructivism in Moral Theory," in *Collected Papers*, 325–26. See also 293, where Rawls indicates that a further reason for publicity is that it educates people to the Kantian conception of the person as a "free and equal rational being."

45 See *Collected Papers*, chapter 11, "Some Reasons for the Maximin Criterion."

46 Rawls does intimate the centrality of these ideas for the difference principle: "What is at issue, then, is. . . whether the difference principle or the principle of restricted utility is more appropriate to the conceptions of citizens as free and equal, and of society as a fair system of cooperation between citizens as so viewed" (JF, 122).

47 This problem becomes all the more pressing when Rawls seems to admit, late in his career, that because of the "burdens of judgment" general agreement on justice as fairness, or on any single liberal conception of justice, among members of any well-ordered society, is unrealistic; more likely citizens will agree upon different liberal conceptions guaranteeing a social minimum, including numerous mixed conceptions, like restricted utility. See Rawls, *Collected Papers*, 582–3, 614 –15. This suggests that, even under the best circumstances, at least some of the more advantaged will reason as the objection suggests.

48 Two ways the difference principle is egalitarian are that (1) it requires that inequalities be justifiable to everyone, beginning with the least advantaged, and (2) as shown by the graph in TJ, sect. 13, figure 6 and in JF, 62, reproduced above p. 191, it requires the distribution of primary social goods at the point on the OP curve that is closest to the equality line.

FIVE JUST INSTITUTIONS

1 In this regard, as a hypothetical inquiry into justice, Rawls's four-stage sequence differs from Jürgen Habermas's ostensibly similar ideal discourse theory. In Habermas's case, evidently, in order for laws to be not only legitimate or just, they must be *actually* agreed to by real persons in the world under certain very stringent conditions enforcing requirements of freedom and equality.

2 Rawls recognizes that there is a range of constitutional "arrangements that are both just and feasible," and the task of constitutional delegates is to choose from within that range "those which are most likely to lead to a just and effective legal order" (TJ, 198/173 rev.).

3 Here I follow Rawls's own account of Locke's social contract doctrine, as presented in his *Lectures on the History of Political Philosophy*, Lecture II on Locke, pp. 122–37.

4 See John Locke, *Second Treatise on Government*, sects. 95–99. Locke says the consent of every individual to a constitution or to specific laws "is next to impossible ever to be had" (sect. 98).

5 See JF, 48. In PL, 230, and the *Restatement* (ibid.). Rawls adds a social minimum to the constitutional essentials. Presumably this requires that in a democracy with judicial review, such as the U.S., the courts have the power to enforce the social minimum against a recalcitrant legislature bent on abolishing social insurance programs.

6 See PL, 230; JF, 48–49. See also TJ, 198/174 rev.

7 It need not be the case that everything in a written constitution is "justiciable" under judicial review. In the U.S. constitution there are several provisions that the Supreme Court historically has left up to the legislative or executive branches for interpretation, on grounds that they raise "political questions" that the Court is not in a position to arbitrate. Rawls's position here may be influenced by the history of judicial review prior to 1940, when a very conservative Supreme Court regularly struck down economic and welfare legislation passed by Congress to meet the exigencies of the Depression in the name of protecting absolute property and contract rights.

8 *National Socialist Party of America v. Skokie*, 432, U.S. Reports 43 (1977).

9 The social and/or political institutions of a society can be democratic in one of these regards, but not in another. Classical liberalism accepts the idea of a democratic society, where all are regarded as equals with equal opportunities and certain equal freedoms, but many classical liberals rejected not just democratic government, but also the idea of a democratic constitution (accepting instead some kind of constitutional monarchy). Also it is conceivable that some moral conceptions (utilitarianism for example) might accept democratic government by majority rule as the best practical method for determining measures that promote greater overall utility in society, but then also reject the idea of a democratic constitution or democratic society as a result of the substantively unequal laws that regularly result from majority rule.

10 See, for example, Jeremy Waldron's *Law and Disagreement*, New York: Oxford University Press, 2001, where he argues for a majoritarian position on grounds of fairness and individual rights. Waldron's position is not, however, welfarist, unlike the utilitarian accounts of democracy discussed above in the text.

11 Of course, many people will privately benefit, depending on their aims, even more from unjust institutions – there's nothing surprising about that, but it does not undermine the basic claim that justice is the common good among reasonable and rational citizens.

12 See Amy Gutmann and Dennis Thompson, *Democracy and Disagreement*, Cambridge, MA: Harvard University Press, 1996.

13 See Rawls's lectures on Marx in his *Lectures on the History of Political Philosophy*. Rawls distinguishes capitalism from a "property-owning democracy," where there is widespread ownership of the means of production, including ownership by laborers themselves.

14 See Branko Horvat, "Labor-Managed Economies," in *Problems of the Planned Economy*, John Eatwell, et al., eds., New York: W.W. Norton, 1990, 122.

15 For an informative discussion about how a market socialist economy should work, see John Roemer, *A Future for Socialism*, Cambridge, MA: Harvard University Press, 1994.

16 Marx argued that markets in factors of production result in "the fetishism of commodities," which is a form of false beliefs ("false consciousness") occasioned by markets that people are led to have about their social and economic relations. See Karl Marx, *Capital III*, on the fetishism of commodities.

17 Robert Nozick, *Anarchy, State, and Utopia*, New York: Basic Books, 1974, ch. 7, part II.

18 Compare Adam Smith's reference to "that universal opulence which extends itself to the lowest ranks of the people" in "a well-governed society," so that the situation of "an industrious and frugal peasant . . . exceeds that of many an African King" (*Wealth of Nations*, New York: Modern Library, 2000, 12, 13).

19 See, for example, Michael Sandel, *Liberalism and the Limits of Justice*, New York: Cambridge University Press, 1983, 1998, 2nd edition.

20 In the United States, the wealthiest 1 percent of households owns roughly 33.4% of the nation's net worth, the top 10% of households owns over 71%, and the bottom 40% of households owns less than 1%. See generally, Edward N. Wolff, "Changes in Household Wealth in the 1980s and 1990s," Working Paper no. 407, May 2004, The Levy Institute of Bard College, at www.levy.org.

21 See Barbara Fried, "Proportionate Taxation as a Fair Division of the Social Surplus: The Career of a Strange Idea," *Economics and Philosophy*, 19, 2, 2003, 211–39.

22 This does not mean that Rawls opposes the minimum wage under less than ideal conditions, such as our own. It may well be the only practicable way in the U.S. to maintain a decent living standard for unskilled workers, given middle-class aversion to public transfer payments to the least advantaged.

23 Rawls cites here Norman Daniels' *Just Health Care*, Cambridge, UK: Cambridge University Press, 1985, chs 1–3.

24 "The principles of justice do not permit subsidizing universities and institutes, or opera or the theater, on the grounds that these institutions are intrinsically valuable, and that those who engage in them are to be supported even at some significant expense to others who do not receive compensating benefits. Taxation for these purposes can be justified only as promoting directly or indirectly the social conditions that secure the equal liberties and as advancing in

an appropriate way the long-term interests of the least advantaged" (*TJ*, 332/291–92 rev.).

25 Here it is important to recall that the "least advantaged" for Rawls are conceived as normal fully functioning citizens, without special disabilities, who are able to engage in remunerative employment. The perpetually infirm and handicapped are a different issue, and are to be provided for independently of the difference principle.

26 See Susan Okin, *Justice, Gender, and the Family*, New York: Basic Books, 1989, 90–93.

SIX THE STABILITY OF JUSTICE AS FAIRNESS

1 "The Independence of Moral Theory," in CP, 294.

2 Sections 3–5, pp. 263–85 are based on my discussion in "Congruence and the Good of Justice," in *The Cambridge Companion to Rawls*, Samuel Freeman, ed., Cambridge, UK: Cambridge University Press, 2003. I am grateful to Cambridge University Press for permission to use this material.

3 Rawls discusses this aspect of Hobbes's account, and the "assurance problem," in *TJ*, 269–70/238 rev. See also Rawls's lectures on Hobbes in his *Lectures on the History of Political Philosophy*.

4 See *TJ*, 240/211 rev., on "Hobbes's Thesis." "Even in a well-ordered society the coercive powers of government are to some degree necessary for the stability of social cooperation. . . . By enforcing a public system of penalties government removes the grounds for thinking that others are not complying with the rules."

5 In *Political Liberalism* (19), Rawls defines the sense of justice in this general way: "A sense of justice is the capacity to understand, to apply, and to act from the public conception of justice . . . a sense of justice also expresses a willingness, if not the desire, to act in relation to others on terms that they also can publicly endorse."

6 See *TJ*, 46/41 rev. "Justice as fairness is a theory of our moral sentiments as manifested by our considered judgments in reflective equilibrium" (*TJ*, 120/104 rev.). Rawls initially developed this idea in his first paper, "Outline of a Decision Procedure for Ethics," (1951) in CP, ch. 1.

7 Alternatively, the sense of justice is "the desire to act in accordance with the principles that would be chosen in the original position" (*TJ*, 312/275 rev.).

8 See Rawls's *Lectures on the History of Political Philosophy*, Hume Lecture II, on the distinction between artificial and natural virtues and sentiments.

9 Rawls explicitly indicates two parts to the stability argument in *Political Liberalism*, 141, though he rephrases the issues there to fit with political liberalism.

10 Rawls uses this term, "limited altruism," taken from Hume's account of justice, to describe the parties in the original position (*TJ*,

146/127 rev.). Special ties of affection and attachments to particular individuals and ends are part of what Rawls calls "the subjective circumstances of justice" (*TJ*, 127/110 rev.).

11 Cf. Rousseau, *Emile*, Allan Bloom, trans., New York: Basic Books, 1979: "But those from whom one expects good or ill by their inner disposition, by their will – those we see acting freely for us or against us – inspire in us sentiments similar to those they manifest toward us. We seek what serves us, but we love what wants to serve us. We flee what harms us, but we hate what wants to harm us." (213).

12 See sects. 69–75 of *Theory*, especially 72 and 74. The three reciprocity principles are (quoting from *TJ* 490–91/429 rev.; note: there is a misprint in the revised edition where part of the first law is mistakenly omitted. It should read the same as in the first edition, as below):

> First law: given that family institutions are just, and that the parents love the child and manifestly express their love by caring for his good, then the child, recognizing their evident love of him, comes to love them.

> Second law: given that a person's capacity for fellow feeling has been realized by acquiring attachments in accordance with the first law, and given that a social arrangement is just and publicly known by all to be just, then this person develops ties of friendly feeling and trust toward others in the association as they with evident intention comply with their duties and obligations, and live up to the ideals of their station.

> Third law: given that a person's capacity for fellow feeling has been realized by his forming attachments in accordance with the first two laws, and given that a society's institutions are just and are publicly known by all to be just, then this person acquires the corresponding sense of justice as he recognizes that he and those for whom he cares are the beneficiaries of these arrangements.

13 For example, Brian Barry says, "My own inclination is to think that the 'Aristotelian Principle' is, as a matter of fact, false of most people most of the time" (*The Liberal Theory of Justice*, Oxford: Clarendon Press, 1973, 29).

14 Rawls's psychological construction draws upon Rousseau, Kant, and Mill, as well as Jean Piaget's work, *The Moral Judgment of the Child*, London: Free Press, 1931. See *TJ*, 459–62/402–5 rev. Piaget distinguishes between the morality of authority and the morality of mutual respect, and Rawls incorporates this distinction into his account of the development of the sense of justice.

15 This psychological law is adapted from Rousseau, *Emile*, 174.

16 Cf. *Emile*, 213.

17 "Thus self-interest is the original motive to the *establishment* of justice: but a *sympathy* with public interest is the source of the *moral approbation*

which attends that virtue" (*A Treatise of Human Nature*, 499–500). "After [justice] is once established by these conventions, it is *naturally* attended with a strong sentiment of morals; which can proceed from nothing but our sympathy with the interests of society" (ibid., 579–80). See also Hume's *Enquiry*, 201. On the sense of justice in Hume, see my paper, "Property as an Institutional Convention in Hume's Account of Justice," *Archiv für Geschichte der Philosophie*, 73, 1990, 20–49.

18 See J.S. Mill, *Utilitarianism*, ch. 3.

19 However, Rawls adds, "a marked capacity for sympathetic identification seems relatively rare" (*TJ*, 500/438 rev.).

20 See *TJ*, 502/439–40 rev., discussing J.S. Mill, *Utilitarianism*, ch. III, par. 10–11. See also Rawls's *Lectures on the History of Political Philosophy*, Lecture II on Mill, pp. 280–84.

21 See Ken Binmore, *Natural Justice*, Cambridge, MA: Harvard University Press, 2006; Allan Gibbard also makes this suggestion in his 2006 Tanner Lectures at Berkeley. Both follow Hume in this respect.

22 See *TJ*, sect. 63 for Rawls's account of these principles of rational choice.

23 See *TJ*, sect. 64 on "Deliberative Rationality." Rawls says a rational plan of life "is the plan that would be decided upon as the outcome of careful reflection in which the agent reviews, in the light of all the relevant facts, what it would be like to carry out these plans and thereby ascertained the course of action that would best realize his more fundamental desires" (*TJ*, 417/366 rev.). Deliberative rationality defines an objective point of view from which to assess a person's good and the reasons he/she has as an individual. The plan of life that a person *would* choose from this perspective is "the objectively rational plan for him and determines his real good" (ibid.). Perhaps we can never really occupy this position, given its idealizations and uncertainty about the future. But with the information we have, we can determine, Rawls says, a "subjectively rational plan," which defines our apparent good.

24 In *Political Liberalism*, xix/xxi, 1996 edition, Rawls distinguishes "the public point of view from the many nonpublic (not private) points of view," which parallels his distinction there between public versus non-public reasons.

25 Henry Sidgwick, *Methods of Ethics*, 7th edition, Indianapolis: Hackett, 1981, 404, 506–09.

26 This does not mean for Rawls that justice is not required by practical reason. The concept of rationality does not exhaust the kinds of reasons we have in his view. Rawls's account of "the reasonable" suggests there are reasons of justice that apply to us, whatever our particular ends or desires. These reasons are "categorical" in Kant's sense, and are established by reference to our considered moral judgments and on the basis of our capacities for practical reasoning. See *PL*, 111f., 115 on objectivity and the reasonable; see also "Kantian Constructivism in Moral Theory," Lecture III, "Constructivism and Objectivity," in Rawls, *CP*, 340–58.

27 "I am not trying to show that in a well-ordered society an egoist would act from a sense of justice. . . . Rather, we are concerned with the goodness of the settled desire to take up the standpoint of justice. I assume that the members of a well-ordered society already have this desire. The question is whether this regulative sentiment is consistent with their good" (TJ, 568/497–98 rev.).

28 Members of a competitive team might have the common aim, not just of winning but winning with the successful participation of each teammate; and even members of opposing teams can have a shared end of engaging in a worthy competition, and appreciate and even enjoy one another's expertise.

29 "From the definition alone very little can be said about the content of a rational plan, or the particular activities that comprise it" (TJ, 423/372 rev.).

30 Other arguments for the good of justice are suggested in sect. 89 of TJ, and include the argument from social union (sect. 79), and an instrumentalist argument (sect. 86).

31 PL, 203 and 203, n. 35.

32 See TJ, 567/497 rev.: "We should like to know that this desire is indeed rational; being rational for one, it is rational for all, and therefore no tendencies to instability exist." See also 568/497 rev. Rawls seems to allow, however, that there may be some in a WOS for whom the sense of justice is not a good (TJ, 575–76/504 rev.).

33 See S. Kierkegaard Either/Or, vol. I, Princeton: Princeton University Press, 1944.

34 See "Kantian Constructivism in Moral Theory," in CP, ch. 16.

35 In "Kantian Constructivism," Rawls refers to the original position as a "procedure of construction." See CP, 340; see also 310–12.

36 Here I interpret the final argument for congruence Rawls suggests in TJ, sect. 86. See especially 572/501 rev., first paragraph, in conjunction with 445/390 rev., 515–16/452–3 rev., then all of sects. 40 and 85, and other pages cited in the text. I provide here only the main strands of argument Rawls weaves together, without detailed elaboration.

37 "The nature of the self as a free and equal moral person is the same for all" (TJ, 565/495 rev.).

38 See also CP, 309.

39 As Rawls makes clearer in "Kantian Constructivism in Moral Theory," the original position can be construed as a "procedural representation" or "modeling" of central features of the conception of moral persons, so that the principles chosen there are determined by these defining features. See CP, 308.

40 Rawls says there is a "practical identity" between these two desires. TJ, 572/501 rev. Cf. "Properly understood, then, the desire to act justly derives in part from the desire to express most fully what we are or can be, namely free and equal rational beings with a liberty to choose" (TJ, 256/225 rev.).

41 See also TJ, 528/462–63 rev.: "When all strive to comply with these principles and each succeeds, then individually and collectively their nature as moral persons is most fully realized, and with it their individual and collective good."

42 Cf. "These principles are then given absolute precedence . . . and each frames his plans in conformity" (TJ, 565/495 rev.).

43 Recall the criticisms that the sense of justice either (a) masks our weaknesses (Nietzsche), or (b) is an outgrowth of envy and jealousy (Freud) (cf. TJ, 539f./472–73 rev.). Or suppose (c) the sense of justice were furtively instilled in us by those in power, to insure obedience to rules designed to advance their interests (cf. TJ, 515/452 rev.).

44 TJ, 505/442 rev., 561/491 rev.; CP, 312–13.

45 "Fairness to Goodness," in CP, 284.

46 See TJ, sect. 77, "The Basis of Equality"; see also CP, 330–33.

47 "[T]he two moral powers [are] the necessary and sufficient conditions for being counted a full and equal member of society in questions of political justice" (PL, 302).

48 As Rawls contends in TJ, sect. 85, "The Unity of the Self," 561–63/491–93 rev.

49 "The Basic Liberties and Their Priority," Lecture VIII, PL, 306. Rawls distinguishes two kinds of autonomy in "Kantian Constructivism," and later in Political Liberalism, each of which is associated with one of the moral powers. "Rational autonomy" is acting on a rational plan of life, hence according to principles of rational choice while pursuing ends that are part of the plan of life one would choose in deliberative rationality. "Moral autonomy" is acting on and from the principles of justice. "Full autonomy" involves the combination of these, where justice is given highest-order priority in regulating one's rational plan. In this regard, full autonomy involves the congruence of the right and the good. See "Kantian Constructivism" (in CP, ch. 17) Lecture I, entitled "Rational and Full Autonomy," esp. 308; PL, 72–81.

SEVEN KANTIAN CONSTRUCTIVISM

1 The first three chapters of Political Liberalism are a substantial revision of the three Dewey Lectures, "Kantian Constructivism in Moral Theory," in CP, ch. 16.

2 See Martha Nussbaum, Frontiers of Justice, Cambridge, MA: Harvard University Press, 2006, ch. 3.

3 J. J. Rousseau, Du contrat social, Paris: Flammarion, 2001, 61 (Bk. I, ch. 8, par. 3).

4 Examples are cultural relativism, some versions of communitarianism, and social constructivism as conceived by social theorists (which is very different from moral constructivism).

5 Of constructivism in moral philosophy and mathematics Rawls says: "In both cases the idea is to formulate a procedural representa-

tion in which . . . all the relevant criteria of correct reasoning – mathematical, moral, political – are incorporated and open to view. Judgments are reasonable and sound if they result in following the correct procedure correctly and rely only on true premises" (PL, 102).

6 See "Kantian Constructivism in Moral Theory," The Dewey Lectures, in John Rawls, Collected Papers, 307.

7 Burton Dreben once made this point in conversation about Rawls's constructivism. Thomas Ricketts makes a similar claim with regard to Frege's understanding of logic.

8 Locke's social contract is the exception, since he grounds the social compact in self-evident moral truths that represent God's natural laws, the main one being that all men are created free and equal, with a duty to preserve themselves and the rest of mankind. On this, see Rawls, Lecture I on Locke in LHPP.

9 Ibid.

10 "Outline for a Decision Procedure in Ethics," from 1951. See Rawls's Collected Papers, ch. 1.

11 The "construction" of value or of "the good" is a subject Rawls only discusses later, in Political Liberalism (Lecture V), and in his Kant lectures, in LHMP.

12 On the division of moral labor between background institutions and individuals, see the paper by Samuel Scheffler, "The Division of Moral Labor: Egalitarian Liberalism as Moral Pluralism," Proceedings of the Aristotelian Society, supp. vol. 79, 2005, 229–53.

13 See Sandel, Liberalism and the Limits of Justice, Cambridge: Cambridge University Press, 1982.

14 In conversations, Rawls said that he thought that both Charles Taylor's and Alasdair MacIntyre's communitarianism were motivated by a kind of perfectionism that stems from their Catholic backgrounds. Rawls has surprisingly little to say about communitarianism in his written works, though he refers to Will Kymlicka's reply in Liberalism, Community, and Culture, Oxford: Oxford University Press, 1989, as "on the whole satisfactory" (PL, 27n.).

15 "The Independence of Moral Theory," Collected Papers, 292–93.

16 See Steven Pinker, The Blank Slate: The Modern Denial of Human Nature, New York: Penguin Books, 2002, 2.

17 Michael Smith, The Moral Problem, Oxford: Blackwell, 1994, 2.

18 See his "Outline for a Decision Procedure in Ethics" (1951), chapter 1 of Collected Papers. This paper was indirectly influenced by Wittgenstein's work, which was popular at the time.

19 Kant's Critique of Pure Reason attempts to show the limits of knowledge accessible to theoretical reason and what we can and cannot know about the universe. It denies the possibility of metaphysical knowledge outside the domains of science (broadly construed).

20 Hare says, "The requirement to universalize our prescriptions, which is itself a logical requirement if we are reasoning morally, demands that we treat other people's prescriptions (i.e. their desires, likings, and

in general preferences) as if they were our own" (R.M. Hare, *Moral Thinking*, New York: Oxford University Press, 1981, 16–17).

21 See Derek Parfit, *Reasons and Persons*, Oxford: Clarendon Press, 1984, part III.

22 Cf. Rawls's discussion in *Political Liberalism* of Kant's Moral Constructivism, 99–101.

23 Rawls's reasons for the fact of reasonable pluralism rest on his account of "the burdens of judgment" (PL, 54–58) which were implicit in his initial account of the subjective circumstances of justice in *Theory* (TJ, 127/110 rev.).

24 For a liberal Thomist position that resembles justice as fairness, see Jacques Maritain, *Man and the State*, Chicago: University of Chicago Press, 1951.

EIGHT POLITICAL LIBERALISM I – THE DOMAIN OF THE POLITICAL

1 This is in fact the third statement of the problem Rawls says *Political Liberalism* is designed to address, and is a "combination" that includes two "fundamental questions." The first "fundamental question" is: "What is the most appropriate conception of justice for specifying the fair terms of cooperation between citizens regarded as free and equal, and as fully cooperating members of a society over a complete life, from one generation to the next?" (PL, 3). The second is: "What are the grounds of toleration so understood and given the fact of reasonable pluralism as the inevitable outcome of free institutions?" (PL, 4).

2 Steven Pinker in *The Blank Slate*, New York: Penguin, 2002, 2, cites even more striking figures from polls taken by Opinion Dynamics, Gallup, and Princeton Survey Research Associates, which are made available through the Roper Center at the University of Connecticut, www.ropercenter.uconn.edu.

3 Is Darwinian evolutionary theory "non-comprehensive" doctrine for Rawls? Most of modern biology depends upon it. As noted earlier, it is not generally accepted as an account of the origin of our species by most Americans, many of whom are "reasonable and rational" according to Rawls's criteria. Since nothing Rawls argues for in *Political Liberalism* significantly depends upon Darwinism, there is no present need to settle this vexing issue, though the question does need to be settled at some point in order to decide the legitimate scope and content of public reason and the considerations that can be invoked in argument in trials and other forums in a democratic society.

4 In "Kantian Constructivism" Rawls said "self-originating" rather than "self-authenticating." The change may be due to Michael Sandel's criticisms that Rawls's conception of the person assumes the liberal illusion that people create their own conception of the good, as if it

were not the product of years of conditioning, education, and social influence. In using "self-authenticating" Rawls signals that he recognizes that we do not form our conceptions of the good *ab initio.* Nonetheless, we do "authenticate" them once we reach maturity, or we often seek to revise them in part and pursue different ends than those we were trained to appreciate.

5 See "Justice and Rights," in Dworkin's *Taking Rights Seriously,* Cambridge, MA: Harvard University Press, 1977.

6 Rawls says: "As a device of representation the idea of the original position serves as a means of public reflection and self-clarification. It helps us to work out what we now think, once we are able to take a clear and uncluttered view of what justice requires when society is conceived as a scheme of cooperation between free and equal citizens from one generation to the next" (PL, 26). Rawls addresses Dworkin more directly in *Collected Papers,* 400–01n.

7 "Outline of a Decision Procedure in Ethics" (1951), *Collected Papers,* ch. 1.

8 See Burton Dreben, "On Rawls and Political Liberalism," in *The Cambridge Companion to Rawls,* Samuel Freeman, ed., Cambridge, UK: Cambridge University Press, 2003, ch. 8.

9 Many think that political liberalism itself is a controversial philosophical position open to reasonable disagreement, but this is a separate issue. Rawls would not dispute this, though he might insist that reasonable disagreement itself does not rule out there being a *most* reasonable position (which he thinks is embodied by political liberalism).

10 See PL, 58–66 on reasonable comprehensive doctrines. There is a peculiar ambiguity in Rawls's idea of "reasonable comprehensive doctrines." On the one hand he defines them epistemically, as doctrines that are responsive to evidence and possess certain other features (PL, 58–66). But on the other hand, he initially characterizes them as "the doctrines that reasonable citizens affirm" (PL, 36) and sometimes reverts to this usage. As we'll see, in order to make sense of Rawls's idea of overlapping consensus, the epistemic version must be relied upon; for if the latter definition applies, overlapping consensus becomes trivial.

11 PL, 49n. Rawls says that reasonableness is closely connected with T.M. Scanlon's contractualist principle of motivation set forth in "Contractualism and Utilitarianism," in Scanlon, *The Difficulty of Tolerance,* Cambridge: Cambridge University Press, 2003, 124–50.

12 Joshua Cohen contends that Rawls's eschewal of the concept of truth within political liberalism is an unnecessary holdover from Kantian Constructivism. Cohen argues that in political liberalism there should be a role for the concept of political truth of first principles within public reason, and that this can be done without subscribing to any metaphysical position regarding the nature of truth. See his paper "Truth Matters," (forthcoming).

13 Philosophers who advocate moral skepticism normally insist that their skepticism has no effect on their moral reasoning or moral sincerity. Moreover, academics in American law schools often profess

to be moral and legal positivists who deny the truth-value of claims of justice; still, as lawyers they reason within the framework of common, statutory, and constitutional law, including the moral concepts laws often employ (reasonable person, due care, equal protection, due process, etc.), and they believe that legal conclusions are more or less reasonable and warranted given the sophisticated framework for legal reasoning.

14 Whether they *are* universally objective or true is not of course a question addressed by political liberalism. Does this suggest that they might *not* be true? It is of course a possibility, but Rawls believes it is highly unlikely that the principles of justice that are in an overlapping consensus among all reasonable doctrines are false. For if any of the reasonable comprehensive doctrines that affirm the political conception is true, then the political conception itself is true (PL, 128). Rawls believes that all reasonable comprehensive liberal conceptions should be able to affirm the political conception of justice, including Kant's and Mill's liberalism, and the liberalism of such contemporary philosophers as Ronald Dworkin and Joseph Raz. Here it is notable that both Dworkin and Raz have challenged Rawls's political liberalism, including the idea of public reason. See my *Justice and the Social Contract*, New York: Oxford University Press, 2007, ch. 8 for a discussion.

NINE POLITICAL LIBERALISM II – OVERLAPPING CONSENSUS AND PUBLIC REASON

1 On the peculiarity of toleration, see T.M. Scanlon, in *The Difficulty of Tolerance*, New York: Cambridge University Press, 2003, ch. 10.

2 See TJ, 490–91/429–30 rev. for a concise statement of the reciprocity principles.

3 Thanks to Gopal Sreenivasan for helping me to clarify this point.

4 "In justice as fairness, then, the guidelines of public reason and the principles of justice have essentially the same grounds. They are companion parts of one agreement" (PL, 226–27).

5 *Political Liberalism*, 217. Rawls's initial statement of the principle is at PL, 137; a later statement is in "Reply to Habermas," PL, 393; Rawls's final statement of the principle in "Public Reason Revisited" is in PL, 446–47, and CP, 578. The latter clearly indicates the relationship between legitimacy and public reason: "Our exercise of political power is proper only when we sincerely believe that the reasons we would offer for our political actions – were we to state them as government officials – are sufficient, and we also reasonably think that other citizens might reasonably accept those reasons." See also the earlier statement of the principle in Rawls's Harvard lecture notes, *Justice as Fairness: A Restatement*, ed. Erin Kelly, Cambridge, MA: Harvard University Press, 2001, 41, 84, 90–91. For a discussion of how political legitimacy is related to but differs from justice, see PL, 427–29.

6 *Political Liberalism*, 217, emphasis added. A duty of civility is in *A Theory of Justice*, but is stated differently: It "imposes a due acceptance of the defects of [just] institutions and a certain restraint in taking advantage of them" (*TJ*, 355/312 rev.). Rawls appealed to this duty to argue for a duty to normally comply with unjust laws provided that they do not exceed certain bounds of injustice.

7 This raises a related issue (discussed in the final section below) regarding the "proviso" that must be satisfied when we argue for political decisions in terms of our comprehensive doctrines. What exactly does the duty of civility require of us when we explicitly appeal to comprehensive reasons?

8 "The Idea of Public Reason Revisited," in CP, 578, also LP, 136–37, PL, 446–47. The criterion of reciprocity is also formulated to say that we are to give "reasons we might reasonably expect that they, as free and equal citizens, might reasonably also accept" (CP, 579). The qualification regarding free and equal citizens is crucial here.

Notice that in the final statement of the principle of legitimacy (in "Public Reason Revisited," CP, 578, PL, 446–47) Rawls says it is "based on the criterion of reciprocity," which applies both at the level of constitutional structure, and to particular statutes and laws. "Our exercise of political power is proper only when we sincerely believe that the reasons we would offer for our political actions – were we to state them as government officials – are sufficient, and we also reasonably think that other citizens might also reasonably accept those reasons" as free and equal citizens. This suggests that, for laws to be legitimate, those voting for them must not simply believe that they conform to a constitution all can reasonably accept, but also believe that particular laws must themselves be justifiable for reasons they can reasonably expect that others, as free and equal citizens, might reasonably also accept (CP, 579, PL, 447). This might make the standard of legitimacy more stringent than Rawls's earlier statements, which refer only to the reasonable acceptability of the constitution. If particular laws must also meet the criterion of reciprocity, then it considerably narrows the range of unjust laws that can be legitimate, and which citizens therefore have a duty to obey. Here it may be relevant that this final statement of the principle of legitimacy incorporates reference to the sincere *beliefs* of citizens, whereas none of the previous statements do. Taking the principles together, they imply at least that for laws to be legitimate (1) those voting for them must sincerely *believe* that they conform to the criterion of reciprocity, and (2) even if particular laws do not so conform, they must at least conform to a constitution that itself conforms to the criterion of reciprocity, and hence is reasonably acceptable to free and equal citizens.

9 Here I follow David Reidy's helpful distinction between reciprocity of advantage and reciprocity of justification, in his paper "Reciprocity and Reasonable Disagreement: From Liberal to Democratic Legitimacy," *Philosophical Studies* (forthcoming 2007).

10 See PL, 393, 427–29. "It is unreasonable to expect in general that human statutes and laws should be strictly just by our lights" (PL, 393n.). See also TJ, sect. 53; Collected Papers, 578.

11 Rawls indicates that the difference principle should not be part of a democratic constitution with judicial review (JF, 162). Since economic decisions are often quite difficult and reasonable people can disagree about policies that conform to the difference principle, judges should not second-guess democratically deliberated decisions. On the other hand, Rawls does see a basic social minimum as judicially enforceable; so a legislature which substantially repeals welfare and social security provisions can be legitimately reversed on judicial review.

12 Does a lack of liberal legitimacy mean these provisions were unjustly enacted? This would seem to depend on the degree of injustice that illegitimate decisions correct for. Surely Lincoln's Emancipation Proclamation, freeing Southern slaves, was not unjust even if not technically legitimate under the Constitution. It might have been better for Lincoln to have sought legislative or constitutional enactments legitimating abolition; but even without that, it is difficult to say that an unauthorized proclamation freeing all the slaves would be unjust. For exercise of political power enforcing slavery cannot be just or legitimate under any circumstances according to Rawls's criteria.

13 "But if each citizen is to have an equal share in political power, then, so far as possible, political power should be exercised, at least when constitutional essentials and questions of basic justice are at stake, in ways that all citizens can publicly endorse in the light of their own reason. This is the principle of political legitimacy that justice as fairness is to satisfy" (JF, 90–91).

14 Political Liberalism, 213; see also CP, 577: "The idea of public reason arises from a conception of democratic citizenship in a constitutional democracy."

15 Rawls in conversation in the 1990s was surprised that others thought that Theory committed him to denying a democratic society the authority to publicly support perfectionist cultural institutions. His position in Theory is not I believe inconsistent with public opera, museums, symphonies, etc. that are supported by "user fees." But given their great costs cultural institutions are rarely supportable by user fees alone.

16 On the resemblance with Rousseau, see PL, 219–20, where Rawls says: "Public reason with its duty of civility gives a view about voting on fundamental questions in some ways reminiscent of Rousseau's Social Contract. He saw voting as ideally expressing our opinion as to which of the alternatives best advances the common good." See David Reidy's "Rawls's View of Public Reason: Not Wide Enough," Res Publica, 6 (2000), 49–72, for the suggestion that political autonomy requires public reason.

17 See Political Liberalism, at xlviii; LP, 49. As mentioned earlier, from "The Idea of an Overlapping Consensus" and Political Liberalism, it is apparent that Rawls sees all liberal political conceptions as protecting basically the same set of abstract basic liberties that he says are protected by his first

principle of justice: namely, liberty of conscience and freedom of thought, freedom of association and equal political liberties, the freedom specified by the liberty and integrity of the person, and the rights and liberties covered by the ideal of the rule of law. See CP, 421, 440 n. 27; PL, 6, 291–94. Since these liberties, along with equal opportunities and adequate all-purpose means, can be understood in different ways, Rawls says there are many liberalisms (ibid. at 6).

18 *Political Liberalism*, lviii–lix.
19 *The Law of Peoples*, at 49.
20 See also LP, 50–51.
21 "Discourse on Political Economy," in Rousseau, *The Basic Political Writings*, Indianapolis, IN: Hackett, 1987, 113.
22 CP, 580.
23 *The Law of Peoples*, 50. For the relationship between public reason and deliberative democracy, see the articles by Joshua Cohen, "Deliberation and Democratic Legitimacy," in *The Good Polity*, Alan Hamlin and Philip Petit eds., New York: Oxford University Press, 1989, 17, 21, 24; "For a Democratic Society," *The Cambridge Companion to Rawls*, Samuel Freeman, ed., Cambridge, UK: Cambridge University Press, 2003, 86.
24 Still, I doubt that Rawls intended to compromise as a condition of political legitimacy the basic requirements on a liberal political conception, including the basic liberties of the first principle of justice, their priority, and the provision of all-purpose means. It is not so clear then how much leeway is envisioned by his claims regarding the flexibility of public reason.
25 That possession of (a capacity for) the moral powers is sufficient for constitutional personhood takes care of the ridiculous argument which says that, "For pro-choice advocates to question the personhood of the fetus is just like supporters of slavery questioning the personhood of slaves." The correct reply is that clearly slaves possess the moral powers and deserve to be treated as persons, and it is not at all clear – indeed all the empirical evidence is to the contrary – whether fetuses do.
26 I am grateful to Joshua Cohen for this argument.

TEN THE LAW OF PEOPLES

1 See Charles Beitz, *Political Theory and International Relations*, Princeton, NJ: Princeton University Press, 1979; Thomas Pogge, *Realizing Rawls*, Ithaca, NY: Cornell University Press, 1989, Part III; K.C. Tan, *Toleration, Diversity, and Social Justice*, University Park, PA: Penn State Press, 2000; Brian Barry, *Theories of Justice*, Berkeley, CA: University of California Press, 1989, 189.
2 See Charles Beitz, "International Liberalism and Distributive Justice: A Survey of Recent Thought," *World Politics*, 51, 1999, 269–96 at 287; and K.C. Tan, *Justice without Borders*, New York: Cambridge University Press, 2004, 10–12.
3 In a well-known review of *A Theory of Justice* Dworkin contends that justice as fairness is really based in this fundamental idea of equal

concern and respect. Ronald Dworkin, "The Original Position," in his *Taking Rights Seriously*, Cambridge, MA: Harvard University Press, 1977, 150–83. Dworkin himself denies that equal concern and respect implies a cosmopolitan position.

4 This is the only entry under "equal respect" in Rawls's thorough index to *A Theory of Justice*. It is noteworthy that there are separate entries for "respect for persons," "mutual respect," and "self-respect."

5 On some metaphysical conceptions which see having a conception of the self as necessary to personality, we are not even persons in the absence of society, but simply members of the human species. Rawls cannot appeal to this within political liberalism to justify giving priority to social justice.

6 Even then peoples and their members can exist and have sometimes even thrived in their own way largely independently from other societies.

7 See, for example, Brian Barry, *Theories of Justice*, Berkeley, CA: University of California Press, 1989, sects. 23, 29, who follows Robert Nozick's attack on Rawls's argument for the significance of social cooperation to justice in *Anarchy, State, and Utopia*, New York: Basic Books, 1974, 183–89.

8 K.C. Tan, in *Justice without Borders*, Cambridge, UK: Cambridge University Press, 2004, has suggested that cosmopolitans can recognize non-instrumental duties towards members of one's own society that are not owed to others in the world.

9 See Kant's essay "Perpetual Peace," in *Perpetual Peace and Other Essays*, trans. Ted Humphrey, Indianapolis: Hackett, 1983, 113.

10 See LP, 36, 48.

11 See, for example, Thomas Pogge, who in "An Egalitarian Law of Peoples," *Philosophy and Public Affairs*, 23, 1994, 195–224, argues that, if given the opportunity, Rawls's parties would choose a global resource tax of 1 percent to be distributed to less advantaged peoples.

12 Rawls's account of a decent society differs in some ways from Avishai Margalit's account in *The Decent Society*, Cambridge, MA: Harvard University Press, 1996. Margalit says a decent society's institutions accord respect to those under its authority, but unlike Rawls, he holds that "The concept of a decent society is not necessarily connected with the concept of rights." Human rights are for Rawls essential to a decent society.

13 This is Thomas Pogge's claim in "An Egalitarian Law of Peoples"; see also K.C. Tan, *Toleration, Diversity, and Social Justice*, 30–31.

14 See David Miller, *Citizenship and National Identity*, Cambridge: Polity Press, 2000, 174.

15 "One aim of the law of nations is to assure the recognition of these [natural] duties in the conduct of states" (TJ, 115/99 rev.).

16 "Thus the complete statement of the difference principle includes the savings principle as a constraint" (TJ, 292/258 rev.).

17 See Brian Barry, *The Liberal Theory of Justice*, 128–33; Charles Beitz, *Political Theory and International Relations*, 127–69; Thomas Pogge, *Realizing*

Rawls, ch. 6; K.C. Tan, Justice without Borders, 7, 55–61; Darrel Moellendorf, Cosmopolitan Justice, Boulder, CO: Westview, 2002, 49.

18 Beitz, Pogge, Tan, and Barry all make the inconsistency argument against Rawls. Of a person born into a country with poor population or bad economic policies, Tan says, "These are mere accidents of birth, and are as morally arbitrary as is being born into wealth or poverty in the domestic context" (Tan, Justice without Borders, 73). See also Beitz, Political Theory and International Relations, 139; Barry, Theories of Justice, 189.

19 See Jon Mandle, Global Justice, Cambridge: Polity Press, 2006, ch. 6 for relevant figures.

20 See TJ sects. 13 and 42; JF, sect. 41.

21 See, for example, JF, 176, 178 where Rawls endorses Mill's idea of worker-owned cooperatives as part of a property-owning democracy. See also LP, 107–8n. on Mill on the "stationary state" and the "labouring class."

22 The extent and powers of global institutions are greatly exaggerated in my view by Rawls's cosmopolitan critics.

23 See, for example, K.C. Tan, Justice Without Borders, 34–35. Much of Thomas Pogge's case for a global distribution principle depends also on abject world poverty and the complicity of advantaged nations in sustaining corrupt rulers. See his World Poverty and Human Rights, Cambridge: Polity Press, 2002.

24 For an informative discussion see Mandle, Global Justice, ch. 7.

25 Thomas Pogge, "Priorities of Global Justice," Metaphilosophy, 32, 2001, 6–24, at 16–17.

26 Cf. Rawls's claim: "It is surely a good for individuals and associations to be attached to their particular culture and to take part in its common public and civic life. . . . This is no small thing. It argues for preserving significant room for the idea of a people's self-determination" (LP, 111).

27 Rex Martin has argued for the appropriateness of a global minimum.

28 I am grateful to Samuel Scheffler and Joshua Cohen for helping me to formulate the ideas in these last paragraphs.

Pages 444–55 of this chapter are adapted from my paper "Distributive Justice and the Law of Peoples," in Rawls's Law of Peoples: A Realistic Utopia?, Rex Martin and David Reidy, eds., Oxford, UK: Blackwell, 2006. I am grateful to Blackwell for permission to use this material.

ELEVEN CONCLUSION

1 G.A. Cohen, one of Rawls's most trenchant and persistent critics says in the Introduction to his forthcoming book on Rawls, Saving Justice from Constructivism: "I believe that there are at most two books in the history of Western political philosophy that are greater than A Theory of Justice, and they are Plato's Republic and Hobbes's Leviathan."

Bibliography

The following bibliography is necessarily selective. Rawls's complete works are cited first. Then follows a list of books and anthologies on Rawls. Most of the bibliography consists of citations of journal articles. The two largest divisions of the bibliography list articles on *A Theory of Justice* and *Political Liberalism*. Other divisions reflect topics of special interest which have stimulated discussions of parts of Rawls's work or its implications.

WORKS BY JOHN RAWLS

"A Study on the Grounds of Ethical Knowledge: Considered with Reference to Judgments on the Moral Worth of Character," Ph.D. Dissertation, Princeton University, 1950, Dissertation Abstracts 15, 1955, 608–09.

"Outline of a Decision Procedure for Ethics," *Philosophical Review* 60, 1951, 177–97.

"A review of Stephen Toulmin's An Examination of the Place of Reason in Ethics," *Philosophical Review* 60, 1951, 572–80.

"A Review of Axel Hägerstrom's Inquiries into the Nature of Law and Morals (translated by C.D. Broad)," *Mind* 64, 1955, 421–22.

"Two Concepts of Rules," *Philosophical Review* 64, 1955, 3–32.

"Justice as Fairness": The first version of this paper, published in *Journal of Philosophy* 54, 1957, 653–62, was read before the American Philosophical Association, Eastern Division Meetings. An expanded version appeared in *Philosophical Review* 67, 1958, 164–94. It is this version that is most frequently anthologized. Another revised version was translated into French by Jean-Fabien Spitz as "La Justice comme équité," *Philosophie* 14, 1987, 39–69.

"Review of Raymond Klibansky, ed., Philosophy in Mid-Century: A Survey," *Philosophical Review* 70, 1961, 131–32.

"Constitutional Liberty and the Concept of Justice," in *Nomos VI: Justice*, C. Friedrich and John W. Chapman, eds, New York: Atherton, 1963, 98–125.

"The Sense of Justice," *Philosophical Review* 72, 1963, 281–305.

"Legal Obligation and the Duty of Fair Play," in *Law and Philosophy*, ed. Sidney Hook, New York: New York University Press, 1964, 3–18.

"Review of Social Justice, ed. Richard Brandt," *Philosophical Review* 74, 1965, 406–09.

"Distributive Justice": The first version of this paper was published in *Philosophy, Politics, and Society*, Third Series, ed., P. Laslett and W.G. Runciman, Oxford: Basil Blackwell, 1967, 58–82. This essay and the essay "Distributive Justice: Some Addenda" were combined to form a second "Distributive Justice" in *Economic Justice*, E. Phelps, ed., London: Penguin Books, 1973, 319–62.

"Distributive Justice: Some Addenda," *Natural Law Forum* 13, 1968, 51–71.

"The Justification of Civil Disobedience," in *Civil Disobedience*, Hugo Bedau, ed., New York: Pegasus, 1969, 240–55.

"Justice as Reciprocity" (written in 1958), in *Mill: Text with Critical Essays*, Samuel Gorovitz, ed., Indianapolis, IN: Bobbs-Merrill, 1971, 242–68.

A Theory of Justice, Cambridge, MA: Harvard University Press, 1971. *A Theory of Justice* has been translated into Chinese, Finnish, French, German, Italian, Japanese, Korean, Portuguese, and Spanish, and twenty other languages. For the first of these, the German translation of 1975, Rawls made some revisions, which have been incorporated into all of the translations.

A Theory of Justice, revised edition, Cambridge, MA: Harvard University Press, 1999. This edition includes the revisions made for the 1975 German translation and the 1988 French translation.

"Reply to Lyons and Teitelman," *Journal of Philosophy* 69, 1972, 556–57.

"Some Reasons for the Maximin Criterion," *American Economic Review* 64, 1974, 141–6.

"Reply to Alexander and Musgrave," *Quarterly Journal of Economics* 88, 1974, 633–55.

"The Independence of Moral Theory," *Proceedings and Addresses of the American Philosophical Association* 48, 1975, 5–22.

"A Kantian Conception of Equality," *Cambridge Review* 1975, 94–99. Reprinted as "A Well-Ordered Society" in *Philosophy, Politics, and Society*, Vol. 5, P. Laslett and J. Fishkin, eds., Oxford: Blackwell, 1979, 6–20.

"Fairness to Goodness," *Philosophical Review* 84, 1975, 536–54.

"The Basic Structure as Subject": The first version was published in the *American Philosophical Quarterly* 14, 1977, 159–65. A revised and expanded version appears in *Values and Morals: Essays in Honor of William Frankena, Charles Stevenson, and Richard B. Brandt*, A. Goldman and J. Kim, eds., Dordrecht: Reidel, 1978, 47–71.

"Kantian Constructivism in Moral Theory: The Dewey Lectures 1980," *Journal of Philosophy* 77, 1980, 515–72.

"Social Unity and Primary Goods," in *Utilitarianism and Beyond*, Amartya Sen and Bernard Williams, eds., Cambridge: Cambridge University Press, 1982, 159–85.

"The Basic Liberties and Their Priority," *Tanner Lectures on Human Values*, Volume III, Salt Lake City: University of Utah Press, 1982, 3–87.

"Justice as Fairness: Political not Metaphysical," *Philosophy and Public Affairs* 14, 1985, 223–251.

"On the Idea of an Overlapping Consensus," *Oxford Journal for Legal Studies* 7, 1987, 1–25.

"The Priority of Right and Ideas of the Good," *Philosophy and Public Affairs* 17, 1988, 251–276.

"Themes in Kant's Moral Philosophy," in *Kant's Transcendental Deductions*, E. Förster, ed., Stanford: Stanford University Press, 1989, 81–113.

"The Domain of the Political and Overlapping Consensus," *New York University Law Review* 64, 1989, 233–55.

"Roderick Firth: His Life and Work," *Philosophy and Phenomenological Research* 51, 1991, 109–18.

Political Liberalism, New York: Columbia University Press, 1993; the revised paperback edition, 1996, includes an additional Preface, and the 1995 paper "Reply to Habermas." The 2005 expanded edition includes the essay "The Idea of Public Reason Revisited."

"The Law of Peoples," in *On Human Rights: The Oxford Amnesty Lectures*, 1993, Steven Shute and Susan Hurley, eds, New York: Basic Books, 1993, 41–82.

"Reply to Habermas," *Journal of Philosophy* 93, 132–80, 1995.

"Fifty Years After Hiroshima," *Dissent*, Summer 1995, 323–27.

"The Idea of Public Reason Revisited," *University of Chicago Law Review* 64, Summer 1997, 765–807.

Collected Papers, Samuel Freeman, ed., Cambridge, MA: Harvard University Press, 1999.

The Law of Peoples, Cambridge, MA: Harvard University Press, 1999, including the paper "The Idea of Public Reason Revisited."

Lectures on the History of Moral Philosophy, Barbara Herman, ed., Cambridge, MA: Harvard University Press, 2000.

"Burton Dreben: A Reminiscence," in Juliet Floyd and Sanford Shieh, eds., *Future Pasts: Perspectives on the Place of the Analytic Tradition in Twentieth-Century Philosophy*, New York: Oxford University Press, 2000.

Justice as Fairness: A Restatement, Erin Kelley, ed., Cambridge, MA: Harvard University Press, 2001.

Lectures on the History of Political Philosophy, Samuel Freeman, ed., Cambridge, MA: Harvard University Press, 2007.

BOOKS ON OR SUBSTANTIALLY ABOUT RAWLS

Barry, Brian, The Liberal Theory of Justice, Oxford: Oxford University Press, 1972.
—— Theories of Justice, Berkeley, CA: University of California Press, 1989, Part II.
Cohen, G.A., Saving Justice From Constructivism, Cambridge, MA: Harvard University Press, forthcoming.
Daniels, Norman, Justice and Justification, Cambridge: Cambridge University Press, 1996.
Freeman, Samuel, Justice and the Social Contract, New York: Oxford University Press, 2007.
Kukathas, Chandran, and Pettit, Philip, Rawls: A Theory of Justice and Its Critics, Stanford, CA: Stanford University Press, 1990.
Mandle, Jon, What's Left of Liberalism?: An Interpretation and Defense of Justice as Fairness, Lanham, MD: Lexington Books, 2000.
Martin, Rex, Rawls and Rights, Lawrence, KS: University of Kansas Press, 1985.
Munoz-Darde, Véronique, La justice sociale: le libéralisme égalitaire de John Rawls, Paris: Nathan University, 2000.
Nussbaum, Martha, Frontiers of Justice, Cambridge, MA: Harvard University Press, 2006.
Pogge, Thomas, Realizing Rawls, Ithaca, NY: Cornell University Press, 1989.
—— John Rawls, His Life and Theory of Justice, Michelle Kosch, trans., Oxford: Oxford University Press, 2006.
Sandel, Michael, Liberalism and the Limits of Justice, Cambridge: Cambridge University Press, 1982; second edition, 1998.
Wellbank, J.H., Snook, Dennis, and Mason, David T., John Rawls and His Critics: An Annotated Bibliography, New York: Garland, 1982.

ANTHOLOGIES ON RAWLS
Arneson, Richard, ed., "Symposium on Rawlsian Theory of Justice: Recent Developments," Ethics, 99, 1989, 695ff.
Blocker, H.G. and Smith, E.H., eds., John Rawls's Theory of Social Justice, Athens, OH: Ohio University Press, 1980.
Daniels, Norman, ed., Reading Rawls, New York: Basic Books, 1975, reprinted with a new introduction by Stanford University Press, 1989.
Davion, Virginia, and Wolf, Clark, eds., The Idea of a Political Liberalism: Essays on Rawls, Lanham, MD: Rowman and Littlefield, 1999.
Fleming, James, ed., Symposium on Rawls and the Law, Fordham Law Review 72, 2004, 1381–2175.

Freeman, Samuel, ed., *The Cambridge Companion to Rawls*, Cambridge: Cambridge University Press, 2003.

Griffin, Stephen, and Solum, Lawrence, eds., Symposium on John Rawls's Political Liberalism, *Chicago-Kent Law Review* 69, 1994, 549–842.

Gaus, Gerald, and Riley, Jonathan, *The Legacy of John Rawls*, Politics, Philosophy, and Economics, 4, 2005, 155–268.

Lloyd, S.A., ed., John Rawls's Political Liberalism, Special Double Issue of *Pacific Philosophical Quarterly* 75, 1994, 165–387.

Martin, Rex, and Reidy, David, eds, *Rawls's Law of Peoples: A Realistic Utopia?* Oxford: Blackwell, 2006.

Reath, Andrews, Herman, Barbara, and Korsgaard, Christine M., eds., *Reclaiming the History of Ethics: Essays for John Rawls*, Cambridge: Cambridge University Press, 1997.

Richardson, Henry, and Weithman, Paul, eds., *The Philosophy of Rawls: A Collection of Essays*, in 5 volumes, New York: Garland, 1999:

volume I: Development and Main Outlines of Rawls's Theory of Justice.

volume II: The Two Principles and Their Justification.

volume III: Opponents and Implications of A Theory of Justice.

volume IV: Moral Psychology and Community.

volume V: Reasonable Pluralism.

ARTICLES ON A THEORY OF JUSTICE

Arneson, Richard, "Primary Goods Reconsidered," *Nous* 24, 1990, 129–54.

Arrow, Kenneth, "Some Ordinalist-Utilitarian Notes on Rawls's Theory of Justice," *The Journal of Philosophy* 70, 1973, 245–63.

Baier, Kurt, "Justice and the Aims of Political Philosophy," *Ethics* 99, 1989, 771–90.

Barber, Benjamin, "Justifying Justice: Problems of Psychology, Politics, and Measurement in Rawls," *American Political Science Review* 69, 1975, 663–74.

Barry, Brian, "Liberalism and Want-Satisfaction: A Critique of John Rawls," *Political Theory* 1, 1973, 134–53.

Bedau, Hugo Adam, "Social Justice and Social Institutions," *Midwest Studies in Philosophy* 3, 1978, 159–75.

——, "Review of Brian Barry's *The Liberal Theory of Justice*," *The Philosophical Review* 84, 1975, 598–603.

Brock, Dan, "John Rawls' *Theory of Justice*," *University of Chicago Law Review* 40, no. 3, 1973, 486–99.

Buchanan, Allen, "A Critical Introduction to Rawls's *Theory of Justice*," in *John Rawls's Theory of Social Justice*, Blocker, H., and Smith, E., eds., Athens, OH: Ohio University Press, 1980, 727–51.

Cohen, Joshua, "Democratic Equality," *Ethics* 99, no. 4, July 1989.

Cohen, Marshall, "The Social Contract Explained and Defended," *New York Times Book Review*, July 16, 1972, 18.

Crocker, Lawrence, "Equality, Solidarity, and Rawls's Maximin," *Philosophy and Public Affairs* 6, 1977, 262–66.

Dworkin, Gerald, "Non-Neutral Principles," *Journal of Philosophy* 71, August, 1974. Reprinted in *Reading Rawls*, Norman Daniels, ed., Stanford: Stanford Univesity Press, 1989.

Dworkin, Ronald, "The Original Position," *University of Chicago Law Review* 40, Spring 1973, 500–33. Reprinted in *Reading Rawls*, Norman Daniels, ed., 16–53.

English, Jane, "Justice Between Generations," *Philosophical Studies* 31, 1977.

Feinberg, Joel, "Rawls and Intuitionism," in *Reading Rawls*, Norman Daniels, ed., 108–23.

—— "Duty and Obligation in a Non-Ideal World," *Journal of Philosophy* 70, 1973, 263–75.

—— "Justice, Fairness, and Rationality," *Yale Law Journal* 81, 1972, 1004–31.

Fisk, Milton, "History and Reason in Rawls's Moral Theory," in *Reading Rawls*, Norman Daniels, ed., 53–90.

Fried, Charles, "Review of Rawls's *A Theory of Justice*," *Harvard Law Review* 85, 1971–72, 169ff.

Galston, William, "Defending Liberalism," *American Political Science Review* 72, 1982, 621–9.

Gauthier, David, "Justice and Natural Endowment: Toward a Critique of Rawls's Ideological Framework," *Social Theory and Practice* 3, 1974, 3–26.

Grey, Thomas C., "The First Virtue," *Stanford Law Review* 25, 1973, 286–327.

Gutmann, Amy, "The Central Role of Rawls's Theory," *Dissent* 36, 1989, 338–42.

Hampshire, Stuart, "A New Philosophy of the Just Society," *The New York Review of Books*, February 24, 1972, 34–39.

Hare, R.M., "Rawls's *Theory of Justice*," *Philosophical Quarterly* 23, 1973, 144–55, 241–51, reprinted in *Reading Rawls*, Norman Daniels ed., 81–107.

Held, Virgina, "On Rawls and Self-Interest," *Midwest Studies in Philosophy* 1, 1976, 57–60.

Kolm, Serge-Christophe, "Equal Liberties and Maximin," in *Modern Theories of Justice*, Cambridge, MA: MIT Press, 1998, 169–208.

Kymlicka, Will, "Rawls on Teleology and Deontology," Philosophy and Public Affairs 17, 1988, 173–190.

Laden, Anthony, "Games, Fairness, and Rawls's A Theory of Justice," Philosophy and Public Affairs 20, 1991, 189–222.

Lyons, David, "Nature and Soundness of the Contract and Coherence Arguments," in Reading Rawls, Norman Daniel, ed., 141–67.

MacCormick, Neil, "Justice According to Rawls," The Law Quarterly Review 89, 1973, 393–417.

MacIntyre, Alasdair, "Justice: A New Theory and Some Old Questions," Boston University Law Review 52, 1972, 330–34.

Mandle, Jon, "Justice, Desert, and Ideal Theory," Social Theory and Practice 23, Fall 1997, 399-425.

Marneffe, Peter de, "Liberalism and Perfectionism," The American Journal of Jurisprudence 43, 1998, 99–116.

Murphy, Liam, "Institutions and the Demands of Justice," Philosophy and Public Affairs 27, Fall 1998, 151–91.

Nagel, Thomas, "Rawls on Justice," Philosophical Review 87, April, 1973, 220–34. Reprinted in Reading Rawls, Norman Daniels, ed., 1–16.

Nielson, Kai, "The Choice Between Perfectionism and Rawlsian Contractarianism," Interpretation 6, 1977, 132–39.

Oberdieck, Hans, "A Theory of Justice," New York University Law Review 47, 1972, 1012–28.

O'Neill, Onora, "The Method of A Theory of Justice," in Otfried Hoeffe, ed., John Rawls: Eine Theorie der Gerechtigkeit, Berlin: Akademie Verlag, 1998.

Ryan, Alan, "John Rawls," in The Return of Grand Theory in the Human Sciences, Quentin Skinner, ed., Cambridge: Cambridge University Press, 1985, 101–20.

Scanlon, T.M., "Rawls's Theory of Justice," University of Pennsylvania Law Review 121, May, 1973, 1029–69, reprinted in part in Reading Rawls, Norman Daniels, ed., 169–205.

—— "Reflections on Rawls's Theory of Justice," Social Theory and Practice 3, no. 1, 1974, 75– 100.

Scheffler, Samuel, "Moral Independence and the Original Position," Philosophical Studies 35, 1979, 397–403.

—— "The Division of Moral Labor: Egalitarianism Liberalism as Moral Pluralism," Proceedings of the Aristotelian Society, supp. vol. 79, 2005, 229–53.

—— "Justice and Desert in Liberal Theory," California Law Review 88, 2000, 965–90.

Sen, Amartya, "Justice: Means versus Freedoms," Philosophy and Public Affairs 19, 1990, 111–121.

Sterba, James, "In Defense of Rawls Against Arrow and Nozick," Philosophia 7, 1978, 293–303.

Strasnick, Steven, "Review of Robert Paul Wolff's Understanding Rawls," Journal of Philosophy 76, 1979, 496–510.

Tattershall, Gerald, "A Rawls Bibliography," Social Theory and Practice 3, 1974, 123–27.

Teitelman, Michael, "The Limits of Individualism," Journal of Philosophy 69, Oct. 5, 1972, 545–56.

Urmson, J.O., "A Defense of Intuitionism," Proceedings of the Aristotelian Society 75, 1974–75, 111–19.

Williams, Bernard, "Rawls and Pascal's Wager," in Moral Luck, Cambridge: Cambridge University Press, 1981, 94–100.

POLITICAL LIBERALISM

Ackerman, Bruce, "Political Liberalisms," The Journal of Philosophy 91, no. 7, July, 1994, 364–86.

Arneson, Richard, "Introduction to a Symposium on Rawlsian Theory of Justice: Recent Developments," Ethics 99, 1999, 695–710.

Baier, Kurt, "Justice and the Aims of Political Philosophy," Ethics 99, 1989, 771–90.

Barry, Brian, "John Rawls and the Search for Stability," Ethics 105, 1995, 874–915.

—— "In Defense of Political Liberalism," Ratio Juris 7, 1994, 325ff.

Brighouse, Harry, "Is There Any Such Thing as Political Liberalism?" Pacific Philosophical Quarterly 75, 1994, 318–32.

Charney, Evan, "Political Liberalism, Deliberative Democracy, and the Public Sphere," American Political Science Review, 92, 1998, 97–110.

Cohen, Joshua, "Moral Pluralism and Political Consensus," in The Idea of Democracy, David Copp, Jean Hampton, and John Roemer, eds., Cambridge: Cambridge University Press, 1993, 270–91.

—— "A More Democratic Liberalism," Michigan Law Review 92, no. 6, May 1994, 1503–46.

—— "Pluralism and Proceduralism," Chicago-Kent Law Review 69, 1994, 589–618.

Dworkin, Gerald, "Contracting Justice," Philosophical Books 36, 1995, 19–26.

Estlund, David, "The Survival of Egalitarian Justice in John Rawls's Political Liberalism," Journal of Political Philosophy 4, 1996, 68–78.

Freeman, Samuel, "Political Liberalism and the Possibility of a Just Democratic Constitution," Chicago-Kent Law Review 69, 1994, 619–68.

Galston, William, "Pluralism and Social Unity," Ethics 99, 1989, 711–26.

Habermas, Jürgen, "Reconciliation Through the Public Use of Reason: Remarks on John Rawls's Political Liberalism," Journal of Philosophy 92, 1995, 109–31.

Hampshire, Stuart, "Liberalism: The New Twist," New York Review of Books vol. 40, Aug. 12, 1993, 43–46.

Klosko, George, "Political Constructivism in Rawls's Political Liberalism," *American Political Science Review* 91, 635–46.

Larmore, Charles, "Political Liberalism," *Political Theory* 18, 1990, 339–60.

—— "The Moral Basis of Political Liberalism," *Journal of Philosophy* 96, 1999, 599–625.

Lehning, Percy B., "The Coherence of Rawls's Plea for Democratic Equality," *Critical Review of International Social and Political Philosophy* 1, 1998, 1–41.

Lloyd, S.A., "Relativizing Rawls," *Chicago-Kent Law Review* 69, 1994, 737–62.

Martin, Rex, "Rawls's New Theory of Justice," *Chicago-Kent Law Review* 69, 1994, 737–62.

Michelman, Frank, "The Subject of Liberalism," *Stanford Law Review* 46, 1994, 1807–33.

O'Neill, Onora, "Political Liberalism and Public Reason: A Critical Notice of John Rawls's *Political Liberalism*," *Philosophical Review* 106, 1997, 411–28.

Nickel, James W., "Rethinking Rawls's Theory of Liberty and Rights," *Chicago-Kent Law Review* 69, 1994, 763–86.

Peffer, Rodney G., "Towards a More Adequate Rawlsian Theory of Social Justice," *Pacific Philosophical Quarterly* 75, 1994, 251–71.

Reidy, David, "Reciprocity and Reasonable Disagreement: From Liberal to Democratic Legitimacy," *Philosophical Studies*, forthcoming 2007.

Rorty, Richard, "The Priority of Democracy to Philosophy," in *Objectivity, Relativism and Truth*, New York: Cambridge University Press, 1991, 175–96.

Sandel, Michael, "Political Liberalism," *Harvard Law Review* 107, 1994, 1765ff.

Scheffler, Samuel, "The Appeal of Political Liberalism," *Ethics* 105, 1994, 4–22.

Solum, Lawrence, "Introduction: Situating Political Liberalism," *Chicago-Kent Law Review* 69, 1994, 549–88.

Waldron, Jeremy, "Disagreements about Justice," *Pacific Philosophical Quarterly* 75, 1994, 372–87.

Weithman, Paul, "Liberalism and the Political Character of Political Philosophy," in *Liberalism and Community Values*, C.F. Delaney, ed., Lanham, MD: Rowman and Littlefield, 1994, 189–211.

Williams, Bernard, "A Fair State," *London Review of Books*, 13 May, 1993.

Young, Iris M., "Rawls's Political Liberalism," *Journal of Political Philosophy* 3, no. 2, 1995, 181–90.

THE LAW OF PEOPLES AND INTERNATIONAL JUSTICE

Beitz, Charles, "Rawls's Law of Peoples," *Ethics* 110, 2000, 669–96.

—— *Political Theory and International Relations*, Princeton: Princeton University Press, 1979, 127–69.

Buchanan, Allen, "Rawls's Law of Peoples: Rules for a Vanished Westphalian World," Ethics, 2000, 697–720.

Caney, Simon, "Cosmopolitanism and the Law of Peoples," The Journal of Political Philosophy 10, 2002, 95–123.

Cohen, Joshua, and Charles Sabel, "Extra Rempublicam, Nulla Justitia?" Philosophy and Public Affairs, 2006, 147–75.

Doyle, Michael, "One World, Many Peoples: International Justice in John Rawls's The Law of Peoples," Perspectives on Politics, 4, 2006, 109–20.

Follesdal, Andreas, "The Standing of Illiberal States: Stability and Toleration in John Rawls' Law of Peoples," Acta Analytica, 1997, 149–60.

McCarthy, Thomas, "Two Conceptions of Cosmopolitan Justice," in Reconstituting Social Criticism, I. MacKenzie and S. O'Neill, eds., New York: St. Martins Press, 1999, 191–214.

Moellendorf, Darrel, "Constructing a Law of Peoples," Pacific Philosophical Quarterly 77, no. 2, June 1996, 132–54.

Nagel, Thomas, "The Problem of Global Justice," Philosophy and Public Affairs 33, 2005, 113–47.

Naticchia, Chris, "Human Rights, Liberalism, and Rawls's Law of Peoples," Social Theory and Practice 24, 1998, 345–74.

Pogge, Thomas, "An Egalitarian Law of Peoples," Philosophy and Public Affairs 23, 1994.

——"Rawls and International Justice," The Philosophical Quarterly, 51, 2003, 25–52.

——"The Incoherence between Rawls's Theories of Justice," Fordham Law Review 72, 2004, 1739–60.

Rawls, John, and Van Parijs, Philippe, "Three Letters on the Law of Peoples and the European Union," in Autour de Rawls, special issue Revue de philosophie économique 8, 2003, 7–20

Tan, Kok Chor, "Liberal Toleration in Rawls's Law of Peoples," Ethics 108, 1998, 276–95.

—— Toleration, Diversity, and Global Justice, University Park, PA: Penn State Press, 2000.

——"Critical Notice of John Rawls's The Law of Peoples," The Canadian Journal of Philosophy 31, 2001, 113–32.

Tasioulas, John "From Utopia to Kazanistan: John Rawls and the Law of Peoples," Oxford Journal of Legal Studies 22, 2002, 367–93.

Wenar, Leif, "Contractualism and Global Economic Justice," Metaphilosophy 32, 2001, 79–94.

RAWLS AND SOCIAL CONTRACT DOCTRINE

Brudney, Daniel, "Hypothetical Consent and Moral Force," Law and Philosophy 10, 1991, 235–70.

Eshete, Andreas, "Contractarianism and the Scope of Justice," Ethics 85, 1974, 38–49.

Freeman, Samuel, "Reason and Agreement in Social Contract Views," Philosophy and Public Affairs 19, 1990, 122–57.

—— "Frontiers of Justice: Contractarianism vs. the Capabilities Approach," Texas Law Review 85, no. 2, 2006, 385–430.

Gauthier, David, "The Social Contract as Ideology," Philosophy and Public Affairs 6, 1977, 130–64.

Hampton, Jean, "Contracts and Choices: Does Rawls Have a Social Contract Theory?" The Journal of Philosophy 77, 1980, 315–38.

Milo, Ronald, "Contractarian Constructivism," Journal of Philosophy 122, 1995, 181–204.

Stark, Cynthia, "Hypothetical Consent and Justification," The Journal of Philosophy 97, 2000, 313–34.

LIBERALISM AND THE PRIORITY OF BASIC LIBERTIES

Barry, Brian, "John Rawls and the Priority of Liberty," Philosophy and Public Affairs 2, 1973, 274–90.

Bowie, Norman, "Equal Basic Liberty for All," in John Rawls's Theory of Social Justice, H. Blocker and E. Smith, eds., Athens, OH: Ohio University Press, 1980, 110–31.

Brighouse, Harry, "Political Equality in Justice as Fairness," Philosophical Studies 86, 1997, 155–84.

Daniels, Norman, "Equal Liberty and Unequal Worth of Liberty," in Noman Daniels, ed., Reading Rawls, 253–81.

Hart, H.L.A., "Rawls on Liberty and Its Priority," University of Chicago Law Review 40, 1973, 534–55. Reprinted in Reading Rawls, Norman Daniels, ed.,

Gutmann, Amy, "Rawls on the Relationship Between Liberalism and Democracy," in The Cambridge Companion to Rawls, Samuel Freeman, ed., Cambridge, UK: Cambridge University Press, 2003, 168–99.

Kymlicka, Will, "Liberal Individualism and Liberal Neutrality," Ethics 99, 1989, 883–905.

de Marneffe, Peter, "Liberalism, Liberty, and Neutrality," Philosophy and Public Affairs 19, Summer 1990, 253–74.

——"Contractualism, Liberty and Democracy," Ethics 104, 1994, 764–83.

Nagel, Thomas, "Rawls and Liberalism," The Cambridge Companion to Rawls, Samuel Freeman, ed., Cambridge, UK: Cambridge University Press, 2003, 62–75.

Raz, Joseph, "Liberalism, Autonomy and the Politics of Neutral Concern," Social and Political Philosophy, Midwest Studies in Philosophy 7, Peter A. French, Theodore Uehlilng, Jr., and Howard K. Wettstein, eds., 1982, 89–120.

Shue, Henry, "Liberty and Self-Respect," Ethics 85, 1975, 68–78.

EGALITARIANISM, DISTRIBUTIVE JUSTICE, AND THE DIFFERENCE PRINCIPLE

Anderson, Elizabeth, "What is the Point of Equality?" *Ethics* 109, Jan. 1999, 287–337.

Buchanan, Allen, "Distributive Justice and Legitimate Expectations," *Philosophical Studies* 28, 1975, 419–25.

Buchanan, James, "A Hobbesian Interpretation of the Rawlsian Difference Principle," *Kyklos* 29, 1976, 5–25.

Cohen, G.A., "On the Currency of Egalitarian Justice," *Ethics* 99, July 1989, 906–44.

—— "Where the Action Is: On the Site of Distributive Justice," *Philosophy and Public Affairs* 26, 1997, 3–30.

Cohen, Joshua, "Democratic Equality," *Ethics* 99, 1989, 727–51.

——"Taking People as They Are?" *Philosophy and Public Affairs*, 30, 2001, 363–86.

Daniels, Norman, "Equality of What?: Welfare, Resources, or Capabilities," *Philosophy and Phenomenological Research* 50, 1990, Supplement: 273–96.

Estlund, David, "Liberalism, Equality and Fraternity in Cohen's Critique of Rawls," *Journal of Political Philosophy* 6, 1998, 99–112.

Freeman, Samuel, "Rawls and Luck Egalitarianism," in *Justice and the Social Contract*, New York: Oxford University Press, 2007, 111–42.

Gibbard, Allan, "Disparate Goods and Rawls's Difference Principle," *Theory and Decision* 11, 1979, 267–88.

Hsieh, Nien-hê, "Rawlsian Justice and Workplace Republicanism," *Social Theory and Practice* 31, 2005, 115–42.

Krouse, Richard, and McPherson, Michael, "Capitalism, 'Property-Owning Democracy', and the Welfare State," in *Democracy and the Welfare State*, Amy Gutmann, ed., Princeton, NJ: Princeton University Press, 1988, 78–105.

Parijs, Philippe van, "Why Surfers Should Be Fed: The Liberal Case for an Unconditional Basic Income," *Philosophy and Public Affairs* 20, 1991, 101–31.

—— "Rawlsians, Christians and Patriots. Maximin Justice and Individual Ethics," *European Journal of Philosophy* 1, 1993, 309–42.

——"Difference Principles," in *The Cambridge Companion to Rawls*, ch. 5, 200–40.

Scanlon, T.M., "Justice, Responsibility, and the Demands of Equality," in *The Egalitarian Conscience*, Christine Sypnowich, ed., Oxford: Oxford University Press, 2006, 70–87.

Schaller, Walter A., "Rawls, the Difference Principle, and Economic Inequality," *Pacific Philosophical Quarterly* 79, 1998, 368–91.

Scheffler, Samuel, "What is Egalitarianism?" *Philosophy and Public Affairs*, 31, 2003, 5–39.

Sher, George, "Effort, Ability, and Personal Desert," *Philosophy and Public Affairs* 8, 1979, 361–76.

Slote, Michael, "Desert, Consent, and Justice," Philosophy and Public Affairs 2, 1973, 323–47.

Strasnick, Steven, "Social Choice Theory and the Derivation of Rawls's Difference Principle," Journal of Philosophy 73, 1976, 85–99.

Tan, K.C., "Justice and Personal Pursuits," Journal of Philosophy 101, 7, 2004, 331–62.

Waldron, Jeremy, "John Rawls and the Social Minimum," in Liberal Rights, Cambridge: Cambridge University Press, 1993, 250–78.

Weithman, Paul, "Waldron on Political Legitimacy and the Social Minimum," The Philosophical Quarterly 45, 1995, 218–24.

Williams, Andrews, "Incentives, Inequality, and Publicity," Philosophy and Public Affairs 27, 1998, 225–47.

Wolff, Jonathan, "Fairness, Respect, and the Egalitarian Ethos," Philosophy and Public Affairs 27, 1998, 97–122.

ON JUSTIFICATION IN MORAL AND POLITICAL PHILOSOPHY: CONSTRUCTIVISM, REFLECTIVE EQUILIBRIUM, AND PUBLIC REASON

Baynes, Kenneth, "Constructivism and Practical Reason in Rawls," Analyse & Critique 14, 1992, 18–32.

Benhabib, Seyla, "The Methodological Illusions of Modern Political Theory: The Case of Rawls and Habermas," Neue Hefte für Philosophie 21, 1982, 47–74.

Bohman, James F., "Public Reason and Cultural Pluralism: Political Liberalism and the Problem of Moral Conflict," Political Theory 23, 1995, 253–79.

Brink, David, "Rawlsian Constructivism in Moral Theory," Canadian Journal of Philosophy 17, 1987, 71–90.

Brower, Bruce, "The Limits of Public Reason," Journal of Philosophy 91, 1994, 5–26.

Cohen, G.A., "Facts and Principles," Philosophy and Public Affairs 31, 2003, 211–45.

Daniels, Norman, "Wide Reflective Equilibrium and Theory Acceptance in Ethics," Journal of Philosophy 76, 1979, 256–82.

—— "Reflective Equilibrium and Justice as Political," in Justice and Justification, Cambridge: Cambridge University Press, 1996, 144–75.

Freeman, Samuel, "The Burdens of Public Justification: Constructivism, Contractualism, and Publicity," Politics, Philosophy, and Economics 4, 2007, 5–43.

George, Robert, "Public Reason and Political Conflict: Abortion and Homosexuality," The Yale Law Journal 106, 1997, 2475–504.

Greenawalt, Kent, "On Public Reason," Chicago-Kent Law Review 69, 1994, 669–89.

Kelly, Erin, and McPherson, Lionel, "On Tolerating the Unreasonable," The Journal of Political Philosophy 9, 2001, 38–55.

Kraus, Jody S., "Political Liberalism and Truth," *Legal Theory* 5, 1999, 45–73.

Larmore, Charles, "Public Reason," in *The Cambridge Companion to Rawls*, 10, 368–98.

Lehning, Percy, "The Idea of Public Reason: Can It Fulfill Its Task?" *Ratio Juris* 8, 1995, 30–39.

Macedo, Stephen, "In Defense of Liberal Public Reason: Are Slavery and Abortion Hard Cases?" in Robert P. George and Christopher Wolfe, eds., *Natural Law and Public Reason*, Washington, DC: Georgetown University Press, 2000, 11–50.

Mandle, Jon, "Having It Both Ways; Justification and Application in Justice as Fairness," *Pacific Philosophical Quarterly* 75, 1994, 295–317.

Marneffe, Peter de, "Rawls on Public Reason," *Pacific Philosophical Quarterly* 75, 1994, 232–50.

O'Neill, Onora, "The Public Use of Reason," in *Constructions of Reason*, Cambridge: Cambridge University Press, 1989, 28–50.

Raz, Joseph, "Disagreement in Politics," *American Journal of Jurisprudence*, 1998, 25–52.

—— "Facing Diversity: The Case of Epistemic Abstinence," *Philosophy and Public Affairs* 19, 1990, 3–46.

Reidy, David, "Rawls's View of Public Reason: Not Wide Enough," *Res Publica* 6, 2000, 49–72.

Richards, David A.J., "Public Reason and Abolitionist Dissent," *Chicago-Kent Law Review* 69, 1994, 787–842.

Scanlon, T.M., "Rawls on Justification," in *The Cambridge Companion to Rawls*, Samuel Freeman, ed., Cambridge: Cambridge University Press, 2003, 139–47.

Solum, Lawrence, "Inclusive Public Reason," *Pacific Philosophical Quarterly* 75, 1994, 217–31.

Weithman, Paul, "Citizenship and Public Reason," in *Natural Law and Public Reason*, Robert P. George and Christopher Wolfe, eds., Washington, DC: Georgetown University Press, 2000, 125–70.

RAWLS'S MORAL PSYCHOLOGY AND THE STABILITY OF JUSTICE AS FAIRNESS

Bates, Stanley, "The Motivation to Be Just," *Ethics* 85, 1974, 1–17.

Darwall, Steven, "Two Kinds of Respect," *Ethics* 88, 1977, 36–49.

Deigh, John, "Shame and Self-Esteem: A Critique," *Ethics* 93, 1983, 225–45.

Gibbard, Allan, "Human Evolution and the Sense of Justice," *Social and Political Philosophy*, *Midwest Studies in Philosophy* 7, Peter A. French, et al., eds., 1982, 31–46.

Hill, Thomas E., Jr., "The Stability Problem in Political Liberalism," *Pacific Philosophical Quarterly* 75, 1994, 332–52.

Hinsch, Wilfried, "Das Gut der Gerechtigkeit," in Otfried Hoeffe, ed., John Rawls: Eine Theorie der Gerechtigkeit, Berlin: Akademie, 1998.

Klosko, George, "Rawls's Argument from Political Stability," Columbia Law Review 94, 1994, 1882ff.

McClennen, Edward F., "Justice and the Problem of Stability," Philosophy and Public Affairs 19, 1990, 122–57.

Sachs, David, "How to Distinguish Self-Respect from Self-Esteem," Philosophy and Public Affairs 10, 1981, 346–60.

RAWLS AND KANT: THE KANTIAN INTERPRETATION AND THE CONCEPTION OF THE PERSON

Buchanan, Allen, "Categorical Imperatives and Moral Principles," Philosophical Studies 31, 1977, 249–60.

Daniels, Norman, "Moral Theory and the Plasticity of Persons," Monist 62, 1979, 267–87.

Darwall, Steve, "A Defense of the Kantian Interpretation," Ethics 86, 1976, 164–70.

—— "Is There a Kantian Foundation for Rawlsian Justice?" in John Rawls's Theory of Social Justice, H.G. Blocker and E.H. Smith, eds., Athens, OH: Ohio University Press, 1980, 311–45.

Davidson, Arnold, "Is Rawls a Kantian?" Pacific Philosophical Quarterly 66, 1985, 48–77.

Doppelt, Gerald, "Is Rawls's Kantian Liberalism Coherent and Defensible?" Ethics 99, 1989, 815–51.

Guyer, Paul, "Life, Liberty, and Property: Rawls and Kant," in Kant on Freedom, Law, and Happiness, Cambridge: Cambridge University Press, 2000, 262–86.

Hill, Thomas E., Jr., "Kantian Constructivism in Ethics," Ethics 99, 1989, 752–70, also in Dignity and Practical Reason, Ithaca NY: Cornell University Press, 1992, 226–50.

Johnson, Oliver, "The Kantian Interpretation," Ethics 85, 1974, 53–66.

Krasnoff, Larry, "How Kantian Is Constructivism?" Kant Studien 90, 1999, 385–409.

Levine, Andrew, "Rawls's Kantianism," Social Theory and Practice 3, 1974, 47–63.

McCarthy, Thomas, "Kantian Constructivism and Reconstructivism: Rawls and Habermas in Dialogue," Ethics 105, 1994, 44–63.

O'Neill, Onora, "Constructivism in Rawls and Kant," in The Cambridge Companion to Rawls, 347–67.

Scheffler, Samuel, "Moral Skepticism and Ideals of the Person," Monist 62, 1979, 288–303.

RAWLS, CONSTITUTIONALISM, AND THE RULE OF LAW

Fleming, Jim, "Constructing the Substantive Constitution," *Texas Law Review* 72, 1993, 211–313.

Freeman, Samuel, "Original Meaning, Democratic Interpretation, and the Constitution," *Philosophy and Public Affairs* 21, 1992, 3–42.

—— "Constitutional Democracy and the Justification of Judicial Review," *Law and Philosophy* 9, 1990–91, 327ff.

Griffen, Stephen, "Reconstructing Rawls's Theory of Justice: Developing a Public Values Philosophy of the Constitution," *New York University Law Review* 62, 1987, 715ff.

Michelman, Frank, "In Pursuit of Constitutional Welfare Rights: One View of Rawls's Theory of Justice," *University of Pennsylvania Law Review* 121, May 1973, 962–1019, also excerpted in *Reading Rawls*, Norman Daniels, ed., 373–46.

Moore, Ronald, "Rawls on Constitution-Making," in *Nomos XX: Constitutionalism*, J.R. Pennock and J.W. Chapman, eds., New York: New York University Press, 1979, 238–68.

Parker, Richard B., "The Jurisprudential Uses of John Rawls," in *Nomos XX: Constitutionalism*, J.R. Pennock and J.W. Chapman, eds., New York: New York University Press, 1979, 269–98.

Sullivan, Daniel, "Rules, Fairness, and Formal Justice," *Ethics* 85, 1975, 322–31.

RAWLS AND UTILITARIANISM

Ball, Stephen W., "Choosing Between Choice Models of Ethics: Rawlsian Equality, Utilitarianism, and the Concept of Persons," *Theory and Decision* 22, 1987, 209–24.

Barry, Brian, "Rawls on Average and Total Utility: A Comment," *Philosophical Studies* 31, 1977, 317–25.

Braybrook, David, "Utilitarianism with a Difference: Rawls's Position in Ethics," *Canadian Journal of Philosophy* 3, Dec. 1973, 303–31.

Freeman, Samuel, "Utilitarianism, Deontology, and the Priority of Right," *Philosophy and Public Affairs*, 1994, 313–49.

Gaus, Gerald, "The Convergence of Rights and Utility: The Case of Rawls and Mill," *Ethics* 92, 1981, 57–72.

Hare, R.M., "Rawls's Theory of Justice," in *Reading Rawls*, Norman Daniels, ed., Stanford, CA: Stanford University Press, 1989, 81–107.

Harsanyi, John, "Can the Maximin Principle Serve as the Basis for Morality? A Critique of John Rawls's Theory," *American Political Science Review* 69, 1975, 694–606.

Kavka, Gregory S., "Rawls on Average and Total Utility," Philosophical Studies 27, 1975, 237–53.

Kymlicka, Will, "Rawls on Teleology and Deontology," Philosophy and Public Affairs 17, 1988, 173–90.

Lyons, David, "Rawls Versus Utilitarianism," Journal of Philosophy 69, 1972, 535–45.

Miller, Richard, "Rawls, Risk, and Utilitarianism," Philosophical Studies 28, 1975, 55–61.

Mulholland, Leslie, "Rights, Utilitarianism, and the Conflation of Persons," Journal of Philosophy 83, 1986, 323–40.

Narveson, Jan, "Rawls and Utilitarianism," in The Limits of Utilitarianism, Harlan B. Miller and William H. Williams, eds., Minneapolis: University of Minnesota Press, 1982, 128–42.

Taylor, Paul W., "Justice and Utility," Canadian Journal of Philosophy 1, 1972, 327–50.

RAWLS, ECONOMICS, AND SOCIAL CHOICE THEORY

Arrow, Kenneth, "Rawls's Principle of Just Savings," Swedish Journal of Economics 75, 1973, 323–35.

Binmore, Ken, "Social Contract I: Harsanyi and Rawls," Economic Journal 99, 1989, 84–102.

Dasgupta, Partha, "On Some Problems Arising from Professor John Rawls's Conception of Distributive Justice," Theory and Decision 11, 1974, 325–44.

Gaa, James, "The Stability of Bargains Behind the Veil of Ignorance," Theory and Decision 17, 1984, 119–34.

Gibbard, Allan, "Disparate Goods and Rawls's Difference Principle: A Social Choice Theoretic Treatment," Theory and Decision 11, 1979, 267–88.

Hammond, P.J., "Equity, Arrow's Theorem, and Rawls's Difference Principle," Econometrica 44, 1976, 793–800.

Howe, R. and Roemer, John, "Rawlsian Justice as the Core of a Game," American Economic Review 71, 1981, 880–95.

Ihara, Craig, "Maximin and Other Decision Principles," Philosophical Topics 12, 1981, 59–72.

Maskin, E., "Decision-Making Under Ignorance with Implications for Social Choice," Theory and Decision 11, 1979, 319–37.

Musgrave, R.A. "Maximin, Uncertainty, and the Leisure Trade-Off," Quarterly Journal of Economics 88, 1974, 625–29.

Sen, A.K., "Rawls versus Bentham: An Axiomatic Examination of the Pure Distribution Problem," Theory and Decision 4, 301–10. Reprinted in

Reading Rawls, Norman Daniels, ed., Stanford, Stanford University Press, 1989, 283–92.

——"Welfare Inequalities and Rawlsian Axiomatics," *Theory and Decision* 7, 1976, 243–62.

Strasnick, Steven, "The Problem of Social Choice: Arrow to Rawls," *Philosophy and Public Affairs* 5, 1976, 241–73.

RAWLS AND COMMUNITARIANISM

Baker, Edwin, "Sandel on Rawls," *University of Pennsylvania Law Review* 133, April, 1985, 895–928.

Buchanan, Allen, "Assessing the Communitarian Critique of Liberalism," *Ethics* 99, 1989, 852–82.

Gutmann, Amy, "Communitarian Critics of Liberalism," *Philosophy and Public Affairs* 14 1985, 308–22.

Kymlicka, Will, "Liberalism and Communitarianism," *Canadian Journal of Philosophy* 18, 1988, 181–204.

Larmore, Charles, "Rawls's Ambiguities and Neo-Romanticism," in *Patterns of Moral Complexity*, Cambridge: Cambridge University Press, 1987, 118–30.

Mulhall, Stephen and Swift, Adam, *Liberals and Communitarians*, Oxford: Basil Blackwell, 1992.

Sandel, Michael, *Liberalism and the Limits of Justice*, Cambridge: Cambridge University Press, 1982, revised edition, 1998.

Schwartzenbach, Sybil, "Rawls, Hegel, and Communitarianism," *Political Theory* 19, 1991, 539–71.

Taylor, Charles, "Cross-Purposes: The Liberal-Communitarian Debate," in *Liberalism and the Moral Life*, Nancy Rosenblum, ed., Cambridge, MA: Harvard University Press, 1989, 159–82.

RAWLS AND FEMINISM

Cohen, Joshua, "Okin on Justice, Gender, and the Family," *The Canadian Journal of Philosophy* 22, no. 2, 1992, 263–86.

Hampton, Jean, "Feminist Contractarianism," in *A Mind of One's Own: Feminist Essays on Reason and Objectivity*, Louise M. Antony and Charlotte Witt, eds., Boulder, CO: Westview, 1993, 227–56.

Kelly, Erin, "Justice and Communitarian Identity Politics," *The Journal of Value Inquiry* 35, 2001, 71–93.

Kittay, Eva Feder, "Human Dependency and Rawlsian Equality," in *Feminists Rethink the Self*, Diana Tietjens Meyers, ed., Boulder, CO: Westview Press, 1997, 219–616.

Lloyd, S.A., "Family Justice and Social Justice," *Pacific Philosophical Quarterly* 75, 1994, 351–71.

Mallon, Ron, "Political Liberalism, Cultural Membership, and the Family," *Social Theory and Practice* 25, 1999, 271–97.

Munoz-Darde, Véronique, "Rawls, Justice in the Family and Justice of the Family," *The Philosophical Quarterly* 48, 1998, 335–8.

—— "Is the Family to Be Abolished Then?" *Proceedings of the Aristotelian Society* XCXIX 99, 1999, 37–56.

Nussbaum, Martha, "Rawls and Feminism," in *The Cambridge Companion to Rawls*, Samuel Freeman, ed., Cambridge: Cambridge University Press, 488–520.

Okin, Susan Moller, "Justice and Gender," *Philosophy and Public Affairs* 16, 1987, 42–72.

—— "Justice as Fairness, For Whom?" in her *Justice, Gender and the Family*, New York: Basic Books, 1989, 89–109.

—— "Political Liberalism, Justice and Gender," *Ethics* 105, 1994, 23–43.

—— "Forty Acres and a Mule for Women: Rawls and Feminism," *Politics, Philosophy, and Economics* 4, 2005, 233–48.

RAWLS, MARX, AND LEFT CRITICISM

DiQuattro, Arthur, "Rawls and Left Criticism," *Political Theory* 11, 1983, 53–78.

Francis, Leslie P., "Responses to Rawls from the Left," in *John Rawls's Theory of Social Justice*, H. Gene Blocker and Elizabeth H. Smith, eds., Athens, OH: Ohio University Press, 1980, 463–93.

MacPherson, C.B., "Rawls's Model of Man and Society," *Philosophy of the Social Sciences* 3, 1973, 341–47.

Miller, Richard, "Rawls and Marxism," *Philosophy and Public Affairs* 3, 1974, 167–91. Reprinted in *Reading Rawls*, Norman Daniels, ed., Stanford: Stanford University Press, 1989, 206–30.

Moulin, Hervé, and Roemer, John, "Public Ownership of the External World and Private Ownership of Self," *Journal of Political Economy* 97, 1989, 347–67.

Nielsen, Kai, "Capitalism, Socialism, and Justice: Reflections on Rawls's Theory of Justice," *Social Praxis* 7, 1980, 253–77.

Reiman, Jeffrey H., "The Labor Theory of the Difference Principle," *Philosophy and Public Affairs* 12, 1983, 133–59.

Wolff, Robert Paul, *Understanding Rawls*, Princeton: Princeton University Press, 1977.

Wolin, Sheldon, "The Liberal/Democratic Divide: On Rawls's Political Liberalism," *Political Theory* 24, 1996, 97–119.

Young, Iris M., "Toward a Critical Theory of Justice," *Social Theory and Practice* 7, 1981, 279–302.

CONSERVATIVE AND LIBERTARIAN CRITICISMS

Bloom, Allan, "Justice: John Rawls vs. the Tradition of Political Philosophy," *The American Political Science Review* 69, 1975, 648–62.

Flew, Anthony, "Rawls's Theory of Justice," in *Contemporary British Philosophy*, H.D. Lewis, ed., London: George Allen and Unwin, 1976, 69–85.

Hospers, John, "A Review of Rawls's *A Theory of Justice*," *The Personalist* 55, 1974, 71–77.

Mack, Eric, "Distributivism vs. Justice," *Ethics* 86, 1976, 145–53.

Nisbet, Robert, "The Pursuit of Equality," *Public Interest* 35, 1974, 103–20.

Nozick, Robert, "Distributive Justice," in *Anarchy, State, and Utopia*, New York: Basic Books, 1974, ch. 7, 149–231.

Rand, Ayn, "An Untitled Letter," *Ayn Rand Letter* 2, no. 9, 1973.

RAWLS AND RELIGION

Franklin, Robert Michael, "In Pursuit of a Just Society: Martin Luther King, Jr, and John Rawls," *Journal of Religious Ethics* 18, 1990, 57–77.

Hollenbach, David, "Contexts of the Political Role of Religion: Civil Society and Culture," *San Diego Law Review* 30, 1994, 879–901.

Jackson, Timothy, "To Bedlam and Part Way Back: John Rawls and Christian Justice," *Faith and Philosophy* 8, 1991, 423–47.

Jones, Gregory, "Should Christians Affirm Rawls's Justice as Fairness?" *Journal of Religious Ethics* 16, 1988, 251–71.

Macedo, Stephen, "Liberal Civic Education and Religious Fundamentalism: The Case of God v. John Rawls?" *Ethics* 105, 1995, 468–96.

O'Neil, Patrick, "The Fate of Theological Facts in the Original Position of Rawls's *A Theory of Justice*," *Dialogue* 28, 1986, 45–56.

Papa, Edward, "Kant's Dubious Disciples: Hare and Rawls," *American Catholic Philosophical Quarterly* 65, 1991, 159–75.

Proudfoot, Wayne, "Rawls on the Individual and the Social," *The Journal of Religious Ethics* 2, 1974, 107–28.

Quinn, Philip L., "Political Liberalisms and their Exclusions of the Religious," *Proceedings and Addresses of the American Philosophical Association* 69, 1995, 35–56.

Sterba, James, "Reconciling Public Reason and Religious Values," *Social Theory and Practice* 25, 1999, 1–28.

Waldron, Jeremy, "Religious Contributions in Public Deliberation," *San Diego Law Review* 30, 1993, 817–48.

Weithman, Paul, "Taking Rites Seriously," *Pacific Philosophical Quarterly* 75, 1994, 272–94.

—— "Rawlsian Liberalism and the Privatization of Religion: Three Theological Objections Considered," *Journal of Religious Ethics* 22, 1994, 3–28, with replies by David Hollenbach, Timothy Jackson, and John Langan, SJ.

Wolterstoff, Nicholas, "Why We Should Reject What Liberalism Tells Us About Thinking and Acting in Public for Religious Reasons," in Paul Weithman, ed., *Religion and Contemporary Liberalism*, South Bend: Notre Dame Press, 1997, 162–81.

MISCELLANEOUS DISCUSSIONS AND REVIEWS

Freeman, Samuel, "John Rawls: Friend and Teacher," *The Chronicle Review: Chronicle of Higher Education*, December 13, 2002; also in Freeman, Samuel, *Justice and the Social Contract*, New York: Oxford University Press, 2007, 325–28.

Hill, Thomas, "Review of John Rawls's *Collected Papers*," *Journal of Philosophy*, 2001.

Larmore, Charles, "Lifting the Veil," *The New Republic*, Feb. 5, 2001, Issue # 4490, 32–37 (a review of Rawls's *Lectures on the History of Moral Philosophy*).

Nussbaum, Martha, "The Enduring Significance of John Rawls," *The Chronicle of Higher Education*, July 20, 2001 issue.

Schneewind, J.B., "What's Fair is Fair," *The New York Times Book Review*, June 24, 2001, 21 (a review of Rawls's *Justice as Fairness: A Restatement*).

Waldron, Jeremy, "The Plight of the Poor in the Midst of Plenty," *London Review of Books* 21, no. 14, July 15, 1999 (review of Rawls's *Collected Papers*).

Index

abortion: and the proviso to public reason 414; right of, and public reason 389, 406–9; right to 84–85
affirmative action 90–91
agency: moral, basis of 288; and moral powers 276–78; and sense of justice 282
altruism 249; limited 253; vs. reciprocity 348, 374–75
Appiah, Anthony 497n33
Aristotelian principle 154, 265, 289, 463; and fair equality of opportunity 91; and the good 269-72; role in congruence argument 272–73
assurance problem 251; and stability 246–48
autonomy 188, 269, 463; constitutive vs. doctrinal 353–56; different senses of 289; full 288; full, defined 290–91; full vs. rational 282, 463, 505n49; of governments and human rights, 436–37; as intrinsic good 276, 282; and liberalism 239; and libertarianism 58; moral 352; moral and political 240–41, 361–63; political, defined 362; political, of peoples, 438, 440, 454; political, and public reason 331; problem with political enforcement of 399; and publicity 309–10; rational 304; rational, defined 297–99; rational, and individuality 289, 337; rational, and priority of liberty 77;

Rawls's Kantian and Millian account 58

background justice 126–27, 463
bargaining 180–81
Barry, Brian 502n13, 512n1, 513n7, 514n17–18
basic institutions: of basic structure listed 101; as essential to social life 102; needed for society 103
basic justice 329; matters of, and constitutional essentials 393–96
basic liberties 464; central range of application of 69–70; and the constitution 205; defined 45–46; fair value of, and difference principle 62; and first principle of justice 44–59; fully adequate scheme of 77–78; grounded in moral powers 55–56; how specified and defined 53; are inalienable 51–52; and liberalism 511n17; multi-tiered account 71–72; none are absolute 52; as political values 396; priority of 200, 206; reasons for restricting 65–66; and self-respect 187; significance of, and moral powers 70; and social minimum 235; specification of 46–51, 73–74, 209–12; specified in four-stage sequence 73–74; summary of 81–84; value of 59–64; worth of 117; *see also* first principle of justice
basic structure of society 202, 332;